Design of a Worker Cooperatives Society

Historical Materialism Book Series

The Historical Materialism Book Series is a major publishing initiative of the radical left. The capitalist crisis of the twenty-first century has been met by a resurgence of interest in critical Marxist theory. At the same time, the publishing institutions committed to Marxism have contracted markedly since the high point of the 1970s. The Historical Materialism Book Series is dedicated to addressing this situation by making available important works of Marxist theory. The aim of the series is to publish important theoretical contributions as the basis for vigorous intellectual debate and exchange on the left.

The peer-reviewed series publishes original monographs, translated texts, and reprints of classics across the bounds of academic disciplinary agendas and across the divisions of the left. The series is particularly concerned to encourage the internationalization of Marxist debate and aims to translate significant studies from beyond the English-speaking world.

For a full list of titles in the Historical Materialism Book Series available in paperback from Haymarket Books, visit: www.haymarketbooks.org/series_collections/1-historical-materialism.

Design of a Worker Cooperatives Society

An Alternative Beyond Capitalism and Socialism, and the Transition Towards It

Geert Reuten

Haymarket Books
Chicago, IL

First published in 2023 by Brill Academic Publishers, The Netherlands
© 2023 Koninklijke Brill NV, Leiden, The Netherlands

Published in paperback in 2024 by
Haymarket Books
P.O. Box 180165
Chicago, IL 60618
773-583-7884
www.haymarketbooks.org

ISBN: 979-8-88890-331-5

Distributed to the trade in the US through Consortium Book Sales and Distribution (www.cbsd.com) and internationally through Ingram Publisher Services International (www.ingramcontent.com).

This book was published with the generous support of Lannan Foundation, Wallace Action Fund, and the Marguerite Casey Foundation.

Special discounts are available for bulk purchases by organizations and institutions. Please call 773-583-7884 or email info@haymarketbooks.org for more information.

Cover art and design by David Mabb. Cover art is a detail of *A pattern of life 6, plan of Letchworth Garden City on William Morris Strawberry Thief fabric*, limited edition of 19 unique linocut prints on fabric (2019).

Printed in the United States.

Library of Congress Cataloging-in-Publication data is available.

Contents

Preface and acknowledgements   VII
About the Author   IX

General introduction   1

PART ONE
Design of the organisation of a worker cooperatives society

1. Preview of the main elements of the design's worker cooperatives society   11

2. Design of the economy of a worker cooperatives society: economic democracy and the organisation of cooperatives   22

3. Design of the state in a worker cooperatives society: democratic governance of the state and the organisation of state institutions   67

4. Municipal and provincial administrations   231

5. International economic relations   238

PART TWO
From modifying capitalism to transition

Introduction to Part Two   243

6. The modification of capitalist practices by 'worker-owned cooperatives' and similar democratic enterprises   245

7. Circumstances just before the transition: financial and real estate markets and the scope of capital flight   298

8. Transition to a worker cooperatives society   307

General summary   396

References 421
Index of names 432
Index of subjects 434
Abbreviations 459
Extended list of contents 460

Preface and acknowledgements

This book sets out an alternative to current capitalism; it does so in considerable detail, so that the reader can judge its feasibility. Specifically, the book sets out a detailed design of a democratic society as organised in worker cooperatives (Part One) and an equally detailed democratic transition to it (Part Two, ch. 8). Although the text on the transition and the movement towards it comprises 40% of the book's core texts, in the lines below I introduce merely Part One.

Full democracy at the level of enterprises is reached by the governance of worker councils that vote on all relevant matters (such as the appointment of removable management, investment and workers' remuneration). The specific legal structure of the worker cooperatives is such that the workers have full rights to the fruits of the cooperative without owning the cooperative, and yet the state does not own the cooperatives either.

Inasmuch as in capitalist society the state is geared to the interests of capitalist enterprises and their owners, the state in the society proposed is geared to the interests of the cooperatives, as well as the households. Democracy at the level of the state is reached, first, by the primacy of the elected parliament in terms of governance, and secondly, within that primacy, by the state institution's workers' councils' decisions regarding the internal work organisation and the remuneration structure. The average remuneration in state institutions (including parliament, government and the judiciary) is equal to the average remuneration in cooperatives.

The general design is such that there is free choice of occupation and of specific consumer goods, and more so in comparison with capitalism.

I am very grateful to Herman van Gunsteren and Dirk Damsma for their important comments on an earlier version of the text. Enormous thanks go to Tony Smith for his extensive critical and stimulating comments on several earlier versions. A discussion that we had in late 2019 on the last two chapters of his 2017 book *Beyond Liberal Egalitarianism* in fact challenged me to write the current book; for that too I am very grateful. For comments on specific parts or chapters of the book I am thankful to Ignacio Bretos and Robert Went. I also thank three anonymous referees for their comments.

The above regards the academic content of the book. English not being my native language, I am very grateful to Simon Mussell for polishing my English. For the material production and publication of the book I thank Danny Hayward (manager of the Historical Materialism book series) as well as the for Brill working staff members Bart Nijsten (production editor) and Debbie de Wit (associate editor). Finally, I thank the (for me) anonymous production workers for materialising the book.

January 2023

About the Author

Geert Reuten taught economics for 35 years at the School of Economics of the University of Amsterdam, where he is currently a guest research associate. From 2007–2015 and 2018–2019 he was a member of the Senate of the Netherlands for the Socialist Party and spokesperson for financial, monetary and economic affairs.

He has authored four academic books, edited six books, and published 80 articles in academic journals and collections (the articles can be accessed at http://reuten.eu). He has also written 75 assessments of Dutch law proposals and published 65 articles in non-academic journals and newspapers.

Books in English by the same author
- *The unity of the capitalist economy and state – a systematic-dialectical exposition of the capitalist system* (Brill, 2019).
- *The culmination of capital: Essays on volume III of Marx's 'Capital'*; editor, with Martha Campbell (Palgrave Macmillan, 2002).
- *The circulation of capital: Essays on volume II of Marx's 'Capital'*; editor, with Christopher Arthur (Macmillan, 1998).
- *Value-form and the State; the tendencies of accumulation and the determination of economic policy in capitalist society*; with Michael Williams (Routledge, 1989).
- *The value-form determination of economic policy: A dialectical theory of economy, society and state in the capitalist epoch*; with Michael Williams (Grüner, 1988).

General introduction

This book sets out the design of a society beyond capitalism and beyond socialism: a society in which 'worker cooperatives' constitute the dominant mode of production. Workers are members of a cooperative, but the cooperative is not their private property, nor is it state-owned. It is democratically governed by the cooperative's workers' council that elects management from its ranks. The workers are the sole beneficiaries of the cooperative's distributable income.

Generally, the worker cooperatives designed in this book differ significantly from those that exist in capitalism. Most briefly: workers are the founders of a cooperative as a legal entity, but once founded it is not allowed to be alienated. The cooperative is the owner of the means of production, but because of the exclusion of alienation this is a restricted ownership. Workers have no direct or indirect ownership in the cooperative; however, collectively they are the cooperative's usufructuary – usufruct combines use right and the fruits right. On the workers' retirement the usufruct succeeds to the next generation of workers. Thus, whereas workers in 'worker-*owned* cooperatives' as existing in capitalism usually have a collective full ownership right, for the proposed cooperatives this is restricted to usufruct rights.[1] One similarity between a capitalist 'foundation' and the designed 'worker cooperative' is that these legal entities have no owners; one relevant distinction is that the cooperative has members, whereas a foundation has no members.

The above constitutes one main distinction between the society to be outlined and, first, a socialist one where the state owns the means of production, and, second, a capitalist one where capitalists own the means of production – either directly or indirectly as in a stock corporation where the shareholders indirectly own the means of production. Contrary to capitalism, the workers in a cooperatives society constitute the single economic class.

Households and cooperatives, and cooperatives mutually, are interconnected via markets – in comparison with capitalism – except for health and education provisions, and for real estate, which are organised via state institutions. Investment loans to production cooperatives are provided by banks that are organised like other worker cooperatives. There is no market for shares or bonds.

---

1 This implies that the book does not propose a variant of a 'property-owning democracy' in the tradition of Meade 1964 and Rawls 2001. For an appraisal of 'property-owning democracy' see Smith 2017, ch. 12.

The design of a worker cooperatives society, set out in the next chapters, constitutes an alternative beyond prevailing ideas of a socialist mode of production, and beyond the existing capitalist mode of production. It will be seen that the design retains some of the latter's elements – especially the free choices of occupation and consumption, and decentralised investment by units of production – whilst overcoming capitalism's: (1) authoritarian relations at the point of production; (2) the property of enterprises in the hands of a few; (3) the highly skewed distribution of income; (4) the even more skewed distribution of wealth; (5) market power generating dominances within markets, including in financial markets; (6) a (often destabilising) real estate market.

The alternative not only overcomes much of the disparities mentioned; foremost it puts democratic decision-making at the front of all of the society's institutions. Next to the Design's democracy at the point of production, democratic decision-making is equally core to the state and state institutions. First, in that the elected parliament is the state's highest legislative and governing body. Second, notwithstanding the former, in that for the internal organisation of state institutions their worker councils play a prominent role.

The income of workers in state institutions, including members of parliament and of the government, is the same as the average realised income of workers in cooperatives – the former is derived from the latter. The primary task of state institutions and their workers is the flourishing and wellbeing of the cooperatives' economy. Given the on average similar income, this stimulates a mutual flourishing. (To put this in economists' terms: it is in the direct interest of state workers that the cooperatives' workers flourish.)

Democracy, and democratisation, is a process. In capitalist nations, democracy is and has been restricted to political democracy (whatever the merits or defects of the specific organisation of that political democracy). In capitalism no democracy, at least no generalised democracy, prevails at the point of production – the place where people during their working life predominantly engage in social relations beyond their intimate ties. When democratic decision-making ends at the factory or office gate – ends, because capitalist legislation generally defines this to be the border separating for-profit rather than for-people activity – disillusion about the scope of democracy is built into the system. However, the experience and learning effects of democratic decision-making at the point of production are likely to permeate political democracy.

This book is not the first to deal with worker cooperatives and the possible future thereof. There is especially a vast literature on the functioning of 'worker-

owned cooperatives' *within* capitalism.² However, a worker cooperatives society, as indicated prior to the last paragraph above, has, as far as I am aware, not been dealt with, at least not in detail.

General accounts or main lines of the organisation of a future society are in my view insufficiently convincing for most people to really see it as an alternative to capitalism – especially in face of the ideological discourse that insists on the opposite: 'there is no alternative to capitalism' (TINA). Hence, for the judgement on the possible functioning of a 'worker cooperatives society' and the adequacy thereof, one needs a design of its full economic and state organisation that is blueprint-like in its detail. Detailed such that the feasibility and consistency of the design can be fully scrutinised. This blueprint-like detail is indeed a main objective of the book.

It will be seen that for the Design's cooperatives economy this does not require more space than about 35 pages (chapter 2). The organisation of state institutions (chapter 3) requires far more space, especially because of their interconnection with the Design's economy.

The latter regards first of all the Design's democratic character of the state's governance. For its design in this book (chapter 3, division 1) I claim that there are more guarantees for democracy than in most current capitalist countries.

Second, quite some attention is devoted to the size of state institutions in terms of their budget and the size of their workforce. In mature capitalist countries on average, state expenditure exclusive of defence amounts around the year 2020 to 41% of GDP.³ In the design it is estimated at 43% of GDP, which includes the fully free of charge health and education provisions, as well as pensions for all individuals at 1⅔ (167%) of the minimum costs of living expenses – the latter three together are estimated at 26% of GDP (Appendix 3A). For all expenditures the design encompasses not only 'hard budget constraints', but also hard constraints regarding the size of the state institutions' workforce (as a percentage of the total workforce).

Furthermore, as already touched on above, the design is such that the income of state workers is a derivative from the average individual income of the cooperatives' workers (it can on average never be above the latter average; workers' councils of state institutions decide, within the average, on the

---

2 See Mellor, Hannah and Stirling 1988, chs. 1–2 for a concise overview from the nineteenth century onwards. See also, for example, Battilani and Schröter (eds) 2012; Dijk, Sergaki and Baourakis 2019; Michie, Blasi and Borzaga (eds) 2017.

3 OECD average for 2019 (OECD, dataset government at a glance, yearly updates; extracted 29 Nov 2021). Reuten 2019 shows the development of this number from 1870 to 2015, and as specified for the various expenditure components (graphically summarised on p. 501).

internal income scales). Therefore, it is in the interest of state workers (including members of the state's governing bodies) to limit state expenditure, because the required taxes for the expenditure are levied as much on their income as that of cooperatives' workers.

So much for the introduction to the design of a worker cooperatives society in Part One of the book. For brevity, this and all the further details about it will henceforth be referred to as 'the Design'.

Arrangement Part One of the book: the Design. Chapter 1 provides a concise overview of the organisation and interconnection of worker cooperatives (the society's economy), as well as of state institutions. Chapter 2 sets out the organisation and interconnection of worker cooperatives in detail. Chapter 3, the longest chapter of the book, presents in detail the democratic governance of the state, as well as the organisation and the tasks of state institutions (ranging from public security, the safeguarding of the cooperative's finance, health and education provision, infrastructure, to public transport and other fields). The final division of this chapter is on the Design's key social-economic policy instruments and on taxation. This is followed by two brief chapters on the municipal and provincial administrations (chapter 4) and on international economic relations (chapter 5).

Part Two of the book: from modifying capitalism to transition. Part Two sets out how we might get to such a society from the womb of current capitalism. Chapter 6 surveys some of the major 'islands' of worker-*owned* cooperatives that currently exist within capitalism.[4] In a review of empirical studies comparing the performance of worker cooperatives with capitalist enterprises in the period 1950 to 2010, Pérotin (2012, pp. 36–38) concludes that 'worker cooperatives perform well in comparison with conventional firms, and that the features that make them special – worker participation and unusual arrangements for the ownership of capital – are part of their strength'. She continues: 'Solid, consistent evidence across countries, systems, and time periods shows that worker cooperatives are at least as productive as conventional firms, and more productive in some areas. The more participatory cooperatives are, the more

---

4 The biggest of those islands is the Mondragon cooperative's federation, mainly located in the Spanish Basque region. In 2020 it encompassed about 100 cooperatives (including a bank) with over 80,000 workers and an annual revenue of over €12 billion. Worldwide cooperatives at large (not just workers cooperatives) reached a number of 3 million in 2020, providing jobs to 10% of the world's employed population.

productive they tend to be'. And: 'profit may not be higher in more participatory cooperatives, but the firms may produce more and preserve their members' jobs better'.

These characteristics of those islands are reason for some optimism about the feasibility of a future generalised worker cooperatives society. Optimism, because they reached this within capitalist surroundings and especially a capitalist state. (In the Design of Part One, state institutions are tailored to meet the requirements of cooperatives, whereas those in capitalism are tailored to capitalist enterprises.) The growth and increase of such islands – and their being a shining example for the workers in capitalist enterprises, as well as for progressive movements and political tendencies – might lead to pressures for capitalist state institutions to gradually turn to backing the current style of cooperatives and other democratic enterprises (chapter 6).

All this regards not a 'transition' to a new world, but rather (to borrow Rostow's terminology) the phase of preconditions for a take-off to it. The borderline for the transition (chapter 8) is the point at which in some country there is a parliamentary majority that is willing to go for the transition to a worker cooperatives society as set out in Part One. That chapter is preceded by a brief chapter that tries to imagine the constellation around two years prior to the transitions, that is, when capitalist enterprises and their owners feel that there might be a reasonable chance that pro-worker-cooperatives political parties will win upcoming elections. It is analysed what effect this might have on the financial and real estate markets and on ensuing capital flight. It is next considered what their effects are on the 'real economy' that will be the inheritance for the transition's actual take off.

The starting point for chapter 8 is the economic inheritance just referred to, but also a confrontation with capitalist vested interests, to which the capitalist state and its legislation is tailored. The core of this legislation regards the capitalist class members' property of the means of production and the entitlement to employ labour as combined with the appropriation of the surplus-value produced by that labour. This capitalist legislation is presented as being in 'the' general interest.[5] Thus a turn will have to be made to an awareness that there might be other 'general' interests than the capitalist general interest. Rather

---

5   On the core legislative part of the capitalist state's tailoring, see Reuten 2019, chapter 6. This regards especially private property and appropriation claims by the capitalist class (property in the earth and the means of production and the entitlement to employ labour as combined with the appropriation of the surplus-value produced by that labour), claims that the capitalist state grants as rights (pp. 303 and 305). On 'the' general interest, see pp. 309–310. https://brill.com/view/title/38778 (open access).

schizophrenic. Part of this turn is a shift from what is considered legal in the previous and the upcoming modes of production. (The (pre-)capitalist ideological view that the state as institution is the result of a 'social contract' will help in this case!)[6]

The transition presented has two broad periods. One in which all of Part One's Design has been put into legislation. Another in which that legislation becomes fully effective in practice in the sense that all of the society's economic domain is organised in Design worker cooperatives. In this last period a capitalist sector might still prevail, but, as will be shown, it will gradually phase out (most within a generation). No pre-transition capitalist enterprise is enforced to legally convert into a cooperative. However, the implementation of the first period's Design legislation will make it increasingly difficult for these enterprises to survive.

The first broad transition period is planned to take five to six years. Here the book's objective is again to set out this transition period in detail. One aim is to reach a sequence of phase-wise constellations in which cooperatives co-exist with pre-transition capitalist enterprises, with the former becoming gradually dominant. The sequence should be such that there is no collapse of the capitalist sector's production and employment, but indeed a gradual transition of it, such that production and work are preserved. The second aim is that all along essential common provisions (pensions and other allowances, and health and educational provisions) are not only maintained at a bare level, but also improved when compared to the pre-transition era.

Parts One and Two together close with a General Summary.

Readers familiar with some of my earlier work will perhaps be surprised not to find any references to Marx in the current book. Marx's mature work is almost exclusively on capitalism. So was my own work (up to and including my 2019 book on the capitalist economy and state) in which I took inspiration from Marx. The latter also applies to the current book in that: 'Conscious change within and beyond the capitalist system requires its comprehension – in this I am an ardent pupil of Marx'.[7]

Character of the book. As indicated, the book aims at a blueprint-like detail of a 'worker cooperatives society'. Detailed such that the feasibility and consistency of the Design can be fully scrutinised. There is a similar aim for the transition

---

6 Cf. Reuten 2019, pp. 308–9 on social contract theory.
7 Reuten 2019, p. 2.

set out in chapter 8. Recall that the latter requires the Design to be actually put into legislation. For these reasons, much of the book's text has the character of points that are preliminary to such legislation, and that can fairly easily be put into the legislative format as customary in specific countries that would transition into a constellation near to the Design. In other words, much of the Design (especially chapters 2–4) has the character of a series of 'explanatory memorandums' that in many countries accompany legislative texts (of Bills).

Although I eagerly defend the book's Design, this might not be the only possibility for a similar society. However, given a number of principles, I have chosen to present just one alternative that is (presumably) feasible and consistent in its interconnections. (Providing alternatives would have made the book much longer than it already is.) The reader will see that I often mention indications of specific numbers, such as for the relative sizes of the cooperatives and the state institutions' sectors, or for required reserves of cooperatives, or for the level of pensions, or for tax brackets – but all these are indeed indications, that together nevertheless constitute a consistency.

Limitations of the book. The scope of the book is limited in two respects. First, I have abstained from any discussion of past actual efforts at, and practices of, a society beyond capitalism. Second – and except for approximately five pages in Division 3 of Chapter 2 – I have abstained from discussing the literature on other alternatives to capitalism (including 'state-planned socialism', 'market socialism' and 'property-owning democracy'; the alternatives that I have seen either lack full democracy at all levels of society and/or are insufficiently detailed for judging their feasibility, and/or are rather cursory about the transition to such a society). Although at some points I included (the beginning of) an Appendix on the prevailing alternatives, the combination of doing justice to the authors (selection already is a problem) and criticising their lack of detail got out of hand in terms of book space. I therefore decided against it.

Had I not imposed these two limitations, the size of the book would easily have doubled. Ultimately decisive was that inclusion of the discussions would not have affected the outlined Design and the current arguments for it.

Format of the book and internal references: Parts, Chapters, Divisions and Sections.
- The two Parts of the book are divided into **Chapters** (all chapters are consecutively numbered 1 through to 8).
- Most chapters are further divided into **Divisions**.
  - In internal cross-references Chapter 1, Division 1 is abbreviated as **1D1** and so on.

- The Divisions are divided into *Sections* (these are consecutively numbered within each chapter).
  - In internal cross-references Chapter 1, Section 1 (§1) is abbreviated as **1§1** and so on.

There are three categories of figures: Schemes, Tables and Graphs. These are consecutively numbered through each chapter (for chapter 2: 2.1, 2.2 and so on).

Appendices are numbered by chapter with a capital letter (for chapter 2: 2A, 2B).

As already mentioned, Part One of the book will be referred to as 'the Design'.

Extended list of contents. At the end of the book the reader will find an extended list of contents which should facilitate the way through the interconnected items especially in the main chapters 2, 3 and 8.

Reading guide. Although the book aims for blueprint-like detail, it is written in such a way that readers can opt to take in main lines and then digest details as and when they choose. The reader could then adopt the following two reading strategies. In face of each of those, all the summaries have been extensively cross-referenced so that the reader can look up details, using the extended list of contents.

1. Moving from the current General Introduction directly to the 25-page General Summary (of Parts One and Two).
2. Moving from the General Introduction to the Part One preview of chapter 1 (11 pages), and next to the introductions and summaries of the main chapters 2, 3, 6 and 8 (together 31 pages).

PART ONE

Design of the organisation of a worker cooperatives society

∵

This part consists of five chapters.
- Chapter 1. Preview of the main elements of the Design's worker cooperatives society (p. 11).
- Chapter 2. Design of the economy of a worker cooperatives society: economic democracy and the organisation of cooperatives (p. 22).
- Chapter 3. Design of the state in a worker cooperatives society: democratic governance of the state and the organisation of state institutions (p. 67).
- Chapter 4. Municipal and provincial administrations (p. 231).
- Chapter 5. International economic relations (p. 238).

CHAPTER 1

Preview of the main elements of the design's worker cooperatives society

Introduction

This brief chapter provides a preview of the two main chapters of Part One: those setting out the organisation of worker cooperatives (ch. 2) and the organisation of the state and state institutions (ch. 3). Division 1 presents the main elements of a constellation in which worker cooperatives are the dominant way of organising production. Division 2 describes headlines of the Design's parliamentary democracy and the organisation of state institutions. Division 3 presents schematically the main income and expenditure flows between aggregates of cooperatives, households and state institutions. Division 4 lists the Design's legal entities.

Division 1. Main elements of the organisation of the worker cooperatives economy

The Design's worker cooperatives economy is such that workers constitute the single economic class. As against capitalism, there is no class of owners of means of production – hence no antagonism between those owners and workers. In contrast with state socialism, the state does not own the economy's reproducible means of production.[1]

1§1   *The cooperative as legal entity and its democratic governance*
A cooperative is a legal entity that is governed by a legal association of which only the workers of the cooperative are members. The association is identical to the cooperative's workers' council, which is the cooperative's highest governing body. Decisions are made on a one person one vote basis. From its ranks it elects one or more managers, the manager(s) being removable by the council.

---

1   The non-reproducible agricultural land, fishery waters and mines can be rented from a state institution. The criterium is that these are 'free gift of nature' that should never be the property of an individual or economic entity.

A cooperative can be founded by two or more workers (see 1§3). Once founded a cooperative shall not be alienated.

The cooperative is the owner of the assets, which because of the non-alienation is a restricted ownership.[2] The workers are collectively merely the unique usufructuaries of the cooperative – thus they have the cooperatives' use right, and the rights to its fruits. They have this right until their retirement or until they move to another cooperative or to a public sector entity. (For comparison: one similarity between a capitalist 'foundation' and a 'Design worker cooperative' is that these entities have no owners; one relevant distinction is that the cooperative has members, whereas a foundation has no members.) Consequently the workers are not the owners of the means of production – nor is any other class.

An important implication of the Design's ownership and usufruct structure is that it eliminates the categories of capital and accumulation of capital (see further 2§10). Because workers constitute the single economic class, and given the ownership-like relations just outlined, there is no means of production owning class that exploits the working class (this is one main distinction from capitalism).

Regarding the workers' collective fruits right (and within the cooperative's required legal reserves constraint – see below) the council sets rules for the individual remuneration of its members.

The council decides on the competences of the management. In any case, that is legally, the council has to approve of, at least:
(a) The internal statute of the cooperative and changes thereof (the internal statute sets rules beyond legal rules) – this statute includes rules for the building up of 'uncommitted' reserves beyond the legally required reserves;
(b) The annual Income account and Balance sheet of the cooperative;
(c) The structure of the individual remuneration levels;
(d) Increases in investments or the workforce, each beyond 5% of the past 5 years' average;
(e) Measures regarding foreseen decreases in the cooperative's 'uncommitted' reserves beyond those due to foreseen retirement or movements (see 1§4 on required and uncommitted reserves);
(f) In case this is opportune or required: a 'restructuring plan' for the cooperative.
(These six points are further detailed in chapter 2.)

---

2 Thus, of the three main elements that define the 'property right' of an entity (use right, right to its fruits, and the right to its alienation), the cooperative holds the first two only.

It can be seen from the preview above that the collective of workers has full democratic powers at the institutional (i.e. cooperative) level. This contrasts with capitalist enterprises where capital shareholders decide, moreover not on a one person one vote basis, but on a capital share basis. Thus, the latter's 'capital-cracy' is indeed turned into 'demo-cracy': given their character persons may not be equal, but they have equal rights. In capitalism persons may have equal political rights (in the best case) but these rights stop at the gate of the enterprise, that is, the place where workers spend most of their daily life. Further, even in those aborted circumstances, a large part of their value-added product accrues to the capital owners, because the capitalist state has granted them the right to appropriate the surplus that labour produces.[3]

1§2 *Markets, types of cooperatives and the 'single person enterprise'*

For their inputs and outputs cooperatives operate on markets, the measure of value being monetary. There are two types of cooperatives: production worker cooperatives (PWC) and cooperative banks (COB). ('Production' is used in the wide sense, as including retail and other services). The term 'cooperative(s)' without specification – as in 1§1 – refers to banking and non-banking cooperatives.

Within the economic domain there are only three legal entities: the two mentioned cooperatives and the 'single person enterprise'. No one is forced to become a member of a cooperative. Within the economic domain the only other possibility is to start a single person enterprise. For the latter, however, 'hiring a worker' is not allowed. The reason is the avoidance of exploitative relations, as in capitalist enterprise–employee relations. A person is not allowed to run such an enterprise and at the same time be a worker in a cooperative or in the public sector (the public sector is introduced in Division 2).

1§3 *Membership of an existing cooperative and the foundation of a cooperative*

A person can become a member of an existing cooperative's association after a successful application for a vacancy. The membership requires no funds of the worker nor a membership fee. A new cooperative can be founded at all times by a group of workers. The foundation requires no funds of the workers. (Details on each of these points are set out in chapter 2.)

---

3 The granting of this right, as well as the right to own much of the Earth, is what a state defines as a capitalist state (Reuten 2019, ch. 6; ch. 1 shows that only labour produces the value-added, that is, the equivalent of wages and the surplus. See more briefly its Glossary entries 'capitalist state' on p. 679 and 'value-added' on p. 692 https://brill.com/view/title/38778 open access).

1§4 Legally required resistance buffer, 'uncommitted' reserves and dividends

Cooperatives are required to build up a 'legally binding resistance buffer', expressed as percentage of the assets. As an indication it is set at 10% for cooperative banks, and at on average 30% for other cooperatives. Prior to having built up this buffer, workers shall receive no more than the minimum wage. (It will be seen in ch. 3 that the minimum wage is 1⅔ (167%) of the minimum costs of living.)

The council of a cooperative decides whether all or part of the end of year disposable surplus is distributed as a dividend to the workers (thus workers receive wages, and at the end of a year they may also receive dividends). The non-distributed part is added to the 'uncommitted reserves' on top of the required buffer of the cooperative. Once the buffer has been reached it is – in face of possible unfavourable market circumstances – in the interest of cooperatives to build up 'uncommitted' reserves beyond the legally required reserves because this may avoid falling back to minimum wages. To stimulate the building up of uncommitted reserves, retiring workers or those that move to another institution, may receive their dated share in the then existing uncommitted reserves, which is in fact a postponed remuneration.

1§5 Credit-debt relation between cooperative banks and other cooperatives

Cooperative banks (COBs) provide credit for investment to production worker cooperatives (PWCs) against an interest that consists of a risk premium, a component that on average covers the COB's material costs and the remuneration of its workers, as well as a component for keeping up the required reserves. (On the interest and debt servicing by PWCs, see 2§6 and 2§8.) The investment loans by COBs are the only way of external finance for the PWCs – notably there is no bonds market.

COBs provide investment loans to PWCs via the ex nihilo creation of new money – this is similar in the case of capitalist banks.[4]

1§6 Competition between cooperatives

In their market, cooperatives compete with other cooperatives. Even with the safety rule of a required resistance buffer and the minimum wage before attainment of the buffer (1§4), competition may ultimately mean that a cooperative goes bankrupt. Jobless allowances apply – it will be seen in ch. 3, 3§18–3§20,

---

4 On the latter see Reuten 2019, ch. 2, pp. 103–5 (more extended pp. 103–20).

that no one is out of work for more than two months ('work' includes permanent jobs and paid traineeships, the latter being a lever to permanent jobs).

The implication is indeed that cooperatives' workers face a risk. Given the issues that a workers' council must approve of (1§1), any decreases in the uncommitted and the committed reserves of a cooperative will usually make workers alert before it is too late.

Further, as will be seen in ch. 2 (2§19) the type of competition between cooperatives is very different from the capitalist type of competition – notably it tends to be non-aggressive. In the same chapter (2§3, 2§4 and 2§14) it will be seen that the market dominance of individual cooperatives is limited by a number of rules, including the rule that cooperatives are not allowed to expand beyond ceilings that in their relevant market would generate market power.

Division 2. Description of the design's parliamentary democracy and state institutions

1§7 *Parliamentary democracy*

The parliament is the highest governing organ of the nation. It has to approve of all legislation as well as of any decrees.[5] There are no exceptions to this power of parliament (as in some capitalist nations, especially those with a presidential system). Parliament is elected on a proportional basis, without an electoral threshold; apart from the principle of proportionality, this has the advantage that minorities can be represented in parliament.

The parliament elects a government that is accountable to the parliament and that is removable by the parliament's majority. There are rules that should prevent monetary means, including gifts, to play a role in the candidacy of parliamentarians (these apply for individuals and for political parties).

1§8 *State institutions and the public sector*

Table 1.1 provides an overview of the public sector institutions. The left part lists the state sector, with in its second column the 'state institutions'; its right part lists the other public sector institutions. The judiciary is a specific state institution (ch. 3, 3§6 sets the appointment rules). All state institutions are internally organised via 'workers' councils' which, among other things, decide on the internal work organisation and the internal wage scales (on the latter see further 1§11).

---

[5] In case of a (defined) high urgency, the government may issue a decree that is legally binding for no more than 15 days; within this period the decree is either repealed or parliament approves of the (amended) decree for a limited period.

TABLE 1.1   *Public sector institutions, with estimates of their assigned state expenditure and workforce*

State sector			This sector constitutes, together with the state sector, the 'public sector'	
Legislation and general governance	*State institutions*	Ch.	*Workers' council governed foundations* (WGFs)	Ch.
• Parliament (highest body)	• The judiciary	3	• *State-financed WGFs*	3
• Government	• Ministries	3	Health sector	
	• Provinces	4	Education sector	
	• Municipalities	4	Part of the culture sector	
	• 18 State agencies	3	• *User charging WGFs*	3
	↓		Rail transport	
	for the internal organisation of all five above: workers' councils†		Essential production/services not undertaken by cooperatives	
Estimated workforce (% of total workforce): 6.5%‡			Estimated workforce (% of tot. workf): 21%	
Estimated state expenditure: 25% of GDP*			Estimated state expenditure: 18% of GDP	

† With competences as set out in 3§3-d.
‡ Cf. Appendix 3A, Table 3A.6.
* Cf. Appendix 3A, Table 3A.1. This is exclusive of the transfers to the state-financed institutions of the upper part of the next column (18% GDP).

Within the officials' organisation (the civil service) there is quite some division of powers. Next to the ministries, there is a key role for 18 state agencies that each have to report annually to parliament. The latter can also adjust the main line of their policies. It will be seen that chapter 3 is mainly organised along these state agencies.

Five of these state agencies are responsible for the sectors listed in the right-hand part of Table 1.1, such as the health and education sectors that provide free of charge services. The institutions that execute the work (such as hospitals and schools) have – within financial, labour force and other constraints – a high degree of autonomy. This is reflected in their legal status of 'worker council governed foundation' (with a prominent role with regard to workers' councils).

1§9 State expenditure and workforce of the public sector

The bottom of Table 1.1 provides estimates of the workforce of and the state expenditure on all these institutions. In can be inferred from the last but one row that the total workforce of the cooperatives economy (division 1 above) is estimated at 73% of the total workforce. Next to the state expenditure on health and education (12% and 6% of GDP) the largest state expenditure is on equal pensions for all (9% of GDP), and full costs covering child costs of living and childcare (5% of GDP).

1§10 Functions of state agencies and the judiciary vis-à-vis cooperatives

After a division on parliamentary democracy and governance, chapter 3 will treat the state agencies as well as the judiciary in priority order. Each of the 18 state agencies will not be listed here (see Appendix 3G). Instead Table 1.2 indicates, group-wise, their functions.

TABLE 1.2 *Functions of state agencies vis-à-vis cooperatives*

	Function	Subject	Agencies	Ch. 3
1	furthering the objectives of cooperatives and workers	• safeguarding the finance of cooperatives and the financial constellation at large	4	3D4
		• job securities	1	3D5
		• income allowances	1	3D6
		• real estate (renting or purchasing), mining and other Earth extractions (licensed renting) and infrastructure	3	3D8
2	constraining cooperatives in the interest of other cooperatives, or of workers and households	• climate and environment protection (incl. via circular production), output safety, work safety, work-time, minimum wages	1	3D3
		• regulation of auditing, patents, copyrights and competition	3	3D10
3	services for which cooperatives' production does not apply because of their character or of free provision	• public security; judiciary	not appl.	3D2
		• health; education; part of culture sector	3	3D7
4	public sector undertaking, either because of its monopoly or oligopoly character, or because of cooperatives' scale or risk constraints	• railway transport (user charged)	1	3D9
		• essential production/services not (yet) undertaken by cooperatives†	1	3D9
				3D9

† Here 'essential' means vital to the functioning of (other) cooperatives or to the welfare of households.

1§11   *Remuneration of public sector workers*
One core part of the Design is that public sector workers – from members of parliament, government and the judiciary to state agencies and workers' council governed foundations – receive a remuneration that is derived from, and per institution *on average equal to, the nationwide average remuneration of cooperatives' workers*.[6] Each institution's workers' council decides on the allocation of that average within the institution (3§3-b).[7] This implies that all these workers have an interest in the flourishing of the cooperatives economy (quite apart from any general social delight they might derive from this).

Other core aspects of the Design are its 'physically circular production' (3§7) and advertisement prohibition (so as to protect consumers and (small) cooperatives) – notably this includes internet advertisement (3§8).

1§12   *Taxation*
State expenditure is generally financed by taxation. There are three taxation categories.

First, for cooperatives. These uniquely pay a turnover tax, one that is based on a 'cascade system' – a system that (contrary to a value-added tax) levies a tax on every transaction in the production process. This taxation system is – in comparison with a value-added tax – not only administratively simple; it also stimulates vertical integration, as a result of which, first, work in a cooperative is more varied, and, second, there is less climate-damaging transport.

This turnover tax should cover the revenue for about 50% of the state expenditure. Its tax rate is uniform and is – depending on the production structure of the country at hand – probably between 5% and 15%

Second, for persons. These pay an *individual income tax* that covers about 50% of the state expenditure. (For the following it is relevant that next to the relatively high state expenditure on health, education, pensions, and costs covering child allowances and childcare allowances – mentioned in 1§9 – there are, amongst others, also expenditures on benefits that are between the minimum costs of living and the minimum wage. It is recalled that the minimum wage is 167% of the minimum costs of living – or, the ratio of the minimum costs of living and the minimum wage is 60%.)

---

6   This average remuneration is made up of wages and dividends, including 'postponed dividends' (2§13.0 and 3§3).
7   However, the members of the parliament, the government and the judiciary each individually receive the cooperatives' average remuneration.

The income tax rates range from 25% (between the minimum costs of living and the minimum wage), via 60% (between one to two times the minimum wage) and further gradually increasing to 95% for incomes above five times the minimum wage. (Note that the latter incomes are most unlikely, given that worker councils decide on the pre-tax income ranges. However, the top income tax rates are relevant for the transition – see Part Two.)

There are no municipal or provincial taxes nor is there a wealth tax (in comparison with capitalist countries, individual wealth will be very minor).

Third, for persons. There is an inheritance tax levied on the receiver, with a tax rate of 50% on the equivalent of between one and two times the annual minimum wage, and 100% above it; there is also a gift tax that is somewhat more complicated and which is not treated here (see 3§46). (The principle point about the – in comparison with capitalism – considerable inheritance tax rate is that the children of all parents deserve an equal start, and that the wealth of their ancestors is not their merit. The tax-free threshold is to cover treasured possessions.)

In face of anticipating behaviour, the inheritance tax revenue is expected to be minor.

Division 3. Macroeconomic income and expenditure flows between cooperatives, households and state institutions

Scheme 1.3 (see page 21) shows the main macroeconomic income and expenditure flows between aggregates of cooperatives, households and state institutions – saving flows are not shown.

(Macroeconomic implies, amongst other things, that the mutual flows between cooperatives – including those between production cooperatives and cooperative banks – are aggregated, and thus are not shown. The households of cooperative workers and of the workers in state institutions are equally aggregated.)

The following are the main monetary income and expenditure flows shown in Scheme 1.3 (p. 21).
- *Cooperatives' income:* consumption expenditure households; material expenditure of the state and state institutions.
- *Cooperatives' expenditure:* wages and dividends (to workers' households). (Investment of cooperatives are an intra-cooperatives flow. Rent payments to state institutions are not shown.)
- *Households' income:* wages and dividends (from cooperatives and state institutions, as including from the 'workers' council governed foundations' that

execute the health and education services); transfers (regarding child allowances and pensions; the quantitively minor transfers are not explicitly shown).
- *Households' expenditure:* consumption expenditure (with cooperatives); charged provisions from or via state institutions (mainly railway transport, and rent of self-occupied dwellings).
- *State (institutions') income:* taxes from cooperatives and households; charged provisions (mainly regarding rented out self-occupied dwellings, and railway transport). (Rents from cooperatives to the state are not shown.)
- *State (institutions') expenditure:* material expenditure (with cooperatives); transfers (to households and to 'workers' council governed foundations' – the latter mainly regarding health and education).

Division 4. The design's legal entities

The Design encompasses the following seven legal entities (as further explained in chapters 2–4):
1. The Cooperative (2§3)
2. The Single person enterprise (2§2.2)
3. The State (3§1)
4. Agency of the state (3§2);
5. The Workers' council governed foundation (3§25)
6. The Province (4§1)
7. The Municipality (4§1)

'State institutions' include: the Judiciary; the ministries of government; the agencies of the state (4); the provinces (6); the municipalities (7).

MAIN ELEMENTS OF THE DESIGN'S WORKER COOPERATIVES SOCIETY 21

SCHEME 1.3 *Main income and expenditure flows between aggregates of cooperatives, households and state institutions (abstracting from savings)*

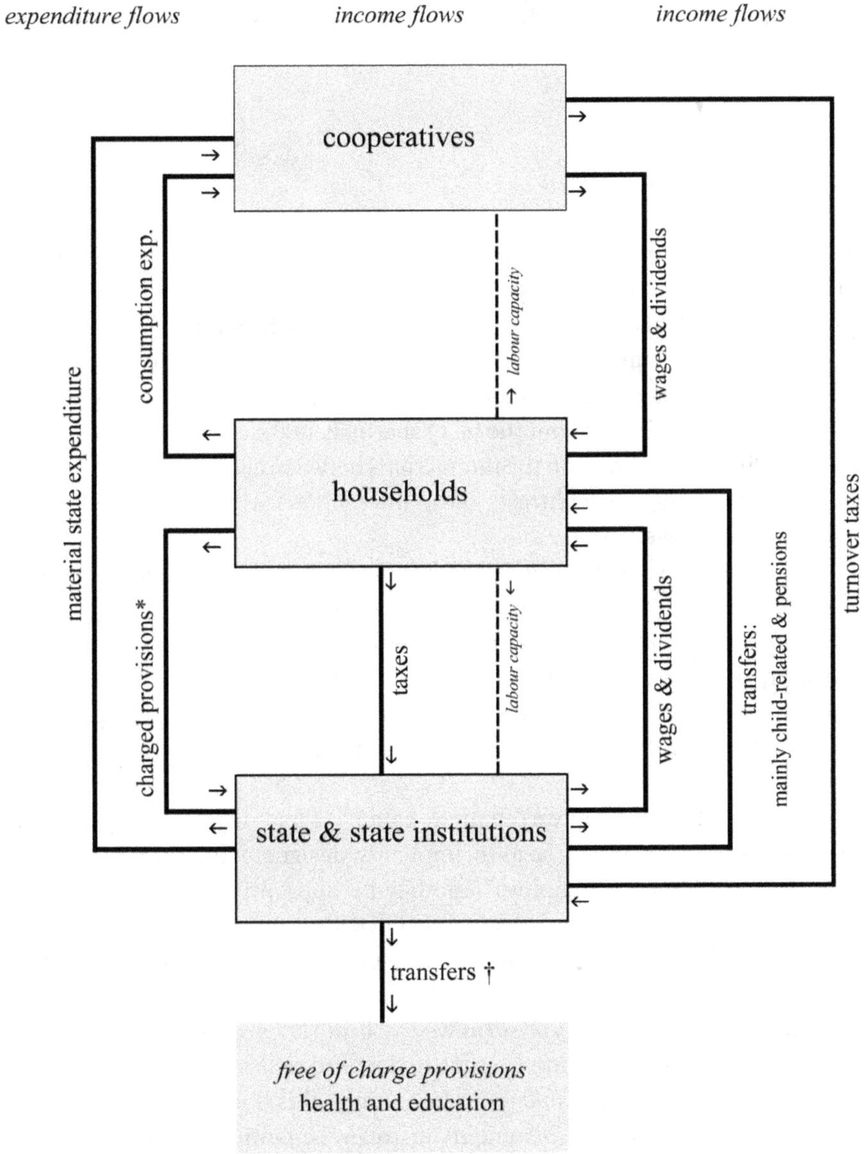

expenditure flows   *income flows*   *income flows*

[Diagram showing flows between three boxes: **cooperatives**, **households**, and **state & state institutions**.

Flows between cooperatives and households: consumption exp., wages & dividends, labour capacity.

Flows between households and state: taxes, wages & dividends, labour capacity, transfers: mainly child-related & pensions.

Flows between state and cooperatives: material state expenditure, charged provisions*, turnover taxes.

From state: transfers † → *free of charge provisions* health and education]

*   Charged provisions: mainly railway transport (other transport is provided by cooperatives).
†   Transfers to the providing 'workers' council governed foundations'.

CHAPTER 2

Design of the economy of a worker cooperatives society: economic democracy and the organisation of cooperatives

Introduction

This chapter presents the organisation of the economy of a worker cooperatives society. This does not take up very much space in this book. Division 1 presents the organisation in itself – further detailing its main elements set out in 1D1. Division 2 sums up the direct support of cooperatives by state institutions and expands on the macroeconomic connections between households and cooperatives. Throughout the text I sparingly make comparisons with capitalism. Division 3 reflects on the interactions between cooperatives and households via markets, and contrasts these interactions with some notions of a socialist alternative.

Regarding the style of especially Division 1, it is recalled from the General Introduction that in face of a transition this text (and others of Part One) has the character of points that are preliminary to transitional legislation, and that can fairly easily be put into the legislative format as customary in specific countries. In other words, the text has the character of a series of brief 'explanatory memorandums' that in many countries accompany legislative texts.

Terminology. In what follows (chapters 2 and 3) I have evaded using the term *employment* for the Design, so as to, implicitly, designate that there is no social class that exploits (i.e. employs) another by appropriating the latter's surplus product. For the same reason I avoided the term 'profit', to the extent that it has a similar connotation, more specifically in the sense of taking profit.

I also avoid the term *enterprise* (as well as 'firm') because of its capitalist connotation; for its Design counterpart I use the term *cooperative*.

When I use the term *economy* or 'economic', this does not imply that the economy is non-political (as some mainstream economists would hold). The Design's economy is as political as the capitalist economy is (regarding e.g. property rights, decision-making at the point of production and the distribution of value-added). The Design's economy refers to the sphere where the cooperatives' organisation predominantly prevails (inasmuch as in the capitalist economy, capitalist enterprises predominantly prevail). (See further the Introduction to chapter 3.)

Below I have maintained the term *surplus* because in any society, producers must yield a surplus beyond what they consume (such as for investment, or for those that cannot produce, or that because of age, or other reasons, are exempted from producing). I use the term '*dividend*' for any part of the surplus that is distributed to workers. For principal reasons I have maintained the term '*interest*' so as to emphasise that in any society, 'roundabout' production, or investment, has a price (investment must in some way be weighed against non-investment). Finally, I have maintained the term '*wage*' for the agreed distributed income that workers can always count on (as against dividends). I use this term for lack of any better one that is not artificial. (The term 'income' tout court will not do, because dividends are also income.)[1] But in case, for some, the term 'wage' would immediately be associated with 'capitalist wage labour' I am happy to replace it with 'advanced income'.

When commenting on capitalist enterprises a distinction is made between 'the capitalist stock corporation' (in brief corporation) as owned by shareholders, and the 'capitalist firm' (in brief firm) as owned by an individual or by partners. The corporation's shareholders are limitedly liable, whereas the owner(s) of a firm are fully liable. (In most countries corporations and firms are also taxed differently.)

Abbreviations and cross-references. I adopt four frequently used abbreviations. On their first use these are underlined and explained; they are also listed at the end of the book. The sections below have numbered subsections (in fact paragraphs) which should facilitate brief cross-references throughout this chapter and the rest of the book. Each section starts with a subsection numbered zero (e.g. 2§2.0) which treats the core of the full section (2§1 has no subsections).

For further information on cross-references between chapters see the General Introduction pp. 7–8.

---

1 Schweickart (2011), for example, explicitly turns away from the term 'wage' (fine), but sees no harm in using instead the term 'distributed profits' as 'the' full workers' remuneration. Apart from my objection to the term 'profits' because of its exploitative connotation (see the main text above) this is somewhat awkward because profits should then be distributed before they are realised (assuming that workers do not have to 'advance' their labour).

Division 1. Organisation of the cooperatives economy

2§1   *General characterisation of the cooperatives economy*

2§1.0. Labour is the sole producer of value-added – this is so for the cooperatives mode of production, outlined below, as much as for the capitalist mode of production.[2] The main economic difference between the two modes of production is that in capitalism the members of the capitalist class appropriate in the form of profit the surplus part of value-added, whereas in the cooperatives mode of production the distributable surplus accrues to the labour that produces it. Because of the capitalist appropriation referred to, the relation between the capitalist and labour class is exploitative.

In the cooperatives economy designed below, workers constitute the single economic class. They do not own the means of production (as in capitalism the capitalist class members do); instead workers are the usufructuaries of the means of production. (Usufruct combines use right and the fruits right – explained in 1§1, and further explained in 2§5.0.) In contrast with state socialism, the state does not own the economy's means of production (except for rented out agricultural land). Instead the cooperative as legal entity holds a restricted ownership of the means of production. Whereas, as explained later on, workers govern the cooperatives, they are as indicated no more, and no less, than the usufructuaries of the cooperative's restricted ownership: they are the sole beneficiaries of the cooperative's distributable income; that is, of wages (far less skewedly distributed than in capitalism) as well as dividends (that in capitalism are received by the capital owners).

Although cooperatives and households are separate entities, there is (as against capitalism) no antagonistic separation between workers' households and enterprises.[3] *Scheme 2.1* shows the main macroeconomic connections between households and cooperatives.

The complete macroeconomic connections between households and cooperatives – as including saving – will be presented in 2§22.

---

2   For capitalism it is shown in Reuten 2019 (pp. 65–71) that labour is the sole producer of value-added, and how the surplus part of value-added is appropriated by the capitalist class (https://brill.com/view/title/38778 open access).
3   On the antagonistic separation within capitalism, see Reuten 2019 pp. 33–4.

SCHEME 2.1 *Macroeconomic connections between households and cooperatives: annual flows (abstracting from saving)*

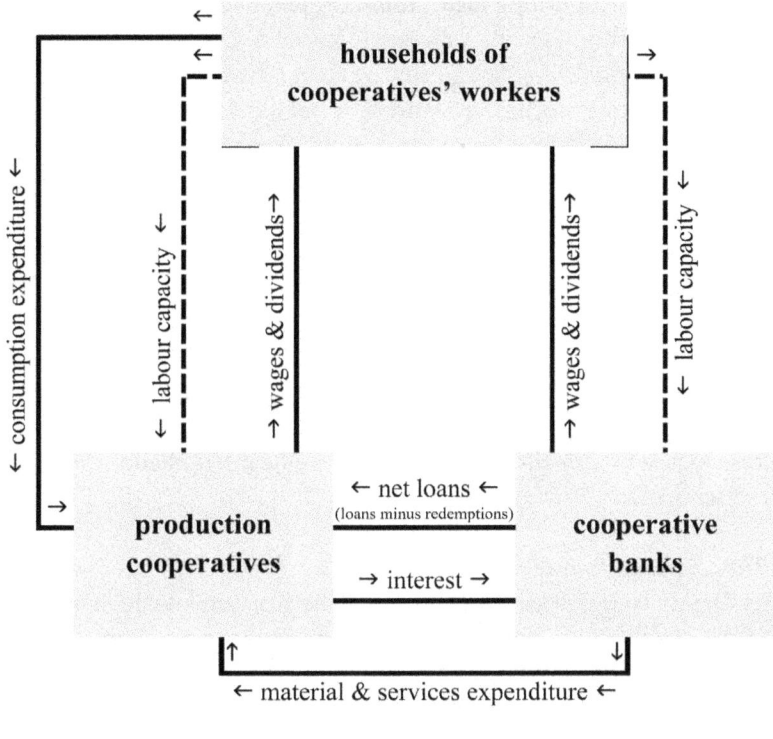

Note: 'Net loans' (stream from cooperative banks to production cooperatives) is the flow of loans minus the flow of redeemed loans.

2§2 *Types of worker cooperatives*

2§2.0. There are two types of worker cooperatives in this economy: production worker cooperatives (PWC) and cooperative banks (COB). ('Production' is used in the wide sense, as including retail and other services. The term 'cooperative(s)' without specification refers to banking and non-banking cooperatives.) For their inputs and outputs cooperatives operate on markets, the measure of value being monetary.

2§2.1. Households and cooperatives, and cooperatives mutually, are interconnected via markets – except for health and education provisions and for real estate that are organised via state institutions (on real estate see also 2§15). COBs provide investment loans to PWCs (see 2§6). With the exceptions mentioned, the organisation of all types of production or services can take the form of a cooperative (similarly to those that in capitalism are organised in firms, corporations, partnerships and foundations).

2§2.2. Although apart from state institutions, cooperatives are the predominant economic organisation entities, no one is forced to become a member of a cooperative. Individuals are free to run by themselves a registered 'Single person enterprise'. However, 'hiring a worker' is not allowed. In the economic domain the only possible legal form for a multi-workers entity is that of a cooperative. The reason is the avoidance of exploitative relations, as in capitalist enterprise–employee relations.[4] A person is not allowed to run such an enterprise and at the same time be a worker in a cooperative or in the public sector (the public sector is introduced in chapter 3).

2§2.3. Individual services for households shall be provided by cooperatives only.[5]

2§2.4. Next to 2§2.2 there are structural or temporary exceptions to the uniqueness of the cooperative organisation of production – see chapter 3, divisions 7 and 9. These regard mainly the fully state-financed health and education sectors, whose services are provided free of charge.

2§3   *The cooperative as legal entity*

2§3.0. The 'Design cooperative' is a legal entity, the structure of which is based on that of the association – the association being its highest governing body. Only the workers of the cooperative can be members.[6] A person can become a member after a successful application for a vacancy. The membership is not bound to refundable or non-refundable dues. The cooperative as legal entity is the owner of the cooperative's assets, though this is a restricted ownership: once founded, a cooperative is not allowed to be sold, nor is it allowed to convert its juridical status into another juridical form.[7] The cooperative's members have no direct or indirect ownership in the cooperative and its assets – notably they own no alienable or non-alienable shares in the cooperative. However, workers are the sole beneficiaries of the cooperatives' distributable income: collectively they are the cooperative's usufructuary.

---

4   I object to Schweickart's idea, of allowing for a labour employing capitalist sector in a 'worker self-management' society (2011 edition, pp. 77–80; the 2002 edition does not mention this).

5   Such services may regard, for example, childcare, cleaning or repair. It will be seen that cooperatives shall pay their workers at least the minimum wage. As a minimum wage does not apply for single person enterprises, rule 2§2.3 implies that for the relevant services households pay at least the minimum wage.

6   The association is similar to a membership association as they exist in most capitalist countries; however, the Design's cooperatives associations pay no membership fee.

7   Thus, of the three main elements that define the 'property right' of an entity (use right, right to its fruits, and the right to its alienation), the cooperative holds the first two only.

Addendum 2§3. One similarity between a capitalist 'foundation' and a 'Design worker cooperative' is that these entities have no owners. One relevant distinction is that the cooperative has members, whereas a foundation has no members.

Because a Design cooperative is not allowed to be sold, it holds a restricted ownership in comparison with a capitalist stock corporation, which holds full ownership of the entity. Because cooperatives' workers own no shares in the cooperative, and because in the economic domain a cooperative is the only possible multi-workers legal entity (2§2.2) there is no shares market.

2§3.1. The prohibition of the selling of the cooperative includes the prohibition of the selling of parts of it such that the income from it accrues as income to the workers. These prohibitions secure the continuity of the cooperative. Workers receive the distributable fruits of the cooperative during their working life. On the workers' retirement the acquirement of the fruits succeeds to the next generation of workers.

2§3.2. When for some reason a cooperative is no longer able to stand on its own, it is allowed to merge with another cooperative (take-overs fall under the selling prohibition).

2§3.3. Cooperatives are organised in no more than a single location (which may consist of several buildings or plants on that location). The main reason for this is that a multitude of locations would dilute the power of the cooperative's council (see 2§5). The combination with the previous point may mean that merged cooperatives have to move to a larger location. (See also 2§14 and 2§15.) Note that the single location rule is not incompatible with large-scale production; depending on the country, a single cooperative might provide jobs to several tens of thousands of workers in a location covering several hundred thousand square metres.

2§3.4. Workers can become members of the cooperative's association after a successful application for a vacancy. The membership shall not require any funds of the worker nor a membership fee. The cooperative's council (see 2§5) may decide to grant memberships after a probation period of maximum two years. Applications are open to all for the vacancy qualified persons, without ethnic, gender, social, political or religious discrimination. (See 2§12.2 on the remuneration of new workers and members).

2§4   *Foundation of cooperatives*

2§4.0. Cooperatives can be founded at all times by a group of workers. The foundation requires no funds of the workers, nor a membership fee. Cooperatives are not allowed to found other cooperatives.

2§4.1. The foundation of a COB is initiated by a 'cooperative bank plan' as drawn up by a group of workers. The foundation of a COB can be assisted by the state's *Guardian Bank* (ch. 3, 3§14). On the foundation see further Appendix 2B. When in case of a COB's bankruptcy there would be insufficient banking capacity for investment loans in a region, the Guardian Bank temporarily stands in until a new COB has been established.

2§4.2. The foundation of a PWC is initiated by the drawing up of a 'cooperative plan' on the basis of which a COB may grant investment loans to the cooperative in formation – see 2§6.0 on investment loans. (Note that in capitalism banks might similarly provide credit based merely on a 'business plan'.) Should no COB be willing to grant credit based on the plan, the initiators can apply with the state's *Investment-credit Guarantee Fund* for the early security of the cooperative (ch. 3, 3§15).

2§5   *Governance of cooperatives*

2§5.0. The highest governing body of a cooperative is its council. The council is formally constituted by the cooperative's association of workers – and exclusively so. Council members have voting rights according to their appointment as a percentage of a full-time one. The council elects from its ranks a management – the management being removable. The council decides on the competences of the management.

> *Addendum 2§5. Comparison of capitalist and cooperatives (non-)ownership relations.*
> • As mentioned, because a Design cooperative is not allowed to be sold, it holds a *restricted ownership* in comparison with a capitalist stock corporation, which holds full ownership of the entity (addendum 2§3).
> • Comparing the highest governing bodies of the two legal entities, the membership of the cooperative council derives from a successful application for a vacancy – the membership not being bound to refundable or non-refundable dues. *Members do not own the cooperative*, instead members collectively are the usufructuaries of the cooperative (2§3.0). The usufruct cannot be alienated, neither collectively nor individually.
> • In a capitalist stock corporation, the general body of shareholders is ultimately the highest body and membership derives from the ownership of shares. *Shareholders own the corporation by owning the shares*. Individually owned shares can be alienated. The majority of shareholders can also decide to sell the corporation (Design cooperative councils cannot decide to sell the cooperative).
> • Whereas the relation between the stock corporation and the labour employed is – within the constraints of the labour contract – an author-

itarian one, the relation between the cooperative and the workers is a democratic one.

2§5.1. (Much of this subsection anticipates what is introduced later.) The elected management deliberates with the council about the general policies of the cooperative, as including the techniques used (the specific inputs mix); the internal division of labour; the planning of investments and the required additional workers in face of expected sales.

In any case, that is legally, the council has to approve of, at least:

(a) The internal statute of the cooperative and changes thereof (the internal statute sets rules beyond legal rules) – this statute includes rules for the building up of 'uncommitted' reserves beyond the legally required reserves (on these reserves see 2§7, 2§9.0 and 2§9.1);
(b) The annual Income account and Balance sheet of the cooperative (see 2§11.0);
(c) The structure of the individual wages and dividend levels (see 2§8.0 and 2§9.0);
(d) Increases in investments or the workforce, each beyond 5% of the past 5 years' average;
(e) Measures regarding foreseen decreases in the cooperative's 'uncommitted' reserves (see 2§9.0) – beyond those due to foreseen retirement or movements (2§13.0);
(f) In case this is opportune or required: a 'restructuring plan' for the cooperative (see 2§14.2).

Any further required approvals are stated in the cooperative's statute.

2§5.2. For large cooperatives the council mentioned so far is called the 'cooperative council'. The latter council can decide to also institute 'departmental councils'. The latter elect the removable departmental management and deliberate over matters that it deems opportune for the operation of the department. In case the cooperative council is so large that most members can merely vote instead of argue, it deliberates over the matters mentioned under 2§5.1 and appoints one or more spokespersons for the cooperative council meetings (which does not interfere with the right of each individual to nevertheless speak at the cooperative council).

2§5.3. The management of the cooperative (and in case its departments) is chosen from the rank and file of the cooperative's workers. It is up to the cooperative council (and in case the departmental council) to decide on who is eligible to be elected as a manager, and if, and how much, managing should be a rotating function. In case of an end of term or in case of removal, the former manager resumes her or his earlier position. (The reason for election from the rank and file of the cooperative's workers is to evade managers of cooperatives to become a separate caste.)

SCHEME 2.2 *The cooperative and its council's rights and main authority*

As a general aside it is mentioned here that within the Design there is no room for 'user cooperatives' (including consumer cooperatives). The reason is that such cooperatives would inevitably restrict the governing competences of the worker councils. (On these user cooperatives and other types of cooperatives as existing in capitalism, see ch. 6, 6§2.)

TABLE 2.3 *Summary memo of 2§3–2§5: legal and effective ownership and governance*

	Capitalist stock corporation	Design worker cooperative
legal form unit of production	stock corporation	cooperative (2§3.0)
foundation unit of production	capital owning shareholders	workers (2§4)
highest governance body	general body of shareholders	cooperative council (2§5.0)
alteration governance body	purchase (and selling) shares	successful application (2§3.4)
legal ownership of assets	corporation: full ownership right	cooperative: no alienation right (2§3.0)
final/effective ownership of entity	shareholders: full ownership	workers: collective usufruct (2§3.0)
appointment (top-)management	body of shareholders	council elects from its ranks (2§5.0)

2§6   Credit-debt relation between cooperative banks and other cooperatives

2§6.0. COBs provide credit for investment to PWCs against an interest that consists of a risk premium and a component that on average covers the COB's material costs, the remuneration of its workers, the interest cost charged by the state's Savings and Loans Bank (2§6.3), a component for keeping up the required reserves. The interest and debt are serviced out of the PWCs' 'surplus' (on the surplus see 2§8.0).

Note. Because of a number of anticipations of sections to come, the following subsections might be difficult. In 2§22 the interconnections will be taken together.

2§6.1. The investment loans by COBs are the only way of external finance for the PWCs – notably there is no bonds market.

2§6.2. COBs provide investment loans to PWCs via the ex nihilo creation of new money – similar to the case of capitalist banks.[8] (For an explanation regarding the Design see 2§22.) The balance sheet assets of PWCs – and/or their assets to be purchased – serve as security for the COB loans.

2§6.3. For their investment loans to PWCs, the state's Savings and Loans Bank (ch. 3, 3§16) can provide collateral secured loans to COBs. (The loans from this fund are indispensable for COBs because they cannot rely on other loans – notably there is no bonds market, nor a savings market – see also 2§16.2 and 2§22).[9]

2§6.4. COBs carry out payment transactions for their clients (PWCs, workers of cooperatives and state institutions, pensioners). Apart from that the COBs' single task is to provide investment loans to PWCs. This means that they shall provide no other loans (especially no loans to households and no mortgage loans to PWCs) and that they shall not engage in insurance provision.[10] (See 2§15.1 on mortgage loans to PWCs.)

2§7   Distribution of income prior to taxation: (a) legally required resistance buffer

2§7.0. Cooperatives are required to build up a legally binding resistance buffer, expressed as a percentage of the assets. As an indication it is set at 10% for COBs

---

8   On the latter see Reuten 2019, ch. 2, pp. 103–5 (more extended pp. 103–20).

9   For the loans by the Savings and Loans Bank to COBs, see also Appendix 2A, 'Income account and balance sheet for a cooperative bank'.

10   For capitalist banks credit provision is merely a matter of profit. The often exceptionally high interest rates on consumer credit are one source of that profit (as well as a cause of financial trouble for the less well-off layers of society). Regarding COBs, however, the point is that other forms of credit or other activities should not hamper their credit potential for investment loans.

and at on average 30% for other cooperatives. Prior to having built up this buffer, workers shall receive no more than the minimum wage. As an indication the minimum wage is 1⅔ (167%) of the minimum costs of living. Levels of buffers and of the minimum wage are set by the state's parliament. (The parliament is elected as set out in chapter 3, 3§1 – and as summarised in 1§7.)

2§7.1. The resistance buffer is built up out of the cooperative's surplus. The buffer may be used only when at some point the cooperative would make losses. (In that case the minimum wage rate rule again applies.)

2§7.2. Since wages can only rise when sufficient reserves have been secured and only while cooperatives operate at a surplus, the councils of all cooperatives have a continuous incentive to see to the cooperative's efficiency.

2§8   *Distribution of income prior to taxation: (b) wages and labour-time*
2§8.0. The value-added of cooperatives consists of the wages and of the surplus. (See *Table 2.4*, rows 1–7 for a conceptual outline.) Workers receive a wage, the wage rate scales being annually decided on by their council. Obviously wages are not allowed to be lower than the minimum wage as set by the state's parliament (ch. 3, 3§11).

> *Addendum 2§8. Likely moderate wage differences compared with capitalism.* The wage rate of workers being decided on by the council of a cooperative, wage rates might differ between workers, especially in case of unpleasant work or in case of an expertise that is (temporarily) scarce. Nevertheless, because of the common decision-making it is not likely for wage differences to be as skewed as under capitalism. It is likely that the cooperative's management makes a wage rate proposal to the council. However, the managers being workers, their voting rights are on a par with all other workers.
>
> In 'worker-*owned* cooperatives' as currently existing within capitalism, the bottom to top salary ratios are far less skewed than in capitalist corporations. (Around 2020 in e.g. the about 100 Mondragon cooperatives the maximum wage differences are 1:9 and in these cooperatives on average they are 1:5 (see 6§6). Although 1:9 is considerable, it regards a constellation surrounded by a capitalist labour market.)

2§8.1. So as to protect workers, a maximum labour-time duration per day, week and year is set by the state's parliament. (Regulation for part-time work is set out in ch. 3, 3§10). The parliament also sets the age at which workers are eligible for a state pension (ch. 3, 3§24).

2§9 *Distribution of income prior to taxation: (c) dividends*

2§9.0. The council of a cooperative decides whether all or part of the end of year disposable surplus is distributed as dividend to the workers. The non-distributed part is added to the 'uncommitted reserves' on top of the required buffer of the cooperative. (See *Table 2.4*, rows 10–13.) No dividends are distributed when the resistance buffer requirement is not met (2§7.0).

TABLE 2.4 *From value-added to disposable surplus and dividends: case of a PWC*

		Example[*]
1	proceeds from sales	1000
2	non-wage current inputs (intermediates' cost)	-425
3	**gross value-added** [= sum rows 1 to 2][†]	575
4	depreciation fixed assets	-50
5	**value-added** (= value-added net of depreciation) [= sum rows 3 to 4][‡]	525
6	wages	-400
7	**surplus** (= operating surplus net of depreciation) [= sum rows 5 to 6]	125
8	net interest paid to bank (COB)	-25
9	amortisation bank loan (COB)	-50
10	surplus destined for building up the legally required resistance buffer[⁑]	-0
11	**disposable surplus** [= sum rows 7 to 10]	50
12	dividends distributed to workers	40
13	disposable surplus-part added to the 'uncommitted reserves'	10

[*] In terms of a non-specified currency.
[†] Macroeconomically this would be GDP.
[‡] Macroeconomically this would be NDP.
[⁑] Relevant for start-ups; established cooperatives will normally have built up this buffer.

2§9.1. Thus for the disposable surplus, workers' councils can alternatively decide for either distribution as dividends or addition to the uncommitted reserves. In order to stimulate the latter, workers hold a claim on the uncommitted reserves (specified in 2§12). It is cautious to keep uncommitted reserves for possible future losses, in face of the rule that when, due to losses, the legally required resistance buffer must be used, workers receive no more than the minimum wage rate (2§7.1).

2§9.2. Given the COB's current costs, its provision on 'bad' loans and its dividends, any of its remaining 'disposable surplus' is a result of its level of interest policy. (See the Income account and balance sheet for a COB in Appendix 2A, Sheets 2A.2).

2§9.3. COBs are prudentially supervised by the state's Central Bank (CB). Prudential supervision includes supervision regarding the soundness of credit policies and reserve ratios (ch. 3, 3§13 on the CB).

2§9.4. In case of wage rate differences within cooperatives, their council might nevertheless decide that any distribution of dividends takes place proportionally to the work-time (FTE or in case part thereof) instead of proportionally to the wage rates.

2§10 Intermediate conclusion: jobs preservation, maximisation value-added, and elimination of capital and the accumulation of capital[11]

2§10.0. The implication of the Design's cooperatives' economy above is that councils of cooperatives tend to aim for the preservation of the cooperative's jobs and for a maximisation of the average value-added per worker (wages and surplus).[12] Given that workers invested no funds in the cooperative (2§4.0), and given that they have no direct or indirect ownership in the cooperative (2§3.0), any enhancement of such funds ('valorisation') can play no role.

2§10.1. This aim contrasts with capitalist enterprises. The capitalist enterprises' aim is a continuous enhancement of the equity capital ('valorisation') through the maximisation of profits. By reinvestment of the latter this results in a continuous accumulation of capital. For these enterprises 'wages' are no aim but rather a cost, nor is 'employment' an aim but merely a profit instrument – thus employment and wages are a capitalist valorisation instrument.

2§10.2. Considering the balance sheets of capitalist enterprises and of Design cooperatives from an accounting perspective, the general structure of these may not seem very different.[13] However, this does not mean that these are conceptually the same. The balance sheet assets of capitalist enterprises are a

---

11 About many points presented in this chapter, but especially those mentioned in 2§10 I have greatly benefitted from intensive discussions with Tony Smith. Often we have still, in mutual respect, disagreements or an open-ended dialogue.
12 Empirical studies on 'workers-owned cooperatives' within capitalism show that these cooperatives tend to adjust pay rather than employment in response to demand shocks (Fakhfakh, Pérotin and Gago 2012, pp. 10–11 and Pérotin 2014, p. 40).
13 For an example of the cooperative balance sheet see Appendix 2A.

capital-form expression; more specifically these show a (e.g. end of year) snapshot of the circulation of capital, which itself results from the capital outlay by owners/financiers and the employment of labour. Each of the latter is absent from Design cooperatives, notwithstanding that the cooperatives' assets are valued in monetary terms. Whereas for capitalist enterprises the assets and the employment of labour are an instrument for the profit part of value-added, the cooperative's assets are an instrument for the value-added per worker.

At the balance sheet's liability side, the cooperatives' reserves might be considered as a counterpart of the capitalist enterprises' equity capital, but again this does not mean that these are conceptually the same. As against equity capital, the reserves of cooperatives are no aim, but an instrument for job preservation.

2§10.3. Sections 2§10.0 to 2§10.2 imply that in the Design's economy the capitalist economic categories of 'capital' and of the 'accumulation of capital' are eliminated – these are eliminated along with the exploitation of labour.

2§10.4. Individual capitalists can be the shareholders in a stock corporation, or the owner(s) of a firm. The former's success measure is the value of the shares together with the rate of return (dividends/individual share capital); for the latter it is the net value of the firm together with the rate of profit on the capital invested. (The 'individual' cooperative worker's success measure is job preservation and individual remuneration – wages and dividends.)

The main conclusions of 2§10 are summarised in Table 2.5.

TABLE 2.5 *Summary memo of 2§10: assets dimension, and aims and instruments of production – comparison capitalist stock corporation and Design cooperative*

	Capitalist stock corporation	Design worker cooperative
dimension assets of legal entity	monetary capital-form	monetary valued (no capital-form)
short-term aim of production	profit[†]	value-added
medium-term aim of production	accumulation of net capital (equity)	work preservation
instrument for aim of production	labour employment and wages (costs)	cooperative assets and reserves
internal finance	capital shareholders	no funds of workers (2§4.0)[‡]
in sum	dominance of capital	dominance of labour; elimination of capital category

[†] Value-added is no aim, merely its profit part.
[‡] Nevertheless the minimum wage related to the legally binding resistance buffer (2§7.0) might be considered as a remote form of internal finance. This buffer cannot be alienated by individual workers, whereas capital shares can.

2§11 Recordkeeping

2§11.0. Cooperatives register their incomes and expenditures in regular bookkeeping, and at the end of the year they shall record an 'Income account' and a 'Balance sheet' of their assets, liabilities and reserves.[14] (See Appendix 2A on the arrangement of the two end of year records.) Each of the latter two shall be approved by an external registered auditor and by the cooperative's council (see 2§5.1 on decisions by the council, and 2§18 on external registered auditors).[15]

2§11.1. An auditor-approved reduced version of the end of year statements (as in Appendix 2A) is sent to the 'General statistical office' (ch. 3, 3§33-B), which serves to determine the average remuneration of public sector workers (see ch. 3). The same reduced version is sent to the ministry of general cooperatives' matters (ch. 3), which checks on the legal resistance buffer and the concomitant remunerations (2§7).

2§12 Change of workforce: (a) additional workers

2§12.0. When a cooperative expands, new workers are allotted a dated share in the uncommitted reserves (2§9.0), with an initial value of zero, that may grow over time.

2§12.1. To keep matters simple, the value of the new workers' dated share (or that of current workers that want to extend or reduce their work-time) is calculated from the year following on the appointment mutation.

2§12.2. Some years after the start-up of a cooperative, it will normally meet the requirement of the legally binding resistance buffer; during this period the workers received no more than the minimum wage (2§7.0). The current workers of a cooperative might consider it unfair if additional workers benefit from the buffer for which the current workers forewent wage increments. In order to prevent cooperatives potentially having to compete on this point, the general rule is that all additional workers start for a period of five years at the minimum wage. (However, if – facing the buffer per current worker – this would mean that new workers over-sacrifice, then the period might be shorter than five years.)

---

14 The 'income account' states the sums of the *flow* of the costs and wages and of the surplus and its allocation. The 'balance sheet' states the *stock* of the assets, liabilities and specified reserves.

15 An auditor is a specialised accountant authorised to examine/verify accounts and accounting records of an institution.

2§13 Change of workforce: (b) retirement or movements

2§13.0. When workers retire (or want to work in another institution) they may receive their dated share in the then existing uncommitted reserves (2§12.0), that is formally paid out as 'postponed dividends'.

2§13.1. This rule (2§13.0) should prevent workers' councils skimping on the formation of uncommitted reserves. Nevertheless it may be the case that at the point of a worker's retirement or movement, the level of the uncommitted reserves was affected by earlier losses.

2§14 Expansion and contraction of cooperatives

• *Expansion*

2§14.0. In order to prevent cooperatives reaching a dominant market power, their allowed expansion is restricted. Expansion limits depend on the size of a country and on the relevant market. (As an indication, in a 'large' country cooperative banks might not be allowed to expand beyond a nationwide market share of 1%. Specific limits for other cooperatives depend on their relevant market – nationwide, regional or local – see further ch. 3, 3§45.)

2§14.1. In face of their expansion, cooperatives can move to a new location (cf. 2§3.3 on 'location'); the old one is then closed, and may be occupied by another moving cooperative, or a newly established one. (All real estate transactions operate via the 'real estate agency of the state' – ch. 3, 3§37.)

• *Contraction*

2§14.2. The core rule that cooperatives are not allowed to be sold in total or in parts (2§3.1) implies that, generally, the selling of assets requires a purchase of assets for at least the same total value. In face of this rule any *contraction* of a cooperative is complicated (that is, in case, contrary to the intention of 2§3.1, any cooperative would try to cash the value of some assets to the benefit of the current workers).[16] This is solved by the following two rules.

• First, in case the selling of assets goes along with less than an equivalent purchase of assets, the revenue must be added to a special 'temporary committed reserves fund' (shown on the end of year Income account and Balance sheet). In some following year this fund can be drawn on *either* for the purchase of additional assets (that thus makes the initial less than equivalent purchase fully or partially undone), *or* for permanent extra jobs.[17] During the time of such mutations two, instead of one, registered external auditors (each of different auditing cooperatives) have to sign for the end of year statements (cf. 2§11.0).

---

16 This contraction referred to might be a contraction of production but also a contraction of the value of the assets because the prices of replacement investments have declined.

17 Then, in effect, (part of) the initial change in the value of assets $\Delta A = (\Delta L)w$.

In case a renewed investment is not a reasonable option, the cooperative might merge with a promising cooperative start-up in which the former brings in its (extended) 'temporary committed reserves fund'. (For the merged entity the single location rule of 2§3.3 applies.)

• Second, in case a cooperative operates for more than three years at losses such that it has to draw on its legally binding resistance buffer (2§7.1), it may – as part of a detailed restructuring plan – sell assets. In a report two registered external auditors (each of different auditor coops) have to sign for the soundness of the plan and the selling. A 'restructuring plan' requires the approval of the cooperative's council.

For each of these two rules applies that in case the two auditors do not agree between them, the opinion of an added third one is decisive – each three nevertheless has to sign, one in case for disagreeing.[18] Such reports of external auditors are sent to the state's 'cooperative restructuring office' – ch. 3, 3§43 (this checks not on the cooperative but rather on registered auditors).

2§15 *Cooperatives' ownership or renting of self-occupied premises*
The rules below avoid a real estate market that speculatively drives up real estate prices.

2§15.0. Cooperatives may own self-occupied premises. They purchase(d) these from the state's Real Estate Agency that owns all other real estate. Alternatively cooperatives may rent premises from that agency. (Ch. 3, 3§37 on the Real Estate Agency.)

2§15.1. For the purchase of the premises cooperatives may get a mortgage loan from the state's Savings and Loans Bank (ch. 3, 3§16).

2§15.2. Workers and pensioners may rent a self-occupied dwelling from the Real Estate Agency.[19]

2§15.3. In case cooperatives or individuals move location, transactions of self-occupied premises or dwellings operate via the Real Estate Agency.

> *Addendum 2§15. No real estate market.* The Real Estate Agency formulates norms for its sales, purchase and rental prices and sets its prices accordingly (3§37). This together with 2§15 implies that there is no real estate market.

---

18   Once an auditor has taken on the task at hand, s/he is not allowed to resign in case of disagreement between one or two of the other auditors.

19   Dwellings are constructed in accordance with acclaimed urban and landscape designs, and provided in a variety of qualities at reasonable rents. All of the designs, the contracting and the building is carried out by a variety of PWCs (3§37).

2§16   Bank payment accounts and their rate of interest

2§16.0. PWCs hold a bank 'payment account' with the COB that grants them investment loans. Individual workers and pensioners hold a 'payment account' with a COB of their preference.

2§16.1. Bank payment-account holders receive a nationwide *uniform* zero rate of interest – or near to zero depending on a rate of inflation/deflation, as specified by the Central Bank (ch. 3, 3§13).

2§16.2. Payment accounts of workers or pensioners (including workers at the public sector institutions as introduced in Chapter 3) should not exceed twice their monthly income. At least amounts exceeding this shall be put on a fully guaranteed savings account with the state's *Savings and Loans Bank* which normally pays interest (ch. 3, 3§16). Primarily this fund provides collateral secured loans to COBs for the latter's investment loans to PWCs (2§6.3).

2§17   Cooperatives specialised in insurance

2§17.0. Qualified cooperatives, having the form of a PWC, set on insurance, such as regarding damage and damage liability. (Health provisions are free of charge – ch. 3, 3D7-A – and at an eligible age all receive a pension – ch. 3, 3§24.)

2§17.1. Licences are provided by the Central Bank that also undertakes the prudential supervision of these PWCs (ch. 3, 3§13).

> *Addendum 2§17. Exclusively financial markets for investment loans and insurances.* It was indicated that in the Design there are no shares and bonds markets (addendum 2§3.0; 2§6.1; 2§6.3) – in ch. 3 it will be seen that nor is there a state bonds market. Section 2§16 implies that there is no market for savings. This means that there are only financial markets for investment loans (provided by COBs to other cooperatives – 2§6.0) and for insurances (2§17).

2§18   Cooperatives specialised in auditing

2§18.0. Specialised cooperatives, having the form of a PWC, set on auditing and in accounting. Among these a licensed category regards the work of 'external registered auditors' (mentioned in 2§11.0). On the latter see further ch. 3, 3§43.

2§19   Competition between cooperatives

2§19.0. In their market cooperatives compete with other cooperatives. Even with the safety rule of a required resistance buffer and the minimum wage before attainment of the buffer (2§7), competition may ultimately mean that a cooperative goes bankrupt. (It will be seen in ch. 3, 3§18, that jobless allowances apply, and that no one is out of work for more than two months – 'work' includes permanent jobs and paid traineeships, the latter being a lever to permanent jobs.)

2§19.1. The implication is indeed that cooperatives' workers face a risk. However, given the issues that a workers' council must approve of (2§5.1), any decreases in the uncommitted and the committed reserves of a cooperative will usually make workers alert before it is too late.

2§19.2. The market dominance of individual cooperatives is limited by, first, the rule that cooperatives shall be organised in no more than one single location (2§3.3), second, the take-over prohibition (2§3.2), third, the rule that cooperatives are not allowed to found other cooperatives (2§4.0), fourth, the rule that cooperatives are not allowed to expand beyond ceilings that in their relevant market would generate market power (2§14.0).

> *Addendum 2§19. Tendency for non-aggressive and non-destructive competitive interaction between cooperatives.* Section 2§10 indicated that the aims of cooperatives are very different from the aims of capitalist enterprises. Cooperatives aim at preservation of jobs and maximisation of the average value-added per worker (VA/L). Capitalist enterprises aim at maximisation of profits over the equity capital (P/EC), where the investment of profits generates enhancement of the equity capital (accumulation of capital); employment is merely a necessary instrument for this process. These differences make that the type of investment decisions, as well as competition processes are utmost dissimilar in the two constellations.
>
> Consider the introduction of a cost price reducing new technique by a cooperative. As in capitalism other units of production in the same branch will usually not immediately follow suit, because they are burdened with the fixed costs of their current means of production. Cooperatives will only scrap the assets that make part of the currently used technique when the new one offers a *net* value-added per worker ('net' that is, taking into account the costs of scrapping) greater than the value-added per worker generated with the current technique on its existing plant.
>
> This means that the cooperative that introduced the new technique has a (temporary) comparative advantage (this is similar for a capitalist and a cooperatives economy).
>
> A capitalist enterprise will often try to use such an advantage for a price competition that squeezes out competitors so as to gain an extra market share. When successful, it can at the increased market share often increase prices to near the previous level. In sum it thus increases its amount of profit, at an increased accumulation of capital.
>
> However, for a cooperative this is not a likely action because with the productivity increase at the current market price, the initiating cooperative will maximise its value-added per worker – which will result in higher wages and/or dividends – leaving the production and jobs of compet-

itors unaffected. In this respect the cooperatives' economic interaction tends to be non-aggressive and non-destructive regarding competitors. Comparatively this tends to result in less technical-change-intermittent joblessness. And to the extent that competitors' physical plants are not scrapped, less dwindling of environmental resources.

Product innovation can, with some adaptation, be analysed similarly.

2§20   *Distribution of wealth prior to taxation*

2§20.0. Given the economic organisation set out above, it is to be expected that the resulting skewedness of the distribution of wealth is very moderate in comparison with the capitalist system.

First, workers are merely the beneficiaries of the cooperatives' distributable income; they do not own the cooperative; they do not own the assets of the cooperative, nor can these assets be alienated (2§3.0); no individual owns the net wealth of a cooperative. (In contradistinction to capitalism's ownership of a firm or of the shares in a corporation.[20] Hence in the cooperatives economy such ownership cannot be inherited by the children or other relatives of rich individuals.)

Second, real estate can also be no source of individual wealth skewedness, because this is owned by a state agency (2§15.0).

Third, workers and pensioners can own material assets and liquidity (only a very moderate amount of these can be inherited – 1§12 and 3§4 Table 3.7). However, as we may expect that the cooperatives' wage rates are far less skewed than under capitalism (addendum 2§8), this also moderates the skewedness of the distribution of these types of wealth in comparison with capitalism. The same applies for dividends, which might even be distributed proportionally per worker (2§9.4).

Division 2. Direct support of cooperatives by state institutions, and the macroeconomic connections between households and cooperatives

After a summing up from Division 1 of the direct support of cooperatives by state institutions (2§21), the macroeconomic connections between households and cooperatives are shown (2§22).

---

20   Regarding the capital that households own in capitalism: for the average of 24 OECD countries in 2019, the top 10% richest households owned 85% of the capital in enterprises – ranging from 63% to 98% for individual countries (Reuten 2023b, §3.5, Graphs 9 and 10).

2§21 The direct support of cooperatives by state institutions

This section sums up the direct support of cooperatives by state institutions as referred to in Division 1. The state institutions themselves will be properly introduced in chapter 3. This direct support regards the following four subjects.

1. Foundation of COBs. It was mentioned in 2§4.1 that the foundation of a COB – after the drawing up of a 'cooperative bank plan' by workers – can be assisted by the state's *Guardian Bank*. (On the latter see ch. 3, 3§14; on the foundation see Appendix 2B.)

2. Foundation of PWCs. For the foundation of a PWC it was mentioned in 2§4.2 that – similarly after the drawing up of a 'cooperative plan' by workers – a COB may grant investment loans to the cooperative in formation. It was also indicated that, should no COB be willing to grant credit on basis of the plan, the initiators can apply with the state's *Investment-credit Guarantee Fund* for the early security of the cooperative (on this fund see ch. 3, 3§15).

3. COBs investment loans to PWCs. In 2§6.3 it was indicated that for their investment loans to PWCs, the COBs can be supported by the state's *Savings and Loans Bank* (SLB) – the latter providing collateral secured loans to COBs (on this fund see ch. 3, 3§16). The reason for such support in the Design is that with the absence of bonds markets, it would otherwise – and with reasonable interests on loans to PWCs – be almost impossible to meet the COBs resistance buffer requirement (2§7).[21] (As will be seen in 3§16 the SLB might, if required, by differentiating the interest rate that it charges, influence investments generally, or encourage certain kinds of investments.)

4. Premises of cooperatives. Cooperatives may either own self-occupied premises, or they may rent their premises from the state's *Real Estate Agency* (2§15.0). (On this agency see ch. 3, 3§37 – rents shall be costs covering and further reasonable in face of their location.) For the purchase of the premises cooperatives may get a mortgage loan from the *Savings and Loans Bank* (2§15.1).

Points 2 and 4 above imply that there is substantial support for start-up PWCs (as including very small ones, also perhaps by a couple of recent graduates in technology fields).

2§22 Macroeconomic monetary connections between households and cooperatives

Scheme 2.1 (2§1) showed the macroeconomic connections between households and cooperatives in abstraction from savings. In 2§16.2 it was indicated that payment accounts of workers (and pensioners) with COBs should not

---

21   For the loans by the fund to COBs, see also Appendix 2A, 'Income account and balance sheet for a cooperative bank'.

THE ECONOMY OF THE DESIGN'S WORKER COOPERATIVES SOCIETY 43

exceed twice their monthly income and that at least amounts exceeding this shall be put on a fully guaranteed savings account with the state's *Savings and Loans Bank*. The previous section indicated under point 3 that the same bank provides loans to COBs, and under point 4 that the SLB provides mortgage loans to cooperatives.

On this basis *Scheme 2.6* shows the full macroeconomic monetary connections between households and cooperatives (now including savings), for which the interconnection with the 'Savings and Loans Bank' must be included.

SCHEME 2.6 *Macroeconomic monetary connections between households and cooperatives, and the interconnection with the state's 'Savings and Loans Bank' (all in terms of annual 'flows')*

interest flows are dotted

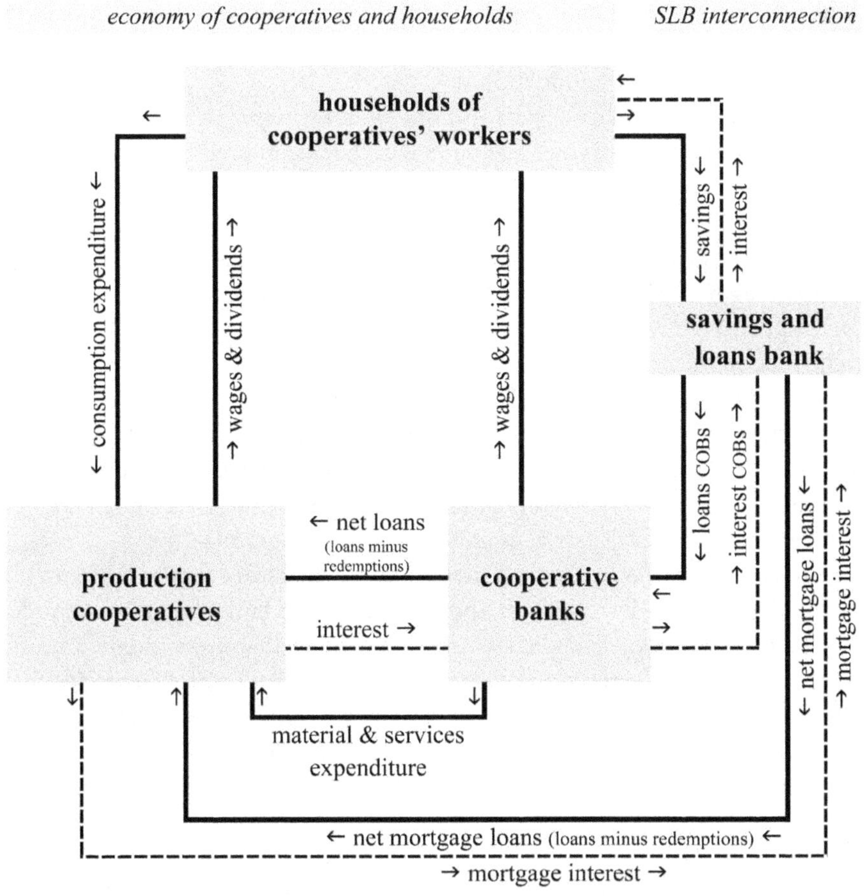

Elucidation Scheme 2.6. (1) 'Net loans' (stream from COBs to PWCs) is the flow of loans minus the flow of redeemed loans. (2) Similarly, the 'net mortgage loans' (stream from SLB to PWCs) is the flow of these loans minus the flow of redeemed mortgage loans. (3) In principle the 'loans COBs' (stream from SLB to COBs) keeps pace with the 'net loans' (stream from COBs to PWCs); the scheme shows the annual flow of these loans.

Note on economic growth and money creation by banks. In a monetary economy, any economic growth must start with money creation by banks. In the previous division it was mentioned that COBs provide investment loans to PWCs via the ex nihilo creation of new money (2§6.2). Such a money-creating loan pre-finances PWCs and anticipates their future production. It is a pre-finance, because after the additional production the debt is serviced out of the PWCs' surplus (together with interest for it). The additional production generates additional income, expenditure and saving. *This saving may, in total or in part, substitute for the bank's pre-finance of the investment.* Thus this is a *substitution 'ex-post'* the additional production.

In capitalism this ex-post substitution out of savings is effectuated via three channels: directly via savings accounts with banks; indirectly via the issue of new bonds or new shares. In the Design the latter two are eliminated, and all savings are collected by the 'Savings and Loans Bank' (SLB). It is thus the latter that ex-post substitutes for the ex-ante COB-finance of production.

Scheme 2.6 is a simultaneous picture rather than sequential one, thus it does not explicitly show the ex-ante and ex-post distinction referred to. The stylised sequence would be: (1) net loans by COBs to PWCs through the banks' ex nihilo money creation; (2) purchase of means of production between PWCs; (3) PWCs production and wages payment; (4) consumption expenditure by households; (5) saving by households collected by the SLB; (6) finally, SLB loans to COBs. Phase (6) then substitutes ex-post for phase (1), either in total or in part. For any remaining part the PWCs remain in debt with the COBs.

Such a sequence is opposite to that of the neoclassical economics' 'loanable funds theory'. One key point of the notions above is that macroeconomically savings do not precede investments, but rather that investments precede savings. This is a Keynesian notion, but in terms of a macroeconomics that includes the by commercial banks ex nihilo creation of money and finance of enterprises, it has been highlighted in the theory of the Monetary Circuit that evolved from about 1980 in France and Italy.[22] Similar ideas have now filtered

---

22   See for example Graziani 1989, 2003 and Bellofiore 1989, 2005, and the introductions and

through circles of bankers. As in a 2015 paper by members of the research departments of the IMF and the Bank of England, Jakab and Kumhof, called 'Banks are not intermediaries of Loanable Funds – and why this matters', its key sentence being: 'Saving does not finance investment, financing does'.[23]

Division 3. The cooperatives economy's markets; and reasons for the book's not taking the 'socialism' road

The General Introduction mentioned that this book presents a form of society beyond capitalism and socialism. So far, I occasionally compared the Design with key aspects of capitalism – especially in some addenda. Until now I have been silent about a would-be socialism that at least combines (and in the ideal case unites) economic and political democracy – 'would-be' because, inasmuch as the Design, it is not, nor has been, actual in my view. In three brief sections I will say something about socialism, but the previous sentence implies that I will have to relate to a shade or angel. More directly I will give reasons for the road not taken in this book.

The first section of this division expands on some relevant implications of the previous division (2§23). After a brief note on collective ownership (2§24), the third section sets out some aims for an outline of socialism (2§25). The final section posits, by way of questions, seven problems that a socialist central planning would have to solve (3§24).

2§23 *The Design's markets and commodification of products*
Early on in Division 1 it was mentioned that 'households and cooperatives, and cooperatives mutually, are interconnected via markets' (2§2.1). The General Introduction mentioned about the Design that individuals have free choice of particular consumption and free choice of occupation, similar as in capitalism.

The Design's economy is for consumers hardly different from capitalist consumer markets, also in that the free choice of particular consumption is limited by income constraints. (Hardly different: in ch. 3, 3§8, it will be seen that cooperatives are not allowed to advertise.) For cooperatives the functioning of markets for means of production (investment goods and intermediate deliveries) and for consumer goods output will equally be similar. To put it straight:

---

contributions in Deleplace and Nell (eds) (1996), Rochon and Rossi (eds) (2003), Fontana and Realfonzo (eds) (2005), Arestis and Sayer (eds) (2006). More references are in the former and Reuten 2019, p. 149.

23   Jakab and Kumhof 2015, p. ii.

the Design will still have commodification of products – I deplore this, but I see no better feasible alternative (see the next sections).

For labour the organisation of production is radically different in comparison with capitalism (2D1). Nevertheless, the free choice of occupation will be as much limited as in capitalism, that is, by the specific labour qualification requirements of cooperatives. A plumber or a medical doctor may not find work in her/his profession if the demand is deficient. Then, s/he still would have to work, though in another profession. In the Design there is as much an enforcement to work as there is in capitalism. (And whatever socialism would exactly look like, there too those who can work will be enforced to work.) This means that the Design does not get beyond the hiring of one's labour capacity. In fact Design cooperative workers are (within an age bound) enforced to become members of an association of workers (2§3.0), and the meaning of a Design 'labour market' is the constellation of a supply and demand for such memberships. However, this does not mean that labour capacity is a commodity as it is in capitalism. Instead, once a worker is a member of an association of workers, they have like all other workers – and within the constraints set by parliament – full say over the product of the cooperative; thus it works for its self-governed collective – not for alien owners of capital as in capitalism. In this sense labour is far from being commodified in the Design.

Cooperatives are superior to capitalist enterprises in that cooperatives will tend to preserve their members' jobs better.[24] Nevertheless, there will still be school-leavers or people temporarily out of work for other reasons. These will have to apply with a cooperative (or with a state institution or a state-financed workers' council governed foundation – ch. 3). Sometimes successful, sometimes not. That regards the quantity aspect of a labour market.

However, the Design has no full-fledged labour market (with quantity *and* price adaptation), because in the Design one potential worker cannot undercut another: the wage is the cooperative's wage, and wage scales are annually fixed. An important side of the quantity aspect is that – as will be seen in ch. 3, division 5 – in the Design no one is out of work for longer than two months – where 'work' includes permanent jobs and paid traineeships, the latter being a lever to permanent jobs.

On markets, finally, recall that in the Design there are only two financial markets, a market for investment loans and a market for insurances (addendum 2§17). On the demand side of the former, non-banking cooperatives (PWCs)

---

24   This is also the experience for worker-*owned* cooperatives existing within capitalism (Pérotin 2012, p. 38).

call for investment loans, and cooperative banks (COBs) compete for these – investment loans are their sole business.[25]

2§24 *A note on the ownership of means of production*
In capitalism, the means of production are privately owned, that is, directly or indirectly by members of the capitalist class. In the Design, the economic domain means of production are restrictively owned by cooperatives (the right of alienation is excluded), without workers having any direct or indirect ownership in these (addendum 2§5). In the remainder of this division, I will suppose that in socialism the means of production are collectively owned. This implies that the socialist collective ownership is effectively the same as the cooperatives' restricted ownership, because there is no party to alienate the collective assets to.

2§25 *Aims for a socialist alternative to the Design*
It seems possible to devise a constellation in which individuals' short-term preferences for specific consumer goods can be signalled to a relevant information collecting office. Perhaps 'iffy' medium-term preferences can also be signalled. (That is not inconsistent with the Design, and the information collecting office could make this information public so that cooperatives can use it. It is also not inconsistent with the Design for cooperatives to engage in some form of 'indicative investment planning' (investment schedules that combine forecasts and planning) that in the 1960s and 1970s was practised in France and Japan.[26] This might result in some coordination of investment, but it would not get beyond product markets and the quantity aspect of a labour market – 2§23.)

Quite another matter for a socialist alternative would be to get from a signalling of individuals' short-term preferences (and 'iffy' medium-term preferences), first, to an actual collective planning of investment and production (this is perhaps feasible), and second, to an actual carrying out of such production (this poses big problems, given the interconnection of sectors and branches of production, and given that even medium-sized economies easily encompass a million enterprises).[27] This takes us to projects outlining a future socialism.

---

25   COBs shall not engage in insurance; savings are collected by the state's 'Savings and Loans Bank' (2§16.2); the interest rate on payment accounts is uniform nationwide (2§16.1); households can get no consumer credit (2§6.4), and any mortgage loans to cooperatives are provided only by the 'Savings and Loans Bank' (2§6.4.).
26   On the French variant see, for example, Dalton (1974, pp. 154–60), Bonnaud (1975, pp. 93–110) and Nielsen (2008). On the Japanese variant see, for example, Caves and Uekusa (1976a; 1976b), Trezise and Suzuki (1976) and Nielsen (2008).
27   The currently common (UN 2008) Standard industrial classification of economic activit-

In principle such a project has my sympathy, provided it improves on the Design in meeting at least the following aims. *First*, it would have to overcome especially the hiring of one's labour capacity such that there is a non-enforced allocation of labour capacity that fares better than the Design regarding the free choice of occupation (I consider this the weak point of the Design). *Second*, it should have a solution for the minimisation, if not the overcoming, of joblessness – also in case a unit of production is deficiently productive. (As indicated, in the Design no one is out of work for more than two months.) *Third*, the organisation of the units of production should be at least as democratic as the Design. *Fourth*, the overall remunerations between the economic and state institutions would have to be at least as equitable as in the Design (details about remuneration in state institutions are presented in ch. 3). *Fifth*, the general constellation should be set out in sufficient detail such that its feasibility can be scrutinised.

I would not exclude that such a constellation can be devised; however, at this point I have not seen a non-iffy one that is sufficiently detailed.

2§26 *Central planning as alternative for the cooperatives' local planning*
Democratic central planning of investment and production might be an alternative for the multiple local democratic planning processes in Design cooperatives. Below I sum up seven main questions for an outline of socialism that encompasses central planning. I will suppose that the governing organs of the state are elected at least as democratically as will be set out in ch. 3, 3§1 (cf., briefly, 1§7). I also suppose that the socialist parliament institutes a 'central planning organ' (CPO) that is accountable to parliament. The CPO devises investment, production and production allocation plans, and is responsible for the overall carrying out of these plans. (Planning and implementation inputs from lower-level democratic organs are not excluded even when these complicate the planning and implementation process.). I leave unspecified if, what for, and to what extent markets are adopted for the implementation process – evidently a feasible project would have to specify this.

1. Democratic character of complex central planning. The central planning of investment and production is a highly complicated technical matter (see also the previous footnote). It is difficult to see how and to what extent this can be

---

ies (SIC) distinguishes at the five-digit level 731 branches in which numerous enterprises are active. Most of these are chain-interdependent regarding their intermediate inputs. Planning and actual production would regard the further digits level of individual enterprises (the number being country dependent, e.g. 5.6 million labour employing ones in the USA 2016; in France 2016, 6.3 million that were employing over 250 people; in the Netherlands 2020, a total of 1.7 million – in a population of 17.3 million.).

democratically scrutinised, apart from the posting of some mainline targets. Parliament (if not the people at large) would have to be confident that it has a thorough, at least indirect, influence on it, and that it could adapt the planning. I would think that this is an immense problem. On the other hand, to the extent parliament could and would have a considerable influence, this may pose legitimation problems in case there turn out to be failures of planning or planning implementation.

2. What are the dimensions of the planning process? Any mode of production must be productive such that outputs > inputs. The inputs are various means of production, that during production are worked up by labour, resulting in the output. Because physical entities cannot be added up in a sufficiently detailed way, I take it that also in a feasible socialism there must be a measure of value similar to, if not necessarily the same as, a monetary measure of value.[28] Thence productiveness requires 'value of current outputs' > 'value of current inputs' – the difference between the two being 'value-added', which is the product of current labour. This productiveness is a macroeconomic requirement, and also a continuity requirement at the micro level of units of production. There so seems to be a generalised requirement of 'valorisation' of the current inputs value in the sense of production of value-added.[29]

3. How to take account of the degree of the roundaboutness of production? Inputs are a 'means of production mixture' of various physical duration. An adequate measure for productiveness requires that these durations are taken account of, so that – for the same output – the costs of one possible mixture can be compared with the costs of another possible mixture. In other words, we need a measure for the degree of 'roundaboutness' of the production (whatever this measure is called; historically 'interest' may be too controversial).

4. What is the criterion for labour's share in the value-added? Someway it must be decided what share of the value-added is distributed to its producers. This would be the part that they can use for consumption and perhaps other private purposes. A related question is if this share is uniform for all workers, and if not, what is the criterion for divergences? Preferably this (or these) distribution criterion (or criteria) should be non-discretionary. The other part of value-added, the 'surplus', will be destined for investment assets and for collective provi-

---

28 This also applies for Saros (2014) although he is somewhat messy about the dimension; in any case, he has prices.
29 A socialist mode of production would seem to have valorisation in this sense in common with the Design mode of production. The capitalist valorisation, which is focussed on the valorisation of capital in the form of the production of surplus-value, is a special case of the production of value-added. See Reuten 2019, p. 62 on the terminology.

sions – including allowances for the young and old aged. A surplus destination to investment assets is no social necessity; however, for a constant real income per head, there would have to be investment in case of population growth. (Assuming that investment is environmentally sustainable.)

5. *How does the CPO get the local production units to do what it had in mind?* If the local production units do what they were assigned to do, how is it avoided that this might be experienced as an alien force? (See further point 7.) In case assignments go along with reward and penalty incentives, we might get to a constellation that mimics market-like incentives. In case the local unit voluntarily and full-heartedly aims to meet the production targets, it may be confronted with suppliers of means of production that did not meet the targets – or with planning mistakes. In case the producer is an intermediate one, this permeates through the production chain; in case it produces consumer goods, it has effect at that end. Each boils down to production losses, and in underproduction or a combination of underproduction and overproduction. I do not argue that this will inevitably go wrong, but rather that it might go wrong. On a small scale the latter is not harmful, but it is when on a large scale.

6. *How will consumer goods be allocated in practice?* Given the value-added share that is distributed to workers for consumption purposes (point 4 above), via what allocation mechanism will it get to the households in their preferred qualities and quantities? – the households that at some point could perhaps express their consumption preferences (quite apart from them possibly having changed their mind).

7. *Central planning versus the local planning by units of production.* The final question is if, and to what extent, the democratic central planning would be experienced as an alien imperative by the units of production and their workers. (That is, hypothetically in comparison with the manifold local democratic planning processes such as in Design cooperatives.) This would require a democratic state administration far beyond the best-practices democracy ever seen in capitalist or other systems. This last point should evidently be the first point as it is a precondition for the rest. A related key question is if, and how, that democracy can be combined with a deep democracy at the level of the units of production.[30] 'Deep' would mean that the decisions at the latter level really

---

30 Suvin (2016, p. 300) remarks in reflection on the practice of socialist Yugoslavia (1943–91): '… even the classical means of production (factories, land, etc.) are not really socialised unless they are managed and determined by a genuine self-government of all the working people concerned. This applies to micro-decisions in each enterprise but then, crucially, also to the economic macro-decisions – setting up the rules of accumulation, organisation, taxation, etc., for the economy as a whole.'

matter in their effect, and such that the experience and learning effects of the latter permeate to the state administration's democracy – in the ideal constellation these would have to constitute a unity that is experienced as a unity (the latter should be the continuous aim).[31]

All these are big questions that I will not be able to answer. I guess that the answers and their elaboration require far more space than was devoted to the Design's economy in Division 1 of this chapter. For a related reason the presentation of the Design's state institutions in the next chapter will take considerable space.

Addendum 2§26. Comments on Tony Smith's proposed form of socialist planning

Of the forms of socialist planning that I have seen, the one proposed by Tony Smith (forthcoming; ch. 4, section 'The investment process') makes most sense to me. Rather than proposing a form of planning aiming at a full matrix including every individual input and every individual output, he proposes a socialist adapted *variant of indicative planning*. Smith posits: 'An indicative plan can effectively direct production to a social goal without having to specify the full range of inputs units of production must mobilize in the production process or the full range of outputs they must produce. Socialist planning is indicative planning on a far more comprehensive scale than capitalist developmental states.' It takes the form of 'establishing general priorities for production, investing in units of production that have the most promise of fulfilling those priorities, allowing those units of production to determine for themselves the best way of meeting the priorities set for them, monitoring their performance, and then favouring enterprises that have furthered social priorities effectively over those that did not.' He adds that we cannot assume 'that the actual needs and wants of social agents in the future, or the products that could then address those wants and needs most effectively, will remain what they were at an earlier point in time. Either the freedom of choice of those using the products would have to be suppressed, or the deviations from the plan would quickly become so extensive the plan was left in shambles.' Smith has indicative plan periods that each last for five years. 'There are two main steps in the allocation of investment. Units of pro-

---

31 Without wanting to open a discussion on the precise meaning and feasibility of a 'free association of producers', I cannot resist to remark that for a road to such or a similar association, a departing from Design cooperatives might be more obvious than departing from state ownership of the means of production and central planning.

duction first formulate investment requests and forward them to local Social Investment Centres. These Centres then evaluate the requests and provide investment funds to units of production on the basis of these evaluations.' (There are also Regional Social Investment Centres.)

Smith does not overcome the first point of 2§25 (the hiring of one's labour capacity), even when he never uses the term labour market for his design of socialism. In my view he is insufficiently specific about the second point of 2§25 (solution for the minimisation, if not the overcoming, of joblessness). However, points three to five of 2§25 do apply for Smith's design, which is quite an achievement.

The remainder of this Addendum refers to 2§26.

Point 1 (central planning). As mentioned, Smith's design of socialism has no central planning. Nevertheless, his sophisticated form of indicative planning (carried out at local, regional and national levels, and when relevant also at an international level) is institutionally rather complex, but thoroughly democratic. Once established after a presumably very complex transition, it seems nevertheless feasible.

Point 2 (dimensions of the planning process). Smith's design has accounting costs and accounting prices. Interestingly he has an accounting value of outputs = accounting value of inputs, whence he evades 'valorisation': The socialist 'production collectives' (enterprises) receive a grant-like investment fund which covers material inputs and the accounting income of their workers (on average the accounting incomes for each production collective are equal);[32] these equal the sum of accounting prices of the output. The accounting input costs and accounting output prices are fixed during the five-year plan period. In case a production collective turns out to be inefficient during this period, it may no longer receive investment funds in a next plan period (this implies that joblessness is not excluded – nor is it in my Design). In my view this means in effect that collectives in the same sector adopt sales quantity competition – presumably by trying to offer a higher quality of products than that of their competitors. Smith does not use the term competition.

Point 3 (degree of the roundaboutness of production). I infer from Smith's text that the institutions that provide investment funds take this into account.

Point 4 (labour's share). See point 2.

---

32   As for my Design's workers' councils, Smith's worker collectives of the production entities can democratically decide for income differences between workers.

Point 5 (implementation of the [indicative] plan). In Smith's design, production collectives are free to decide on the implementation of production – given the investment fund that they received. In case of inefficiency the possible 'penalty' is the withholding of investment funds in the next plan period (see point 2).

Point 6 (allocation of consumer goods). For the consumer goods that are not allocated via the fully democratic elected governmental institutions (i.e. the non-collective ones), Smith has in fact consumer goods markets – without him using that term – in which consumers buy products of their preference against per plan period fixed accounting prices. Given the goods offered by production collectives (point 2) consumers will presumably first go for the highest quality goods offered. In case qualities would be rather diverse, this implies in my view – given the fixed prices – that there will be a queuing for the top-quality goods, and that consumers next have to go for their second-best options. (In my view this is rather defective, but once consumers are accustomed to it, it is nevertheless feasible.)

Point 7 (central planning experienced as an alien imperative). This does not apply *at all* for Smith's indicative planning. Prior to an indicative plan period, agents (both consumers and production collectives) have *plenty* of opportunities to express their needs (consumers and material production inputs for production collectives) and to express how they plan to carry out the production (production collectives).

In sum. Smith's variant of indicative planning has some defects (my Design proposed in the current book also has defects), but Smith's form of socialist planning is the best I have seen.

Concluding summary chapter 2

In the Design's cooperatives economy, workers constitute the single economic class. As against capitalism, there is no class of owners of means of production – hence no antagonism between those owners and workers. In contrast with state socialism, the state does not own the economy's means of production – except for rented out agricultural land. Below five main further characteristic of the Design's cooperatives economy are summarised.

1. Democracy at the point of production. Worker cooperatives constitute the units of production – production in the wide sense, as including retail and other services. Core of the Design is the democratic decision-making at the point of production by the workers who carry out the production – the cooperative's workers' council being the highest governing body. The council elects the management from its ranks, and can also remove the management. Democratic decision-making regards: (a) the policies of the cooperative, as including the techniques used (the specific inputs mix), the internal division of labour; (b) the planning of investments and the required additional workers in face of expected sales; (c) the determination of the internal wage scales (in case these are not uniform in face of unpleasant work, or an expertise that is (temporarily) scarce, or for other reasons that the council deems opportune); (d) the allocation of the cooperative's surplus, including the distribution of dividends.

2. Ownership-like characteristics. The cooperative as legal entity holds a restricted ownership of the cooperative's assets – the right to alienation of the cooperative is excluded. This should guarantee that cooperatives are continuous between generations of workers. A cooperative is founded by a group of workers; the foundation requiring no own funds of the workers. Whereas workers collectively are the sole beneficiaries of the cooperative's distributable income – they are the usufructuaries of the cooperative – they have no direct or indirect ownership in the cooperative and its assets; nor is the membership of a cooperative bound to refundable or non-refundable dues. Because workers constitute the single economic class, and given the ownership-like relations just outlined, there is no means of production owning class; by implication no class that exploits the working class (this is one main distinction from capitalism). One similarity between a capitalist 'foundation' and a 'Design worker cooperative' is that these legal entities have no owners. One relevant distinction is that the cooperative has members, whereas a foundation has no members.

3. Tendential aim of cooperatives' councils; elimination of the categories of 'capital' and 'accumulation of capital'. 'Value-added' is the sum of wages and the surplus. Given the Design's interconnections, councils of cooperatives tend to aim for, first, the preservation of the cooperative's jobs and, next, for a maximisation of the average value-added per worker – furthermore, the last can increase by expansion investments and workforce increases. The reserves of cooperatives are no aim, but an instrument for job preservation; the cooperative's assets are an instrument for the value-added per worker. Because, as just mentioned (point 2), workers have no direct or indirect ownership in the cooperative, nor invested funds in the cooperative, any aim of enhancement of such funds ('valorisation') can play no role. These considerations imply that the Design eliminates the capitalist economic categories of 'capital' and of the 'accumulation of capital' (2§10).[33] They also imply that the type of investment decisions by cooperatives are significantly different from those of capitalist enterprises.

Table 2.7 lists the Design's economic characteristics mentioned above (points 1–3), as well as some other ones – each in comparison with a capitalist economy.

TABLE 2.7   *Key distinctions between the capitalist and the Design cooperatives economies*

Production relations	Capitalist economy	Design economy
economic classes	capitalist and labour	labour (single class) (2§1.0)
relation to means of production	property by members capitalist class	usufruct by labour (2§1.0; 2§3.0)
economic class relation	exploitative	not applicable: single class (2§1.0)
organisation units of production	authoritarian	democratic (addendum 2§5)
measure of value†	monetary	monetary (2§2.0)
general form efficient production	value output > value input	value output > value input (2§26 sub 2)
result of efficient production	value-added (VA)	value-added (VA) (2§1.0; 2§8.0)
producer of value-added	labour	labour (2§1.0)
core economic category	capital	labour; category capital eliminated (2§10.3)
aim of production	profit and accumulation of capital	work preservation and VA (2§10.0)
instrument for aim of production	labour employment and wages (costs)	cooperative assets and reserves (2§10.2)
internal finance	capital shareholders or owner(s) firm	no funds or dues of workers (2§3.0; 2§4)‡

---

[33] The aim of capitalist enterprises is to accumulate capital and to maximise the profits as calculated over the equity capital – the profit rate. At a given profit rate, the accumulation of capital also maximises absolute profits. For these enterprises 'wages' are no aim but rather a cost, nor is 'employment' an aim but merely a profit instrument – thus employment and wages are a capitalist valorisation instrument.

TABLE 2.7   *Key distinctions (cont.)*

Ownership and governance	Capitalist stock corporation	Design worker cooperative
legal form unit of production	stock corporation	cooperative (2§3.0)
foundation unit of production	finance-capital-owning shareholders	workers (2§4)
funds required for foundation	finance capital of shareholders	none (2§4)
highest governance body	general body of shareholders	cooperative council (2§5.0)
alteration governance body	purchase (and selling) shares	successful application (2§3.4)
legal ownership of assets	corporation: full ownership right	cooperative: no alienation right (2§3.0)
final/effective ownership of entity	shareholders: full ownership	workers: collective usufruct (2§3.0)
appointment (top-)management	body of shareholders	council elects from its ranks (2§5.0)

† This regards the means of payment for – and the means of circulation of – commodities or other entities.
‡ Nevertheless the minimum wage related to the legally binding resistance buffer might be considered as a form of internal finance. This buffer cannot be alienated by individual workers, whereas capital shares can.

4. Free choice occupation, specific consumption and cooperative's investment. Predicated on the Design's commodity markets for consumer goods, individuals have free choice of specific consumption. Predicated on the quantity aspect of a labour market (2§23), individuals have a free choice of occupation, somewhat akin to a full-fledged capitalist labour market. Predicated on commodity markets for means of production, cooperative councils have a free choice of (specific) investment and techniques – constrained by investment loans from cooperative banks.

5. Market dominance, technical change and competition. In the Design the possible market dominance of individual cooperatives is restricted by four rules: first, they shall be organised in no more than a single location;[34] second, they are not allowed to found other cooperatives; third, they shall not take over other cooperatives; fourth, they shall not expand beyond ceilings that in their relevant market would generate market power (as an indication, for cooperative banks in a 'large' country the ceiling might be nationwide market share

---

34   The primary reason for this rule is that a multitude of locations would dilute the power of the cooperative's council. The rule also affects potential market power.

of 1%).[35] Nevertheless these rules are not incompatible with large-scale production; country dependent a single cooperative might provide jobs to several tens of thousands of workers in a location of several hundred thousand square metres.

These restrictions – together with the aforementioned (under 3) council's aims of preservation of the cooperative's jobs and of a maximisation of the average value-added per worker – mean that technical change has a very different role in comparison with capitalism. Whereas capitalist enterprises tend to use technical change as an instrument to squeeze out competitors, it is for cooperatives primarily an instrument for increasing their per worker value-added, leaving the production and jobs of competitors unaffected. In this respect the cooperatives' economic interaction tends to be non-aggressive and non-destructive regarding competitors. Comparatively this tends to result in less technical-change-intermittent joblessness; and to the extent that competitors' physical plants are not scrapped, less dwindling of environmental resources. (2§19 addendum.)

The restrictions mentioned under (5), together with other restrictions for cooperatives or their councils, are listed in *Table 2.8*.

TABLE 2.8   *Main requirements or restrictions for cooperatives and councils*

	Foundation of cooperatives	
1	cooperatives are founded by workers; cooperatives shall not found cooperatives	2§4.0
2	foundation of cooperatives requires no funds of the workers	2§4.0
	Cooperatives	
3	a founded cooperative shall not be sold; nor shall it convert its juridical status	2§3.0
4	take-overs are prohibited (implied by the previous point)	2§3.2
5	cooperatives are organised in no more than a single location	2§3.3
6	cooperatives pay at least the minimum wage (set by parliament)	2§8.0
7	a maximum labour-time duration per day, week and year applies (parliament sets)	2§8.1

---

35   All nationwide ceilings are indeed dependent on the size of a country. See further ch. 3, 3§45.

TABLE 2.8   *Main requirements or restrictions (cont.)*

Cooperatives

8	cooperatives shall build up a legally binding resistance buffer, expressed as a percentage of the assets – 10% for COBs and on average 30% for other cooperatives; before meeting it, workers are paid no more than the minimum wage[36]†	2§7.0
9	in face of market dominance, the cooperatives' expansion is restricted	2§14.0
10	cooperatives shall register their incomes and expenditures, and annually record an 'Income account' and a 'Balance sheet'	2§11.0

Additional workers

11	positions shall not be denied on ethnic, gender, social, political or religious grounds	2§3.4
12	any probation period for new workers is maximum two years	2§3.4

Cooperative banks, specifically

13	besides servicing payments, COBs uniquely provide investment loans to PWCs†	2§6.4

Councils

14	membership of councils is not bound to refundable or non-refundable dues	2§3.0
15	only the cooperative's workers can be members of its council	2§3.0
16	the council elects the management (removable) from its ranks	2§5.0
17	the council must approve of at least five key issues listed in 2§5.1, including the internal structure of the wages and dividend levels, and increases in investments or in the workforce, each beyond 5% of the past 5 years average	2§5.1

† COB: cooperative bank. PWC: all other cooperatives (production worker cooperatives; including services production).

---

36   On the percentages see further 3§13-l.

THE ECONOMY OF THE DESIGN'S WORKER COOPERATIVES SOCIETY 59

So far, it seems, there is a sensible alternative (TISA) to at least a capitalist economy. However, that is of little worth without a sensible design of state institutions accommodating that economy – and effectively as well as efficiently so, and at least as democratically organised as cooperatives. This is the subject of the next chapter.

∴

Appendices chapter 2. Here follow two appendices. The first regards the Income accounts and the Balance sheets of cooperatives. The second regards the foundation of a cooperative bank.

Appendix 2A. Examples of Income accounts and Balance sheets for cooperatives

This appendix provides examples of the two required end of year statements of cooperatives: the Income account and the Balance sheet (referred to in 2§11.0). Those for production worker cooperatives (PWCs) are taken first, followed by those for cooperative banks (COBs). Note that in all of the income accounts, wages as well as dividends are an expenditure for the cooperative, but not *costs* as each of these are *aims* for the cooperative. (In capitalist enterprises, wages are costs.)

SHEETS 2A.1 *Income account and balance sheet for a production worker cooperative*

Income account pwc			
Expenditure		**Income**	
current material inputs	a	sales revenue	p
current external services inputs	b		
workers' wages	c		
direct expenses (a to c)	d	*gross operating surplus (p-d)*	q
depreciation fixed means of production†	e	*net operating surplus (q-e)*	r
interest to bank (COB)	f		
amortisation bank loan (COB)	g		
total expenses (d to g)	h	*disposable surplus (r-f-g)*	s
workers' current dividends	i	added to reserves (s-i-j)	t
workers' postponed dividends‡	j		
Memorandum items⁂			
number of workers in FTE	k		
average wage and dividend per worker*	l		

† In case of rented premises, rent appears below item g.
‡ See 2§13.0.
⁂ This information serves to determine the average remuneration of public sector workers.
* Regards items c, i and j.

THE ECONOMY OF THE DESIGN'S WORKER COOPERATIVES SOCIETY

Balance sheet pwc			
Assets		Liabilities	
premises		loan from bank (COB)	
fixed equipment			
input stocks			
work in progress			
output stocks			
commercial claims		commercial debts	
bank accounts (COB)			
*Total assets**	A	*Total liabilities*	B
		legally binding buffer (30% A)	
		uncommitted reserves	
		Total reserves	A–B
* in estimated current value		*Liabilities + reserves*	A
Memorandum item			
List of workers' shares in the uncommitted reserves (attached)			

SHEETS 2A.2 *Income account and balance sheet for a cooperative bank (COB)*

Income account cob			
Expenditure		Income	
current material inputs	a	net interest income ⁂	p
current external services inputs	b		
workers' wages	c		
direct expenses (a to c)	d	*gross operating surplus (p-d)*	q
depreciation non-financial fixed assets†	e	*net operating surplus (q-e)*	r
write-down on loans	f		
total expenses and provisions (d to f)	g	*disposable surplus (r-f)*	s
workers' current dividends	h	added to reserves (s-h-i)	t
workers' postponed dividends‡	i		
Memorandum items⁑			
number of workers in FTE	j		
average wage and dividend per worker*	k		

†   In case of rented premises, rent appears below item f.
‡   See 2§13.0.
⁑   This information serves to determine the average remuneration of public sector workers.
*   Regards items c, h and i.
⁂   Interest paid to Savings and Loans Bank, see 3§16-c, and interest received from PWCs (the interest on payment accounts is normally zero).

Blance sheet cob				
Assets			Liabilities	
*Non-financial assets**	A	*Non-financial debts*		D
• premises				
• fixed equipment				
• commercial claims		• commercial debts		
*Financial assets**	B	*Financial debts*		E
• clearing claim on CB†		• clearing debt to CB		
• investment loans: high security		• Loan from SLB⁑		
• investment loans: guaranteed‡		• PWC account holders		
• investment loans: low security		• household account holders		
• other loans to PWCs				
Total assets (A+B)	C	*Total liabilities (D+E)*		F
		legally binding buffer (10% C)		
		uncommitted reserves		
		Total reserves		C–F
* in estimated current value		*Liabilities + reserves*		C
Memorandum item				
List of workers' shares in the uncommitted reserves (attached)				

† Central Bank, see ch. 3, 3§13 f.
‡ Guaranteed by the 'Investment-credit Guarantee Fund', see ch. 3., 3§15b–c.
⁑ Savings and Loans Bank, see 3§16-c.

Because COBs cannot borrow in the form of bonds, and in face of the rule that savings must be stalled with the 'Savings and Loans Bank' (SLB), the loans from the latter (row 7 on the liabilities side) are a substitute for bonds and savings. For these loans the SLB requires an assignment of the collateral that the COB required for the investment loans.

Appendix 2B. Foundation of a cooperative bank

This appendix explains the process of the foundation of a cooperative bank (COB) by some of its (prospective) workers after the latter drew up a 'cooperative bank plan', referred to in 2§4.1. The state's *Guardian Bank* (GB, introduced in ch. 3, 3§14) may assist the foundation. As will be seen, the foundation of a bank is not a big problem; the problem is to get clients (this is similar for the foundation of a capitalist bank). For the success of the bank, it is essential that the founding (prospect) workers have a cooperative plan, the most important part of which is an amount of reasonable commitments by PWCs that they might likely bank with the COB once it is founded.[37] In case this cooperative plan is sound, the GB temporarily provides guarantees for the foundation (it will be seen below that it only in effect provides guarantees). The GB provides these temporarily, that is until the COB has been fully established.

The actual process of founding a COB involves three logical steps that are not fundamentally different from those of founding a capitalist bank.[38] The following two balance sheets show the results of the key bookkeeping acts for the foundation.

(a) *Foundation of a COB in terms of its balance sheet.* In 'bookkeeping act one' the COB provides a money-creating loan to the Guardian Bank. It results in *Sheet 2B.1*.

SHEET 2B.1   *COB founding balance sheet: money-creating loan to the Guardian Bank*

Balance sheet cob: day one 12:00 hrs			
Assets		Liabilities	
Non-financial assets	0	*Non-financial debts*	0
Financial assets		*Financial debts*	
• loan to Guardian Bank	€x	• current account Guardian Bank	€x
		Reserves	0

---

37   Such commitments might be likely in case PWCs are not happy with their current COB, or in case in a town or in (the district of) a region there is no COB as yet.
38   See Reuten 2019, pp. 167–70.

The point here is that by way of the loan of the COB in foundation *to* the Guardian Bank, the GB pays in no funds (at least no net funds).

In bookkeeping act two, the GB pays in from its account the initial reserves of the COB (*Sheet 2B.2*). This reveals the risk that the GB takes. Because in case the banking project is going to fail, it will be in debt with the COB for the amount of the loan €x. Thus the involvement of the GB boils down to the provision of a guarantee. (To keep the presentation simple, I omit any possible mutual interest agreements between the GB and the COB.)

SHEET 2B.2   *COB founding balance sheet: initial reserves of the COB*

Balance sheet cob: day one 12:01 hrs			
Assets		Liabilities	
Non-financial assets	0	*Non-financial debts*	0
Financial assets		*Financial debts*	
• loan to Guardian Bank	€x	• current account Guardian Bank	€0
		Reserves (paid in by Guardian Bank)	€x

Regarding capitalism, Lavoie remarks about a bank's own capital (equivalent to the reserves in Sheet 2B.2): 'The own capital of the bank constitutes a liability to itself. It represents the funds which the firm [the bank] owes to its owners [here the non-owning GB]. In general, the own funds [reserves] play a role similar to deposits that would be in the hands of the owners. ... The own funds [reserves] are an accounting entry, but in contrast to deposits they cannot be drawn on by the owners'.[39]

(*b*) *Period of transition from founding of COB to its full establishment.* At this point (*Sheet 2B.2*) the COB has 100% reserves (the required reserves are 10% of the assets). It now rents its premises and uses some of the reserves to purchase assets. It starts its (further) banking by providing investment loans to PWCs. Given that the COB requires a legally binding reserves buffer of 10% of its assets, *the pace* at which it can provide loans depends on the sum that the GB paid in as reserves (sheet 2B.2).

In the course of time, and out of its disposable surplus, the COB gradually buys in the reserves provided by the GB (€x in balance sheet 2B2); the loans to

---

39   Lavoie 2003, p. 512.

the GB (€x) decrease at the same pace. In this transitional period an (abbreviated) balance sheet might look like *Sheet 2B.3*.

SHEET 2B.3 *COB balance sheet during its transition to full establishment*

Balance sheet cob			
Assets		Liabilities	
*Non-financial assets**	A	*Non-financial debts*	D
• premises (rented in)	€0		
• fixed equipment			
• commercial claims		• commercial debts	
*Financial assets**	B	*Financial debts*	E
• clearing claim on CB†		• clearing debt to CB	
• investment loans to PWCs		• Loan from SLB‡	
• loan to Guardian Bank (GB)	€½x	• account holders	
Total assets (A+B)	C	*Total liabilities* (D+E)	F
		legally binding buffer (10% of C)	
		uncommitted reserves	€0
		reserves paid in by GB	€½x
		Total reserves	C–F
* in estimated current value		*Liabilities + reserves*	C

† Central Bank, see ch. 3., 3§13 f.
‡ Savings and Loans Bank, see 3§16-c.

(c) The COB as fully established. Only when the COB has fully bought in the reserves provided by the GB (yet €½x in *Sheet 2B.3*) is it fully established such that it fully owns its assets. The COB balance sheet would then be as the one shown in Appendix 2A, *Sheets 2A.2*.

This concludes the Appendices of Chapter 2.

CHAPTER 3

Design of the state in a worker cooperatives society: democratic governance of the state and the organisation of state institutions

Introduction

In any stable mode of production, 'the state' (or whatever a similar body is called) must be tailored to meeting the requirements of its particular economy. Thus the two spheres must constitute a unity.

Mature capitalism has succeeded very well in this.[1] The capitalist state applies on the capitalist enterprises' claims of entitlement to the private property of much of the earth; their claims of entitlement to private property in means of production other than for production by the claimant; and their claims of entitlement to employ labour as combined with the appropriation of the surplus-value (profit) produced by that labour. The state as an extraordinary institution *grants* these claims in the form of capitalist legal rights. Because and to the extent that the state grants *these* rights in particular, it is identified as a capitalist state, which constitutes a unity with the capitalist economy. All of that state's actions actualise the coming to fruition of these rights, especially in that this state not only furthers the accumulation of capital, but also seeks the legitimation for the granted rights and the accumulation of capital – as including the resulting skewed distribution of income and wealth that goes along with it.[2]

Its counterpart in the Design's worker cooperatives society is presented in the current chapter. Here the unity lies first of all in the common interest between the economy's cooperatives and the institutions of the state, and between each of their workers. An important Design element is that the per state institution average remuneration of workers is the same as – and derived

---

1 Whereas *generalised* capitalist production started to emerge around 1800 (Great Britain, France), a sophisticated version of the unity dates from 150 years later. (See Bavel 2016 on early forms of capitalist production.)
2 See the systematic exposition of the capitalist system in *The unity of the capitalist economy and state* (Reuten 2019). The exposition of the state in that book covers 225 pages (pp. 295–522.) For a worker cooperatives society, we evidently lack a mature existence as well as empirical data, whence, in my view, it cannot be presented as a proper systematic exposition – I nevertheless do the best I can.

from – the nationwide average remuneration in cooperatives. (We will see that state institutions have workers' councils, and these councils decide on the internal wage scales, just as the councils of cooperatives decide on the internal wage scales.) This means that state institutions and their workers have a direct interest in the flourishing of the cooperatives economy. In line with this, the former have a direct interest in the tailoring of state regulation to the prosperity of cooperatives and their workers. We will encounter this in each of the separate state institutions that are the subject of the divisions of the current chapter.

This chapter is fairly long (about 110 pages; 164 pages including the appendices). In the remainder of this introduction I will not introduce the content of each of its 11 divisions. For a four-page overview of these divisions the reader can turn back to 1D2. The division order is a priority order, but in the end it is their interconnection that matters.

Below I present a brief conceptual taxonomy – focussing on types of regulation and on production – that underlies the chapter's divisions. Division 1 presents the general organisation of the state: its democratic and legislative organs and its further organisation in state institutions. Division 2, 3§6, presents the Judiciary, that has a special status.

Except 3§6, Divisions 2–10 present concrete *regulation in the broad sense*, that is, of legislation and its implementation, the latter by ministries of the government and by 'state agencies'.

Relevant is, first, that parliament and government *legislate* in the form of acts of parliament (an act is identical to a law).[3] Second, those acts might *delegate* 'the authority of *regulation*' to a government ministry or to a state agency, the scope of the regulation being specified in the act. Inasmuch as acts, regulation is binding for all. (The last two sentences are also common for many capitalist states.) Third, acts of parliament might also delegate the authority of *implementation* (the execution and the supervision) of regulation to, usually, a state agency. (Parliament can also withdraw the delegated authority.)

Thus 'regulation' is different from local 'instructions' that a cooperative might impose on its workers or clients, or that a state institution might impose ('in this building do not use elevators on Sundays').

---

3   A term that will not be used is 'the law' (as opposed to 'a law'). Those that use the term 'the law' usually refer to the total of the current paragraph. I sparingly use the term Bill which is the proposal for an Act/Law before it has been accepted by parliament.

The 'regulation broadly' that will be presented in Divisions 2–10 is *produced* by state workers (including members of parliament and of government), and it generates value-added in the form of wages.[4]

The general Design tenet is that any production beyond this (as including also of the material inputs for state institutions, such as the construction of buildings, computers and roads, but also of services such as auditing) is carried out by Worker cooperatives (ch. 2). This is a key rule for understanding the general line of the chapter. However, it is a general rule with two main exceptions; the reasons for the exceptions will be set out in the relevant division.

In Division 7 (on the health, education and culture sectors) and in Division 9 (mainly its section on railway transport) we will see that there is also production *beyond* 'regulation broadly' that is carried out by so-called 'Workers' council governed foundations'. The workers staffing these foundations (such as medical and educational workers) are not state workers and these foundations are not part of the state sector, but rather of the public sector at large (nevertheless these workers are remunerated similarly as state workers – derived from the cooperatives' remuneration). It should be mentioned that this is not a minor detail. The workforce of these foundations is estimated at about 21% of the total workforce of the society. (This is far more than the workforce share of about 6.5% for the state sector – the latter including municipalities and provinces.)

The taxonomy above is summarised in *Table 3.1*.

TABLE 3.1 *Types of production in the state sector and in a specific public sector institution*

	Institution	Production of[†]	Division
1	parliament and government	legislation	3D1
2	judiciary	trials and judgements	3D2: 3§6
3	ministries and state agencies	regulation broadly; together with its implementation and maintenance	3D2: 3§5 3D3–3D10
4	workers' council governed foundations	specific public services (mainly health and education)	3D7; 3D9

† For the institution below, all material production inputs are produced by worker cooperatives (ch. 2).

---

4 The latter is not different from how it is accounted for in the *System of National Accounts* (UN 2009).

The production by 'workers' council governed foundations' is a separate category of production (non-regulative), but it is nevertheless part of the state's total expenditure, to the extent that the foundations' services are provided free of charge – notably health and education. (See also Scheme 1.3 in chapter 1.) Formally these foundations are part of the public sector. Provinces and Municipalities are state institutions that are treated in chapter 4. However, some of the specific regulation in the current chapter will regard 'state institutions' in general, thus including municipalities and provinces.

Table 3.2 list the Design's legal entities that were covered in chapter 2, together with those that will be covered in the current chapter

TABLE 3.2   *The Design's economic and public sector legal entities*

	Economic and public sector legal entities		1	2	3	4
1	cooperatives†	ch. 2				
2	single person enterprises	2§2.2				
3	workers' council governed foundations	3§25				
4	state (parliament and government)	3§1				
5	judiciary	3§6	state institutions	general state*	public sector	Design society
6	ministries	3§2				
7	*state agencies*	3§2				
8	provinces	ch. 4				
9	municipalities	ch. 4				

†   Banking as well as non-banking cooperatives.
*   In the column numbered (2) the term 'general state' is used. In statistics this term is contrasted with the 'central state', which is the sum of my rows 4–7.

In Table 3.2 note the distinction between 'state institutions' (the column numbered 1) and its subcategory 'state agencies' (row 7). When in this chapter I use the term 'state' without further specification, I refer to 'the state as legal entity' as governed by parliament and government (row 4).

The Design's size of the state sector, as measured by its *workforce* as a percentage of the total workforce of society, is estimated to be smaller, rather than larger, than the average of mature capitalist countries (2020). In terms of *state expenditure*, however, there are four expenditure categories that make a difference. In quantitative order: first, the free of charge health services for all; second, the pensions for all; third, the free of charge education for all; and fourth, the child allowances for all relevant. (Quantifications will be provided in the relevant sections later on.) Apart from pensions (part of these if we calculate insurance premiums for those that can afford these in capitalism), the counterpart is that households have fewer expenditures. But even including all these different state expenditures, their total is not much above the average of mature capitalist countries. This is amplified on in Appendix 3A.

In this context it is to be mentioned that the Design includes not only 'hard budget constraints', but also workforce constraints for all state institutions as well as for the 'workers' council governed foundations' (3§2).

Regarding the style of this chapter, it is recalled from the General Introduction that in face of a transition this text (and others of Part One) has the character of points that are preliminary to transitional legislation, and that can fairly easily be put into the legislative format as is customary in specific countries. In other words, the text has the character of a series of brief 'explanatory memorandums' that in many countries accompany legislative texts.

A reading guide. The chapter encompasses 11 divisions (as mentioned), with in total 47 sections. The extended list of contents at the end of the book enumerates these. Depending on the size of a division these start with an introduction of between 50 and 270 words, which most often also highlights key items. This should facilitate the reader's choice of reading a division thoroughly or skimming or skipping it. Most often the latter can be done without losing the thread (especially because there are many references to earlier sections which should facilitate looking up something). However, Division 1 (about 15 pages) provides key information for all of the following divisions. Difficult to skip would also be 3§16 on the Savings and Loans Bank, which is one of the most prominent economic policy institutions, that is often referred to (just over one page). Nevertheless, for a general gist of the chapter, the reader might also immediately turn to its seven-page summary.

Terminology of state workers and civil (service) workers. State workers are all persons that work for/at the state and the central state institutions (that is, state institution except provinces and municipalities). These include, first, elected workers (members of parliament and members of the government) and, second, appointed workers which are called 'civil service workers' or in brief 'civil workers'. Judges are state workers with a special status which is reflected in their appointment procedure.

Note on the fractional precision of estimates. The source and procedure regarding my quantitative estimates in this chapter (expenditure in % of GDP; workforce in % of total workforce) is provided in Appendix 3A. In the main text the estimates are often rounded off to whole numbers, and sometimes to one fractional decimal. Estimates are indeed estimates and not facts, even if these are based on current facts. When it is stated, for example, that the workforce of the public sector is estimated at 27.5% of the total workforce, whence that of cooperatives at 72.5% of the total, I might as well have indicated margins (25–30%, and 70–75%). This would become awkward when we consider the disaggregates of such numbers, for example for the branches of the health sector or the education sector. When stating these in whole numbers, these would often not exactly add up to the aggregate, which might be confusing for the reader, whence for details of sectors and its branches, I often state these in one or two decimal fractions. However, this does not take away that all these are rough estimates, and the reader should take them as such.

Division 1. The state's democratic organs and the general organisation of state institutions

This division presents the democratic organisation of the state. Its first section (3§1) sets out the democratic organs and how these are elected, as well as their tasks and powers. The state is internally organised in state institutions, as including ministries and state agencies. (State agencies constitute the main subcategory of state institutions; divisions 2–10 expand in detail on these.) The second section (3§2) presents the general organisation of state institutions, as including their budget and amount of workforce (3§3). State institutions are again internally organised via workers' councils. The latter are outlined in the next section (3§4) that also sets out the remuneration of these state workers. A final section (3§5) introduces the finance of the state and state institutions.

It will be seen: *first*, that the elected parliament has supreme powers over the government (there is no separate president with independent or delegated political powers); *second*, that rules prevent monetary means, including gifts, to play a role in the candidacy of parliamentarians; *third*, that there are hard budgetary and amount of workforce constraints for all state institutions; *fourth*, that all state institutions are internally organised via workers' councils; and *fifth*, that the remuneration of state workers (including parliamentarians and members of government) is, per state institution, on average equal to the nationwide average remuneration in cooperatives, the state's workers' councils deciding on the internal wage scales.

All this would in principle not be incompatible with a (reorganised) capitalist state or with a future socialist state.

3§1 *The democratic organs of the state*
The state is a juridical entity that is organised as set out in this section.
• *Democratic organs of the state*
(a) *Parliament highest governing body.* The parliament is the highest governing organ of the nation. It has to approve of all legislation, as well as of decrees. There are no exceptions to this power of parliament (as in some capitalist nations, especially those with a presidential system).[5,6]
(b) *Election of parliament.* Once every four years the eligible voters of the nation elect the parliament. It is elected on a proportional basis, without an electoral threshold. Apart from the very principle of proportionality, this has the advantage that minorities can be represented in parliament.[7] (The government cannot dissolve parliament; however, parliament itself might do so with a two-thirds majority, upon which new elections are held.)
(c) *Election of government.* The parliament elects a government that is accountable to the parliament and that is removable by the parliament's majority.[8] The government consists of ministers, each heading a ministry; minsters may, but need not, be elected from the parliamentary ranks. When one is, s/he resigns as parliamentarian. Initially a government is elected in toto.[9]

---

5   It might be argued that in case a president is democratically elected, there is no harm in her/his having absolute power over, for example, the military or foreign policy matters. First, however, it is not wise to grant one person absolute power in one or several fields. Second, a president is rarely elected for merely these powers – they are mostly a by-product of her/his being elected for other reasons.
6   In case of a (defined) high urgency the government may issue a decree that is legally binding for no more than 15 days; within this period the decree is either repealed or parliament approves of the (amended) decree for a limited period – see further Appendix 3C (Constitution) Division 2, article 14.
7   This implies that if a parliament has e.g. 150 seats, a seat is determined by 0.67% of the voters. Proportionality not only has the advantage that it reflects voters rather than the contingent composition of voting districts. The representation of minorities is good in itself; however, when minorities grow, it potentially also increases the political dynamism.
8   Together with the previous point's proportionality, this implies that governments are most often coalition governments.
9   The procedure for the election of the government is as follows. First, parliament elects a candidate prime minister. Second, the latter constitutes a team of candidate ministers, which is proposed to parliament as the new government during parliament's term, which is also

(d) *Candidates for parliamentary elections.* As an aside to its other political party work, each political party constitutes an 'association of electors' that has regional branches. Its main function is to draw up a list of candidates for parliamentary elections. An eligible voter of the nation may become a member of *one* such association without any discrimination and without membership fee;[10] the membership is continuous until the member resigns. The branches delegate members to the association's *electoral college*, which draws up the association's list of candidates. (Each association of electors is free to determine if and how their candidate parliamentarians reflect the country's regions, and/or other nation characteristics and/or or other qualities.)[11]

The per party lists of candidates are assembled on a single list, from which voters sub (b) vote.

(e) *Rules for (candidate) parliamentarians, ministers and political parties.* Parliamentarians shall act, speak and vote independently and shall not be bound by any mandate or instruction. Parliamentarians, candidate parliamentarians, ministers, associations of electors and political parties are not allowed to accept gifts. Political parties can raise an annual membership fee of no more than 0.5% of the statutory annual minimum wage. None of those mentioned in the previous two sentences is allowed to raise money via the organisation of any sort of event or in any other way. Nor are they allowed to promise to anybody any office or the promotion of it, or to promote the award of public contracts to a specific cooperative; or to create the semblance of these. Nor shall they in any way abuse their power, or create the semblance of it. Appendix 3D treats the judicial proceeding in case of breaking these rules.

(f) *President of parliament and ceremonial president.* Members of parliament elect from their ranks a President of Parliament. One year after taking office they elect, external to their ranks, the nation's ceremonial president, who has no political powers. The latter extends office until one year after the next election, and is re-electable.

---

the (prospective) government's term. Third, in case each candidate has the confidence of the parliamentary majority, parliament votes on the proposed new government. When during its term a minister no longer has the confidence of parliament, a motion of no-confidence is directed at the relevant minister whence s/he has to resign.

10   Political parties receive a compensation for the costs of the elections.
11   It might be argued that representation on basis of ethnicity, gender, religion or region etc. are all forms of de-politicisation that should be avoided. Moreover, such criteria might lead to proportional candidacies at nauseam. However, because positive discrimination is sometimes of importance, the matter is left with political parties – where it belongs anyway.

(g) *Rights of parliamentarians and ministers on office termination.* Cooperatives or other institutions shall not prevent in any way parliamentarians or ministers from taking on their function or the candidacy for it. After the termination of their office, parliamentarians and ministers have the right to a paid sabbatical of five months, and immediately after this period they have the right to return to their previous position in a cooperative or other institution (see Appendix 3F about the compensation regarding cooperatives or other institutions).[12]

Scheme 3.3 summarises the above points (a)–(d) and (f).

SCHEME 3.3 *Democratic organs of the state and their election*

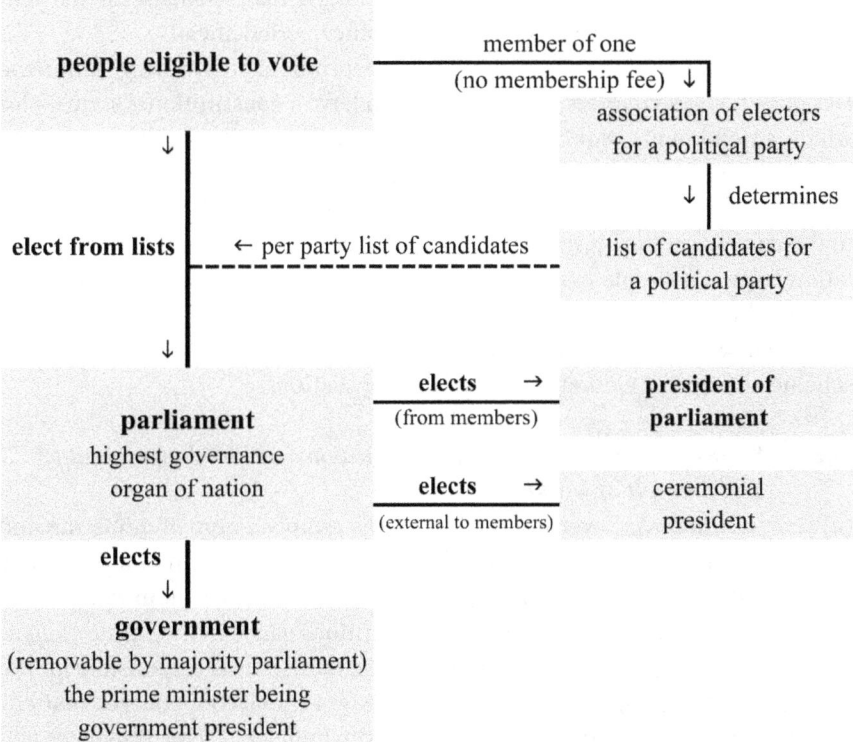

• *Main task and powers of parliament and government*
(h) *Parliament sets agenda.* Parliament sets the agenda for its relations with the government. On request of parliament, government members as well as

---

12 The same applies for the assistants of parliamentarians that come and go with their being in office, though with a sabbatical of two months only.

directors-general and secretaries-general of ministries and state agencies (see 3§3c–d) have to appear in parliament for briefings or interrogation. They shall provide parliament, orally or in writing, with any information requested by one or more members. The information shall be complete in the sense that no information is withheld that might be expected to be relevant.[13]

(i) *Proposals of laws and budget.* Government proposes to parliament: laws or their amendment, and a yearly state *budget, specified per ministry and per state institution*, as well as, similarly specified, their amount of workforce *in FTE* (see also 3§2d). Parliament has to approve all of these, or can do so after its amendment. Parliamentarians can also propose laws themselves. Along with the budget, the government outlines its intended main policies for the year ahead. At its taking office it does so for the office period ahead.

(j) *Constitutional legislation.* Parliament or government puts into legislation the Design set out in chapters 2–3. Part of it can have a constitutional status – for which amendments require a 2/3 parliamentary majority. This should apply especially to the economic design elements about the cooperative as legal entity (2§3.0) and about the governance of cooperatives (2§5.0–5.1), as well as to the current section 3§1(a–c, h–i). Amendments of non-constitutional legislation require a simple majority. Appendix 3C sets out fundamental constitutional rights and the main other constitutional elements.

Scheme 3.4 (p. 77) summarises points (h)–(j) above. The bottom of the scheme anticipates elements of the next two sections.

3§2 State agencies and other state institutions: establishment, budget and amount of workforce

(a) *State institutions.* Government initiates the establishment of ministries and of other 'state institutions', the establishment having the form of a law – thus requiring the approval of parliament. Parliament can also itself initiate the establishment of state institutions. State institutions each have *separate budgets and maintain separate accounting*. One of the ministries is responsible for the overall state budget and for taxation, and one for general cooperatives' matters. Next to ministries the state institutions are the Judiciary (3D2), Provinces and Municipalities (ch. 4) and State Agencies. (The outline of the latter constitutes the main part of the current chapter – divisions 3–10.) See Table 3.5 (p. 77).

---

13   'Complete information' includes any underlying documentation as specified by Act of Parliament. The information shall be provided within 20 days after the request. (They may request exemption for the public conveyance of specific information. It is regulated by Act of Parliament how parliament weighs such requests and how parliament shall be informed in an alternative non-public way.)

SCHEME 3.4 *Main tasks and powers of parliament and government*

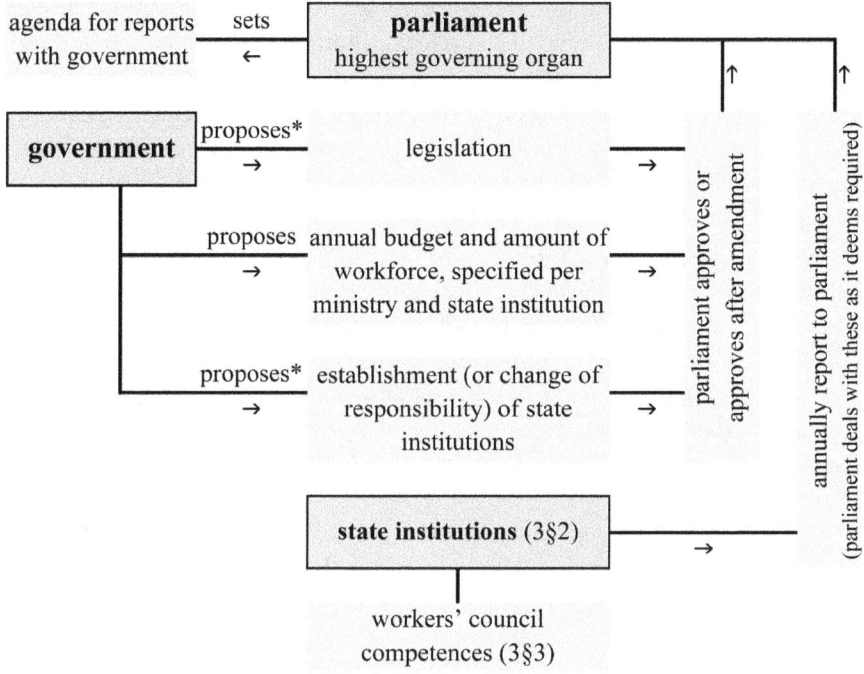

* parliamentarians can equally make such a proposal

TABLE 3.5   *State and state institutions*

State as legal entity		State institutions	
parliament†	3D1	judiciary‡	3D2: 3§6
government	3D1	ministries	3D1
		state agencies	3D2–3D10
		provinces and municipalities	ch. 4

† The parliament as organisation (assisting parliamentarians) is internally organised as a state agency.
‡ The judiciary is subdivided into courts. The judiciary as organisation (assisting judges) is internally organises as a state agency.

(b) *Legislation regarding state institutions.* The legislation referred to under (a) sets out what responsibilities are exactly delegated to these institutions; how they at least annually report to the relevant minister and to parliament; and how parliament can adjust the main line of their policies (the latter except for the judiciary). Parliament deals with these annual reports as it deems required. To the extent that ministries or state agencies own assets, this shall be understood as a delegated ownership, the ownership ultimately resting with the state as legal entity.

(c) *Special status of the parliament as organisation.* The parliament as organisation is treated as a special state institution that assists the collective of parliamentarians with their work, as including the seeking of all the information that they require. (In this and the following section it is abbreviated as PO.) It is a special state institution in order to guarantee its independency. The PO aims at a fixed amount of workforce as per mill of the total workforce of society. Any decision regarding the parliament itself requires a two-thirds parliamentary majority.

(d) *Budget of state institutions and their amount of workforce.* State institutions are each committed to a budget and an amount of workforce in FTE (3§1-i). *Together*, they are committed to a fixed expenditure budget as % of GDP, and to a *fixed amount of workforce* as a percentage of the total workforce of society.[14] The government allocates the fixed budget and workforce (exclusive that of the parliament as organisation) over the ministries and other state institutions (as indicated in 3§1-i, parliament has to approve of this).

(e) *Record keeping.* State institutions register their incomes and expenditures in regular bookkeeping, and at the end of the year they record an Income account and a Balance sheet of their assets, liabilities and reserves. Each of the latter two is to be approved by two external registered auditors (see 3§43) – each of different auditing cooperatives.[15] Together with a general explanatory memorandum, the end of year records are sent to parliament that deals with these as it deems necessary.

(f) *Establishment of other institutions.* Government initiates the establishment of municipalities, provinces (ch. 4) and of 'workers' council governed founda-

---

14　An exception *may* relate to the budget and workforce segment of formal education – as explained in subdivision 7B.

15　External registered auditors work at licensed PWCs. In case the two auditors do not agree, the opinion of an added third one is decisive – all three nevertheless have to sign, one in case for disagreeing. Once an auditor has taken on the task at hand, s/he is not allowed to resign in case of disagreement between one or two of the other auditors.

tions' (3§25). These are legal entities, their establishment having the form of a law. Municipalities and provinces receive a per capita budget. 'Workers' council governed foundations' (mainly these carry out the health and education provisions that are provided free of charge) fall under the responsibility of a State Agency and are financed by these, but they are formally not part of the state sector, but rather of the 'public sector at large'; they receive a population dependent budget and are committed to a population dependent amount of workforce. (Note that this is not a subordinate category as their total workforce is estimated at 21% of the nation's workforce; that of the state institutions at 6% – Appendix 3A, section 3A-5.)

(g) *Borderline for production by worker cooperatives and by state institutions.* Acts of parliament delegate specific responsibilities to ministries, state agencies, provinces and municipalities (b above). Most often these regard the delegated authority of specific regulation in a field, as well as the delegated authority to implement that regulation – together called 'regulation broadly'. Economically this 'regulation broadly' is produced by the relevant civil service workers.

A general Design rule is that any production beyond this (as including also of the material inputs for state institutions, such as the construction of buildings, computers and roads, but also of services such as auditing) is carried out by Worker cooperatives (ch. 2). However, it is a general rule with two main exceptions; the reasons for the exceptions are explained in the relevant Division 7 (on the health, education and culture sectors) and in Division 9 (mainly its section on railway transport). This production is carried out by 'Workers' council governed foundations' (f above), be it that all their material inputs are again produced by Worker cooperatives.

(h) *Hard budget constraints and workforce constraints.* Points (d) and (f) above (summarised in *Table 3.6*) make sure that there are not only hard budget constraints but also workforce constraints for state institutions and other state-financed institutions. This counterposes what in the literature is known as 'soft budget constraints'.[16]

---

16 Kornai 1979; 1986; Kornai, Maskin and Roland 2003.

TABLE 3.6   *Budget and workforce constraints*

State institutions	Workers' council governed foundations state-financed (3§25); mainly regarding free Health and Education (3D7)
budget: fixed % GDP workforce: fixed % L	budget: population dependent % GDP workforce: population dependent % L

Note: L stands for the total nationwide workforce.

In Divisions 2 to 10 a distinction will be made – when relevant – between annual budget and workforce constraints (these are always hard) and structural (long-term) budget constraints that are most often population growth dependent.

3§3   Councils of state institutions and remuneration of parliamentarians, ministers and state workers

(a) *Remuneration of parliamentarians and ministers*. Members of parliament and members of the government receive individually a remuneration equal to the nationwide average wages and dividends of cooperatives in FTE (as including their 'postponed dividends' – 2§13.0).[17,18] In addition they may receive a compensation of expenses as laid down by a two-thirds majority requiring Act of Parliament.

(b) *Wages sum of state institutions*. As an earmarked part of their budget, each state institution receives collectively a wages sum equal to their workforce in FTE times the average wages and dividends of the nation's cooperatives in FTE (as including their 'postponed dividends – 2§13.0). See (d) on the distribution of these wages.

(c) *Ministries' and state agencies' coordination of political matters*. For each ministry and state *agency* the government appoints a Director General who is responsible for matters of political content and their coordination within the institution. S/he is either directly accountable to a minister (for ministries), or confers with the relevant minister (state agencies); s/he can be requested for briefings or interrogations by parliament (3§1(h)). Together with the Secretary General (mentioned in the following point d) the Director General is also

---

17   The same applies for the assistants of parliamentarians that come and go with their being in office.
18   Mutations are implemented with some time lag, given the required end of year calculations.

responsible for the drawing up of the institution's end of year records including its general explanatory memorandum as mentioned in 3§2e.

(d) *Workers' council of state institutions*. Workers of state institutions (including ministries and state agencies) constitute a council, that has five main competences.

First, it elects a management, including a Secretary General; the management is removable by the council, and is revolving or re-elected at intervals of no more than five years. The Secretary General is responsible for organisational matters. S/he is directly accountable to the council, but can be requested for briefings or interrogations by parliament (3§1(h)).

Second, it deliberates (perhaps delegated) with the management about the work organisation, as including procedures for applications and other workforce changes.

Third, it deliberates (perhaps delegated) with the Secretary General about the annual 'general explanatory memorandum' of end of year records (point c above, last sentence).

Fourth, annually it has to approve of the internal structure of the wages scales.

Fifth, annually it has to approve of the Income account and the Balance sheet, mentioned in 3§2e.

(e) *Political content of work*. As in other politico-economic systems (such as capitalism) some friction is inevitable between the political content and the work organisation of civil service workers (civil servants in capitalism). Above this has been made explicit in the functions of the Director General and the Secretary General. In case frictions become disturbing, these two are the first to seek solutions for them, and if required to get into deliberation with the council and the politically relevant minister.

(f) *Council(s) of large state institutions*. (The following point is analogous to 2§5.2.) For large state institutions – which will most often be the case – the council mentioned so far is called the 'institutional council'. This council can decide to also introduce 'departmental councils'. The latter elects the removable departmental management and deliberates over matters that they deem opportune for the operation of the department. In case the institutional council is so large that most members can merely vote instead of argue, the departmental council deliberates over the matters mentioned under 3§3d, and appoints one or more spokespersons for the institutional council meetings (which does not interfere with the right of each individual to nevertheless speak at the institutional council).

(g) *Comment on the remuneration of state workers*. When we get to the specific tasks of state agencies in Divisions 2–10 of the current chapter, it will be seen that their primary task is the flourishing and wellbeing of the cooperatives' economy. Given the on average similar income of the state institutions' and cooperatives' workers, this ensures that a mutual flourishing is pursued. Nevertheless, it cannot be excluded that in bad times cooperatives have to use up part or all of their resistance buffer, and then are paid no more than the minimum wage (2§7); it also cannot be excluded that a cooperative goes bankrupt. However, ebbs and flows for cooperatives equally affect the income of state workers – on average at least. It will be seen in Division 5 that there are quite some measures to avoid, or at least mitigate joblessness. It will also be seen that the burden of those measures is equally shared by workers of cooperatives and state institutions.

(h) *Improper behaviour by state workers.* State workers shall not accept gifts, or promises of these, in any form; they shall not promote the award of public contracts to a specific cooperative or favour specific cooperatives in any form when applying the law; nor shall they favour specific individuals when applying the law. Generally they shall in no way abuse their power. Generally they shall also not create the semblance of all the above. Appendix 3D treats the judicial proceeding in case of breaking these rules.

3§4   *Finance of the state and state institutions*
• *Income and expenditure of the state: main line*
(a) The state's budget (3§1-i), and thus its expenditure, is generally financed by taxation.
(b) Only the central state levies taxes.
(c) The state's main current expenditures regard:
• wages to civil service workers and purchases from cooperatives;
• transfers to state institutions.
• *Borrowing by, and bank overdrafts of, the state and state institutions*
(d) The state can sell short-term or long-term debt paper to the 'Central Bank' (see 3D4), though not to any other institution (including cooperatives), nor to individuals, nor to foreign institutions or individuals.
(e) State institutions are allowed to borrow from the state in case of emergency (if the state consents) but not from any other institution or individual.
(f) The state and state institutions are not allowed to run a bank overdraft.
(g) Points (e) and (f) also apply to institutions that are fully financed by the state (Workers' council governed foundations mentioned in 3§2-f).

The reason of these points is to keep 'hard budget constraints' (see 3§2-h), thus keeping the non-taxation finance of the state clearly structured and without unexpected gaps. Regarding (g) above, the point is also to evade that some state-external finance in one year would have to be compensated by less services in another year – think of health and education.

Regarding point (d) above, the selling of debt paper, it is to be remarked that in the Design's 'worker cooperatives society' there is no a priori reason for the state to run a budget deficit (normally all current expenditures are financed by taxation). It might nevertheless run a short-term deficit in case of business-cycle-like recessions with dampening tax receipts – these would then be offset in an upswing (see further 3§19, 3§20 and 3§42).

Table 3.7 (p. 84) presents the taxation categories and tax rates of the Design. Here this merely serves as a preliminary impression for the reader. The argumentation for these categories and rates is given in 3§46. There are two main taxation categories.

First, a *turnover tax* (cascade system) that should cover the revenue for about 50% of the state expenditure. Its tax rate is between 5% and 15% depending on the production structure of the country at hand (3§46 argues why this is to be preferred to a value-added tax).

Second, an *individual income tax* that covers about 50% of the state expenditure (cf. Appendix 3A, section 3A-4). The income tax rates range from 25% (between the minimum costs of living and the minimum wage), via 60% (between one to two times the minimum wage) and further gradually increasing to 95% for incomes above five times the minimum wage. (Note that the latter incomes are most unlikely, given that worker councils decide on the pre-tax income ranges. However, the top income tax rates are relevant for the transition – Chapter 8.)

On top of these two there are inheritance and gift taxes, the revenues of which are expected to be minor in face of anticipating behaviour.

The table's columns 3 to 5 show an example of the taxation effect on individual incomes in case a country's annual minimum wage would be €20,000. This figure is not essential: when in face of the country's purchasing power structure, the nominal minimum wage would be higher or lower, the taxation revenue would be proportionally higher or lower (as would be the money-level of the required state expenditure).

TABLE 3.7 *Overview of the tax categories and tax rates*

	(1)	(2)	(3)	(4)	(5)
	Category	Tax rate on bracket	Average tax rate	Tax sum (top of bracket)	After-tax income (top bracket)†
1	(MiW = annual minimum wage)		at MiW = €20,000‡		
2	Taxation cooperatives*				
3	Turnover tax: cascade system**	5% to 15%‡			
4	Income tax individuals††				
5	to 60% MiW (costs of living threshold)	0%	0.0%	€ 0	€ 12,000 [0.7]
6	from off € 60% MiW – 1× MiW	25%	10.0%	€ 2,000	€ 18,000 [1.0]
7	from off € 1× MiW – 2× MiW	60%	35.0%	€ 14,000	€ 26,000 [1.4]
8	from off € 2× MiW – 3× MiW	70%	46.7%	€ 28,000	€ 32,000 [1.8]
9	from off € 3× MiW – 4× MiW	80%	55.0%	€ 44,000	€ 36,000 [2.0]
10	from off € 4× MiW – 5× MiW	90%	62.0%	€ 62,000	€ 38,000 [2.1]
11	above € 5× MiW	95%			
12	example of € 5× MiW – 10× MiW	95%	79.0%	€ 157,000	€ 43,000 [2.4]
13	Wealth tax individuals	nil			
14	Inheritance tax, levied on the receiver‡‡				
15	over € 0 – MiW	0%			
16	over € MiW – 2× MiW	50%			
17	above 2× €MiW	100%			
18	inheritance tax spouse/partner	0%			
19	Gift tax (on annual gifts; levied on receiver)♣				
20	over € 0–10% MiW	0%			

THE STATE AND THE STATE INSTITUTIONS OF THE DESIGN 85

TABLE 3.7 *Overview of the tax categories and tax rates (cont.)*

	(1)	(2)	(3)	(4)	(5)
	Category	Tax rate on bracket	Average tax rate	Tax sum (top of bracket)	After-tax income (top bracket)†
21	above 10% MiW	100%			
22	Municipal and provincial taxes	nil			

†   The outer end of column (5) shows the ratio of the after-tax income differences (€18,000 = 1). (For 60% MiW = 12,000 = 1, and from 60% MiW to 5× MiW, the ratio's run from 1 to 3.2.)
‡   The figure of €20,000 is not essential: when in face of the country's purchasing power structure, the nominal minimum wage would be higher or lower, the taxation revenue would be proportionally higher or lower (as would be the money-level of the required state expenditure). The tax rates of column (2) are essential.
*   Cooperatives pay no surplus tax.
**   A different regulation applies for 'single person enterprises' – see Appendix 3E.
‡   Dependent on the production structure of the country concerned.
††   The income tax rates might be considered substantial, but this is required to finance pensions for all, the free health and education services as well as child and childcare allowances (see 3D6 and 3D7). The wages supplements for evening and night shifts are taxed according to the bracket rate before these supplements.
‡‡   Maximum 15 receivers. Apart from row 18, no differentiation regarding the relation between testator and receiver.
***   A gift by a parent to a child is twice exempted for 50% MiW. The reason is assistance for a child who is starting to live on their own (this is turned into a general rule).

Addendum 3§4. Summary of the general regulation for state agencies. For future reference this addendum summarises the regulation for state agencies from sections 3§2 to 3§4.
(1) On the initiative of government or parliament they are established in the form of a law, which sets out what responsibilities are exactly delegated to these agencies, how they at least annually report to the relevant minister and to parliament and how parliament can adjust the main line of their policies; any ownership of state agencies shall be understood as a delegated ownership, the ownership ultimately resting with the state as legal entity (3§2-a;b).
(2) They receive a separate budget, maintain a separate accounting, register their incomes and expenditures in regular bookkeeping, and at the end of the year they record an Income account and a Balance sheet – the records requiring approval by two external registered auditors (3§2d–e). They are not allowed to borrow, nor to run a bank overdraft; though they are allowed to borrow from the state in case of emergency (3§4-e).

(3) They are committed to an amount of workforce in FTE specified together with the budget (3§2-d). An earmarked part of the budget consists of a wages sum equal to their workforce in FTE times the average wages and dividends of the nation's cooperatives in FTE (3§3-b). Workers of an agency constitute a council that (amongst other competences) elects a management and annually has to approve of the internal structure of the wages scales (3§3-b;d).

Division 2. Institutions safeguarding public security and justice

This division sets out the main lines of the organisation of public security (3§5) and of the judiciary and of administrative prosecution (3§6). The first section presents not much new. The second section presents a specific way of appointment of the judiciary and of administrative prosecutors which builds in some distance from political appointments.

3§5 *Public security*
The safeguarding of 'public security' encompasses the following subjects. First, the protection against fire and atmospheric elements. Second, the protection against offences and crimes. The annual budget and workforce constraints for these public securities are hard. There is no reason to expect a structural growth above population growth.

• *Fire and atmospheric elements*
(a) *Protection against fire.* Municipalities are responsible for local fire brigades (4§3-c). The minister of home affairs is responsible for multi-purpose fire-combatting units that are regionally and inter-regionally available; as well as for the design and implementation of various fire-combatting scenarios (such as for forest fires).
(b) *Protection against open water.* Provinces are responsible for provincial waterways and dykes – in coordination with other provincial administrations (4§5-c). Some minister (perhaps a minister of infrastructure and public works) is responsible for sea dykes and other sea walls.
(c) *Protection against other atmospheric elements.* Required protection, or warning, against other atmospheric elements depends on the geography of a country (e.g. tropical cyclones).

- *Protection against offences and crimes*
(d) *Police.* Municipalities are responsible for the local police (here lies the main weight qua amount of police force) – 4§3-c. Provinces are responsible for cross-municipal police tasks (4§5-b). A minister of national public security is responsible for cross-regional and special police services.
(e) *Public prosecution.* The minister of national public security is responsible for public prosecution. (The specific category of 'Administrative prosecution' is treated in the next section.)
(f) *Case under judicial consideration.* When a case is under judicial consideration, as including being in treatment by a prosecutor, members of the democratic organs of the state (3§1), provinces (4§4) or municipalities (4§2) shall not interfere with the case, nor create the perception of any interference.
(g) *Penitentiaries.* The minister of national public security is responsible for the penitentiaries. S/he may delegate the execution of relevant penitentiaries to provincial or municipal authorities.

- *Workers' councils and remuneration*
(h) *Workers' councils.* Workers of fire brigades, the police and penitentiaries constitute councils, similar to those for (other) state institutions (3§3-d).
(i) *Remuneration.* Fire brigade, police officers and prison guards are remunerated similar to all state workers (3§3-b). However, those that run evening, night and weekend shifts receive an 'unsocial hours wages supplement'. Prosecutors are remunerated equally and similar to all state workers.

- *A note on defence against possible international aggression*
It would be naïve to ignore that there might be international aggression towards the society being outlined, especially from the side of some capitalist countries that fear a spread of the cooperatives' organisation to their nation. I have no sound answer to the question of how especially military aggression should be responded to. It depends also on whether the country that is making, or has made, a transition to a cooperatives society had a (considerable) defence force prior to the transition. The following alternatives – which are not mutually exclusive – might be considered. (1) The relying on the United Nations organisation, and hope for the best. (2) The concluding of non-aggression pacts with relevant countries (knowing that international treaties can be broken). (3) The seeking of alliances with countries that adopt a similar or nearby economic organisation; or, more generally, with peaceful nations. (4) Providing defensive civil training in underground resistance or guerrilla resistance. (There is at least one big military force in the world that does not look back with joy at such resistances.)

In any case it is not wise to delegate the command of any armed forces to one person, and therefore it shall be delegated to at least a triumvirate.[19]

3§6 The judiciary, and administrative prosecution
• *The judiciary*

The judiciary is an extraordinary state institution. The combination of a deemed independent judiciary together with politically decided appointments of the judiciary is rather precarious (in some capitalist nations more than in others). A moderate solution for this problem is set out below.

(a) *The judiciary committee: appointment of judges.* Parliament institutes a standing 'judiciary committee' that selects – and has the ceremonial president (3§1-e) appoint – the resigning judges of the 'supreme court' and of the 'courts level just below it'. These are appointed for until the legal retirement age.

(b) *Composition of the judiciary committee.* The judiciary committee consists of 16 members and is composed of, each for one quarter: former judges, lawyers, former ministers, former parliamentarians.

(c) *Resigning members of the judiciary committee.* A quarter of this committee resigns every fourth year (thus a committee member sits for a maximum of 16 years), though must resign five years prior to the current average death age, in which case more than a quarter may resign.

(d) *Appointment of new members of the judiciary committee.* One year after taking office, parliament elects and appoints a quarter of the standing committee, having heard without commitment the sitting committee (or in case the age clause under 'c' applies, accordingly more than a quarter).

(e) *Appointment of lower-level judges (third, and in case, fourth level).* Sitting judges in the courts level just below the supreme court (second level) organise between them a procedure of co-opting judges in the lower courts, though taking account of a spread of the latter's age distribution. These too are appointed for until the legal retirement age.

(f) *Courts judging on administrative prosecution.* One second-level court of the nation has a chamber that judges the prosecuted administrative cases (see 'g' below and the next • marked heading). Appeal is possible with (a chamber of) the supreme court. These courts also judge on conflicts between administrations.

(g) *Courts judging on abuse of power by authorities and state workers.* There are special rules and courts for the trial of the abuse of power and other improper

---

19 The constitution (Appendix 3C) mentions this, and also that the declaration of a state of war shall not be made without the prior approval of parliament (its division 5, articles 34 and 35).

behaviour by parliamentarians, ministers, others state workers and political parties – see Appendix 3D.

(h) *Number of judges*. The nationwide number of judges is a fixed percentage of the labour population, initially calculated over a five-year period in which they could properly do their work without arrears.

(i) *Remuneration of judges*. Judges receive the same remuneration as members of parliament and the government (thus they receive individually a remuneration equal to the nationwide average wages and dividends of cooperatives in FTE – 3§3-a).

(j) *Budget of courts*. For the costs of the courts assisting staff and other expenses, the judiciary receives a budget that grows proportionally to the full state budget. Amendment of this requires a two-thirds parliamentary majority by two subsequently elected parliaments. The initial budget is calculated over a five-year period in which courts could properly do their work. A subsequently elected parliament has to confirm this.

(k) *Workers' councils and remuneration of courts staff*. The staff of courts is organised in councils in similar way as set out in 3§3-d;f. They are remunerated similar to all state workers (3§3-b).

(l) Judges are member of a nationwide association that is organised as decided by the association. In a way as it deems appropriate it annually reports to parliament over matters that it deems opportune. Parliament deals with the report as it deems required.

The annual budget and workforce constraints for the judiciary are hard. There is no reason to expect a structural growth above population growth.

• *Administrative prosecution*
Administrative prosecution regards the behaviour of elected political officers and of other state workers (national, provincial or municipal) that is deemed against the law (such as misuse of power, or the acceptance of gifts or the raising of money mentioned in 3§1-e and 3§3-h). Experience in many capitalist countries shows that this prosecution falling under the responsibility of a minister (or a parliamentary chamber) is not appropriate, because of possible conflicting personal or political interests. Such prosecution, therefore, requires to be carried out by an organ at distance from administrations. Therefore, the standing 'judiciary committee' (see the previous subsection) selects – and has the ceremonial president (3§1-e) appoint – one or more 'administrative prosecutors' (depending on the size of the country; again, depending on the size of the county this may be a full-time or a part-time function). Administrative prosecutors receive the same remuneration as judges.

Division 3. Protecting constraints: environment; safety output and work; work-time; minimum wages

This division sets out constraints for cooperatives regarding environmental aspects of their production (3§7) and the safety of their output (3§8); as well as constraints for cooperatives and state institutions regarding the safety at work (3§9), the work-time (3§10) and the minimum wages of their workers (3§11). Inspectorates see to the compliances (3§12).

It will be seen in the first section (3§7) that if the climate and other environment aims would require mitigation of growth, the state's 'Savings and Loans Bank' (see 3§16) could play a rather direct role in the mitigation of investment. Within capitalism such a mitigation would require, if possible at all, profound regulations. Section 3§8 indicates that the Design prohibits advertisement. In capitalism this would be seen as encroachments on the freedom of enterprise. The rest of the division seems compatible with capitalism (compatible: for some perhaps grudgingly).

3§7 *Physically circular production*
(a) The cooperatives' economy is vitally a physically circular one; each cooperative is required to further optimise it. As much as is possible, the production is located near to where it is used, which saves on transport of freight and on commuting. As based on input from the 'National institute for the advance of physically circular production' (3§33-B), legislation sets rules for such production, as including sector-specific rules for the location of production near its use.
(b) In case the economy is not yet physically circular when the transition (ch. 8) takes off, the requirement is to reach this as soon as possible. The latter not via subsidies, but via rules setting out a time path of duties and interdictions. When required, legislation also sets out the relevant time paths.
(c) Should the climate and other environmental aims require mitigation of growth, then a cooperative economy is much better equipped to reach this than a capitalist one. We have seen that the 'Savings and Loans Bank' (SLB) provides loans to cooperative banks, such loans being essential for the provision of the latter's investment credits to non-bank cooperatives (2§6.3 and 2§21, point 3) – hence such loans are essential for economic growth. As we will see in 3§16-d, the SLB could in principle mitigate its loans to cooperative banks, so as to mitigate macroeconomic investment and growth, or even that of specific sectors.

Related to physically circular production are 'mining and other extractions from the Earth', which are treated in 3§38.

THE STATE AND THE STATE INSTITUTIONS OF THE DESIGN   91

3§8 *Safety of, and information about, output*
Cooperatives are responsible for safe and healthy products. Regarding the latter a designated minister initiates legislation setting out a combination of duties and interdicts. However, such legislation does not withstand the ultimate responsibility and liability of the producer as well as the wholesaler and retailer for the safety and health that is not, or insufficiently, covered by the legislation.

So as to protect consumers and (small) cooperatives, cooperatives are not allowed to advertise in any form (to be sure, this includes internet advertisement). Instead there are output information services that are set up under the responsibility of a minister and/or by a consumer association. Cooperatives can inform the information provider about product changes or new products, but the information provider deals with it as it deems appropriate and is fully responsible for the information provided.

So as to protect the privacy of individuals, it is not allowed to collect personally identifiable data via internet cookies, or to ask consent for these. To be sure, this applies to cooperatives as well as to state institutions.

Addendum 3§8. Note on the consequences of advertisement prohibition. In comparison with a constellation in which advertisement prevails, the effect of non-advertisement is a cost price reduction of most output, whence consumption prices decrease (note that this includes the sales of personal internet data to advertisers). Nevertheless, for some sectors, revenues are negatively affected. Some main sectors are listed below together with the consequence.
- Broadcasting (TV and radio) → pay TV/radio.
- Newspapers and magazines → subscription price increase (probably about 20%).
- Various internet sites (no personalised adds) → subscription.
- Various sports events → price increase.
- Cinema → price increase.
- Municipalities (revenue of street advertisement) → tax increase (state level).
- Development of advertisement and advertisement campaigns → loss of current job.
- Development of internet data collection on individuals → loss of current job.

The absence of advertising will not only reduce the general consumer price level, but also considerably increase individual consumer choice. This is so because with advertisement the advertiser decides which specific branches/sectors 'deserve' advertisement; a lower price for the products of such branches might be considered welcome, but it also applies for those which particular consumers are not interested in, whilst these nevertheless increase the price of their consumer basket. Moreover, the absence of street/city advertisement will considerably change the street scene. Last but not least, the prohibition will take out the gist of the massive internet data collection on individuals.

3§9   Safety at work

Cooperatives and state institutions are responsible for safe and healthy work conditions. Regarding the latter a designated minister initiates legislation setting out a combination of duties and interdicts. However, such legislation does not withstand the ultimate responsibility and liability of cooperatives and state institutions for the safety and health that is not, or insufficiently, covered by the legislation.

3§10   Work-time

(a) *Determination of a full-time work position.* The state's parliament sets the number of work hours per year that defines a 'full-time position' (cf. 2§8.1). The considerations for it relate to demography, the actual workforce and state finance. The number of hours is at least revised every 10 years and may be revised once a year.

A general aim is that the *average* productivity increase that is realised by cooperatives and state institutions is at least partly translated into a decrease in the number of work hours per year. (The latter, instead of a full translation into wages and concomitant consumption increase, also contributes to saving the environment. In the last but one sentence the phrase 'at least partly' should for High Income Countries be substituted by 'predominantly'.)

(b) *Maximum work-time.* The number of hours of work per year that defines a 'full-time position' is also the maximum work-time in hours per year. Notwithstanding that maximum the state's parliament also sets a maximum work-time per day and week. (The first maximum is the point of departure; the daily and weekly maximums can to some degree take account of seasonal work and temporary understaffing.)[20] The maximums are at least revised every 10 years and may be revised once a year.

Overtime is not paid, but in time compensated for within no more than a year. Because the maximum work-time should protect workers, the overtime compensation in time is its logical consequence. The maximum work-time and

---

20   On seasonal work see also Appendix 3F.

the overtime rule should also contribute to the aim of continuous sufficient work for all – see 3D5. (At the other end of the latter matter, the maximum work-time and the overtime rules should also prevent the economy from 'overheating'. Investment should serve workers, instead of workers serving investment.)

(c) *Minimum work-time*. In principle the number of hours of work per year that defines a 'full-time position' is also the minimum work-time in hours per year. The minimum work-time should contribute to an equivalency of tax contribution,[21] given that all, or most, benefit from provisions such as healthcare, education, child allowances and pensions (together these are estimated at 31% of GDP; summarised in Appendix 3A, Table 3A.1).

(d) *Temporary part-time position*. However, workers who wish so can at some time opt to work part-time for the maximum of a total equivalent of 10 years at 50% of the full-time (to be sure, during such times wages are reduced proportionally – parental leave is treated separately in 3§22). This total might be spread over more than 10 years at less than 50%, but not over less than 10 years at more than 50%. (The reason for the latter is that this way they keep seriously in touch with their cooperative or state institution, and also do not lose qualifications.) However, there can be a one-time exception that extends to 100% for half a year, and a long-time 100% exception for the period just before retirement. Any period, and rate, of part-time work should annually be mentioned in the appropriate box of the tax return form (3§46). The part-time option above is a 'right in principle', to the extent that the exact part-time period(s) should be well planned and be in agreement with the management and the council of the cooperative or other institution in face of the internal staff capacity – this is especially important for small cooperatives (see Appendix 3F on possible stand-ins for those working part-time and the costs thereof). The long-time period just before retirement requires no agreement, but has to be announced four months in advance.

In principle there is no echelon in the Design's society that continuously merely works part-time. The person who works part-time under the conditions indicated above remains fully associated with a cooperative or a state institution.

Here, and under (c) above, the term 'in principle' is used. A conscientious objector to the minimum work-time – beyond the temporary part-time possibilities – might be granted the right to work less than the minimum work-time,

---

21   As indicated in 3§4, the remuneration of workers contributes to about 50% of the taxation revenue.

provided that in case her/his taxes do not cover the average state expenditure per income receiver, the taxes paid are supplemented by premiums that cover the average state expenditure on: child-related allowances (3§22), pensions (3§24), health provisions (3D7-A) and formal education (3D7-B).

3§11   *Minimum wages*
The state's parliament enacts a 'minimum wage'. It is accounted in the going FTE per year. (Whence the minimum wage rate is the minimum wage divided by the full-time number of hours per year.)

The minimum wage (MiW) is a derivative of the 'minimum costs of living' (MCL), which is based on a costs of living basket, as calculated by the General statistical office (3§33-B). As an indication the pre-tax MiW is one and two-thirds (167%) of the MCL (MCL/MiW = 60%). It will be seen later on that various allowances are in between the two.[22]

The 'minimum costs of living' and the minimum wage are adapted for inflation or deflation every year. The content of the costs of living *basket* is revised at intervals of five years.

3§12   *Inspectorates*
For all of the items in the current Division, the state institutes 'inspectorates' that see to the relevant compliances. In case of an offence, inspectors can impose fines. Institutions or individuals can also complain with inspectorates in case of offences.

Together the inspectorates constitute a state agency, which is administered and organised as summarised in Addendum 3§4.

Budget and workforce constraints. Sections 3§7–3§11 regard rules initiated by a ministry. The annual budget and workforce constraints for the inspectorates are hard. There is no reason to expect a structural growth above population growth.

Division 4. Institutions safeguarding the finance of cooperatives and the financial constellation at large

This division presents four state agencies that should safeguard the finance of cooperatives, as well the financial and payment system at large in case cooperative banks should get into trouble. The Central Bank (3§13) takes on

---

22   Summarised in 3§24, Table 3.9.

the prudential supervision of cooperative banks and insurance cooperatives. It is also the bank of all state institutions and, given the rules for this bank (see below), it performs a main function for the keeping of 'hard budget constraints' of state institutions (3§2h). The Guardian Bank (3§14) is a bank that is 'dormant' most of the time, but that in case of financial calamities could be activated so as to keep the payment system going and to temporarily stand in for failed cooperative banks. The Investment-credit Guarantee Fund (3§15) may help start-up cooperatives that for some reason cannot get sufficient credit from a cooperative bank. The Savings and Loans Bank (3§16) provides loans to cooperative banks, as well as mortgage loans to cooperatives.

As mentioned, the Central Bank functions as gatekeeper for the 'hard budget constraints' of state institutions. Apart from that, however, the Savings and Loans Bank is one of the most prominent economic policy institutions of the Design, as it can *directly* affect macroeconomic investment as well as the investment of specific sectors.

3§13 *The Central Bank*
The state institutes a Central Bank (CB), that is administered and organised as summarised in Addendum 3§4. The CB has the following tasks and delegated authority.

• *Regarding the state and state institutions*
(a) Being the bank of the state, the state institutions and workers' council governed foundations (3§25). This means that all of these have one or more accounts with the CB, and that all their transactions are handled by the CB. These include transfers from the state to state institutions, from state institutions to workers' council governed foundations, as well as transfers between all of the former and account holders with COBs, as including all tax payments. (This is the main reason for calling this bank the Central Bank.)
(b) The purchase of short-term or long-term debt paper from the state – cf. 3§4-d. (This means that the state can get credit from the CB against a security, similarly as the credit from COBs to other cooperatives.) It finances the state in no other way. The CB is not allowed to purchase debt paper from any other institution (including provincial and municipal administrations). Nor is it allowed to let any payment account be overdrawn (cf. 3§4-f).
(c) Coordination of the policies of the four banking or fund institutions of the state, though without interfering with the responsibilities of the other institutions (hence this is a sophisticated coordination directed at mutual information and deliberation). Representatives of these institutions meet at least every quarter.

• *Regarding COBs*
(d) The issuing of licences to be a money-creating bank to COBs (in formation).
(e) Prudential supervision of COBs (cf. 2§9.3). In case COBs do not comply with the rules set by the CB, the licence can ultimately be withdrawn.
(f) Clearing of the payments between COBs – each COB holds an account with the CB. Any non-cleared payments are settled by the CB at some rate of interest, though such that there are no direct debt–credit relations between COBs.
(g) Specification of the nationwide *uniform* zero, or near to zero, rate of interest that 'payment account holders' receive from their COBs (2§16.1). The 'near to zero' should account for inflation or deflation.
(h) Setting a nationwide maximum market share limit for COBs such that no COB reaches a dominant market power (measured in terms of their financial assets); at this limit they are not allowed to grow further (2§14.0). Market share limits are dependent on the size of a country. As an indication the limit might for a 'large' country initially be set at a structural market share of 1%.[23] For a period of maximal six months it can release COBs from this rule. Via the relevant minister the CB can propose parliament to structurally adapt the rule upwards or downwards; or to extend the six-month period mentioned above. For the releases or the structural proposal mentioned, the CB consults with the Competition Authority (3§45).
(i) In case a COB should go bankrupt, the CB compensates the households' payment-account holders with this COB (recall that the accounts of workers or pensioners shall not exceed twice their monthly income – 2§16.2).

• *Regarding insurance*
(j) The issuing of licences to cooperatives that engage in insurance (2§17) – COBs are not allowed to engage in insurance (2§6.4).
(k) Prudential supervision of insurance cooperatives. In case the latter do not comply with the rules set by the CB, the licence can ultimately be withdrawn.

• *Regarding all cooperatives*
(l) In case the CB deems this required, it proposes to parliament sector-specific *rates* of the legally binding resistance buffer of cooperatives (2§7.0), or an adaptation of the sector-specific rates. (The initial buffer rate is set at 10% for COBs and at 30% for other cooperatives.)

---

23   For very small countries in which there is no room for more than, say, ten banks, the maximum market share would be near to 10%.

• *General remarks on the Central Bank*
The Central Bank is not more or less 'independent' than other state institutions (introduced in this Division or elsewhere in this chapter). State institutions are a matter of organisation of the division of labour, and the policies of all state institutions ultimately require the consent of the democratically elected parliament (3§2-a;b). All state institutions must be independent in the sense that their policy rules are applied non-discriminatorily vis-à-vis the subjects concerned. This regards for example the inspectorates mentioned in 3§12, and no more or less the licensing and supervision of banking and insuring cooperatives. As indicated, the main reason of maintaining the name CB is that all the transactions of the state and state institutions are handled by this bank. Notably it does not intervene in financial markets other than regarding the banking COBs and insurance cooperatives – to the extent that there are no other financial markets (there are no shares or bonds markets).

3§14 *The Guardian Bank*
COBs are crucial for the other cooperatives (as banks are crucial, in another form, for a capitalist system). In case a COB should go bankrupt, the affiliated cooperatives are in great trouble. The state therefore institutes a *'Guardian Bank'* (GB), that is administered and organised as summarised in Addendum 3§4. The GB has the following tasks and delegated authority.
(a) The GB is usually dormant but may become active when required. It has branches in each region and big city. Each cooperative and each worker or pensioner must have a dormant account with this bank.
(b) In case of a COB's bankruptcy, the GB keeps at least the payment system going.
(c) When in case of bankruptcy there would be insufficient banking capacity for investment credits in a region, the GB temporarily stands in until a new COB has been established. It never competes with COBs.
(d) The GB assists the establishment of new COBs (see Appendix 2B).
(e) Normally the GB branches can do with a small office and a one person staff. The GB has a movable office for the calamities cases.

3§15 *The Investment-credit Guarantee Fund*
The state institutes an *Investment-credit Guarantee Fund* (IGF) that has branches in the nation's regions and large cities. It is administered and organised as summarised in Addendum 3§4. The IGF has two main tasks. One regarding PWC's in formation, and one regarding regional discrepancies (in case there are such discrepancies in the country at hand).

• PWCs in formation
(a) As indicated in 2§4.2 the foundation of a new PWC is initiated by the drawing up of a 'cooperative plan' on the basis of which a COB may grant investment credit to the cooperative in formation. Should no COB in a region be willing to grant credit on the basis of the plan, the initiators may apply to the IGF for a security guarantee that might temporarily take away some or all of the risk for a COB.
(b) The IGF weighs the plan in face of the competitive circumstances as well as the possible joblessness in the region. After an initial positive assessment of the plan by the IGF, one or more initiators and a functionary of the IGF and a COB enter into consultation about a degree of guarantee by the IGF for the repayment of the credit.
(c) The guarantee holds for a limited time (usually five years). The interest risk premium that the COB normally charges (cf. 2§6.0) is paid to the IGF.
(d) For each quarter of the year the total size of these guarantees issued is limited (published at the start of each year). The degree to which guarantees issued result in actual claims on the fund by COBs is likely to be constant in the long run. The total of the guarantees is an economic policy matter in face of the general economic situation.

• Regional discrepancies
(e) In the country at hand there may be an unwanted uneven production and jobs distribution over regions (including migration or commuting undesired by workers). If in that case existing PWCs want to expand whereas no COB in the region is willing to grant new investment credit, similar procedures as under (a) to (c) apply. Regarding point (d) above there is a separate quarterly budget for the regarding discrepancies.

However, it is also possible that existing PWCs see no opportunities for additional investment in their region. For such a case of 'regional stagnation', policy measures are set out in 3§42 under (f).

3§16   The Savings and Loans Bank

The state institutes a national *Savings and Loans Bank* (SLB) that has branches in the nation's regions and large cities. It is administered and organised as summarised in Addendum 3§4. The SLB has the following tasks and delegated authority.
(a) It collects the savings from individuals, 'workers' council governed foundations' (on the latter see 3§25), and in case also state institutions. These savings are fully state guaranteed, and the SLB normally pays an interest on the savings.

As indicated in 2§16.2, payment accounts of workers or pensioners should not exceed twice their monthly income. Apart from that amount, the SLB is the only institution where savings can be stalled. Savings are repayable on demand within the constraint mentioned in the previous sentence.
(b) To the extent that the rate of interest affects savings (at least the degree is doubtful) the SLB might – in consultation with the Central Bank – use this interest rate as a policy instrument so as to influence the consumption expenditure by households.
(c) It provides loans to COBs for their investment loans to PWCs. For these loans the SLB requires either an assignment of the collateral that the COB requested for the investment loans, or some general security that the COB can provide. (These loans make it that the SLB is one of the most prominent economic policy institutions. Note that, in the absence of these SLB loans, and given point (a) above, COBs would be ineffective – see their balance sheet in Appendix 2A, Sheets 2A.2 – because in the Design there are no shares and bonds markets.)
(d) In consultation with the Central Bank and the (for the SLB) relevant minister, it can propose to parliament for a temporarily granted authority to provide the loans sub (c) selectively, either as an economic policy instrument so as to stimulate specific kinds of investments in face of social priorities, or as an instrument to reach particular macroeconomic objectives (including environment related ones – 3§7-c). These policies can either take the form of interest rate variations between branches, or the form of direct interventions regarding (types of) investment (the latter by mitigating or withholding loans for particular branches). Parliament or the government may also take the initiative for the policies above. The SLB requires parliamentary approval for such a policy because it has an effect on the potential expansion of particular cooperatives.
(e) It provides mortgage loans to COBs and PWCs. Newly founded cooperatives can get a 100% mortgage which must be reduced to 90% within 10 years and to 80% within 15 years. (An alternative for such loans is to rent premises from a state agency – see 3§37.)
(f) The rates of interest charged include a risk surcharge, as well as a surcharge that on average covers the SLB's material costs and wages.

The above points (a) through (f) mean that the SLB is one of the most, or perhaps the most, influential economic policy institution of the Design (see also 3§47-a-first).

Budget and workforce constraints Division 4
3§13. *The Central Bank.* The annual budget and workforce constraints for the CB are hard. Over time its work regarding the banking and the insurance cooper-

atives will increase with their number; regarding the CB's other tasks, the structural budget and workforce can be pretty constant.

3§14. The Guardian Bank. In normal times the budget and workforce for the GB will be very moderate. When a cooperative bank should go bankrupt, its work and required budget suddenly increases.

3§15. The Investment-credit Guarantee Fund. The annual budget and workforce constraints for the IGF are hard. Structurally the budget and workforce will grow with the average rate of economic growth of the cooperatives sector, though within that with fluctuations.

3§16. The Savings and Loans Bank. Normally the annual budget and workforce constraints for the SLB are hard (this may be different in case of the special policies of 3§16-d). Qua budget it structurally runs on a break-even basis.

Table 3.8 summarises all of the various rates of interest prevalent in the Design.

TABLE 3.8   *Summary of the Design's various rates of interest*

Interest receiver	Interest payer	Interest rate	Section
COBs for investment credit	PWCs for investment credit	variable†	2§6.0
PWCs and individuals on payments account (for individuals max. two months income)	COBs	zero or near zero, specified by CB: nation-wide uniform	2§16.1 2§16.2 3§13-g
Individuals, WGFs* and state institutions; all on their saving account (in case they save)	Savings and Loans Bank	variable	2§16.2 3§16-a
Savings and Loans Bank	COBs for investment credit	variable†	3§16-c
Savings and Loans Bank	Cooperatives for mortgages self-occupied premises	variable†	3§16-e

† Costs and risks covering.
* Workers' council Governed Foundation (3§25).

Division 5. Job securities, jobs shortages and restricted abilities to work

In capitalism (and any mode of production) being jobless is a great social-economic evil. Whereas capitalist enterprises require a degree of unemployment so as to press down wages, no institution in the Design has a similar interest – on the contrary. In face of the Design's free choice of occupation and the hiring of labour capacity (2§23), it gives high priority to evading joblessness.

This Division first introduces a state agency that is responsible for job securities and the minimisation of joblessness (3§17). The next sections set out: how joblessness due to an inadequate match between jobs and workers' qualifications is minimised (3§18); how recessional joblessness is dealt with (if such joblessness would prevail in the Design society); how the policies countering the aforementioned joblessness types are articulated (3§20); and how workers with restricted physical or mental abilities get a regular job (3§21).

It will be seen that these measures impose, in varying degrees, an administrative burden on cooperatives and public sector institutions. However, the result is that (apart from those unable to work) no one is out of work for longer than two months – where 'work' includes permanent jobs and paid traineeships, the latter being a lever to permanent jobs (3§20).

Depending on the reader's background, the sections 3§18–3§20 may be more demanding than other sections of the book.

3§17 *Job securities and jobs shortage agency*
The state institutes a *Job securities and jobs shortage agency* (JSA) that has local and regional branches. It is administered and organised as summarised in Addendum 3§4. The JSA has the following tasks and delegated authority.
(a) Generally its task is to minimise any jobs shortage.
(b) Quarterly registration of the jobs and the total wages sum in cooperatives and public sector institutions (in FTE and persons) – on the basis of quarterly reports by the entities. The reports should distinguish between the wages for workers with regular positions, and the compensation for trainees (this last category will be introduced in 3§18).
(c) Registration of the municipal and nationwide joblessness – as reported by individuals.
(d) Registration of the municipal and nationwide vacancies – as reported by cooperatives and public sector institutions.
(e) Before anything else, it tries to match (c) and (d): joblessness and vacancies (this is not different from what is customary in many capitalist nations).

(f) Registration of the persons with restricted physical or mental abilities to work (the relevance is indicated in 3§21).[24] Quarterly registration of the cooperatives and public sector institutions that provide a position to such workers (in FTE and persons) – on the basis of quarterly reports by the entities.

(g) The authorisation to impose on cooperatives and public sector institutions with a workforce of more than 50 workers in FTE, the requirement of, first, continuously offering *potential* traineeship positions of, as an indication, 5% of their workforce, second, reporting to the JSA when an *actual* traineeship has started and ended – each as set out in 3§18. The JSA may, when required, adapt the 5% figure.

(h) The authorisation to impose on cooperatives and public sector institutions temporary work-time reductions as set out in 3§19.

(i) The authorisation to impose on cooperatives and public sector institutions the requirement to temporary provide a position to currently jobless workers, as set out in 3§19.

(j) Exempted from (h) and (i) are: the parliament as organisation (3§2-c), public security institutions (3§5), the judiciary (3§6), health institutions (3D7-A) and educational institutions (3D7-B).

3§18   *Qualifications mismatch and other non-recession joblessness*

Introduction to all types of joblessness. Three types of (potential) workers may be jobless. *First*, school-leavers. *Second*, those who had a job, but are now out of work because of qualifications mismatches, or because of the restructuring of a cooperative or public sector institution, or because of the bankruptcy of a cooperative. These two are treated in the current section. *Third*, those who had a job, but are now out of work because of an economic recession (treated in 3§19). The three types are treated in different sections because their counteraction requires different policy measures.

Qualifications mismatch and other non-recession joblessness. (In this and the following two sections MiW abbreviates the minimum wage. MCL abbreviates the minimum costs of living. As mentioned in 3§11, the MiW is as an indication 1⅔ (167%) of the MCL, whence MCL/MiW = 60%.)

(a) Everyone out of work has, during two months, the right to a job search allowance, provided s/he indeed actively seeks work. The allowance is 60% of the

---

24 On the basis of a statement by the person or a general practitioner. Persons with restricted abilities are medically examined regarding their abilities to work at a defined quality, speed and work-time. The medical examiner reports this to the JSA together with a statement if and where the person works. On the basis of this information, the JSA determines the number of persons that could in principle work if they were offered a job.

MiW for school-leavers and for those who had a job for in total less than two years.[25] The allowance is 85% of the MiW (142% MCL) for those who had a job during two years or more (this is independent of any payments that might have been agreed with the institution at which the person worked – this also applies to those who worked less than two years).

(b) In case a person during these two months found no work, s/he is required to take on a paid traineeship, which is part of a traineeship programme as set out below. The traineeship programme has two purposes. First, for the trainee, to gain additional qualification as well as work experience. Second, for the provider of the traineeship, the programme offers an easy way to find new workers: next to the qualifying training the traineeship functions as a probation without commitment – traineeships are thus a lever to regular jobs.

(c) All cooperatives and public sector institutions with a workforce in FTE of 50 or more should continuously offer *potential* traineeship positions of (as an indication) 5% of their workforce.[26] Those with a workforce of less than 50 may, but are not required to, offer traineeships. (Below all these are called 'the providers'.) The traineeships should provide on-the-job training, and be *representative* for a regular job with the provider. The offered potential trainee positions are registered at the JSA with a brief indication of the kind of traineeship. The latter makes these publicly available (as including on a well searchable website).

(d) From the offered potential traineeships, the jobless make their preferences known to the JSA, whereupon the JSA allots *actual* traineeships to the jobless (without interference of the providers, and for the jobless without any guarantee of a preferred traineeship). It does so such that the providers take a proportionally equal share in the actual traineeships. During the traineeship, trainees should keep on searching for a regular position, either with the provider or elsewhere.

(e) The duration of one actual traineeship is a maximum of one year. Providers shall pay the trainees a compensation of 60% of the MiW (100% of the MCL). For those who had a job (or jobs) for at least two years, the JSA makes this up to 85% MiW (142% MCL).

---

25 The period of two years relates to their total working past. It takes account of a job with a probation period, the latter being a maximum of two years – 2§3.4 – and that in effect might be a period of a couple of months. The 60% MiW allowance is the same as what school-leavers received when still at school (cf. 3§23).

26 As a rough estimate, the institutions with a workforce of more than 50 workers encompass 56% of the total workforce. This implies that the mentioned 5% of the institutions' workforce traineeships may account for an *annual* traineeships amount of 2.8% of the labour population (see further point h below).

(f) The provider, as well as the trainee, reports to the JSA when a traineeship has started and ended. When after a one-year traineeship someone is still out of regular work, s/he is required to adopt a new traineeship with another provider.

The relevant (councils of) cooperatives and public sector institutions might consider the traineeships and the compensation for these as a financial burden. However, in the absence of traineeship programs, the burden might even be higher in the form of the taxation to finance jobless allowances, and in the latter case without the traineeship advantages for the entities.

It is estimated that the number of people out of work is on an *annual* basis 1.1% of the available workforce – this regards the two months sub (a) on an annual basis.[27] Thus this is the estimated rate of joblessness. It is also estimated that – *initially* (the inflow) – a maximum of 3% of the available workforce consists of job searching school-leavers, and that on average a maximum of 4% of the available workforce consists of non-school-leavers that initially participate in a traineeship programme.[28] However, it is expected that the participation in a traineeship programme will be on average far less than a full year – though some might need a full year (or even longer).

(g) Should the amount of people without a *regular* job on an *annual* basis structurally turn out to be more than, say, 2.5% of the available workforce, then a general work-time reduction (decided on by parliament, 3§10-a) should bring the figure down (such that the duration of actual traineeships is on average no more than a couple of months).

3§19 *Recessional joblessness*

In capitalism the cyclically recurrent recessional unemployment is mainly caused by prior macroeconomic over-investment (in the upturn) as resulting in macroeconomic over-capacity.[29] It is difficult to foresee whether recessional joblessness will occur in a cooperatives economy and, if so, as frequently and deeply as in a capitalist economy. Recall that cooperatives' councils must approve of investment increases beyond 5% of the past five-year aver-

---

27 Appendix 3A, Table 3A.5.
28 The total potential workforce regards the number of people within some age bound, for example 15 to 65. It is composed of three categories: (1) people being formally educated; (2) people not available for work because of incapacity or long illness; (3) **the available workforce**. The latter is subdivided into: (3a) the **actual workforce** (those actually having a position as including those on short-term sick leave or parental leave); (3b) the **jobless workforce**. The **rate of joblessness** equals the jobless workforce over the available workforce (3b/3).
29 Outlined in Reuten 2019, pp. 256–79.

age (2§5.1c). In case it does occur, the recessional joblessness hits school-leavers as well as dismissed workers. In a recession under capitalism, enterprises might lay-off current workers whom they are not fond of. In a cooperatives economy it is less likely that councils will vote out some of their colleagues for reasons of an economic recession. (It will be seen in chapter 6 that in a recession the 'worker-*owned* cooperatives' as existing in capitalism tend to adapt the wages of workers rather than the number of workers.)

The economic policy instrument introduced below applies on a similar solidarity between workers, here for the economy at large.

First of all, the JSA has to find out the character of any prevailing joblessness as either resulting from qualifications mismatches (3§19), or from a general recession, and it does so with the assistance of the *National institute for economic analysis and forecasts* (3§33-B).

For the total joblessness, as well as separately for the non-recessional and recessional joblessness, the rates of joblessness can be calculated. The 'rate of recessional joblessness' is the 'recessional joblessness' over the 'available workforce' (see the last but one footnote).

Below the policy instrument for countering recessional joblessness will be outlined in two stages. The first stage is outlined in the rest of the current section: it abstracts from any remnants from mismatches joblessness (3§18). The second stage – outlined in 3§20 – considers the articulation of the two forms of joblessness. In that section it will also be clarified why the much simpler policy instrument of 3§18 is inadequate during a recession.

Recessional joblessness in abstraction from qualifications mismatches remnants. For any recessional joblessness, the countering policy instrument implies that the recessional joblessness is allocated over *all* workers, instead of, as in capitalism, merely the jobless. The instrument consists of four steps.

1. Announcement step. When according to specified statistical indicators there is a recession – and hence actual recessional joblessness – the 'Job securities and jobs shortage agency' (JSA) makes a formal *announcement* about it to cooperatives and the relevant public sector institutions. The announcement refers to their last reported jobs account (3§17-b), which is now called the 'reference labour force'. Recall that the public sector institutions mentioned in 3§17-i are exempted from the measures below.

2. Intermediate matching period. Intermediate matching period of three months, elucidated after step 3.

3. Step of work-time reduction and temporary work provision. Step 3A. Three months after the announcement (sub 1), *all* cooperatives and the relevant public sector institutions are required to introduce, at the going wage-*rates*, a work-time reduction for all their regular (non-trainee) workers at 0.5% points above the rate of joblessness. This means – so far – that their wages sums decrease (in case the rate of joblessness is for example 4%, the wages sum decrease would be 4.5%).

Step 3B. Concomitantly the cooperatives and relevant public sector institutions are required, for the duration of the recession, to provide a *temporary position* to jobless persons – proportionally to their workforce *at the point of* the JSA's recession announcement (the 'reference labour force' of step 1). The compensation for these additional workers is, as a preliminary indication, 85% of the minimum wage (142% of the minimum costs of living) – on this indication see further 3§20-h. This means that there will still be a wages sum reduction (at least so in the abstract account of the current section). The temporary workers do not make up part of workers' councils, and they do not share in dividends (in a recession there are on average not likely to be substantial dividends).

The key point is that for step (3) it is the JSA that allocates the jobless over the cooperatives and the relevant public sector institutions (though, if feasible, it might take account of their earlier announced vacancies (cf. 3§17-d)). Obviously, cooperatives and these institutions do not like such enforced allocation. It is therefore in their interest to use the intermediate three-month period after the announcement (step 2) to themselves search for people for the additional number of workers of step (3). A similar seeking argument applies for the jobless. This may mean that at least part of the problem is resolved, in a rather brief period of time, and without the JSA's enforcement of step 3 – although step 3 is required for the non-resolved part.

In the case that the recession becomes prolonged with extra jobless, the JSA makes a new announcement, upon which a similar step 2 three-month process develops as set out above.

4. *End of recession announcement.* The JSA also announces when the recession is over (perhaps when the rate of joblessness is below 1–2%). Three months after this announcement, the general work-time reduction ends, as does the temporary contract of the formerly jobless. However, in a gradually up-swinging conjuncture, together with their hardly interrupted work experience, it will – in comparison with capitalism – not be extremely difficult to find permanent work. It is not unlikely that parts of the temporary appointments are turned into permanent ones with the same cooperative or public sector institution.[30]

---

[30] For recessions in capitalism there has been a longstanding debate about the efficacy of so-called macroeconomic cyclical 'fine-tuning' – via macroeconomic state expenditure (Snowdon and Vane 2002, pp. 19–20 and their references). One main point being that

The following two conclusions are drawn. First, the measures for countering recessional joblessness amount to a tempering of the joblessness and a different distribution of its burden in comparison with capitalism.

Second, all workers take some of the burden of the recessional joblessness, but still those actually out of regular work do so the most. For the latter, nevertheless, the jobless period is far less than is common in capitalism: in the current stage's account, at most the three months of the step 2 intermediate matching period (it will be seen in 3§20c–d that the maximum is rather two months). In case of a prolonged recession, it is recurrently a new group of jobless that takes on the extra burden. Another burden for the extra hit is that the work that they do get during the recession may not be near their preference.

3§20   *The articulation of joblessness due to qualifications mismatches and to recessions, and conclusions on joblessness in general*

Recessional joblessness does not occur in a void of non-prevalence of mismatches joblessness, as was assumed in the previous section. The current section sets out from any prevailing mismatches as outlined in 3§18 – and hence from prevailing mismatches countering traineeships – and outlines its articulation with the 3§19 policy measures.

(a) First of all, it is likely that in the period just prior to the recession announcement (3§19), the number of the 3§18 traineeships expanded – this is an indication of an upcoming recession. As will be seen under (b), the expansion of traineeships is the reason why the fairly simple design of 3§18 is inadequate in a situation of recessional joblessness, that is, at much higher joblessness rates.

(b) The burden of the traineeship programmes was taken on by, mainly, cooperatives and public sector institutions with a workforce of more than 50 workers (3§17-g and 3§18-c). At an increasing joblessness the traineeship burden for the cooperatives concerned becomes quite high, depending on the proportion of cooperatives with more than 50 workers (which is difficult to estimate before a Design society exists). However, at least in the capitalist enterprises around 2019 in Upper-middle income and High income countries on average, the enterprises that employ 50 or more persons cover just over 40% of these countries' total employment by enterprises; in Low income and Lower-middle income

---

because of various time lags between the detection of recessional problems and the actual implementation of extra state expenditure, the latter may work countercyclically. That policy instrument is (was) regarding employment an *indirect* one (extra state expenditure) hoping that it would affect employment. The policy instrument outlined above indeed 'fine tunes', but regarding the workforce it does so directly, and it cannot work countercyclically because there is a definite start (step 1) and end (step 4).

countries this is far less.[31] This was one reason for the design of 3§19. The following points set out the previous two sections' articulation proper.

(c) Taking recessions to be exceptional, the constellation with actual traineeships is 'normal'. This also means that no one is out of work (any kind) for more than two months (3§18-b) – also if articulated with a recession.

(d) In the first three months after the announcement of a recession, nothing might change for those under a traineeship (step 2 of 3§19). However, anticipating step 3 (including the Job securities and jobs shortage agency's (JSA) allocation of workers without a regular job over the cooperatives and relevant public sector institutions) part of the trainees may be offered a regular position or a temporary position. This will foremost be trainees that already worked in the regarding institution.

(e) After this period (entering step 3 of 3§19) all going traineeships are transferred into *temporary positions*, at a higher compensation than the one for traineeships – obviously this is an advantage for the former trainees (that is, for the duration of the recession).

Recall that, amongst the public sector institutions, traineeships are offered by the parliament as organisation, and most of the public security institutions, of the courts, and of the health and education (3§17-a), whereas the mentioned public sector institutions are exempted from the recession work-time reduction, as well as (in case) from the requirement to offer extra positions as measured by the reference labour force (3§17-j and 3§19–3B). Nevertheless (for equity among trainees) their going traineeships are for the duration of the recession transferred into temporary positions. The extra compensation is, via the JSA, made up by the state via deficit financing (this boosts macroeconomic expenditure).

(f) At this point it is clear for the cooperatives and the relevant public sector institutions what their temporary positions target is, which is derived from the 'reference labour force' (step 1 of 3§19). However, new school-leavers and newly dismissed workers may enter the jobless workforce. In order to keep the mentioned targets clear, these persons are proceeded with as in 3§18, that is, after a two-month job search period they have to take on a traineeship under the 3§18 conditions.

---

31   ILO 2019, p. 3. In Low and Lower-middle income countries on average, one person enterprises are dominant (50–60% of the labour force of enterprises) and enterprises with more than 50 workers constitute no more than 7–10% of the total. This means that for a transition (ch. 8) of these countries, the 50 worker number (3§18) has to be adapted. Alternatively, and as long as the mentioned proportions prevail, the 3§18 measures might be omitted – in which case the current section is irrelevant.

(g) Should the recession prolong (see the last sentence of step 3 of 3§19) then the JSA makes a new recession announcement, based on an updated 'reference labour force'. Then, again after a three-month intermediate period, the new traineeships are transferred into temporary positions, as mentioned under (e) above.

(h) This final point is on the compensation of workers with a temporary position. The compensation should be such that *for cooperatives* the sum of the regular wages and this compensation should hardly change in comparison with the start of the recession. (A decrease would have a negative effect on aggregate demand and sales; an increase would have a negative effect on the surplus of cooperatives and so on their room for investment.) Thus this final point seeks a finely tuned policy to reach this.

The compensation of workers with a temporary position was (as mentioned in 3§19 under step 3B) as a preliminary indication set at 85% of the minimum wage. The definite percentage, now called the *'target percentage'*, is to be determined in face of the percentage of the wages sum reduction for regular workers of 0.5% points above the rate of joblessness (3§19, step 3B). The point of departure for the determination of the 'target percentage' is the 'reference labour force' (3§19, step 1), more specifically, the for *cooperatives* average of (a) the wages of regular workers and (b) the compensation paid for traineeships. The 'target percentage' is set such that there is hardly any change in the average payment to labour, as mentioned in the first paragraph (of h). Not much more can be said about it now, because the target percentage is to be set on the basis of empirical information at the point of a recession in a future society.[32] The target percentage has to be determined by the JSA, as assisted by the 'National institute for economic analysis and forecasts' (3§33-B).

Concluding summary of sections 3§18–3§20
(1) In combination the measures of 3§18–3§20 imply that school-leavers and those that had a job before may be out of work for a maximum period of two months. Apart from this period, everyone either has a regular job, or has temporary work (during a recession), or participates in a traineeship; the latter being a lever to regular jobs.

(2) New school-leavers and newly dismissed workers have, during two months, the right to an allowance; in this period they are required to actively search for

---

32   What can be mentioned is that in the hypothetical situation in which there would be no mismatches joblessness at the start of a recession, then a compensation *at the minimum wage* for temporary workers would nearly reach the target.

a regular job. For school-leavers and those that had a job before for less than two years, the allowance is 60% of the minimum wage (equal to the minimum costs of living). For those that, during their total working past, had a job for two years or more, the allowance is 85% of the minimum wage (142% of the minimum costs of living).

(3) If during this two-month period (sub 2) the persons concerned (sub 2) found no regular job, they have to take on a traineeship (as outlined in 3§18). Traineeship providers shall pay a compensation of 60% of the minimum wage. For those that had a job for two years or more, the JSA makes this up to 85% of the minimum wage. During the traineeship period, trainees shall actively search for a regular job.

(4) In case a recession should emerge (3§19) the traineeships (sub 3) are transferred during the recession into 'temporary jobs' (as outlined in the first part of 3§20). The persons with these temporary jobs receive a compensation of 85% of the minimum wage; 85% being a preliminary indication as set out in 3§20-h.

3§21 *Restricted abilities to work, and sickness payments*

Restricted abilities to work. Around 2020 the population with restricted abilities to work may – depending on specific country definitions – comprise 10% of the total potential workforce (the population between age 15 and the pension age). It is important that these people are socially part of the working community according to their abilities.

In the Design, therefore, proportional to their workforce, cooperatives and public sector institutions are required to provide work to those with restricted physical or mental abilities to work. Their workers' council decides on the wage, but they shall be paid at least 150% of the minimum wage (exclusive of their dividends).[33] This figure takes account of extra expenditure for transport and provisions at home and the possibility of some saving for after their pension age (it will be seen in 3§24 that pensioners receive 100% of the minimum wage).

The rule at hand increases the wages sum, but in comparison with many current mature capitalist countries it reduces taxes that finance the allowances for these persons. It may well be the case that due to this kind of social integration, or due to other factors, the abilities of a category of these persons moves to near average. They are therefore medically re-examined every five or ten years.[34]

---

33 Given that these people are generally worse off than the average worker, my initial idea was that they should receive (a percentage of) the average remuneration of the institution at hand. Its disadvantage would be a diverse remuneration depending on the institution.

34 The 10% – or whatever the exact number may be – referred to in the first paragraph implies

There will be a remaining category of disabled persons who are hardly able to work (defined at 80% inability to work; estimated at 4% of the population between 15 and 65 years). Most of these will live in a nursing (care) home; some looked after by family or friends. These persons, or those caring for them, receive a social security allowance of 120% of the minimum wage (this is exclusive of all medically prescribed extra provisions). These allowances are paid out of the general taxation means. The state expenditure on these allowances is estimated at 1.3% of GDP (cf. Appendix 3A).

Sickness payments. Payments for short sickness (less than one month) are paid out of the entities' wage bill. For any longer sickness cooperatives as well as 'workers' council governed foundations' (3§25) with fewer than 100 workers are required to take out a sickness insurance with an insurance cooperative (institutions with more than 100 workers may do so). It is supposed that state institutions take on the risk collectively. (On any stand-ins for sick workers see Appendix 3F.)

• *Budget and workforce constraints Division 5*
For its registration tasks the JSA (3§17) requires an annual moderate budget and workforce that structurally grows with the workforce. The budget and workforce ceilings for these tasks are hard.

The action required by the JSA for recessional joblessness (3§19) is irregular. Regarding the 'qualifications mismatch joblessness' (3§18) some mismatch between jobs offered and (potential) workers' qualifications is probably permanent; however, irregularly the mismatch may be larger than normal. The work for the JSA regards mainly registration matters, and next to that the (one-sided) matching of traineeship preferences of the jobless to the traineeships offered. On top the JSA should, on a sample basis, check on the actual quality of the traineeships offered. The duration of joblessness allowances is a maximum of two months and these are financed out of the general taxation means of the state (the same applies for 25% MiW traineeship supplements).

Regarding the restricted abilities to work (3§21) the measures mainly regard one-off rules.

---

that there is a threshold problem that may be solved by bonuses in between the thresholds. Thus a small cooperative with e.g. seven workers receives a bonus when as an eighth person it provides a position to a worker with restricted abilities – etc.

Division 6. Income allowances (exclusive work-related allowances)

This Division presents: child-related allowances – child's costs of living allowances, childcare allowances and parental leave allowances (3§22); allowances for students (3§23); and equal pension allowance for all (3§24). Their levels are set by parliament. The granting is implemented by an executive *Pensions and child allowances agency* that is assigned a budget and an amount of workforce in FTE for the agency itself, as well as separately a budget for the allowances that it pays. The agency is administered and organised as summarised in Addendum 3§4.

A table at the end of the Division summarises all income securities and allowances, as including the work-related allowances.

3§22 *Child-related allowances*
The argument for child allowances is based on an equity principle. Everybody is free not to have children. However, to the extent that a larger part of the population would refrain from having children, the fewer adults can care for the old (including for those that freely decided not to have children). It is therefore fair that, within a population reproduction bound, parents are compensated for child expenses.

(1) Child's costs of living allowances. Until a juvenile reaches age 18 (or if this is earlier, until the juvenile starts working) the caring parent receives, for up to three children, age-dependent child's costs of living allowances (as based on costs of living baskets and indexes).

As an indication the annual per child allowances amount age dependently from 14% to 22% of the minimum wage. The state expenditure for this is estimated at 1.5% of GDP (see also Appendix 3A).

(2) Childcare allowances. Childcare is carried out by licensed cooperatives. Until a juvenile turns 18 (or if this is earlier, until they start working) the caring parent receives, for up to three children, age-dependent costs covering childcare allowances. Until age 5 this regards a full working day allowance, and from age 5 onwards one for outside school hours and the school holidays beyond the parent's holidays. The annual costs per child are estimated at 74% of the minimum wage until age 5, and at 34% afterwards. The state expenditure for this is estimated at 3.8% of GDP (see also Appendix 3A). The parent can opt for day care by a cooperative or any other way of care, including by her/himself (in the latter case s/he would have to use up part of the 'temporary part-time' option – 3§10-d).

(3) Parental leave allowance. Before and after the birth of a child a period of parental leave is paid by the state at 100% of the minimum wage (it is up to

the councils of cooperatives and public sector institutions to make this up to a larger amount). The mother is eligible to an allowance of 16 weeks around birth (of which at least four weeks prior to birth), and of another nine weeks any time during the child's first three years. The partner (in case) is eligible to an allowance of one week immediately after birth, of two weeks any time during the child's first half year, and of three weeks any time during the child's first three years. This makes together 31 weeks. A single parent is eligible to 31 weeks.

The annual state expenditure for this allowance is estimated at 0.25% of GDP (see also Appendix 3A).

(*4*) *Orphan allowances.* Foster parents or adoptive parents of domestic orphans receive annually twice the child's costs of living allowances under (1), though for siblings the three children limit does not apply. Relatively this makes up a small category. The relevant state expenditure is estimated at 0.001% of GDP (see also Appendix 3A).

Because each of these four child allowances are, with some lag, roughly proportional to population growth – hence with some time lag to the working population growth – there is for these, roughly, a budget ceiling as percent of GDP.

3§23   *Costs of living allowances for students*

From age 18 onwards, students receive, for usually a maximum of six years, costs of living allowances (of 60% of the minimum wage for students living away from home). PhD students receive in addition a similar allowance for a maximum of four years. A part-time student receives a part-time allowance. (In international classifications each of these allowances are usually subsumed under education.)

The state expenditure on these allowances is estimated at 1.3% of GDP (see also Appendix 3A). For these allowances there is no structural budget ceiling, as their budget grows with the average number of schooling years.

3§24   *Pensions*

Parliament determines at which age workers are eligible for a pension. Pensions are state provided, uniformly at (as an indication) 100% of the minimum wage, as decided on by parliament (recall that, as an indication, the minimum wage is 167% of the minimum costs of living).

It is fair, first, to make the eligible pension age dependent on the number of years that a person worked (this implies that those who followed a tertiary education are eligible at a later age than those who did not). Second, to bring forward the eligible pension age for those with a physically heavy profession.

Regarding the finance of pensions, a structural budget ceiling as percent of GDP would need to bring the average number of retirement years in line with the average number of working years (meaning that with an ageing population the pension age is proportionally postponed).[35]

For the type of finance for pensions the general rule is that pensions are 'pay-as-you-go' financed (that is, from going tax receipts). In case of an expected ageing population (this can be demographically foreseen) pensions in the Design are in part (to the extent of the ageing) financed on the basis of funding. This fund also originates from taxes, though from taxation preceding the ageing. This should prevent that a relatively small working population is taxed in full for a relatively large pensioner population. (In effect the system is such that the part of taxes that is destined for pensions is more or less constant per generation.)

Workers who reached the pension age are free to continue working when, and as long as, there is no joblessness. This does not affect their pension (however, they will reach a higher income tax bracket – 3§46).

The pension allowance leaves unaffected that workers might want to save for their retirement via the Savings and Loans Bank (3§16).

The state expenditure on pensions is estimated at 8.5% of GDP – it is the Design's second largest state expenditure category after health at 12% of GDP (Appendix 3A, Table 3A.1).

Table 3.9 summarises all of the income securities and income allowances prevalent in the Design.

TABLE 3.9   *Summary of the Design's income securities and income allowances*

	Category	Indication of level (before tax)†	Sect.
1	minimum costs of living (MCL)	costs of living basket	3§11
2	minimum wage in FTE (MiW)	set by parliament; indication: 167% MCL	3§11
3	MCL/MiW	60%	3§11
Required remunerations (by cooperatives and state institutions)‡			
4	at least the minimum wage	see above	3§11
5	traineeships	60% MiW (= 100% MCL)	3§18

---

35 That is, given that pensions are linked to the minimum wage (as an indication at 100%). The level of the minimum wage is itself a policy variable (it includes a costs of living component plus an additional component as discussed in 3§47-e). Parliament might decide to keep the retirement age fixed, even with an ageing population, but this would 'merely' mean that a larger share of the after-tax income of those that work goes to the retired.

TABLE 3.9   *Summary of the Design's income securities (cont.)*

Category	Indication of level (before tax)†		Sect.
6	recessional work-time and wage reduction	wage reduction equivalent to 0.5%-points above the rate of recessional joblessness		3§19
7	recessional additionally appointed workers	85% MiW (preliminary indication; cf. 3§20-h)		3§19
8	workers with restricted abilities	150% MiW (= 250% MCL)		3§21
State provided income allowances			% GDP	
9	job search school-leavers (max. 2 months)*	60% MiW (= 100% MCL)	0.1%	3§18
10	job search after a 2y job (max. 2 months)	85% MiW (= 142% MCL)	0.1%	3§18
11	trainees after having had a two-year job	25% (→ 85% MiW = 142% MCL)‡	0.2%	3§18
12	more than 80% inability to work	120% MiW (= 200% MCL)	1.3%	3§21
13	child costs of living (for up to 3 children <18y)	age dependent; average 18% MiW	1.6%	3§22
14	childcare (for up to 3 children <18y)	age dependent; average 47% MiW	3.8%	3§22
15	parental leave (31 weeks for parents together)	100% MiW	0.3%	3§22
16	students (usually max. 6 years)	60% MiW (= 100% MCL)	1.3%	3§23
17	pensions	100% MiW (= 167% MCL)	8.5%	3§24

† No taxes are levied on the minimum costs of living (MCL).
‡ Including 'workers' council governed foundations' (introduced in 3§25).
* The same applies for those that had a job for less than two years. If unsuccessful followed by a traineeship (row 7).
⁂ 60% MiW is paid by traineeship providers (row 5); the JSA makes this up to 85% of the MiW.

Division 7. Wellbeing institutions: health, education, culture

This Division treats the health, education and culture sectors in three subdivisions. With its about thirty pages (including an appendix), this is the largest Division of this chapter. Health provisions (subdivision 7A) constitute by far the largest state expenditure category (estimated at nearly 12% of GDP, and 28% of total state expenditure). The provision of education (subdivision 7B) constitutes – after pensions – the next largest expenditure category (estimated at nearly 6% of GDP, and 13% of total state expenditure).[36] In terms of expenditure the culture sector (subdivision 7C) is relatively a minor one.

---

36   Appendix 3A, Table 3A.1.

(Recreation and sports facilities are not treated in this Division because these are carried out by cooperatives.)[37]

The three sectors are coordinated by three state agencies. The executing health, education and culture institutions themselves (hospitals, schools and so on) have the legal form of a 'Workers' council governed foundation'. The Division's first section (3§25) sets out the organisation of these state-financed institutions.

Health and education provisions are free for all (financed out of taxation). There is no additional market for these. Health and education workers shall work in licensed institutions only, and they are remunerated similar as state workers (in case with an 'unsocial hours' wages supplement). Given these points, the organisation of these sectors – as including the planning for future capacity – seems rather straightforward. Nevertheless their outline below is detailed given blue-print character of this book and given the relative size of these sectors. (Without losing the further thread of the book, readers might merely skim the regarding subdivisions 7A and 7B.)

The culture sector (subdivision 7C) is for one part organised in state-financed 'workers' council governed foundations', and for another part taken on by cooperatives (for which municipalities receive an earmarked subsidy budget).

Especially for this Division the reader should recall the last paragraph of the Introduction to chapter 3: 'Note on the fractional precision of estimates'. Even when I state estimates in decimal fractions, this does not take away that all these are rough estimates, and the reader should take at that.

3§25 *Workers' council governed foundations*
(a) A *'Workers' council governed foundation'* (WGF) is a foundation that is governed by an association of which the institution's workers are the members. The association's membership is identical to the membership of the institution's workers' council.
(b) The foundation's premises and fixed equipment are owned by a relevant state agency that rents these out to the WGF. The foundation is the owner of the other assets. (Given that a WGF uses collective means, a state agency being the owner of the premises and fixed assets is a security in case of bankruptcy of a WGF; the services could then be taken on by a new WGF.)

---

37   Individually operating top athletes who gain less than the minimum wage may receive a grant.

(c) The foundation receives a budget from the relevant state agency. The foundation may be committed to constraints regarding the amount of its workforce as decided on by the relevant state agency.

(d) The budget includes a sum for its wages, the wages sum being equal to its workforce in FTE times the average wages and dividends of the nation's cooperatives in FTE. (In case of evening, night and weekend work-time shifts – such as in medical institutions – the regarding workers also receive a compensating wages supplement.)

(e) The foundation is not allowed to borrow, including by way of a bank overdraft.

(f) The foundation registers its incomes and expenditures in regular bookkeeping, and at the end of the year it records an Income account and a Balance sheet of their assets, liabilities and reserves. Unless otherwise indicated, each of the latter two is to be approved by an external registered auditor (see 3§43).

(g) The institutional council has the following main tasks and competences.

First, it elects a management that is removable by the council and that is revolving or re-elected at intervals of no more than five years.

Second, annually it has to approve of the institution's internal structure of the wage scales.

Third, it has to approve of the foundation's annual Income account and Balance sheet.

Fourth, in case of a large institution it may decide to introduce departments (see further point h). Along with it, an initial amount of staff and budget is allocated over these. The amount of staff and the budget normally change with the institutional staff and budget. The per department allocation may be revised every five years. The institutional council may also decide to merge departments.

(h) (The following point is analogous to 2§5.2 and 3§3-f.) In case of departments, each one constitutes a 'departmental council'. The latter elects the (removable) departmental management and deliberates over matters that it deems opportune for the operation of the department. In case the institutional council is so large that most members can merely vote instead of argue, the departmental council deliberates over the matters mentioned under (g), and appoints one or more spokespersons for the institutional council meetings (which does not interfere with the right of each individual to nevertheless speak at the institutional council).

(i) Workers can become member of the WGF's association after a successful application for a vacancy. The council may decide to grant memberships after a probation period of maximum two years. Applications are open to all for the vacancy qualified persons, without ethnic, gender, social, political or religious discrimination.

(j) WGFs are, even when fully financed by a state agency, no part of the state sector, but rather of the public sector. WGF workers are not civil service workers. (This is mainly relevant for statistical matters of international comparison.)

(k) Most often WGFs provide their services free of charge on basis of their budget sub (c) above – see the subdivisions below. However, Division 9 introduces WGFs that charge for their services (such as for railway transport). Their budget takes account of these charges. For these WGFs all other rules above apply, as including the determination of their wages sum according to sub (d) above and the allocation of the wages sum sub (g-second) above.

Subdivision 7A. The health sector

In the Design all health services are free of charge provisions that are fully state-financed out of taxation. The argument for it is as follows. Whereas the before and after-tax distribution of income in the Design is far less skewed than in capitalism, it is most probably not an equal one. A relatively high income may give more contentment, but that is fundamentally different from the health provision related inherent quality of life, or even its length. Moreover, there is a considerable difference in reversibility (next time I buy a fancier bicycle, versus next time I have my leg amputated by a better physician). These are two main reasons for having health provisions equally and freely available for all. (Evidently these are normative arguments, but all choices in the Design are normative.)

As mentioned, state expenditure on the health sector is estimated at nearly 12% of GDP and at 28% of total state expenditure.

Health services are organised as set out in this subdivision that subsequently treats: the tasks and delegated authority of the National Health Agency (3§26); primary medical treatment and prevention (3§27); hospitals (3§28); and care institutions (3§29). Here the last three sections are kept relatively brief, details of the organisation of these institutions being relegated to an Appendix at the end of the current subdivision.

3§26   *National Health Agency: tasks and delegated authority*

The state institutes a *National Health Agency* (<u>NHA</u>), that has regional branches. It is administered and organised as summarised in Addendum 3§4. It is assigned a budget and an amount of workforce in FTE for the NHA itself, as well as separately for the medical institutions for which it is responsible (see below). The NHA has the following tasks and delegated authority.

(a) Coordination of the nation's medical institutions (see 3§27–3§29). All medical institutions have the legal form of a 'Workers' council governed foundation' (3§25).
(b) Budget and workforce allocation over the nation's medical institutions.
(c) The issuing of licences to be a medical practitioner, pharmacist or other medical worker, and to be a medical institution. Medical practitioners, pharmacists and medical staff cannot freely establish. Instead they have to associate with alternatively: primary medical treatment clinics (3§27); hospitals (3§28); care institutions (3§29). All these (the workers and the medical institutions) shall – on risk of a fine or losing their licence – not require or accept any form of fees, payments in monetary form or in kind, gifts, or promises. (This rule should prevent uneven access to medical services.)
(d) Registration of all medical workers (including school-leavers) according to their formal education and later training for their specialisms, as well as their foreseen date of retirement.
(e) Long-term planning of medical workers' capacity in coordination with the *National Education Agency* (3§30). (In case of a foreseen insufficient capacity – perhaps because of the toughness of the profession, as including night shifts – it can, for specific professions, institute a medium-term work-time reduction at the going full average wage, as adapted every 10 years.)[38]
(f) Drawing up of peer group-informed and patient-informed medical quality standards, and the supervision of the medical institutions on basis of these standards.
(g) Carrying out of patient surveys and ratings of medical institutions, and their publication on a well accessible and searchable site.
(h) Registration of potential patients. For planning purposes all inhabitants are required to be registered with the NHA for a 'primary medical treatment clinic' (3§27) and a 'general multi-specialisation hospital' (3§28) of their choice (this applies from their birth onwards – until age 16 of their parents' choice). In case they are no longer happy with their choice they can quarterly register for another one. The NHA communicates this registration with the relevant clinics and hospitals.
(i) Drawing up of a long-term budget planning (25 years) – this long period is required for the establishment of especially new hospitals, residential care centres and nursing homes – that is adapted every five years. If required, the NHA takes the initiative to found the new institutions mentioned in the previous sentence.

---

38 The going average wage is the take-home wage; in effect this means an increased wage rate per hour.

(j) Drawing up of five-year indicative budgets (revised each year), and of one-year definitive budgets, as including their allocation over the medical institutions. Items (i) and (j) are communicated to the institutions and are also publicly available.

(k) Regarding the long-term budget planning (i) and the five-year indicative budgets (j) the NHA confers with the relevant minister.

(l) Owning the premises and the fixed equipment of the medical institutions; it rents these out to the latter (as mentioned in 3§2-b, this is a delegated ownership, the ownership ultimately resting with the state as legal entity). The purchase of new premises and fixed equipment takes place in close consultation with the medical institutions, the latter via the NHA's branches. (Regarding the fixed equipment this has the advantage of more or less collective purchases, and of the concentration of expertise for it.)

(m) The provision and finance of a nationwide net of ambulances. Preferably it licenses these facilities to cooperatives. In the relevant cases of non-precarious patient transport, taxi cooperatives may do the job.

(n) The issuing of licences for the production of pharmaceutics and of key medical instruments to the relevant cooperatives. The licence conditions include not only quality guarantees but also extra financial conditions regarding failure risks, as well as the monitoring of these.

3§27 *Primary medical treatment and prevention*

Primary medical treatment and prevention is divided into three categories: (1) primary medical treatment clinics; (2) auxiliaries for these; (3) prevention. Together these constitute 12% of the labour force of the total health sector. (All numbers mentioned here and in the next two sections are summarised in Table 3.10, that is placed after 3§29.)

The main part of the primary medical health service is organised in 'Primary medical treatment clinics' (MTCs). Their legal form is that of a 'Workers' council governed foundation' (WGF) (3§25). These clinics provide the medical – non-medical-specialist – treatment that is locally readily available for all. Their staff ranges from general practitioners, obstetricians, nurses, physiotherapists and dentists to pharmacists and various assistants. In terms of number of workers this primary treatment is estimated to make up about 9.5% of the total health sector. An appendix to the current subdivision sets out details of a possible organisation of such clinics.

Primary auxiliary institutions include ambulances and various services for the MTCs such as laboratories (the latter have the legal form of a WGF).

Other WGFs are responsible for various preventive measures, such as population screening and screening programmes; vaccination and other prevent-

THE STATE AND THE STATE INSTITUTIONS OF THE DESIGN 121

ive interventions; public information on diseases (including research on all of these) as well as for reintegration services.

3§28 Hospitals

Hospitals have the legal form of a WGF (3§25), and together these are estimated to make up 33% of the total health sector. There are four types of hospitals.

(1) 'General multi-specialisation hospitals' provide general diagnostic and medical treatment (both surgical and non-surgical) to patients with a wide variety of medical conditions, either for outpatients or inpatients. They encompass all standard medical specialisations.

(2–3) 'Single specialisation hospitals' (SSH) and 'University hospitals' (UH) provide diagnostic and medical treatment (both surgical and non-surgical) for patients with a special (SSH) or a complex (UH) medical condition, either for outpatients or for inpatients.[39] All these pertain to somatic treatment.

(4) 'Psychiatric hospitals' specialise in mental treatment (8% of the health sector).

An appendix to the current subdivision sets out details of a possible organisation of all of these hospitals.

3§29 Care institutions

The qua labour force largest part of the health sector category consists of care institutions (55%) which again have the legal form of a WGF. These include: care for physically or/and mentally disabled persons (14%); nursing institutions (28%) – mainly for elderly (hereunder is also included 9% for home healthcare). All these provide care, and in relevant cases medical treatment. Finally, this category includes social care, including youth care (11%).

An appendix to the current subdivision sets out details of a possible organisation of these institutions.

Table 3.10 summarises various quantifications of the health sector. It can be seen that the state expenditure for this sector makes up about 12% of GDP (column 2), its share of societies' labour force makes up about 15% (column 4). Column 6 shows an indicator for the relative labour intensity of the three main subsectors (given that the average workers remuneration of each one institution is equal).

---

[39] SSHs regard hospitals such as those for the unique treatment of cancer, burns, eye defects or a category such as young children.

TABLE 3.10   *Estimates of the state expenditure on, and the labour force of, the health sector*

(1)	(2)	(3)	(4)	(5)	(6)
	Expenditure in % GDP	Exp. share of health institutions	Labour force in % total labour force	Labour force in % labour force health institutions	Column (4) / (2)
Primary medical treatment and prevention	**2.25%**	**19.1%**	**1.8%**	**12.0%**	0.79
Primary medical treatment clinics (MTCs)†	1.85%			9.5%	
Primary auxiliaries‡	0.10%			2.5%	
Prevention (public health services)*	0.30%				
Hospitals	**4.35%**	**36.9%**	**4.9%**	**33.2%**	1.12
General multi-specialisation hospitals	2.00%			25.1%	
University hospitals	1.00%				
Specialising hospitals: somatic	0.50%				
Psychiatric hospitals	0.85%			8.1%	
Care institutions	**4.85%**	**41.1%**	**8.1%**	**54.8%**	1.66
Institutions for care disabled	1.65%			14.0%	
Nursing institutions (mainly for elderly)	2.50%			28.3%⁑	
Social care, including youth care	0.70%			11.5%	
Medical devices for individuals⁂	**0.35%**	**3.0%**			
Total of health institutions (WGFs)	**11.80%**	**100%**	**14.7%**	**100%**	1.25
Administration NHA	0.10%		0.1%	0.8%	
Total of health sector incl. NHA	**11.90%**		**14.8%**		

† Including pharmacies and pharmaceutics.
‡ These include ambulances; laboratories for MTCs; blood banks.
* Including population screening and screening programmes; vaccination and other preventive interventions; public information on diseases; research on all of these; reintegration services.
⁑ Of which home healthcare 9.4%.
⁂ Including prostheses, individual special means of transport for disabled, and home adaptations for disabled.

Appendix to subdivision 7A: Details of a possible organisation of the health sector

This appendix sets out details of a possible organisation of the health sector. Details are first of all opportune in face of the inherent importance of the sector for people's wellbeing, but also because of the state expenditure associated with this sector, which is, as mentioned, estimated at nearly 12% of GDP. The appendix is organised in the same order as the previous three sections.[40]

7A-1. Primary medical treatment and prevention. Primary medical treatment and prevention is divided into three categories: (1) primary medical treatment clinics; (2) auxiliaries for these; (3) prevention. Here the focus is on the primary medical treatment clinics (MTCs), which are estimated to make up 9.5% of the total health sector's labour force.
(a) *MTC task, staff and juridical form.* MTCs provide the medical – non-medical-specialist – treatment that is readily available for all. If required they are also responsible for the referral of patients to specialised medical and care institutions (3§28; 3§29 and 7A-2; 7A-2 below). An MTC is organised in units of about 50 staff, that serves about 10,000 inhabitants (see *Table 3.11*, middle column). Their legal form and internal administration is that of a 'workers' council governed foundation' (WGF, 3§25).

TABLE 3.11   *Composition of a primary medical treatment clinic (MTC); per about 10,000 inhabitants*[†]

	Normal composition	Minimum composition[‡]
general practitioners	5	4
obstetricians	1	1
nurses	3	2
district nurses*	4	2
physiotherapists*	8	5
speech therapists	2	1
psychologists and psychotherapists	6	3
dentists	4	3

---

40   The sector includes the following entries of the 'Standard industrial classification of economic activities' (UN 2008), here subsumed under the categories in bold. **Primary medical treatment** (3§27): General medical practice activities (86210); Dental practice activities (86230). **Hospitals** (3§28): Hospital activities (86101); Specialists medical practice activities (86220). **Care institutions** (3§29): ~~Child day-care activities (88910)~~ [carried out by cooperatives]; Medical nursing home activities (86102); Residential nursing care facilities (87100); Residential care activities for learning difficulties, mental health and substance abuse (87200); Residential care activities for the elderly and disabled (87300); Social work activities without accommodation for the elderly and disabled (88100).

TABLE 3.11 *Composition of a primary medical treatment clinic (cont.)*

	Normal composition	Minimum composition[‡]
dental assistants (general)	4	3
oral hygienists	2	1
pharmacists	1	1
pharmaceutic assistants	6	3
secretaries and general assistants	6	4
total number of staff (FTE)	52[*]	33

[†] An in-house pharmacist is the starting point for the unit's composition (the number of other staff per category is derived from it).
[‡] For MTCs being founded or being phased out (rough minimum, to be accorded with the NHA).
[*] Including for patients released from hospital.
[⁂] 31% of these are professionally educated for five years or more.

The organisation in such units has advantages for patients and for the staff. The staff can use collegial consultations, and directly refer a patient to a colleague with short information lines. Patients benefit from the latter, and the concentration of services may reduce their travelling time.

(b) *Council.* The MTC council elects among the staff a part-time manager – revolving or re-elected at intervals of no more than five years. (On the council see further 3§25.)

(c) *Work shifts.* Together with about 16 other MTCs, the evening, night and weekend shifts are regulated.[41] The staff members for which these shifts apply, receive an 'unsocial hours wages supplement'.

(d) *Pharmacy.* The MTC pharmacy delivers only to its MTC patients, and solely for MTC prescriptions. (In case a patient is referred to a specialised medical institution, that institution's pharmacy delivers any prescriptions by specialists.)

(e) *Finance.* As indicated (3§26-l), the clinic's premises and fixed equipment are rented from the NHA. For their current purchases, wages and unsocial hours compensation, MTCs receive from the NHA a quarterly lump-sum payment.

(f) *No borrowing.* Because MTCs are not allowed to borrow (3§25-d) they will continuously have to keep a reserve for not precisely plannable expenditures

---

41   For thinly populated areas this number is adapted.

(as including pharmaceutical purchases).[42] The quarter-based lump sum may contribute to this.

(g) *Recordkeeping*. MTCs register their incomes (e), expenditures and patient visits in regular bookkeeping. At the end of the year they record an income account and a balance sheet; as well as summary statements of their registered potential patients (3§26-h) patient visits, wages and wages supplement expenditures per staff member, and of any staff mutations.[43] The end of year statements are sent to the NHA and are discussed with a NHA official (the latter may require the statements to be approved by an external registered auditor – paid by the NHA).

(h) *Adapted composition of a MTC*. In face of their patients' background (including their ages) an MTC may, in deliberation with the NHA, change the composition of its staff, provided that all professions remain represented.

(i) *Disturbed continuity*. In case of a considerable quality drop (see 3§26-f;g), and in case the number of registered patients considerably drops due to demographic or other reasons, the council devises a restructuring plan on which it deliberates with a NHA official. The NHA may also take the initiative. Depending on for what reason the plan is initiated, the plan may range from quality-improvement measures, to adaption of the number of staff, to association with another MTC, and – when the latter is not feasible – ultimately the closing of an MTC. The latter when all professions can no longer be represented.

(j) *Founding of MTCs and staff mutations*. In consultation with the NHA individual medical professionals (school-leavers or any other) can take the initiative to found a new MTC, provided that it can be fully staffed and that there is qua

---

42 The latter is a limited problem because, as indicated under (e), the pharmacy delivers solely for MTC prescriptions.

43

	INCOME ACCOUNT		BALANCE SHEET	
Expenditure	Income		Assets	Liabilities
rent for premises	lump sums:		COB: payment account	none
rent for fixed equipment	• current purchases		SLB: reserves account*	
current purchases	• wages†		pharmaceutics stock	
wages (specified per worker)	• wages suppl.‡		other stocks	reserves
wages supplement (idem)				
surplus: added to reserves				

† Includes dividends (see 3§25c).
‡ Unsocial work hours.
* SLB: Savings and Loans Bank (3§16).

number of patients room for it in a city or region. The NHA provides information on the latter and can also mediate for additional staff. In case of (foreseen) vacancies in MTCs, the NHA can also mediate; the same applies for MTC staff that wish to move.

Conclusion on the financing of Primary medical treatment clinics. The annual budgets for MTCs are hard. The above organisation of MTCs makes sure that there is a structural budget ceiling as percent of GDP. The lump-sum financing according to the number of staff per, normally, 10,000 patients, as well as the preclusion of borrowing, realises this. In the aggregate the structural budget is population based – hence also working population based – instead of being (far more complicated) specific treatment based.[44] Via a parliamentary decision the lump-sum level may be adjusted.

7A-2. Hospitals. As mentioned, four types of hospitals are distinguished: General multi-specialisation hospitals; Single specialisation hospitals; University hospitals; and Psychiatric hospitals. Together these are estimated to make up 33% of the total health sector. This section starts with a point (a) that differs for the different types of hospitals; this is followed by points that are common for all.

• *General multi-specialisation hospitals* (GSH)
(a-1) *GSH tasks.* GSHs provide general diagnostic and medical treatment (both surgical and non-surgical) to patients with a wide variety of medical conditions, either for outpatients or inpatients. They encompass all standard medical specialisations. Generally, patients require a referral from their MTC, except in case of casualties or other urgent medical treatment (see d).

There is one GSH on about 300,000 inhabitants, each with about 3,000 total staff (including medical specialists, nurses, assistants, secretaries). Thus on average one GSH covers the patients of 30 MTCs, and they are accordingly spread over regions and cities. In thinly populated regions a GSH encompasses one or more outpatient-policlinics.

• *Single specialisation hospitals and university hospitals* (SSH and UH)
(a-2/3) *SSH and UH tasks.* SSHs and UHs provide diagnostic and medical treatment (both surgical and non-surgical) for patients with a special (SSH) or a complex (UH) medical condition, either for outpatients or for inpatients.[45]

---

44   It is 'also' working population based provided that with an ageing population the pension age is proportionally postponed (3§24).

45   SSHs regard hospitals such as those for the unique treatment of cancer, burns, eye defects or a category such as young children.

Generally patients require a referral from their GSH (see m), except in case of casualties or other urgent medical treatment (see d).
• *Psychiatric hospitals* (PH)
(a-4) *PH tasks.* PHs provide mental treatment either for outpatients or inpatients. Generally these patients require a referral from their GSH (see m), except in case of casualties or other urgent medical treatment (see d).
• *All hospitals*
(b) Their *legal form and internal administration* is that of a 'workers' council governed foundation' (WGF, 3§25).
(c) *Departments.* Hospitals are divided into Medical Departments according to the specialisations (consisting of medical specialists, nurses, assistants, secretaries).[46] See 3§25-f on departmental councils.
(d) *Pharmacy and urgent medical treatment unit.* GSH's include a pharmacy for their outpatients. GSHs and PHs must, and the other hospitals may, include a 'urgent medical treatment unit' (24/24 hrs., all days). This unit is constituted by the departments together, and is coordinated by the hospital's management.
(e) *Work shifts.* It is inherent to hospitals that most of the staff has to rotate in day, evening, night and weekend shifts. The staff members for which these shifts apply, receive an 'unsocial hours wage supplement'.
(f) *Number of staff.* The number of staff of each hospital is fixed as a percent of the nation's workforce. Thus the staff increases (or decreases) directly with the total workforce and indirectly with the total population. (University hospitals have next to their medical treatment function, research and student-training functions. The NHA – in coordination with the *National Education Agency* (3§30) – decides which average staff percentage is allotted to medical treatment. The same applies for UH premises and fixed equipment. What follows about the UH finance and its allocation, regards their medical treatment function.)
(g) *Finance.* As indicated (3§26-l), the premises and fixed equipment of hospitals are rented from the NHA. The NHA finances the hospitals via a quarterly lump sum that is composed as follows. *Basis wages:* the number of staff (see f) times the nationwide average wages and dividends of cooperatives (3§25-c). *Supplement wages:* a wages supplement for the average number of staff participating in work shifts (e) – calculated as a supplement-percent on the

---

46   When for a GSH there are 25 departments, then the average size of a department consists of 120 staff (usually departments such as internal medicine, paediatrics and anaesthesia are far above average). The staff of the under (a-1) mentioned GSH outpatient-policlinics, formally makes part of the Medical Departments according to the policlinic's specialisations.

basis wages.[47] *Budget for current equipment and other expenses:* calculated as a supplement-percent on the basis wages. (Note that other ways of distribution, such as based on the number and kind of treatments, will lead to enormous time-taking administrative burden – and irritation along it – without being waterproof.) Hospitals also receive (have received) a one-time reserve allowance of 5% of the wages sum that is owned by the hospital as foundation (the WGF).

(h) *No borrowing.* As indicated, WGFs (thus hospitals) are not allowed to borrow (3§25-d). Therefore they will continuously have to keep a reserve for not precisely plannable expenditures. Next to the reserve allowance (g), the quarter-based lump sum (g) may contribute to this. The reserve allowance may be drawn on only temporarily, after which it has to be made up to the normal level.

(i) *Recordkeeping.* In regular bookkeeping hospitals register their incomes (g), expenditures, patient visits, beds-capacity and their utilisation – all separately for each department. At the end of the year they record an income account and a balance sheet for the hospital at large; as well as summary statements per department of patient visits, beds-capacity and their utilisation, wages and wages supplements, as well as of workers mutations.[48] The end of year records and statements require approval by an external registered auditor and by the hospital's council.[49] After having been sent to the NHA, these are discussed with a NHA official. (The details above facilitate the inter-hospital comparison of departments.)

---

47 Some of a 'unsocial hours' compensation is included in the cooperatives average – regarding cooperatives that work in shifts.

48

INCOME ACCOUNT		BALANCE SHEET	
Expenditure	**Income**	**Assets**	**Liabilities**
rent for premises	lump sums:	COB: payment accounts	*none*
rent for fixed equipment	• current purchases	SLB: reserves account*	
current purchases	• wages: basis†	pharmaceutics stock	
wages: basis	• wages: suppl.‡	other stocks	reserves (allowance)
wages: supplement			other reserves
surplus: added to reserves			

† Includes dividends (see 3§25c).
‡ Unsocial work hours.
* SLB: Savings and Loans Bank (3§16).

49 See 3§43 on external registered auditors.

(j) *Quality drop.* In case in of a considerable quality drop of a department (see 3§26-f;g), the departmental council together with the hospital management devises a restructuring plan on which they deliberate with one or more NHA officials. The NHA may also take the initiative. This plan focusses on quality improvement measures. In case of insufficient results, a subsequent restructuring plan comprises adaption of the staff.

(k) *Vacancies.* For vacancies of a medical department its council may decide for a probation period of a maximum of two years. Applications are open to all for the vacancy qualified persons, without ethnic, gender, social, political or religious discrimination. Further the council adopts procedures that it seems fit. (Recall that the NHA registers the medical workers – 3§26-d.)

(l) *Second opinion for patients.* In case of a proposed treatment with alternative high risks, patients (or in case their guardian) can get a second opinion from a specialist of another hospital.

(m) *Referral.* A medical specialist of a 'General multi-specialisation hospital' (GSH) may refer a patient to a Single specialisation hospital, a University hospital, or a Psychiatric hospital. This requires prior consent between, first, the specialists of the two hospitals, and second, the patient and the GSH specialist.

Conclusion on the financing of hospitals. The annual budgets for hospitals are hard. The above organisation of hospitals makes sure that there is a structural budget ceiling (as percent of GDP). The lump-sum financing according to the number of staff of hospitals as a fixed percent of the nation's workforce, as well as the preclusion of borrowing, realises this. In the aggregate the budget is population based instead of specific treatment based (which would be far more complicated).[50] In comparison with an insurance-based system, medical staff – instead of insurance institutions – ultimately decide on the rationing of treatments. Via parliamentary decisions the fixed percent and/or the lump-sum level may be adjusted; this regards the degree of the rationing, not its content.

(It might be thought that with an ageing population the number of medical treatments increases. That is so for the average number of treatments, however, the top number of treatments tends to occur in the last three years of a persons' life. Thus when the average life expectancy increases, the top number of treatments moves to a later age.)

---

50   The budget is population based, and therefore also working population based provided that with an ageing population the pension age is proportionally postponed (3§24).

7A-3. **Care institutions.** As mentioned, in terms of number of staff the care institutions (CI) are estimated to make up 55% of the total health sector. These institutions include: (1) the care of physically or/and mentally disabled persons (14%); (2) nursing institutions (28%) – mainly for elderly (hereunder is also included 9% for home healthcare). All these provide care, and in relevant cases medical treatment. Finally this category includes social care, including youth care (11%).

Below the four tasks or rules different from those of hospitals are marked •
(a) • *CI tasks.* CIs provide care – and in relevant cases medical treatment – to persons under the categories mentioned above. Generally patients/persons require a referral from their MTC or a medical specialist of a hospital.
(b) Their *legal form and internal administration* is that of a 'workers' council governed foundation' (WGF, 3§25).
(c) • *Departments.* CIs are divided into Departments according to the CI's organisation (depending on the CI consisting of medical specialists or general practitioners, therapists, nurses, assistants, secretaries). See 3§25-f on departmental councils.
(d) • *Urgent treatment unit.* Especially social care institutions may include an 'urgent medical treatment unit' (24/24 hrs., all days).
(e) *Work shifts.* It is inherent to CIs that most of the staff has to rotate in day, evening, night and weekend shifts. The staff members for which these shifts apply, receive an 'unsocial hours wages supplement'.
(f) *Number of staff.* The number of staff of each CI is fixed as a percent of the nation's workforce. Thus the staff increases (or decreases) directly with the total workforce and indirectly with the total population. (Regarding (nursing) homes for the elderly this assumes that aging goes along with a postponement of the number of years that persons cannot care for themselves.)
(g) *Finance.* As indicated (3§26-l), the premises and fixed equipment of CIs are rented from the NHA. The NHA finances CIs via a quarterly lump sum that is composed as follows. *Basis wages:* the number of staff (see f) times the nationwide average wages and dividends of cooperatives. *Supplement wages:* a wages supplement for the average number of staff participating in work shifts (e) – calculated as a supplement-percent on the basis wages.[51] *Budget for current equipment and other expenses:* calculated as a supplement-percent on the basis wages. (Note that other ways of distribution, such as based on the number and kind of treatments, will lead to enormous time-taking administrative bur-

---

51   Some of a 'unsocial hours' compensation is included in the cooperatives' average – pertinent to cooperatives that work in shifts.

den – and irritation along it – without being waterproof.) CIs also receive (have received) a one-time reserve allowance of 5% of the wages sum that is owned by the institution as foundation (the WGF).

(h) *No borrowing*. As indicated, WGFs (thus CIs) are not allowed to borrow (3§25-d). Therefore they will continuously have to keep a reserve for not precisely to plan expenditures. Next to the reserve allowance (g), the quarter-based lump sum (g) may contribute to this. The reserve allowance may be drawn on only temporarily, after which it has to be made up to the normal level.

(i) *Recordkeeping*. In regular bookkeeping CIs register their incomes (g), expenditures, patient visits, beds capacity and their utilisation – all separately for each department. At the end of the year they record an income account and a balance sheet for the CI at large;[52] as well as summary statements per department of patient visits, beds capacity and their utilisation, wages and wages supplements, as well as of workers' mutations. The end of year records and statements require approval by an external registered auditor and by the CI's council.[53] After having been sent to the NHA, these are discussed with a NHA official. (The details above facilitate the inter-CI comparison of departments.)

(j) *Quality drop*. In case of a considerable quality drop of a department (see 3§26-f;g), the departmental council together with the CI management devises a restructuring plan on which they deliberate with one or more NHA officials. The NHA may also take the initiative. This plan focusses on quality improvement measures. In case of insufficient results, a subsequent restructuring plan comprises adaption of the staff.

(k) *Vacancies*. For vacancies of a department its council may decide for a probation period of maximum two years. Applications are open to all for the vacancy qualified persons, without ethnic, gender, social, political or religious discrimination. Further the council adopts procedures that it seems fit. (Recall that the NHA registers the medical workers – 3§26-d.)

(l) *Second opinion for patients*. In case of a proposed treatment with alternative high risks, patients (or in case their guardian) can get a second opinion from a specialist of another CI or of a hospital.

(m) • *Referral*. A general practitioner of a CI may refer a patient to a hospital. This requires prior consent between, first, a hospital specialist and the general practitioner, and second the patient (or its guardian) and the general practitioner.

---

52   For an example see 3§28, hospitals, under (i) the first footnote.
53   See 3§43 on external registered auditors.

- *Conclusion on the financing of CIs.* The annual budgets for CIs are hard. The above organisation of CIs makes sure that there is a structural budget ceiling (as percent of GDP). The lump-sum financing according to the number of staff of CIs as a fixed percent of the nation's workforce, as well as the preclusion of borrowing, realises this. In the aggregate the budget is population based instead of specific treatment based (which would be far more complicated).[54] Via parliamentary decisions the fixed percent and/or the lump-sum level may be adjusted.

Subdivision 7B. The education sector

In the Design all primary, secondary and tertiary education is provided free of charge, their provision being fully state-financed out of taxation. The normative argument for it is as follows. More than any other good or service, formal education is – irreversibly – determining for the course of one's life. Therefore, everybody should be put in the position to enjoy a formal education in accordance with their potential capacities – the education not being conditioned by the income of one's parent or parents, nor by the student's post-education income. Whilst this is desirable for individuals, it is equally socially desirable that all can develop their capacities during the formal education period.

Formal education is organised as set out in this subdivision that subsequently treats: the tasks and delegated authority of the National Education Agency (3§30); pre-primary education (3§31); primary, secondary and tertiary education (3§32); research by universities and by other state-financed institutions (3§33).[55]

---

54   The budget is population based, and therefore also working population based provided that with an ageing population the pension age is proportionally postponed (3§24).

55   The sector includes the following entries of the 'Standard industrial classification of economic activities' (UN 2008). **Pre-primary education** (85100); **Primary education** (85200); **Secondary education** (85310, General secondary education; 85320, Technical and vocational secondary education; 85410, Post-secondary non-tertiary education); **Tertiary education** (85421, First-degree level higher education; 85520, Cultural education; 85510, Sports education; 85422, Post-graduate level higher education).

3§30   *National Education Agency: tasks and delegated authority*
The degree of detail below has to do with the inherent wellbeing importance of the education sector, as well as with its state expenditure size – as mentioned, estimated at nearly 6% of GDP, and 13% of total state expenditure.

The state institutes the *National Education Agency* (NEA), that has regional branches. It is administered and organised as summarised in Addendum 3§4. It is assigned a budget and an amount of workforce in FTE for the NEA itself, as well as separately for the educational institutions for which it is responsible (see below). has the following tasks and delegated authority.

• *Educational institutions at primary, secondary and tertiary level*
(a) Coordination of the nation's educational institutions at primary, secondary and tertiary level. This education is provided free of charge, as financed out of taxation.
(b) Budget allocation and quantitative workforce allocation over the educational institutions sub (a).
(c) The institutions sub (a) have the legal form of a 'Workers' council governed foundation' (3§25). The NEA owns the premises and the fixed equipment of the educational institutions; it rents these out to the latter (as mentioned in 3§25-b, this regards a delegated ownership, the ownership ultimately resting with the state as legal entity). The purchase of new premises and fixed equipment takes place in close consultation with the educational institutions, the latter via the NEA's branches. (For the fixed equipment this has the advantage of more or less collective purchases, and of the concentration of expertise for it.)
(d) Only licensed institutions are allowed to provide the education sub (a); licences are issued by the NEA. Licences may be revised every five years. These institutions shall – on risk of a fine or losing their education licence – not require or accept entrance or enrolment fees in any form. (This rule should prevent uneven access to the institutions.)

• *Teachers at primary, secondary and tertiary level*
(e) Determination of the minimum qualifications for teachers at the various levels sub (a).
(f) Registration of all teachers sub (a) (including school-leavers) according to their teaching qualifications, as well as their foreseen date of retirement.
(g) Long-term planning of the teaching workers capacity.

• *Quality of teaching programs and of teaching*
(h) Determination of the attainment targets for primary, secondary and tertiary education; as well as broad per year attainment levels such that pupils and students can horizontally switch between institutions.

(i) Establishing the curriculum of educational institutions as well as (when relevant) various learning pathways. These result from the regular set up of committees for the curriculum development and their reports; these committees should communicate with the workers in the field, at least via platforms.

(j) Drawing up of peer group-informed and student-informed teaching quality standards, and the supervision of educational institutions on basis of these standards.

(k) Carrying out of student surveys (for primary education also parent surveys) and ratings of educational institutions, and their publication on a well accessible and searchable site.

- *Medium- and long-term planning*

(l) Drawing up of a long-term budget planning (25 years) – this long period is required for the establishment of new educational institutions – that is adapted every five years. If required, the NEA takes the initiative to found the new institutions mentioned in the previous sentence.

(m) Drawing up of five-year indicative budgets (revised each year), as including their allocation over the primary, secondary and tertiary school levels and the individual educational institutions. Items (l) and (m) are communicated to the institutions and also publicly available.

(n) Regarding the annual budgets (b), the long-term budget planning (l) and the five-year indicative budgets (m) the NEA confers with the relevant minister.

- *Pre-primary education institutions and teachers*

(o) The non-compulsory pre-primary education is carried out by cooperatives that require a licence from the NEA. The institutions are supervised by the NEA, especially in case of complaints.

(p) Determination of the minimum qualifications for pre-primary teachers.

(q) Carrying out of parent surveys and ratings of pre-primary educational institutions, and their publication on a well accessible and searchable site.

3§31   *Pre-primary education*

As indicated, the non-compulsory 'pre-primary education' is provided by licensed cooperatives (3§30-o). (See also 3§22 on child allowances and childcare allowances.)

3§32   *Primary, secondary and tertiary education*

(For the costs of living allowances for tertiary students see 3§23.)

(a) General quantitative indicators for the three main levels of educational institutions are stated in Table 3.12.

TABLE 3.12 *Educational institutions qua level: spread, size and student/staff ratio*

(1)	(2)	(3)	(4)	(5)	(6)	(7)
Level	Spread	Number of students (rough indicative)	Average class size	Student/ staff ratio[c]	Number of staff per institution[e]	Relative total staff (estimate)[g]
primary	neighbourhood	200–500[b]	20	15[d]	13–33	37%
secondary	local	1000–5000	20	15	67–333	38%
tertiary	cities[a]	10,000–30,000		15	667–2000[f]	25%[h]

(a) Regionally spread.
(b) A smaller number for villages and for special schools (the latter for children with special needs).
(c) Including non-teaching staff.
(d) Special schools have a lower student/staff ratio.
(e) Columns (3) divided by (5).
(f) For universities exclusive of research.
(g) This relates to the staff of all educational institutions together (adding up to 100%).
(h) Inclusive universities' research.

(b) The *legal form and internal administration* of educational institutions is that of a 'workers' council governed foundation' (WGF, 3§25).

(c) *Departments*. Secondary level institutions are divided into departments according to learning pathways. Tertiary level institutions are divided into departments per teaching programme and/or professional group. Departments include assistants and secretaries. See 3§25-f on departmental councils.

(d) *Number of staff*. The number of staff of the institutions is determined on basis of student/staff ratios (see Table 3.12, column 5). These ratios are an average; at the institution's level the staff includes teachers, assistants and secretaries. (See 3§33 on the research function of universities and the staff-time allocated to it.)

This staff determination implies that, contrary to all other state institutions (including the health sector), educational staff is not a fixed percent of the working population; it is related, first, to the population of younger than, say, 25 years and, second, the average number of years of schooling. Especially the latter may mean that teaching staff as percent of the working population gradually increases (though foreseeable so).

(e) *Finance*. As indicated (3§30-c), the premises and fixed equipment of educational institutions are rented from the NEA. The NEA finances the institutions via a quarterly lump sum that is composed as follows. *Wages:* the number of staff (see d) times the nationwide average wages and dividends of cooperatives. *Budget for current equipment and other expenses:* calculated as a supplement-percent on the wages. Institutions also receive (have received) a one-time reserve allowance of 5% of the wages sum that is owned by the institution as foundation (the WGF).

(f) *No borrowing.* As indicated WGFs (thus educational institutions) are not allowed to borrow (3§25-d). Therefore they will continuously have to keep a reserve for not precisely to plan expenditures. Next to the reserve allowance (e), the quarter-based lump sum (e) may contribute to this. The reserve allowance may be drawn on only temporarily, after which it has to be made up to the normal level.

(g) *Recordkeeping.* In regular bookkeeping institutions register their incomes (e), expenditures and number of students – in case of departments, separately for each department (c on departments). At the end of the year they record an income account and a balance sheet for the institution at large;[56] as well as summary statements of the number of students and of workers' mutations. The end of year records and statements require approval by an external registered auditor and by the institution's council.[57] After having been sent to the NEA, these are discussed with a NEA official. (The details above facilitate inter-institutional comparisons.)

(h) *Quality drop.* In case of a considerable quality drop of an institution or a department thereof (see 3§30-h to k), the council (or in case the departmental council) together with the institutional management devises a restructuring plan on which they deliberate with one or more NEA officials. The NEA may

---

[56]

INCOME ACCOUNT		**BALANCE SHEET**	
Expenditure	**Income**	**Assets**	**Liabilities**
rent for premises	lump sums:	COB: payment accounts	*none*
rent for fixed equipment	• current purchases	SLB: reserves account‡	
current purchases	• wages†	stocks	reserves (allowance)
wages			other reserves
surplus: added to reserves			

† Includes dividends (see 3§25-c).
‡ SLB: Savings and Loans Bank (3§16).

[57] See 3§43 on external registered auditors.

also take the initiative. This plan focusses on quality-improvement measures. In case of insufficient results, a subsequent restructuring plan comprises adaption of the staff.

(i) *Vacancies.* For vacancies of an institution (in case, of a department), its council (departmental council) may decide for a probation period of a maximum of two years. Applications are open to all for the vacancy qualified persons, without ethnic, gender, social, political or religious discrimination. Further the council adopts procedures that it seems fit. (Recall that the NEA registers all teachers – 3§30-f.)

• *Conclusion on the financing of educational institutions.* The annual budget and workforce ceilings are hard. Structurally the above organisation of educational institutions deviates from the general rule that the workforce of state institutions constitutes a fixed percent of the nation's workforce. In the aggregate the budget and workforce for educational institutions is based on, first, the segment of the population younger than, roughly 25 years old, and second, changes in the duration of their schooling. Given those, the structural budgets and workforce of these institutions are semi-ceiled. Via parliamentary decisions the student/staff ratios for educational levels may be adjusted.

3§33   *Research by universities and by other state-financed institutions*
Although universities' research is properly not 'education' it is institutionally part of it, and university education and research are closely linked. Qua systematic it is then adequate to also treat other state-financed research in this section.

In the Design, fundamental and applied research is carried out by the following institutions.
• Universities: fundamental and applied research;
• State-financed research institutes: applied research;
• Specialised cooperatives: applied research for other cooperatives;
• Other relevant cooperatives: own applied technique related research (R&D).

Below only the first two are treated.

The workforce of universities is estimated at 0.6% of the total workforce, and the part devoted to research at 0.25% of the total workforce (all in FTE). This includes university hospitals and medical research.

3§33-A. Universities and university research. (a) All individual university teachers are required to combine teaching and research. Research time is separately financed and is calculated as a supplement-percent on the teaching time, such that all individual staff can devote 60% of their work-time to teaching and

40% to research (the latter is assessed on basis of publications output). Thus each staff member must be qualified for both of the tasks. This way students benefit from teaching that is directly research informed.[58]

(b) Point (a) implies that the departmental organisation of research coincides with the educational organisation (cf. 3§32-b;c).

(c) Staff members are free to choose the subject of their research. They can, but are not enforced, to participate in research programmes. The only criterion is that they regularly publish in scientifically recognised media, though without neglecting propagation of their research for a wider public.

(d) University departments annually report their research output. It is regularly reviewed by committees of other universities.

(e) Staff members that (at some point) turn out to be reluctant or unable to combine high standard teaching and research are required to seek a position with (as the case may be) specialised research institutions, or non-research tertiary education institutions.

3§33-B. State-financed research institutes. The state establishes at least four applied research institutes. First, a *General statistical office*. Second, a *National institute for the environment and public health*. The latter researches and reports on: general environmental issues as well as the state of the circular production (3§7); the safety of output (3§8); the safety at work (3§9); epidemiological exposures and prevention (3§27). Third, a *National institute for the advance of physically circular production*. This institute focusses on technology and applied technique development that optimises the physically circular production (3§7). Fourth, a *National institute for economic analysis and forecasts*.

These institutes have the legal form of 'Workers' council governed foundations' (3§25). Their workforce is a fixed permille of the total workforce and their budget a fixed permille of the state budget. They are regularly reviewed by committees of similar institutes in other countries.

One task of the 'General statistical office' is to determine the annual average remuneration of the cooperatives' workers in FTE, which serves to determine the average remuneration of public sector workers. The office does this on basis of the reduced end of year statements that cooperatives are required to send to the office (2§11.1), either by way of a sample or of the integral information.

---

58 A moderate degree of 'specialisation' in either teaching or research inevitably leads to non-moderate degrees in skewedness of the one or the other, as research requires time to mature.

Subdivision 7C. Cultural heritage and contemporary creative arts and arts performance

This subdivision treats the organisation of the 'cultural heritage' and of contemporary creative arts and arts performance. It is divided in three sections: the 'Culture and cultural heritage agency' (3§34); cultural heritage (3§35) and contemporary creative arts and arts performance (3§36).[59]

3§34 *Culture and cultural heritage agency: task and delegated authority*
The state institutes a *Culture and cultural heritage agency* (CHA). It is assigned a budget and an amount of workforce in FTE for the CHA itself, and separately for the cultural heritage institutions for which it is responsible (see below). The CHA is administered and organised as summarised in Addendum 3§4. It has the following tasks and delegated authority.
(a) Budget and workforce allocation over the National Library and the State Museums.
(b) Owning the premises and the fixed equipment of these institutions (a); it rents these out to the latter. (As mentioned in 3§2-b, this regards a delegated ownership, the ownership ultimately resting with the state as legal entity.)
(c) Owning the collections of these institutions (a); it rents these out to the latter.
(d) Determination as to whether cultural heritage objects may be exported, and if so the laying down of rules for it that may be different for state museums, other museums, galleries and individuals.

3§35 *State and non-state museums, and the national library and archives*
Before treating below the organisation of museums, I begin with a note on the monetary value of cultural heritage and contemporary arts objects. In capitalism much of these objects function as (speculative) wealth portfolio assets for the rich, which drives up their market prices. Because it is to be expected that in a worker cooperatives society the skewedness of the distribution

---

59 The culture sector includes the following entries of the 'Standard industrial classification of economic activities' (UN 2008). 1. **Artistic creation** (90030): authors, composers, visual artists; 2. **Performing arts** (90010; performing artists of music, theatre, film; orchestras, music companies (music groups), theatre companies); 3. **Support activities to performing arts** (90020): ateliers, studios; production houses, producers (of theatre, film); galleries (visual arts); 4. **Operation of arts facilities** (90040): concert halls, theatre halls (theatre rooms); 5. **Cultural heritage**: Libraries (91011); Archives (91012); Museums (91020); Operation of historical sites and buildings (91030): Botanical and zoological gardens and nature reserves activities (91040).

of wealth is very moderate in comparison with capitalism (2§20), and because bequests are heavily taxed (3§4, Table 3.7 and 3§46), it is likely that the market prices of these cultural objects will radically fall in comparison with capitalism. Amongst other, this means that the owning of objects of art becomes available for a wider public – that is, to the extent that at least during the transition (ch. 8) there is a ban on the export of objects of art.

(*a*) *Libraries and archives.* There is a *National Library* that has the legal form of a Workers' council governed foundation (3§25).[60] It stores all culturally, socially and scientifically relevant publications and archives (the latter in auxiliary branches). All these are digitalised and five years after their publication freely available via its website. (After five years all digital copyrights expire.) It has an indicative budget of 0.02% of GDP.

(*b*) *Museums.* All museum collections are digitally archived by the *National library*. There are two categories of museums: 'state museums' – a limited number – and 'other museums' that are run by cooperatives. Each category regards cultural heritage and contemporary visual arts, though a museum may specialise in one of these.

(*c*) *State museums.* State museums (SMs) have the legal form of a Workers' council governed foundation (3§25). SMs have a permanent 'key collection' and a non-permanent 'variable collection'.

All of the '*key collection*' is exhibited at least once in every seven years, and prominently so for at least two months – this defines the key collection. (Exceptionally, and in close consultation between an SM and the 'Culture and cultural heritage agency' (CHA), it is possible to substitute between the key collection and the variable collection.)

For the '*variable collection*' the SM decides if, and how often, it is exhibited. In case an SM wants to add to this collection, or to the key collection, via purchases, it must sell some of the other variable collection for the equivalent in monetary value. (The key reason of this rule is that it does not seem to make sense to endlessly accumulate objects of art that are never shown to the public.) Intended sales must be offered, first, to other state museums, and secondly to non-state museums ('d' below). The SM informs the CHA about sales and purchases.

SMs pay to the CHA a rent for their collection, no less than such that non-state museums can compete (see 'd' below). Current expenditures of SMs (rent, wages and other current costs) are covered by museum entrance fees – though for visitors below 18 years the entrance is free.

---

60 Municipalities are responsible for local public libraries (4§3-f).

(Explication. Entrance fees for state museums might be considered unfortunate. The reason for it is that non-state-owned museums will most often have to raise entrance fees for at least adults. Without entrance fees for state museums, it would be hard for non-state museums to survive.)

(d) *Non-state museums.* Non-state museums, as including such galleries, are run (and owned) by cooperatives – without state finance. Intended sales by these must be offered, first, to state museums, and secondly to other non-state museums.

(e) *Historical sites and buildings.* These fall under the responsibility of municipalities (4§3-g) and provinces (4§5-e).

3§36   Contemporary creative arts and arts performance

All cooperatives mentioned below have the form of a production worker cooperative (PWC). Like all cooperatives they either own their premises, or rent these from the 'National real estate agency' (see 3§37). When below it is mentioned that an activity is carried out by a cooperative, an alternative is always that an activity is run by a 'single person enterprise' (2§1.2) which may be relevant for artistic creations and performances by individuals.[61]

(a) *Concert halls, theatre halls, cinemas.* (Concert and theatre halls include opera houses as well as small scale rooms.) All these activities are undertaken by cooperatives that derive their income from entrance fees.

(b) *Reproduction of artefacts: arts publishing (literature and other), film, television and radio.* This paragraph is about the reproduction of artefacts (the artistic creations are treated in the following paragraph). These reproductions are undertaken by cooperatives that derive their income either from sales (to individuals for literature and pay-TV/radio; to arts performers for scores and scripts; to cinemas for film). For television and radio it is recalled from 3§8 that cooperatives are not allowed to advertise.

(c) *Artistic creations and performances.* (1) Orchestras, music and ballet companies, theatre companies (all cooperatives) sell their performances either to (intermediating) cooperative production houses, or directly to the under (a) mentioned concert and theatre halls. (2) Artistic creators cooperatives of composers and authors sell their product either to the under (1) mentioned institutions, or/and to the under (b) mentioned arts publishers. (3) Cooperatives producers of film, television and radio (including documentaries) sell their

---

61   Recall 2§2.2: 'Individuals are free to run by themselves a registered "Single person enterprise". However, "hiring a worker" is not allowed. In the economic domain the only possible legal form for a multi-workers' entity is that of a cooperative.'

product to the under (b) mentioned institutions. (4) Visual artist cooperatives sell their product to contemporary art museums or galleries, and – via art galleries or directly – to individuals.

Table 3.13 summarises the above in case there would be no subsidies (cf. point d below).

TABLE 3.13 *Final finance of contemporary arts (column 5) in case of absence of subsidies*

	(1)	(2)	(3)	(4)	(5)
	Initial artist	Sold to	Purchased by	Final performance	Final finance
1	composer music score	publisher*	orchestra etc.†	music hall etc.‡	entrance fee
2	composer theatre script	publisher*	theatre company†	theatre hall etc.‡	entrance fee
3	author film script		film producer**	cinema††	entrance fee
4	author TV script		TV producer	TV broadcast	fee of pay-TV
5	author literature	publisher		individual‡‡	selling
6	visual artists		museum	museum	entrance fee
7	idem		gallery / individual	individual	selling

* In addition the publisher may sell scores or scripts to individual musicians or readers.
† With permanent workers (musicians/actors and other workers). Outside workers are not excluded; this may regard hiring either from a cooperative set up by such workers, or by a 'Single person enterprise' set up for this purpose (see the previous footnote).
‡ Perhaps via production houses.
** Actors and other workers subcontracted from specialising cooperatives or single person enterprises.
†† After a lapse of time film rights may be sold to pay-TV broadcasters.
‡‡ Or individual via library or other lending right fee.

(*d*) *General on subsidies for contemporary creative arts and arts performance.* Of the budget that municipalities receive from the state, an earmarked part is destined for subsidies of the contemporary arts. On top of that, municipal councils may decide for extra subsidies (ch. 4, 4§3-f).

The allocation of such subsidies is rather complicated because it usually requires non-obvious selection criteria. The least (but still) complicated would be to subsidise music and theatre halls as well as museums – assuming that cinemas survive without subsidies. But least complicated is not always the best. However, the more one moves down to sizable cooperatives (orchestras and theatre companies) and to small cooperatives (such as those of authors and visual artists), the complication of selection procedures multiplies.

THE STATE AND THE STATE INSTITUTIONS OF THE DESIGN   143

Table 3.14 summarises the organisation of cultural heritage (3§35) and of the contemporary arts and arts performance (3§36).

TABLE 3.14   *Summary of the organisational form and the current expenditure finance of cultural heritage and of the main contemporary creative arts and arts performance (3D7-C)*

	Legal form	Current expenditure finance	Subsidy provider
Libraries and museums (3§35)			
(a) National library	WGF	state	
(a) Municipal public libraries	WGF	municipalities	
(b) State museums	WGF	entrance fees	
(b) Non-state museums	PWC†	entrance fees	
Contemporary creative arts and arts performance (3§36)			
(a) Music and theatre halls	PWC	entrance fees	municipalities
(b) Reproduction of artefacts*	PWC	sales	
(c) Artistic creations and performances	PWC‡	sales	municipalities

† Possibly a one person undertaking in the case of galleries.
* Arts publishing (including literature), film and television.
‡ Possibly a 'single person enterprise'.

The subsidies of the last column of Table 3.14 regard mainly earmarked transfers from the central state to municipalities that are estimated at 0.15% of GDP. For municipal and provincial libraries and the maintenance of historical sites and botanical gardens 0.03% of GDP is transferred. Earlier 0.02% of GDP was mentioned for the National library and archives. This means that apart from the expenditure on the administration of the 'Culture and cultural heritage agency' the total state expenditure on this sector is 0.20% of GDP. This relatively minor figure reflects that the main part of the culture sector is undertaken by cooperatives. Recall that purchases of cultural objects by state museums balance sales of such objects.

Division 8. Real estate, mining and infrastructure

This Division sets out how the Design deals with the society's surface and subsurface land and waters ('free gifts of nature'), the extractions from these, as well as the structures built on, or in, the surfaces and sub-surfaces. This is critical to the extent that surface and subsurface land and waters are inherently part of the category of the physically most commune of all communalities, whence no institution or person should have any priority ownership in these.

The Design deals with this as follows. First, dwellings of workers and pensioners are owned by the *National Real Estate Agency* (REA) and rented out to the former. It is also responsible for the construction of dwellings. Cooperatives can in principle own *self-occupied* premises as including the plot of land on which these are build (this is a practical matter to the extent that these buildings must fit the cooperative's size and its particular means of production). All other land (including agricultural land) and the waters are owned by the REA. It is also the only one institution from which or to which premises can be purchased or sold. This agency also rents out premises and land to cooperatives – including to agricultural cooperatives. (All treated in 3§37.)

Second, another state agency has the task to determine the limits of the yearly mining and other extractions from the Earth that are sustainable. Within those limits, cooperatives can tender for a concession to engage in those activities, for which they pay a rent-like fee (3§38).

Third, still another agency coordinates the national, provincial and municipal infrastructures, and is responsible for its national part (3§39). This agency owns the infrastructural interurban networks, and notably also the nationwide digital and non-digital networks for communication, information and energy.

3§37 *Housing, real estate and the tasks and delegated authority of the 'national real estate agency'*

The state institutes a *National Real Estate Agency* (REA), that has regional branches. It is administered and organised as summarised in Addendum 3§4. The REA has the following tasks and delegated authority.

• *General tasks*
(a) Ownership and management of the nation's real estate, except the real estate that is owned by other state institutions or the self-occupied premises that are owned by cooperatives. (The REA ownership is, as mentioned in 3§2-b for all state agencies, a delegated ownership, the ownership ultimately resting with the state as legal entity.)

THE STATE AND THE STATE INSTITUTIONS OF THE DESIGN   145

(b) Selling of self-occupied premises to cooperatives that seek such ownership.
(c) Renting out of self-occupied premises to cooperatives, and of self-occupied dwellings to individual workers or pensioners.
(d) Renting out of land to agricultural cooperatives.

• *Regarding the construction of rental premises and dwellings*
(e) Estimation of the long-term, medium-term and short-term demand for rental premises and dwellings – with the help of research institutes and statistical bureaus.
(f) On basis of (e) being the contracting authority for the architectural design and for the contracting of the construction of rental premises and dwellings. These should be designed and constructed in accordance with acclaimed architectural, urban and landscape designs – perhaps also via national and international design contests – and be provided in a variety of qualities. For the designs the REA deliberates also with the regarding municipalities (ch. 4). All of the designs, the contracting and the building is carried out by a variety of cooperatives.

• *Regarding renting out*
(g) Owner-relevant maintenance of premises and dwellings rented out (c).
(h) Rents (c) shall be costs covering (costs of the object's construction and maintenance and of average vacancy rates) and further reasonable in face of their location.
(i) Rents of land for agricultural cooperatives (d) should be reasonable in face of the fertility of the land and its location.

• *Regarding sales and purchases*
(j) The sale of the premises (c) to the occupying cooperatives in case these wish so. That is, in case these regard separate buildings, or units of buildings that are divided, or that can be divided against a reasonable price. Land is not for sale.
(k) In case the cooperatives that own their self-occupied premises want to move to another location (2§14.1), the REA purchases these against a reasonable price. In case cooperatives wish so, the REA also sells premises at a new location, if available, against a reasonable price. Instead, cooperatives might decide to rent-in premises; however, for cooperatives it is normally not allowed for this to involve an assets decrease (cf. 2§14.2).
(l) Cooperatives can undertake the construction of (to be) self-occupied premises via architect and building cooperatives. These should be constructed in accordance with acclaimed urban and landscape designs. The building plot for these is purchased from the REA.

(m) Should a cooperative go bankrupt, then the REA purchases the real estate at hand against a reasonable price.

- *Norms, publication and appeal regarding rents and real estate prices*
(n) The REA formulates norms for the rents (h-i) and the sales and purchasing prices (j-m), and publishes these.
(o) The REA publishes past and actual rents and sales and purchasing prices on a well accessible and searchable site.
(p) Regarding actual rents, and the proposed before-sale or before-purchase real estate prices, the party concerned can go in appeal with a standing committee of three experts, its costs being met by the unsuccessful party.

- *Implications regarding the impact of the REA.*
(q) • First. The Design of the REA makes that there is no (speculative) real estate market.
• Second. The construction tasks of the REA (in accordance with acclaimed urban and landscape designs) makes that it has a huge impact on the beauty of cities, towns and villages.[62]
• Third. Because in its function of contracting authority the REA (besides the previous point) bases itself on long-term and medium-term planning, it does not act pro-cyclically whence is operates as a stabilising agent for the economy's construction sector.
• Fourth. The REA covers an enormous amount of economic wealth. It is estimated that apart from the real estate owned by state institutions other than REA, the relevant total *value of real estate per million inhabitants* amounts to €145 billion (prices of 2019). Of this sum dwellings make up €118 billion and agricultural land €6 billion. The remaining part of €22 billion (15%) is either owned by cooperatives or rented out to cooperatives by REA.

- (r) *Conclusion regarding the income and expenditure of the REA.* Regarding the construction and renting-out of premises and dwellings the REA structurally runs on a break-even basis. This also applies for the selling of premises,

---

62 The REA might be assisted by a regularly revolving committee of top architects. Generally evolutionary architectural design change should fit with existing designs – each in country-wide varieties. Given that dwellings mostly last 100–250 years, there will have to be regular renovations, but in face of diversity these should relate to the inside rather than the outside of buildings. Another point is that for people to have a real choice of dwellings, there should continuously be some degree of unoccupied dwellings.

though for the plot on which structures are built the REA runs a surplus. The latter also applies for the selling of building plots and for the renting out of agricultural land. Each stems from 'free gifts of nature'. These surpluses annually accrue to the income of the state and are used for infrastructural works (3§39).

3§38 *Concessions for mining and other extractions from the Earth*
'Mining and other extractions from the Earth' ranges from professional marine and freshwater fishing to all kinds of mining and extractions such as crude petroleum and natural gas. Similar as is the case for land (3§37, conclusion), mining and other extractions regard 'free gifts of nature', in the current case usually exhaustible ones.

The state institutes a *Mining and other Earth extractions agency* that is administered and organised as summarised in Addendum 3§4. It has the following tasks and delegated authority.
(a) Determination of the limits of yearly extractions that are sustainable. This regards mining for which there are no substitutes, and for example the amount of fishing that conserves fish stocks, whilst also maintaining marine and freshwater ecosystems and biodiversity. For the scientific underpinning of such limits this agency collaborates with the *National institute for the advance of physically circular production* (3§33-B).
(b) Within the limits, the Agency provides extraction concession. Such extractions still regard 'free gifts of nature'. Therefore cooperatives that – via tender procedures – are granted a concession to engage in such extractions, shall pay a rent in the form of a one-off moderate tender amount, as well as annually a percent fee on their sales. These accrue to the annual income of the state and are in part used for finance of the *National institute for the advance of physically circular production* (3§33-B) and in part deposited in a fund for future environment protecting infrastructural constructions (see 3§39 on infrastructure).

3§39 *Infrastructure and the 'national infrastructure agency'*
Infrastructure is vital for the functioning of an economy and for the welfare of people. A distinction can be made between 'infrastructural networks' and 'infrastructural supply' (plant). These are briefly introduced in the two paragraphs below – thereafter it is indicated how the Design deals with these.
• *Infrastructural networks*. Infrastructural networks include networks for: (a) water; (b) the transport of vehicles (for people and freight), including their critical nodes – more specifically roads, waterways, railways, air-facilities, bridges and viaducts; (c) communication, information and energy; and (d) waste (in-

cluding sewers). (Protection against open water, including dykes, is treated under 'public security' – 3§5.)
• *Infrastructural supply (plant)*. In many cases the supply of the goods transported via infrastructural networks has itself a so-called infrastructural character tending to (regional) monopoly or oligopoly of the supplier (for example water resources, mass energy generation, communication, train connection). When in addition there are no ready (regional) substitutes for these, the possible bankruptcy of the supplier would jeopardise the reproduction of the (regional) economy.
• In order to further an adequate infrastructure, the state institutes a *National Infrastructure Agency* (NIA), that has regional branches. It is administered and organised as summarised in Addendum 3§4. The NIA has the following tasks and delegated authority.

• *General tasks*
(a) Coordination of national, provincial and municipal infrastructure.
(b) Responsibility for the national part of infrastructure (investment and maintenance – see below).
(c) Drawing up of a long-term budget planning (25 years) for investment in infrastructure, that is adapted every five years. These include projects for environment protecting infrastructure. Apart from the latter it considers for transport infrastructure that in terms of greenhouse gas emissions in CO_2 equivalents, emissions intensities increase in the order: waterway transport, railway transport, road transport, air transport (as measured around 2020).
(d) Drawing up of five-year indicative budgets for investment and maintenance (revised each year).
(e) Regarding budget planning (c and d) the NIA confers with the for the NIA relevant minister.

• *Transport networks*
(f) Ownership of the infrastructural transport networks of *interurban* waterways, railways, and roads, as well as the bridges, viaducts, railway stations and waterway ports. (As mentioned in 3§2-b, this is a delegated ownership, the ownership ultimately resting with the state as legal entity – the same applies for point h below.) Airports are owned by licensed PWCs – via tendered concessions. (Municipal and provincial authorities are responsible for the local and regional networks – chapter 4, 4§3 and 4§5.)
(g) Infrastructural transport investment projects and the maintenance of transport networks (sub f) are carried out by PWCs via tender procedures.

• *Networks for communication, information and energy*
(h) Ownership of nationwide digital and non-digital networks for communication, information and energy. (On digital communication see also 3§8.)[63]
(i) Investments projects for these networks (h) as well as the maintenance of these networks are carried out by PWCs via tender procedures.
(j) The management of these networks (h). In the relevant cases this includes the charging of users. The charging of users is carried out by PWCs via tender procedures. (Municipal authorities are responsible for the networks for water and for waste, as including sewers, as well as waste processing. See chapter 4, 4§3-d.)

• *Infrastructural supply (plant)*
(k) Interurban rail transport is treated in 3§40. Municipal authorities are responsible for urban rail transport (see chapter 4, 4§3).
(l) Municipal authorities are responsible for water resources (see chapter 4, 4§3).
(m) Under responsibility of the NIA, mass energy generation is carried out by licensed PWCs via tender procedures. The NIA sees to, first, their interconnection via mass transport networks and, second, that these together have sufficient overcapacity such that the lot can take over the provision when one fails for technical or financial reasons.

• *Conclusions on the NIA expenditure.* The NIA's main expenditure regards infrastructural investment and maintenance (g and i). Apart from planning, tendering procedures and supervision it requires hardly any staff. The average annual expenditure of the NIA is estimated at 2% of GDP (the infrastructural expenditure of the NIA together with that of provinces and municipalities is estimated at 2.3% of GDP).

Division 9. User charged production and services undertaken by 'Workers' council governed foundations'

The 'Workers' council governed foundations' (WGFs) presented so far are state-financed and without charging the user of the service (the one semi-exception

---

63 The first sentence has 'ownership of nationwide'; not '*the* nationwide'; the NIA digital network ownership regards at least one free of charge digital network. Recall that 3§8 mentions the prohibition of advertisement.

is state museums that cover their current expenditure with an entrance fee – 3§35; all other WGFs were presented in the same 3D7).

This Division presents WGFs that fully charge for the costs of their production or services. Normally this regards railway transport only (3§40). However, in case for some production or service that is essential for the functioning of cooperatives or for the welfare of households, the required scale of production and/or the risk turns out to be too large for being undertaken by cooperatives, this is undertaken by a charging WGF (3§41). The Division's final section sets out precautionary measures in case a stagnation-like constellation ever arises. Among these, a measure of last resort could be that charging WGFs *temporarily* take on stagnation countering production (3§42).

3§40 *Public transport and the special treatment of railway transport*

Much of the public transport can be provided by licensed cooperatives. Although these could be able to also provide railway transport, such transport has to a large extent a monopoly or oligopoly character, and working with concessions would not take away that the possible bankruptcy of the supplier would jeopardise the reproduction of the economy (cf. 3§39 under 'infrastructural supply'). Moreover, experience in a number of capitalist counties has shown that several railway transport companies operating on the rail network is inconvenient for users. Such transport, therefore, is provided by a single WGF per relevant rail category.

Railway transport falls under the responsibility of an authority at the level of the state or a municipality (ch. 4), and it is carried out by a WGF. All other passenger public transport is carried out by licensed PWCs. See *Table 3.15*.

The remainder of this section treats row 1 of *Table 3.15*. The other rows are dealt with in Chapter 4 (municipal and provincial administrations).

The interurban railway service is carried out by a full costs charging WGF. Firstly, because different users may prefer different means of transport (including cars) and, secondly, to make it possible for cooperatives to compete with the railway transport. (However, it is not excluded that, at some point, for environmental reasons the charges are reduced, perhaps even to nil. This might also be a consideration for the municipal railway transport.)

The state institutes the *National Public Transport Agency* (NTA) which maintains a separate accounting. It is administered and organised as summarised in Addendum 3§4. The NTA has the following tasks and delegated authority.
(a) The institution of a National Railway Company (below 'the Company') that has the legal form of a 'Workers' council governed foundation' (WGF – 3§25) for which it is responsible, and that carries out the interurban railway transport for passengers and freight.

THE STATE AND THE STATE INSTITUTIONS OF THE DESIGN   151

TABLE 3.15   *Public transport: responsible administration, and carriers*

	Transport category	Responsible	Carrier[†]
1	interurban railway transport: passenger and freight	state administration	one WGF[‡]
2	urban and suburban railway transport: passenger	municipal admin.	one local WGF[‡]
3	interurban bus services: passenger	state administration	licensed coops
4	provincial bus services: passenger	provincial admin.	licensed coops
5	municipal bus services: passenger	municipal admin.	licensed coops
6	all other transport: passenger	relevant authority	licensed coops
7	all other transport: freight		cooperatives[*]

[†]   Supervised by inspectorates (3§12).
[‡]   WGF: Workers' council governed foundation (3§25).
[*]   Licensed for air carriers (see the current section under f below).

(b) Owning the premises and the fixed equipment of the Company; it rents these out to the latter. The Company transfers its annual surplus to the NTA, out of which the current and future investments are financed. The purchase of new premises and fixed equipment takes place in close consultation with the Company. (Comment. Like for all WGFs, there is here the safety measure that the responsible state institution owns, and rents out, the premises and the fixed equipment. Apart from that, the NTA functions in fact as a supervisory board for the Company.)
(c) The Company charges customers at average costs covering prices, that is, such that its current costs as well as its investment costs are covered. (The Company competes with PWCs – *Table 3.15*, rows 3 and 7.)
(d) The annually drawing up and establishing the budget of the Company in close consultation with the latter.
(e) The Company draws up a long investment term planning (25 years) that is adapted every five years. It also draws up five-year indicative investment plans (revised each year). The Company confers about these with the NTA.
(f) The issuing of licences to cooperatives that want to be a carrier for air transport or for interurban passenger transport.

3§41   *Essential production or services that might possibly not be taken up by PWCs*

This section regards the production or the service that is essential for the functioning of cooperatives or for the welfare of households. It cannot be excluded that for some of such production or services, the required scale of production and/or the risk is too large to be undertaken by cooperatives – especially in the early years after the transition to a worker cooperatives society (on the latter see Chapter 8). Examples might be mass energy generation or damage insurances and damage liability insurance.[64] (Any insurance that is undertaken is offered by non-COB cooperatives.)

For these cases (and cases treated in the next section) the state institutes an *Agency for temporary workers' council governed foundations* that is administered and organised as summarised in Addendum 3§4. This agency sets up WGFs (3§25) that fully charge for the costs of their production or services – though no more than the costs, thus without generating a structural surplus above normal WGF dividends (included in WGF wages). Once these are sufficiently running, they can be sold – or in the relevant cases rented out – to new cooperatives.[65] It is also possible that the foundation is legally converted into a cooperative.[66]

3§42   *Possible stagnant underinvestment by PWCs*

It cannot be excluded that a stagnation-like constellation ever arises, such that PWCs do not dare to invest (perhaps also in merely one or more regions). In that case five measures can be taken.

(a) One is via the *Real Estate Agency* (3§37) by its bringing forward planned building of new dwellings to rent out. That is usually efficacious because of the high multiplier effect of the building sector.

(b) In case there is a housing overcapacity, an alternative is that the *National Infrastructure Agency* (3§39) brings forward planned infrastructure projects – these usually also have high multiplier effects.[67]

(c) A next possibility is that the *Investment-credit Guarantee Fund* (3§15) provides more investment-credit guarantees, even if this means that it has to take more risks.

---

64   Other usual insurances in capitalism, such as for pensions, health (cure and care), and disability to work are covered in the Design by income allowances (3§24, Table 3.9) or by free provisions in kind (3D7).

65   Regarding insurance an alternative might be that cooperatives and households set up mutual insurance *user* cooperatives (a legal form not introduced so far). However, the workers of such cooperatives should have rights similar to those of WGFs.

66   When the WGF has reserves, then – for equivalency reasons with cooperative start-ups that have to build up a resistance buffer (2§7.0) – the workers of the converted entity will have to pay the equivalent sum of the reserves within a to be agreed number of years.

67   For this and the previous case these institutions should have ready plans on their shelves that can be implemented in the short run.

(d) Still another way is that the *Agency for temporary workers' council governed foundations* (3§41) sets up WGFs (3§25) for activities that have not been undertaken by production cooperatives.[68] These sell on a cost price basis. Once sufficiently running, they can be rented out or sold to new PWCs.

(e) A final, less attractive, possibility of last resort is that the Agency just mentioned sets up extra WGF units of production in branches where cooperatives are already (moderately) active, with again the aim of, once running, their being rent out or sold to new cooperatives. This is only a last-resort possibility because this way WGFs compete with cooperatives (such WGFs must be committed not to under-price the existing cooperatives). But perhaps such WGFs can be established in underdeveloped regions that do not host this kind of production, and regarding developed regions in sectors for which the transport cost would be high enough to not effectively compete with relevant cooperatives.

(f) Stagnation may also have a regional character as resulting in regional discrepancies (cf. 3§15 under (e), on the Investment-credit Guarantee Fund). In that case (d) and (e) above can be applied regionally. The multiplier effects of the investment by WGFs should after some time encourage existing cooperatives to expand their investment.

Division 10. Regulation of auditing, of patents and copyrights, and of competition

This Division takes together three issues that are not directly interconnected. However, devoting separate Divisions to each would not contribute to a clearer structure of the chapter. The first one regards the regulation and supervision of registered external auditors, and the cooperatives into which these are organised; this is imperative because these perform a key task for guaranteeing the adequacy of the recordkeeping of 'cooperatives', 'state institutions' and 'workers' council governed foundations' (3§43). The second one is about patents and copyrights (3§44). The final one regards the cooperatives' competition and the prevention of their reaching a 'dominant market power' (3§45).

3§43 *Auditing rules and the supervision of registered auditors*
Cooperatives, state institutions and 'workers' council governed foundations' are required to register their incomes and expenditures in regular bookkeeping, and at the end of the year they shall record an 'Income account' and a 'Bal-

---

68   The previous footnote is here also applicable.

ance sheet' (2§11.0; 3§2-e; 3§25-e).[69] These are usually recorded by an internal accountant or by an accountant of a specialised accounting cooperative, that each usually serve the interests of the institution at hand.

However, the two end of year statements also have to be checked, and in the end approved of, by one or more registered auditors (one or more as indicated in the references above).[70] Thus these registered auditors play a key role for the accuracy of the recordkeeping. Therefore the state institutes a *Registered Auditors Authority* which is an agency that is administered and organised as summarised in Addendum 3§4. It has the following tasks and delegated authority.

(a) Devising of rules to which registered auditors have to comply.
(b) Licensing of individual auditors and of the cooperatives into which these auditors must be organised. These cooperatives are allowed to do only this external kind of work (it may not be combined with any paid or unpaid advice to cooperatives, state institutions or workers' council governed foundations).
(c) Supervision of individual auditors and their cooperatives. In case of malfunctioning (to be specified) the licence is withdrawn. (Thus this supervisor supervises the auditors that in effect supervise the internal accountants.)
(d) Part of the authority is a 'cooperative restructuring office' that checks on the registered auditors reports on cooperatives that are in a process of economic contraction (as mentioned in 2§14.2).

(Besides, not instead, of this auditing structure, the state might also institute a general Court of Auditors for the state administrations.)

3§44   *Patents and copyrights*

The state institutes a *Patents and copy rights authority* which is an agency that is administered and organised as summarised in Addendum 3§4. It decides whether patent applications by cooperatives (or individuals) are substantial enough, as well as sufficiently in the interest of households, to grant these. Seeds or similar natural origins shall not be put under patent. Patents usually expire after 5–10 years. For the granting of patents the authority may make a distinction between the national and the international jurisdiction. Universities and state research institutions (or their current or former workers) are not

---

69   The 'income account' states the sums of the *flow* of the costs and the surplus and the allocation of the surplus. The 'balance sheet' states the *stock* of the assets, liabilities and specified reserves.
70   An auditor is specialised accountant authorised to examine/verify accounts and accounting records of an institution.

eligible for patents (at least not for patents within the national jurisdiction). Users of an invention that was put under an expired patent, are required to acknowledge the inventor.[71]

Copyrights for the digital reproduction of artefacts or for artistic creations (3§36-b) expire after five years. Copyrights for workers at universities or state research institutions expire after one year. For any type of reproduction of an expired copyright, the original creator or author must be acknowledged.

3§45   Competition and market power

In principle cooperatives compete in the markets relevant to them. This should be such that none reaches a 'dominant market power', whence prices could (implicitly) be dictated, or such that entry in the market of new cooperatives is inhibited. The same applies for agreements between a number of cooperatives that result in a similar effect. This section sets out how in the Design a dominant market power is avoided.

The state institutes a *Competition authority* (CA) which is an agency that is administered and organised as summarised in Addendum 3§4. The CA has the following tasks and delegated authority.

(a) Generally, preventing cooperatives to reach a constellation of 'dominant market power' (as defined above).

(b) Supervision of the rules that cooperatives shall be organised in no more than one single location and shall not take-over other cooperatives (2§3.3 and 2§3.4). (In comparison with capitalism, these rules considerably temper the possibility for cooperatives to reach a dominant market power.) Note that the rules under (a) and (b) are not incompatible with large-scale production; country dependent a single cooperative might provide jobs to several tens of thousands of workers in a location of several hundred thousands of m^2.

(c) The setting of, and the supervision of, sector specific *maximum market share rules* for PWCs. (Recall from 3§13-h that the Central Bank sets market share limits for COBs.) As a general indication the market share ceilings for medium-sized countries might on average be 1–5% nationwide and 10% in a local relevant market. Especially the nationwide ceilings depend on the size of a country. In a relatively small country there might, for example, be no efficient room for seven producers of mass energy generation, in which case their average market share would be about 15% (a ceiling would also depend on alternatives, in

---

[71]   In face of this, universities and state research institutions (or their current workers) could formally apply for patents.

this case energy alternatives). One of the complications is to properly define a 'relevant market'. For example, consider the number of pubs that a person might visit in their neighbourhood. In case there would be no more than five pubs these would constitute the 'relevant market' each with an average market share of 20%. In general, the possible market entry of a new competitor in a relevant market is also a consideration. (In the example just given, the average market share of 20% might not inhibit a new competitor to enter the market.)

The implication of the market ceilings set by the Competition Authority, is that when a cooperative reaches the ceiling, it is not allowed to further expand its production or services capacity, including its amount of workforce. However, within the ceiling cooperatives can still have labour productivity growth – including beyond competitors. This would mean relative increases in value-added per worker and in wage rates or dividends.

(d) Maximum market share rules do not apply for the 'Workers' council governed foundations' treated in 3D9 that charge for their services (3§25-h), as their point is a degree of monopoly. (Non-charging foundations, as in the health sector, do not operate in a market.)

(e) State institutions shall not issue concessions to cooperatives that would result in a surpassing of the market share ceilings. In case a concession holder reaches a market ceiling it shall act as indicated in the last paragraph under (c).

(f) In case the production technique in some sector is inherently a large-scale one that, given the size of the country, would lead to a dominant market power of the producer, or some producers, it acts as follows.

(f-1) For production that is essential for the functioning of other cooperatives or for the welfare of households, it proposes to parliament, via the for the CA relevant minister, to undertake the production by way of a user charging 'Workers' council governed foundation'.[72]

(f-2) For production that is *not* essential for the functioning of other cooperatives or for the welfare of households, it proposes to parliament, via the for the CA relevant minister, a restructuring plan that gradually phases out the sector at hand.[73]

---

72   The proposal encompasses possible details for the conversion of the juridical status of a regarding existing PWC into a WGF (an exception to 2§3.o) such that their workers are only moderately affected.

73   Gradually, such that, first, workers have sufficient time to seek other work, secondly, much of the PWCs investments are earned back. Part of the restructuring plan might be that the gradual phasing out is accomplished by a temporary WGF via a conversion as mentioned

THE STATE AND THE STATE INSTITUTIONS OF THE DESIGN 157

(g) The prohibition of price and quantity cartels – as including for tenders – and the setting out of criteria that cooperatives must adhere to, notwithstanding their own responsibility to adhere to the intention of the prohibition.

(h) The setting up of, and publication of, the fines for non-compliance to the relevant rules above; and in case the actual fining of non-complying cooperatives.

Division 11. Taxation, and key macroeconomic and other social-economic policy instruments

This final Division of chapter 3 consists of two sections. The first one sets out how state expenditure is financed by taxation; it provides arguments for the taxation categories and the taxation rates. The second section infers from the previous Divisions the Design's key macroeconomic and other social-economic policy instruments.

3§46   *Taxation*

Taxation is carried out by the taxation authority, which is a separate accounting maintaining institution under responsibility of a minister. It is administered and organised as summarised in Addendum 3§4 (for state agency read taxation authority).

This section sets out how state expenditure is financed by taxation. It provides arguments for the taxation categories and tax rates. *Table 3.7* reproduces the taxation table that was shown early on in this chapter (3§4). Before commenting on this table I begin with four principles.

First, regarding the taxation of cooperatives. There is a turnover tax (see below) but no tax on the net income of cooperatives, nor other taxes. All of the distributed income of cooperatives (wages and dividends) accrues to cooperative workers' households. Workers of state institutions and of 'workers' council governed foundations' receive on average a similar income (wages and dividends) as the cooperatives' workers. Therefore there is not much point in taxing the surplus of cooperatives separately (a surplus tax would be analogous to a profits tax in capitalism).

---

in the previous footnote. Generally the reason for the phasing out is that state entities and other public sector entities should be restricted to socially necessary functions.

TABLE 3.7 *Overview of the tax categories and tax rates (repeat from 3§4)*

	(1) Category	(2) Tax rate on bracket	(3) Average tax rate	(4) Tax sum (top of bracket)	(5) After-tax income (top bracket)†
1	(MiW = annual minimum wage)		at MiW = €20,000‡		
2	Taxation cooperatives*				
3	Turnover tax: cascade system**	5% to 15%‡			
4	Income tax individuals††				
5	to 60% MiW (costs of living threshold)	0%	0.0%	€ 0	€ 12,000 [0.7]
6	from off € 60% MiW – 1× MiW	25%	10.0%	€ 2,000	€ 18,000 [1.0]
7	from off € 1× MiW – 2× MiW	60%	35.0%	€ 14,000	€ 26,000 [1.4]
8	from off € 2× MiW – 3× MiW	70%	46.7%	€ 28,000	€ 32,000 [1.8]
9	from off € 3× MiW – 4× MiW	80%	55.0%	€ 44,000	€ 36,000 [2.0]
10	from off € 4× MiW – 5× MiW	90%	62.0%	€ 62,000	€ 38,000 [2.1]
11	above € 5× MiW	95%			
12	example of € 5× MiW – 10× MiW	95%	79.0%	€ 157,000	€ 43,000 [2.4]
13	Wealth tax individuals	nil			
14	Inheritance tax, levied on the receiver‡‡				
15	over € 0 – MiW	0%			
16	over € MiW – 2× MiW	50%			
17	above 2× €MiW	100%			
18	inheritance tax spouse/partner	0%			
19	Gift tax (on annual gifts; levied on receiver)♣				

TABLE 3.7 *Overview of the tax categories and tax rates (cont.)*

	(1)	(2)	(3)	(4)	(5)
	Category	Tax rate on bracket	Average tax rate	Tax sum (top of bracket)	After-tax income (top bracket)†
20	over € 0–10% MiW	0%			
21	above 10% MiW	100%			
22	Municipal and provincial taxes	nil			

† The outer end of column (5) shows the ratio of the after-tax income differences (€18,000 = 1). (For 60% MiW = 12,000 = 1, and from 60% MiW to 5× MiW, the ratio's run from 1 to 3.2.)
‡ The figure of €20,000 is not essential: when in face of the country's purchasing power structure, the nominal minimum wage would be higher or lower, the taxation revenue would be proportionally higher or lower (as would be the money-level of the required state expenditure). The tax rates of column (2) are essential.
* Cooperatives pay no surplus tax.
** A different regulation applies for 'single person enterprises' – see Appendix 3E.
⁑ Dependent on the production structure of the country concerned.
†† The income tax rates might be considered substantial, but this is required to finance pensions for all, the free health and education services as well as child and childcare allowances (see 3D6 and 3D7). The wages supplements for evening and night shifts are taxed according to the bracket rate before these supplements.
‡‡ Maximum 15 receivers. Apart from row 18, no differentiation regarding the relation between testator and receiver.
⁂ A gift by a parent to a child is twice exempted for 50% MiW. The reason is assistance for a child who is starting to live on their own (this is turned into a general rule).

Second, regarding the income taxes. Even when the Design's distribution of income will be far less skewed than in capitalism, taxation might undo any remaining skewedness. This poses a potential conflict, because non-proportional taxation affects the democratic decisions of councils. However, for taxation there also counts the normative principle that 'the strongest bodies have to shoulder the heaviest burden'. Progressive income tax rates are therefore taken as a fairness principle. (Note that top incomes listed in Table 3.7 are most unlikely, given that worker councils decide on the pre-tax income ranges. However, the top income tax rates are relevant for the transition – Chapter 8.)

Third, regarding the transparency of the income taxation. The individual income tax assessment should be transparent as to the average tax rate that each person pays, as well as to the major expenditure destinations of the tax (see further below). Apart from transparency for the individual, there should also be social transparency. Therefore information about all of society's incomes and tax assessments should be publicly available on a website (this is customary in Norway and Finland).[74]

Fourth, regarding wealth taxes. In the Design wealth differences are going to be minor, and immensely minor in comparison with capitalism (2§20), therefore there are no lifetime taxes on wealth or the income from it. Nevertheless, regarding the inheritance of any wealth, there is still the principle point that the children of all parents deserve an equal treatment and that the wealth of their ancestors is not their merit (if a merit at all). This, in brief, provides an argument for having a considerable inheritance tax.

The Design includes four taxation categories. Relatively the taxation revenue from the inheritance taxes is expected to be minor because of anticipation behaviour. About half of the revenue is to be covered by the income taxes (cf. Appendix 3A, section 3A-4) and the other half by a tax on the turnover of cooperatives.

(1) *Taxation of cooperatives: turnover tax (cascade system)*. This turnover tax sets a uniform tax rate on the *output* of cooperatives. A main argument for this type of taxation is that its administrative burden for cooperatives (and also for the fiscal authority) is minor in comparison with a value-added tax (VAT). However, there are further advantages. It does (as against a VAT system) stimulate vertical integration, which has two results. First, the work within a single cooperative is more diverse, and secondly there is less environment damaging transport (this thus fits a physical circular economy that is geared at production near to where it is used). Another advantage of a cascade turnover tax is that it is probably less sensitive to fraud than a VAT. (Remarkably, proponents of a VAT within capitalism see the cascade turnover tax's stimulation of vertical integration as a disadvantage.)

If this turnover tax is to cover about 50% of the taxation revenue, then the tax rate would probably have to lie somewhere between 5% and 15%, its more exact percentage depends on the production structure of the regarding country. The taxes are due quarterly.

Although the starting point for a turnover tax is a uniform tax rate, it is possible to diversify the rate in view of the environment. For example, as long as the greenhouse gas emissions from aviation continue to be by far the highest among the means of transport, a relatively higher tax rate might be levied on

---

74   https://theculturetrip.com/europe/norway/articles/norway-country-public-tax-returns/

aviation. (Note that as such higher rates aim to affect the production structure, these should not be counted as structurally extra taxation revenue.)

(2) *Income tax, levied on the income of workers and pensioners. Tax rates.* There is a general tax exemption for the income below the 'costs of living threshold' (3§47-e): as an indication this is at 60% of the minimum wage (MiW). Above it, tax rates gradually increase progressively (see Table 3.7, rows 4–12). *Tax base.* Apart from the exemption, income taxes are raised on wages and dividends, pension income and the other allowances, except child cost of living allowances (childcare allowances are taxed).[75] The wages supplements for evening and night shifts are taxed according to the bracket rate before these supplements, because otherwise the compensation objective would be reduced. Interest on savings is not taxed because, if not expended later, these end up as taxed bequests (see below).

The tax rate on wages and dividends is the same, because a distinction would probably affect the distribution between the two in cooperatives.

The specific income tax rates are listed in Table 3.7. The outer end of its column (5) shows that the after-tax income differences might amount to a ratio of 1:2.1 – exceptionally 1:2.4.

(3) *Inheritance tax, levied on the receiver.* See Table 3.7, rows 14–18. Inheritance taxes are levied on the receiver; the number of receivers is maximal 15 (the reason for this limit is that these taxes are to contribute to the total state expenditure, even if probably moderately). There is a tax exemption equivalent to a year's minimum wage (this is to cover treasured possessions). Above the exemption the tax rate is 50% on an equivalent of twice the minimum wage, and beyond it 100%. The partner of a deceased is exempted from inheritance tax (her or his bequest will be taxed when s/he deceases). There is no other differentiation regarding the relation between testator and receiver.[76]

(4) *Gift tax.* See Table 3.7, rows 19–21. A logical consequence of an inheritance tax is that gifts during life will also have to be taxed. The maximum annual number of receivers is again 15. Gifts during life, regardless of to whom they are given, are exempted from taxation up to 10% of the minimum wage. However,

---

75 The difference between the latter two were explained in 3§22. For the principle reasons indicated in that section, the costs of living based child allowances are not taxed; childcare allowances are taxed because of the principle of progressive income tax rates, given that these allowances are also received by parents with a relatively high income.

76 In case the testator has made no notarial will, the only receiver is the testator's surviving partner/spouse, and in case the partner/spouse is deceased the only receivers are in the following priority order of up to 2xMIW: (1) her/his children; (2) her/his grandchildren; (3) her/his living parent(s).

a gift by a parent to a child is twice exempted for 50% MiW. The reason is assistance for a child starting living on its own (this is turned into a general rule). Gifts beyond these thresholds must be declared to the tax authority and are taxed at a rate of 100%. (This is not watertight, but so be it in face of non-complexity.)
(5) *No other taxes.* Given the inheritance tax, a wealth tax does not seem required, all the more so because wealth differences are probably going to be moderate. There are no municipal or provincial taxes. (Note that because there are no net income (surplus) taxes for cooperatives, the – in comparison with capitalism – complexity and fraud sensitivity of corporate profit taxes is also absent.)

Institutional prepayment of income taxes. So as to make sure that individuals receive approximately a take home remuneration that they can spend, cooperatives, state institutions, workers' council governed foundations and for pensions the 'pensions and child allowances agency' are required to withhold expected taxes from the remuneration that they pay out. They receive simple instructions for this from the taxation authority. They monthly pay the deducted taxes to that authority. (Withholdings are settled with the annual final tax assessment. Everybody, even those on a low income, is required to file an annual tax return.)

Transparent income tax assessment. Given the principle that the income tax assessment should be transparent as to the average tax rate that each person pays, as well as to the major expenditure destinations of the tax, *Table 3.16* provides an example of an income tax assessment sheet. The information mentioned regards rows 12 and 17 to 22 of this table.

TABLE 3.16 *Example of an income tax assessment sheet*

	Income statement		
1	income from [institution]		€ a
2	income from [institution] {in case of movement during the year}		€ b
3	allowance from [institution] {in case}		€ c
4	total income (1 to 3)		€ d
	taxes due	*rate*	*tax*
5	over 60% MiW (costs of living threshold)	0%	nil

TABLE 3.16 *Example of an income tax assessment sheet (cont.)*

		Income statement		
6	from off € 60% MiW – 1× MiW		25%	€ e
7	from off € 1× MiW – 2× MiW		60%	€ f
8	from off € 2× MiW – 3× MiW		70%	€ g
9	from off € 3× MiW – 4× MiW		80%	€ h
10	from off € 4× MiW – 5× MiW		90%	€ i
11	*total taxes due (5 to 10)*			€ j
12	average tax rate € j over € d (row 11 over row 4)		x%	
	yet to pay or to receive			
13	total taxes due (row 11)			€ j
14	prepaid taxes via [institution; regards row 1]			€ k
15	prepaid taxes via [institution; regards row 2 or 3] {in case}			€ l
16	yet to pay {or to receive} (€ j – € k – € l)			€ m
	main destination of the taxes			
	the following estimates over year [year] apply: in quantitative order		in your case this is	
17	n% of taxes finance health service			€ n
18	o% of taxes finance pensions			€ o
19	p% of taxes finance education			€ p
20	q% of taxes finance child-related allowances			€ q
21	r% of taxes finance the administration of ministries and state agencies			€ r
22	s% of taxes finance the administration of municipalities			€ s

3§47   *Key macroeconomic and other economic policy instruments*

(*a*) *Macroeconomic policy instruments*. In capitalism the main macroeconomic policy instruments are 'government (state) expenditure' and 'taxation', as well as the rate of interest, the latter via the Central Bank's purchasing or selling of bonds.[77] Government expenditure has a direct effect on macroeconomic expenditure; for the taxation and interest rate instruments it can merely be hoped that these influence the investment of enterprises and/or the consumption of households.

In the Design the bonds trade policy is impossible because there are no bonds markets (2§17, addendum). Because of its 'hard budget constraints' (3§2-h) the Design severely restricts the state and state institutions' expenditure. Cooperatives pay no net income (surplus) tax, and each of the by cooperatives paid turnover tax and the by workers and pensioners paid income tax are no discretionary policy instrument and these rather function as an automatic stabiliser in case of business-cycle-like recessions with dampening tax receipts – that are offset in an upswing.

However, this does not imply that the Design's state has no macroeconomic policy instruments. On the contrary it has such instruments that operate far more directly and far more effectively than the capitalist ones.

First. We have seen that for the cooperative banks' investment loans to other cooperatives, the loans to the banks by the Savings and Loans Bank (SLB) are indispensable (2§6.3; 3§16-c). Therefore the SLB, by varying the rate of interest on these loans, can have rather promptly effect on the macroeconomic investment. Thus whereas capitalist CBs can only indirectly affect the rate of interest that banks charge to enterprises, the SLB can directly affect the interest that COBs charge to non-banking cooperatives, which may again affect the degree of the latter's investment. (The same instrument can be used mesoeconomically – heading c below.)

Second. For the countering of especially labour qualifications mismatches, there is a general traineeship programme which makes it that no one is out of work for longer than two months – where 'work' includes permanent jobs and paid traineeships, the latter being a lever to permanent jobs (3§18).

---

[77] Many macroeconomic textbooks hold that the central bank can influence, or even determine, the amount of money in circulation. Bindseil and König (2013) argue that even if economics textbooks such as those of Ball, Mankiw, or Mishkin still explain the money supply by means of the multiplier process and proceed under the assumption that the central bank controls the supply of money, 'central bankers have by now largely buried this "verticalism", at least when it comes to monetary policy implementation'. (Expanded on in Reuten 2019, p. 113.).

Third. There is an instrument to counter recessions and joblessness (3§19 and 3§20). This instrument and the first act far more directly than the conventional capitalist supposed 'fine-tuning' manipulation of macroeconomic expenditure and taxation.[78] They also work very fast (the duration of recessional joblessness for a worker will not be longer than two months). Moreover, the design of the Real Estate Agency makes it that in recessions it acts as a stabilising agent for the economy's construction sector – 3§37-q.

Fourth. To the extent the rate of interest affects savings (at least the degree is doubtful), the Savings and Loans Bank might, as an additional countercyclical instrument, adapt the interest rate on savings so as to influence consumption expenditure (3§16-b).

(b) *Stagnation countering instruments.* The instruments referred to in the previous subsection (a) would seem to be sufficient for the cases referred to. If a stagnation-like constellation would ever arise there are the stagnation countering measures set out in 3§42 (the most direct of these are investment by the 'Real Estate Agency' or the 'National Infrastructure Agency' – usually efficacious because of the high multiplier effect of the building sector).

(c) *Social priorities of particular investments.* Because of the way in which the 'Savings and Loans Bank' finances cooperative banks, this finance might be used to stimulate investments that have social priority (including for environmental reasons) and to curb other – that is, in case parliament approves such policies, or itself initiates these (3§16-d).

(d) *Maximum and minimum work-time.* Overall work-time variation is a general social-economic policy instrument (cf. 3§10).[79] Especially the rate of population growth is insecure. At a prevailing work-time, population growth might at one extreme result in labour shortage, and at the other in labour abundance. In each of these cases a general adaptation of the work-time is an important instrument (see 3§10 for the considerations of why the maximum work-time should, in principle, also be the minimum work-time).

(e) *Level of the minimum wage.* (Section 3§11 merely indicates that the minimum wage level is set by parliament as some derivative of the minimum costs of living.) The level of the minimum wage is a key factor by itself (see below),

---

78   Cf. the last footnote of 3§19 on cyclical fine-tuning.
79   This is how it was introduced: 'The state's parliament sets the number of work hours per year that defines a "full-time position". The considerations for it regard demography, the actual workforce and state finance. The number of hours are at least revised every 10 years, and may be revised once a year.'

   A general aim is that the *average* productivity increase that is realised by cooperatives and state institutions is at least partly translated into a decrease in the number of work hours per year.

but also in that it affects several to it linked allowances (see 3§24, Table 3.9), especially pensions – the one but largest state expenditure category.

Costs of living threshold. The bottom line for the minimum wage is that it should cover the costs of living expenses, which is rather indefinite, but it should at least include the means to fully participate in society's culture and communication in a wide sense. Because anybody will at some point be eligible to the for all equal pension (3§24), everyone – including parliamentarians – has an interest that the minimum wage is defined adequately.

Minimum wage: threshold plus supplement. It will be seen later on that the annual *average* before-tax wage is estimated at 3.5 times the minimum wage (Appendix 3A, section 3A-4). The actual minimum wage consists of the costs of living plus some supplement, the latter being a policy matter (the indication as provided in 3§11 was set at 167% of the minimum costs of living threshold). Given the threshold bottom line, the level of the minimum wage should be set such that it is no bottleneck for the majority of cooperatives (that seems evident), but also not for start-up cooperatives. These of course must pay the minimum wage, but continuously so until they have met the legal requirement of the 30% of the assets resistance buffer (2§7). If the minimum wage is too high to build up this buffer, then some setback may cause their failure. (At a lower minimum wage, they can spend less, but by earlier building up the buffer, their position is more secure.)

Thus the level of the minimum wage requires a fine balance between the two points mentioned above. It also requires a balance, thirdly, with the raising of feasible taxes such that – apart from all other necessary state expenditure (see this chapter's previous Divisions) – expenditures for pensions, and other to the minimum wage related allowances, can be met. Nevertheless, even if allowances are linked to the minimum wage, the size of the link need not be a fixed one: given the bottom line threshold, the minimum wage might be lowered along with an increase in pensions to, say, 105% of the minimum wage instead of the 100% indication in 3§24 (or the other way around).

This triple aim is a matter of delicate policy, one that should, moreover, be sufficiently stable (in the sense that it does not result in continuous fits and starts). I see this as a key policy challenge for the Design's cooperatives society. Because this delicate policy must be based on future empirical facts, I can say no more about it.

General Addendum. An evaluation of chapter 3 in the perspective of chapter 2

This addendum presents a perhaps unusual evaluation by the author of his own work. I convey to the reader, first, the targets I had in mind when starting the work and, second, what I myself consider strong, good and weak points of the result. The reader may of course have different objectives and different opinions about the results.

A   *The initial goals and their implementation*

1. *Economic democracy* at the point of production, and autonomy at the point of production where possible. (Economic democracy, and any democracy, is limited by what can be governed on.) I think that this is reasonably realised in the Design's councils of worker cooperatives.[80]

2. *Political democracy* in general, and *democracy for state workers within their institution*. I think that the first of these aims has been reasonably guaranteed in the Design. There is ample room for the second of these aims to clash with the first one. This has been moderately resolved by giving the councils of state institutions the governance over the work organisation (including the election of management) and over the wage-scales distribution of their wages budget, but not over the objectives of the institution which is the exclusive power of parliament. A similar division of governance applies for the councils of 'workers' council governed foundations'.

3. *The overcoming of the exploitation of one class by another*. I think the legal structure and the organisation of worker cooperatives has realised this in the Design.

4. *The prevention of joblessness*. In the Design this has been realised considerably, but not fully (no one is out of work for longer than two months – where 'work' includes permanent positions, paid traineeships, and during recessions temporary positions).

5. *Little skewedness in the distribution of income and wealth*. Although there are no absolute guarantees for it, it is at least within the democratic powers of the councils to prevent a skewed distribution of remunerations. Because in the Design there is no income from property, the former is the only one wealth source. Taxation could minimise or even undo any skewedness. Given point 1 there is a potential conflict here, because non-proportional taxation undoes

---

80   Cf. 2§5 in connection with the constraints of 2§3, of ch. 2 *passim*, and of 3D3, 3§38, 3§44 and 3§45.

the democratic decisions of councils. However, for *taxation* there also counts the normative principle that 'the strongest bodies have to shoulder the heaviest burden'.

6. *Equal pensions for all*. The Design realised this.
7. *Freely available health provisions for all*. The Design realised this.
8. *Freely available education provisions for all*. The Design realised this.
9. *Evading discrimination and corruption*.[81] Regarding discrimination and corruption there are duties and interdictions, and for corruption and abuse of power by authorities and state workers also judicial proceedings.[82] However, these do not guarantee their non-occurrence.

B   From deemed strong to weak points

B1. Deemed strong points

1. The specific design of cooperatives as legal entity (restricted ownership) and cooperatives' workers as usufructuaries (2§3).
2. The remuneration of public sector workers (including members of parliament and of government) as on average derived from the remuneration of cooperatives workers (3§3).
3. The specific way of counteracting joblessness, as well as the regular jobs for those with restricted capacities (3D5).
4. The large macro- and meso-economic policy potential of the Savings and Loans Bank regarding especially investment (3§16).
5. The design of the Real Estate Agency resulting in: the elimination of a (speculative) real estate market; its huge impact on the beauty of cities, towns and villages; its stabilisation of the economy's construction sector (2§5 addendum and 3§37-q).
6. The restrictions on, and the concessions for, mining and other extractions from the Earth (3§38).

B2. Deemed good points

1. The relation between parliament and government (3§1).
2. Budget and workforce constraints for state institutions (3§2-h).
3. The ban on subsidies (including taxation subsidies), with one exception (see B3–5).

---

81   Added after the first draft.
82   Appendix 3D.

THE STATE AND THE STATE INSTITUTIONS OF THE DESIGN   169

4. The specific design of the appointment of judges and of administrative prosecutors (3§6).
5. The specific design of market share ceilings; the single location of cooperatives; and the ban on take-overs (2§3.2, 2§3.3, 2§14.0 and 3§45).
6. The rather simple taxation system, including for cooperatives a cascade turnover tax instead of an administratively burdening value-added tax (3§46).

B3. Deemed imperfections and weak points
1. Joblessness is considerably but not completely eliminated (3D5): one can still be out of work during two months, and the Design requirement of a traineeship programme (3§18) seems an inevitable imperfection.
2. The possible bankruptcy of cooperatives (even with the build-in precautions of 2§19.1).
3. The limited free choice of occupation in case of an inadequate match between jobs and workers' qualifications (3§18).
4. There is no completely equal distribution of income (this is a weak point except regarding unpleasant work and wages supplements for evening and night shifts).[83]
5. The culture sector is, regarding the contemporary arts, probably still subsidy dependent, and it is extremely difficult to devise criteria for such subsidies – the Design leaves the latter casually to the elected councils of municipalities (3§36). Within the Design, the specific design of the contemporary arts was for me one of the very difficult ones given that in case arts products were *free goods/performances*, there would have to be not only workforce constraints (that also applies for the health and education sectors), but also allocation constraints over households/individuals (for the health sector the latter task is allotted to the medical professionals).[84]
6. The casual treatment of the boundaries between, and the interconnections of, the police services: municipal, provincial and the national cross-regional and special police services (3§5-d).
7. The casual treatment (in effect non-treatment) of defence against possible international aggression (3§5).

---

83   With some more administrative burden these wages supplements might be replaced by an overall work-time reduction for those concerned. The same applies for unpleasant work (in case this cannot be made more pleasant) or of an expertise that is temporarily scarce (2§8, addendum).
84   Could this be analogous for the contemporary arts? For example, it is most difficult, first, to determine who is deemed a visual artist, second to get these organised and have them constrain *their* number, third to get the reduced number of artists to decide on the allocation of their products. There are similar difficulties for writers and performing artists.

Concluding summary chapter 3

This concluding summary highlights a restricted number of subjects. These are the following eight: (1) the chapter's types of institutions; (2) the parliamentary democracy; (3) the remuneration of public sector workers; (4) the unity of the worker cooperatives society's economy and state; (5) further important characteristics; (6) taxation; (7) the hard budget and workforce constraints; (8) a classification of state agencies according to their expenditure.

1. Types of institutions, workforce and expenditure. Next to the parliament and the government, five types of state institutions are distinguished: the judiciary, ministries of the government, state agencies and provinces and municipalities (the latter two are treated in chapter 4). These together produce the legislation and regulation as well as their implementation. Besides these institutions there are 'workers' council governed foundations' (WGFs). These do not regulate but carry out collective or communal functions without being part of the state sector – together with the state sector they are part of the public sector at large. *Table 3.17* lists these, together with estimates of their workforce as a percentage of the total workforce, and estimates of the required state expenditure for these in percent of GDP (more detailed estimates are in Appendix 3A).

All material inputs for the public sector (such as the construction of buildings, medical instruments, computers and roads) are produced by Worker cooperatives (ch. 2). Whereas most WGFs are state-financed, they have a high degree of autonomy, even if their autonomy may be constrained (constraints also apply for cooperatives).

2. Parliamentary democracy. The parliament is the highest governing organ of the nation. It has to approve of all legislation as well as of any decrees.[85] There are no exceptions to this power of parliament (as in some capitalist nations, especially those with a presidential system). Parliament is elected on a proportional basis, without an electoral threshold. The parliament elects a government that is accountable to the parliament and that is removable by the parliament's majority. Section 3§1e set rules that should prevent monetary means, including gifts, to play a role in the candidacy of parliamentarians. Schemes 3.1 and 3.2 (3§1) summarise the election of the democratic organs of the state, and the main tasks and powers of parliament and government, as including the establishment (or change of responsibility) of state institutions.

---

85 In case of high urgency, the government may issue a decree that is legally binding for no more than 15 days – see further Appendix 3C (Constitution) Division 2, article 14.

TABLE 3.17 *Public sector institutions, with estimates of their assigned state expenditure and workforce*

State sector		This sector constitutes together with the state sector the 'public sector'	
Legislation and general governance	*State institutions*	*Workers' council governed foundations* (WGFS)	
• Parliament (highest body)	• The judiciary	• ***State-financed WGFs***	
• Government	• Ministries	Health sector	3D7-A
	• Provinces†	Education sector	3D7-B
	• Municipalities†	Part of the culture sector††	3D7-C
	• 18 State agencies‡	• ***User charging WGFs***	
	↓	Rail transport	3§40
	for the internal organisation of all five above: workers' councils*	Essential production/services not undertaken by cooperatives	3§41 3§42-e
Estimated workforce (% of total workforce): 6.5%⁑		Estimated workforce (% of total wf.): 21%⁑	
Estimated state expenditure: 25% of GDP⁎⁑		Estimated state expenditure: 18% of GDP	

† Treated in chapter 4.
‡ Listed in Appendix 3G (and in Table 3.19 below).
* With competences as set out in 3§3-d.
⁑ Cf. Appendix 3A, Table 3A.6.
⁎⁑ Cf. Appendix 3A, Table 3A1. This excludes the transfers to the state-financed institutions of the upper part of the next column (17.6% GDP).
†† See Table 3.14 (3§36).

Within the officials apparatus (the civil service) there is quite some division of powers, given that, next to the ministries, there is a key role for eighteen state agencies (see *Table 3.17*) that each have to report to parliament. The latter can also adjust the main line of their policies (3§2-a;b). Chapter 3, Divisions 4–10, was organised along these state agencies.

3. Remuneration of public sector workers. One core of the Design is that public sector workers (from members of parliament, government and the judiciary to state agencies and workers' council governed foundations) receive a remuneration that is derived from, and per institution on average equal to, the nationwide average remuneration of cooperatives' workers. Each institution's workers' council decides on the allocation of that average within the institution. This implies that all these workers have an interest in the flourishing of the cooperatives economy (quite apart from any general social delight they might derive from this).

4. Unity of the worker cooperatives society's economy and state. It was mentioned in the chapter's Introduction that in any stable mode of production, the economic sphere and the sphere of the state must constitute a unity, notably in that state institutions must be tailored to meeting the requirements of its particular economy. The previous point 3 makes that all state workers – including members of the parliament and the government – have a direct interest in optimally tailoring state institutions to the prosperity of cooperatives and their workers.

The chapter's division order has been a priority order, whence it started with the democratic organisation of the state, followed in the subsequent division by public security and the judiciary and so forth. *Table 3.18* schematically present a divisions order that runs alongside that priority order – one that focusses on the mentioned tailoring of the state institutions.

TABLE 3.18 *Functions of state institutions vis-à-vis cooperatives*

	Function	Subject	Ref.
1	furthering the objectives of cooperatives and workers	• safeguarding the finance of cooperatives and the financial constellation at large	3D4
		• job securities	3D5
		• income allowances	3D6
		• real estate (renting or purchasing), mining (renting) and infrastructure	3D8
2	constraining cooperatives in the interest of other cooperatives, or of workers and households	• environment, output safety, work safety, work-time, minimum wages	3D3
		• regulation of auditing, patents, copyrights and competition	3D10

TABLE 3.18 *Functions of state institutions vis-à-vis cooperatives (cont.)*

	Function	Subject	Ref.
3	services for which cooperatives production does not apply because of their character or of free provision	• public security; judiciary	3D2
		• health; education; part of culture	3D7
4	public sector undertaking, either because of its monopoly or oligopoly character, or because of cooperatives' scale or risk constraints	• railway transport (user charged)	3D9, §40
		• essential production/services not undertaken by cooperatives†	3D9, §41 3D9, §42

† Here 'essential' means vital to the functioning of (other) cooperatives or to the welfare of households.

5. Further important characteristics. This section briefly lists further important characteristics of the Design (in the chapter's sections order).
• Judges of the 'supreme court' and of the 'courts level just below it', as well as administrative prosecutors, are appointed by a judiciary committee of 16 members composed of – each for one quarter – former judges, lawyers, former ministers, former parliamentarians (3§6).
• Physically circular production (3§7) and sustainable extractions from the Earth (3§38).
• The large macro- and meso-economic policy potential of the Savings and Loans Bank regarding especially investment (3§16 under c and d; 3§47 under a-first and c).
• No one is out of work for more than two months, where 'work' includes permanent jobs and paid traineeships – during recessions the latter are replaced by temporary jobs (3§17–3§20).
• Permanent jobs for workers with restricted physical or mental abilities – spread over all cooperatives and state institutions (3§21).
• Equal pensions for all (3§24); child's costs of living allowances, cost covering childcare allowances, and parental leave allowances (3§22); allowances for tertiary students (3§23).
• Free for all health and education provisions (subdivision 7A and 7B).
• The elimination of a (speculative) real estate market; all can rent within a variety of qualities against reasonable prices. Within the Design's alternative there is also a huge impact on the beauty of cities, towns and villages, as well as a stabilisation of the economy's construction sector (3§37).
• Special judicial proceedings regarding the abuse of power and other improper behaviour by parliamentarians, ministers, others state workers and political parties (Appendix 3D)

• The administrative burden for cooperatives is (qualitatively estimated) probably less than that for capitalist enterprises (Appendix 3B).

6. *Taxation*. State expenditure is generally financed by taxation. There are two main taxation categories. First, a *turnover tax* (cascade system) that should cover the revenue for about 50% of the state expenditure. Its tax rate is between 5% and 15% depending on the production structure of the country at hand (3§46 argued why this is to be preferred in comparison with a value-added tax). Second, an *individual income tax* that covers about 50% of the state expenditure. On top of these two there are inheritance and gift taxes, the revenue of which are expected to be minor in face of anticipating behaviour. (This issue and the ones below are treated in 3§46, unless indicated otherwise.)

For the income taxes it is recalled that there are costs covering child allowances and childcare allowances, that education and health services are free of charge and that everybody has the right to a pension of around the minimum wage. The minimum wage is 1⅔ (167%) of the minimum costs of living (or the ratio of the minimum costs of living and the minimum wage is 60% – 3§11 and Table 3.9 of 3§24). The income tax rates range from 25% (between the minimum costs of living and the minimum wage), via 60% (between one to two times the minimum wage) and further gradually increasing to 95% for incomes above five times the minimum wage. (Note that the latter incomes are most unlikely, given that worker councils decide on the pre-tax income ranges.)

There are no municipal or provincial taxes nor is there a wealth tax. However, the on the receiver levied inheritance tax rate is (in comparison with most capitalist countries) considerable: 50% over an inheritance equivalent between one and two times the minimum wage, and 100% above it. (The principle point about this tax rate is that the children of all parents deserve an equal treatment and that the wealth of their ancestors is not their merit. The tax-free threshold is to cover treasured possessions.)

In Appendix 3A-4 the revenue from the income tax is estimated.

7. *Hard budget constraints and workforce constraints*. A main theme throughout the chapters' Divisions 1–10 is the setting of not only 'hard budget constraints' but also workforce constraints for ministries, state agencies and workers' council governed foundations (first introduced in 3§2h). These constraints are twofold.

First, the yearly budgets consist of a separate sum for wages (including a dividends equivalent) and a sum for material expenses (as well as, when relevant, a budget for the payment of allowances). Because borrowing, including by bank overdraft, is prohibited, the budget ceiling is hard (thus this requires a tight planning of expenses).[86]

Second, regarding structural (long-term) budgets, the rules for provisions are such that, in general, there is a budget ceiling as percent of GDP and a workforce ceiling as percent of the total workforce. For this second constraint I below go through the three in this respect difficult provisions (pensions, health and education) that also happen to be the quantitively main state expenditure categories.

First pensions. For these only a budget ceiling is relevant. In case the average number of retirement years is continuously brought in line with the average number of working years (meaning that with an ageing population the eligible pension age is proportionally postponed) there is an adequate structural budget ceiling, in the sense of a constant percent of GDP.

Second health provisions. The Design's organisation of the health sector (carried out by workers' council governed foundations) is such that there is a structural budget ceiling as percent of GDP as well as a structural ceiling for the number of staff as a fixed percent of the nation's workforce. In the aggregate the budget is population based instead of specific treatment based (which would be far more complicated). However, relevant for the budget ceiling is, next to the population base, that it is also working population based – which is the case provided that with an ageing population the pension age is proportionally postponed (see the previous paragraph). In comparison with an insurance-based system, medical staff – instead of, as in many capitalist countries, insurance corporations – ultimately decide on the rationing of treatments. In practice the required degree of rationing depends on the mentioned medical workers fixed percent of the workforce, as well as on a lump-sum finance that the medical institutions receive. Via parliamentary decisions each of the latter might be adjusted, in case health provisions are prioritised over other provisions – which evidently would imply a budget ceilings reordering.

Third education provisions. These provisions are the main exception to the two structural ceilings. There are fixed student/staff ratios, but given those the aggregate structural number of staff and the aggregate structural budget depends on, first, the segment of the population younger than, roughly, 25 years old, and second, changes in the duration of their schooling. Especially the duration tends to increase over time. (This would similarly be the case for any other – non-cooperatives – mode of production.) Quite apart from the latter, the student/staff ratios might be adjusted via parliamentary decisions, which, given the schooling duration, would imply a budget ceilings reordering.

---

86   The institutions receive their budget on their account at the Central Bank, which is not allowed to grant overdrafts. This bank is the only bank they can bank with.

8. Classification of state agencies by their expenditure. A few state agencies run a surplus and a few are responsible for very large expenditures (and constitute the major part of state expenditure). *Table 3.19* classifies the agencies in groups along this continuum. (More detailed state expenditure estimates are presented in Appendix 3A, sections 3A-2 and 3A-3.)

TABLE 3.19 *Classification of state agencies by their expenditure: from surplus-running to big spending ones*

	State Agency	From surplus to large expenditure	
1	Real estate agency (3§37)	surplus	
2	Mining and other Earth extractions agency (3§38)	surplus	
3	Savings and Loans Bank (3§16)	break-even	
4	National public transport agency (3§40)	break-even	
5	Central bank (3§13)	low	
6	Guardian bank (3§14)	low	
7	Culture and cultural heritage agency (3§34)	low	
8	Agency for temporary WGFs (3§41)	low	each < 0.5% GDP
9	Registered external auditors authority (3§43)	low	
10	Patents and copy rights authority (3§44)	low	
11	Competition authority (3§45)	low	
12	Inspectorates – regarding various safeties (3§12)	considerable	
13	Investment-credit guarantee fund (3§15)	considerable†	each 0.5% – 2% GDP
14	Job securities and jobs shortage agency (3§17)	considerable‡	
15	National infrastructure agency (3§39)	large*	2% – 5% GDP
16	National education agency (3§30)	very large**	
17	National health agency (3§26)	very large‡	each 5% – 15% GDP
18	Pensions and child allowances agency (3D6, intro)	very large⁂	

† Though policy dependent.
‡ Allowance payments for: qualifications mismatch joblessness (0.3% GDP), and those at more than 80% inability to work (1.3% GDP).
* 2.1% GDP.
** 5.7% GDP, including allowances for students aged 18–25 (1.3% GDP).
‡ 11.9% GDP.
⁂ 14.0% GDP. Of which: pension allowances at 8.5% GDP; and the sum of allowances for child costs of living, childcare, and parental leave at 5.6% GDP.

THE STATE AND THE STATE INSTITUTIONS OF THE DESIGN   177

Appendices to chapter 3. Here follow seven appendices.
- 3A. Estimates of state expenditure, of taxation revenue and of the state's labour force.
- 3B. Estimates of the administrative burden for cooperatives in comparison with capitalist enterprises.
- 3C. Constitutional rights and main other constitutional elements.
- 3D. Abuse of power and other improper behaviour by parliamentarians, ministers, others state workers and political parties: judicial proceedings.
- 3E. Regulation of the turnover tax for 'Single person enterprises'.
- 3F. Stand-in work as organised in 'stand-in cooperatives', and the prevention of casual inferior jobs.
- 3G. List of separate accounting maintaining state agencies and other state institutions.

Appendix 3A. Estimates of state expenditure, taxation revenue and the state's labour force

This appendix comprises five sections: • Introduction and method; • Summary of the Design's state expenditure; • State expenditure according to the international 'classification of the functions of government' (COFOG); • Taxation revenue from the income tax; • Labour force of the public sector.

3A-1 *Introduction and method*
The Design should be applicable to any country at some stage in the future. In this appendix I am therefore considering an empirically non-existent constellation. The most important problem is the 'broad demography' of such a constellation, by which I understand not only the population and its growth and the pension age, but also the proportion of the population that pursues the various levels of education (whence they are not part of the active labour force), the general health condition of the population (as affecting the utilisation of health services as well as the inability to work) and similar characteristics of the population.

I have 'solved' this problem by modelling the Design's features (chapters 2 and 3) on the population characteristics and various economic characteristics of one single existing country, for which I have taken the Netherlands, simply because I know most about this country and because it has a very good statistical bureau. The relevant data are drawn from *Statistics Netherlands*.[87] In capitalist terms it is a rather advanced country.[88]

However, for the estimates in this appendix the demographical characteristics are far more important than the economic characteristics. Next to the labour force, my main units of measurement are percentages of GDP, and percentages of the minimum wage. Although in the model I use some money level of the minimum wage, this can, without loss of information, be replaced with another level (this would, for example, proportionally affect the revenue from taxation, which would affect the money level of the state expenditure out of taxation). Alternatively, the minimum wage might have been expressed as a percentage of NDP (but this would have made my examples less transparent). Note that out of the Design's minimum wage (whatever its level) no expenses have to be paid for health and education (because these are free for all), nor for pension provisions, child cost of living and childcare (because these are compensated by uniform allowances – provisions and allowances are financed out of taxation).

For the demography and other characteristics, I have used the year 2019, that is the year just prior to the COVID-19 turbulences.

When in this appendix the term 'state' is used without specification, this refers to *the general state* which is the sum of the 'central state' (for federal states this is the federal central state) and the provincial and municipal administrations (for federations including the local states). The 'general state' is the most reliable category for international statistical comparisons because different countries have different allotment principles for what is carried out at the central, regional and local levels. Although provincial and municipal administrations are dealt with only in Chapter 4, their expenditure is thus included in the current appendix (in the Design only the central state levies taxes).

The reader should recall the last paragraph of the Introduction to chapter 3: 'Note on the fractional precision of estimates'. Even when I state estimates in decimal fractions, this does not take away that all these are rough estimates, and the reader should take at that.

---

87   https://opendata.cbs.nl/#/CBS/nl/ (Netherlandic). Only a limited amount of data are available in English: https://opendata.cbs.nl/statline/#/CBS/en/.

88   World rank GDP per capita in 2019: 14 (in PP $). World rank GDP in 2019: 28 (in PP $). https://knoema.com/sijweyg/world-gdp-per-capita-ranking-2019-data-and-charts https://knoema.com/nwnfkne/world-gdp-ranking-2019-gdp-by-country-data-and-charts Annual minimum wage 2019: €21,069. https://stats.oecd.org/Index.aspx?QueryId=64622 Annual minimum wage 2018 in US$ 1,882; world rank 5. https://ilostat.ilo.org/topics/wages/

3A-2 *Summary of the Design's state expenditure*

Before getting to further details, *Table 3A.1* (p. 180) summarises the main categories of the state expenditure which regards the Design's allowances and the sectors of health and education. Together these cover 77% of the total state expenditure. Column (3) is derived from the underlying model; it expresses the absolute state expenditure (2019) per million of inhabitants of a country. Health and education were explained in Division 7. The allowances were explained in Divisions 5 and 6 – the relevant section references were indicated in Table 3.9 (end of 3§24).

TABLE 3A.1 *Summary of the annual state expenditure*

		(1)	(2)	(3)	(4)	(5)
	Demography dependent (see the main text)	Level in % minimum wage (for allowances)	Estimated % of people (for allowances)	Expenditure per million population, in million €[†]	Share of total state expenditure	State expenditure in % GDP
	ALLOWANCES (excl. allowances for students)					
1						
2	pensions (estimated for an average of 20 years)	100%	20% of population	€3,961	19.7%	8.45%
3	*child-related allowances*					
4	child costs of living (age dependent, until max. age 18)[‡]	from 14% to 22% per child	20% of population	€725	3.6%	1.55%
5	childcare (age dependent, until max. age 18)[‡]	from 74% to 34% per child	20% of population	€1,772	8.8%	3.78%
6	parental leave (31 weeks for the parents together)	100%	1.0% of population (birth/pop.)	€117	0.6%	0.25%
7	foster/adoptive parent of domestic orphans	twice the allowance row 4	0.02% of population age 0–18	€0.3	0.0%	0.001%
8	*joblessness*					
9	job search allowance school-leavers (max. 2 months)[*]	60%	0.5% of available workforce[*]	€32	0.2%	0.07%
10	job search allowance after had a 2y job (max. 2 months)[*]	85%	0.6% of available workforce	€55	0.3%	0.12%
11	for the latter, traineeship supplement (on top of 60%)[*]	25%	2.7% of available workforce	€72	0.4%	0.15%

THE STATE AND THE STATE INSTITUTIONS OF THE DESIGN

TABLE 3A.1 *Summary of the annual state expenditure (cont.)*

	(1) Level in % minimum wage (for allowances)	(2) Estimated % of people (for allowances)	(3) Expenditure per million population, in million €†	(4) Share of total state expenditure	(5) State expenditure in % GDP
	Demography dependent (see the main text)				
12 allowance for those at more than 80% inability to work‡	120%	4.0% of population 15–65y	€ 622	3.1 %	1.33 %
13 total of allowances (excl. allow. for students)			€ 7,356	36.6 %	15.70 %
14 MAIN PROVISIONS					
15 health (incl. care disabled)			€ 5,581	27.8 %	11.90 %
16 education (primary, secondary, tertiary)			€ 2,682	13.3 %	5.72 %
17 of which allowances students (usually max. 18–24y)	60%	5.6% of population	€ 593	3.0 %	1.27 %
18 total of main provisions			€ 8,263	41.1 %	17.62 %
19 total of allowances and main provisions			€ 15,526	77.7 %	33.32 %
20 all other state expenditure (exclusive defence)			€ 4,488	22.3 %	9.35 %
21 Total state expenditure (sum of rows 19–20)			€ 20,108	100 %	42.67 %

Prices 2019.

† The figures include families with more than 3 children (though for more than 3 children there is no eligibility)
‡ After 2 months followed by compulsory traineeship; the percentage in the 3rd column regards 2 months on annual basis.
* The available workforce equals the 'potential workforce' (= the population age 15–65) minus those pursuing formal education, and minus those at more than 80% inability to work (row 12).
** This is a maximum amount, assuming, first, that the job search period had no result, and, second, a full year traineeship. Most often this will be less (that is, when they found a new job).

3A-3 State expenditure according to the international 'classification of the functions of government' (COFOG)

This section categorises the Design's state expenditure in terms of the international 'classification of the functions of government' (COFOG). This is a classification in ten categories, each with further subdivisions (for a brief explanation see Eurostat 2020 and for a longer one Eurostat 2019). Table 3A.2 shows the Design's estimated first digit of this classification, in comparison with the OECD average.

TABLE 3A.2 *Estimate of the Design's state expenditure in comparison with the OECD average for 2019: COFOG 1st digit in % GDP*

		Design†	Design†	OECD‡	Difference D–O
	Category	share total exp.	% GDP	% GDP	% GDP
1	General public services	7.6 %	3.25 %	5.30%	-2.05%
2	Defence	not classified	not classified	1.45%	not included
3	Public order and safety	4.3 %	1.85 %	1.64%	0.21%
4	Economic affairs	6.0 %	2.55 %	4.48%	-1.93%
5	Environmental protection	3.4 %	1.45 %	0.70%	0.75%
6	Housing and community amenities	0.1 %	0.05 %	0.54%	-0.49%
7	Health	27.9 %	11.90 %	6.57%	5.33%
8	Recreation, culture and religion	0.5 %	0.20 %	1.27%	-1.07%
9	Education	13.4 %	5.72 %	5.12%	0.60%
10	Social protection	36.8 %	15.70 %	15.66%	0.04%
	Total			42.45%	
	Total exclusive defence	100 %	42.67 %	38.92%	1.67%

† Model basis 2019.
‡ Source: https://stats.oecd.org/; OECD average (as calculated by the OECD for 2019).[89]

---

89 OECD.stat, dataset Public sector, taxation and market regulation / Government at glance / Government at glance – yearly updates / Government at glance / General government expenditures by function.
https://stats.oecd.org/# (Last updated: 11 May 2021; extracted 29 Nov 2021).

It can be seen from the last row of *Table 3A.2* that in comparison with the OECD average the total Design state expenditure is moderately higher (1.67 percent point). Especially the row 7 category Health is considerably higher (5.33 percent point). Note that for most categories the compositions are different; this regards especially the row 10 Social protection (for which the Design's pensions and child-related allowances are considerable, and other items relatively minor).

Table 3A.3 (9 pages) lists estimates of the Design's state expenditure in terms of the COFOG classification's second digit level. (The abbreviations referred to in the table's 4th column are listed on p. 192).

TABLE 3A.3 *Estimate of the Design's state expenditure: COFOG 2nd digit in % GDP*

COFOG category	Expenditure in % GDP	Expenditure subcategories in % GDP	Design's state agency [abbreviations written out at end of table]	Division or section ch. 3	Remark
1. General public services	**3.25%**				
1.1 Executive and legislative organs; financial, fiscal and external affairs.		2.10%	see remark	3D1; 3D4; 3§46	3D4 includes CB, GB, IGF and SLB
1.2 Foreign economic aid [0.7% NDP, country dependent]		0.60%			Tinbergen norm
1.3 General services		0.15%			
• incl. below not specified non-transfer budgets of agencies					
1.4 Basic research		0.40%			regards research for all categories
1.5 R&D general public services		nil			
1.6 General public services n.e.c.		nil			
1.7 Public debt transactions		nil			State may borrow from CB only
1.8 Transfers between levels of government.		nil			consolidated general government
2. Defence	**not classified**				3§5: Note on defence
3. Public order and safety	**1.85%**		see remark	3D2	ministry (no agencies)
3.1 Police services [including prosecution]		0.90%		3§5	

TABLE 3A.3 *Estimate of the Design's state expenditure: COFOG 2nd digit in % GDP (cont.)*

COFOG category	Expenditure in % GDP	Expenditure subcategories in % GDP	Design's state agency [abbreviations written out at end of table]	Division or section ch. 3	Remark
3.2 Fire-protection services	0.20%			3§5	
3.3 Law courts	0.40%			3§6	
3.4 Prisons	0.30%			3§5	
3.5 R&D Public order and safety	0.05%				
3.6 Public order and safety n.e.c.	nil				
4. Economic affairs	2.55%		see also remarks	3D3; 3D10	see also 3D4 (classified under cat. 1)
4.1 General economic, commercial and labour affairs	0.25%				
• safety of, and information about, output[90]		0.09%		3§8	ministry of cooperatives affairs
• labour affairs (regulation only) including on safety at work, work-time and minimum wages		0.01%		3§9, 3§10, 3§11	ministry of labour affairs
• inspectorates on the above		0.10%		3§12	incl. on physical circ. production. (5.4)
• market power, patents and auditing affairs		0.05%		3§43–3§45	
4.2 Agriculture, forestry, fishery, and hunting	nil		f, f, h: MEA	3§38	MEA runs a surplus

---

90 The costly part is the information in face of the advertisement prohibition (including internet advertisement).

TABLE 3A.3 *Estimate of the Design's state expenditure: COFOG 2nd digit in % GDP (cont.)*

COFOG category	Expenditure in % GDP	Expenditure subcategories in % GDP	Design's state agency [abbreviations written out at end of table]	Division or section ch. 3	Remark
4.3 Fuel and energy	nil		MEA	3§38	MEA runs a surplus
4.4 Mining, manufacturing and construction	nil		mining: MEA	3§38	MEA runs a surplus
4.5 Transport [infrastructure]	2.10%		NIA[91]	3§39	see also 3§40
4.6 Communication [including internet]	0.20%		NIA	3§39	
4.7 Other industries	nil				
4.8 R&D Economic affairs	nil				
4.9 Economic affairs n.e.c.	nil				
5. **Environmental protection**	**1.45%**		see remarks		
5.1 Waste management		0.50%		4§3	carried out by municipalities
5.2 Waste water management		0.40%		4§3	carried out by municipalities
5.3 Pollution abatement		0.30%		3§7	together subsumed under physically circular production (3§7)
5.4 Protection of biodiversity and landscape		0.15%		3§7	

[91] Provincial and municipal authorities are responsible for the local and regional infrastructural networks.

TABLE 3A.3 *Estimate of the Design's state expenditure: COFOG 2nd digit in % GDP (cont.)*

COFOG category	Expenditure in % GDP	Expenditure subcategories in % GDP	Design's state agency [abbreviations written out at end of table]	Division or section ch. 3	Remark
5.5 R&D Environmental protection	0.10%			3§33-B	5.5. by the 'National institute for the advance of phys. circular production'
5.6 Environmental protection n.e.c.	nil				
6. Housing and community amenities	0.05%		REA	3D8; 3§37	REA runs a (moderate) surplus
6.1 Housing development	nil			3§37	responsibility of REA
6.2 Community development	nil			3§37	responsibility of REA
6.3 Water supply	0.03%			4§3	carried out by municipalities
6.4 Street lighting	0.02%			4§3	carried out by municipalities
6.5 R&D Housing and community amenities	nil			3§37	responsibility of REA
6.6 Housing and community amenities n.e.c.	nil				
7. Health	11.90%		NHA	3D7-A	3§26–3§29
7.1 Medical products, appliances and equipment	0.90%				in the Design subsumed under Primary medical treatment clinics and Hospitals

TABLE 3A.3 *Estimate of the Design's state expenditure: COFOG 2nd digit in % GDP (cont.)*

COFOG category	Expenditure in % GDP	Expenditure subcategories in % GDP	Design's state agency [abbreviations written out at end of table]	Division or section ch. 3	Remark
• of which pharmaceutics public pharmacies		0.55%			
7.2 Outpatient services [primary medical treatment]	1.20%				Primary medical treatment clinics
7.3 Hospital services	8.50%				in the Design divided in 3 categories
• of which general multi-specialisation hospitals		2.00%			
• of which university hospitals		1.00%			
• of which other hospitals and clinics (somatic)		0.50%			
• of which psychiatric hospitals and clinics		0.85%			
• of which institutions for care disabled		1.65%			
• of which other care institutions		2.50%			
7.4 Public health services	0.45%				Design: 'preventive and auxiliary inst.'
7.5 R&D Health	0.05%				
• excl. research by hospitals and prevention institutions					
7.6 Health n.e.c.	0.80%				
• social care including youth care		0.70%			

THE STATE AND THE STATE INSTITUTIONS OF THE DESIGN 189

TABLE 3A.3 *Estimate of the Design's state expenditure: COFOG 2nd digit in % GDP (cont.)*

COFOG category	Expenditure in % GDP	Expenditure subcategories in % GDP	Design's state agency [abbreviations written out at end of table]	Division or section ch. 3	Remark
• administrative matters		0.10%			regarding the NHA and its branches
8. Recreation, culture and religion	0.20%		CHA	3D7-C	3§34
8.1 Recreational and sporting services	nil				undertaken by cooperatives
8.2 Cultural services	0.20%				
• National library and archives		0.02%		3§35	
• Municipal subsidies contemporary arts		0.15%		3§36; 4§3	
• Municipal/provincial libraries and historical sites etc.		0.03%		3§35; 4§3; 4§5	
8.3 Broadcasting and publishing services	nil				see category 4.6
8.4 Religious and other community services	nil				
8.5 R&D Recreation, culture and religion	nil				
8.6 Recreation, culture and religion n.e.c.	nil				
9. Education	5.72%		NEA	3D7-B	
9.1 Primary education	1.44%			3§32	see 3§31 on pre-primary (by coops)

TABLE 3A.3 *Estimate of the Design's state expenditure: COFOG 2nd digit in % GDP (cont.)*

COFOG category	Expenditure in % GDP	Expenditure subcategories in % GDP	Design's state agency [abbreviations written out at end of table]	Division or section ch. 3	Remark
• including school transport		0.01%			
9.2 Secondary education	1.82%			3§32	
• including school transport		0.01%			
• incl. cooperatives' costs of training secondary students		0.04%			
9.3 Post-secondary non-tertiary education	nil				
9.4 Tertiary education	1.11%			3§32	
Allowances students age 18–25	1.27%				
9.5 Education not definable by level	nil				
9.6 Subsidiary services to education (see 9.4 allowances)	nil				
9.7 R&D Education	0.03%				
9.8 Education n.e.c. [administrative matters]	0.05%				regarding the NEA and its branches
10. Social protection	15.70%			3D5 and 3D6	
10.1 Sickness and disability	1.33%				
• allowances for those at >80% inability		1.33%	see remark	3§21	carried out by a ministry

TABLE 3A.3 *Estimate of the Design's state expenditure: COFOG 2nd digit in % GDP (cont.)*

COFOG category	Expenditure in % GDP	Expenditure subcategories in % GDP	Design's state agency [abbreviations written out at end of table]	Division or section ch. 3	Remark
• sickness on an insurance basis		nil		3§21	
10.2 Old age [pensions]	8.45%		PCA	3§24	
10.3 Survivors	0.001%		PCA	3§22	
• regards extra child benefits for foster/adoptive parents					
10.4 Family and children	5.58%				
• child costs of living		1.54%	PCA	3§22	
• childcare		3.78%	PCA	3§22	
• parental leave		0.25%	PCA	3§22	
10.5 Unemployment	0.34%				
• job search allowance school-leavers (max. 2 months)		0.07%	JSA	3§18 and 3§20	
• job search allowance after had a 2y job (max. 2 months)		0.12%	JSA	3§18 and 3§20	
• for the latter, traineeship supplement		0.15%	JSA	3§18 and 3§20	
10.6 Housing	nil				housing is carried out by REA (cat. 6)

TABLE 3A.3 *Estimate of the Design's state expenditure: COFOG 2nd digit in % GDP (cont.)*

COFOG category	Expenditure in % GDP	Expenditure subcategories in % GDP	Design's state agency [abbreviations written out at end of table]	Division or section ch. 3	Remark
10.7 Social exclusion n.e.c.	nil				
10.8 R&D Social protection	nil				
10.9 Social protection n.e.c.	nil				
Sum (exclusive defence)	**42.67%**				

Abbreviation of relevant state agencies

CA	Competition Authority		NEA	National Education Agency
CB	Central Bank		NHA	National Health Agency
JSA	Job Securities and jobs shortage Agency		NIA	National Infrastructure Agency
GB	Guardian Bank		NTA	National public Transport Agency
IGF	Investment-credit Guarantee Fund		PCA	Pensions and Child allowances Agency
CHA	Culture and cultural Heritage Agency		REA	Real Estate Agency
MEA	Mining and other Earth extractions agency		SLB	Savings and Loans Bank

THE STATE AND THE STATE INSTITUTIONS OF THE DESIGN   193

3A-4   Taxation revenue from the income tax

An estimate of the revenue from the income tax is acquired in the following four steps.

(1) Calculation of the average taxable income. Because public sector workers receive on average the same remuneration as the average remuneration of workers in cooperatives, the average taxable income of workers can be calculated as in *Table 3A.4*. It is assumed that the Design's cooperatives economy is equally productive as a capitalist economy (though it is likely more productive, because the cooperatives' workers work for themselves instead of for an employer).[92]

TABLE 3A.4   *From GDP to the average taxable income: estimates*

	Category	Remark	2019 size per mil population, in mil €	In % GDP
1	GDP		€ 46,884	100%
2	depreciation of fixed investment		€ 7,718	16.46%
3	NDP = value-added	rows 1–2	€ 39,166	83.54%
	allocation of value-added			
4	net investment (cooperatives and state)		€ 2,260	4.82%
5	value-added (total) minus net investment cooperatives and state	rows 3–4	€ 36,906	78.72%
6	net investment all cooperatives		€ 777	1.66%†
7	net investment non-bank cooperatives		€ 732	1.56%‡
8	risk premium on net investment by non-bank coops for bank loans and state guarantees (together 3%)*	3% row 7	€ 22	0.05%
9	cooperatives addition to required resistance buffer (30% of net investment)	30% row 6	€ 233	0.50%
10	**Value-added available for distribution to workers = total taxable primary income (annual)**‡	rows 5–8–9	€ 36,651	78.17%

---

92   As will be seen in ch. 6 (6§3), empirical research regarding 'worker-*owned* cooperatives' within capitalism shows that the latter are at least as productive as conventional capitalist enterprises, and more productive in some areas (Pérotin 2012, p. 37).

TABLE 3A.4 *From GDP to the average taxable income: estimates (cont.)*

	Category	Remark	2019 size per mil population, in mil €	In % GDP
	average taxable income		↙ dimensions of next column	
11	total taxable primary income	in mil €	€ 36,651	
12	available labour force	in 1000	527	
13	**average taxable primary income (annual)** ⁂	in one €	€ 69,028	

† This is 3.2% of the value-added of all cooperatives. Their gross investment is 17.8% of their gross value-added.
‡ This is 3.3% of the value-added of non-bank cooperatives. Their gross investment is 18.4% of their gross value-added.
* It is assumed that this corresponds to the loans and guarantees that are actually written off.
⁑ Exclusive interest on savings.
⁂ This is the average taxable income paid to workers of cooperatives and state institutions; it thus excludes taxable allowances such as pensions.

It can be seen from row 13 of *Table 3A.4* that at an annual minimum wage (MiW) of €20,000 (the example that I have used so far, and that I will use later on) the annual average taxable income is near to 3.5 times the MiW.[93]

(2) *Calculation of the number of income tax payers*. Table 3A.5 (p. 195) shows how from the potential and the available labour force, the number of income tax payers is calculated (this regards primary and secondary incomes, the latter in the form of allowances).

Explanatory remark on *Table 3A.5*. Row 5: These persons (except prisoners) receive an income that is included in the other categories. Rows 3 and 15: Parents of those pursuing formal education (row 3) receive until age 18 a child costs of living allowance, which is part of their taxable income (classified under some other category of the table). From age 18 pursuers of formal education receive themselves an allowance (row 15).

---

93 In the Netherlands (year 2018) for employees between age 15–75, the average primary income, as scaled to FTE, is €63,700. This is exclusive primary income from wealth. https://opendata.cbs.nl/statline/#/CBS/nl/dataset/83686NED/table?dl=43F5B.

TABLE 3A.5 *Calculation of the number of income receivers*

	Category (1)	% of total population (2)	Absolute per mil population (3)	In % available labour force (4)	Fixed income receivers (5)	Other income receivers (6)	% of all income receivers (7)
1	Potential labour force (PLF) = population age 15–65	64.5%	645,037				
2	PLF not available for work (age 15–65)	11.8%	117,927				
3	of which PLF pursuing formal education	8.6%	85,716				
4	of which PLF at more than 80% inability to work†	2.6%	25,732		25,732		3.2%
5	of which PLF in institutions (mainly care)	0.6%	6,480				
6	Available labour force (ALF)	52.7%	527,109	100%			
7	of which ALF with regular position	49.2%	491,652	93.3%			
8	workers with restricted ability‡	2.1%	20,686	3.9%	20,686		2.6%
9	other workers with regular position	47.1%	470,966			470,966	59.2%
10	of which ALF with traineeship position	3.0%	29,885	5.7%			
11	School-leaver trainees‡	1.6%	15,622	3.0%	15,622		2.0%
12	trainees after having a two-year position‡*	1.4%	14,264	2.7%	14,264		1.8%
13	of which ALF without work (max. 2 months)†	0.6%	5,595	1.1%			
	Other categories						
14	Pensioners (population > age 65)†	19.7%	196,622		196,622		24.7%
15	students aged 18–25†	5.2%	52,014		52,014		6.5%
16	**Total of income receivers**				324,939	470,966	100% 795,906
17	Total income receivers in % total population				32%	47%	80%⁑

† Receivers of an allowance (fixed income).
‡ Receivers of a fixed income from cooperatives or state institutions.
* On top of the fixed income from cooperatives or state institutions (60% MiW), these receive an allowance of 25%.
⁑ This regards the total population above age 18.

(3) *Calculation of the income tax brackets and the average tax rates.* Table 3.7 (see 3§4 or 3§46) showed the Design's income tax rates. *Table 3A.6* shows their application to the fixed incomes, and Table 3A.7 the application to the other incomes.

TABLE 3A.6   *The average tax rate on the fixed incomes*

(1)	(2)	(3)	(4)	(5)	(6)	(7)	(8)	(9)
			→	at MiW = € 20,00†				←
	% MiW	Tax rate	Income	Bracket	Tax on bracket	Sum of tax	After-tax income	Average tax rate
minimum allowances‡	60%	0%	€ 12,000	€ 12,000	€ 0	€ 0	€ 12,000	0.0%
trainees after 2y job	85%	25%	€ 17,000	€ 5,000	€ 1,250	€ 1,250	€ 15,750	7.4%
pensioners	100%	25%	€ 20,000	€ 3,000	€ 750	€ 2,000	€ 18,000	10.0%
inability allowance	120%	50%	€ 24,000	€ 4,000	€ 2,000	€ 4,000	€ 20,000	16.7%
restricted ability	150%	50%	€ 30,000	€ 6,000	€ 3,000	€ 7,000	€ 23,000	23.3%

† The figure of €20,000 is not essential: when in face of the country's purchasing power structure, the nominal minimum wage would be higher or lower, the taxation revenue would be proportionally higher or lower (as would be the money-level of the required state expenditure). The proportions of column (2) and the tax rates of column (3) are essential.
‡ Mainly students aged 18–24 and school-leavers.

In step (4) the taxation revenue will be estimated via the median average tax rate of income classes. Therefore *Table 3A.7* calculates these medians (the non-median table rows serve as clarification).

TABLE 3A.7   *The average of the (median) tax rate on the fixed incomes*

(1)	(2)	(3)	(4)	(5)	(6)	(7)	(8)	(9)
			→	at MiW = € 20,00†				←
	% MiW	Tax rate	Income	Bracket	Tax on bracket	Sum of tax	After-tax income	Average of (median) tax rate
60% MiW	60%	0%	€ 12,000	€ 12,000	€ 0	€ 0	€ 12,000	0.0%
median 60% MiW–MiW	80%	25%	€ 16,000	€ 4,000	€ 1,000	€ 1,000	€ 15,000	6.3%
MiW	100%	25%	€ 20,000	€ 4,000	€ 1,000	€ 2,000	€ 18,000	10.0%
median 1–2 MiW	150%	60%	€ 30,000	€ 10,000	€ 6,000	€ 8,000	€ 22,000	26.7%
2 MiW	200%	60%	€ 40,000	€ 10,000	€ 6,000	€ 14,000	€ 26,000	35.0%
median 2–3 MiW	250%	70%	€ 50,000	€ 10,000	€ 7,000	€ 21,000	€ 29,000	42.0%

THE STATE AND THE STATE INSTITUTIONS OF THE DESIGN   197

TABLE 3A.7 *The average of the (median) tax rate on the fixed incomes (cont.)*

(1)	(2)	(3)	(4)	(5)	(6)	(7)	(8)	(9)
			→		at MiW = € 20,00†			←
	% MiW	Tax rate	Income	Bracket	Tax on bracket	Sum of tax	After-tax income	Average of (median) tax rate
3 MiW	300%	70%	€ 60,000	€ 10,000	€ 7,000	€ 28,000	€ 32,000	46.7%
median 3–4 MiW	350%	80%	€ 70,000	€ 10,000	€ 8,000	€ 36,000	€ 34,000	51.4%
4 MiW	400%	80%	€ 80,000	€ 10,000	€ 8,000	€ 44,000	€ 36,000	55.0%
median 4–5 MiW	450%	90%	€ 90,000	€ 10,000	€ 9,000	€ 53,000	€ 37,000	58.9%
5 MiW	500%	90%	€ 100,000	€ 10,000	€ 9,000	€ 62,000	€ 38,000	62.0%

† See note † of Table 3A.6.

(4) Estimate of the taxation revenue from the income tax. The final step estimates the revenue from the income tax. This is not difficult for the fixed incomes (Table 3A.8). However, as we will see the revenue from the non-fixed incomes (Table 3A.9) depends on the behaviour of the councils of the various institutions.

TABLE 3A.8 *Taxation revenue from the receivers of fixed incomes*

	(1)	(2)	(3)	(4)	(5)	(6)	(7)
		→		at MiW = € 20,00			←
		Annual income in % MiW	Annual income in €	Average tax rate	Number per mil population	Number in % of all fixed incomes	Revenue in € million (per mil population)
	source	Table 3A.6	Table 3A.6	Table 3A.6	Table 3A.5	Table 3A.8	column 3*4*5
1	students aged 18–25	60%	€ 12,000	0.0%	52,014	16%	€ 0.0
2	School-leaver traineeships	60%	€ 12,000	0.0%	15,622	5%	€ 0.0
3	traineeships after a two-year position	85%	€ 17,000	7.4%	14,264	4%	€ 17.8
4	Pensioners	100%	€ 20,000	10.0%	196,622	61%	€ 393.2
5	persons unable to work	120%	€ 24,000	16.7%	25,732	8%	€ 102.9
6	restricted ability (workers)	150%	€ 30,000	23.3%	20,686	6%	€ 144.8
7	Total				324,939	100%	
8	**Total revenue from fixed incomes**						€ 658.8

TABLE 3A.9 *Taxation revenue from the receivers of non-fixed incomes (primary income, except income from savings): at an assumed distribution of income as decided on by workers' councils – alternative 1*

	(1)	(2)	(3)	(4)	(5)	(6)	(7)
				→	at MiW = € 20,00		←
		Annual income in % MiW	Annual income in €	Average tax rate	Assumed % distribution of income	Resulting number per mil population	Revenue in € million (per mil population)
	source	Table 3A.7	Table 3A.7	Table 3A.7		Table 3A.5†	column 3*4*6
1	MiW	100%	€ 20,000	10.0%	15%	70,645	€ 141.3
2	median 1–2 MiW	175%	€ 35,000	26.7%	20%	94,193	€ 879.1
3	median 2–3 MiW	250%	€ 50,000	42.0%	30%	141,290	€ 2,967.1
4	median 3–4 MiW‡	350%	€ 70,000	51.4%	30%	141,290	€ 5,086.4
5	median 4–5 MiW	450%	€ 90,000	58.9%	5%	23,548	€ 1,248.1
6	Total				100%	470,966	
7	**Total revenue non-fixed incomes**						€ 10,322.0

† Total of column (in bold).
‡ 3.5 MiW is the average income (see Table 3A.4, last row).

Tables 3A.8 and 3A.9 result in the income taxes coverage of total state expenditure as indicated in *Table 3A.10*. Recall that (as an indication), the 'turnover tax' – the Design's other main tax – is to cover about 50% of state expenditure.

TABLE 3A.10 *Coverage of state expenditure by income taxes: alternative 1*

		in million €
1	total revenue income taxes (source: Tables 3A.8 and 3A.9, sum last row)	€ 10,981
2	total state expenditure per mil population (source: Table 3A.1, row 21)	€ 20,108
3	percent of state expenditure covered by income taxes	55%

THE STATE AND THE STATE INSTITUTIONS OF THE DESIGN   199

In the Design the state's parliament decides on the tax rates, but given those rates it cannot affect the pre-tax income distribution (column 5 of Table 3A.9) as only the worker's councils of cooperatives and public sector institutions decide on this distribution. In case parliament is not happy with the resulting revenue from the income taxes, then it has to adapt the tax rates for a following year. At the same tax rates as in Table 3A.9, the following *Table 3A.11* shows an example of the sensitivity of the taxation revenue for a pre-tax distribution of income that is less skewed than alternative 1.

TABLE 3A.11 *Taxation revenue from the receivers of non-fixed incomes (primary income, except income from savings): at an assumed distribution of income as decided on by workers' councils – alternative 2*   *changed percentages*

	(1)	(2)	(3)	(4)	(5)	(6)	(7)
		→			at MiW = € 20,00		←
		Annual income in % MiW	Annual income in €	Average tax rate	Assumed % distribution of income	Resulting number per mil population	Revenue in € million (per mil population)
	source	*Table 3A.7*	*Table 3A.7*	*Table 3A.7*		*Table 3A.5†*	*column 3*4*6*
1	MiW	100%	€ 20,000	10.0%	15%	70,645	€ 141.3
2	median 1–2 MiW	175%	€ 35,000	26.7%	20% → 25%	117,742	€ 1,098.9
3	median 2–3 MiW	250%	€ 50,000	42.0%	30% → 35%	164,838	€ 3,461.6
4	median 3–4 MiW‡	350%	€ 70,000	51.4%	30% → 25%	117,742	€ 4,238.7
5	median 4–5 MiW	450%	€ 90,000	58.9%	5% → 0%	0	€ 0.0
6	*Total*				100%	470,966	
7	**Total revenue non-fixed incomes**						€ 8,940.5

† Total of column (in bold).
‡ 3.5 MiW is the average income (see Table 3A.4, last row).

In this case, the coverage of the income taxes is as in Table 3A.12.

TABLE 3A.12 *Coverage of state expenditure by income taxes: alternative 2*

		in million €	revenue and coverage alternative 1
1	total revenue income taxes (source: Tables 3A.8 and 3A.11, sum last rows)	€ 9,599	€ 10,981
2	total state expenditure per mil population (source: Table 3A.1, row 21)	€ 20,108	
3	percent of state expenditure covered by income taxes	48%	55%

This concludes the section on the 'taxation revenue from the income tax'.

3A-5   *Estimate of the labour force of the public sector*

The labour force of the public sector depends (as alluded to in the Introduction to this appendix) on 'broad demographic' factors. This applies especially for the health and education sectors, which also constitute by far the two largest components of the public sector. *Table 3A.13* provides estimates of the labour force of the Design's public sector and its components as based on 2019 figures.

TABLE 3A.13 *Estimate of the labour force of the public sector, in % of the total labour force*

		All in full-time equivalents	In % of the total available labour force†		
1		Labour force of the state and state institutions	6%	6.35%	
1a		of which the judiciary		0.08%	
1b		of which the police		1.04%	
2		Labour force non-state public sector (the WGFs)	21%	21.26%	
2a		Labour force health institutions (WGFs)		14.72%	
2b		Labour force education institutions (WGFs)		6.19%	
2c		Labour force national rail transport (WGF)‡		0.35%	
3		**Total of the public sector (sum of rows 1 and 2)**	**28%**	**27.61%**	
4		By implication: labour force cooperatives	72%		
		Specification health sector	in % total LF health sector	section ch. 3	section sums
		(exclusive the NHS, which is included in row 1)			
H1		Primary medical treatment*	12.0%	3§27	12.0%
H2		Hospitals: somatic treatment and care ‡	25.1%	3§28	
H3		Psychiatric hospitals and clinics	8.1%	3§28	33.2%
H4		Care physically disabled	14.0%	3§29	
H5		Nursing and care	29.3%	3§29	
		including home healthcare	9.4%	3§29	
H6		Social care including youth care	11.5%	3§29	54.8%
			100%		*100%*
		Specification education sector	in % total LF education sector	section ch. 3	
		(exclusive the NEA, which is included in row 1)			
E1		Primary education	37.3%	3§32	
E2		Secondary education	38.2%	3§32	
E3		Tertiary education	24.6%	3§32	
			100%		

† Defined in Table 3A.5 (ALF). Defence is not included in the total, nor in the figure of row 1.
‡ This is exclusive of any local rail transport.
* MTCs, the auxiliary services for these, and preventive healthcare.
‡ General multi-specialisation hospitals; Single specialisation hospitals; and University hospitals.

Comments on *Table 3A.13*. Whereas the labour force of the state and its institutions encompasses 6.35% of the total, their expenditure is 42.67% of GDP (Table 3A.2). Whilst the labour force of the health institutions encompasses 14.72% of the total, the state expenditure on these institutions is 11.90% of GDP (Table 3A.2, category 7). The labour force of the education institutions encompasses 6.19% of the total, whilst the state expenditure on these is 5.72% of GDP (Table 3A.2, category 9).

For comparison. The OECD publishes data of the number of persons (non-FTE) that are employed in the composite of the sectors 'public administration', 'compulsory social security', 'education' and 'human health'. For the year 2019, this composite as percent of the total of employed persons (non-FTE) makes up:

- 27.0% for the unweighted average of 29 OECD countries that reported this composite (ranging from 20.6% for Luxembourg to 34.7% for Sweden); this average is hardly different from the somewhat different composite of row 3 of Table 3A.13;
- 25.9% for the European Union;
- 19.0% for the unweighted average of the four non-OECD countries that reported (Bulgaria, Costa Rica, Romania and South Africa).[94]

This concludes Appendix 3A.

Appendix 3B. The administrative burden for cooperatives in comparison with capitalist enterprises

This appendix compares the administrative burden for cooperatives with those for enterprises in many or most current capitalist nations. The comparison regards qualitative estimates. Burdens that are obviously the same as in capitalism are not mentioned (such as a wages administration, the purchasing/selling /renting of premises, or the application for licences and the taking part in tenders). After showing a summarising table, the regarding burden increases and decreases will be briefly mentioned in reference to chapters 2 and 3. It will be seen that the differences are not large; probably the burden for cooperatives is somewhat less.

---

94   OECD.stat, https://stats.oecd.org/Index.aspx?QueryId=268 (accessed 26 Nov 2020). These are quarterly data, and I have taken the average of the four 2019 quarters.

TABLE 3B.1 *Number of administrative burden increases and decreases for cooperatives in comparison with capitalist enterprises: qualitative estimate*

	Number of burden increases	Number of burden decreases
minor change	3	1
moderate change	2	2
considerable change	1	1
vast change	1	2

A *Burden increases: cooperatives versus capitalist enterprises*

Minor increases

• All cooperatives, annually: sending of a reduced version of the end of year statements to the 'General statistical office' and to the 'Ministry of general cooperatives' matters' (2§11.1). Capitalist statistical offices gather similar information, perhaps sampling based.
• All cooperatives, annually: determination of the dated shares of workers in the uncommitted reserves (2§12.0 and 2§13.0).
• All cooperatives, quarterly: statement of jobs of persons with physical or mental abilities to work (3§17 f.).

Moderate increases

• All cooperatives, continuously: proportional to their workforce, to provide work to those with restricted physical or mental abilities to work (3§21). This is not an administrative burden; it is questionable if and to what extent this is a burden at all once this is an integral part of the work organisation (moreover, the effect is less payment of taxes by workers).
• All cooperatives, occasionally: actions in case of contraction of a cooperative (2§14.2).

Considerable increase (cyclically)

• All cooperatives, cyclically at intervals of (perhaps) some eight years: to introduce, at the going wage-*rates*, a work-time reduction for all their workers at 0.5% points above the rate of recessional joblessness; and, concomitantly, to *temporarily* provide work to the jobless – proportionally to their workforce (3§19, points 2 and 3, and 3§20). (Classified 'considerable' on average; at the time it is a vast burden increase. The effect is reduction of recessional joblessness to maximum two months; the likely effect is a decrease in the length of recessions.)

Vast increase
- Cooperatives with a workforce of more than 50 workers, continuously: the requirement of, first, to continuously offer potential traineeship positions of 5% of their workforce, second, to report to the 'Job securities and jobs shortage agency' when an actual traineeship has started and ended (3§17-j; details in 3§18).

B Burden decreases: cooperatives versus enterprises
Minor decrease
- All cooperatives, continuously: no take-overs (2§3.2) – hence no irregular defence strategies or worry about it.

Moderate decreases
- All cooperatives, continuously: single location (2§3.3), hence no coordination between locational branches of an entity.
- All cooperatives, continuously: no advertisement (3§8). (Perhaps this should be classified as a considerable decrease.)

Considerable decrease
- All cooperatives, annually: no income and property taxes (Table 3.7). The decrease regards especially the often very complicated seeking of evading profit taxes by capitalist enterprises.

Vast decreases
- In comparison with capitalist countries with a value-added tax. All cooperatives, daily and quarterly:[95] no VAT burden (Table 3.7 and 3§46). This indeed regards the administrative burden, not the tax.
- All cooperatives, annually or irregularly: with one small exception there is no regulation via subsidies – notably including via subsidy-like tax reductions. In comparison with many capitalist nations this makes an enormous difference in subsidy applications and settlements. The exception regards cooperatives in the sector 'artistic creations and performances' that may (usually on application) receive a subsidy from municipalities (4§3, f-g).

C Main burden mutation for workers or households
Minor burden increase for workers
- Workers for which this is applicable, annually: mentioning of the period, and rate, of part-time work in the appropriate box of the tax return form (3§10d).

Moderate burden decrease for workers or households
- Because pensions are equal and sufficient for all and on individual (not household) basis (3§24), no administrative burden for pensions, life insurances or other retirement provisions.

---

95 Quarterly, assuming that the final tax form is due quarterly.

• The income tax return is right out simple.
Considerable burden decrease for workers or households
• Regarding health and education provisions: no insurances (Subdivisions 7A and 7B).
• Regarding education provisions: no fees, loans and loan repayments (Subdivision 7B).

D   *Burden mutation for ministries and state agencies*
Whereas the organisation of the ministries and state agencies is often different (with an emphasis on the latter) *the total* administrative burden for the public sector in the Design in comparison with many or most current capitalist nations, is not much different.

Especially for the *health sector* quite some organisation is undertaken by the National Health Agency, but this seems to balance against a lesser burden for the public sector medical institutions (WGFs).

In the case of *real estate matters*, quite some organisation is undertaken by the National Real Estate Agency; for one part this weights against 'state domains'/'state territories' institutions in capitalist countries; for another part it weights against private real estate institutions (trade and rent) and private real estate management.

The taxation authority (often a main employer in capitalist countries) has a very considerably lighter job in the Design: no income and property taxation for units of production and financial institutions (hence also no regarding tax exemptions or tax subsidies); no value-added taxes; for individuals no property and other wealth taxes; simple individual income taxes.

The competition authority also has a somewhat lighter job: no market-power affecting take-overs, and for other potential market power there are general, though branch specific rules, with little case supervision and juridical case disputes.

Appendix 3C. Constitutional rights and main other constitutional elements

This appendix is composed of seven Divisions. The articles of the first Division are separately numbered; those of the other Divisions continuously.
1.   Constitutional rights: articles 1–24;
2.   The parliament and the government: articles 1–21;
3.   The judiciary: articles 22–28;
4.   Miscellaneous institutions and provisions: articles 29–32;

5. International matters: articles 33–35;
6. Worker cooperatives, Single person enterprises, and individual services for households: articles 36–39;
7. Revision of the Constitution: article 40.

(The phrase 'main ... elements' in the Appendix title refers to the first section of Division 4, where for the sake of non-repetition of chs. 3–4, especially the legislation of state agencies, municipalities and provinces has been relegated to non-constitutional legislation.)

Division 1. Constitutional rights

Revision of the constitution requires a two-thirds parliamentary majority by two subsequently elected parliaments. For this reason, many rights formulated below are cast in fairly general terms and in reference to non-constitutional ordinary Acts of Parliament that require a one-time simple majority. The rights are formulated in 24 articles.[96]

Article 1. Equal treatment and non-discrimination
1. All inhabitants and worker cooperatives shall be treated equally in equal circumstances. Discrimination on the grounds of ethnicity, gender, social background, political opinion, religion, belief, or on any other grounds whatsoever shall not be permitted.
2. It is regulated by Act of Parliament how violation of the above rights can be established, and what in case of a sentence the penalties or penalty limits are.

Article 2. Slavery and employment
1. Nobody shall be kept in slavery.
2. No cooperative or other institution shall employ workers unless the workers collectively, can decide on the distribution of the total value-added generated by the cooperative or other institution. The same applies for the use of an outside worker or outside workers. Each as further specified by Act of Parliament.
3. Individual services for households (excluding health and education) shall be provided by cooperatives only.
4. The slaveholder or the employer, or in case of an institution its manager,

---

[96] For this Division the relevant chapter in the constitution of the Netherlands (Government of the Netherlands 2012) was used as an initial template which was adapted for the purposes of the Design (such as for example the inclusion of article 2). For the other Divisions some articles have been taken over from the same source.

that is sentenced for violating a right mentioned in the preceding paragraphs shall be penalised by compensating the person whose right was violated as well as by imprisonment, each as laid down by Act of Parliament.

Article 3. Nationality and international migration
1. Nationality shall be regulated by Act of Parliament.
2. International migration shall be regulated by Act of Parliament.
3. Extradition may take place only pursuant to a treaty that requires a two-thirds parliamentary majority. Further regulations concerning extradition shall be laid down by Act of Parliament.
4. Everyone shall have the right to leave the country, except in the cases laid down by Act of Parliament. [For such an exception see 5§1, regarding compensation for formal education. Another one may regard persons that are sentenced to imprisonment.]

Article 4. Equal right to elect and be elected
All nationals shall have an equal right to elect the members of the general representative bodies and to stand for election as a member of those bodies, subject to the limitations and exceptions prescribed by Act of Parliament. ['Nationals' contrasts with temporary residents. Limitations regard age and may regard persons sentenced for abuse of power as laid down in Appendix 3D.]

Article 5. Equal eligibility for appointment to public service
All nationals shall be equally eligible for appointment to public service, subject to the limitations and exceptions prescribed by Act of Parliament. [Limitations may regard persons sentenced for abuse of power as laid down in Appendix 3D.]

Article 6. Right to petition
Everyone shall have the right to submit petitions in writing to the competent authorities.

Article 7. Right to publication
1. No one shall require prior permission to publish thoughts or opinions through the press, without prejudice to the responsibility of every person under the law.
2. Rules concerning radio, television and digital communications shall be laid down by Act of Parliament. There shall be no prior supervision of the content of these.

3. No one shall be required to submit thoughts or opinions for prior approval in order to disseminate them by means other than those mentioned in the preceding paragraphs, without prejudice to the responsibility of every person under the law.
4. The preceding paragraphs do not apply to commercial advertising. [Which the Design bans (3§8).]

Article 8. Right to freely profess religion or belief
1. Everyone shall have the right to profess freely her/his religion or belief, either individually or in community with others, without prejudice to her/his responsibility under the law.
2. Rules concerning the exercise of this right may be laid down by Act of Parliament for the protection of health, in the interest of traffic and to combat or prevent disorders.

Article 9. Right to economic and non-economic association
1. Persons have the right to economic association in either 'worker cooperatives' (2§2) or 'workers' council governed foundations' (3§25).
2. The right of non-economic association shall be recognised. This right may be restricted by a two-thirds majority Act of Parliament in the interest of public order.

Article 10. Right to assembly and demonstration
1. The right of assembly and demonstration shall be recognised, without prejudice to the responsibility of everyone under the law.
2. Rules to protect health, in the interest of traffic and to combat or prevent disorders may be laid down by Act of Parliament.

Article 11. Right to privacy and to information of, and correction of, data recorded
1. Everyone shall have the right to respect for her/his privacy, without prejudice to restrictions laid down by Act of Parliament.
2. Rules to protect privacy shall be laid down by Act of Parliament in connection with the recording and dissemination of personal data.
3. Rules concerning the rights of persons to be informed of data recorded concerning them and of the use that is made thereof, and to have such data corrected, shall be laid down by Act of Parliament.

Article 12. Right to inviolability of person
Everyone shall have the right to inviolability of her/his person, without prejudice to restrictions laid down by Act of Parliament.

Article 13. Home privacy
1. Entry into a home against the will of the occupant shall be permitted only in the cases laid down by Act of Parliament, by those designated for the purpose by Act of Parliament.
2. Prior identification and notice of purpose shall be required in order to enter a home under the preceding paragraph, subject to the exceptions prescribed by Act of Parliament.
3. A written report of the entry shall be issued to the occupant as soon as possible. If the entry was made in the interests of state security or criminal proceedings, the issue of the report may be postponed under rules to be laid down by Act of Parliament. A report need not be issued in cases, to be determined by Act of Parliament, where such issue would never be in the interests of state security.

Article 14. Privacy of correspondence
1. The privacy of correspondence shall not be violated except in the cases laid down by Act of Parliament, by order of the courts.
2. The privacy of the telephone, telegraph and electronic mail shall not be violated except in the cases laid down by Act of Parliament, by or with the authorisation of those designated for the purpose by Act of Parliament.

Article 15. Taxation and expropriation
1. Taxes are levied only by the state and shall be laid down by Act of Parliament.
2. Expropriation may take place only in the public interest and on prior assurance of reasonable compensation, in accordance with regulations laid down by Act of Parliament.
3. Prior assurance of reasonable compensation shall not be required if in an emergency immediate expropriation is called for.
3. In the cases laid down by Act of Parliament there shall be a right to full or partial compensation if in the public interest the competent authority destroys property or renders it unusable or restricts the exercise of the owner's rights to it.

Article 16. Deprivation of liberty
1. Other than in the cases laid down by Act of Parliament, no one may be deprived of her/his liberty.
2. Anyone who has been deprived of her/his liberty other than by order of a court may request a court to order her/his release. In such a case s/he

shall be heard by the court within a period to be laid down by Act of Parliament. The court shall order her/his immediate release if it considers the deprivation of liberty to be unlawful.
3. The trial of a person who has been deprived of her/his liberty pending trial shall take place within a reasonable period.
4. A person who has been lawfully deprived of her/his liberty may be restricted in the exercise of fundamental rights in so far as the exercise of such rights is not compatible with the deprivation of liberty.

Article 17. Offences under the law
No offence shall be punishable unless it was an offence under the law at the time it was committed.

Article 18. Assignment of a court
No one may be prevented against her/his will from being heard by the courts to which s/he is entitled to apply under the law.

Article 19. Legal representation
1. Everyone may be legally represented in legal and administrative proceedings.
2. Rules concerning the granting of legal aid to persons of limited means shall be laid down by Act of Parliament.

Article 20. Sufficient jobs and right to a free choice of work
1. The state shall be committed to a strong effort to realise sufficient jobs in cooperatives and in or via state institutions, each as laid down by Act of Parliament.
2. All inhabitants shall have the right to free choice of work, without prejudice to the restrictions laid down by Act of Parliament.

Article 21. Right to a pension and to at least costs of living allowances
1. All inhabitants have the right to at least costs of living allowances as specified by Act of Parliament, without prejudice to the restrictions regarding prisoners laid down by Act of Parliament.
2. Rules concerning entitlement to costs of living allowances shall be laid down by Act of Parliament.
3. All national inhabitants have the right to a pension from off the legal retirement age as laid down by Act of Parliament. Non-national inhabitants may have the right to a pension from off the legal retirement age as laid down by Act of Parliament.

Article 22. Protection and improvement of the environment
The state shall be committed to a strong effort to keep the country habitable and to protect and improve the environment, as laid down by Act of Parliament

Article 23. Housing, health, formal education and culture
1. The state shall be committed to a strong effort to provide to be rented living accommodation according to the quality preferences of inhabitants, as laid down by or pursuant to Act of Parliament.
2. All inhabitants have free and equal access to health provisions, as regulated by Act of Parliament.
3. All young people have according to their capacities free and equal access to primary, secondary and tertiary education, as regulated by Act of Parliament.
4. The state shall promote the preservation of the cultural heritage, and promote the contemporary creative arts and arts performance as including by subsidies, each as laid down by or pursuant to Act of Parliament.

Article 24. Right to complain about the maintenance of rights
Anyone who has a complaint about the maintenance of her/his rights, or about the manner in which public sector authorities fulfil their statutory responsibilities, can lay down complaints with an investigator: the National Ombudsperson. The latter's specific tasks and authority shall be regulated by Act of Parliament. [See also Division 4, art. 32.]

Division 2. The Parliament and the Government
This Division is divided in five sections: Election and composition of the parliament (2.1); Parliamentary procedures (2.2); The government (2.3); Legislation (2.4); Relations between the parliament and the government (2.5) – together 21 articles.

Section 2.1. Election and composition of the parliament
Article 1. Parliament: representation and election
1. The parliament shall represent the entire people of the nation.
2. The parliament shall consist of X members.
3. The members of parliament shall be elected for four years.
4. The members of parliament shall be elected by proportional representation, without an electoral threshold. [3§1b]
5. Elections shall be by secret ballot.
6. Matters pertaining to the specific election date and the election procedures shall be laid down by Act of Parliament.

Article 2. Electorate of parliament
1. The members of parliament shall be elected directly by nationals who have attained the age of 18, with the exception of any nationals who may be excluded by Act of Parliament by virtue of the fact that they are not resident in the nation.

Article 3. Eligible members of parliament
1. To be eligible for membership of the parliament, a person must be a national and must have attained the age of 18 years.
2. Disqualified from eligibility are those former members of parliament or of a former government that were sentenced accordingly by an 'Extraordinary supreme court' or by the 'Supreme court' for abuse of power or other improper functional behaviour. [Appendix 3D]
3. Disqualified from eligibility are those state workers or former state workers that were sentenced accordingly by a court for abuse of power or other improper functional behaviour. [Appendix 3D]

Article 4. Actual members of parliament
1. A member of the parliament may not simultaneously be a member of the government, an Auditor that audits Ministries or State Institutions, member of the Supreme Court, an Administrative prosecutor (3§6), National Ombudsperson.
2. Notwithstanding the above, a member of the government who has offered to tender her/his resignation may combine the said office with membership of the parliament until such time as a decision is taken on such resignation.
3. Other public functions which may not be held simultaneously by a person who is a member of the parliament may be designated by Act of Parliament.
4. The temporary replacement of a member of the parliament during pregnancy and maternity, paternity or partner leave or during illness shall be regulated by Act of Parliament.
5. Parliament shall examine the credentials of its newly appointed members as related to paragraphs 1 and 3 and article 3, and shall decide with due reference to rules to be established by Act of Parliament any disputes arising in connection with the credentials or the election.
6. Upon accepting office members of parliament shall make an affirmation and promise before parliament in the manner prescribed by Act of Parliament that they have not done anything which may legally debar them from holding office, and shall also promise allegiance to the Constitution and that they will faithfully discharge their duties.

Article 5. Chair and Clerk of Parliament; Ceremonial President
1. Parliament shall elect a President of Parliament from among its members.
2. Parliament shall appoint a Clerk who shall not be a member of the parliament.
3. One year after taking office parliament shall appoint a Ceremonial President who shall not be a member of the parliament.
4. The procedures for the appointments shall be laid down by Act of Parliament.

Article 6. Remuneration Parliamentarians, Clerk of Parliament and Ceremonial President
1. The remuneration for the members of the parliament and the persons mentioned in article 5, paragraphs 2 and 3 is equal to the nationwide average wages and dividends in FTE of the Worker cooperatives [3§3a].
2. In addition they may receive a compensation of expenses as laid down by Act of Parliament, the latter requiring at least a two-thirds majority.

Article 7. Dissolution of a sitting parliament
1. Parliament can vote itself out of office with an at least a two-thirds majority, upon which new elections are held.
2. The newly elected parliament takes office within three months after the elections.
3. The dissolution of the parliament, shall take effect on the day on which the newly elected parliament meets.
4. The previous two paragraphs equally apply for a regular four-year termination of the office.

Section 2.2. Parliamentary procedures
Article 8. Sittings, deliberations, decisions and voting of or by the parliament
1. The sittings of the parliament shall be held in public.
2. The sittings shall be held in camera if one tenth of the members present so require or if the President of Parliament considers it necessary.
3. The parliament may deliberate or take decisions only if more than half of the members are present.
4. Decisions shall be taken by majority unless otherwise laid down in articles above or below.
5. The members shall not be bound by a mandate or instructions when casting their votes.
6. Voting on matters not relating to specific individuals shall be either by sitting and standing or electronically; if requested by one member voting

is by roll call. Voting on matters relating to specific individuals shall be either by written vote or by anonymised electronic vote.
7. Parliament shall draw up further rules of procedure.

Article 9. Right of inquiry
Parliament shall have the right of inquiry to be regulated by Act of Parliament.

Section 2.3. The government
Article 10. The election of the government by the parliament
1. The parliament elects the government; it is accountable to the parliament and it is removable by the parliament.
2. The government consists of ministers, each heading a ministry. One minister is the 'Prime Minister' that acts as head of the government. It may be established by Act of Parliament that next to ministers there are also deputy ministers that work under the final responsibility of a minister; for their tasks deputy ministers are nevertheless accountable to the parliament; in case there are deputy ministers, paragraphs 3 to 5 below equally apply to these.
3. Minsters may but need not be elected from the parliamentary ranks. When one is, s/he resigns as parliamentarian.
4. The procedure for the election of the government is as follows. First, parliament elects a candidate prime minister. Second, the latter constitutes a team of candidate ministers, which is proposed to parliament as the new government during parliament's term, which is also the (prospect) government's term. Third, in case each candidate has the confidence of the parliamentary majority, parliament votes on the proposed new government. When during its term a minister has no longer the confidence of parliament, a motion of non-confidence is directed at the regarding minister whence s/he has to resign [3§1c]. Further details of the procedure may be laid down by Act of Parliament.
5. The government shall consider and decide upon the overall government policy and shall promote the coherence thereof, notwithstanding the accountability of the government to the parliament.

Article 11. Formal appointment and dismissal of ministers.
1. Upon the parliament's decisions, ministers (and, in case, deputy ministers) are formally appointed and dismissed by the Ceremonial President (art. 5).
2. Upon accepting office Ministers (and, in case, deputy ministers) shall make an affirmation and promise in the presence of the Ceremonial Pres-

ident, in the manner prescribed by Act of Parliament, that they have not done anything which may legally debar them from holding office, and shall also promise allegiance to the Constitution and that they will faithfully discharge their duties.

Article 12. Remuneration of ministers
1. The remuneration of ministers (and, in case, deputy ministers) is equal to the nationwide average wages and dividends in FTE of the Worker cooperatives [3§3a].
2. In addition they may receive a compensation of expenses as laid down by Act of Parliament.

Article 13. Public information
In the exercise of their duties, government bodies shall observe the right of public access to information in accordance with rules to be prescribed by Act of Parliament.

Section 2.4. Legislation
Article 14. Acts, Decrees and Orders in council
1. Acts of Parliament and Orders in Council, as laid down in articles 15 and 16, are normally the only generally binding regulations established by the State.
2. In case of high urgency in the interest of the protection of health, in the interest of traffic and to combat or prevent disorders, the government may issue a Decree that is legally binding for no more than 15 days without possibility of extension or reissue. In the meantime, government proposes to parliament an Emergency Law that may more or less cover the Decree and that parliament may approve of with or without amendment. Parliament decides on the date of expiration of the Emergency Law, which shall be within two months. Parliament may also request the government a to be proposed revised Emergency Law before the said date of expiration; that revision shall expire not later than after two months. Further procedures regarding Decrees and Emergency Laws shall be regulated by Act of Parliament.
3. The previous paragraph's rules about 'high urgency' equally apply for a 'state of emergency'.

Article 15. Bills and acts
1. A Minster, or ministers, propose(s) bills to parliament. Parliamentarians equally have the right to propose bills to parliament. Bills can be

amended by parliament. After written and/or oral deliberation parliament votes on a bill; on a majority voting the bill becomes an Act of Parliament.
2. Annual estimates of the State's revenues and expenditures have the form of a bill. The same applies for the forms of taxation and the annual tax brackets.
3. A Bill may be withdrawn by or on behalf of the proposer until such time as it is passed by the parliament.
4. A Bill shall become an Act of Parliament once it has been passed by the parliament and has been signed by the President of Parliament.
5. The publication and entry into force of Acts of Parliament shall be regulated by Act of Parliament. They shall not enter into force before they have been published.
6. Rules relating to the management of the State's finances shall be prescribed by Act of Parliament. [3§4]
7. Annually an audited statement of the actually realised revenues and expenditures of the State shall be presented to parliament in accordance with the provisions of the relevant Act of Parliament.
8. Civil law, criminal law and civil and criminal procedure shall be regulated by Act of Parliament in general legal codes without prejudice to the power to regulate certain matters in separate Acts of Parliament.
9. General rules of administrative law shall be laid down by Act of Parliament.

Article 16. Orders in council
1. 'Orders in council' may regulate specific details of an Act. The act shall mention which details are delegated to a by name mentioned Order in council.
2. Orders in council are proposed by a minister or by the government. They require the approval of parliament and can be amended by parliament.
3. Orders in council shall be established by signature of the President of Parliament.
4. Any regulations to which penalties are attached shall be embodied in such orders only in accordance with an Act of Parliament. The penalties to be imposed shall be determined by Act of Parliament.
5. Publication and entry into force of orders in council shall be regulated by Act of Parliament. They shall not enter into force before they have been published.

THE STATE AND THE STATE INSTITUTIONS OF THE DESIGN 217

Section 2.5. Relations between the parliament and the government
Article 17. Statement of policy to be pursued by the government
A statement of the policy to be pursued by the government shall be given when the government enters into office and again annually, each during a parliamentary meeting as prescribed by Act of Parliament.

Article 18. Agenda and briefings or interrogation
1. Parliament sets the agenda for its relations with the government.
2. On request of parliament, government members shall appear in parliament for briefings or interrogation.
3. On request of parliament, Directors-general and Secretaries-general of ministries and state agencies shall appear in parliament for briefings or interrogation. [3§3, c–d]
4. By Act of Parliament it is regulated which other functionaries shall appear on request in parliament for briefings or interrogation.

Article 19. Information obligation
1. Members of the government shall provide parliament, orally or in writing, with any information requested by one or more members. The information shall be complete in the sense that no information is withheld that might expected to be relevant. 'Complete information' includes any underlying documentation as specified by Act of Parliament. The information shall be provided within 20 days of the request.
2. The government may request exemption for the public conveyance of specific information. It is regulated by Act of Parliament how parliament weighs such requests and how parliament shall be informed in an alternative non-public way.

Article 20. Right of government members to attend sittings of the parliament
1. Members of the government shall have the right to attend sittings of the parliament. They may take part in the deliberations within the constraints determined by the President of Parliament.
2. They may be assisted at the sittings by persons nominated by them, within the constraints determined by the President of Parliament.

Article 21. Non-liability during sittings of parliament and for related written submissions
Members of the parliament and members of the government and other persons taking part in deliberations may not be prosecuted or otherwise held liable in law for anything they say during the sittings of the parliament or of its committees or for anything they submit to them in writing.

Division 3. The judiciary

Article 22. The judiciary
1. The adjudication of disputes shall be the responsibility of the judiciary.
2. The trial of offences shall be the responsibility of the judiciary.
3. Different rules may be established by Act of Parliament for the trial of cases outside the nation and for martial law.
4. Capital punishment may not be imposed.

Article 23. Courts of the judiciary
1. The courts which form part of the judiciary shall be specified by Act of Parliament, one court being the Supreme Court.
2. The organisation, composition and powers of the judiciary shall be regulated by Act of Parliament.
3. In cases provided for by Act of Parliament, persons who are not members of the judiciary may take part with members of the judiciary in the administration of justice.
4. The supervision by members of the judiciary responsible for the administration of justice of the manner in which such members and the persons referred to in the previous paragraph fulfil their duties shall be regulated by Act of Parliament.

Article 24. Appointment and remuneration of the judiciary
1. The members of the courts shall be appointed as regulated by Act of Parliament [see 3§6].
2. Members of the judiciary shall be appointed for until the general statutory retirement age as determined by Act of Parliament. They cease to hold office on resignation.
3. In cases laid down by Act of Parliament such persons may be suspended or dismissed by a court that is part of the judiciary and designated by Act of Parliament.
4. Members of the judiciary are remunerated equal to the nationwide average wages and dividends in FTE of the Worker cooperatives.

Article 25. The supreme court
1. In the cases and within the limits laid down by Act of Parliament, the Supreme Court shall be responsible for annulling court judgments which infringe the law.
2. Additional duties may be assigned to the Supreme Court by Act of Parliament.

Article 26. Offences by authorities, political parties and civil service workers
1. Present and former members of parliament and of the government shall be tried for offences committed while in office as laid down in Appendix 3D.
2. Political parties shall be tried for offences as laid down in Appendix 3D.
3. Civil service workers shall be tried for offences committed while in office as laid down in Appendix 3D.

Article 27. Administrative prosecution
1. The prosecution for offences mentioned in article 26 shall be undertaken by an Administrative Prosecutor.
2. Article 24 is equally applicable for administrative prosecutors.

Article 28. Publicness of trials and judgements
Except in cases laid down by Act of Parliament, trials shall be held in public and judgments shall specify the grounds on which they are based. Judgments shall be pronounced in public.

Division 4. Miscellaneous institutions and provisions
Section 4.1. State agencies and other state institutions
Article 29. State agencies and other state institutions
1. On the initiative of the government, or of one or more members of parliament, State Agencies and other State Institutions are established by Act of Parliament.
2. The tasks, the delegated authority, the organisation and the budget of State Agencies are regulated by Act of Parliament, part of the organisation being their workers' councils.
3. Other State Institutions include the Parliament as organisation, the Judiciary as organisation, Ministries, Municipalities and Provinces. The tasks, the competences, the organisation and the budget of State Institutions are regulated by Act of Parliament, part of the organisation being their workers' councils.
4. Part of the budget for State Agencies and other State Institutions is their wages sum, which equals their workforce in FTE times the nationwide average wages and dividends of cooperatives in FTE. Given this wages sum, their workers' councils decide annually on the internal wage scales.

Section 4.2. Workers' council governed foundations
Article 30. Workers' council governed foundations
1. All health provisions, all the primary, secondary and tertiary education provisions are state-financed and exclusively organised in 'Workers' coun-

cil governed foundations' as regulated by Act of Parliament. Other designated services that might or might not be state-financed, may be organised in such foundations as regulated by Act of Parliament.
2. A 'Workers' council governed foundation' is a legal entity that is administered by an association of which the institution's workers are the members; the association's membership is identical to the membership of the institution's workers' council; each as regulated by Act of Parliament [3§25].
3. The finance of these foundations, the competences of the workers' councils and other rules for the foundations are regulated by Act of parliament. The average remuneration of the workers of these foundations is equal to the nationwide average wages and dividends in FTE of the Worker cooperatives, the foundations' workers' councils decide on the internal wage scales, as regulated by Act of Parliament. [3§25]

Section 4.3. Audit
Article 31. Audit of state and state institutions
1. Licensed Auditors that are part of specific licensed Worker cooperatives shall be responsible for the examining of and the reporting on the State's and the State Institution's revenues and expenditures. The licensing, examination and reporting shall be regulated by Act of Parliament.
2. On top of the required auditing referred to in the previous paragraph, there may be audit by a Court of Audit as regulated by Act of Parliament. By Act of Parliament additional duties may be assigned this court.

Section 4.4. National Ombudsperson
Article 32. Tasks and authority of the National Ombudsperson
1. The National Ombudsperson shall investigate, on request or of her/his own accord, actions taken by administrative authorities of the State and other administrative authorities designated by Act of Parliament.
2. The National Ombudsperson shall be appointed by parliament for a period to be determined by Act of Parliament. The powers and methods of the National Ombudsperson shall be regulated by Act of Parliament. The recommendations made by the National Ombudsperson shall be made public according to rules to be laid down by Act of Parliament.

Division 5. International matters
Article 33. Treaties
1. The nation shall not be bound by treaties, nor shall such treaties be denounced, without the prior approval of an at least two-thirds parliamentary majority.

2. Treaties shall not be inconsistent with the Constitution. In case after signing a treaty there nevertheless proves to be an inconsistency the Constitution has priority. In this case a treaty may be denounced with a simple parliamentary majority. In case 30 percent of the members of parliament dispute the said (in)consistency mentioned in one of the first two sentences, the matter is adjudicated by the Supreme Court as regulated by Act of Parliament.
3. Provisions of treaties that may be binding on the nation's persons or institutions by virtue of their contents shall become binding after they have been published.
4. Resolutions by international institutions that are inconsistent with the Constitution shall not be binding for the nation's persons or institutions. In case 30 percent of the members of parliament dispute the said (in)consistency, the matter is adjudicated by the Supreme Court as regulated by Act of Parliament.
5. Resolutions by international institutions which may be binding on the nation's persons or institutions and that are inconsistent with a non-constitutional Act of Parliament can only be actually binding in case the parliamentary majority explicitly so consents. The procedures for such a consent, as including cases of disputes over the (in)consistency, are regulated by Act of Parliament.
6. Resolutions referred to in the previous paragraph shall become binding after the regarding Resolution has been published, and, in case this is required, after the relevant Act or Acts of Parliament have been amended and published.

Article 34. Declaration of war
A declaration that the nation is in a state of war shall not be made without the prior approval of parliament.

Article 35. Armed forces and civil defence
1. There may be armed forces for the defence and protection of the interests of the nation, and in order to maintain and promote the international legal order, as laid down by Act of Parliament.
2. The armed forces shall consist of volunteers and may also include conscripts.
3. Compulsory military service and the power to defer the call-up to active service shall be regulated by Act of Parliament.
4. Duties may be assigned for the purpose of civil defence in accordance with rules laid down by Act of Parliament.

5. Each of the political and the military command of armed forces shall be delegated to at least a triumvirate, as further laid down by Act of Parliament.

Division 6. Worker cooperatives, Single person enterprises, and individual services for households

Article 36. Non-public economic legal entities
1. There are two non-public economic legal entities, the Worker cooperative and the Single person enterprise. Other non-public economic entities are prohibited. (The 'Workers' council governed foundation' treated in article 30 is a public entity.)

Article 37. The worker cooperative
1. The Worker cooperative (below 'cooperative') is an association of which only the workers of the cooperative can be members as regulated by Act of Parliament [2§3]. Cooperatives include cooperative banks.
2. The Cooperative has a restricted ownership in the cooperative's assets as regulated by Act of Parliament [2§3]. The cooperative's members are collectively the cooperative's usufructuary as regulated by Act of Parliament [2§3], hence they have no direct or indirect ownership in the cooperative and its assets.
3. The cooperative is founded by workers, and a cooperative shall not found a cooperative as regulated by Act of Parliament [2§4].
4. A cooperative shall not be alienated as regulated by Act of Parliament [2§4].
5. A cooperative is organised in no more than one single location as regulated by Act of Parliament [2§3].
6. The highest governance body of a cooperative is its council. The council is formally constituted by the cooperative's association of workers. Council members have voting rights according to their appointment as percent of a full-time one. The council elects from its ranks a management – the management being removable. Details regarding this paragraph are regulated by Act of Parliament [2§5].
7. Other rules regarding the cooperative are laid down by Act of Parliament [Chapter 2, Table 2.8].

Article 38. The Single person enterprise
1. No one is forced to become member of a cooperative. Individuals are free to run by themselves a registered 'Single person enterprise' as regulated by Act of Parliament [2§2.2 and Appendix 3E].

2. A Single person enterprise shall not hire a worker [2§2.2].
3. It is regulated by Act of Parliament that as long as a person runs a Single person enterprise s/he is eligible for child and pension allowances [3§22 and 3§24] but not for any other allowances, nor for traineeships [3§18]

Article 39. Individual services for households
Any individual services for households shall be provided by Worker cooperatives or by 'Workers' council governed foundations' only.

Division 7. Revision of the Constitution
Article 40. Revision of constitutional rights and other articles of the constitution requires a two-thirds parliamentary majority by two subsequently elected parliaments. Further procedures are laid down by Act of Parliament.

Appendix 3D. Abuse of power and other improper behaviour by parliamentarians, ministers, other state workers and political parties: judicial proceedings

This appendix sets out the judicial procedures in case of abuse of power and other improper behaviour by parliamentarians, ministers, others state workers and political parties (3§1e and 3§3h).[97,98]

In all cases the *prosecution* is carried out by an administrative prosecutor (3§6) on its own initiative or after a report or complaints by institutions or individuals. The judicial process and verdict are executed by courts as specified below. It will be seen that the sanctions may be severe; this is because the public should rely on impeccable public administration.

---

97 From 3§1e: *Rules for (candidate) parliamentarians, ministers and political parties.* Parliamentarians shall act, speak and vote independently and shall not be bound by any mandate or instruction. Parliamentarians, candidate parliamentarians, ministers, associations of electors and political parties are not allowed to accept gifts. Political parties can raise an annual membership fee of no more than 0.5% of the statutory yearly minimum wage. None of the aforementioned is allowed to raise money via the organisation of any sort of event or in any other way. Nor are they allowed to promise to anybody any office or the promotion of it, or to promote the award of public contracts to a specific cooperative; or to create the semblance of these. Nor shall they in any way abuse their power, or create the semblance of it.

98 The first two sections are in part based on mixtures of UK Parliament 2010 and Government of the Netherlands 2012 (constitution 2008, art. 119).

(a) *Prosecution of sitting individual parliamentarians or ministers*

The court that judges on alleged abuse of power or other improper behaviour of sitting individual parliamentarians or ministers is called the 'Extraordinary supreme court' which is an ad hoc court consisting of eleven members that is formed as follows. (1) Parliament elects from its ranks six members of the court. Three must be of an opposition party and three must be of the party or parties that voted the government into power. (2) Five members are supreme court judges, determined by lot.

The prosecutors' final indictment, the proceedings and verdict are public; judges of this court individually vote publicly on the guilty or non-guilty.

Sanctions for the sentenced are the following. In all cases: immediate expulsion from office, exclusion from re-election in any public office and confiscation of advantages. On top the following separately or in combination as determined by the court: imprisonment; a fine; and confiscation of future remunerations above the minimum wage – during some period or lifelong.[99]

Because the trust in parliamentarians or ministers is at issue, the procedure should not only be careful but also most speedy. As an indication: prosecution 4 weeks (all other prosecution matters by the team of administrative prosecutors are postponed to later); preparation of defence 2–4 weeks (determined by the court); court procedure maximum 6 weeks. It is left to the prosecuted whether s/he suspends office during this period.

(b) *Prosecution of individual parliamentarians or ministers out of office*

Here the court is the supreme court or a chamber of it. The prosecutor's final indictment, the proceedings and verdict are public; judges of this court individually vote publicly on the guilty or non-guilty.

Sanctions for the sentenced: in all cases, exclusion from re-election in any public office, and confiscation of advantages. On top the following separately or in combination as determined by the court: imprisonment; a fine; and confiscation of future remunerations above the minimum wage – during some period or lifelong.

(c) *Prosecution of political parties*

(See the first footnote of this appendix, p. 223.) Here the court is the supreme court or a chamber of it. The prosecutors' final indictment, the proceedings and verdict are public; judges of this court individually vote publicly on the guilty or non-guilty.

---

99 The point is (also) that there may not be much to fine immediately.

THE STATE AND THE STATE INSTITUTIONS OF THE DESIGN   225

Sanctions for the sentenced: in all cases confiscation of advantages. On top the following separately or in combination as determined by the court: a fine for the party; fines or/and imprisonment of one or more party leaders; the highest sanction is the exclusion of the party for one electoral period – in case of recidivism more than one period or forever.

(d)   *Prosecution of state workers (civil service)*[100]

The court is (a chamber of) the courts level below the supreme court. The prosecutors' final indictment, the proceedings and verdict are public.

Sanctions for the sentenced: in all cases confiscation of advantages. On top the following separately or in combination as determined by the court: a fine; imprisonment; confiscation of future remunerations above the minimum wage of future wages and dividends above the minimum wage (during some period); exclusion from election in any public office (during some period or lifelong); exclusion from civil work (during some period or lifelong).

Appendix 3E. Regulation of the turnover tax for 'Single person enterprises'

This appendix sets out how 'Single person enterprises' (SPES) should contribute to taxation.

In the previous chapter (2§2.2) it was stated: 'Individuals are free to run by themselves a registered "Single person enterprise". However, "hiring a worker" is not allowed. In the economic domain the only possible legal form for a multi-workers entity that of a cooperative. The reason is the avoidance of exploitative relations, as in capitalist enterprise–employee relations.' We saw in 3§10 (c) that the reason for a minimum work-time rule lies in an equivalency of tax contribution to the state expenditure on provisions and on allowances such as pensions, given that all benefit from provisions such as healthcare, education and pensions. Even a person that earns merely the minimum wage (MiW) would at an MiW of €20,000 still contribute €2,000 to the taxes; at twice the MiW this would be €14,000 (Appendix 3A, section 3A-4).

---

100   From 3§3h. *Improper behaviour by state workers.* State workers shall not accept gifts or promises of these in any form; they shall not promote the award of public contracts to a specific cooperative or favour specific cooperatives in any form when applying the law; nor shall they favour specific individuals when applying the law. Generally, they shall in no way abuse their power. Generally, they shall also not create the semblance of all the above.

However, it cannot be excluded that the person running a SPE purposefully slows down, and keeps its income below the MiW. This would be unfair in comparison with cooperatives that in case of a purposeful slow down still would have to pay the MiW.

Therefore, the general regulation on taxation includes the clause that '*in case the income of a SPE is less than the MiW, the SPE has to pay a turnover tax of 20% on top of the regular turnover tax, which is accounted for on the annual tax assessment*'.

In case the regarding SPE would have little or no input costs (and while the person works from home), then at an income of 60% MiW (on which no income taxes are paid) this 20% would generate a tax revenue of €2,400. With input costs the tax assessment would be accordingly higher. (The average income receiver contributes €25,122 to the income taxes – calculated from Table 3A.9.)

The reason for this rule is not to capture the odd exception, but rather to prevent that the regarding 'slow down' SPE category develops into a relatively large one. It is assumed that quite some SPEs will rather choose for this legal form because in this way they expect to make an income well above the MiW (or because they abhor cooperatives).

Regarding SPEs it is further regulated that as long as a person runs a SPE, s/he is eligible for child and pension allowances (3§22 and 3§24) but not for any other allowances, nor for traineeships (3§18).

Appendix 3F. Stand-in work as organised in 'stand-in cooperatives', and the prevention of casual inferior jobs

This appendix is about the undesired case in which cooperatives or public sector institutions would try to get around providing permanent jobs to workers, substituting those for an echelon of workers with casual inferior jobs.

Cooperatives and public sector institutions provide in principle permanent jobs for workers, with the possible exceptions of: (1) a probation period for new workers (maximum two years); (2) temporary traineeships; and (3) when as result of a restructuring of an institution jobs cannot be maintained. Jobs are in principle also full-time jobs, with the possible exception of a voluntary period at less than full-time (maximally for an equivalent of 10 years at 50% of a full-time position – 3§10-d).

Regarding the prevention of casual inferior jobs there are four problems for the Design: (1) cooperatives with a seasonable work concentration; (2) cooperatives and public sector institutions that are confronted with sickness of their workers for more than a brief period; (3) the provision of parental leave for more than a brief period; (4) cooperatives and public sector institutions of which one or more workers have been elected into a public office; (5) cooperatives and public sector institutions of which workers make use of a period of less than full-time work.

Apparently these are no or less of a problem in capitalism because of the use of institutions such as temporary work agencies that often provide employment on demand with the worker rather than the employer taking the risk.

For the five cases above, the following paragraphs provide a (imperfect) solution, that should at least prevent that temporary work is used more widely than in the cases mentioned in the second paragraph above, whence there might structurally develop two echelons of workers, with one benefitting from the other.

Stand-in cooperatives (SICs)
Legislation establishes a special category of cooperatives, called the 'Stand-in cooperative' (SIC). These cooperatives are organised like all other cooperatives (ch. 2) but their output regards a special service for other cooperatives that is bound to a specific rule – the service being the standing-in for, or temporary replacing, workers of other cooperatives or of public sector institutions. (Below the latter are indicated as 'the seeker'.) Like for all cooperatives SIC jobs are in principle permanent ones. The main specific rule for SICs is that for the replacement or standing-in they are required to charge the seeker *at least* 150% of the seeker's average wage as indicated in the latter's last audited annual report. The seeker is required to mention the annual amount and payments for replacements in each (following) annual report.

It is also enacted that only SICs (thus no other cooperatives nor 'single person enterprises') are allowed to provide the stand-in service.

An auxiliary rule is that for persons elected in a public office (parliamentarians, ministers, provincial and municipal councillors and board members) the state pays 50% of the officer's former wage to the regarding cooperative or public sector institution.[101]

Any charging and payment above the mentioned 150% is a matter of supply (number and size of SICs) and demand (amount of seeking). The following sections A–C set out the consequences for the seekers, for the SIC and for the SIC workers.

---

101   The same applies for a limited number of parliamentary and ministerial assistants that come and go with the parliamentary or minister.

A. *Consequences for the replacement seekers*
(*1*) *Season work.* It is up to the regarding cooperative whether it is prepared to pay at least 50% extra wages to season workers from SICs. Alternatively it increases its permanent workforce and makes use of the possibility of some variation in the maximum work-time within a year (3§10-b – in that section it was also mentioned that overtime is not paid, but in time compensated for within no more than a year). All cooperatives with a seasonable work concentration are confronted with the same choice, and each choice will affect output prices.
(*2*) *Sickness of workers for more than a brief period.* It was mentioned in 3§21 that cooperatives as well as 'workers' council governed foundations' with less than 100 workers are required to take out a sickness insurance with an insurance cooperative (institutions with more than 100 workers may do so). It is now manifest that in case the institution intends to seek stand-ins with a SIC, this insurance should cover the wage supplement (50% or more). Because this category cannot be planned, there may be shortages with SICs.
(*3*) *Parental leave.* As mentioned in 3§22–3 the state pays parental leave at the level of the minimum wage for in total 31 weeks (leaving it to the institutional councils to make this up to a higher amount). Parental leave can be planned (from off pregnancy). The brief parental leave periods for each of the parents during the child's first three years (15 weeks) can probably be overcome within the institution's work schemes. For small institutions this may be different for the mother's leave of 16 weeks around birth. In case a stand-in is sought, the extra payment for the stand-in has to be brought up by the institution (alternatively a general insurance is taken out).
(*4*). *Election into a political office.* Recall from 3§1-g that on the office termination of persons that were elected to a political office, these have the right to return to their previous position in a cooperative or other institution, whence the latter will usually seek a stand-in (it will be seen in ch. 4 that the same applies for provincial and municipal offices). The election of particular persons cannot be planned, but on the other hand the duration is usually four years or more. As mentioned the state compensates 50% of the officer's former wage to the regarding cooperative or public sector institution (in case this does not cover the SIC costs of the seeker, the latter can apply for an extra compensation).
(*5*) *Cooperatives and public sector institutions of which workers make use of a period of less than full-time work.* This is the most difficult problem. It was mentioned in 3§10-d that 'the part-time option .... is a right in principle, to the extent that the exact part-time period(s) should be well planned and be in agreement with the management and the council of the cooperative or

public sector institution in face of the internal staff capacity – this is especially important for small cooperatives (the long-time period just before the retirement requires no agreement, but it has to be announced four months in advance).' For persons that make use of the option there seems to be no fair possibility other than that these themselves pay the 50% supplement out of their savings (this does not apply for the period just before the retirement).

B. Consequences for the stand-in cooperatives
Stand-in cooperatives shall explicitly be registered as such. As mentioned SICS are organised like all other cooperatives (ch. 2). Notably SICS shall have a permanent workforce. Thus, as against what is often the case with capitalist employment agencies, workers are not 'employed' on demand, and the revenues form seekers are collective revenues, the individual wages scales and the dividends being decided on by the SIC's council.

The required SIC's charge to the seeker of *at least* 150% of the latter's average wage, aims to prevent the emergence of a cooperative's echelon (SICS) that might ultimately pay its workers no more than the minimum wage as a result of competition. The charge is a net charge that includes turnover taxes. The remaining part of the supplement of 50% (or more) serves to fill gaps in the demand from seekers, given that the demand from seekers is probably irregular.

So as to fill the gaps, it is up to the SIC to combine its main service of standing in with other work that can be delivered on demand (for example advice or repair work).

C. Consequences for the workers of stand-in cooperatives
SIC workers may find the relatively large diversity of work in various seeking cooperatives attractive. They might also find the gaps attractive (in case the SIC does not combine its main service with other work). For some the downside might be that there is hardly a career perspective, and that there are hardly enduring ties with colleagues.

Appendix 3G. List of separate accounting maintaining state agencies and other state institutions

Here follows a list of the state agencies and the other state institutions that maintain a separate accounting. See also the alphabetical list of abbreviations at the very end of the book.

3D1
• The parliament as organisation; central state ministries; the taxation authority; provincial and municipal administrations.
3D2
• The judiciary (3§6)
Below the 18 state agencies are listed.
3D3
• Inspectorates – regarding various safeties (3§12)
3D4
• Central bank (3§13)
• Guardian bank (3§14)
• Investment-credit guarantee fund (3§15)
• Savings and Loans Bank (3§16)
3D5
• Job securities and jobs shortage agency (3§17)
3D6
• Pensions and child allowances agency (3D6, intro)
3D7
• National health agency (3§26)
• National education agency (3§30)
• Culture and cultural heritage agency (3§34)
3D8
• Real estate agency (3§37)
• Mining and other Earth extractions agency (3§38)
• National infrastructure agency (3§39)
3D9
• National public transport agency (3§40)
• Agency for temporary workers' council governed foundations (3§41)
3D10
• Registered external auditors authority (3§43)
• Patents and copyrights authority (3§44)
• Competition authority (3§45)

This concludes the Appendices of Chapter 3.

CHAPTER 4

Municipal and provincial administrations

Introduction

Next to the administration of the state (ch. 3), municipalities constitute the main administrations of the society of worker cooperatives. These regard the municipality of a city or town, villages being part of such a municipality. (In case of large areas without a city or town, a large group of villages may together constitute a municipality.) They carry out local public services. There are also provincial administrations, that perform cross municipal border public services.

The sections 4§1 (budget) and 4§6 (workers' councils) apply to both municipalities and provinces. The sections in between treat their democratic organs (4§2 and 4§4) and their tasks (4§3 and 4§5) separately.

Terminology. Only in 4§6 the term 'workers' council' is used (always with the adjective 'workers'). When in the preceding sections the term 'council' is used (without adjective) this refers to the by citizens elected governing political body.

4§1   *Establishment and budget of municipalities and provinces*
(a) *Establishment.* Municipalities and provinces are separate accounting maintaining legal entities that are established by the state in the form of a law (3§2-f).
(b) *Budget.* Municipalities and provinces shall not impose taxes on cooperatives or inhabitants. They receive a nationwide uniform per capita budget (proportional to the municipal or provincial inhabitants) that is different for municipalities and provinces (cf. 3§2-f). The elected councils of municipalities and provinces decide on the allocation of the budget over the institution's tasks (see 4§3-a and 4§5-a). However, there are three allocation constraints. First, regarding remunerations: municipal workers on average, and provincial workers on average, receive a remuneration equal to the nationwide average wages and dividends of cooperatives in FTE. Second, regarding the amount of workforce: each of the municipal and of the provincial workforce in FTE is not allowed to grow by more than an annually set percentage. (This percentage is equal to the average FTE growth of state institutions exclusive of the education sector; the reason for the latter is that within the total state budget, the education sector might grow above average – 3§32, last para–

graph.)¹ Third, regarding arts subsidies: an earmarked part of the municipalities budget shall be destined for subsidies of contemporary creative arts and arts performance (3§36-d).

(c) *Borrowing restrictions*. Each municipality and province holds one or more accounts with the Central Bank. In case of emergency they can borrow from the state (if the state consents) but they are not allowed to borrow from any other institution or individual – including by way of bank overdraft (cf. 3§4). The reason of this points is to keep 'hard budget constraints' (3§2-h).

(d) *Record keeping*. Municipalities and provinces register their incomes and expenditures in regular bookkeeping, and at the end of the year they record an Income account and a Balance sheet of their assets, liabilities and reserves. The latter two are sent to the minister of home affairs, after their approval by, first, two external registered auditors (see 3§43) – each of different auditing cooperatives,² and, second, their workers (see 4§6). The minister sends a summarising report to parliament that deals with it as it deems required.

4§2 *Municipal democratic organs*

The main part of this section regards the democratic organs of a municipality, and its structure is analogous to the first part of 3§1 (the democratic organs of the state).

(a) *Election of municipal council*. Once every four years the eligible voters of a municipality elect a municipal council that is the municipality's highest governance body. It is elected on a proportional basis, without an electoral threshold.³

(b) *Election of municipal executive board*. The municipal council elects a municipal executive board that is accountable to the council and that is removable by the council's majority.⁴ The chair of this board has the title of 'municipal

---

1 Thus, indicating the budget by B, the average workers remuneration by w and the maximum amount of workforce by L^{max}, then the total remuneration share in the budget is $(wL^{max}) / B$.
2 In case the two auditors do not agree between them, the opinion of an added third one is decisive – each three nevertheless has to sign, one in case of disagreement. Once an auditor has taken on the task at hand, s/he is not allowed to resign in case of disagreement between one or two of the other auditors.
3 This implies that if a municipality has e.g. 40 seats, a seat is determined by 2.5% of the voters. Proportionality has not only the advantage that it reflects voters rather than the contingent composition of voting districts, it also has the advantage that small parties can gain seats (which increases the political dynamism) and that minority tendencies can feel themselves represented.
4 Together with the previous point's proportionality, this implies that municipal executive boards governments are most often coalition boards.

mayor'. The members of the board may, but do not need to be elected from the council's ranks. In case a councillor is elected as board member, s/he resigns as councillor.

(c) *Candidates for municipal elections.* As an aside to its other political party work, each political party constitutes an *association of electors* that has local branches. Its main function is to draw up a list of candidates for the municipal elections. (The association is the same as the one mentioned in 3§1-d for parliamentary elections.) An eligible voter of the municipality may become member of *one* such association without any discrimination and without membership fee;[5] the membership is continuous until the member resigns. The branches delegate members to the association's *electoral college*, which draws up the association's list of candidates. (Each association of electors is free to determine if and how their municipal council candidates reflect the city or town districts and the villages.)

The per party lists of candidates are assembled on a single list from which voters sub (a) vote.

(d) *Rules for (candidate) councillors and political parties.* Municipal councillors shall act, speak and vote independently and shall not be bound by any mandate or instruction. Councillors, candidate councillors, associations of electors and political parties are not allowed to accept gifts. Political parties can raise an annual membership fee of no more than 0.5% of the statutory yearly minimum wage. None of the in the previous two sentences mentioned is allowed to raise money via the organisation of any sort of event or in any other way.

(e) *Chair of council and ceremonial mayor.* Municipal councillors elect from their ranks a chairperson. One year after taking office they elect, external to their ranks, a ceremonial mayor, which has no political powers. The latter extends office until one year after the next elections, and is re-electable.[6] Ceremonial mayor might be a part-time function.

(f) *Village mayor.* Inhabitants of villages elect a part-time mayor for the rapports with the municipality; for their joint interests the village majors may constitute a committee that confers with the municipality.

---

5   Political parties receive a compensation for the costs of the elections.
6   The ceremonial mayor is similar to the ceremonial president at the state level. The point is that in each case (state and municipality) the by the population elected organ (parliament or municipal council) is the highest legislative and administrative body. A parallel by the population elected top person risks to lead to autocratic powers for a single person and to a diffusion of the collective power of the elected body (parliament or municipal council).

(g) *Work-time of councillors and executives.* Membership of the executive board is a full-time function. Except for very large municipalities, the councillorship is a part-time function.

(h) *Remuneration of councillors and executives.* Proportional to their work-time, councillors and executives receive a remuneration equal to the nationwide average wages and dividends of cooperatives in FTE.

(i) *Rights of councillors and executives.* Cooperatives or other institutions shall not prevent in any way councillors and executives to take on their function or the candidacy for it. After the termination of their office, fulltime working councillors and executives have the right to a paid sabbatical of two months, and immediately after this period they have the right to return to their previous position in a cooperative or other institution. Councillors that worked part-time have the right to return to their previous full-time position in a cooperative or other institution. Any part-time political work, including the sabbatical, does not count to the part-time limit mentioned in 3§10-d.

4§3   Tasks and authority of the municipal administration

(a) *General responsibility and budget allocation.* • Responsible for municipal public services. • Institution of municipal acts that are in the direct interest of the inhabitants and that may not be inconsistent or in conflict with legislation of the state and of the municipal's province. The municipal council decides on the allocation of the budget (4§1) over the municipality's tasks (see below) as well as on any municipal acts – each as proposed by the municipal executive board. The council may amend such proposals.

(b) *Registration.* Keeping of: a population register; a register of dwellings; a register of cooperatives.

(c) *Public security.* Responsible for fire brigades and the local police (the latter in coordination with the provincial administration that is responsible for the provincial police – 4§5-b).

(d) *Infrastructure.* Responsible for: water networks and water supply (via one or more licensed PWCs); for waste processing (including sewers); construction and maintenance of city/town and intra-village roads and streets as well as bicycle tracks (the provincial administration is responsible for inter-village roads); housing amenities; parks. All these are carried out by PWCs.

(e) *Transport.* (1) Responsible for (in case) urban and suburban passenger railway transport (carried out by one local 'workers' council governed foundation' (WGF) that charges customers; the rules for the latter are similar as for the national railway transport – 3§40). (2) Responsible for municipal bus services and taxis – carried out by licensed PWCs. (The provincial administration is responsible for inter-village and provincial bus services.) (3) Responsible for adequate connections of the municipal passenger transport with the national and provincial transport (in consultation with the municipal carriers).

(f) *Public library and contemporary creative arts and arts performance.* (1) Responsible for at least one public library (carried out by a local WGF). (2) Provision of subsidies for contemporary creative arts and arts performance out of the for it earmarked budget (4§1-a). (3) Depending on the council's view on the adequacy of the regarding service by PWCs: the possible extra subsidising of halls and rooms and of artistic creations and performances (see 3§36, Table 3.14).

(g) *Cultural heritage and nature reserves.* Responsible for the operation of municipal historical sites and buildings; botanical gardens and nature reserves activities. If possible these activities are carried out by PWCs, if not by local WGFs.

(h) *Charges for services.* As mentioned, municipalities shall not impose taxes; nor shall they charge inhabitants or cooperatives for general services; however, they may charge for non-general services, that is those that benefit specific categories of users (for example, car parking and parking places, or encroachments on, over and under public land and water).

4§4   *Provincial democratic organs*

Because the tasks of the provincial administrations are rather restricted and often require coordination with the municipalities (4§5), the main governance organ of the province is indirectly elected by the province's municipal councillors that so function as an electoral college.[7]

(a) Via the procedure analogous as set out under 4§2-c, a list of candidates for the provincial council is drawn up (in the current case municipal councillors are member of the association of electors).

(b) The municipal councillors in a province constitute an *electoral college* that once every four years elects from the list under (a) the *provincial council*. It is elected on a proportional basis, without an electoral threshold. The elections are held half a year after the councillors have entered office. (This is to give them time to grow in their function.)

(c) The provincial council is the province's highest governance body. The council elects a *provincial executive board* that is accountable to the council and that

---

7   Moreover, given the tasks of the provinces (4§5), it is likely that many inhabitants will not be eager to bring out a vote in provincial elections. In this case an indirect election seems better than a direct one.

is removable by the council's majority. The members of the board may, but need not be elected from the council's ranks. In case a councillor is elected as board member, s/he resigns as councillor.

(d) Councillors elect from their ranks a chairperson.

(e) Councillors shall act, speak and vote independently and shall not be bound by any mandate or instruction. Councillors, candidate councillors, associations of electors and political parties are not allowed to accept gifts. Political parties can raise an annual membership fee of no more than 0.5% of the statutory yearly minimum wage. None of the in the previous two sentences mentioned is allowed to raise money via the organisation of any sort of event or in any other way.

(f) *Work-time of councillors and executives*. Membership of the executive board is a full-time function. The councillorship is a part-time function.

(g and h) Regarding the 'remuneration of councillors and executives', and the 'rights of councillors and executives', 4§2 (h) and (i) apply.

4§5   *Tasks and authority of the provincial administration*

(a) *General responsibility and budget allocation.* •Responsible for public services beyond those of municipalities, and that are not part of the responsibilities of the state. •Institution of provincial acts that are in the direct interest of the province's inhabitants and that may not be inconsistent or in conflict with state legislation. The provincial council decides on the allocation of the budget over the province's tasks (see below) as well as on any provincial acts – each as proposed by the provincial executive board. The council may amend such proposals.

(b) *Public security*. Responsible for the provincial police (in coordination with the municipalities which are responsible for the municipal police – 4§2-b).

(c) *Infrastructure*. Responsible for: the construction and maintenance of provincial roads (as including bicycle tracks and inter-village roads); provincial waterways and dykes (in coordination with other provincial administrations). All these works are carried out by PWCs.

(d) *Transport*. Responsible for provincial passenger bus services, carried out by one or more licensed PWCs.

(e) *Cultural heritage and nature reserves*. Responsible for the operation of provincial historical sites and buildings; botanical gardens and nature reserves activities. If possible these activities are carried out by PWCs, if not by local WGFs.

(f) *Land use and planning*. Determines whether cities, towns and villages are allowed to expand, and (in consultation with the relevant municipalities) where business areas and industrial zones can be situated. Determines the areas that are reserved for agriculture, nature conservation, woods and forests, and recreation.

(g) *Charges for services.* As mentioned, provinces shall not impose taxes; nor shall they charge inhabitants or cooperatives for general services; however, they may charge for non-general services, that is those that benefit specific categories of users (for example, to the extent that the user-charged railway transport increases, provincially residing users of provincial roads may be charged).

4§6   *Workers' councils of municipal and provincial institutions*
Similar as for state institutions, municipal and provincial institutions or divisions are internally organised via workers' councils. See 3§3: for 'state institution' read municipal or provincial institution; for 'member of parliament' read member of municipal or provincial council; for 'members of the government' read members of the municipal or provincial executive board.

CHAPTER 5

International economic relations

Introduction

This very brief chapter sets out some headlines of the Design's international economic relations. Main other international matters, such as treaties, are included in Appendix 3C (Constitution, Division 5).

5§1   *International migration*
• *International immigration* is free for immigrants eligible under the international 'Convention relating to the status of refugees'. Other immigration permission is dependent on the degree of actual or expected joblessness.
• *International emigration.* Given that formal education – as well as up to about 25 years of costs of living allowances – is free (that is, financed out of the tax receipts), inhabitants that emigrate within ten years after having completed their formal education are required to return in instalments an amount to be specified. (This is a compensation for the taxes that all inhabitants pay for the educational system. The point is that in countries where education is not free, students build up a student debt, but on average pay lower taxes on future wages.)

5§2   *International trade*
Generally, in order to keep international independence, imports should not exceed exports; in case they are this is regulated via import duties. (This may be different for low-income countries that receive compensating international aid or transfers.)
• *Commodity trade.* In face of the environment, freight transport and hence the international trade of commodities is best to be minimised (cf. 'physically circular production', 3§7-a).[1] This implies an aim for maximal self-sufficiency (generally not only internationally, but within a nation also regionally).[2]

---

[1] Taking account of both production effects and transport effects, Cristea et al. 2013, p. 13, show that ¾ of the world international trade results in increasing greenhouse gas emissions; the International Transport Forum (ITF 2019, p. 53) projects that, in comparison with 2015, international trade transport CO_2 emissions, instead of the required decrease, will have grown by 157% in 2050, even in the case of no new free trade agreements coming forward.

[2] I wrote the draft of this text prior to the outbreak of COVID-19 around 2020. That showed, apart from the arguments above, that international dependency for medical supplies, as well as for food and essential non-food supplies, is not wise.

• *Services trade*. It is likely that the international services trade, mainly regards international travel and stay (including tourism), and work for international organisations.

5§3 *International ownership titles*
Because worker cooperatives and single person enterprises are the only one economic legal entities, foreign multinational enterprises can have no enterprise ownership in a Design country. Other international ownership titles generally regard those of, first, financial ownership titles (shares, bonds and their derivatives, as well as loans including savings with banks), and, second, of real estate. In the Design there are no markets for these and all individual's savings above two months income are stalled with the Savings and Loans Bank. Therefore foreigners can own no such titles in a country that adopts the Design. However, the rules so far do not exclude that cooperatives or individuals purchase international ownership titles or borrow abroad (which would disturb the home financial circuits, and possibly also the international balance of payments – see the next section). Appendix 5A sets out rules to prevent this; it also amplifies on import duties.

5§4 *International balance of payments*
The previous two sections (together with the implementation of Appendix 5A) imply that the Design's balance of payments regards the unavoidable international trade of commodities, as well as services, and the sum of the former two on the so-called 'capital account'.

5§5 *International development transfers*
In case the Design is actualised in a High Income Country (according to the World Bank definition) it would be appropriate if any surplus on the balance of payments (thus far) would be expended on especially formal education in Low and Lower-Middle Income countries. (This counts all the more for High Income Countries with a colonial or imperialist past, and/or those that have structurally taken advantage from their international terms of trade.)

Appendix 5A. Regulation of international ownership titles and of import duties

International ownership titles
Cooperatives, single person enterprises (2§2.2), and households/individuals are prohibited:

- To borrow abroad (recall that this also applies for the state);
- To purchase, or otherwise own, foreign financial titles (shares, bonds and their derivatives), or to lend out abroad, as including to save with foreign banks.
- To purchase, or otherwise own, foreign real estate or other property, either directly or indirectly.

The rules above also apply for national non-resident households/individuals that are – or in the future want to be – eligible for an allowance (especially pension). Probably this mainly regards pensioners and persons that work for international organisations.

International trade by cooperatives and single person enterprises
International trade transactions have two-sided branch codes (from–to). For their foreign transactions cooperatives and single person enterprises have to open a separate account with their cooperative bank (COB), the transactions requiring codification. The COB quarterly reports the sums of these transactions to the Central Bank. On the basis of it, the latter advises the taxation authority whether import duties should be adapted.

International purchases by households/individuals
International purchase transactions have a simple branch code (such as textiles or books). For their foreign transactions households/individuals have to open a separate account with their COB that is associated with a separate payment card. The transactions require codification. The COB quarterly reports the sums of these transactions to the Central Bank. On the basis of it, the latter advises the taxation authority whether import duties should be considered. If so, individuals have to pay these above a certain annual threshold.

PART TWO

From modifying capitalism to transition

∴

This part consists of three chapters.
- Chapter 6. The modification of capitalist practices by 'worker-owned cooperatives' and similar democratic enterprises (p. 245)
- Chapter 7. Circumstances just before the transition: financial and real estate markets and the scope of capital flight (p. 298)
- Chapter 8. Transition to a worker cooperatives society (p. 307)

Introduction to Part Two

This part is about the transition in some country from the capitalist mode of production to a worker cooperatives mode of production as set out in Part One. Most of the text of this part is indeed on the transition itself (chapter 8), rather than on the period preceding it (that is, from to date onwards, as outlined in chapters 6–7). To the extent that Part One has been fairly detailed, the chapter 8 outline of the transition can also be detailed. The two go together. The writing of this book is based on the conviction that the prospect of a radical progressive change of society is served by not only the outline of feasible details of a future society but also feasible details of the transition.

The main chapter 8 of Part Two takes off at the point when in a particular country there is a parliamentary majority that aims to go for the transition to a society as set out in Part One. As will be seen, its main problematic is to reach an actual transition during which existing capitalist enterprises keep functioning along with a gradually increasing Design cooperatives sector (increasing both absolutely and relatively). The point is the maintenance throughout the transition of a high level of production and work. That requires a rather finely balanced series of legislation aiming at a gradual emergence of Design cooperatives – building on the then existing worker-owned cooperatives and similar democratic entities – together with a gradual evanescence of capitalist enterprises.

This legislative period is planned to take five to six years, and during these years a great deal of the gradual emergence and evanescence can already be reached. It will be seen that the main legislative means to reach this are the Design's taxation and competition legislations (there are also some auxiliary ones). Apart from those legislative social forces – forces that also exist within capitalism, though tuned to capitalist enterprises – no capitalist enterprise will be enforced to legally convert into a cooperative. At the end of this legislative period, all of the Design's main provisions (health, education and the reduction of joblessness to two months) and its allowances (pensions and child-related) will be realised.

The full actual completion of the transition's gradual emergence of Design cooperatives and gradual evanescence of capitalist enterprises (after the mentioned five to six years) is based on the same legislative instruments. This completion will be reached within one generation.

Chapter 8 on the transition is fairly detailed, taking a space of about 80 pages (apart from an appendix with some summarising tables). This chapter is preceded by a rather brief chapter 7 that tries to imagine – and on that basis to analyse – the circumstances during about two years just before the start of the transition, that is, when owners of capitalist enterprises perceive it likely that there might be a transition (a perception based on the previous elections and polls about the forthcoming elections). It will be seen that matters such as so-called 'capital flight' are hardly worrying, because this regards monetary matters (hardly any physical enterprises can be 'exported'). The main problem of this period is that – because the relevant actors perceive insecurities about the future – capitalist enterprises will stop investing. As a result, it is likely that the transition (chapter 8) will take off in a recession.

The depth of that recession depends on the relative sizes (during the chapter 7 period) of the sector of capitalist enterprises in comparison with the sector of worker-owned cooperatives and similar democratic entities that had emerged within the capitalism of those days. In principle there might be a transition with only a relatively small worker-owned cooperatives sector, but, as said, this affects the depth of the recession at the transition's start.

Chapter 6 treats the current modification of capitalist practices by 'worker-*owned* cooperatives' and similar democratic enterprises. It sets out the current size and the employment (world-wide) of worker-owned cooperatives, and how these compare with conventional capitalist enterprises – other democratic enterprises will be treated cursorily. This is an empirical matter (and I am grateful to the scholars who in the past decade engaged with research about it). The future development of the democratic enterprises sector is a matter of speculation. But it can be hoped that the facts of the comparison – which are by social and economic measures in favour of the cooperatives – will contribute to their absolute and relative growth. Besides, other empirical facts – especially those regarding the increasing skewedness in the distribution of income and wealth within, and stemming from, the capitalist sector – tends to make a relative growth of the democratic enterprises sector rather likely. If so, this would contribute to the preconditions for a take-off to a transition.

CHAPTER 6

The modification of capitalist practices by 'worker-owned cooperatives' and similar democratic enterprises

Introduction[1]

The main part of this chapter is about worker cooperatives as existing within current capitalism. These are almost inevitably worker-owned, and so they are distinct from the Design cooperatives as outlined in the previous chapters – the core distinction being that in Design cooperatives workers are not owners but usufructuaries. The main aim of this chapter is to outline the characteristics of these 'worker-owned cooperatives' (WOCs) in comparison with conventional capitalist enterprises. It will be seen that WOCs engender an important modification of capitalist practices, not least because of their democratic character and their general way of prioritising employment rather than capital. The WOCs' transitory 'beyond capitalism' potential will be referred to only in the chapter's conclusions.

The chapter encompasses three Divisions. Division 1 is about WOCs generally. Division 2, the lengthiest one, discusses the case of the Spanish Mondragon cooperatives (in 2020 about 100 cooperatives, employing over 80,000 workers, that together constitute the Mondragon federation, the world's largest of its kind). The focus is on this case, not only because of the available large amount of quantitative information, but especially because it reveals the complexities of maintaining its cooperative ideals in face of globalising capitalist competition. The relatively brief Division 3 broadens the picture to what since about 1980 is called the 'social and solidarity economy' which encompasses among others: WOCs, other cooperatives, mutual societies, and most recently 'social enterprises'. These entities have in common that they adopt an inclusive and participatory governance model, ideally a one member/stakeholder, one vote kind.

---

1   A version of Divisions 1 and 2 of this chapter was published in the *Journal of Labor and Society* (Reuten 2023a).

Division 1. Worker-owned cooperatives within capitalism up to 2020: number and performance

The first section of this Division briefly sets out four general characteristics of 'worker-owned cooperatives' existing within capitalism (6§1). The second section starts by setting out general distinctions between these cooperatives and the main other cooperatives types; this is followed by their quantification on a world and continental level (employment and the number of cooperatives' members), and some quantitative information on worker-owned cooperatives in individual countries (6§2). After this cursorily general overview, the third section provides information on the performance of worker-owned cooperatives in comparison with conventional capitalist enterprises (6§3).

6§1 *Worker-owned cooperatives (wocs) and similar legal entities: general characteristics*

In this section, and all of ch. 6, the single term 'worker-owned cooperative' (WOC) is used for legal entities that in the literature may also be indicated by names such as 'worker cooperative', 'labour-managed enterprise', 'employee-owned enterprise' and 'democratic enterprise'.

The WOC's exact legal form and its specifics diverge widely across the worlds' countries. I focus on the following four general characteristics.

1. Democratic decision-making. The legal entity is democratically governed by its worker-members, which directly or indirectly appoint the entity's management on a one person one vote basis. The other coverage of the democratic decision-making (for example regarding the annual wage scales) varies by the specific statute of the entity. Main lines may also have been legislated.

2. Ownership. The legal entity is owned by the worker-members of the cooperative. When they become a member, they most often have to pay into a fund, either directly or via a deduction from their remuneration in the early years of their membership. This fund functions as a reserve of the cooperative. Most often all or part of this fund is refundable when workers retire or move to another enterprise. Often the ownership is restricted by so-called 'asset locks' which means that a specific part of the asset value shall not be sold – this should secure the long-term survival of the cooperative.

3. Non-members. Often the statute allows for the employment of some percentage of non-members; this may include workers who refrain from paying in to the fund mentioned under 2. This may be regarded as a defect, depending on the rights of these employees concerning the democratic decision-making, and on their remuneration.

4. Surpluses. The statute of an entity may prescribe that a part of the annual surpluses is not distributed to the workers, but be added to the common reserves to which workers can make no individual claim (as against the funds under 2, or part thereof). In some countries this is legislated.

I remark that the world-wide divergence of the exact legal form of what I denote by WOC poses statistical problems when quantifying their occurrence (section 6§2).

6§2 Worker-owned cooperatives and other cooperatives: terminology and quantifications

This section provides general information on the distinction between WOCs and other types of cooperatives. Next to WOCs the two other main types of cooperatives are 'producer-serving cooperatives' and 'user-serving cooperatives' (the latter include consumer cooperatives). *Table 6.1* provides a classification of the three types. The classification is, with some rephrasing of the terminology, in keeping with that of CIPOCA (2017a) so that I can use its empirical data in the remainder of this section.

TABLE 6.1   *Classification of cooperatives as functioning within capitalism*

	All cooperatives below provide jobs to workers		
	Worker cooperatives (WOCs)	Producer-serving coops (PSCs)	User-serving coops (USCs)
1	workers are its members, though there may be non-member workers	independent producers are its members	users are its members; though they might also provide services for non-members†
2	in principle one member one vote	in principle one member one vote	in principle one member one vote
3	most often owned by the workers or a subset of these‡	most often owned by these members or a subset of these	often owned by these users or a subset of these
4	depending on country legislation and/or the statute of a coop, these coops might also employ non-members*	provide services directly related to the jobs of the regarding producers‡	provide services not directly related to the jobs of the regarding users

TABLE 6.1   *Classification of cooperatives (cont.)*

	All cooperatives below provide jobs to workers		
	Worker cooperatives (WOCS)	**Producer-serving coops (PSCS)**	**User-serving coops (USCS)**
5	*qualification* worker cooperatives may make use of producer-serving cooperatives and be their member (next column), such as regarding finance; and they might also own these, for example a cooperative bank.	*subsets (non-exhaustive)* production cooperatives (e.g. dairy, fishery products); purchasing cooperatives; marketing and sales coops; financial coops.∗∗	*subsets (non-exhaustive)* consumer coops (retail); housing coops; financial coops.
			Especially for insurance, a specific subset regards '*mutual coops*' (or mutual societies)[2]
	A category that I will not further refer to in the current Division is a 'hybrid cooperative' (or 'mixed cooperative' or 'multi-stakeholder cooperative') which combines two or more of the three types above, each type being represented in the governance structure of the cooperative.		

† Sometimes at prices that are different from those for members.
‡ The ownership is one major difference between these cooperatives and Design cooperatives.
* In the Design this is possible only during a probation period of maximum two years – as well as during general recessions.
‡ To the extent that the independent producer-members are in fact dependent on producer-serving coops, the borderline between 'worker cooperatives' and 'producer-serving cooperatives' blurs (see CICOPA 2017a, p. 34; see also p. 37).
∗∗ CICOPA (2017a) classifies all financial coops under user cooperatives.

On basis of Table 6.1's classification, *Table 6.2* (p. 249) provides a quantification of the world-wide employment within cooperatives and of the members of cooperatives (based on data of 156 countries). For the employment an important question is whether the employment of the *members* of 'producer-serving cooperatives' (PSCs) should be counted to the overall cooperative employment. Most often these members are self-employed individual producers, the vast

---

2 Like for all cooperatives, these are owned by the members. The distributable profits are either paid out in the form of dividends or destined to reduce the members' premiums.

majority being in agriculture. Roelants, Eum and Terrasi (2014) and CICOPA (2017a) argue that employment of these producers should be counted to the cooperatives employment, because most of the members of PSCs cannot survive without the PSC. In *Table 6.2*, row 11, this employment is called 'employment within the scope of cooperatives'.

TABLE 6.2   *World employment in or within the scope of cooperatives around 2016*[†]

		in million	In % of the world's employed population
	Types of cooperatives and their members		
1	number of cooperatives (all three types of Table 6.1)	2.94	
2	members of 'worker-owned cooperatives'	11.15	
3	members of 'producer-serving cooperatives'	252.20	
4	members of 'user cooperatives'	954.11	
5	total number of cooperatives members [2+3+4]	1,217.46	
6	world population age 15–65[‡]	4,861.01	
	Employment in or within the scope of cooperatives		
7	member-workers of 'worker-owned cooperatives' [WOCs]	11.15	0.38%
8	non-member employees of cooperatives (all three coop types)	16.05	0.54%
9	total workers in cooperatives [7+8]	27.20	0.92%
10	member-workers of 'producer-serving coops'*	252.20	8.54%
11	total employment in coops or their scope [9+10]	279.39	9.46%
	Estimated total workers in 'worker-owned cooperatives'		
12	estimated non-member employees of WOCs [‡]	1.21	0.04%
13	estimated total workers in 'worker-owned cooperatives' [7+12]	12.36	0.42%
14	estimated workers of producer-serving and user coops [9–13]	14.84	0.50%
15	total workers in cooperatives [13+14 = 9]	27.20	0.92%

† Based on data of 156 countries. Some data are from 2017, the others from 2016 or the latest year available. The data of worker-owned cooperatives are available for only 51 out of 156 countries (see Table 6.4)
‡ Row 5 divided by 6 is 25%, but people may be member of more than one cooperative.
* These members are mainly self-employed individual producers, the vast majority being in agriculture (CICOPA 2017a, pp. 21, 24, 25 n. 2, and 33).
[‡] The estimate is based on CICOPA 2017b, Table 1 (p. 9), where for worker-owned cooperatives [WOCs] in the industry and service sectors together, employees constitute a factor 0.11 of the worker members.
Data sources. Rows 1–5 and 7–11: CICOPA 2017a, Executive summary, p. 12, and Table 1, p. 25.[3] Row 6: World Bank, database World Development Indicators, population ages 15–64, year 2016, Last updated: 19 March 2021. https://databank.worldbank.org/reports.aspx?source=world-development-indicators&l=en

3   https://www.ica.coop/sites/default/files/publication-files/cooperatives-and-employment-second-global-report-625518825.pdf.

Using the same systematic as Table 6.2, *Table 6.3* indicates the world cooperative employment proportions by continent (row numbers 1–11 refer to the former).

TABLE 6.3   *Continental employment in or within the scope of cooperatives around 2016†*
(WOC = worker-owned cooperative; PSC = producer-serving coop; USC = user coop.)

		(1) World in million*	(2) Africa	(3) Americas	(4) Asia	(5) Europe	(6) Oceania
			in % of column (1)*				
1	number of cooperatives	2.937	13%	6%	73%	8%	0%
2	members of WOCs	11.149	0.3%	8.8%	76.9%	13.9%	0.0%
3	members of PSCs	252.199	8.1%	1.3%	86.9%	3.6%	0.1%
4	members of USCs	954.110	3.5%	43.8%	33.6%	15.9%	3.2%
5	total members cooperatives [7+8+9]	1,217.458	4.4%	34.6%	45.0%	13.4%	2.5%
7	member-workers of WOCs	11.149	0.3%	8.8%	76.9%	13.9%	0.0%
8	non-member employees of coops (all types)	16.049	12.1%	11.8%	46.3%	29.4%	0.5%
9	total workers in cooperatives [7+8]	27.198	7.3%	10.6%	58.8%	23.0%	0.3%
10	member-workers of PSCs	252.199	8.1%	1.3%	86.9%	3.6%	0.1%
11	total employment in coops or their scope [9+10]	279.387	8.0%	2.2%	84.2%	5.5%	0.1%
15	number of countries dataset	156	35	39	33	37	12
16	total labour force dataset countries (2016)	3,029.994	12.1%	14.8%	61.3%	11.2%	0.6%

† See the notes of Table 6.2.
* Except row 15.
Data sources. Rows 1–11: CICOPA 2017a, p. 25, Table 1 (percentages calculated); Row 16: World Bank, labour force, total; last updated 16-12-2020.[4]

Row 16 of *Table 6.3* serves to interpret the continental proportions of the table. The large employment shares of, for example, Asia are co-determined by its relatively large total labour force.

The remainder of this section focusses on WOCs only. A general problem is that the data on WOC's are scarce. This also applies for the CICOPA dataset

---

[4] https://data.worldbank.org/indicator/SL.TLF.TOTL.IN?view=chart (shown excel, dataset countries 2016).

that I have referred to above. Although it has data from 156 countries (71% of all countries), within those data the data on WOCs specifically are relatively under-represented – as is shown in *Table 6.4*.

TABLE 6.4　*Scarceness of data on WOCs around 2016*

		World	Africa	Americas	Asia	Europe	Oceania
1.	number of countries dataset CICOPA 2017a	156	35	39	33	37	12
2.	number of country data on WOCs†	51	3	14	14	19	1
3.	available country data on WOCs [2/1]	33%	9%	36%	42%	51%	8%

† When the dataset mentions that there are no WOCs in a country I have included these in the row 2 numbers.
Data source. Calculated from CICOPA 2017a, Annex 1 on individual countries, pp. 101–10.

It can be seen from *Table 6.4* that quite some data on WOCs are lacking in the 2017 CICOPA dataset. This is no criticism of its author, but rather reveals the lack of consistent WOC data generally.

An earlier report on cooperatives by Grace (2012), with data from 142 countries, which at the time claimed to be 'the most comprehensive data set on cooperatives' (p. 1), makes no distinction between types of cooperatives at all.[5]

Regarding WOCs *Table 6.5* shows from the CICOPA dataset the top-10 countries in terms of relative employment as % of a country's labour force (column 4), as well as in terms of absolute employment (column 5).

TABLE 6.5　*Country-wise employment in WOCs around 2016: world top-10's relative and absolute rank (out of 51 countries)*

(1)	(2)	(3)	(4)	(5)	(6)
Country	Amount employment	% labour force	Relative rank, top-10	Absolute rank, top-10	Continent
Italy	1,017,663	3.9%	1	2	Europe
Malaysia	524,713	3.5%	2	4	Asia
Sweden	96,552	1.8%	3	11	Europe
India	6,845,701	1.4%	4	1	Asia

5　The same (no distinction) applies for Cooperatives Europe (2015). This was their latest report of key figures on cooperatives when I accessed their website on 9 January 2021.

TABLE 6.5   Country-wise employment in wocs around 2016 (cont.)

(1)	(2)	(3)	(4)	(5)	(6)
Country	Amount employment	% labour force	Relative rank, top-10	Absolute rank, top-10	Continent
Spain	230,000	1.0%	5	7	Europe
Argentina	177,568	0.9%	6	8	S-America
Costa Rica	18,021	0.8%	7	21	N-America
Iran	162,287	0.6%	8	9	Asia
Paraguay	18,939	0.6%	9	20	S-America
Uruguay	9,345	0.5%	10	35	S-America
Colombia	117,622	0.5%	12	10	S-America
Bangladesh	268,556	0.4%	14	6	Asia
Brazil	291,046	0.3%	17	5	S-America
China	650,000	0.1%	26|[6]	3	Asia

Data sources. Row 2 CICOPA 2017a, Annex 1, pp. 101–10. Underlying data row 3: World Bank, labour force, total, last updated 16 December 2020 (see previous footnote).

It can be seen from column (3) of Table 6.5 that WOCs constitute as yet no threat to conventional capitalist enterprises.

The following information regards a class more encompassing than WOCs, namely 'majority-employee-owned enterprises' (all legal forms), though only those with more than 100 workers. In 2019 there were within 32 European countries (the European Union plus Iceland, Norway, Serbia, Switzerland, and the UK) 338 of such enterprises (of which 168 WOCs). Together these employed 486,000 workers, which is on average 1,438 workers per enterprise. The amount increased from 271 in 2010 to 338 in 2019. The largest proportion (90%) of these 338 enterprises are located in France (108), the UK (90), Spain (55), Italy (26), and the Czech Republic (19). All of the 168 WOCs are located in France (74), Spain (41), Italy (26), the Czech Republic (19), and the UK (3).[7]

---

[6] Of the dataset countries with a 2016 labour force > 30 million, the UK ranks relatively 18th (0.3%) and absolutely 12th (94,049); Vietnam 24th (0.1%) and 14th (51,066); France 25th (0.1%) and 17th (27,330); Japan 32nd (0.04%) and 18th (25,373); USA 33rd (0.03%) and 13th (55,140); Turkey 39th (0.01%) and 32nd (3,556). In the same category Thailand has no WOCs, and there are no WOC data for Ethiopia, Germany, Indonesia, Mexico, Nigeria, and the Russian Federation.

[7] Data from EFES 2020, Tables 31 and 32.

6§3 *The performance of worker-owned cooperatives: some key results of empirical research*

Standing out in a comparison of worker-owned cooperatives (WOCs) and 'conventional capitalist enterprises' (CCEs) is the difference in *institutional democracy* (this regards democracy at the level of the legal entity). WOCs are democratic, with a 'one person one vote' democracy for the cooperative's members. Legally this democracy is most often vested in the cooperative's council. In CCEs (these include stock corporations and firms) there is a peculiar kind of aborted 'democracy', first in that workers have no decisive vote at all, second in that suffrage is restricted to the shareholders/capital owners, and third in that the suffrage is not person based but rather amount of capital based. Instead of demo-cracy this comes down to capital-cracy: the rule of capital. Thus democratically CCEs do not perform at all. (Within CCEs there may be an organ where workers can voice their opinion, but this organ is – to date – never decisive in the CCE's governance.)[8]

When, as for the governance of a state, the democracy, or the degree of democracy, is the major normative principle of judgement, there is nevertheless more to say on the functioning of the legal entities. The two subsections below briefly expand on this functioning. First a general summary of the economic performance of WOCs; second, studies of French and Italian WOCs, specifically regarding their productivity and investment performances.

(1) A general summary of the economic performance of WOC. A comparison between WOCs and CCEs is hampered, or complicated, in face of their different objectives. Quite apart from the mentioned democratic strivings, the objective of WOCs is the preservation of employment and (subsidiary) the maximisation of value-added. However, as already mentioned in ch. 2, employment is no objective of CCEs but rather an instrument for their aims. Nor is value-added an aim for CCEs, but rather one part of it, namely profit, wages being the cost for the profit aim. More specifically profit is measured against the financial investment (WOCs would measure the total of value-added against the financial investment). Further, whereas for CCEs and their owners profit contributes to the general aim of the accumulation of capital, for WOCs the company's assets contribute to the mentioned employment and value-added aims.

---

8 In principle a capitalist state has the power to legislate full institutional-economic democracy. The non-actualisation of this power, together with rights that is does grant to conventional capitalist enterprises and capital owners, defines a state to be a capitalist state.

Nevertheless WOCs and CCEs can be compared on many performance indicators. In 2012 Pérotin published a review of empirical studies comparing the performance of worker cooperatives with capitalist enterprises in the period 1950 to 2010. She mentions that large representative data sets on WOCs have only recently become available. Her review covers about seventy empirical studies. Below I present her main conclusions. To these I have added on some conclusions from her 2014 paper.

1. Pérotin's general conclusion is that 'worker cooperatives perform well in comparison with conventional firms, and … the features that make them special – worker participation and unusual arrangements for the ownership of capital – are part of their strength' (2012, p. 36).

2. 'Worker cooperatives are present in most industries, are not always less capital-intensive and tend to be larger on average than their conventional counterparts, and survive at least as well' (2014, p. 35).

3. 'Solid, consistent evidence across countries, systems, and time periods shows that worker cooperatives are at least as productive as conventional firms, and more productive in some areas. The more participatory cooperatives are, the more productive they tend to be' (2012, p. 37). 'Participation' regards the degree of workers actually taking part in the democratic structure, thus the degree in which they use their rights.

4. Whereas it is often assumed that worker cooperatives under-invest, 'no rigorous empirical evidence can be found in support of the under-investment hypothesis' (2014, p. 38).

5. 'The temptation to consume capital accumulated by previous generations, demutualize, sell out successful cooperatives to conventional owners, or degenerate by restricting membership …, all have solutions that were adopted by different types of worker cooperatives around the world, assisted by legislation' (2012, p. 37).

6. 'Among the possible solutions [sub 5] are measures like asset locks and collective accumulation of capital … Such measures do not seem to hamper productivity by dampening incentives – some of the same cooperatives that have adopted these particular measures are found to be more productive (as the French cooperatives) or to preserve jobs better (as the Italian cooperatives) than conventional firms' (2012, p. 37).

7. 'Employment in a labour-managed firm is not the same thing as employment in a conventional one. In a labour-managed firm, members participate in the decisions that affect their unemployment and income risks. They are considerably better protected against the moral hazard potentially attached to management decisions over investment, strategy, or even human resource policies' (2012, pp. 37–8).

8. 'Profit may not be higher in more participatory cooperatives, but the firms may produce more and preserve their members' jobs better' (2012, p. 38).
9. 'Workers' participation in profit and in decisions makes it possible for worker cooperatives to adjust pay rather than employment in response to demand shocks' (2012, p. 38). Whereas conventional enterprises primarily adjust employment, worker cooperatives primarily adjust remuneration (2014, p. 40).
10. Recessions increase the number of firm *closures* among conventional and labour-managed enterprises alike. However, recessions decrease the number of *creations* among conventional enterprises, whereas the creations of worker cooperatives increases – that is, when the risk of job loss increases in conventional enterprises (2014, p. 41).[9]
11. 'The density of worker cooperatives in an area, year and/or industry is an important determinant of further cooperative creation' (2014, p. 43; see also Pérotin 2016, p. 17).

Drawing on over 100 studies across many countries, many of the points above are confirmed in a summary paper by Kruse (2016). A well-documented analytical literature review of the performance of WOCs, especially in face of economic globalisation, is provided by Bretos and Marcuello (2017).

(2) The productivity and investment performances of WOCs. Much of the conventional economic literature hypothesises that worker-owned cooperatives would underinvest and so generate a lower labour productivity in comparison with conventional capitalist enterprises. Because this is an important issue, this subsection presents the results of two econometric studies on the productivity and investment performances of WOCs. The first one studies the case of French cooperatives (Fakhfakh, Pérotin and Gago 2012), and the second one the case of Italian cooperatives (George, Fontanari and Tortia 2020). In my rendering of the results of these studies I adopt a mixture of implicit citations combined with terminological adaptations.

- *Fakhfakh, Pérotin and Gago 2012: Productivity, capital and labour in French labour-managed and conventional firms.* These authors compare the productivity of WOCs and CCEs using two panel data sets covering about 7,000 enterprises from France in manufacturing and services, including representative samples of CCEs and all WOCs with 20 employees or more (about 500). They present estimates of production functions industry by industry for WOCs and

---

9 On this point see more extensively Pérotin 2006.

CCEs and test for the equality of their total factor productivities. They also allow 'systematic differences in scale and technology to be determined by the ownership form'. Their method also allows 'returns to scale to vary with input levels, which makes it possible to disentangle embodied incentive effects from systematic differences in scale due to underinvestment' by WOCs. (From the abstract and introduction.)

On basis of their econometric analysis the authors draw the following conclusions.

1. WOCs are at least as productive as CCEs. However, the two types of enterprises organise production differently. WOCs use their capital and labour more effectively than CCEs. With their current levels of inputs, WOCs produce at least as much with the technology they have chosen as they would if they were using the CCE's technology. In contrast, in several industries CCEs would produce more with their current inputs if they were organising production as WOCs do.

2. The authors find no evidence that systematic differences in input levels cause the WOCs to produce at inefficiently small scale. Using the same technology, the returns to scale parameter is significantly lower in WOCs than CCEs in some industries, and both groups of enterprises operate at constant or decreasing returns in most industries. (Increasing returns to scale points at a small scale of production.)

3. Differences in the average returns to scale of both groups of enterprises between the two sample periods, which cover different parts of the business cycle, suggest both groups adjust scale in the same direction as growth slows down.

4. Univariate comparisons indicate for all industries that WOCs are not smaller or less capitalised than CCEs, that they expand their capital at least as fast and grow at least as fast as CCEs.

5. Capital intensity is often the same in the two groups of enterprises, and they adjust their capital intensity at the same rate in all industries.

6. No evidence is found of under-investment among WOCs.

7. Employment may be more stable in WOCs over the business cycle, but the differences with CCEs are only weakly significant.

(From the abstract and the conclusions.)

- *George, Fontanari and Tortia 2020: Finance, property rights and productivity in Italian cooperatives.* Regarding WOCs conventional economic theory 'predicts that the accumulation of capital by means of indivisible reserves would lead to underinvestment and undercapitalisation, due to the truncated temporal horizon of worker-members'. 'An inefficiently low stock of capital would imply, other things being equal, lower labour productivity.' (In the introduction to their paper the authors remark that Fakhfakh, Pérotin and Gago (2012) is 'one of the few contributions that have tested productivity in a systematic way.')

The authors test 'the real effects of collective capital on productivity, using a large panel of Italian worker and social cooperatives.'[10] Enterprise-level balance sheet data are used to 'estimate the effects of collective and individual reserves of capital on total factor productivity'. 'Social security data on employment contracts in all Italian enterprises' are used to measure enterprise-level full-time employment. (From the abstract.)

On basis of econometric analysis, the authors find that 'collective ownership [WOCS] and total factor productivity are positively and significantly related after controlling for factor productivity, individual capital ownership and other standard enterprise-level and sector controls. This result is robust to different specifications of the model and suggests a positive role of collective capital in strengthening financial sustainability, patrimonial and employment stability in the long run'. (From the abstract.)

More specifically the authors do 'not find that collective capital engenders under-capitalisation in terms of a too low scale of production (increasing returns to scale).' Quite the contrary: they find that 'cooperatives operate either at constant or decreasing returns to scale (they are not undercapitalised). Furthermore, correlation analysis shows that older co-ops are more capitalised than younger ones, and this implies that cooperatives do indeed increase capitalisation over long spells of time'. The authors also find that 'the correlation between collective capital and fixed assets is itself positive, implying that collective capital does not hamper the accumulation of fixed assets. Quite the contrary, it looks like that more abundant collective capital favours more investments and capitalisation, probably due to the availability of more collateral guarantees that allow the attainment of cheaper borrowing from financial institutions.' (From the Conclusions.)

---

10 11,289 cooperatives, of which 52% worker cooperatives and 48% social cooperatives (p. 13). Italian social cooperatives are multi-stakeholder cooperatives. 'Stakeholders can include paid workers, volunteers (up to 50% of cooperative members), some public institutions, outside investors (without control rights) and, importantly, beneficiaries of the cooperatives activities. ... Control rights are exercised on a one vote per member basis.' (p. 11)

Division 2. Complexities of worker-owned cooperatives' functioning within globalising capitalism: the case of Mondragon

This Division is on the Mondragon Corporation, which is the umbrella organisation for (in 2020) nearly 100 separate self-governing worker-owned cooperatives. It is the world's largest WOC group in terms of annual turnover (14.4 billion US$ in 2018, with about 81,000 employees).[11] It is the tenth-largest company in Spain and the leading one in the Basque region. The group's cooperatives operate throughout the world, with 141 production plants in 37 countries, commercial business in 53, and sales in more than 150 countries.[12]

I begin by mentioning that from the rather extensive literature on Mondragon that I have seen, I gather that all the cooperatives' characteristics that were listed in 6§3 (subsection 1, Pérotin 2012 and Pérotin 2014) generally also apply to the Mondragon cooperatives – and I will not repeat these below.

My general approach in most of this Division is to start by presenting quantitative information in the form of graphs and tables as based on the Mondragon Annual Reports 1998–2019 (from 2010 onwards the amount of information in these reports ever more decreases). The outline is restricted to observations (indirect ones as based on the Mondragon annual reports and the literature that I have seen) without normative judgement.

I will not go into the early history of Mondragon, and merely note that its first cooperative was founded in 1956. (See further Mondragon n.d., and for example Bretos, Errasti and Marcuello 2019a, pp. 10–15, extending to the after 2005 period on pp. 15–18; a briefer account is Barandiaran and Lezaun 2017, pp. 280–2.) The Division focusses on some aspects of Mondragon's development in the first two decades of the twenty-first century, and especially its (way of) employment. To put this into perspective, three brief sections set out: the organisational structure of Mondragon and its cooperatives (6§4); the ten Mondragon core principles (6§5); some general information as including on salary differences between cooperative worker-members (6§6). This is followed by three core sections: a general quantification of the amount of Mondragon employment 1983–2019 (6§7); its sales 1996–2019 (6§8); Mondragon's way of employment 2001–2019 in face of globalising capitalism's competition (6§9). This last section closes off with a 2001–2019 comparison of Spain's employment with the Mondragon employment in Spain.

---

11 See ICA and Eurice (2021, p. 62), which is about the world's top 300 cooperatives. (The worker-owned enterprise John Lewis Partnership PLC (UK) ranks second.)
12 https://www.mondragon-corporation.com/en/about-us/ (accessed 18 January 2021).

It will be seen that two important aspects of the Mondragon employment in the twentieth century are, first, its adoption of non-member workers in the Spanish cooperatives and, second, the establishment of non-cooperative foreign subsidiaries. The last two sections' considerable degree of detail serves to present a balanced account of these aspects. The chapter's concluding summary states that whereas worker-owned cooperatives are an enormously progressive phenomenon within capitalism, the capitalist surrounding limits that progression as revealed in the two mentioned aspects.

6§4 *The organisational structure of individual Mondragon cooperatives and of the Mondragon umbrella*

Mondragon consists of about 100 individual worker-owned cooperatives (around 2020) and an umbrella organisation which is also a cooperative, the individual cooperatives being its members. This umbrella organisation has formally the somewhat confusing name of 'Mondragon Corporation'. Following Ugarte, the former president of Mondragon International, I will often use the term 'Mondragon federation' (White 2015).

Each individual cooperative is an autonomous and legally independent entity; its membership of the Mondragon federation is a voluntary choice. Worker-members of individual cooperatives create the entity, or join it, by contributing an amount of capital. The amount of contribution is decided by each cooperative's General Assembly and it varies by cooperative. *Scheme 6.6* and *Scheme 6.7* set out the organisational template for the individual Mondragon cooperatives and of the Mondragon federation.

SCHEME 6.6 *The organisational structure of individual Mondragon cooperatives (↓e stands for elect; ↓a stands for appoint)*

General Assembly of worker-members (GA) supreme body; one member one vote
competences:
• formulation of the cooperative's strategy;[13]
• election of the three bodies below.†

↓e **Governing Council (GC)** • worker-members elected by the GA; • the standing governing body of the coop; • makes important decisions in consultation with the SC (see right-hand side). *tasks:* • overseeing the fulfilment of the policies agreed by the GA; • selection and appointment of the management.	↓e **Social Council (SC)** • worker-members elected by the GA; • represents the interests of coop members as employees. *tasks/competences:* • consultative body for the GC; • counterbalances the managerial focus of the GC and the MC. (The SC's strength varies per cooperative.)
↓a **Management council (MC)** (multi-person body; for small coops one general manager) • in many cases recruited from an external (sometimes non-cooperative) institution.‡	

↓e

Monitoring Committee
supervisory body; tasks: arbitration and auditing

† 'With the exception of the most senior executive position, all the other members of these bodies are elected on an unpaid basis and for a specific term of office.' (Mondragon 2009, p. 53)
‡ Recall that in Design cooperatives the management is always elected from the ranks of members (2§5.0).

Source: Compiled on basis of Mondragon, Annual Report 2009, p. 53, and Barandiaran and Lezaun 2017, p. 283.

---

13 'Every significant strategic or social issue – such as an acquisition, extended work hours, or a salary reduction in an economic downturn – must be voted on in the General Assembly.' (White 2015, p. 2.)

SCHEME 6.7 *Main organisational structure of the Mondragon Corporation (from 1991)* (↓e *stands for elect;* ↓a *stands for appoint*)

Mondragon Corporation		Sector groups of individual coops
Cooperative Congress (CC) • body that ultimately decides on the Mondragon policy; • meets at least once every four years; • the 650 delegates to the CC are chosen by the members of the individual cooperatives.		An individual cooperative's membership of Mondragon is a voluntary choice; it is also free to quit.
		The Governing councils of individual coops (Scheme 6.6) elect a '**sector council**' (sectors such as construction, industrial automation or retail).‡
		↓e
Standing Committee of Mondragon (SCM)† • oversees the implementation of the policies agreed by the Congress; • appoints the council below.	←e ←a	**Sector councils** • joint councils elect SCM members (at least 50%) and appoint other members.
		Sector groups are organised in four **divisions** (finance, industry, retail, knowledge).
↓a **Mondragon General Council** • executive body of Mondragon; • consists of a president, of vice-presidents representing the divisions, and of managing directors.		
↓a **Operational Management**		

† In 2019 it had 19 voting members (Mondragon Annual Report 2019, p. 8).
‡ The councils also appoint a management of the sector group (manages central services for a group).
Source: Compiled on basis of Mondragon, Annual Report 2009, p. 52; Barandiaran and Lezaun (2017, p. 283); Surroca, Garcia-Cestona and Santamaría (2006, p. 8).

6§5 The ten 1987 principles of Mondragon

At Mondragon's Cooperative Congress of 1987 the federation's 'basic principles' were approved.[14] Below these are taken over from Barandiaran and Lezaun (2017, pp. 281–2, with some textual changes).

1. *Free membership:* for cooperatives that want to be part of Mondragon there are no barriers to membership, provided they respect its basic principles;
2. *Democratic organisation:* equality of worker-members, expressed in the election of the cooperative's representative bodies (one member, one vote);
3. *Sovereignty of labour:* labour is the transformative factor in society and in human beings and is therefore the basis for the distribution of wealth;
4. *The instrumental and subordinated character of capital:* capital is an instrument, and should be subordinated to labour;
5. *Self-management:* worker-members should be provided with opportunities and mechanisms to participate in the management of the cooperative;
6. *Pay solidarity:* a fair and equitable return for labour;
7. *Inter-cooperation:* a commitment to cooperation among the individual cooperatives;
8. *Social transformation:* a commitment to transform society by pursuing a future of liberty, justice, and solidarity;
9. *Universalism:* the Mondragon constellation is part of the broader search for peace, justice, and development of the international cooperative movement;
10. *Education:* a commitment to dedicate the necessary human and economic resources to cooperative education.

Barandiaran and Lezaun (2017, p. 282) remark that 'while the founding generation saw these ten principles as the enunciation of a lived experience of cooperative life, younger cohorts of worker-members increasingly treat them as part of Mondragon's corporate self-presentation.'

6§6 Worker-member salaries and paid-in capital, and inter-cooperative solidarity funds

The first three points below regard worker-*members* of the Mondragon cooperatives (6§9 expands on non-members). As in most of this Division, I begin with information from inside Mondragon. The information below is from a 2015 interview with Josu Ugarte, at the time the president of Mondragon International (Pizzigati 2015).

---

14 Mondragon (n.d.), history.

- The maximum salary differences within the individual Mondragon cooperatives amount to 1:6.[15] (For the corporations listed in the Spanish IBEX 35 stock market index the average compensation difference is 1:105 [around 2015].)
- The lowest paid Mondragon associate makes in 2015 about €28,000 [in 2015 this was three times the Spanish minimum wage].[16]
- The maximum compensation difference *between* cooperatives is 38%. This implies that between cooperatives the compensation difference for a top manager cannot exceed 38%.

    Interviewer: 'So where do your executives come from?' Ugarte: 'we give a lot of training for our people ... In this environment, we get all our executives from inside. We promote from within.[17] We have more than 100 Mondragon cooperative companies and over 240 associated entities, so we have a lot of opportunities in different companies to promote. We have many people moving inside Mondragon.' Interviewer: 'Mondragon operates within a globalized world economy. What would happen if executives within Mondragon started arguing that your enterprise could no longer be globally competitive with a one-to-six pay gap?' Ugarte: 'To modify the gap would take a vote in the General Assembly, our cooperative's congress. So it would not be easy to have the congress of Mondragon approving this kind of modification.'
- To become an associate of a cooperative a worker-member has to pay-in capital. 'We are all owners. As cooperativists, we all have capital, equity, in our company. This equity starts now with 15,000 euros [2015].' Cooperatives allow this sum to be paid in 24 monthly instalments from the worker's salary.[18] 'This

---

15 According to Barandiaran and Lezaun (2017, p. 284) the maximum ratio is 9:1 in gross terms, the after-tax ratio being close to 1:6.5. According to Herrera (2004, p. 7) the before-tax ratios range from 3:1 to 9:1 in different cooperatives and average 5:1. Flecha and Santa Cruz (2011, p. 161) write: 'Currently, the top salary at MC is six times that of the lowest worker, except that a few CEOs may earn up to 9 times the salary of the ordinary worker. At most of the cooperatives the ratio is far lower.' Arando, Freundlich, Gago, Jones and Kato (2011, pp. 30–1) write that from 2002 the maximum ratio is 8.9:1 but that most cooperatives maintain 5:1 as a maximum.

16 In 2015 the Spanish annual minimum wage stood at €9,080. https://www.citizensadvice.org.es/faq/minimum-wage-for-2015-2016-2017-2018-2019-2020/.

17 See also Arando, Freundlich, Gago, Jones and Kato (2011, pp. 35–7). However, Bretos, Errasti and Marcuello (2019b, p. 13) mention that from about 1990 onwards, 'many Mondragon cooperatives have hired external managers who are more committed to efficiency than to the cooperative culture and social objectives'.

18 These contributions are decided on by a cooperative's General Assembly and vary by cooperative.

equity grows over time, as our enterprises within Mondragon have profits. So we have, in effect, three kinds of income at Mondragon: our salaries, the growth in our equity in the company, and the interest Mondragon pays on that equity.'[19]

The next information is similarly from a 2015 interview with Josu Ugarte (White 2015).

• One quarter of the profits of each member-cooperative is used to support the well-being of the entire Mondragon federation. Of which 3/5 is used to compensate losses experienced by other members, 1/5 is used to support innovation by funding technology centres and university education, and 1/5 supports an Investment Fund that helps members to internationalise their business. (The technology centres operate as cooperatives and help members to compete in an increasingly technology-driven global economy.) Between cooperatives there is a commitment to employment relocation in case a cooperative would go bankrupt.[20,21]

6§7 The course of Mondragon's employment: general quantification 1983–2019

Mondragon is organised in four main divisions: industry, retail, finance, and knowledge. Qua employment the first two are the major ones (in 2019 together 96% of the total). Many industrial cooperatives encompass – gradually increasing from 1989 – production plants abroad (6§8–6§9).

So as to put the next sections into perspective, the following two figures present for the period 1983–2019 Mondragon's total employment and its Spanish employment, in comparison with the employment of Spain and the aggregate of OECD countries.

Thus whereas in the period 1983–2019 the Mondragon employment *in Spain* outran that of Spain by a factor of 3.4, it outran that of the OECD countries by a factor of 6.3.

Comparatively this is rather successful. Mondragon also created employment abroad (*Table 6.8*, rows 1 minus 2), but to an unknown extent this also applies for Spain and the other OECD countries.

---

19   When a member-worker retires, the nominal value of the capital paid-in is reimbursed.
20   On the 'profit pooling' and the employment relocation see also Arando, Freundlich, Gago, Jones and Kato (2011, pp. 33–5).
21   Next to the profit allocation above, there are also general rules for the allocation of the remaining part of profits within individual cooperatives – the largest part of these profits stays in the cooperatives (Flecha and Santa Cruz 2011, p. 160).

TABLE 6.8 *Employment of Mondragon, Spain and the aggregate of OECD countries: growth 1983–2019*

		1983	2019	Growth
1	Mondragon total employment	18,744	81,507	335%
2	Mondragon employment in Spain†	18,744	67,052	258%
3	Employment Spain (× 1000)	11,323	19,779	75%
4	Employment OECD countries (× 1000)‡	316,570	447,623	41%

† In 1983 all Mondragon employment was employment in Spain.[22]
‡ Regards the 21 countries that were OECD member in 1983, and for which OECD data are available for the full period.[23]
Data sources columns 1983 and 2019. Rows 1–2: compiled from Mondragon (1998–2019); Rows 3–4: OECD Statistics.[24]

Graph 6.9 (p. 266) shows the development of Mondragon's total employment from 1983, together with Spain's employment calibrated on 1983.[25]

It can be seen from *Graph 6.9* that compared with Spain, Mondragon took longer to recover from the international banking crisis and its aftermath, which has to do with the different sector composition of the Spanish economy and Mondragon (see the first sentence of the current section).

For the next section it is relevant to distinguish the total Mondragon employment by its divisions – see *Graph 6.10*. (The financial division includes banking, insurance and social security, and the corporate division includes technology centres as well as other knowledge related cooperatives including a university.)

---

22 Mondragon's first production plant abroad dates from 1989 (Luzarraga 2008, p. 82). In 1995 there were five plants abroad (Errasti, Heras, Bakaikoa and Elgoibar 2003, p. 558) and up to 2019 their number had grown to 141. In 2019 82% of the total Mondragon employment is employment in Spain.
23 These 21 countries are Australia, Austria, Belgium, Canada, Denmark, Finland, France, Germany, Greece, Iceland, Ireland, Italy, Japan, Netherlands, New Zealand, Norway, Portugal, Spain, Sweden, UK and USA. For individual countries the growth percentages range from 8% (Finland) to 113% (New Zealand), Spain ranks with 75% in the top 6. The countries that were member in 1983 but for which early data are missing are Luxembourg, Switzerland and Turkey.
24 https://stats.oecd.org/ (accessed 13-05-2021): Labour/Labour force statistics/Annual LFS/Summary tables/Employment.
25 The first Mondragon cooperative was founded in 1956 and in 1968 the group's then existing co-operatives encompassed about 6,000 worker-members (Mondragon, n.d., history). Thomas and Logan (1982, pp. 46–7) provide data on the employment in industrial cooperatives in the period 1956–1977.

Note that the employment downturn after 2007 is a result of the international banking crisis and its aftermath (for Spain also visible in Graph 6.9).

GRAPH 6.9 *Total employment Mondragon in comparison with that of Spain: 1983–2019*

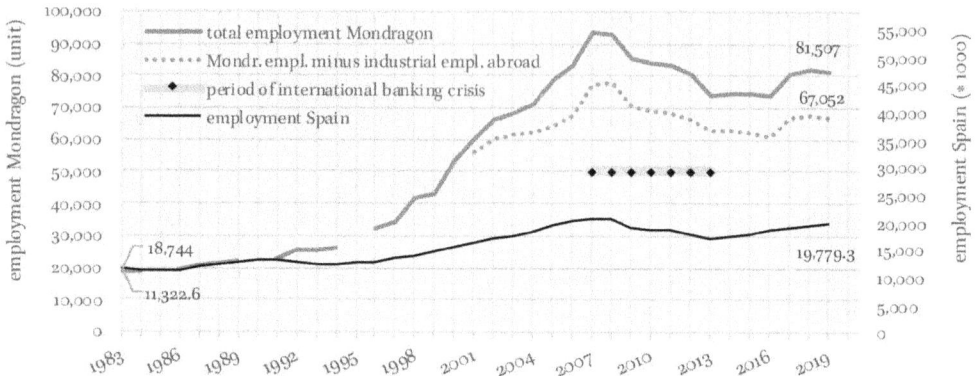

The total Mondragon employment includes employment abroad (expanded on below). The dotted line shows the total minus the industrial employment abroad. Note that because the scale of Spain's employment is 1,000 times larger than Mondragon's, Spain's variations are less visible.
Data sources. Employment Mondragon. Compiled from Mondragon (1998–2019); annual reports. Data from before 1998 were collected from these reports when they were given, whence before 1998 there are some data gaps. *Employment Spain.* OECD Statistics (as for Table 6.8).

GRAPH 6.10 *Employment Mondragon Corporation by divisions 1996–2019*

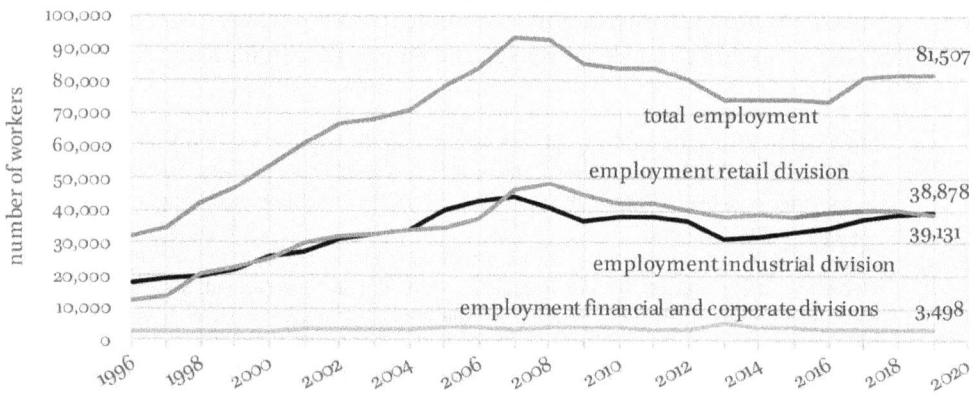

Data source. Compiled from the annual reports Mondragon Corporation 1996–2019. The figures for the financial and corporate divisions are derived (total minus retail and industrial). The figure for the retail division 2016 has been interpolated because for that year the annual report provides no datum.

6§8   Mondragon's sales 1996–2019

This section provides information on the sales of Mondragon's retail and industrial divisions. *Graphs 6.11 and 6.12* show their sales from 1996–2019, focussing especially on the international sales, which in the Mondragon annual reports includes not only exports but also the sales by subsidiaries abroad.[26] Throughout this period many of the industrial cooperatives increasingly opened subsidiary production plants abroad.

GRAPH 6.11   *Mondragon total sales and its industrial international sales 1996–2019*

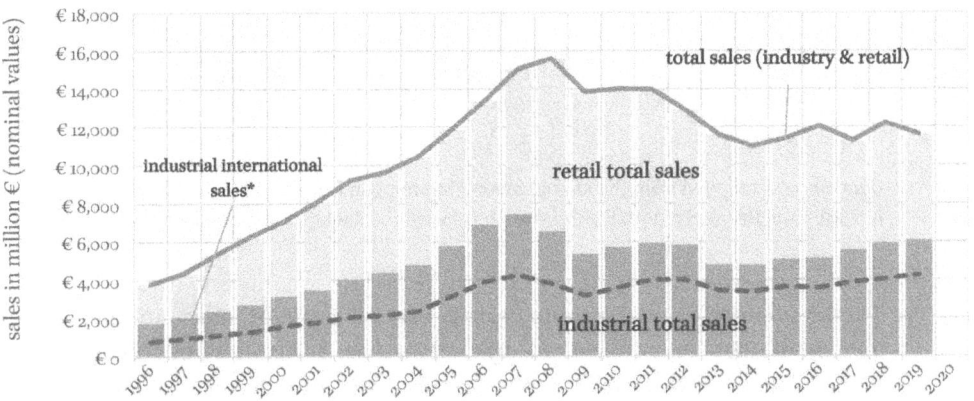

* Industrial international sales regard exports plus sales generated from production plants abroad.
Data source: see Graph 6.12.

The top line of *Graph 6.11* shows the downturn in the total Mondragon sales during the international banking crisis (starting end 2007); it is reflected in the employment fall that was shown in *Graph 6.10*. It should be noted that especially in the Eurozone (EMU) of the European Union, the banking crisis of 2007–2013 moved over to a (sovereign) debt crises with a recessive government expenditure cutback aftermath, which resulted in a continuation of the home downturn in sales (2014–2016). It will be seen in 6§9 why the sales of the retail division slugged beyond this period.

Graph 6.12 shows that from 1996–2019 Mondragon's proportion of the industrial international sales (exports, and sales of subsidiaries abroad) in the total industrial sales considerably increases. For exports this trend set in during the

---

26   See, e.g., the annual report 1998, p. 17.

run-up to the 1986 Spanish membership of the European Union (at the time the 'European Economic Community'); foreign subsidiaries were opened from 1989.

GRAPH 6.12   *Mondragon's industrial international sales proportions 1996–2019*

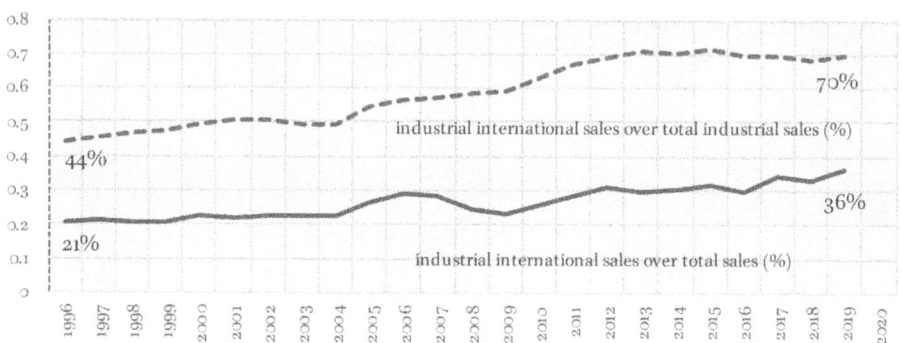

Date source: Compiled from the annual reports Mondragon Corporation 1998–2019. Data 1996–1997 are from the 1998 report. For the year 2007 I used the data as revised in the annual report of 2008.

The Mondragon annual reports provide alas no separate information on the *amount* of sales (or employment) by cooperatives, as distinct from their subsidiaries. *Table 6.13* collects all the available information in the annual reports on the *number* of Mondragon cooperatives and subsidiaries (the 2016–2019 reports provide no information on this). Foreign subsidiaries (column 3) regard mainly industrial production plants.[27] Home subsidiaries regard mainly retail entities.

Table 6.13 shows that from 1998–2015 the number of production plants abroad (subsidiaries) increased by a factor 13 (from 17 to 128), exceeding the total number of cooperatives (industry and retail) from 2013. The table also shows, perhaps more remarkably, the large number of subsidiaries in Spain (columns 2 minus 3), of which a large amount are subsidiaries of the retail cooperative Eroski.[28]

---

27   In 2012 – the last year for which this information is available – the retail division had no subsidiaries abroad; during some time earlier, it had 22 establishments in France.
28   In 2019 the number of its subsidiaries amounted to 27 (Eroski Group 2020, p. 15). In that year the group encompassed 36% of the total Mondragon employment. (For comparison: this is as much as 74% of the employment of the national and international industry division.)

TABLE 6.13 *Number of Mondragon cooperatives and subsidiaries 1998–2020*

	Cooperatives	Subsidiaries (columns 2 to 5)			
		Total: national & international[29]	Production plants abroad	Proportion foreign over total	Proportion total over no. cooperatives
	(1)	(2)	(3)	(4)	(5)
1998	note[30]		17[31]		
1999			23		
2000			26		
2001			34		
2002					
2003			38		
2004			48		
2005	108	138	57	41%	128%
2006	107	126	65	52%	118%
2007	106	136	69	51%	128%
2008	106	129	73	57%	122%
2009			75		
2010			77		
2011	111	143	94	66%	129%
2012	110	147	105	71%	134%
2013	103		122		
2014	103		125		
2015	101[32]		128		
2020	96		141		

Data sources: 1998–2015, compiled from the annual reports Mondragon Corporation 1998–2020 (no information for 2016–19); 2020, Mondragon n.d., *About us.* https://www.mondragon-corporation.com/en/about-us/ (accessed 5 March 2021).

29   Some of the national subsidiaries are 'mixed cooperatives' – see Flecha and Ngai (2014, pp. 673–6) and Bretos, Errasti and Marcuello (2019a, p. 16). A 'mixed cooperative' is in principle self-governing, but the parent cooperative is a shareholder (which should safeguard its original financial investment).
30   Luzarraga (2008, p. 144) mentions that 14 industrial cooperatives were founded during 1956–1966, and 80 during 1965–1983.
31   Mondragon's first production plant abroad dates from 1989 (Luzarraga 2008, p. 82). In 1995 there were five (Errasti, Heras, Bakaikoa and Elgoibar 2003, p. 558).
32   Bretos and Errasti (2018, p. 5) mention that in 2015 the *industrial division* alone consisted

Regarding the number of cooperatives in column 1: one main cooperative went bankrupt – Fagor Electrodomésticos in 2013; other declines in the number may result from mergers between cooperatives, or from cooperatives leaving Mondragon. Errasti, Bretos and Nunez (2017, p. 4) mention that prior to the Fagor case the Mondragon group 'had an excellent survival record of firms with practically no demise'.

6§9   Mondragon's way of employment in face of globalising capitalism's competition

This section – the core one of this Division – returns to the Mondragon employment. Its focus is quantitative, complemented by qualitative information from the literature. As before, the quantitative information is mainly based on the Mondragon annual reports. Although, in terms of employment (and most of the time also in terms of sales) the retail and industry divisions are about equally large, for a to me unknown reason the reports devote relatively minor space to the retail division – also regarding data. The section is devised in four subsections.
(1)   Types of employment by the Mondragon entities.
(2)   Retail cooperatives: worker-members and other employment.
(3)   Industrial cooperatives: worker-members and other employment.
(4)   Comparative employment performance of Spain and aggregate Mondragon entities in the first two decades of the twenty-first century.

(1) Types of employment by the Mondragon entities. As an introduction to, and organising framework for, the remainder of this section, *Table 6.14* outlines Mondragon's main legal entities and their types of employment. The legal entities range from 'straight worker-owned cooperatives' and 'hybrid cooperatives' to 'non-cooperative subsidiaries'. The types of employment range from those of 'worker-members' to various kinds of 'temporary employment'.

---

of 68 cooperatives of which about half controlled a total of 128 subsidiaries abroad, all of which are non-cooperative entities. Bretos, Errasti and Marcuello (2019a, p. 7) indicate for the year 2016 the same number of industrial cooperatives as controlling 140 subsidiaries abroad.

TABLE 6.14 *Main Mondragon legal entities and their types of employment* †

Employment by legal entity	Possible types of employment					
	Full or partially worker-owned					Subs.
	(1)	(2)	(3)	(4)	(5)	(6)
	Ownership related: worker-members	Voluntary non-members	Aspirant worker-members on probation	Temporary worker-members	Other temporary employment by cooperatives	Fixed or temporary employment by subsidiaries
WOCs (straight) and hybrid cooperatives						
1 straight worker-owned cooperatives (WOCs)	x	x	x	x	x	
2 hybrid worker- and consumer-owned co-operatives: applies to most of the retail division	x	x	x	x	x	
3 hybrid worker-owned cooperative: mixed parent WOC-owned and local worker-owned	x	x	x	x	x	
subsidiaries of WOCs						
4 *partial subsidiary:* mixed ownership by parent WOC and other (non-worker) co-owning financiers						x
5 *full subsidiary:* parent WOC-owned						x
6 *full subsidiary variant:* idem, with local workers' participation in the management						x

† Rows 2 and 3 show the main cooperative mixtures.

Remarks on Table 6.14.
• *Row 1. Straight worker-owned cooperatives (WOCs).* Applies (around 2020) only to cooperatives in Spain.

• *Row 2. Hybrid worker- and consumer-owned cooperatives.* Applies to the major part of the retail division (Spain), specifically to the Eroski Group, which in 2019 employed together with its subsidiaries 36% of the total Mondragon employment (Eroski Group 2020, pp. 11 and 15).

• *Row 3. Hybrid worker-owned cooperatives: mixed parent woc-owned and local worker-owned.* Applies currently only to (part of the) cooperatives in Spain. These mixed cooperatives are in principle self-governing, but the parent cooperative is a shareholder – which should safeguard its original financial investment (Flecha and Ngai 2014, pp. 673–6).[33]

• *Row 4. Partial subsidiary: mixed ownership by parent woc and other (non-worker) co-owning financiers.* These co-financiers can also be (non-parent) other Mondragon cooperatives. Applies to domestic subsidiaries, though currently mainly to industrial subsidiaries abroad (Arando, Freundlich, Gago, Jones and Kato 2011, pp. 28–9).

• *Row 5. Full subsidiary: parent woc-owned.* Applies to domestic subsidiaries, though from about 2011 predominantly to industrial subsidiaries abroad.

• *Row 6. Full subsidiary: parent woc-owned;* variant with local worker's participation in the management. Regards domestic and foreign subsidiaries, in application of Mondragon's 'corporate management model' (Flecha and Ngai 2014, pp. 676–8; regarding foreign subsidiaries see also Bretos and Errasti 2018, p. 10).

• *Column 1. Ownership related: worker-members.* The next two subsections expand on the proportion of worker-members.

• *Column 2. Voluntary non-members.* Workers may refrain from membership in face of the capital to be paid in, and other cooperative duties such as payment reduction in an economic downturn. Fixed contracts for these non-members are not excluded (this is practice in especially the retail division).

• *Column 3. Aspirant worker-members on probation.* This is a functional type of employment, as aspirant worker-members have to fit the collaborative and governance culture of the regarding cooperative (mentioned by Flecha and Santa Cruz 2011, p. 161; see also Arando, Gago, Jones and Kato 2015, pp. 6–7). In periods of considerable employment growth (such as from 1999–2007) this category will be substantial.

• *Column 4. Temporary worker-members.* This category was created in 1993. The duration of this membership is maximum five years, and no more than 20% of a cooperative's full membership can consist of temporary members. These

---

33 The authors remark that 'the creation of mixed cooperatives brings the Mondragon cooperatives closer to their aim of not only expanding their economic activities but also their cooperativist values and culture.' (p. 674.)

have most of the same rights as full members (they share in surpluses based on the individual's salary, and may vote for and can serve on elected bodies) – their membership fee is 10% of the full membership fee. However, they do not have job security. (Arando, Freundlich, Gago, Jones and Kato 2011, p. 32; Flecha and Santa Cruz 2011, p. 161.)

• *Column 5. Other temporary employment by cooperatives* – mentioned by, e.g., Barandiaran and Lezaun 2017, p. 287. This category, and the following one, has evoked quite some critical attention from inside Mondragon[34] and from other commentators.[35]

• *Column 6. Fixed or temporary employment by subsidiaries*. There is an enormous amount of literature on this category. Some of it will be referred to in following two subsections.

Generally a handicap for the current section is that on the column categories above 'precise longitudinal data are hard to come by' (Arando et al. 2011, p. 17).

The following two subsections take retail and industrial cooperatives separately. On the two together, the authors just quoted mention that by 1990 non-member workers in cooperatives comprised 10% of the total (p. 18), and that, at least by 2011, these 'receive an annual profit share of, at a minimum, 25% of the share a worker-member at the same pay grade would receive' (p. 18).

(2) *Retail cooperatives: worker-members and other employment.* Mondragon's retail division consists of two cooperative groups: the Erkop Group and the Eroski Group.[36] In face of the available data I focus below on the latter, which around 2020 encompasses about 75% of this division's employment. Herewith Eroski is the largest cooperative group of Mondragon in toto (in 2019 it employed 36% of Mondragon's total employment). In Deloitte's world top 250 largest retailers it ranks 193rd with in 2018 a revenue of $5.3bn. (Deloitte 2020, p. 19).[37] Eroski is a hybrid worker- and consumer-owned cooper-

---

34 Referred to by e.g. Arando, Freundlich, Gago, Jones and Kato (2011, pp. 18–19).
35 See the references by Heras-Saizarbitoria (2014, p. 4), and more recently Kasmir (2016a and 2016b) – see also the comment on her 2016b by Santa Cruz and Alonso 2016.
36 In the academic literature that I have seen, there is hardly any information on the Erkop Group apart from that it operates in the agri-food and services sectors. Its website mentions that it encompasses four cooperatives with a total employment of 9,500 persons (https://erkop.coop/; accessed 20 February 2021).
37 In that year it ranked as the 5th largest retailer in Spain. In 2009 it was the 3rd largest in Spain, with a 76th place on the Deloitte ranking (Arando, Freundlich, Gago, Jones and Kato 2011, p. 9).

ative.[38] Its Governing Council is made up of 12 members elected by the General Assembly; six of these come from the group of consumer-members, and the other half from the group of employees. The General Assembly is composed jointly by 250 Consumer Partner representatives and 250 Employee Partner representatives. (Eroski Group 2020, p. 26.)

Whereas the Mondragon annual reports from 2006 present information on the percentage of cooperative worker-members of the *industrial* division (see the next subsection), the information on worker-members in cooperatives of the retail division is most scarce.[39] For this division only four data on the proportion of worker-members are provided (2002 and 2003 each 41%; and 37% in 2005; for 2013 there is one datum on the Eroski group: 34%).

GRAPH 6.15   *Proportion of worker-members in the retail division employment: Eroski Group, 2000–2019*

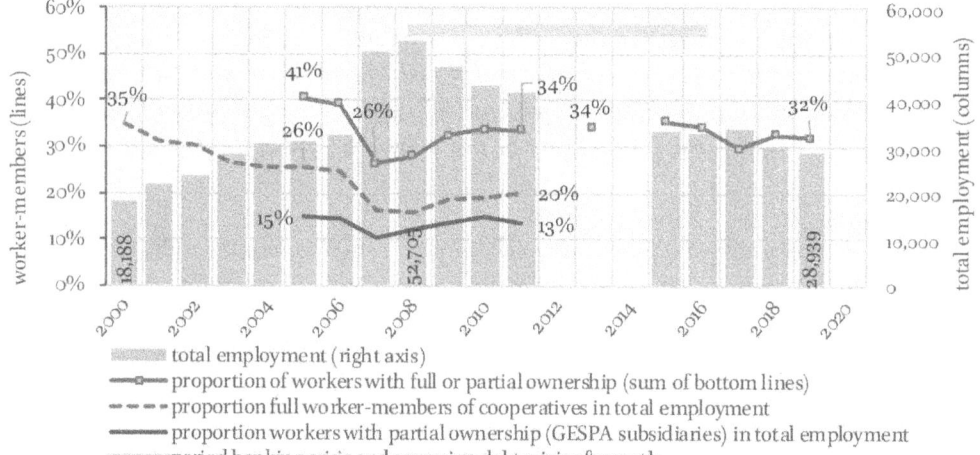

total employment (right axis)
—□— proportion of workers with full or partial ownership (sum of bottom lines)
– – – proportion full worker-members of cooperatives in total employment
——— proportion workers with partial ownership (GESPA subsidiaries) in total employment
period banking crisis and sovereign debt crisis aftermath

Data sources. 2000–2011: Storey, Basterretxea and Salaman (2014, p. 12); 2015–2019: Eroski Group, annual reports.[40] The 2013 datum is from the Mondragon annual report.

Graph 6.15 presents – based on other sources – information on the proportion of worker-members in Eroski's total employment. The incomplete top line of this graph is the sum of the two bottom lines (also incomplete). Before comment-

38   Though it tends to advertise itself as consumer cooperative. Which is not odd given that (in 2019) it had next to 9,258 'Employee Partners', 1,228,830 'Consumer Partners' (Eroski Group 2020, p. 24).
39   As already mentioned, the information in the annual reports on the retail division is generally minor relative to the industrial division.
40   After comparing the Storey et al. data for the total employment (columns) with those of

ing on these, it is relevant to note first that the Eroski Group was heavily hit by the 2007/08 banking crisis and its aftermath (that applies to most enterprises) especially because of its enormous amount of debt-financed acquisitions just prior to it – the burden of which required 15 years of continuous restructuring (reflected in the employment downfall shown in the blue columns of the graph).[41]

Along with the mentioned acquisitions (mainly non-cooperative subsidiaries) the proportion of the worker-members dropped from 41% in 2005 to 26% in 2008 – see the top line. The acquisitions accelerated in 2007–08, but had continuously moved up in the period before it – see the blue columns 2000–06. Arando, Freundlich, Gago, Jones and Kato (2011, p. 19) mention that the acquisitions (starting in the 1990s) were a 'response to competitive pressures, especially from large French chains', whence 'the need to expand quickly and substantially ... was pressing' and that 'Eroski felt it was potentially too slow, risky, and complicated to expand by using cooperative legal structures'.

Next to the regular (full) worker-owners/members of its cooperatives (the dotted line in Graph 6.15), Eroski established in the late 1990s a voluntary, partial employee-ownership structure – called GESPA (see the bottom line of the graph) – aiming for these to become full members at a later stage (Arando et al. 2011, p. 20).[42] The year 2017 was the last time that in the Eroski annual reports the GESPA category was mentioned (with a minor number of 486), which – given the worker-member percentages of the (broken) top line of Graph 6.15 – probably means that the former partial members have become full members (as was the intention). Flecha and Ngai (2014, p. 676) mention that in face of concern about worker participation in its subsidiaries, it was decided at the group's 'General Assembly in 2009, by a vote of 77.5%, to offer all workers at its

---

the total Retail Division as stated in the Mondragon annual reports (in FTE), it seems that the Storey et al. data are in 'persons' rather than FTE. (For a number of years – e.g. 2008, p. 29 – the Mondragon reports provide both data, each for Eroski and Erkop separately.) Supposing that the Storey et al. membership data are also in persons, this may not very much affect the membership percentages.

41 The debt finance was in 2019 still a big problem. The Eroski annual report 2019 (p. 22) mentions 'a restructuring agreement for its financial debt to banks' giving 'financial coverage until 2024 ... without the obligation to make divestments'.

42 Arando, Gago, Jones and Kato (2015, pp. 8–9) mention that the (non-full) GESPA members require a membership capital stake that is about half as large as in a cooperative; this represents about 25% of the average annual earnings for workers in a GESPA store. They also mention that 'membership in GESPA, as with membership in cooperatives, provides what is effectively 100% job security – no GESPA members have ever been laid off, and in the few instances of GESPA store closures, members have always been offered alternative employment nearby.'

related capitalist companies [subsidiaries] the opportunity to become worker-owners in mixed cooperatives'. (According to the annual report 2019 all the Eroski cooperatives are mixed worker-consumer cooperatives.)

I consider that this opportunity for all workers to become worker-owners in the mixed cooperatives is an important principle, one that does not apply for much of the industrial division. Nevertheless the current worker-member percentage of just over 30% seems very low. This may have to do with the branch and with the capital that full members have to pay-in (which in 2009 amounted to about 30% of the average annual remuneration in an Eroski store – Arando, Gago, Jones and Kato 2015, p. 7). But even in case the latter would be no hindrance, given that Eroski allows the capital to be paid in five-year instalments, general risk aversion – as including the for members possible wage decreases in an economic downturn – might be a hindrance.

Finally, I mention from the annual report 2019 that 76% of the employees had a permanent contract; that the salary range of the group was 1:8.2; that the minimum salary was 8.6% higher than the minimum inter-professional salary in Spain; and that there is no salary difference between men and women. (Eroski Group 2020, pp. 56–9 and 64–5.)

(3) Industrial cooperatives: worker-members and other employment. In 1989 two Mondragon industrial cooperatives started to locate production abroad and since then their number and the number of foreign locations has steadily increased (6§8, Table 6.13, column 3). Before getting to the proportion of worker-members in the industrial cooperatives some preparatory information is provided.

National and international employment of the industry division. Graph 6.16 (p. 277) shows the national and international employment of Mondragon's industry division from 2001–2019. The reason why this graph does not (and cannot) provide information on employment within industrial *cooperatives* will be explained later on.

It can be seen from the percentages at the bottom of Graph 6.16 that in 2006 and 2007, just prior to the banking-induced recession, the international industrial employment share stood at 37% (1 -63%). During the recession period it increased to a maximum of 40% (2011). From 2017–2019 it is back to the 37% level. Thus in a way the international subsidiaries modified the recession's employment downturn for Mondragon as a whole (there are quite some subsidiaries in countries that were not/less hit by the banking crisis) – at least until 2013. From 2007 to 2013 the industrial employment abroad dropped from 16,580 to 11,012 (-34%). In the same period home employment dropped from 27,700 to 19,889 (-28%).

GRAPH 6.16 *National and international employment of Mondragon's industry division 2001–2019*

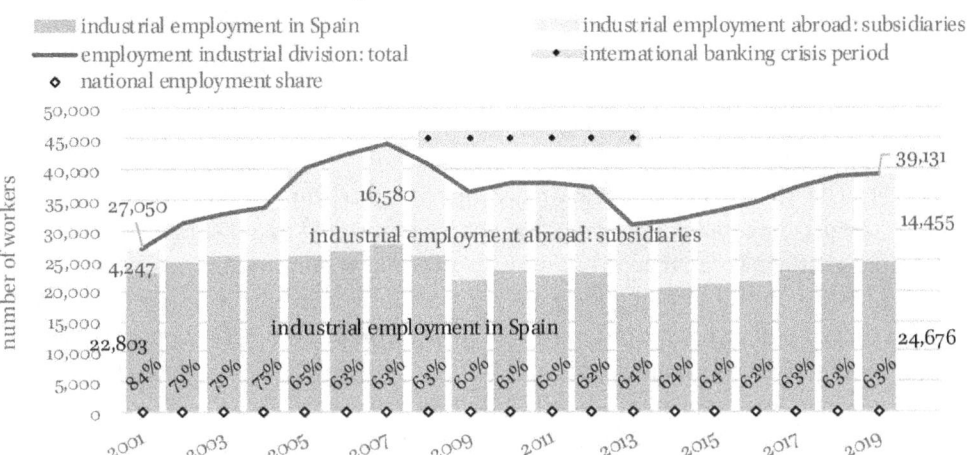

Note on 'Industrial employment abroad'. These data are available for 2012–2019. However, for 2001–2011 there are data on the total employment abroad. I have used these as a proxy for the industrial employment because the foreign retail employment is relatively minor.[43]

Data source. Compiled from the annual reports Mondragon Corporation 2001–2019. The data for the year 2007 are those as revised in the annual report of 2008.

International employment strategy in face of economic globalisation. The total industrial employment increased by 45% from 2001 to 2019. In the same period the national Mondragon industrial employment increased by 8%, and the international employment more than tripled (growth 240%). These figures reveal the employment strategy in this period by about half of the industrial cooperatives, that is, to found or acquire subsidiary companies abroad, with the intention of maintaining the home cooperative employment. This strategy was quite independent of the 'great recession', as can be seen from the run-up to the foreign top employment in 2007 (16,580 workers). It was rather the general response – from the last decade of the twentieth century – of multi-nationalising cooperatives to international competitive pressures in face of economic globalisation.[44] Ugarte, the former president of Mondragon Interna-

---

43 Moreover, I have adopted the information provided by Bretos and Errasti (2018, p. 5) that there are no Mondragon cooperatives abroad (only subsidiaries). However, at least in the annual reports this is never *explicitly* stated (nor denied).

44 Two cooperatives multi-nationalised in 1989, and in 2006 their number had grown to 25 (Luzarraga 2008, pp. 81–2). In 2015 'about 30 industrial co-ops (out of a total of 68) are multinational companies that control 128 productive subsidiaries abroad, all of which are non-cooperative firms' (Bretos and Errasti 2018, p. 5).

tional, remarks about it in a 2015 interview: 'We have compared our companies that invest abroad with the companies that stayed in the Basque country. Our multi-localised companies increased all their figures, and the companies that did not multi-localize lost employment at home.' [45,46] Being questioned about the salaries of these workers abroad, Ugarte replies: 'For the worker salaries, we pay higher than the local society norm. We always pay higher than the prevailing wage.' (Interview by Pizzigati 2015, p. 4.)

The objective of the Mondragon international employment in function of the parent cooperatives' employment is often stated as a distinguishing characteristic in comparison with multi-nationalising mainstream capitalist enterprises – the latter being indifferent as to where workers produce the surplus that capital owners appropriate. Obviously worker-owners of cooperatives are not indifferent, as relocation would affect their job (the same applies for workers in mainstream enterprises, but they do not decide).

Ugarte: 'Employment creation and preservation, at whatever scale, is deeply embedded in the culture of coops. When workers are owners, closure of any operation – even one with limited profitability – is a last resort, pursued only when a facility endangers the survival of the larger enterprise. (…) When opportunities arise in another country, Mondragon's strategy is not to relocate an existing facility there, but, instead, to maintain the Spanish operation and to acquire or build a new facility abroad. This is quite different from the behaviour of US and UK companies, for example, which have been moving domestic operations overseas for decades.' (Interview by White 2015, pp. 3–4.) Errasti, Bretos and Nunez (2017, p. 8) confirm that mostly only production that was no longer profitable or feasible in the parent cooperative was transferred to foreign subsidiaries. Similarly Bretos and Erasti (2018, p. 8) indicate that 'unlike the offshoring model practiced by many capitalist multinationals, the Mondragon cooperatives have expanded … [in] new emerging markets, without that meaning the closure of plants and the destruction of jobs in the Basque Country.'

On this multi-national employment strategy see also Luzarraga (2008, conclusions pp. 408–24); Flecha and Ngai (2014, pp. 668–9) and Bretos, Errasti and Marcuello (2019b, pp. 5–6, 10–11 and 17).

---

45   Flecha and Ngai (2014, p. 670) mention that between the periods 1990/95 and 2005/10 employment in non-internationalising cooperatives decreased by 11%, whereas it increased by 170% in the home cooperative of internationalising cooperatives.
46   It will be seen later on that in 2006 the proportion of worker-members in industrial cooperatives was 82%. In reference to Ugarte's statement of the relative performance of

Non-cooperative international subsidiaries. In principle multi-nationalising parent cooperatives might have, for the legal structure of the foreign settlements, the four options indicated in rows 3–6 of Table 6.14 (current section, subsection 1). It is understandable that worker-owners of the parent cooperative (these decide on a foreign settlement) wish to safeguard their original financial investment. That might be the case when the settlement's legal structure has the form of a mixed cooperative that is jointly owned by the parent cooperative and the local workers (row 3 of Table 6.14) – which would contribute to the Mondragon principle of 'development of the international cooperative movement' (6§5, 9th principle).

Nevertheless, towards the end of the twenty-first century's second decade no foreign settlement has a cooperative form (Bretos and Errasti 2018, p. 5). Apart from the possibility that some cooperative would not care for the 9th principle, two issues might hinder the foundation of a hybrid worker-owned cooperative (row 3 of Table 6.14). The first one is that many countries lack legal cooperative structures similar to those that apply for the Mondragon cooperatives' ownership and governance. The second – in case the first does not apply – is that in a culture where worker-cooperatives are uncommon, the paying in of capital and the possibility of wage decreases in an economic downturn (and other cooperative duties) is even more of an obstacle than it is for quite some workers in a culture where worker-cooperatives are common, such as in Spain and the Basque Region specifically. (On each of these hindrances see Flecha and Ngai 2014, pp. 671–2; Barandiaran and Lezaun 2017, pp. 286–7; Bretos, Errasti and Marcuello 2019b, pp. 15–16.)

Cooperative worker-members in the industrial division. Graph 6.17 (p. 280) shows the percentage of worker-members in industrial cooperatives from 1995 to 2019. The annual reports of Mondragon from 2006 mention these percentages under its 'basic data' (for a reason unknown to me these are not given for the retail division). However, the amount of employment in cooperatives is never stated (the same applies for the employment in subsidiaries), and therefore the proportion of worker-members in the total industrial employment cannot be calculated (comparable to Graph 6.15 for the retail division). Of the literature on Mondragon that I have seen, Luzarraga 2008 is the only one author that traced the amount of employment in industrial cooperatives for a couple of years between 1999 and 2006. Combining this with data on the amount of worker-members (Luzarraga, Aranzadi and Irizar 2007) the resulting three odd

---

multi-localising cooperatives it is very interesting that Luzarraga (2008, p. 178) finds for this year (the single one studied) that the multi-localising cooperatives outperform the non-multi-localising ones in worker-membership: 84% versus 75%.

data are given at the bottom of *Graph 6.17*.[47] Given that in 2006 and 2019 the amount of each of the Mondragon industrial employment in Spain (-7.5%) and abroad (-8.2%) do not deviate very much, the graph's 45% of 2006 might be used as a very rough indicator for 2019.

GRAPH 6.17 *Proportion of worker-members in industrial cooperatives 1995–2019 (with an indication of their proportion in the total industrial employment)*

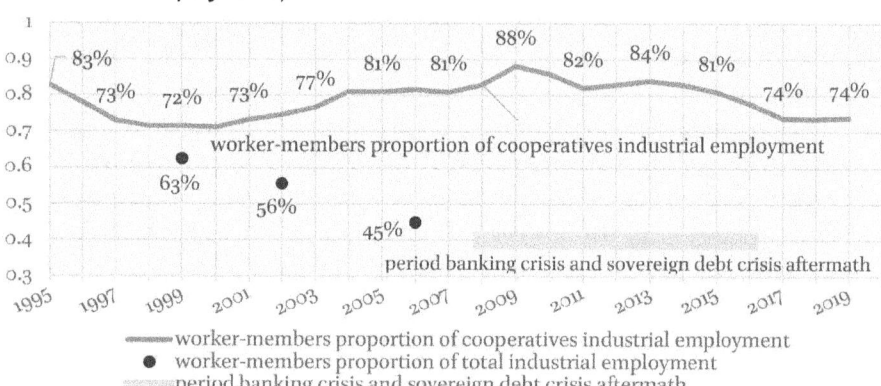

———worker-members proportion of cooperatives industrial employment
● worker-members proportion of total industrial employment
———period banking crisis and sovereign debt crisis aftermath

Data sources. Top line 1995–2005: Arando, Freundlich, Gago, Jones and Kato 2011, p. 19; 2006–2019: Mondragon annual reports 2006–2019. Data for 'worker-members proportion of total industrial employment': compiled from Luzarraga 2008, p. 70 and Luzarraga, Aranzadi and Irizar 2007, p. 21.

Regarding the top line of Graph 6.17 (the complement of which is the proportion of temporary workers and perhaps workers with a fixed contract), Arando, Freundlich, Gago, Jones and Kato (2011, p. 19) mention that during the 1990s the industrial cooperatives group 'began to emphasize the importance of minimizing the use of temporary workers and set a goal that a minimum of 85% of the coops' internal work force should be made up of worker-members'.[48] This goal was reached in 2009, but it is not unlikely that this was triggered by the 'great recession'-induced redundancy of temporary workers instead of their adopting membership (from 2007 to 2009 the division's employment in Spain dropped

---

47 Luzarraga (2008, p. 144) mentions that in 1994 (not shown in Graph 6.17) 85% of the total industrial workforce consisted of members.
48 At the time the authors' last datum was for 2009, whence it was understandable that they observed a 'steady if modest improvement in the membership ratio beginning early in this decade and continuing through 2008, when the group approached its 85% membership goal' (p. 19).

by 21% – cooperatives plus subsidiaries).[49] By 2017 the percentage of worker-members was back to the 2002 level, well below the intended minimum level of 85%.

Both from the side of the Mondragon federation and from the side of quite some individual cooperatives, the amount of temporary workers in cooperatives as well as the legal form of subsidiaries has been considered as conflicting with Mondragon's initial cooperative values, or at least as second-best practices in face of finding a modus between competitive pressures and the maintenance of employment within cooperatives (see for example Bretos, Errasti and Marcuello 2019a – for an overview their table on p. 9).

(4) Comparative employment performance of Mondragon, Spain and the aggregate of OECD countries: 2001–2019. This subsection compares the employment performance of aggregate Mondragon entities with Spain's employment performance. Many commentators assert that Mondragon has on average succeeded in maintaining the employment in its cooperatives (cf. the heading 'International employment strategy' of the previous subsection). Although this is plausible, at least the Mondragon annual reports provide no quantitative evidence for this thesis. It is most remarkable that these reports, as mentioned, never state the amount of employment in cooperatives. They state the amount of employment of the sum of the cooperatives and their subsidiaries for each of the retail and industrial divisions. For a quantitative analysis this lack has many repercussions (as mentioned one regards the amount of worker-members). Because only for a restricted period (2001–2019) the reports mention the amount of Mondragon employment in Spain (cooperatives plus their subsidiaries) this period is taken as basis for the comparative performance.

Table 6.18 (and two more specific graphs that follow it) shows the results – the long-term perspective was shown in Graph 6.9. The period 2001–2019 covers one 'normal' cyclical recession (2001–2002 – for Spain a relatively minor one with no employment fall) and the 'great recession' (Spain 2008–2013) with, in the EU, its sovereign debt crisis aftermath.

---

49   As indicated, the annual reports never mention the amount of employment in *cooperatives*; however, from 2001 the total industrial employment *in Spain* (cooperatives plus subsidiaries) is either directly mentioned, or it can be derived from other data. (It runs from 22,803 in 2001 to 24,676 in 2019.)

TABLE 6.18 *Comparison of the Mondragon employment in Spain, with that of Spain and the aggregate of OECD countries: 2001–2019*

	Employment†	(1) 2001	(2) 2019	(3) Growth	(4) Mondragon's growth minus Spain's growth
1	Mondragon: Spain & foreign subsidiaries	60,200	81,507	35%	pro memory
2	Mondragon industrial: Spain & for. subs.	27,050	39,131	45%	pro memory
3	Mondragon: Spanish (sum rows 6, 8, 10)	55,191	67,052	21%	-2%
4	total Spain (× 1000)	16,146	19,779	23%	
5	total OECD (× 1000)‡	503,068	592,656	18%	
	employment by Mondragon's divisions				
6	Mondragon retail (Spanish)*	30,158	38,878	29%	10%
7	Spain retail (× 1000)	1,597	1,908	19%	
8	Mondragon Spanish industrial	22,803	24,676	8%	28%
9	Spain industrial (× 1000)	5,053	4,041	-20%	
10	Mondragon financial and corporate div.	2,230	3,498	57%	

† All Mondragon figures are in FTE and those of Spain and the OECD in persons. (Spain and OECD figures are in persons × 1000.) The data of the for this table relevant row 7 are only available from 2001–2019.
‡ Excluding countries that were not member in 2001 (Chile, Colombia, Estonia, Israel, Latvia. Lithuania).
* From 2012 the retail division had no subsidiaries abroad; earlier it had 22 establishments in France.
Data sources columns 1–2. Rows 1–3, 6, 8 and 10: compiled from Mondragon annual reports 2001–2019. *Rows 4–5 and 9*: OECD Statistics;[50] *Row 7*: Eurostat.[51]

Comments on *Table 6.18*. Row 1 regards the total Mondragon employment, which includes foreign subsidiaries, whilst the total of Spain and the OECD do not include the employment of corporate subsidiaries. For the comparison, therefore, the Mondragon Spanish employment has been used (rows 3–9). The comparison of rows 3–4 (Spain and Mondragon Spanish) is only moderately relevant because of the sectoral differences between Spain and Mondragon. Rows 6–9 therefore focus on the Mondragon and Spain's retail and industry sectors. This comparison shows (column 4) that Mondragon did much better than the Spanish averages, especially for the industrial division.

50 https://stats.oecd.org/ (accessed 13 May 2021): Labour/Labour force statistics/Annual LFS/ Summary tables/Employment.
51 2001–2007: https://ec.europa.eu/eurostat/databrowser-backend/api/query/1.0/LIVE/xlsx

The following two graphs show in more detail the development, and comparison, of the retail and industrial divisions in the period covered by Table 6.18. (Similar as for Graph 6.9, in *Graphs 6.19* and *6.20* Spain's variations are less visible than Mondragon's because its employment scale is 1000 times larger than Mondragon's.)

GRAPH 6.19 *Comparison of Spain's retail employment with Mondragon's: 2001–2019*

Data sources: see Table 6.18.

The shaded area in *Graph 6.19* marks the, what later turned out to be, choking acquisitions of the Eroski Group – mentioned in subsection 2 (when I compiled Graph 6.15 (Eroski) I had not expected that it outperforms the average Spanish retail). Note that not all of the employment downfall resulted in lay-offs. Part of the acquisitions were sold, and for another part Eroski developed a franchise system (in 2019, on top of the graph's employment, franchise holders employ about 3,400 people).

It can be seen from *Graph 6.20* that Mondragon's industrial employment outperformed Spain especially in the four recession years 2010–2013. One main reason is that during recessions cooperatives foremost tend to adapt wages, and employment only if inevitable.

/en/download/49f69dfc-567b-4306-ad80-d0abd794a5c4 (last updated 26 March 2020, accessed 23 February 2021); 2008–2019: https://ec.europa.eu/eurostat/databrowser/bookmark/17e0d63c-bfe6-48b6-b832-e7ab333bf2ee?lang=en (last updated 11 November 2020; accessed 23 February 2021).

GRAPH 6.20 *Comparison of Spain's industrial employment with Mondragon's industrial employment in Spain: 2001–2019*

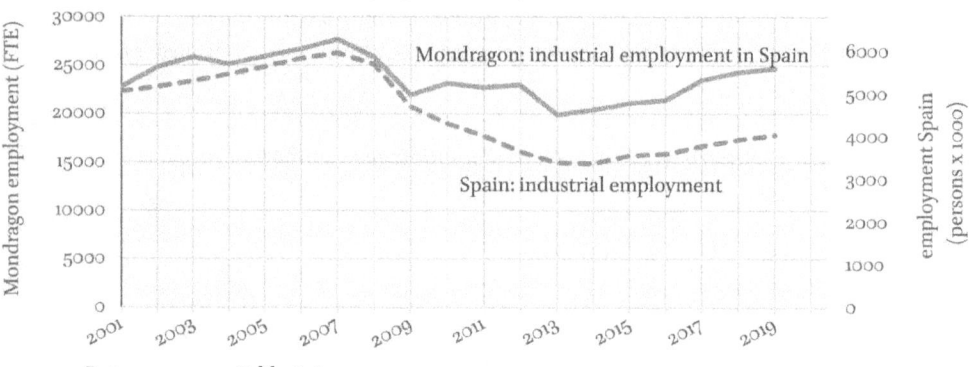

Data sources: see Table 6.18.

In 2019 the retail division's employment is back beyond the 2006 level and the industrial division's employment in Spain is back at the 2004 level.

In sum, qua overall employment the Mondragon retail and industrial divisions performed much better than Spain from 1983 until 2001 (Graph 6.9). In the predominantly recessive period 2001–2019 period Mondragon lost employment that was built up until 2007, but comparatively the Mondragon divisions also outperformed Spain in this period. In terms of employment quality and payment, members of cooperatives are much better off than workers in mainstream capitalist enterprises. I have seen little quantitative information on the payment of other Mondragon workers, however, on basis of the information that has been quoted, these other workers (be it in cooperatives or subsidiaries) are on average better paid than workers in mainstream capitalist enterprises.[52]

Division 3. Cooperatives as subcategory of 'social and solidarity economy entities'

The so far presented worker-owned cooperatives, as subclass of cooperatives, are part of the wider range of entities that are covered by the term 'social and solidarity economy' (SSE). This term and its concept gradually emerged from the late 1970s. It encompasses both long-established social economy entities –

---

52 The regarding quotes are in 6§9: end of subsection 1; end of subsection 2; subsection 3 quote from Ugarte.

cooperatives, mutual benefit societies and a subclass of associations – and newer solidarity entities that nowadays are called 'social enterprises' (SES).

This brief Division first delineates the categories just mentioned (6§10) and next provides a geographically limited quantification of the employment by SSES (6§11).

6§10 Social and solidarity economy entities

Before expanding on the SSE categories, *Table 6.21* sets out the historical emergence of the relevant entities

TABLE 6.21 *Social and solidarity economy entities as prevalent within capitalism: end of the second decade of the twenty-first century*

Entity	Emergence
1 membership association (voluntary association)†	ancient; proliferated 19th cent.‡
2 cooperative	mid-19th century
3 mutual benefit society	2nd half 19th century
4 SSE foundation	late 1970s
5 social enterprise	late 1970s

† ILO term: association and community-based organisations.
‡ Proliferation at first in Europe and North America.
Sources. Row 1: Anderson 1971, pp. 215–16. Rows 2–5: ILO 2011, pp. 1–5.

Delineation and elucidation of main SSE categories

• *Entities comprising the 'social and solidarity economy' (SSE)*
SSE entities 'produce goods, services and knowledge while pursuing economic and social aims and fostering solidarity'; they include 'cooperatives, mutual benefit societies, associations, foundations and social enterprises' (ILO 2011, pp. i, 2 and 5). On the terminological issues, see also ILO 2020, pp. 10–14.
• *Cooperative*[53]
• According to the International Co-operative Alliance 1995: an 'autonomous association of persons united voluntarily to meet their common economic, social and cultural needs and aspirations through a jointly owned and democratically controlled enterprise'.

---

53 The definitions below for 'cooperative' are taken over from European Commission 2020, pp. 161–2 (authored by Borzaga, Galera, Franchini, Chiomento, Nogales and Carini).

- According to the ILO Recommendation 193 of 2002: a legal form that is broadly characterised by the following features:
    - jointly owned and democratically controlled by the people who work in it, trade through it or use its products or services ('members');
    - can pursue almost any purpose, traditionally subject to the requirement that there should be a common economic, social or cultural need or interest shared by members of the cooperative;
    - can in principle distribute profits to members; however, there can be limitations to the distribution of profits, i.e., notably in those legal systems that have strengthened cooperatives' social function.
- *Worker-owned cooperative and other cooperative subcategories*
See 6§1 and 6§2, Table 6.1 (Classification of cooperatives as functioning within capitalism).
- *Mutual benefit society*
An organisation whose objective is to provide social services for their individual members and their dependants; provides services through a mechanism where risks are shared and resources are pooled. As against a classical insurance company it has no profit aim and it does not select its members, nor does it calculate members' premiums on the basis of their individual risks. (ILO 2011, p. 2.)
- *SSE foundation*
On the problem of delineating the category, see ILO (2011, p. 5). An SSE foundation might be delineated as a membership foundation with a democratic structure that produces goods and/or services and/or knowledge while pursuing economic and social aims and fostering solidarity.
- *SSE association*
An association generally provided in many countries the basic juridical framework for all current SSE entities. An SSE association aims to produce goods or services by or for its members on a continuous basis without being primarily focused on profit (ILO 2011, pp. 2–3).
- *Social enterprise*[54]
As indicated, the 'social enterprise' is a fairly recent phenomenon. Whereas all the entities mentioned above promote mainly the interest of their members – thereby having only an indirect impact on the society or a community at large – a 'social enterprise' pursues an explicit social aim in the interests of the society or a community. This aim can be the provision of general interest

---

54   Most of the elements stated below have been taken over from European Commission 2020, pp. 26–32 (authored by Borzaga, Galera, Franchini, Chiomento, Nogales and Carini).

services or, for example, the facilitation of work integration of disadvantaged persons.
• Generally a social enterprise (SE) has a social aim; it adopts specific restrictions regarding the distribution of profits and about its governance.
• It runs commercial activities in order to achieve a social or societal common good and has an organisation or ownership system that reflects its mission. It may, but need not be, collectively owned.
  - Regarding the commercial activities it engages in a market-oriented stable and continuous production of goods and services. Revenues are generated mainly from both the direct sale of goods and services to private users or members and public contracts. In addition to earned incomes it may rely on a mix of resources: voluntary work, donations and grants.
  - Regarding the organisation it adopts an inclusive and participatory governance model: all concerned stakeholders are involved, regardless of the entity's legal form. Depending upon the type of SE, ownership rights and control power can be assigned to one single category of stakeholders (users or workers) or to more than one category at a time.[55]
  - Regarding the continuity of production, it adopts profit distribution constraints and asset locks, guaranteeing that its social purpose is safeguarded.
• These characteristics separate the SE from the public sector as well as from traditional non-profit organisations.
• The legal form of a SE is country dependent. As yet the majority of SEs uses a legal form that is also used by non-SEs, especially that of a cooperative, mutual society, foundation, association or also that of a conventional enterprise.[56]

6§11   *Employment by SSE entities – a geographically limited account*

Aggregate data on the employment in the SSE beyond single countries are rather scarce. The most encompassing (though yet limited) are those for cooperatives: see the data by continent of Table 6.3 (6§2).

For the other SSE categories I have not seen any world scale employment data.[57] However, for the category of 'social enterprises' (SE) an indicator can be

---

[55] On differences of democratic governance between especially North American and European Union approaches, see EESG/CIRIEC 2017, pp. 23–5.
[56] For an overview within the EU countries see European Commission 2020, pp. 108–18. For a comparison of the legal form of SEs in the USA and the EU see Kerlin 2006, pp. 253–4.
[57] Borzaga, Salvatori and Bodini (2017, pp. 14–15) indicate that there are very little reliable

constructed for the dispersal of SEs by world regions. These are shown in *Graph 6.22*. Its underlying data are based on 2015 interviews with 167,793 adults in 58 countries, as reported in Bosma, Schøtt, Terjesen and Kew (2016, the authors also report the country data).

GRAPH 6.22 *Persons that lead a 'social enterprise' as indicator for the dispersal of SEs: world regions estimates 2014–15*

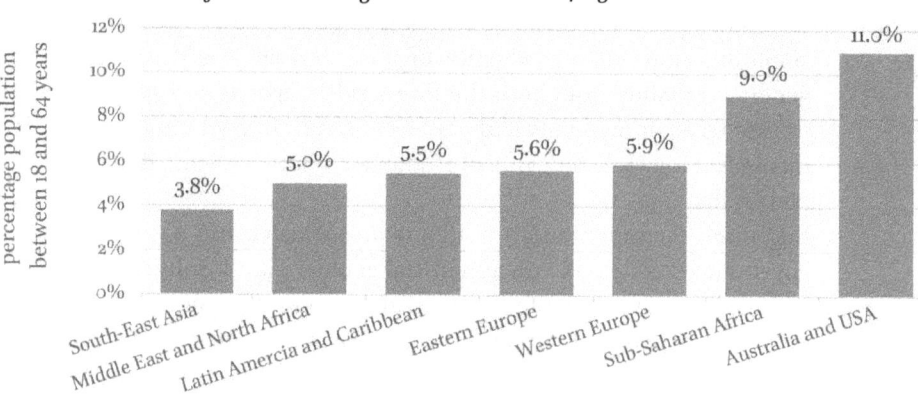

Measured is the percentage of the population that leads a SE: alone or with others. This provides an indicator for the dispersal of SEs in a region on the assumption that the average ratio of single to joint leadership is uniform across countries.
Data source: Bosma, Schøtt, Terjesen and Kew 2016, p. 13.

The most comprehensive SSE employment data that I have seen are of the European Union (EU), as reported by EESG/CIRIEC (2017). On its basis *Graph 6.23* (p. 289) shows for the period 2002–2015 the employment growth of SSEs in comparison with the total employment growth within the EU (only data for three sets of years are available: 2002/03. 2009/10, 2014/15). *Table 6.24* (p. 289) shows some more aggregate details.[58] Note that the last set of data (2014/15) regards the international banking crisis period. The EU regards 28 countries (EU-28) – at the time including the UK.

SSE data and mention (without data) that 'the rise of social enterprises has been the most significant and widespread in Europe, Asia and North America'. Grigore 2013 provides useful information on these and other regions/countries, though without employment data. In their book on the social economy in the USA Mook, Whitman, Quarter and Armstrong (2015) have data on cooperatives (p. 222), but apart from those they merely mention that non-profit organisations in the USA employed in 2010 about 10 percent of the workforce (p. 221).

58   EESG/CIRIEC 2017, pp. 68–95 provide the underlying country data.

GRAPH 6.23 *Employment growth in SSE entities within the EU in comparison with the total EU employment growth: 2002–2015*

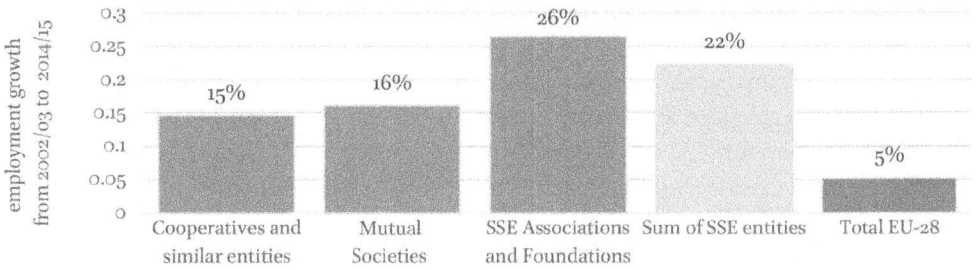

Data source: see Table 6.24.

It can be seen from *Graph 6.23* and *Table 6.24* that in the covered period the SSE-sector has a much better employment record than the conventional entities – mainstream capitalist enterprises and the public sector together. This is one main reason why the EU seeks to stimulate the SSE sector (EESG/CIRIEC 2017, p. 47).

TABLE 6.24 *Employment and employment growth in SSE entities within the EU in comparison with the total EU employment: 2002–2015*

		(1)	(2)	(3)	(4)
	Annual number of employees (columns 1–3 of rows 1–5)	2002/03	2009/10	2014/15	Growth 2002/03 to 2014/15
1	Cooperatives and similar entities	3,663,534	4,551,959	4,198,193	15%
2	Mutual Societies	351,291	364,221	407,602	16%
3	SSE Associations and Foundations	7,128,058	9,221,038	9,015,740	26%
4	Sum of SSE entities	11,142,883	14,137,218	13,621,535	22%
5	Total employment EU-28	203,505,000	213,369,500	214,031,000	5%
6	SSE/total EU employment [row 4/5]	5.5%	6.6%	6.4%	16%
7	SSE A&F / Sum SSE [row 3/4]	64%	65%	66%	

Data sources. Rows 1–4, columns 1–3: EESG/CIRIEC (2017, Tables 7.1 and 7.4). Row 5, columns 1–3: Eurostat.[59]

---

[59] Employment and activity by sex and age, employed population between 15 and 65 years. https://appsso.eurostat.ec.europa.eu/nui/show.do?dataset=lfsi_emp_a&lang=en (last updated 8 February 2021). Averages of the paired years calculated.

The democratic-enterprise and employment potential of cooperatives and other SSE entities has been noticed by not only the EU but also by other supranational organisations such as the United Nations and the OECD.[60] Among the policies that might further the proliferation of SSEs the most important one is that, in comparison with mainstream capitalist enterprises, their special character is recognised and that, in face of this, they are not disfavoured to the conventional entities.[61] Amongst others this may require: measures accommodating SSE access to funding; specific tax treatments; the formation of federations (such as between WOCs) that are at least as permissive as those for private capitalist holdings; the insertion of social clauses in public procurement procedures; recognition of the social economy in regional policy; incentives for the retiring owner of a firm to transfer the entity to the employees.

Concluding summary chapter 6

The chapter descended from cooperatives in general, to worker-owned cooperatives (WOCs) in general (Division 1) and to the specific case of the Mondragon cooperatives (Division 2). Division 3 again moved up, placing cooperatives within the broad category of 'Social and solidarity economy entities'. This concluding summary is divided in five parts. (1) The number and the general performance of WOCs up to 2020; (2) Complexities of WOCs' functioning within globalising capitalism: the Mondragon case; (3) Reflection on WOCs within capitalism as significant modification of capitalist practices; (4) Cooperatives as subcategory of 'social and solidarity economy entities'; (5) Future growth of the number of WOCs and other SSE entities within capitalism.

---

60   • On cooperatives in general: United Nations General Assembly (2013). • On the social economy: OECD 1996–2020 http://www.oecd.org/cfe/leed/social-economy.htm. • On social economy enterprises ('organizations based on the primacy of people over capital ... such as cooperatives, mutual, foundations and associations as well as newer forms of social enterprises'): European Council (2015). • On social economy enterprises: European Parliament (2015). • On the promotion of employee ownership and participation: European Commission (2014). • On social economy enterprises: European commission (n.d.), 'Social economy in the EU'. • On cooperatives: European commission (n.d.), 'Cooperatives'. • On worker-participation and EU legislation about it see https://www.worker-participation.eu/About-WP/About-this-website.

61   See also EESG/CIRIEC 2017, pp. 39–43.

1. The number and the general performance of WOCs up to 2020 (Division 1). The first sections of Division 1 outlined general characteristics of WOCs as functioning within capitalism (6§1) and their distinction from other types of cooperatives (6§2, Table 6.1).

World-wide data on WOCs are scarce: a 2016 dataset of 156 countries on all types of cooperatives includes only for 51 countries information on WOCs (6§2, Table 6.4). In these 51 countries 11 million people worked in WOCs – 0.4% of all of the world's employed population (6§2, Table 6.2).[62] However, even in the top-five countries qua relative WOC employment (Italy, Malaysia, Sweden, India and Spain) the WOC employment ranges around 2016 from no more than 3.9% to 1.0% of their labour force (Table 6.5). This means that, as yet, WOCs constitute on average no threat to conventional capitalist enterprises.

Nevertheless WOCs outperform conventional capitalist enterprises (CCEs) not only in their institutional democracy (mainstream enterprises are governed by way of capital-cracy), but also on the following main points each one of which regards empirical comparisons between WOCs and CCEs (from 6§3, subsection 1, based on a review of empirical studies in the period 1950 to 2010 by Pérotin 2012).

1. WOCs are present in most sectors of the economy; on average WOCs are larger than CCEs, and they survive at least as well.

2. WOCs are at least as productive as CCEs, and more productive in some areas.

3. Profit may not be higher in WOC than in CCEs, but WOCs may produce more and preserve their members' jobs better.

4. Regarding unemployment and income risks, workers in WOCs are considerably better protected than workers in CCEs against the moral hazard potentially attached to management decisions over investment.

5. When faced with demand shocks CCEs primarily adjust employment whereas WOCs primarily adjust remuneration.

6. Recessions increase the number of firm *closures* among CCEs and WOCs alike. However, recessions decrease the number of *creations* among CCEs, whereas the creation of WCCs increases.

Focussing particularly on matters of, or related to, the comparative productivity in WOCs and CCEs, econometric country studies for France and for Italy (each quoted in 6§3, subsection 2) found, among other issues, the following.

---

62 A number of 252 million people (8.5% of the world's employed population) were members of 'producer-serving cooperatives' – these members are mainly self-employed individual producers (6§2, Table 6.2).

France. WOCs are at least as productive as CCEs, however, WOCs use their capital and labour more effectively than CCEs. Using the same technology, the scale of production is significantly larger in WOCs than CCEs in some industries, and similar in most industries. For all industries applies that WOCs are not smaller or less capitalised than CCEs, and that WOCs expand their capital at least as fast and grow at least as fast as CCEs.[63]

Italy. The WOCs' collective ownership and total factor productivity are positively and significantly related after controlling for factor productivity, individual capital ownership and other standard enterprise-level and sector controls. This suggests a positive role of collective capital in strengthening financial sustainability and employment stability in the long run. The WOCs' collective capital favours more investments and capitalisation. Generally WOCs are not undercapitalised and they increase capitalisation over long spells of time.[64]

2. Complexities of WOCs' functioning within globalising capitalism: the Mondragon case (*Division 2*).

Division 2 outlined the constellation of Mondragon, a cooperative federation with in 2019 about 100 individual worker-owned cooperatives that employ over 81,000 workers, including in 140 production plants abroad. Based on the Mondragon annual reports and the literature that I have seen, the outline focussed on Mondragon's employment performance as summarised in the following points.

1. In comparison with CCEs the core characteristic of the Mondragon cooperatives is – as for all WOCs – the democratic decision-making at enterprise level by the workers, that is, the worker-members (6§4). (On non-members see point 6.)

2. The in comparison with CCEs very moderate intra-cooperative income differences are remarkable – by 2019 a before-tax ratio of maximum 1:9, and for individual cooperatives on average about 1:5 (6§6). This is a shining example for CCEs: Mondragon shows that the latter's income differences are a matter of economic power rather than (alleged) scarcity of managers or of efficiency requirements.

3. The comparative quantitative employment record of Mondragon is impressive. From 1983–2019 its total employment grew by 335%, and its comparatively relevant employment in Spain by 258%. In the same period Spain's employment grew by 75%, and that of the aggregate of OECD countries by 41% (6§7, Table 6.8 and Graph 6.9; for specifically 2001–2019 see 6§9, Table 6.18 and Graphs 6.19 and 6.20).

---

63 From Fakhfakh, Pérotin and Gago 2012.
64 From George, Fontanari and Tortia 2020.

4. The group's survival record of almost 65 years is outstanding – the major exception being the 2013 bankruptcy of Fagor Electrodomésticos (6§8, last paragraph).

5. The inter-cooperative solidarity is striking. One quarter of the profits of individual cooperatives is used to support the well-being of the entire Mondragon federation – of which 3/5 is used to compensate losses experienced by other cooperatives, 1/5 supports innovation, and 1/5 supports internationalisation – and between cooperatives there is a commitment to employment relocation in case a cooperative would go bankrupt (6§6). It seems that for the long-term survival of worker-owned cooperatives it makes sense to collaborate.

The next three issues (6 to 8 below) – mostly gradually emerging or increasing during 1990–2018 – in part result from international competitive pressures. Both from the side of the Mondragon federation and from the side of quite some individual cooperatives, these issues are considered as conflicting with Mondragon's initial cooperative values, or at least as second-best practices in face of finding a modus between competitive pressures and the maintenance of employment within cooperatives (6§9, end of subsection 3).

6. A considerable proportion of workers *within cooperatives* are non-members (6§9, Graphs 6.15 and 6.17; for the rest of the current point and the following one see Table 6.14 and the remarks on it). In quite some cases the non-membership is voluntary in face of the capital to be paid in, and of other cooperative duties such as payment reduction in an economic downturn. In case the non-membership is involuntary, it makes a difference whether these workers have the prospect of membership within a preset reasonable time. This is usually the case for aspirant members on probation, but the prospect of membership is also relevant for other workers that aspire membership. Without this prospect they are in fact temporary workers (perhaps on a limited fixed contract). For these it makes again a difference whether they receive wages similar to worker-members and also share in the profits. If they do, the motive of worker-members is probably their own job guarantee in case the cooperative would run into bad market conditions. If they don't, the just mentioned motive may be in play, but they also appropriate part of the surplus produced by these workers. (The aspiration by some cooperatives to restrict the proportion of temporary workers lessens the effects just mentioned, without undoing them.)[65]

---

65 Recall that in Design cooperatives there can be a temporary probation period but no structural temporary work. When there is unemployment, the State may *impose* traineeships or

7. Mondragon cooperatives can found or acquire subsidiary companies.[66] At best these have the legal form of a 'hybrid worker-owned cooperative' with a mixed ownership by the parent cooperative and by the local workers (6§9, Table 6.16 row 3). Other cases regard 'partial or full subsidiaries' (6§9, Table 6.16 rows 4–6); how in these cases the workers are treated depends on the parent cooperative. At best most of the latter workers have a well-paid permanent position. For these, as well as for temporary workers, the same applies as stated in the last four sentences under point 6.

8. This point refers to 2019. Of the total employment by the retail Eroski Group, 32% regards cooperative worker-members – 6§9, Graph 6.15. (Eroski encompasses 75% of the total retail employment and 36% of the Mondragon total employment.) Of the industrial cooperatives 74% regards cooperative worker-members; a very rough estimate (2006-based) is that worker-members make up 45% of the total industrial employment – cooperatives plus subsidiaries (6§9, Graph 6.17).

9. Generally, members of worker-owned cooperatives are far better off than workers in mainstream capitalist enterprises, and even non-members are on average better paid than workers in mainstream capitalist enterprises.[67]

3. Reflection on WOCs within capitalism as significant modification of capitalist practices. The capitalist criterion for success is ultimately rather simple: profit measured over capital, and amount of profit increase via the accumulation of capital. Labour employment is an inevitable means for this aim. The enormously progressive character of WOCs consists in their reversal of the capitalist aim and its instrumental means – as made explicit in the Mondragon 1987 principles (6§5). Nevertheless WOCs have to function within the capitalist competitive contest. (It is like functioning within a hurdle race wherein participants who opt for elegance over speed end up losing the contest.) The point is that worker cooperatives within capitalism do not set the competitive rules. They have their own normative cooperative rules, and they must seek to combine these with the dominant capitalist profit rules of competition. (The hurdler who seeks to combine some elegance with the decisive speed criterion.)

---

    temporary jobs on these cooperatives proportional to their workforce (3§18–3§20). When cooperatives require temporary replacement or seasonable work, this is serviced by special cooperatives, the workers of which have a permanent position that is not paid less than the cooperatives for which they temporarily work (Appendix 3F).

66 Recall that for Design cooperatives this is impossible: these cooperatives are the only one possible multi-worker legal entity (2§2.2) and they are prohibited to take-over other cooperatives (2§4.0).

67 The last phrase of this sentence is based on little information (see the last footnote of 6§9).

Quite some commentators consider the Mondragon cooperatives and worker-owned cooperatives generally as an alternative to the mainstream capitalist practices. I suppose that the detection of the limits of WOCs in actual practice has contributed to the often heated debates about the Mondragon case in particular – debates between and among insiders and outsiders.

Indeed the Mondragon case shows both the merry excitement about WOCs – until at least the turn to the twenty-first century – and, depending on the commentator the, or some, pessimism later on, especially about points 6 and 7 of the previous heading (non-members and subsidiaries). Regarding Mondragon's functioning within capitalism a key point is the 4th 1987 principle (6§5): '*The instrumental and subordinated character of capital:* capital is an instrument, and should be subordinated to labour.' This is a most sympathetic assertion, and its actualisation would be an enormous step forwards. However, the within capitalism inevitable dilemma is that capital is still an instrument, which, to begin with, is revealed in the worker-owners paying-in of capital (6§6). Taking Mondragon's annual reports, and the 'highlights'/'basic data' mentioned at the beginning of each report, it is revealing that the instrumental matters always come first (sales, equity, investment and financial results) and only after that the amount of workforce.

The means of production of WOCs take indeed the form of capital and even when merely instrumental, capital is not abolished (contrary to the Design). This is not a criticism but rather an observation (and within capitalism the non-abolishment seems inevitable).

The Mondragon cooperative's international and local subsidiaries show what cooperatives can and what they cannot reach within capitalism, and the same applies for part of the tiered workforce (members and non-members) within cooperatives. More specifically, the rise and the 2013 demise of Fagor Electrodomésticos, once Mondragon's largest industrial cooperative (as narrated by Errasti. Bretos and Nunez 2017), is most sad as well as enlightening as to what WOCs can(not) attain within globalised capitalism (in this case in the oligopolistic surrounding that Fagor was part of). Nevertheless I am an advocate for the Mondragon and other WOCs, because – in the combination of their virtues and their defects within a capitalist surrounding – they are a most important lever to the required 'beyond capitalism'.

I am convinced that a beyond capitalism cannot be reached without (defective) islands that modify capitalism or capitalist practices, and WOCs are currently a very important instance of such islands. They reveal that there is a *potential* feasible alternative to capitalism. One that could be actualised with a State that is tailored to meeting the requirements of worker-cooperatives rather than capitalist enterprises (cf. Ch. 3, Introduction, first three paragraphs).

Some enthusiasm about WOCs is appropriate in my view. However, because they have to function within capitalism, their non-capitalist reach is limited. A 2020 *New York Times* article on Mondragon was headed 'Coops in Spain's Basque Region soften capitalism's rough edges' (Goodman 2020). This seems a good way of putting it.[68]

4. Cooperatives as subcategory of 'social and solidarity economy entities' (Division 3). Cooperatives, as including WOCs, are part of the encompassing category of 'social and solidarity economy entities' (SSES). Generally these produce goods, services and knowledge while pursuing economic and social aims and fostering solidarity. Cooperatives, mutual benefit societies and production/service associations do so for their members – thereby having only an indirect impact on the society or a community at large. A fairly recent category (late 1970s) is the 'social enterprise' (SE) which pursues an explicit social aim in the interests of the society or a community. Like the earlier mentioned categories, it runs market-oriented production activities, and it likewise adopts an inclusive and participatory governance model.

Regarding the number of SEs there is some rough indication that their prevalence by world regions is largest in Australia and the USA, followed by Sub-Saharan Africa (6D3, Graph 6.22).

Regarding the employment performance of all of the SSEs, data for cooperatives are available on a world scale (though still limited – 6D1). Aggregate data beyond a single country are much more limited for the other categories. However, there are encompassing data for the European Union from 2002–2015 which show that in this period the aggregate employment performance of SSEs outran that of the EU at large by a factor 4.4; concomitantly the share of SSEs in the total EU employment increased from 5.5% to 6.4% (6D3, Table 6.24).

---

[68] Goodman observes, among other characteristics: 'In a world grappling with the consequences of widening economic inequality, cooperatives are gaining attention as an intriguing potential alternative to the established mode of global capitalism. They emphasize one defining purpose: protecting workers. (…) They elevated workers into owners – partners is the term of art – with each gaining a single vote in a democratic process that determines wages, working conditions and the share of profits to be distributed each year. (…) In the United States, the chief executives of the largest 350 companies are paid about 320 times as much as the typical worker (…). At Mondragon, salaries for executives are capped at six times the lowest wage. The lowest tier is now €16,000 a year (about $19,400), which is higher than Spain's minimum wage. Most people earn at least double that, plus they receive private healthcare benefits, annual profit-sharing and pensions.'

5. Future growth of the number of WOCs and other SSE entities within capitalism. The democratic-enterprise and employment potential of SSE entities has been noticed by supra-national institutions, such as the United Nations, the OECD and the EU (end of 6§11). However, legislation that would further the quantity of these entities within capitalism depends on the willingness of the specific states.

Within capitalism the whole private sector could in principle be organised by way of WOCs and similar democratic enterprises. Pending such a constellation, and if states would take the advantages of the democratisation of enterprises seriously, legislation could impose on mainstream enterprises an 'extensive and statutory employee involvement in strategic and day-to-day decisions at all levels, as well as provisions for sharing profit with employees' (Pérotin 2016, pp. 2–3). This would then also apply to non-member workers of WOCs and to the subsidiaries of cooperatives. Currently, however, the prevalence within mainstream capitalist enterprises of employee governance involvement and of employee-profit-sharing is very moderate. Regarding the latter France is a main exception.[69]

In comparison with capitalist enterprises, the employment record of WOCs – and of other worker-owned entities, as well as of 'social and solidarity economy' entities generally – is outstanding. The further growth of SSE entities might lead to a gradual expansion of the current islands of such entities and, similarly as mentioned above for WOCs, this expansion would be an important lever to a 'beyond capitalism'. Whether the success of SSE entities would gradually undermine the legitimation for conventional capitalist enterprises is bare speculation. Anyway, the next two chapters assume that the SSE has expanded substantially (say to near one third of the employment in the private sector – although this number is no condition for the chapter 8 transition) and that along with it the said legitimation has indeed been undermined.

---

69 For decades, profit-sharing in France has been mandatory for enterprises with more than 50 employees; recent (2019) legislation is available at: https://www.lexology.com/library/detail.aspx?g=453c69e4-c618-42cf-b5f6-b184cffcc005. Information for other EU countries can be found at: https://www.worker-participation.eu/National-Industrial-Relations/Compare-Countries. For the USA see Monaco 2020.

CHAPTER 7

Circumstances just before the transition: financial and real estate markets and the scope of capital flight

Introduction

Relevant to the point at which the transition takes off (ch. 8) is the size of the 'worker-owned cooperatives' sector reached within capitalism in comparison with the conventional capitalist sector. For that take off, however, it is also important to have an idea about the economic and political constellation immediately before the take off. This brief chapter tries to imagine that constellation. It starts from the point at which capitalist enterprises and their owners feel that there might be a reasonable chance that pro-worker cooperatives political parties are going to win the next elections. It is analysed what effect this might have on the financial and real estate markets and on an ensuing capital flight. It is next considered what their effects are on the 'real economy' that will be the inheritance for the transition's actual take off.

7§1   *The 'critical period' just before the transition*
The year in which a parliamentary election results in a majority that is willing to implement the Design is indicated by (t). It is assumed that *at least* two years earlier (t-2), many become aware that the majority referred to might not be unlikely – perhaps the elections in year (t-4) might already point in that direction. I call the period of such awareness until the implementation (t), the 'critical period'.

7§2   *The value of financial assets in the critical period*
After the full transition, shares, bonds and the markets for these will no longer exist; notably this includes state bonds and its market (2§17, Addendum; 3§4-d). Because of anxiety among owners of these financial capital assets, their prices will deeply fall. Some might regard state bonds to be still the safest heaven, but assuming that the latter are also traded on international markets, the value of the local state bonds will anyway go down internationally, and via arbitrage this will also result in state bonds price decrease in the local market.

Graph 7.1 provides information on the distribution of net wealth and of financial assets for the average of 24 OECD countries around 2019. It shows that financial assets, including ownership in enterprises, are predominantly owned by the top of the wealth distribution.

GRAPH 7.1   *Distribution of net wealth, financial assets and capital ownership assets: average of 24 OECD countries around 2019, shares of quintiles and top 10%*

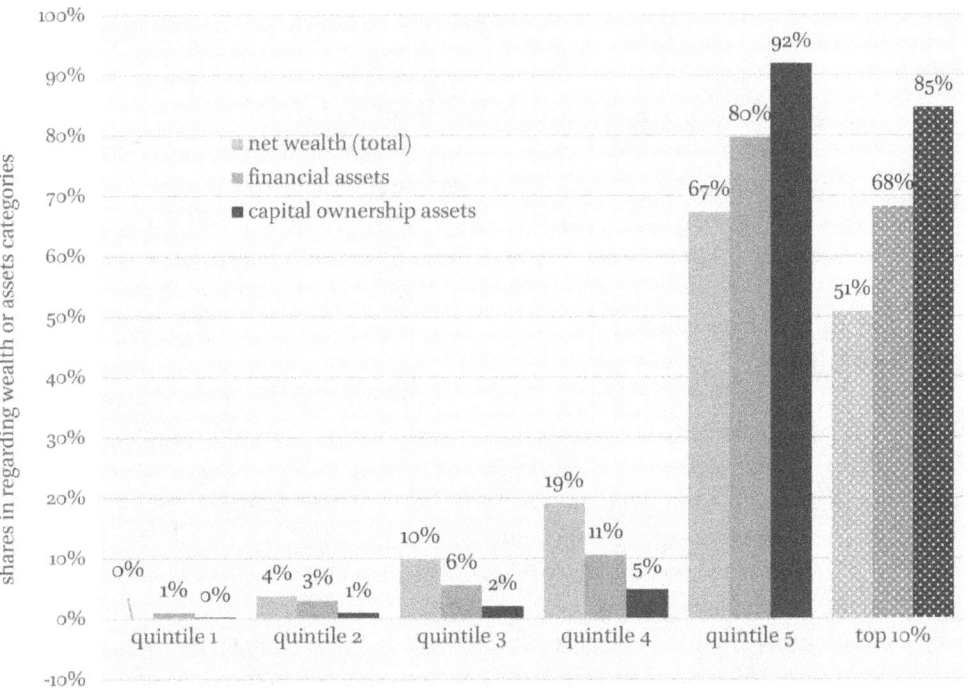

Notes: 'Capital ownership assets' are a sub-category of the 'financial assets'. 'Capital ownership assets' include: net equity in own unincorporated businesses; shares and other equity (including shares in banks and pension companies); mutual funds and other investment funds. Thus bonds (and bank accounts) are included in the main category of 'financial assets'. For other OECD countries than these 24, the data are not sufficiently detailed.
Source: Compiled from data of OECD 2022. Source of graph: Reuten 2023b (its Graph 10).

Decreasing shares and bonds prices will affect:
- the big financial capital owners (rich individuals);
- middle-class financial capital owners that possess such financial assets, including for pension purposes;
- financial assets of banks;
- financial assets of pension funds (most often these have a mix of national and international assets);

- financial assets of insurance corporations (most often these have a mix of national and international assets);
- financial assets of mutual insurance associations/companies.

Because shares and bonds price decreases occur via (effort at) selling, the question is if anyone is still willing to purchase. Some might perhaps speculate that the transition is not going to occur. However, most likely is that once the (effort at) selling sets in, the prices' fall will be steep, and end up near zero. Note that at this point we are still fully within capitalism and capitalist legislation. What would the Central Bank and government do in this case? I postpone this question until section 7§6.

7§3   *The value of real estate in the critical period*

Recall that after the *full transition*, cooperatives that wish so can own self-occupied premises, and that all other real estate will be owned by the National real estate agency. This agency rents out (1) dwellings for self-occupation to households; (2) premises to cooperatives; (3) land to agricultural cooperatives. There will no longer be a real estate market (3§37). Recall also that mortgage loans will be provided by the Savings and Loans Bank only, and to cooperatives only (3§16).

Generally the effect will be a sharp fall in the prices of immovable property, with distinctive effects for owner-occupied dwellings, for rented out dwellings and for other real estate. These regard anticipations of the following points.

- *Owner-occupied dwellings in general.* It will be seen in chapter 8 (8§9, Table 8.2) that the inheritors of these dwellings are heavily taxed, but that during the lifetime of these owners the regarding wealth taxes are nil.
- *Owner-occupied dwellings without mortgage loan.* The previous point implies that during the lifetime of the owners that have no (longer) mortgage loans, there is no effect on the usage of the property, even when the value of the dwelling falls.
- *Owner-occupied dwellings with mortgage loan.* In case the value of the dwelling drops below the mortgage loan there is no effect on the usage of the property, that is, in case there would be no action from the side of the mortgagee (a bank or other institution). However, as long as the mortgagor pays the interest and instalments as before, then action of the mortgagee is not likely. (In the circumstance of generally falling dwelling prices the execution of the collateral – in case the agreement would allow for this – is not likely to be in the interest of the mortgagee.)
- *Ownership by rich individuals of rented out real estate (dwellings, premises and land).* The before-tax income from these rents is not affected. However, it will be seen in chapter 8 (8§9, Table 8.2) that incomes above 5 times the per annum minimum wage are taxed at 95% (taxes on the regarding wealth are nil).

CIRCUMSTANCES JUST BEFORE THE TRANSITION   301

• *Ownership by pension funds and insurance companies of rented out real estate (dwellings, premises and land)*. During the transition the pre-transition pension funds and insurance companies pay no more than pre-transition taxes so that they can meet their obligations. This means that their before and after-tax receipts from tenants are not affected; nevertheless, the value of their assets will decline because of the general fall in real estate prices.
• *Ownership by other enterprise of rented out real estate (dwellings, premises and land)*. It will be seen in chapter 8 (8§9, Table 8.2) that the taxation of this ownership is very substantial, and such that these enterprises will have to sell most of their real estate. However, because most potential purchasers fall under the same tax rates, the price/value of such real estate sharply drops. Nevertheless, at declined prices there might be demand from the side of pension funds and insurance companies and perhaps also from the side of tenants.

7§4   *Country dependent effect on taxation revenue*
The above-mentioned anticipations on the transition result during the critical period in falls in the prices of financial assets and real estate. However, during the critical period these will by themselves not affect their owners' income from these, hence also not the taxation revenue from these *incomes*. Nevertheless, depending on the taxation structure in a 'near to transition country' regarding the taxation of various *wealth* categories, there might be downward effects on the wealth taxation revenue.

7§5   *The value of other real assets (non-real-estate) in the critical period*
Given that in the markets for shares, bonds and immovable property the prices will fall sharply with hardly any trade (thus it is rather the *expected* value of these assets that falls), microeconomically (and macroeconomically) not much additional money will end up in current and savings accounts. The question then is what will happen with the stock of money on current and savings accounts. Because their owners will consider what can be bought with it after the full transition to be insecure, they might want to purchase real assets such as precious metals and objects of art on the local market (international markets are considered in the next section). However, to the extent that all consider this, there is not likely to be much trade in such assets, and the little trade that there is will be highly speculative. Thus there may be some price movement, but with a slack volume of trade.[1]

---

1   As an aside I mention that there might be consumer goods hoarding in the critical period, but as always this has only temporary effects.

7§6 *Capital flight in the critical period*

In the critical period there is surely going to be capital flight. There are two possible forms of this: emigration, or international movement of assets without emigration.

I take the latter first. Note that this and the aforementioned market turbulences are likely to happen simultaneously once it sets in for one. Given the turbulences at generally slack trading volumes, there is not much value of home assets to substitute into foreign assets. Therefore, the first relevant movement is the ownership in foreign titles that people already possessed. They might transfer these titles to a foreign bank or trust. Note that this does not affect the home economy at all. Second, they might similarly transfer the money in their saving accounts to a foreign bank. Apart from an effect on international currency exchange rates, this also does not affect the home economy (regarding banks these savings liabilities are substituted by a liability to a foreign bank). For each – foreign titles and monetary savings – the income from these will be taxed after the transition, and inheritances considerably so (3§4, Table 3.7, and 3§46).[2]

Emigration. Like the category above, these persons will move their ownership in foreign titles and their monetary savings to a foreign bank, with little (currency exchange rates) or no effect on the home economy, though there will be an effect on taxation revenue. Here, however, two other assets categories are also relevant. First, they have to sell their self-occupied dwelling at a dropped price. The second relevant category is their possible ownership in a firm (that is, a non-incorporated enterprise). They need to sell this. But given that after the full transition all enterprises will have been converted into worker cooperatives, the price that they will get for the firm (or their part in case of a partnership) will be minor. This selling has no effect on the real economy because the firm as structure cannot be moved abroad (though some precious means of production or stocks might be shipped abroad, where these might be sold at second-hand prices).[3]

7§7 *Direct effects of changes in assets value and capital flight*

Table 7.2 summarises the main direct effects during the 'critical period' of the turbulences in the financial and real estate markets – as well as the effect

---

2 Perhaps some of these might be held 'black', which would mean that the income from these would have to be expended abroad (as long as the blackness can prevail).

3 In case they held ownership in objects of art they might also ship that ownership – that is, in case the country at hand has no ban on the export of such objects. In case there is such a ban they will have to sell these objects (for various reasons at relatively low prices, one reason being the Design inheritance taxes).

of capital flight. It would seem that there is no direct effect on the production of enterprises (including that of pre-transition worker-owned cooperatives).

TABLE 7.2 *Effects of turbulences financial and real estate markets during the 'critical period'*

Change of	Selected direct effects on					
	Production of enterprises†	Labour income†	Average value major assets of			
			Banks‡	Pension funds	Insurance corp.	Capital owners
7§2 value fin. assets	none	pensions ↓*	↓	↓	↓	↓
7§3 value real estate	none	none	none	↓	↓	↓
7§6 capital flight	none	none	none	none	none	none

† Including pre-transition worker-owned cooperatives.
‡ Including worker cooperatives owned banks. The latter are not likely to much engage in proprietary trading for their own account.[4]
* Contract dependent.

Any indirect effect from the provision of investment credit by banks, depends on the degree in which they engaged in financial assets trading for their own account (as affecting their reserves). Regarding the income of labour (or the population at large) the main effect regards pension allowances from pension funds or insurance institutions, depending on the type of contracts people had with these funds/institutions.

7§8 Turbulences' investment effects on production, employment and incomes

However, apart from the pensions, rather more important is that capitalist firms and corporate enterprises will probably stop investing in face of the insecure future. Taken by itself this would set in motion a serious recession. On the other hand, worker-owned cooperatives (WOCs) would go on investing and on top they might profit from the downsizing activity of the former mentioned

---

4 Laboral Kutxa 2019 [Mondragon bank], p. 1 (after the eight auditor pages).

firms and corporates. How this is going to weigh up is much dependent on the now reached size of the WOC sector (ch. 6).

It is important (also for the start of the transition – ch. 8) to characterise this recession. It is not a structural underinvestment, and clearly it is neither a cyclical overinvestment recession, nor a qualifications mismatch problem. It is rather a recession caused by an uncertainty investment-strike. *Table 7.3* outlines the key effects of the latter.

TABLE 7.3 *Turbulences' investment effects on production, employment and incomes: non-WOC sector*

Effects on:	Construction of buildings; including dwellings	Other investment: plant and equipment
production of enterprises	↓	↓
employment	↓	↓
wages	↓	↓
profits	↓	↓
taxation revenue	↓	↓

7§9 *Reactions: the central bank, government and 'the public vote'*

Could and would the country's government and the central bank do anything in this situation? In capitalism the main policy instrument of the central bank regards (the effort at) influencing the rate of interest via open market trade in financial assets. However, given the degree of the prices' fall in the financial markets set out above, it is most unlikely that it could even try to adopt this policy effectively. The only other action that the central bank might take is to soften the prescribed reserve ratios of banks hoping that this would keep their investment credit going. But if capitalist enterprises do not want to invest this does not help. (Worker cooperatives owned banks are not likely to soften their reserve ratio's even if they are allowed so.) Thus it seems that the central bank is paralysed during the sketched 'critical period'.

What about the government? It could buy (very cheaply!) financial and real estate assets, trying to put floors in these markets. But even when this might be effective (which is doubtful) it is not likely that a pro-capitalist government would do this. First, because it might think that this would facilitate the transition for a future pro-worker cooperatives government. Second, because it might believe that maximum turbulences now might turn away a transition. The latter is a tricky strategy that much depends on the ideological climate in the critical period. The government in charge is responsible for its (non-)actions, but it will probably utter aloud that the 'pro-worker cooperatives' parties are responsible for the turbulences – even when at this point these have not acted apart from communicating their future plans.

It is likely that, for gaining the general 'public vote', the ideological battle in the press and other media releases during this period is going to play a dominant role.[5] Its outcome cannot be predicted. But it can be predicted that the distinction between the for the majority important facts, less important facts, and fiction is going to play an important role. The next section makes some remarks about this.

7§10 *A concluding appraisal of the critical period*

I would think that the character of the ideological battle during the critical period much depends on the size reached by the worker-owned cooperatives (WOC) sector. By character I mean here the degree of distinction between the for the majority important facts, less important facts, and fiction.

The turbulences on the financial and real estate markets predominantly directly affect capital owners and to a much lesser extent the workers (though during this period it may hit the pensions of retired workers). The part of the press and other media that believes that a capitalist world is the best forever, will undoubtedly highlight the turbulences as a doom for a non-capitalist future (even if this is counterfactual because the turbulences are capitalist facts).

Based on the outline of the critical period in this chapter, there are two important issues for the majority of the people, each one conditional. The first one – as an upshot of the financial and real estate markets turbulences – is, as mentioned, the possible effect on pensions. This effect depends on the type of contract people had with the allowance providing institutions. The second important issue is the 'investment strike' by capitalist firms and corporations which might give rise to a considerable recession. The degree of severity of such a recession depends on the at the time relative size of the WOC sector. In case the latter would be nearly dominant, the recession might be moderate, but qua unemployment still affect the workers in capitalist firms and corporations. Nevertheless, because WOCs would still be expanding, some of the unemployed might find work in the WOCs.

---

[5] Klikauer and Simms 2020 argue in a review of Adler 2019 that the latter undervalues the role of the media in capitalism. 'The media is an important gatekeeper in society linking the individual to society.' True, but in this case the gate is not a static element. When worker-owned cooperatives have become more dominant and more accepted in society than in 2020, it is not unlikely that at least an important echelon of the 'keepers' moves along this trend.

To the extent that capitalist firms and corporations foresee this duality (and to the extent that they coordinate their actions via employers' organisations) this poses quite an ideological problem. Because when in the critical period capitalist firms and corporations decay, whereas WOCs expand, the public vote might lean towards political parties that seek to generalise a worker cooperatives mode of production.

If, against their inclinations, capitalist firms and corporations would massively decide not to go for an investment strike, then the general effect of the 'critical period' on production and employment will be rather steady, and put little in the way of the political parties seeking a transition to a Design worker cooperatives mode of production.

It will be seen in the next chapter that in the transition's phase 1 a floor will be put in for the pensions. Because the outcome of the last two paragraphs above is insecure, the transition's phase 1 will, if required, also immediately adopt recession-countering measures.

CHAPTER 8

Transition to a worker cooperatives society

Introduction

As indicated, the start of the transition outlined in this chapter is the point at which in a particular country there is a parliamentary majority that is willing to go for the transition to a worker cooperatives society as set out in Part One.

The aim of this chapter is to show that a transition might be feasible in a democratic and peaceful way. However, I see it as my self-imposed task to not merely set out principles or headlines of a transition, but to present a rather detailed path of how this might be reached. Reached such that along the path the economy keeps functioning, with 'pre-transition worker-owned cooperatives' and emerging Design cooperatives on the one hand, and a gradually decreasing capitalist sector on the other.

Because I will only sparingly repeat some of the Part One content, the text below will be rather demanding for the reader – and in case the difficulties of the puzzle referred to in the previous sentence is not obvious, the text may not be exciting for some readers.

For the transition path that I present, choices are made. I do not claim that my choices are the only possible ones. My only objective is to show that there is at least one feasible transition path.

The transition below takes two broad periods. The first period takes five to six years, during which all of the Part One's Design has been put into legislation, and during which a great deal of the transition will already be reached in practice (Divisions 1–5 of this chapter). Another in which that legislation becomes fully effective in practice in the sense that all of the society's economic domain is organised in Design worker cooperatives (Division 6). In this last period a capitalist sector might still prevail, but, as will be shown, it will gradually phase out (within one generation). No pre-transition capitalist enterprise is enforced to legally convert into a Design cooperative. However, the implementation of the first period's Design legislation will make it increasingly difficult for these enterprises to survive.

The first broad period is, as mentioned, planned to take five to six years. The objective for this period – itself organised in five legislative phases (Divisions 1–5) – is twofold. One aim is to reach a sequence of phase-wise constellations in which cooperatives co-exist with pre-transition capitalist enterprises, with the former becoming gradually dominant. The sequence should be such that there is no collapse of the capitalist sector's production and employment, but, as indicated, indeed a gradual transition of it, such that production and work is preserved. The second aim is that all along essential common provisions (pensions and other allowances, and health and educational provisions) are not only maintained at a bare level, but also improve in comparison with the pre-transition era. It will be seen that these two aims require a punctual interconnection of the legislation for each one of the five transitional phases. Thus 'phase 1' must be self-contained coherent, and after that the same must apply for phases 1 and 2 together, and so forth.

It will be seen that for the mentioned coherences it does not matter too much how big the pre-transition worker-owned cooperatives sector and the capitalist sector are. Nevertheless, these determine how long the second, above-mentioned, broad period (Division 6) will last.

However, as indicated in Chapter 7, for the economic conditions at the start of the transition the relative sizes of the two sectors are important. In any case the transition starts with the enactment of pension provisions and minimum costs of living allowances as well as other recession countering measures regarding construction and other investment. At the end of phase 2 – this is well before the next parliamentary elections – not only the mentioned allowances but also health and education provisions for all will have been established, as well as an after-tax far less skewed distribution of income than before the transition (as in the chapter 3 Design the income tax rates will be such that the after-tax income ratio's range from 1:3.2.). However, as in the Design, there will be no wealth tax for individuals, though an inheritance tax of inheritance taxes of 100% above an equivalent of twice the annual minimum wage. Thus apart from the income tax there is no intention to further affect people's way of life as they used to. During the transition people can keep on inhabiting the self-occupied dwelling that they owned before the transition.

In line with what was mentioned above about 'the first broad period' of the transition, the systematic order of the current chapter is one of the priorities during the transition, and this systematic differs from the systematic order of Part One. Readers that would wish to see the correspondence between the two orders, might consult Table 8.22 in Appendix 8A that shows at what transition phase parts of, and finally the total of, the Part One Design is enacted.

Ideology of the 'general interest'. At the end of chapter 7 I referred to the (presumed) ideological battle during the critical period before the start of the transition. It is likely that much of this battle continues in at least the early phases of the transition. This will regard the functioning of the existing capitalist enterprises versus the existing worker-owned cooperatives and the emerging Design cooperatives. It will also regard the state's parliament's legislation of rights. As mentioned in the General Introduction, the capitalist state's legislation grants the members of the capitalist class's the right to property of the means of production and the entitlement to employ labour as combined with the appropriation of the surplus-value produced by that labour. This capitalist legislation is presented as being in 'the' general interest.[1] In the Design no right to private (or state) property in the economy's means of production exists, nor a right to employ labour. Much of the ideological battle, therefore, will be about the turn in the consciousness that there might be other 'general' interests than the capitalist general interest.

Almost all of the current chapter is about legislations. The text of the chapter will only sparingly refer to this ideological battle, but it is most likely that each of the legislations presented will evoke debate on 'the' general interest: in parliament, the media, at kitchen tables and so forth.

Terminology and general matters
• *'Full enactment'*. This term refers to the full legislation of, usually, a section of the Design. When appropriate this term appears in the section headings of the current chapter.
• *'Phase x–y'*. Often the 'full enactment' is legislated in phases or via a temporary legislation. In this case the heading of a section mentions the legislative phases in which that legislation applies. (For such legislation there will in a later phase always be a 'full enactment'.)
• The sections of this chapter include required enactments and introductions and comments on these. Required enactments are preceded by the bullet •.
• *Entry into force of an enactment*. At the end of each legislative section below it is mentioned when an act enters into force (without repeating this, it refers to a date after publication of the act.) This entry into force is also preceded by the bullet •. The publication of acts should be widely communicated, especially to those directly concerned. Table 8.20 in Appendix 8A list the entry into force of all legislation.
• *Pre-transition capitalist enterprises/entities*. This refers to capitalist corporations and firms. A firm refers to a non-incorporated enterprise, including an enterprise run by one individual or by two or more partners.

---

1 Reuten 2019, chapter 6. On the state's granting of core capitalist right see pp. 303 and 305. On 'the' general interest see pp. 309–10. https://brill.com/view/title/38778 (open access).

- *Pre-transition worker-owned cooperatives* (WOCs). Contrary to Design cooperatives, the in capitalism existing cooperatives are most often 'worker-owned cooperatives'. These might be non-banking and banking ones. However, banking cooperatives might also be owned by WOCs.
- *Pre-transition enterprises/entities*. The entities under the two previous points taken together.

Table 8.1 summarises the Design legal entities (Part One), together with the pre-transition economic legal entities. During the transition these coexist.

TABLE 8.1   *Legal entities during the transition: Design and Capitalist legal entities*

	Legal economic and public sector entities		1	2	3	4	5
1	**Design legal entities**						
2	cooperatives (Design cooperatives)†	ch. 2					
3	single person enterprises	2§2.2					co-existing during the transition
4	workers' council governed foundations	3§25				Design society	
5	the state (parliament and government)	3§1					
6	the judiciary	3§6	state institutions		public sector		
7	ministries	3§2		general state			
8	*state agencies*	3§2					
9	municipalities	ch. 4					
10	provinces	ch. 4					
11	**Capitalist economic pre-transition entities**						
12	Worker-owned cooperatives (WOC)†						
13	Capitalist enterprises (firms and stock corporations)†						

† Banking as well as non-banking entities.

Recall the distinction between 'state institutions' (right-hand side column 1) and its subcategory 'state agencies' (row 8).

Reading guide. The reader that merely requires a general gist of the chapter, might turn to 8§22 (on the transition in general) and 8§23 (on the transition strategy) and to the chapter's concluding summary (together 13 pages).

Division 1. Transitional legislation phase 1: transition foundations

This Division sets out the legislation of the basic framework for the transition, as well as of elementary social-economic provisions. In terms of space this is the chapter's largest Division (nearly 40 out of nearly 80 pages). It is composed of four subdivisions:
- 1A. Institutional changes and regulation in the public sector domain (nine sections);
- 1B. Regulation of social-economic provisions (four sections);
- 1C. Institutional changes and regulation in the economic domain (five sections);
- 1D. Recession policy, the general transition strategy and concluding matters phase 1 (six sections).

The legislation time is estimated at just over one year, as explained in Subdivision 1D. The objective of phase 1 is to find a balance between substantial changes and keeping the inherited existing economy's production and employment going, thus evading a collapse of the pre-transition capitalist sector. Along with it there should be recession countering policies.

Thinking quite some decenniums ahead, it would be useful regarding the future implementation of what this Division sets out, if transition-promoting political parties would already have drafted the main legislation of phase 1 (and 2) according to the legislative standards in the country at hand.

Subdivision 1A. Institutional changes and regulation in the public sector domain

The first five sections of this subdivision set out legislation about the democratic organs of the state and about administration of the state and state institutions (8§1–8§5). Its last four sections (8§6–8§9) present main instruments for the transition: taxation, competition policy, and the competences of the 'Agency for temporary workers' council governed foundations' (it will be shown in subdivision 1D how these three interact as main levers for the transition).

8§1 *Democratic organs of the state (cf. 3§1) – full enactment*
• Legislation enacts the Design's outline of the 'democratic organs of the state and their election' (3§1). Depending on the Constitution of the country at hand, some of it may only enter into force after the next elections.

It will be a difficult task in quite some countries to get parliament early on in the transition to the top of the state's administration, and on basis of proportional elections (cf. 3§1). This applies especially for countries with a presidential system and those with elections on basis of districts. The point is that these changes most often require a change of the constitution. When on top of this, traditional country cultures would be in the way of this, pragmatics may, during some time, have to rule over principles, as long as this does not prevent the transition to the rest of the Design. Therefore the following might be considered.

(a) *Presidential systems.* In case the presidential system is such that the president could in principle block the parliament's proposals for changes, then a change of the constitution is set in motion. Often this will require a next round of parliamentary elections (sometimes a referendum might be a possibility). The change of the constitution may then enter into force after the next elections (or after the referendum). In case the sitting president and parliament fruitfully collaborate, the as yet not changed constitution is not in the way of the legislation set out in the rest of this division and chapter.

(b) *Systems on basis of district elections.* For systems on basis of district elections that do not end up in nationwide proportionality, a change of the constitution should equally be set in motion.

(c) *Other systems.* Other systems should bring the primacy of the parliament's powers vis-à-vis the government to the front (cf. 3§1), if this is not already the case. In case of two parliamentary chambers instead of one, its change into a single one is not urgent as long as each of the two chambers are elected on a nationwide proportional basis.[2]

In the rest of this division and chapter it is assumed that for presidential systems the sitting president will be in agreement with parliament about the urgency and the purport of the transition.

• In sum, all of the 3§1 legislation will be enacted, but some of it may only enter into force after a referendum or after the next national elections.

• Other elements of the existing constitution, including the constitutional rights, are brought in line with the Design's constitution as set out in Appendix 3C. It is (re)voted on after the next elections.

8§2   Competences of the judiciary – phases 1–3

During phases 1–3 the judiciary and its organisation is left unchanged, though with two exceptions.

• First. In countries with a constitutional court, a temporary law will set out that until the constitution has been changed, no court is eligible to assess ordinary laws against the current constitution.

---

2   Although monarchies are rather anachronistic, their elimination is also not urgent in case the monarch has no more powers than a ceremonial president, and is not remunerated more than the latter (which is the same as parliamentarians or members of government), and pays taxes like anybody else.

Nevertheless parliament is required to respect the current constitution. (Thus this temporary law excludes that in the *interpretation* of the constitution and ordinary laws, the judgement of courts has priority over the judgement of the elected parliament.)
• Second. No court is eligible to assess laws against current international treaties.

In case a relevant international organisation considers that a law passed conflicts with a treaty, the country will resign from that treaty – but the effectiveness of such resignation often takes time.
• The legislation enters into force immediately after the enactment.

8§3   *Ministries and state agencies (cf. 3§2) – full enactment*
• Legislation establishes 3§2 regarding ministries and state agencies. Some clauses of 3§2 enter into force at the point indicated below (clauses indications, such as (d), refer to 3§2).
(d) On their budget and amount of workforce in FTE: for state agencies this enters into force when the regarding institution is enacted. (In the current and subsequent divisions state agencies according to the Design will gradually be introduced. Until the explicit introduction of these, ministries and the relevant currently existing state agencies – or similar organs – keep on being organised as they are.)
(e) On the record of an Income account and a Balance sheet and their approval by two external registered auditors: this enters into force when the regulation on auditors and audit companies has been enacted – phase 2, 8§32. (For the approval the Design text refers to 'auditing cooperatives'; depending on the amounts of such cooperatives at this point, the audits might also be commissioned to pre-transition auditing companies, or be carried out by a court of audit.)
(f) On municipalities and provinces: this enters into force when these have been enacted – phase 5, 8§56.

For ministries and state agencies the 3§3 matters regarding their average wages, their council and the latter's decision on wage scales are only introduced later (8§26 and 8§49), and enter into force at that point.
• Legislation establishes that all transactions of the state, of state institutions and of workers' council governed foundations operate uniquely via the Central Bank (see 8§5). This enters into force two months after the enactment. Regarding any borrowing by the state 3§4-d applies (borrowing uniquely from the Central Bank). This enters into force immediately after the enactment. Existing state bonds will be paid off at the date due, or be bought back at an earlier date.

- Legislation establishes all of the Design's state agencies (see Appendix 3G). At this point the establishment goes along with merely a most brief general description of their Design tasks (ch. 3). However, each has the transitional task to *prepare* for the Design tasks that will formally be allotted to them upon legislation during phases 1–5.[3] The full establishment of many of these agencies goes along with a reorganisation of a perhaps similar currently existing institution, or of a split-off from a department of a current ministry. The agency established also has the transitional task to prepare such reorganisation in deliberation with the existing entities. The regarding preparation tasks enter into force three months after the enactment (so as to give time to appoint a, perhaps temporary, director general and other staff.)
- Regarding cultural heritage objects it is enacted that until the 'Culture and cultural heritage agency' sets rules about this (phase 5, 8§53) the export of such objects is prohibited. This enters into force immediately after the enactment.

8§4 *Unchanged municipal and provincial administrations – phases 1–4* {requires no legislation}

During phases 1–4, all provincial (or regional) and municipal (or local) and similar administrations and their tasks, are left unchanged. They keep on being financed as they were, in case including by way of regional/local taxes. The elections for these organs also stays as they are in case there are such elections before phase 4 (in phase 3 the election procedure will be adapted).

8§5 *The four banking and fund agencies – full enactment*

The four banking and fund agencies mentioned in 3D4 (Central bank; Guardian bank; Investment-credit guarantee fund; Savings and Loans Bank) were formally established in 8§3. Legislation now establishes their 3D4 tasks and competences.
- The establishment of the Central Bank (CB) regards a conversion of the current one. To the enactment of 3§13 articles are added setting out that during the transition the CB also supervises non-cooperative banks and insurance institutions.
- Regarding the 'Guardian Bank' 3§14 is enacted, as well as the transition rule that also pre-transition enterprises must have a dormant account with this bank.

---

3   Those enacted early on in the transition will be given more time to implement their tasks than those enacted later on.

TRANSITION TO A WORKER COOPERATIVES SOCIETY 315

• The task of the 'Investment-credit Guarantee Fund' are equally enacted (3§15). Its tasks regarding regional discrepancies enter into force from Phase 5. (Recall that its other main task is to help cooperatives in formation in the case no cooperative bank would be willing to provide investment credit on merely a business plan. The Fund may then (cautiously) provide an investment-credit guarantee to a cooperative bank for a limited time.)

To the legislation of this fund the transitional rule is added that in case there is a severe recession at the start of the transition, the fund is allowed to also cautiously provide investment-credit guarantees for Design cooperatives (when established) and to pre-transition 'worker-owned cooperatives'. (See further 8§20 on 'recession-countering policies'.)

• The 3§16 tasks of the 'Savings and Loans Bank' (SLB) are enacted. It is also enacted that during the transition the SLB can (next to COB's), up to its discretion provide securitised loans to non-cooperative banks for their investment loans to cooperatives, and – when sufficient savings are forthcoming – also for their investment loans to non-cooperative enterprises (specified in 8§17 below). It is enacted too that, first, also savings accounts with non-cooperative banks must be terminated and that their credit balance must be transferred to a savings account with the SLB; secondly that payment accounts of workers or pensioners should not exceed twice their monthly income (cf. 3§16-a.)

• The legislation enters into force four months after the enactment.

Subdivision 1C will introduce the gradual legal conversion of pre-transition enterprises into Design cooperatives. The current subdivision 1A ends with four sections (8§6–8§9) setting out essential instruments for that conversion.

8§6   Competition and the 'competition authority' – full enactment

The Design's 'Competition Authority' (CA) was formally established in 8§3. In many countries a similar authority currently exists; after an adaptation of the rules the same personnel can do the work.

It will be seen that the to be enacted market power related rules play an important role for the transition.

• Legislation enacts the 3§45 tasks of the CA. Generally to the rules is added that as long as pre-transition enterprises exist, the CA rules also apply to the latter.

• (a) The prohibition of take-overs is enacted.

• (b) Maximum market share rules are enacted. (Depending on the size of country, nationwide maximum market shares might vary from 1–5% – 3§45-c.)

- During the transition the following entities are exempted from the maximum market share rules: pre-transition pension funds and life insurance companies (cf. 8§27), as well as specific other insurance companies to be specified in 8§12 (for their awarded health sector tender).

The market share rules imply that entities that surpass the limits will have to break up into two or more independent smaller legal entities.
- To the maximum market share rules is added that when entities surpass these limits, they have to report this to the CA (the CA itself also supervises this), together with a plan of how they will separate the entity into legally independent entities within, ultimately, one year.
- **(c)** To the market share rule the transitional clause is added that it overrules any pre-transition existing licences, concessions or related contracts (cf. 3§45-e). A similar clause is added for patents and copyrights.[4] Within one year after the enactment of the authority, the holders of licences or concession shall report to the authority how they will go about the expiring licences or concessions.[5]
- *Entering into force.* The legislation under (a) enters into force immediately after the enactment; that under (b) one year after the enactment. The legislation under (c) enters into force three years after enactment (thus this is the point of expiration of those licences, concessions, patents and copyrights that surpass the market share limits). However, in case the (phases 4–5) legislation of 8§39 (mining), or 8§40 (infrastructure), or 8§54 (railway transport) enter in force later than after the three years sub (c), the expiration is postponed until the mentioned phase 4–5 legislation.

8§7   Workers' council governed foundations – phases 1–4

- Legislation establishes the *'Workers' council governed foundation'* (WGF) as legal entity, together with its statute as set out in 3§25. When an existing entity is legally converted into a WGF, then until phase 5 (8§49) clause 3§25-d does not apply (that clause regards the remuneration of WGF workers).
- The legislation enters into force immediately after the enactment.

8§8   'Agency for temporary workers' council governed foundations' – full enactment

The 'Agency for temporary workers' council governed foundations' (ATF) was formally established in 8§3.

---

[4] Aspects relevant to patents and copyrights qua expiration are stated in 3§44.
[5] It will be seen that this is especially relevant for the phases 4 and 5 legislation on mining and other Earth extractions (8§39), infrastructure (8§40) and railway transport (8§54).

- Legislation enacts 3§41(d-e). It is added that during the transition the ATF can (on a larger scale than after the transition), temporarily establish Workers' council governed foundations (WGFs, 3§25); once these are sufficiently running, the foundation's assets can be sold (or temporary rented out) to a new cooperative. It is also possible that the foundation is legally converted into a cooperative.
- It is also enacted that during the transition the ATF is allowed to purchase or sell corporate shares with a view to legally converting an entity into a Design cooperative (directly so or via the stage of a WGF). It is equally enacted that when during the transition corporate shares, or a firm, are part of a bequest, the agency has a pre-emptive right to purchase these – against reasonable prices. (It will be seen in 8§9 that the transition inheritance taxes are the same as in the Design.)[6]
- It is also enacted that, during the transition, on the retirement of the (main) owner of a non-incorporated enterprise – and on the initiative of the latter or the ATF – the ATF may bargain to purchase the entity, paying by way of 'lifelong consols' (consols are a specific type of perpetual bonds, here lifelong ones) that are on name and non-tradable.[7] The interest rate is 2.5% (annually plus or minus the rate of inflation or deflation).[8]

The reasons for, and the effects of, this last rule and others are amplified on in 8§23. In brief: it may be wise to purchase an entity when it is still vital (vital to be continued as a cooperative).

- The legislation enters into force immediately after the enactment.

8§9 Taxation during the transition – permanent transition legislation

At the start of the transition the income and wealth distribution will still be very skewed. When gradually more capitalist enterprises are legally converted into cooperatives (see Subdivision 1C) and when the taxation presented in Table 8.2 (pp. 318–19) increasingly becomes effective, these distributions will become less skewed.

---

6   The working children of a deceased person working in a firm (or in a small corporation) will be offered a position in an entity that is legally converted into a WGF or cooperative.
7   The same applies for an enterprise as owned by a single owner or a few partners that has been incorporated.
8   The alternative for the (main) owner is to sell the business to a third party, on the proceeds of which income taxes have to be paid.

TABLE 8.2 *Overview of tax categories and tax rates during the transition*

	(1) Category	(2) Tax rate on bracket	(3) Average tax rate	(4) Tax sum (top of bracket)	(5) After-tax income (top bracket)*	(6) Remark
1	(MiW = annual minimum wage)		at MiW = €20,000**			
2	**Production and/or consumer goods taxes**					
3	pre-transition enterprises	maintained				
4	Design cooperatives: turnover tax (cascade)	5% to 15%				a
5	**Income tax individuals**					
6	to 60% MiW (costs of living threshold)	0%	0.0%	€ 0	€ 12,000 [0.7]	
7	from off € 60% MiW – 1× MiW	25%	10.0%	€ 2,000	€ 18,000 [1.0]	
8	from off € 1× MiW – 2× MiW	60%	35.0%	€ 14,000	€ 26,000 [1.4]	
9	from off € 2× MiW – 3× MiW	70%	46.7%	€ 28,000	€ 32,000 [1.8]	
10	from off € 3× MiW – 4× MiW	80%	55.0%	€ 44,000	€ 36,000 [2.0]	
11	from off € 4× MiW – 5× MiW	90%	62.0%	€ 62,000	€ 38,000 [2.1]	
12	above € 5× MiW	95%				
13	example of € 5× MiW – 10× MiW	95%	79.0%	€ 157,000	€ 43,000 [2.4]	
14	**Wealth tax individuals**	nil				
15	**Inheritance tax, levied on the receiver**†					b
16	over € 0 – MiW	0%				
17	over € MiW – 2× MiW	50%				
18	above 2× €MiW	100%				
19	inheritance tax (non-recent) spouse/partner	0%				
20	**Gift tax (on annual gifts; levied on receiver)**†					c
21	over € 0–10% MiW	0%				
22	above 10% MiW	100%				
23	**Tax rental property owned by enterprises**‡					d
24	over property < 50× MiW	20%				
25	over property > 50 × MiW	40%				

TABLE 8.2   Overview of tax categories and rates during the transition (cont.)

	(1)	(2)	(3)	(4)	(5)	(6)
	Category	Tax rate on bracket	Average tax rate	Tax sum (top of bracket)	After-tax income (top bracket)*	Remark
26	Income and property taxes economic entities					d
27	pre-transition entities	maintained‡				
28	Design worker cooperatives	0%				
29	**Municipal and provincial taxes**					d
30	for pre-transition entities	maintained⁂				
31	for Design worker cooperatives	nil				

*   The outer end of column (5) shows the ratio of the after-tax income differences for MiW= €18,000 = 1. (For 60% MiW = 12,000 = 1, and from 60% MiW to 5× MiW, the ratio's run from 1 to 3.3.)
** The figure of €20,000 is not essential: when in face of the country's purchasing power structure, the nominal minimum wage would be higher or lower, the taxation revenue would be proportionally higher or lower (as would be the money-level of the required state expenditure). The tax rates of column (2) are essential.
†   Maximum 15 receivers.
‡   With the exception of pre-transition pension funds and insurance companies (in face of their commitments). This tax enters into force in the first calendar year after the full enactment of the 'Real estate agency' – phase 3, 8§38.
♯   Except rental property that is taxed differently (see row 23).
⁂   These taxes are maintained during about five years. In phase 5 these will be abolished.
a. The tax rate depends on the production structure of the regarding country (after the transition the revenue from this tax should be about 50% of state expenditure). For Design 'single person enterprises' the regulation of Appendix 3E is enacted.
b. As in the Design: apart from the partner exemption, row 19, no differentiation regarding the relation between testator and receiver. (The qualification 'non-recent' in row 19 regards a marriage/partnership for the sake of tax evasion.)
c. As in the Design: these gifts must be declared to the tax authority; a gift by a parent to a child is twice exempted for 50% MiW (this is the general rule, but its mean reason is assistance for a child starting to live on its own).
d. This is a transition tax; it is no Design tax.

- The country's taxation legislation is adapted according to the relevant passages in 3§46 and to *Table 8.2* (including its notes); the latter sets out the tax categories and their tax rates during all of the transition period.

Apart from transitional matters, the main line of the taxation is similar to the Design taxation (Table 3.7). The tax rates and the tax brackets are provisional

and are to be adapted to the required taxation revenue. The state expenditure and tax revenue will be commented on in 8§21.
- *Production taxes* and/or consumer goods taxes – such as VAT (table row 2). For pre-transition enterprises these will be maintained as they were at the start of the transition (table row 3). For Design cooperatives a turnover tax (cascade system) will apply; its tax rate depends on the production structure of the country at hand (after the transition the revenue from this tax should cover about 50% of state expenditure).[9] One reason to have different production/consumption taxes is that introducing a VAT for cooperatives during the transition period would mean an enormous administrative burden for these (for other entities it is a burden that they are accustomed to).
- The *income tax for individuals* (row 5) is considerable – as in the Design. It can be seen from the table's row 12 that from an annual income of five times the minimum wage, the average tax rate steeply increases. (Recall from 3§46 that economic and public sector entities are required to withhold expected taxes from the remuneration that they pay out. This also applies for pensions. The entities receive simple instructions for this from the taxation authority. They monthly pay the deducted taxes to that authority. This should make sure that individuals receive approximately a take home remuneration that they can spent.)[10]

It may be noted that with this tax, parliamentarians are to vote about a considerable decrease in their own after-tax remuneration (that is, in many countries). This positively affects the nationwide legitimation for the income taxes.
- There are, as in the Design, no *taxes on the wealth of individuals* (row 15) even when during the transition wealth differences will still be considerable.
- All the income from wealth elements falls under the income taxes, as does the proceeds from the sale of wealth elements – this also applies for objects of art and for the received pay-off of loans, including from bonds. However, the annual proceeds from the sales of wealth elements, may be set off against the annual purchases of wealth elements – financial and non-financial wealth taken together – this is called the 'wealth netting rule'. (The burden of proving the details of correct netting is on the taxpayer. During the transition individuals shall specify their wealth elements, and the mutations thereof, on their annual tax return.)

---

9   For after the start of the transition established 'single person enterprises' the turnover tax (cascade system) will apply as specified in Appendix 3E.
10 During the transition a flat tax withholding of 60% applies for dividends and interest on bonds. All withholdings are settled with the final tax assessment.

The point about this is that the income and inheritance taxes (see below) are based on Design principles, but that there is no intention to further affect people's way of life as they used to. For this reason also – as will be seen later – people can during the transition keep on inhabiting the self-occupied dwelling that they owned before the transition. (In case they want to move, the wealth netting rule applies. This is indeed a transition rule: after the transition dwellings can be rented only – as in the Design.)

• About the substantial *inheritance tax* (row 15 – the same as in the Design) it should be communicated widely that these regard the principal point that all children deserve at least materially an equal treatment, and that inheritances are no merit of children.

Recall from ch. 3 that there shall be no more than 15 inheritors, and that apart from the spouse/partner exemption (row 19) there is no differentiation regarding the relation between testator and receiver.

• Contrary to the Design, row 19 of Table 8.2 has the qualification 'non-recent' spouse or partner; this regards a marriage/partnership for the sake of tax evasion.[11]

Recall from 8§8 that when during the transition corporate shares or a firm are part of a bequest the 'Agency for temporary workers' council governed foundations' has a pre-emptive right to purchase these.

• *Gift taxes* are as in the Design (row 20).

• The *tax on rental property owned by enterprises* (row 23) is a transition tax because there is no such property in the Design. Pre-transition pension funds and insurance companies are – in face of their commitments – exempted from this tax. The tax implies that it will be hardly profitable for (other) pre-transition enterprises to maintain such ownership. This tax has two purposes. One is to make pre-transition enterprises focus on production and employment. The second is that it prepares the rental Design tasks of the 'Real estate agency' (phase 3, 8§38).

• The *income and property taxes for pre-transition enterprises* (row 27) are maintained as they were before the transition, though except for rental property (the previous point).

---

11 Generally, 'recent' may be specified as 'from the start of the transition'. However, for later marriages/partnerships the regulation should be such that the spouse/partner can keep on living in the dwelling with its furnishings. Nevertheless corporate shares or a firm that are part of the bequest will be fully taxed, and these fall under the 8§8 rule that the 'Agency for temporary workers' council governed foundations' has a pre-emptive right to purchase these.

- The income tax rate of 0% for Design cooperatives (row 28) is in line with the Design. (Note that these cooperatives only gradually emerge – see 8§18 and 8§23.)
- *Municipal and provincial taxes* are no Design category. In case there were such taxes before the transition (row 29), these are maintained during about five years: in phase 5 these will be abolished. However, Design cooperatives pay no such taxes.

The result is that during the transition there are different taxation regimes for different legal entities. Note that also in capitalist countries this is not uncommon (corporations, firms, foundations, cooperatives etc.).

- *Entering into force*. The inheritance tax and the gift tax (rows 15 and 20) enter into force immediately. The tax on 'rental property owned by enterprises' (row 23) enters into force in the first full calendar year after the full enactment of the 'Real estate agency' (phase 3, 8§38). All other taxes enter into force in the first full calendar year that starts nine months after the enactment (briefly this is the calendar year that starts twelve months after the start of phase 1; thus if the enactment is in the first quarter of the year, it enters into force in the next calendar year; if the enactment is in a later quarter of the year, it enters into force on the second 1 January thereafter).

It will be seen that for health and education provisions and for pension and child allowances (8§12, 8§13, 8§27, 8§28) the entry into force is similar as in the previous sentence. In fact the entry into force of the taxation is derived from the latter. The reason is that especially the bottom half of the income distribution should not be heavily taxed before the provisions mentioned are in force, thus when the provisions counterpart of the taxes is experienced.

Subdivision 1B. Regulation of social-economic provisions

This subdivision comprises four sections that regard permanent or temporary legislation of elementary provisions. These include a minimum wage, minimum costs of living allowances, ceilings on the rental price for dwellings, and free health and education provisions for all. In phase 2 provisions will be extended to other fields.

8§10   *Minimum wage – full enactment – and temporary 'minimum costs of living allowances' – phases 1–3*

- *The minimum wage and the minimum costs of living*. Legislation enacts the determination of the minimum wage (3§11).

As an indication parliament sets the pre-tax minimum wage (MiW) at 167% of the 'minimum costs of living' (MCL), whence MCL/MiW= 60%. Recall that the MCL is based on a costs of living basket; that the MCL and the MiW are adapted for inflation or deflation every year; and that the content of the costs of living *basket* is revised at intervals of five years. (See also 3§47-e for the policy considerations regarding the percentages above.)

• The following transition legislation is also enacted. First, during the transition the content of the costs of living basket, as well as the prices thereof, may be revised each year. Second. In case the pre-transition minimum wage is higher than the one as calculated above, the pre-transition level is maintained in phase 1 of the transition. Third, in case the pre-transition minimum wage is below the one as calculated above, it is forbidden to lay off minimum wage earners – unless the employer can show that an intended lay off is caused by other reasons and has gotten permission for the lay-off.

Comment on the transitional change of the monetary MCL and MiW at constant purchasing power. The costs of living basket, as well as the prices thereof – and thence the minimum wage, will vary during the transition for the following two reasons.

First, early on in the transition (after about a year after the start of the transition) health and education provisions will become free for all – that is, financed out of taxation (at that point they are no longer part of the costs of living basket); similarly pensions for all will be financed out of taxation (whence premiums for pensions are no longer part of the basket).

Second, after phase 3 the average costs of housing will *gradually* decrease.

Summing this up: during the transition the composition and monetary value of the costs of living basket (the MCL) will gradually decrease, and derived from it the monetary minimum wage (MiW). Note that the real purchasing power of the MCL and the MiW are not affected by this. Declining monetary minimum wages, or allowances, at a constant purchasing power is nevertheless a psychological problem because of the associated money wage illusion. Therefore it should repeatedly be widely communicated *why* the MCL and the MiW minimum wage gradually decrease.

Note that the taxation table (Table 8.2) gave the *example* of a minimum wage at €20,000; the latter would decline pari passu the above. Note also that the decline of the MiW above, has nothing to do with the sales (thence the wages sum) of the cooperatives/enterprises. Thus when the MiW declines, more workers have an above MiW income, whence (cet. par.) there is no effect on the total taxation revenue. In fact the MCL and MiW matter is about an index for the determination of the MCL and MiW levels.

• *Temporary 'minimum costs of living' allowances.* The pre-transition income allowances are maintained until the regarding Design allowances (3§24, Table 3.9) have been introduced. It is enacted that in case in the country at hand

pensioners or people out of work receive no allowances at all, these can apply for 'minimum costs of living' allowances that are provisionally set at 60% of the minimum wage (the MCL). In case pre-transition income allowances would be lower than this level, the MCL level will apply. The level is set by parliament and may be changed each subsequent year.
• This rule is implemented by municipalities (in case in the country at hand these do not so already, this is an exception to 8§4). Those that consider themselves eligible shall one time apply for these allowances. Between the application and the temporary granting there might be a delay of up to one months (with retroactive payment as per the application date), the detailed eligibility being assessed later.
• *Entry into force*. The transition rule about non-lay-offs ('third' under the second bullet) enters into force immediately. All other legislation above enters into force two months after the enactment.

8§11   Housing legislation: rental dwellings – permanent transition legislation; and rental dwellings construction – phases 1–2

This section presents two housing legislation subjects.
• (a) *Rented out dwellings owned by enterprises or individuals*. It is enacted that rents of dwellings owned by enterprises or individuals may be changed, but they shall not increase by more than the general rate of inflation (consumer price index of the previous year). When at the start of the transition the economy is in recession (by standard definition) rents shall not increase at all. During the transition this legislation is permanent and it enters into force immediately after the publication of the enactment.
• (b) *Real estate agency*. The 'Real estate agency' (REA) was formally established in 8§3. It is enacted that until phase 3 (8§38) this agency has only the following two tasks.
• In case the pre-transition inheritance is such that there is a shortage of dwellings for rent at reasonable rents, the REA immediately starts an emergency building programme for to be rented out dwellings. These dwellings should be easily removable qua location, and be depreciated in about twenty to thirty years. The design and building are carried out by pre-transition enterprises on basis of a curtailed tender procedure. (In the likely case that the economy is in a recession such building would also be production stimulating.)
• In case of a foreseeable future shortage of dwellings for rent, the REA (also) starts a programme of building permanent dwellings, constructed in accordance with acclaimed urban and landscape designs, and provided in a variety of qualities (cf. 3§37-f).

• The legislation enters into force immediately after the enactment. On each of these two REA programmes see further 8§20 on recession countering policies.

8§12 Health provisions: temporary regulation – phases 1–4

The transition of the health sector is among the most complicated ones; it is postponed to phase 5 (8§50).
• Prior to it, the following temporary legislation is enacted.
(a) All medical institutions, medical practitioners, pharmacists and other medical workers (including medical school-leavers) shall register with the National Health Agency (the agency was established in 8§3) or with a currently existing institution that already undertakes such registration. All medical institutions and the individuals mentioned above require a licence (that may already be the case).
(b) There is a medical insurance for all, for which the premiums are paid by the state out of the income taxes that it receives.
(c) The payment to the under (a) mentioned is carried out by one or more insurance companies that have experience with this kind of insurance. From off the start of phase 1 these can give notice to the Ministry of Health that they are interested to do this, and three months after the start of phase 1 (this is at the time of the current enactment) they can, during two months, tender for a minimum five-year contract.[12] This contract enters into force at the time indicated at the end of the current section. The ministry shall award the contract to the tenderer which submitted the best tender on the basis of the award criteria set out in the contract notice. (In case no insurance company meets the criteria, the ministry caries out the payment to the health institutions.)
(d) There will be a ceiling for the premiums that is based on, first, similar premiums prevailing in the country at hand, and second deliberation between the ministry, the insurer(s) and representatives of the medical sector.
(e) Persons that already are insured, and that can submit evidence from their insurer that the insurance level is not lower than that of the collective insurance, can apply for a tax reduction on their annual tax return (the reduction being 90% of the premium under b). Early on they will have to report this to the insurer, who reports this to the ministry of health.
(f) No new health insurance contracts shall be entered on.
(g) Besides the payments by insurance companies, none of the under (a) mentioned shall – on risk of a fine or losing their licence – require or accept any

---

12 The Design health sector will be enacted in phase 5; should this enactment or its entry into force be delayed, then the contract is extended, and the regarding insurance companies should commit themselves to carry out a possible extension to more than five years.

form of fees, payments in monetary form or in kind, gifts, or promises. (This rule should prevent uneven access to medical services. The implication of the clauses above is that all necessary health treatment is paid by the insurance companies.)[13]

Already at this point medical institutions and pharmacies should be informed that entities with more than ten workers that (will) receive reimbursement via the collective medical insurance, shall, around two years after the start of the transition, introduce workers' councils with (at that point) restricted competences – as indicated in 8§26.

• *Entry into force.* The legislation under (c) about insurance tender and contracts enters into force immediately. That under (a) enters into force three months after the enactment. The other clauses enter into force in the first full calendar year that starts nine months after the enactment (briefly this is the calendar year that starts 12 months after the start of phase 1; thus if the enactment is in the first quarter of the year, it enters into force in the next calendar year; if the enactment is in a later quarter of the year, it enters into force on the second 1 January thereafter). Note that the entry into force of the income taxation legislation (8§9) should run analogous.

8§13   Education provisions: temporary regulation – phases 1–4

The 'National Education Agency' (NEA) was formally established in 8§3, and given the tasks of, first, preparing for a reorganisation of a perhaps similar currently existing institution, or of a split-off from a department of a current ministry of education, and, second, preparing for the execution of the regulation set out in the current section.

This section sets out temporary regulation of the education sector that is to be executed by the NEA. The full regulation of the sector will be enacted in phase 5 (8§51).

• The following legislation (1–10) is enacted.

1. The NEA is annually assigned a budget for itself. For the internal organisation and remunerations of the agency 8§3 applies.
2. The NEA is annually assigned a budget for the educational institutions for which it is responsible; until phase 5 there are no workforce targets.
3. All primary, secondary and tertiary education will be provided free of charge (tertiary education up to and including a masters level).[14] The provision is fully state-financed out of taxation. (Cf. 3§30-a.)

---

13   During the transition there may nevertheless be a degree of unequal access due to the existing insurances mentioned under (e).
14   The PhD level is enacted in phase 5.

4. Budget allocation over the educational institutions (3§30-b, exclusive workforce allocation).
5. Only NEA-licensed institutions are allowed to provide the education sub (3). In case there does not already exist a licence register in the country at hand, the institutions should apply for a licence with the NEA. Licences may be revised every five years. Education institutions shall – on risk of a fine or losing their licence – not require or accept entrance or enrolment fees in any form. (This rule should prevent uneven access to the institutions.) (Cf. 3§30-d.)
6. The NEA determines minimum qualifications for teachers at the various levels sub (3). (Cf. 3§30-e.)
7. All teachers sub (3), including school-leavers, should register with the NEA according to their teaching qualifications, as well as their foreseen date of retirement (3§30-f).
8. Determination of the attainment targets for primary, secondary and tertiary education; as well as broad per year attainment levels such that pupils and students can horizontally switch between institutions (3§30-h).
9. Various issues regarding the quality of teaching programmes and of teaching (3§30-i, j, k).
10. *Specific temporary rules.*
• For their staff budget educational institutions will be financed on the basis of the student/staff ratios of Table 3.12, column 5 (3§32). These ratios are targets. In case an institution feels that it cannot adhere to the target, it can, substantiated, request a temporary exception. The institutions will receive lump sum finances for fixed and other equipment as well as other expenses (based on averages of five years prior to the transition).
• Currently 'for profit' educational institutions will receive no more budget than non-profit institutions.[15]
• In case institutions foresee that potential enrolments are larger than the places, they should deliberate with the NEA that might ultimately decide that enrolment is allocated on a lottery basis.
• The non-compulsory pre-primary education is offered by licensed educational cooperatives or other currently existing educational entities. (These are not financed by the NEA or other state institutions.)
• For their PhD programmes and for their research, universities keep on being financed as they currently are.

---

15 This means that these are often better off when they legally convert into a foundation. (In phase 5, 8§51, this will have to be a 'Workers' council governed foundation' – 3§25 – at that point only these WGFs will be financed.)

- *Entering into force.* The legislation enters into force as follows.
Points 1 and 7. Four months after the enactment.
Points 2–5 and 10. The first school/academic year that starts nine months after the enactment (briefly this is the school year that starts twelve months after the start of phase 1; thus if the enactment is in the first quarter of the year, it enters into force just before/after the next school year; if the enactment is in a later quarter of the year, it enters into force on the second school year).[16] Note that the entry into force of the income taxation legislation (8§9) should run analogously.
Points 6 and 8. One year after the enactment. It is applied in the second school/academic year after this date.
Point 9. Two years after the enactment. It is applied in the second school/academic year after this date.

Subdivision 1C. Institutional changes and regulation in the economic domain

This subdivision comprises five sections regarding: the transition's core legislation of Design cooperatives (8§14 and 8§15); regulation of financial markets (8§16); the accommodation of banks' investment loans (8§17); and the legal conversion of pre-transition entities into Design cooperatives – the conversion of Worker-owned cooperatives in particular (8§18). Herewith, and together with the last four sections of Subdivision 1A, the transitional foundations of the economic domain will be laid.

8§14   *The Design's cooperative as legal entity; unique form for newly established multi-worker legal entities in the non-public sector domain – full enactment*

The following three sets of rules are key ones for the transition.
- The Design's cooperative as legal entity is enacted (2§3); all rules set out in chapter 2 are also legislated, though those mentioned in 8§15 with a postponed entry into force.
- Regarding take-overs it is enacted that during the transition only, a newly founded cooperative may purchase part or all of the pre-transition entity where the founders were employed at the time of, or just prior to, the foundation of the cooperative. (The reasons for this temporary rule are indicated in 8§23, under its last sections A and B.)

---

16   This is for countries in which the school/academic year starts around September or October.

• It is also enacted that regarding the economic domain (the non-public sector domain) no legal entity shall be established other than a Design cooperative, except for: (a) a 'single person enterprise'; (b) enterprises that are legally enforced to break up into two or more entities (because of their market ceiling, 8§6, or because – in phase 3 – the single location requirement). Also enacted is that the only one allowed non-public sector legal conversion of an entity is that into a Design cooperative.
• *Entry into force.* The legislation above enters into force immediately after the enactment.

8§15 *Temporary exceptions for the Design's cooperatives – phases 1–2*
In comparison with the Design, cooperatives established may apply the following two rules, but temporarily are not required to do so (enforced application will be required in phase 3; 8§35).
• 2§3.4. Cooperatives are organised in no more than one single location.
• 2§7.0. The rule that cooperatives are required to build up a legally binding resistance buffer of 30% of the assets *does* apply. However, the rule that prior to having built up this buffer, workers receive no more than the minimum wage is relaxed to twice the minimum wage. Nevertheless, in face of phase 3, cooperatives would be wise to go for less than twice.

When these rules enter into force (phase 3), similar rules will also apply for all pre-transition enterprises. In phase 1 this should be publicly announced so that these enterprises, and the Design cooperatives, can already prepare for it.

8§16 *Financial markets legislation: shares, bonds, mortgages, consumer credit and savings – permanent transition rules*
All of the legislation set out in this section regards implicit or explicit Design rules. Their enactment here makes that these rules also apply to pre-transition financial and non-financial enterprises. For these entities the rules may limit their expansion (rules a and b), or – for banks – focus the expansion on investment credit (rules c and d), or (the other rules) increase the monetary and financial policy scope. Some of the rules are put in the form of 'no *new*' bonds etc. so as to accommodate a gradual transition.
• The following seven rules are enacted.
(a) Enterprises (including when relevant Worker-*owned* cooperatives) shall not issue new shares or bonds; nor shall they place new private loans. (As including such issue to, or placement with, foreign institutions or individuals.) During the transition, markets for *existing* shares and bonds keep existing. (See 8§17 for loans from banks.)

(b) No new contracts for pensions or life insurances shall be entered on (see also 8§27).
(c) No new mortgage loans shall be provided by banks (including by cooperative banks) or by other enterprises. (New mortgage loans for Design cooperatives are provided by the 'Savings and Loans Bank' – cf. 3§16-e; this bank was enacted under 8§5.)
(d) No new consumer credit shall be provided by banks or other institutions (2§6.4; the reason is indicated in 2§6.4 footnote).
(e) Bank savings accounts in any form (such as term deposits) shall be terminated. Holders of these accounts shall transfer their credit balance to a savings account with the 'Savings and Loans Bank' (2§16.2).
(f) Bank payment accounts of individuals shall not exceed twice their monthly income (2§16.2).
(g) Bank payment-account holders receive a nationwide *uniform* zero, or near to zero, rate of interest as specified by the Central Bank (2§16.1)
• *Entry into force.* The first four rules (a-d) enter into force immediately after the enactment, and the last three (e-g) two months after the enactment. Note that in case 8§5 (on the four banking and fund agencies) was already enacted, some of these rules already apply or enter into force soon.

8§17 Accommodation by the SLB of banks' investment credit – permanent transition rules

In in face of the rules about shares and bonds (8§16-a) and savings accounts (8§16-d), banks are – for the provision of investment credit to cooperatives and enterprises – increasingly dependent on loans from the 'Savings and Loans Bank' (SLB – 8§5). The 'increasingly' pertains to pre-transition banks that can initially still rely on existing shares and bonds.
• The following legislation is enacted (this regards a specification of that for the SLB as set out in 8§5).
(a) The SLB can provide securitised loans to banks in the priority order below; at its discretion it sets the loan quantities, the required type of securities and the further loan conditions including the interest rate.
(1) Loans to cooperative banks for their loans to cooperatives.
(2) Loans to non-cooperative banks for their loans to cooperatives.
(3) Loans to non-cooperative banks for their loans to non-cooperatives. The extent of such loans by the SLB is co-dependent on the degree in which sufficient savings are forthcoming.
(b) For non-cooperative banks (pre-transition capitalist banks) applies that in order to be eligible for these loans, they are required to legally separate the entity into a part that services the investment credit to cooperatives (as

including the payment accounts of their workers), and a part for all their other activities.[17]
• *Entry into force.* The legislation above enters into force immediately after the enactment.

8§18 *Conversion of the legal form of pre-transition entities (those of WOCs in particular) into Design cooperatives – phases 1–3 and permanent transition rules*

At this point there are yet no Designs cooperatives, but from now on workers might found a Design cooperative, and pre-transition 'worker-owned cooperatives' (WOCs), or other pre-transition entities, might legally convert into a Design cooperative.[18]

Existing entities might wish to go for a legal conversion in consideration of economic democracy and for strategic considerations. Apart from this, there are three main fiscal advantages of a conversion. *First*, Design cooperatives pay a simple turnover tax, instead of (depending on the country) one with a high administrative burden such as the VAT (Table 8.2, rows 3–4). *Second*, Design cooperatives pay no income and property taxes, whereas pre-transition entities may have to pay such taxes (Table 8.2, rows 27–28). *Third*, whereas during about five years from the start of the transition, pre-transition entities have to pay municipal and provincial taxes as before the transition, Design cooperatives pay no such taxes (Table 8.2, rows 30–31).

The legally converting entities are supposed to use the competitive advantage (at least for some period) for: the conversion costs, the resistance buffer requirement, and the single location rule (the latter from off phase 3 – cf. 8§15). Note that most entities will have reserves similar to a resistance buffer.

Legislation regarding the legal conversion of 'Worker-owned cooperatives'. In most, or many, WOCs the workers deposited with the entity a sum of money, or held a share in that entity, that according to the entity's rules is all or in part returnable at some point – usually at their retirement. Such deposits or similar requirements shall not be required for Design cooperatives (2§3.4; 2§4.0).

• In order to compensate the workers of legally converting WOCs for their deposits, it is enacted that these workers are during ten years after the conversion exempted from income taxation over the second bracket (€ 60% MiW –

---

17 The bank might decide to legally convert the first part into a cooperative bank (which, amongst other things, has taxation advantages). If it does not decide to do so, the bank's shares are partitioned according to the entities.
18 For existing medical or educational partnerships it is mentioned that in phase 5 these shall be organised as 'workers' council governed foundations' – 8§50 and 8§51.

1xMiW; Table 8.2, row 7; this tax exemption adds up to a sum of 1xMiW), provided that the conversion takes place within two years from off the start of transition phase 1. (The reason for the time limit is that after the second year of the transition, the taxation revenue gradually decreases – 8§21.) The tax exemption also applies for workers that during the mentioned ten years would retire. The regarding converting WOCs shall provide the tax authority with an audited list of the workers that qualify for the tax exemption. On their tax return the regarding workers shall, in reference to the just mentioned list, indicate the current year of exemption (1–10).

The compensation is thus uniform for all WOCs. For the WOC as entity, the implication is that the earlier paid in funds/deposits can be transferred into the required resistance buffer or into non-committed reserves.

woc-owned banks. A group of WOCs might own a cooperative bank.
• It is also enacted that in case a group of WOCs (now Design cooperatives) is the owner of a cooperative bank (non-Design) these are required to legally convert that bank into a Design bank (COB) within five years. Alternatively these WOCs might bargain to sell the entity to the 'Agency for temporary workers' council governed foundations' (8§8), with all the bank workers keeping their position (in due time the Agency converts the entity into a Design cooperative bank). Over the proceeds from the selling no taxes are due.

Note regarding the legal conversion of pre-transition banks into a Design cooperative bank. Design cooperative banks focus on providing investment credit to non-bank cooperatives, and apart from that only provide the service of payment accounts for cooperatives and individuals. Therefore, a pre-transition bank that wishes to legally convert part of its activities into a Design bank, shall first legally separate its activities into one entity suited for Design bank activities, and a second one for all its other activities (which may keep the legal form of a capitalist stock corporation).
• *Entry into force*. The legislation under the two bullets above enters into force immediately after the enactment.

Subdivision 1D. Recession policy, the general transition strategy and concluding matters phase 1 {requires no legislation}

This subdivision is divided into six sections. The first one makes some general comments on phase 1 (8§19). The second one (8§20) is on recession countering policies (recall that it is almost sure that the transition starts in a recession as inherited from the pre-transition turbulences – cf. ch. 7). The third one is on the state expenditure and taxation revenue due to the phase 1 legislation (8§21). The following two sections are on the transition in general (8§22) and on the transition strategy for the gradual legal conversion of pre-transition capitalist enterprises into Design cooperatives (8§23). The final section provides an estimate of the amount of legislative work during phase 1. On basis of it – and of similar estimates for the next phases – an estimate is made of the total duration of the legislative phases 1–5 (8§24).

8§19 *General comments on phase 1*

At the end of phase 1 the transition has been set in motion. However, the economic structure is as yet left rather unchanged.

There are minimum wages, and minimum costs of living allowances for all people out of work. For tenants of dwellings there is a ceiling on the rent. For all there is at the start of year two after the transition the prospect of full healthcare and education provisions. (How much all of these count for the majority depends on what is inherited from the pre-transition constellation.).

In this respect the start is rather cautious, also in face of insecurities about the inherited taxation revenue at the start of phase 1 (see also 8§21). The income taxation enactment (8§9) is planned to enter into force together with the health and education provisions and the (in the in phase 2 to be enacted) pension and child allowances; together these provisions and allowances constitute (and will constitute) the by far largest share of total state expenditure.

The before-tax wages and other incomes of the pre-transition enterprises and public sector institutions will until phase 5 not be affected by legislation (however, from year two onwards, the after-tax distribution of income and wealth will considerably be affected by the taxation legislation). In phase 5 legislation will adapt the before-tax remuneration of workers in the public sector institutions.

8§20 *Recession-countering policies*

It is almost certain that at the start of the transition the country at hand is in a recession, as caused by an uncertainty investment-strike (7§8). By the start of the transition (and the programme for it) uncertainty turns into rather certain changes (see 8§23 below). This section sets out three fields that on basis of the Division 1 legislation either does counter the recession, or that may be set to counter the recession. A fourth measure is independent of the legislation.

(1) *Consumption expenditure floor*. The legislation under Subdivision 1B puts a floor in the potential level of consumption expenditure: minimum wages and the minimum costs of living allowances (each entering into force soon after the enactment); and the ceiling on the rent for tenants of dwellings (entering into force immediately after the enactment).

(2) *Construction and maintenance of buildings.* What construction and maintenance of buildings will there be going on immediately after the transition's start?

• Owner-occupied dwellings: necessary maintenance, but hardly any new construction (the latter in face of the regulation on mortgages and on inheritance taxes).

• Rented-out dwellings: necessary maintenance, but hardly any new construction (in face of the taxes on income, and for enterprises in face of the tax on rental property – Table 8.2, row 24).

• Maintenance of premises: necessary maintenance.

• Construction of premises: by 'workers-owned cooperatives' (WOCs) according to the size of the WOC sector; probably none by capitalist enterprises.

Hence it is most likely that – aside from the WOC premises part – the construction sector reached near to a standstill (see also Table 7.3). It is therefore important that the 'Real estate agency' (REA) as soon as possible sets up a dwellings construction programme (cf. 8§11) – thus the regarding enactment should have high priority (there are many priorities in phase 1!) Recall from 3§37-r that, regarding the construction and renting-out of dwellings, the REA structurally runs on a break-even basis. However, at the current point of the transition it requires a pre-finance of its construction expenditures via borrowing from the state. The state itself receives additional taxation revenues only with a delay from off about year t+1, thus for financing the REA it must now borrow from the Central Bank (see further 8§21). It seems reasonable to do so because of the high multiplier effect of the construction sector on the total economy. The REA undertakes the following two construction programs, each for to be rented out dwellings.

(2-a) *Emergency programme of dwellings construction.* This regards the construction of prefabricated transportable and re-transportable dwellings in modules of about 30–40 m², in prices of 2020 costing around €70,000 to €100,000, each lasting about 30 years. The time between the start of the construction and the delivery is about five months.[19] Especially such a relatively short construction time is relevant. The design and building are carried out by pre-transition enterprises on basis of a curtailed tender procedure.

The programme has three purposes. First, the supply of dwellings for rent in case there is currently a general shortage. Second, use for unexpected future

---

19   Aedes 2020, pp. 5, 10 and 7. For especially modular construction Aedes refers in this report to experiences in Japan, the Netherlands, the Scandinavian countries, and the UK.

shortages. Third, use for temporary housing in case of future renovation of existing dwellings.

(2-b) *Regular dwellings construction program.* At the same time the REA sets in motion a programme of building permanent dwellings, constructed in accordance with acclaimed urban and landscape designs, and provided in a variety of qualities (cf. 3§37-f). Apart from the important design phase, the construction takes probably a year. However, in terms of a 'recession-countering policy', the very start of the construction already has multiplier effects. The more the transition proceeds in the following years, the more emphasis there should be on acclaimed urban and landscape designs – and varieties therein – perhaps also via national and international design contests.

(3) *Policies regarding non-construction investment.* For such policies the focus should be on the investment by sectors/branches that have a relative high multiplier effect and that are relatively labour intensive. In the current transition phase 1, two agencies have been established that in principle might support such investments: the 'Savings and Loans Bank' (SLB, 8§5) and the 'Investment-credit Guarantee Fund' (IGF, 8§5). For the regarding investments the SLB can temporally decrease the rate of interest that it charges to banks (cf. 8§5, last but one paragraph), on the condition that the banks pass on this rate to the enterprises (on which banks have to report to the SLB). In case this insufficiently boosts investment, the IGF could, with the same focus mentioned above, selectively provide investment-credit guarantees for cooperatives (including pre-transition workers-owned cooperatives) – for which these cooperatives have to apply with the IGF.

(4) *Forwarding of infrastructural projects.* (The following measure is independent of Design legislation.) It would be appropriate to legislate early on in phase 1 the forwarding of already planned infrastructural projects. (It will be seen in 8§24 that the first ten weeks after the start of the transition are reserved for general legislative preparations by civil service workers. This time might be used for the mentioned forwarding and similar economy stimulating measures.)

8§21   *State expenditure and taxation revenue due to phase 1 legislation*
Before getting to the State expenditure due to phase 1 legislation, *Table 8.3* lists the expected extra transition taxation revenue in comparison with the Design.

It can be seen from *Table 8.3* that from off the second calendar year after the start of the transition there will be quite some extra taxation revenue in comparison with the Design. However, during the transition this extra gradually decreases.

TABLE 8.3 *Extra taxation revenue due to phase 1 legislation in comparison with the Design*

Row Table 8.2	Tax category†	Phase 1	Further transition	Extra after full transition
5	income tax	+ top incomes from capitalist enterprises	→ share of these enterprises gradually decreases	none
5	income tax	+ rental income + income shares and bonds + net selling of wealth	→ idem; gradually decreasing along with bequests	none
15	inheritance tax	+ rented out wealth + wealth shares, bonds, firms + owner-occupied housing	→ idem; gradually decreasing along with bequests	none
23	rental property tax enterprises*	enters into force in phase 3 in year after full enactment Real estate agency (8§38)	main revenue in the first three years after its entering into force	none
27	income and other property taxes of pre-trans. enterprises	pre-transition tax maintained; extra is country dependent	gradually decreasing along with conversion into Design coops	none

† The revenue from municipal and provincial taxes has no effect, because when these taxes are abolished (phase 5) these are replaced by transfers from the state to these institutions.
* Except pension funds and insurance companies.

State expenditure. With four exceptions the first phase of the transition is 'merely' legislative. This legislation takes an effort from parliament and ministries, but this can probably be done with no more than the current staff of these – whence this will not result in extra state expenditure in comparison with the pre-transition period. The five exceptions are listed below (recession-countering policies are based on legislation).
• 8§10. *Minimum costs of living allowances.* Whether, and to what extent, these result in extra state expenditure depends on the pre-transition inheritance.
• 8§11. *Housing legislation: construction dwellings.*
• 8§20. Recession-countering policies (these are not legislative).
• 8§18. *Legal conversion wocs.* Formally this is not an expenditure, but what is sometimes called a 'taxation expenditure' (tax reduction).
• 8§8. *Legal conversion non-incorporated enterprises (i.e. firms) via lifetime consols after retirement.* This regards an expenditure by the 'Agency for temporary workers' council governed foundations'. It is further explained in 8§23 under its last subheading.

Table 8.4 lists these state expenditures together with their way of finance in phase 1 and in the further phases of the transition.

TABLE 8.4 *State expenditure due to phase 1 legislation*

Expenditure category	Finance of expenditure†		
	Phase 1	Further transition	After transition
general state administration‡	permanent taxes	permanent taxes	permanent taxes
Savings and Loans Bank (8§5)	savings of households and interest from banks		
temporary allowances (8§10)*	permanent taxes	permanent taxes	N.A.
construction dwellings (8§11)	borrowing⸸	inheritance taxes⁂	none: break even
health provisions (8§12)	N.A.	permanent taxes††	income taxes
education provisions (8§13)	N.A.	permanent taxes††	income taxes
recession measures (8§20)	borrowing⸸	→ idem phase 2	N.A.
legal conversion WOCs (8§18)	N.A.	temporary reduction revenue from income taxes	N.A.
legal conversion firms via lifetime consols (8§8 and 8§23)	N.A.	interest serviced from inheritance tax	N.A.

N.A. = not applicable.
† 'Permanent taxes' are mainly the turnover/production tax and the income tax.
‡ This includes the internal organisation of the state agencies introduced in phase 1, excluding their payment of allowances or other transfers.
* Gradually replaced by other (higher) allowances.
⸸ Borrowing from CB via the state. Repayment out of taxes rental property enterprises (see last but one row of Table 8.3).
⁂ Gradually income from rent of dwellings.
†† The expenditure enters into force together with that of the taxation.

8§22 *Note on the transition in general in face of the 'phase 1 taxation measures'*

This section regards the transition in general. The taxation measures (8§9, Table 8.2) include considerable inheritance taxes. This tax (with, as in the Design, a top bracket of 100% above twice the minimum wage) implies that after a generation the private property ownership, in multi-person enterprises, shares, bonds and real estate will have evanesced.[20] (It will always remain pos-

---

20 Shares and bonds will no longer exist, and real estate (except premises of cooperatives) will be owned by the 'National Real Estate Agency' (3§37; 8§38).

sible to own a 'single person enterprise' for one generation – 2§1.2).[21] Hence ultimately within one generation the capitalist sector will have faded away.

The above is, apparently, the 'simple' part of the transition. Generally the transition strategy should be that well before this ultimate point – and from phase 1 onwards – there is a *gradual* conversion of pre-transition entities into Design cooperatives such that production and jobs are preserved. This is not complicated for pre-transition 'worker-owned cooperatives' (cf. 8§18). Whence, again, the relative size of this sector in comparison with the pre-transition capitalist sector is important. A gradual legal conversion of pre-transition capitalist entities is more complicated – and this is the aim of the next transition phases (next to a gradual transition of the public sector institutions). The following section provides a preview of the legal conversion of these enterprises.

8§23 The transition strategy for the gradual legal conversion of pre-transition capitalist enterprises into Design cooperatives

This section is divided into the following four subjects: 1. the effect of the transition on the owners of capitalist enterprises; 2. a comparison between cooperatives and capitalist enterprises during the transition; 3. the general strategy of the transition; 4. transition differences between stock corporations and firms.

1. How the transition impacts on the owners of pre-transition capitalist enterprises during their lifetime
(a) The income tax is, measured by capitalist standards, considerably progressive (even if owners of capitalist enterprises would believe that there are good reasons for a skewed distribution of income, they might also consider that there is no good economic reason for a specific degree of skewedness).[22]
(b) The income tax affects their material way of living. On the other hand, this tax finances also for them:
• free health services (from about year two onwards).
• free education for their children (from about year two onwards).

---

21   One generation because of the inheritance tax.
22   Cf. Schumpeter 2003 [1943], p. 208: 'In capitalist society, social recognition of performance or social prestige carries a strongly economic connotation ... pecuniary gain is the typical index of success (...) the prestige motive, more than any other, can be molded by simple reconditioning: successful performers may conceivably be satisfied nearly as well with the privilege – if granted with judicious economy – of being allowed to stick a penny stamp on their trousers as they are by receiving a million a year. Nor would that be irrational.'

• (a floor in) their pensions (phase 2; from about year two onwards);
• child benefits; and cost of living benefits for their studying children (each from phase 2 onwards);
(c) Qua housing their way of life is not affected, because during the transition there are no property or wealth taxes on owner-occupied dwellings.
(d) The substantial inheritance taxes do not affect the current owners, but rather their children; but they might consider that an equal start for children in terms of wealth is a virtue (inheritances are no merit of children).

Regarding these four points (a-d) there might be a mixed (dis)satisfaction for the material circumstances of the capital owners personally, but perhaps they might derive satisfaction from an increased material equality for all (including for future generations).

2. Transition comparison between capitalist enterprises and cooperatives
The general strategy of the transition is one of non-enforcement – that is, given the income and inheritance taxes (these are Design taxes, also qua tax brackets). However, the capital owners are also, though during the transition most often moderately, affected by the prosperousness of the enterprises that they own ('moderately' because of the income taxes: mediocre or very high dividends, for example, do not make a big after-tax difference). Below I expand on the (for the owners) relevant prosperity of the enterprises in comparison with cooperatives.

Especially medium-sized and big corporations will have to split into two or several entities in face of their market share and in face of the single location rule (the same applies for worker-owned cooperatives – market share rules are enacted in phase 1 and the single location rule in phase 3; cf. 8§14 and 8§15). This may but need not affect their prosperity. The reason for these splits is to create an equal level playing field with Design cooperatives (these are similarly bound to a single location and market share ceilings). The prosperity of the capitalist enterprises, or at least their possible expansion, is further affected by the ban on the issuance of new shares and bonds and the placement of new private loans. (This is again a matter of equal level playing field with Design cooperatives.)

'Worker-owned cooperatives' that convert into Design cooperatives face adaptation problems, whereas the capitalist enterprises maintain their general structure. Therefore, as an equal playing field compensation, the pre-transition income and property taxation for capitalist enterprises is maintained, whereas cooperatives fall under the Design's zero taxation (Table 8.2, rows 26–28). Further, on one financial point the capitalist enterprises face a possible disadvantage in comparison with cooperatives, which is that the former are last in row regarding bank loans for expansion investments (8§17, point 3).

All these are indeed constraints for capitalist enterprises. But these might also be interpreted positively, in that it is up to the capitalist enterprises to show that (presumably in their view) they are more efficient than Design cooperatives.

The above regards efficient production and the resulting output prices. The labour market is equally important. Because, as judged by pre-transition practices, the workers of the capitalist enterprises – whilst working in authoritarian relations – get less paid than cooperatives' workers (the latter also having more secure jobs), these enterprises will tend to see their workers gradually move to cooperatives, which will affect the capitalist enterprises' production and the amount of profits that they can make. This point reveals the paradox that in case the capitalist enterprises – in order to prevent this movement – would start paying their workers better, they will equally see their profits decrease.

3. General strategy of the transition

Given the constraints mentioned under the previous heading, the first principle for the transition is that no pre-transition enterprise (banking or non-banking) is enforced to legally convert into a Design cooperative. The general strategy of the transition is one of gradual change such that the capitalist enterprises keep functioning as long as they can, in face of on the one hand their competition with cooperatives, and on the other the inheritance taxes. The objective of this gradual change is job-preservation.

Whereas taxation (especially the inheritance tax) and the mentioned market competition rules (single location and maximum market share) are *necessary* instruments for the transition, these alone are *not sufficient* to bring about a gradual change such that production and jobs are preserved. For the latter the competences of the 'Agency for temporary workers' council governed foundations' are essential (8§8). These are expanded on under the next heading (4).

4. Transition differences between stock corporations and firms

We have seen that inheritances above two times the minimum wage are taxed at 100% (except for a surviving spouse/partner). It was indicated in 8§8, first, that on the death of the owner of a firm or of the owner of corporate shares the 'Agency for temporary workers' council governed foundations' (ATF) has a pre-emptive purchase right of the firm or the shares (against reasonable prices); and, secondly, that on the retirement of the (main) owner of a firm, the ATF may bargain to purchase the entity, paying by way of 'lifelong consols'.

For the transition there is an important difference between firms as run by one owner or a partnership, and corporations that are ultimately owned by a group of more or less anonymous shareholders. The survival of these corporations is independent of who owns the shares. The survival of a firm is dependent on whether it can be sold to a successor at the retirement or death of the (main) owner.[23] This succession is often also a problem within capitalism.

Table 8.5 and *Table 8.6* list the main differences regarding, first, the transition in general and, second, the transition repercussion of bequests. It will be seen that the continuation of a firm is more problematical than that of a corporation

4-A. Medium to large stock corporations. This category regards medium and large sized stock corporations that are owned by a multitude of more or less anonymous shareholders (*Table 8.5* – p. 342). These are burdened by the constraints listed in rows 1–7 of the table. Special mention deserves that for corporations that issued bonds, their pay-off might be problematical because they cannot refinance this by the issue of new bonds (rows 2 and 7). (However, they might get an agreement with bondholders to pay-off in tranches – which for the bondholders makes a gigantic difference in income taxes – and in the case of tranches bargain to pay only part of the principal sum.)[24] Apart from that, the corporations could, in principle, survive much of the transition, though probably with little expansion (row 3). Note though that they could keep on investing out of depreciation allowances (which usually is the main source for the finance of investments).

---

23 In case an enterprise as owned by a single owner or a few partners has been incorporated, the same problem applies as for firms. Below, therefore, such an enterprise is treated in a similar way to firms.

24 As an aside this means that anyway (tranches or no tranches) bond prices will fall towards their pay-off maturation. Thus the value of bonds approaches the present value of the interest – with only a minor element for the principal sum.

TABLE 8.5 *Stock corporations (including banks): taxation, expansion, break up and continuity*

		Corporation	Share- and bondholders
1	taxes during transition	corporate property & income taxes (maintained; with separate tax for rental property)	dividend and interest: substantial income taxes
2	shares, bonds, private loans	no new issuance	trade shares/bonds permitted
3	expansion during transition	hard (8§16-a; 8§17)	
4	prohibition take-overs	phase 1: immediately	
5	maximum market share rule	phase 1; one year after enactment*	
6	single location rule	phase 3: 6 months after enactment*	
7	pay off bonds†	problematic in face of non-refinance	bondholders pay income tax
8	market-value shares‡		present value of expected future dividends (after individual tax and during lifetime of holder)
9	on death of a share-holder		shares purchased by ATF⸸
10	on death of a bond-holder		bonds sold by inheritors
11	continuity	in principle continuous: if it survives competition and as long as the shareholders majority decides so	within one generation the ATF owns the majority of shares and will set on legal conversion

* Whence for many: enforced break up into two or more independent smaller legal entities (shares are partitioned according to the entities). A legally split off entity might be sold in tranches to the entity's workers who found a cooperative. See the main text for the considerations.
† See the main text on how the problem mentioned in the next two columns might considerably be circumvented.
‡ See footnote 24 for the market-value of bonds.
⸸ ATF: 'Agency for temporary workers' council governed foundations' (8§8) which has a pre-emptive purchase right.

Before returning to issues at the top of *Table 8.5*, I turn to the bottom rows of the table (8–11). Given the considerable inheritance taxes, the market-value of shares (row 8) is not determined by the corporations' equity (and prospects) but by the present value of the expected future dividends during the lifetime of the average shareholder (an individual shareholder will calculate her/his expected lifetime, as well as the individual marginal tax rate). On the death of a shareholder (row 9) the 'Agency for temporary workers' council governed foundations' (ATF) will most often use its pre-emptive purchase right (mentioned at the opening of the current sub-section 4). For the inheritors this is not interesting, but for the corporation this implies that the ATF becomes an increasingly large shareholder. Once it is the majority shareholder it could insist on a legal conversion of the corporation into a cooperative (perhaps via the temporary stage of a workers' council governed foundation). Prior to that conversion, the prospect of it may have a downward effect on the market-value of shares.

This might mean that at an earlier stage (I now return to the top of the table) the shareholders might be better off when they sell one or more locations of the initial corporation to their workers. Many corporations will be enforced to split up in face of the maximum market share rule (row 5) and the single location rule (row 6) – in that case the corporate shares are partitioned according to the new corporate entities. Whether it is interesting for the shareholders of an entity to sell it to the entity's workers (that found a cooperative) depends on a rather complicated calculation, one part of which regards the (future) market-value of shares mentioned in the previous paragraph. The other part depends on how the workers pay. Payment in one go is not interesting for the shareholders because of the income taxes (nor is payment in one go feasible for the workers). Workers may therefore propose to pay in a number of tranches that are agreed to be paid out of the cooperative's surplus.[25] In face of the income taxes the shareholders on average have an interest in spreading the sale over many tranches (this is different for old-aged shareholders). A risk for the shareholders is that payment of the tranches is dependent on the cooperative's surplus.

As indicated, the calculation of the total of considerations is complicated. Anyway, even without selling one or more entities to the workers, legal conversion of the corporations will emerge within a generation.

4-B. Firms (i.e. non-stock corporations) and limited-owner incorporates. It will be seen that this category of (often) small enterprises, is from the side of the ATF treated differently than medium- and large-sized corporations (4-A). The reason is that the former's continuity is at risk when the (main) owner retires or deceases.

---

25 With the help of an accountant – paid by the ATF – the workers decide on whether the project is feasible. The advantage for these workers is the democratic decision-making, the jobs continuation and possibly there is a sufficient resistance buffer (whence they do not have to start at minimum wages).

TABLE 8.6 *Firms and limited-owner incorporates: taxation, expansion and legal conversion upon retirement of owner*

		Firms (non-incorporated)	Owners of limited-owner incorporates*
1	taxes during transition	property taxes (maintained; with separate tax for rental property)	corporate property & income taxes (maintained; with separate tax for rental property)
2	taxes during transition	substantial income tax	dividends: substantial income tax
3	single location rule	phase 3: enters into force 6 months after enactment‡	
4	expansion during transition	hard (8§16-a; 8§17)	hard (8§16-a; 8§17)
5	retirement (main) owner	• liquidation or selling to third party; income is taxed • alternative: appoint manager. • alternative: sell to workers or to ATF†	sell shares to third party or parties (if market); income is taxed • alternative: appoint manager. • alternative: sell to workers or to ATF†
6	death (main) owner before retirement	ownership to surviving spouse; spouse may consider alternatives of previous row	shares to surviving spouse; spouse may consider alternatives of previous row
7	death surviving spouse (in case s/he still holds ownership)	firm purchased by the ATF‡	shares purchased by the ATF‡

* Enterprises as owned by a single owner or a few partners that has been incorporated
‡ An incorporated business is required to legally separate locations (shares are partitioned according to the entities). A firm is required to adopt a ring-fenced bookkeeping for each location.
† See the main text for the alternatives. ATF: 'Agency for temporary workers' council governed foundations'.
‡ The ATF has a pre-emptive purchase right (8§8).

Firms and limited-owner incorporates (*Table 8.6*) can in principle survive until the retirement of the (main) owner or – in case of a partnership – the retirement of the youngest partner; though probably with little expansion. (See the first four rows of the table.) Regarding the single location rule (row 3) an incorporated business is required to legally separate locations (shares are partitioned according to the entities). A firm is required to adopt a ring-fenced bookkeeping for each location.

I further focus on the case of a *single* owner of a firm (non-incorporated). At the point of retirement (row 5) the owner can try to sell the firm to a willing person with sufficient means (bank credit might be problematical). If the owner does not succeed (or shrinks from the income tax upon sale), there are three alternatives.

• One is to appoint a manager until the owner's (or her/his spouse's or life partner's) death. At this point the inheritance tax is relevant. So as to secure the firm's continuation the ATF can use its pre-emptive right to purchase the firm. (The ATF will convert the entity into a cooperative.)[26]

• A second alternative is that the retiring owner sells the firm (or locations of it) in a number of to be agreed tranches to the firm's workers, who found a Design cooperative. The tranches are agreed to be paid out of the cooperative's surplus. The advantage for these workers is the democratic decision-making, the jobs continuation and possibly there is a sufficient resistance buffer (whence they do not have to start at minimum wages). The advantage for the owner is that this evades possible conflicts with the manager of the first alternative. In face of the income taxes, the owner has an interest in many tranches spread over the owner's expected lifetime. The owner's disadvantage is that the tranches are surplus dependent. (With the help of an accountant – paid by the ATF – the workers decide on whether the project is feasible.)

• A third alternative is that the ATF purchases the firm, paying by life-long consols (see the opening of the current main sub-section 4). The amount of consols is a matter of bargaining, also in face of the relative vitality of the firm/future cooperative. The advantage for the owner is that these consols are more secure than the tranches of the second alternative (but possibly less in value amount).

8§24 Amount of legislative work in phase 1, and the duration of the legislative transition phases 1–5

Table 8.7 provides a rough estimate of the amount of legislative work during phase 1. The estimate is measured in what I call 'sequential weeks', that regard the unlikely case in which each one legislative process would be fully carried out before the next one starts. In the usual parliamentary practice, many legislative processes are carried out simultaneously. Sequential is only the very last stage of the processes, that is the parliament's legislation debate followed by the voting on the bill and its enactment.

---

26 Perhaps via the temporary stage of a 'workers' council governed foundation'.

TABLE 8.7 *Indication amount of legislative work phase 1: sequential measure (in weeks)*

	Subject		Indication	Wk.
	general legislative preparations by civil service workers			10
8§1	state's democratic organs	full legis.	much†	5.5
8§2	judiciary		minor	1.5
8§3	ministries and state agencies (elementary)		moderate	3.5
8§5	four state's banking and fund agencies	full legis.	much	5.5
8§6	competition and competition authority	full legis.	moderate	3.5
8§7	workers' council governed foundations		moderate	3.5
8§8	agency for temporary workers' council governed foundations	full legis.	moderate	3.5
8§9	taxation		much	5.5
8§10	minimum wage; minimum cost of living allowances		minor	1.5
8§11	housing legislation		minor	1.5
8§12	health sector, temporary		moderate	3.5
8§13	education sector, temporary		moderate	3.5
8§14	Design ch. 2	full legis.	very much	9.0
8§15	idem, temporary exceptions		minor	1.5
8§16	financial markets		minor	1.5
8§17	accommodation banks' investment credit to cooperatives		minor	1.5
8§18	conversion legal form into Design coops (esp. WOCs)		minor	1.5
	total weeks in the non-likely case of a complete sequential treatment			67.0
	total weeks in terms of the simultaneous measure (2/3 previous row)			44.7

† A revision of the constitution is not included in this amount (country dependent).

The last two columns of *Table 8.7* (except the last row) indicate an estimate for the amount of legislative work in weeks by parliamentarian spokespersons, including written interchange with the responsible minister and a legislation debate with other spokespersons and the responsible minister. This is what above was called the *sequential* amount of time. (For different terrains this is usually done by different spokespersons.) 'Minor' indicates on average 1½ full-time weeks; 'moderate' 3½ weeks; 'much' 5½ weeks; 'very much' 9 weeks. The drafting of an act could be done in twice the amount of weeks if a sufficient number of civil service officers work on it. (Apart from the beginning of phase 1 – see row 1 – which prepares for phase 1 only, it is assumed that groups of civil officers in a field work concurrently on all of the five phases' bills in that field.)

TABLE 8.8 *Indication of the duration of the legislative transition phases 1–5 (repeat from 8§24)*

Phase	Duration in weeks		Duration in years
	Sequential	Simultaneous 2/3 previous column	Simultaneous at 40 weeks per year
(1)	(2)	(3)	(4)
1 *after the first transition elections*			
2 transition legislation phase 1	67.0	44.7	1.1
3 transition legislation phase 2	23.5	15.7	0.4
4 transition legislation phase 3	31.5	21.0	0.5
5 *overrun and adaptation period*†			2.0
6 *subtotal*			4
7 *after the second transition elections*			
8 transition legislation phase 4	12.5	8.3	0.2
9 transition legislation phase 5 (final)	36.0	24.0	0.6
10 *overrun period*			0.7
11 *subtotal*			1.5
12 *total number of weeks*	170.5	113.7	
13 *total number of years*			5.5

† In case there is no overrun, an adaptation period of nearly two years is nevertheless required in view of phases 4–5. Thus phase 4 (row 8) should start after 4 years.

At the end of each of the following divisions (and phases) a table similar to Table 8.7 will be shown. These tables together provided the information for *Table 8.8*. As mentioned, in practice several enactment processes will be going on at the same time. Column 2 of *Table 8.8* shows the *sequential* estimate, with in column 3 a more realistic *simultaneous* estimate (2/3 of the former; but it is probably a smaller fraction – however, other than transitional legislation may also go on). In this case the duration of phase 1 would be 1.1 year (last column).

If my estimate is adequate, the total of the transitional legislation would take 5.5 years (row 13), taking account of a possible overrun of the legislative processes as shown in rows 5 and 10. However, even if there would be no overrun during phases 1–3, there must after these phases still be an adaptation period of nearly two years in view of the legislation of phases 4–5 (this will become clear when we get there).

Readers who at this point might be interested in the order in which all of the Part One Design will be implemented during the five legislative phases, might glance at Table 8.22 in Appendix 8A.

Division 2. Transitional legislation phase 2: completion of elementary transition

This Division sets out legislation on: the maximum work-time (8§25); workers' councils of the public sector (8§26); pension allowances for all (8§27); additional elementary allowances (8§28–8§29); preparatory regulation about jobs (8§30); and a cluster around end of year Income and Balance sheet reports (8§31–8§33).

8§25 *Full-time position and maximum work-time – full enactment*
• Legislation establishes the number of hours that defines a 'full-time position' and sets the maximum work-time accordingly as set out in 3§10-a;b (amongst other: the number of hours of per year that defines a 'full-time position' is also the maximum work-time in hours per year; notwithstanding that maximum, a maximum work-time per day and week is equally enacted). Parliament may adapt the maximum work-time annually. The rules apply for cooperatives, state institutions and 'workers' council governed foundations' as well as for all pre-transition entities.
These rules, first, aim to protect of workers and, secondly are an instrument for reaching an equitable distribution of work (by varying the maximum work-time).
• *Entry into force.* The legislation enters into force three months after the enactment.

8§26 *Workers' councils public sector, except remuneration matters – phases 2–4*
• Except its last paragraph, all of the following is enacted.
• Legislation establishes workers' councils for all state institutions (the judiciary, ministries, state agencies, municipalities and provinces), state-financed cultural heritage and arts performance institutes, state-financed research institutes, as well as for the health sector and education sector institutions – in the country at hand the latter may (yet) not be part of the public sector, but these shall nevertheless introduce workers' councils. Until phase 5 (8§49) their competences may, but need not, include remuneration matters (as determined by each single institution). More specifically the enactment regards the following section clauses.

- Workers' councils and other internal organisation of the judiciary, ministries and state agencies: 3§3, (c), (d), (e) except 'fourth', (f).
- Workers' councils and other internal organisation of municipalities and provinces: 4§6.
- Workers' councils and other internal organisation of the institutions of the health sector, the education and the culture sector at large: 3§25, *only* its clauses (g) except 'second' and (h).
- For small institutions the management may be a part-time management (to decide by the council). Until phase 5, institutions with fewer than 10 workers may, but are not required to introduce councils.
- The current legal form of the health, education and culture institutions remains unaffected until phase 5 (8§50 and 8§51); however, the introduction of workers' councils and their competences is a condition for the institutions being financed by or via state, in any form.
- *Entry into force.* The legislation enters into force one year after the enactment (this is about two years after the start of the transition; or, towards the end of phase 3).

Note. After the entering into force, the institution requires time to adapt to the new relations. This is one main reason why there should be a considerable time between the end of phase 3 and the start of phase 5 (Table 8.8) when the councils will have full competences.

8§27   *Pension allowances – full enactment*

The *'Pensions and child allowances agency'* was formally established in 8§3.
- Legislation enacts the agency's pension tasks as set out in 3§24. The following transition regulation is also enacted.
- Parliament sets the retirement age; it regularly adapts the age when required. Initially the 'standard level of pensions' paid by the agency – in full or supplemented (see below) – is provisionally set at 100% of the minimum wage.
- During the transition there will be a mixed private–public finance of pensions.
- Current pension funds and life insurance companies annually pay out the allowances (in monthly instalments) that they would have paid prior to the transition – if required recalculated for the set retirement age.
- In the relevant cases the *Pensions and child allowances agency* increase these allowances to the going standard level of pensions (100% of the minimum wage). All other persons that reach the retirement age receive the going standard pension.

As already mentioned in (8§16), no new contracts for pensions or life insurances shall be entered on. This implies that these pension funds and the regarding insurance company branches gradually phase out.

- *Entry into force.* The legislation enters into force when the income taxation enters into force (8§9), though not earlier than three months after the current enactment.[27] With the entering into force any 'minimum costs of living allowances' (8§10) expire for pensioners.

8§28   Child-related allowances – full enactment

- The following child allowances of 3§22 are enacted. Their granting is implemented by the *'Pensions and child allowances agency'* (cf. 8§27).
- *Child's costs of living allowances.* Until a juvenile's aged 18 (or if this is earlier, until the juvenile starts working) the caring parent receives, for up to three children, age-dependent child's costs of living allowances (as based on costs of living baskets and indexes).
- *Childcare allowances.* Until a juvenile's aged 18 (or if this is earlier, until the juvenile starts working) the caring parent receives, for up to three children, age-dependent costs covering childcare allowances (for details see 3§22–2).
- *Parental leave allowance.* Before and after the birth of a child a period of parental leave is paid by the state at 100% of the minimum wage for a total of 31 weeks as specified in 3§22–3.
- *Orphan allowances.* Foster parents or adoptive parents of domestic orphans receive annually twice the child's costs of living allowances (first bullet; though for siblings the three children limit does not apply).
- *Entry into force.* The legislation enters into force when the income taxation enters into force (8§9). It replaces existing similar allowances or tax reductions.

8§29   Costs of living allowances for students – full enactment

- The costs of living allowances for students are enacted (3§23). Their granting is implemented by the *'Pensions and child allowances agency'* (cf. 8§27). Students shall one time apply for these allowances. Between the application and the granting there might be a delay of up to two months (with retroactive payment as per the application date).

---

27   The entering into force act mentions that in case of lack of sufficient information about pensions eligibility, persons may receive their pensions with some delay. (Meanwhile the allowances of 8§10 apply, and these shall be returned to the municipality when the pension is received.)

Details of the pensions' regulation. On basis of the country's (or municipals') population register the Agency determines the eligibility for the standard pension. Pension funds and life insurance companies are required to inform the Agency about their payments in the categories 'below standard pensions' and 'at to above standard pensions'. From the start of the transition, a relevant ministry sets up a computer program and starts collecting this information.

- *Entry into force.* The legislation enters into force when the income taxation enters into force (8§9). It replaces any existing similar allowances or state-provided loans.

Appendix 8A, Table 8.19, lists all provisions together with the allowances and their level.

8§30   Preparatory regulation on job securities – phases 2–3

The 'Job securities and jobs shortage agency' (JSA) was formally established in 8§3. In phases 2–3 the JSA has a restricted number of tasks as indicated below.
- The following tasks are enacted together with the mentioned obligations for economic domain and public sector entities as well as individuals. (All of the registrations below prepare for the 3§17 full task of the JSA as enacted in phase 4, 8§43.)
- (a) All currently existing public sector entities – and those to introduce later on – as well as all of the economy's legal entities (including firms) shall register with this agency. The registration must include: (1) their number of jobs (in FTE and persons); (2) their vacancies; (3) the number of people with restricted physical or mental abilities to work that have a position in the entity (in FTE and persons). The entities shall update this information at the end of each quarter.
- (b) All currently existing public sector entities – and those to introduce later on – as well as all of the economy's legal entities, each with an FTE workforce of 50 or more, shall continuously offer *potential* traineeship positions as indicated in 3§17 and 3§18.

Only after follow-up legislation in phase 4 (8§43), actual traineeships will be allocated by the JSA proportional to the size of the entities. The entities are warned that in case of an actual traineeship the entity shall pay the trainee 60% of the minimum wage.
- (c) The JSA registers the municipal and nationwide joblessness – as reported by individuals.
- (d) The JSA registers, the municipal and nationwide, persons with restricted physical or mental abilities to work that either have a position, or/and that have no (full-time) position, or/and that receive an allowance – as reported by the individuals or a general practitioner.
- (e) (For the following task 3§21, on restricted abilities to work, is relevant.) All persons under (d) are medically examined regarding their abilities to work at a defined quality, speed and work-time. The medical examiner reports this to the JSA together with a statement if and where the person works. On basis of this information the JSA determines the number of persons that could in principle work if they were offered a job. Combining this with the information under (a),

the JSA determines in what proportions the public sector's and the economy's legal entities should provide work to persons with restricted abilities to work – that is, at the point when this becomes an obligation (phase 4, 8§44).
• (f) The JSA has the task of informing all relevant entities that early phase 4 (this is in about 2½ years) intended legislation will establish the requirement of the traineeships sub (b), as well as the requirement to provide regular work to persons with restricted physical or mental abilities to work on top of their other workforce (the latter is provisionally estimated at 5% of the workforce).
• *Entry into force*. The registration and information requirements under (a), (c–d) and (f) enter into force six months after the enactment; the registration requirement under (b) enters into force three years after the enactment.

8§31   *Auditing – full enactment*
The 'Registered external auditors authority' was formally established in 8§3. In many countries a similar authority currently exists, whence merely some rules have to be adapted, and the same personnel can do the work.
• Legislation enacts this agency conform 3§43a–d. It is added that the authority's rules also apply to non-cooperative auditors/accountancy companies and to auditors working for these.
• *Entry into force*. The legislation enters into force three months after the enactment.

8§32   *Legal separation audit and accountancy companies – full enactment*
• It is enacted that auditors/accountancy companies, including existing cooperatives, are required to legally separate their activities into the following two.
• External auditing (also called 'certified public accountancy'); this entity shall not undertake any advisory or consultancy activities.
• All other accountancy and auditing work, as including advisory or consultancy activities and accountancy work for enterprises (as including for cooperatives).
• *Entry into force*. The legislation enters into force six months after the enactment. (Thus at that point the legal separation will have to be effective. The relevant companies should be informed that phase 3 includes the rule that entities shall be organised in no more than one single location – 8§35; each one shall not combine external auditing and other work.)

8§33   *End of year income account and balance sheet of economic domain entities – permanent rules*
• Legislation establishes that all economic domain entities shall deliver an end of year Income account and Balance sheet that is approved by an external aud-

itor. (This already applies for ministries and state agencies on basis of 8§3, and for 'workers' council governed foundations' on basis of 8§7.)
• The income account should include a memorandum item about the entity's number of workers in FTE and the average remuneration of workers in FTE (for Design cooperative this already applies on basis of 8§14).[28] In a reduced format similar as in Appendix 2A, all these entities (including Design cooperatives) shall send the statements – within four months after the end of the regarding year – to a to be specified department of the General statistical office (3§33-B) or its current equivalent. The reduced format should equally have been approved by the external auditor. (This information serves to determine the average remuneration of public sector workers – see phase 5, 8§49.)
• *Entry into force*. The legislation above enters into force one year after the enactment of 8§32.
• Legislation also enacts that one task of the General statistical office (enacted in 8§52) – or its current equivalent – is to annually determine the economic domain's average remuneration of workers in FTE on basis of the end of year statements. The office does this either on basis of a sample, or on basis of the integral information. The calculated average should be communicated as soon as possible, but not later than 1 October of each year.
• This enactment enters into force on 1 October after the entering into force of the previous enactment of the current section.

8§34   *Conclusions on phase 2 and phases 1–2 together*
• *General comments on phases 1–2*. According to the Table 8.8 estimate (8§24) about 1½ years have now passed since the start of the transition. At this point all elementary income allowances, including pensions for all, child-related allowances, as well as health and education provisions for all, have been enacted. And, next to those in cooperatives, there will be workers' councils in all of the public sector, even if the latter's full competences must await phase 5. This means that the vast majority of the population may already perceive the emergence of social progress (the extent depends on the pre-transition constellation).

Persons who are immediately affected by the pension allowances and the child-related allowances, especially those in the lower half of the income distribution, will probably expend more than before, which has a positive effect on production and the getting out of the perhaps still remaining recessive circum-

---

28   Recall that for Design cooperatives the remuneration regards wages as well as current and postponed dividends.

stances. In case of an inherited, and continued, structural unemployment a, at least temporary, general work-time reduction would be appropriate (via a maximum work-time reduction – 8§25), and together with a temporary increase in the minimum wage *rate* level such that the minimum wage per year/month remains constant (8§10).

• *State expenditure and its finance due to phase 2 legislation*
Table 8.9 lists the state expenditure due to the phase 2 legislation, together with its way of finance in phase 2 and in the further phases of the transition. (This is a continuation from a similar table in 8§21 – Table 8.4.)

TABLE 8.9   *State expenditure due to phase 2 legislation*

Expenditure category	Finance of expenditure†		
	Phase 2	Further transition	After transition
general state administration‡	permanent taxes	permanent taxes	permanent taxes
pensions (8§27)‡	permanent taxes	permanent taxes	permanent taxes
child-related allowances (8§28)*	permanent taxes	permanent taxes	permanent taxes
allowances students (8§29)*	permanent taxes	permanent taxes	permanent taxes

† 'Permanent taxes' are mainly the turnover/production tax and the income tax.
‡ This includes the internal organisation of the agencies introduced in phase 2, excluding their payment of allowances or other transfers.
* The expenditure relevant part of the legislation enters into force together with that of the taxation.

• *Amount of legislative work in phase 2.* Table 8.10 provides an indication of the sequentially measured amount of legislative work in phase 2. The simultaneously measured legislation time for phase 2 is 15 weeks or 0.4 year (at 40 weeks per year) – see Table 8.8, 8§24.

TABLE 8.10   *Indication amount of legislative work phase 2: sequential measure in weeks*[29]

Subject			Indication	Wk.
8§25	full-time position and maximum work-time	full legis.	minor	1.5
8§26	workers' councils public sector inst. (restricted)		moderate	3.5

29   [The following explanatory note is abbreviated from a note to the phase 1 Table 8.7.] It

TABLE 8.10 *Indication of legislative work phase 2: sequential measure (cont.)*

	Subject		Indication	Wk.
8§27	pension allowances	full legis.	moderate	3.5
8§28	child-related allowances	full legis.	moderate	3.5
8§29	costs of living allowances students	full legis.	minor	1.5
8§30	preparatory regulation about job securities		moderate	3.5
8§31	registered external auditors authority	full legis.	minor/mod	2.5
8§32	audit/accountancy companies separation	full legis.	minor	1.5
8§33	end of year statements economic domain entities	permanent	minor/mod	2.5
	total weeks in the unlikely case of a complete sequential treatment			*23.5*
	total weeks in terms of the simultaneous measure (2/3 previous row)			*15.7*

Division 3. Transitional legislation phase 3: preconditions for mature transition

Thirteen subjects are to be legislated in phases 3 and 4 together, and ten in the final phase 5. The legislation order for phases 3 and 4 is not determined by their inherent importance, but rather by the following two considerations. The first one is that most of the subjects of phase 5 must be legislated at the same time. The second one is that the first subject of phase 3, and three subjects of phase 4 cannot be placed earlier or later for various reasons. The other nine subjects of phases 3 and 4 simply have to be placed in one of these phases.

Table 8.11 summarises the phases duration in years.

Division 3 (phase 3) starts with economic domain legislation that has an important effect on the position of the pre-transition capitalist entities, because they will have to break up in single location entities (8§35). It is a main lever of the transition, next to the phase 1 legislation on competition, taxation, and financial markets (8§6, 8§9, 8§16). The Division's second subject (8§36) regards production safeties (circular production, safety at work and safety of output). So far it was assumed that in the pre-transition period of the country

---

is assumed that several enactments are in process at the same time. 'Minor' indicates on average 1½ full-time weeks; 'moderate' 3½ weeks; 'much' 5½ weeks; 'very much' 9 weeks. The drafting of an act could be done in half the time if a sufficient number of civil service officers work on it. It is assumed that groups of civil officers in a field work concurrently on all of the five phases' acts.

TABLE 8.11 *The transition phases duration in years*

	Transition phase	Duration in years	(Sub)total years
after the first transition elections	phase 1	1.1	
	phase 2	0.4	
	phase 3	0.5	
	overrun and adaptation period	2.0	4
after the second transition elections	phase 4	0.2	
	phase 5 (final)	0.6	
	overrun period	0.7	1.5
	total number of years		**5.5**

at hand these reached at least the qualification 'sufficient'. Should this not be the case then this legislation must be put forward. The third subject regards the municipal and provincial democratic organs (8§37) which should in the ideal case be enacted before their first elections after phase 1, but this is no absolute requirement. For the rest of Division 3 there is some subjects-coherence for the legislation on real estate, earth extractions and infrastructure (8§38–8§40), though not for the last section on patents and copyrights (8§41).

8§35 *Design cooperatives: termination of exceptions 8§15; rules for pre-transition entities – full entry into force Design ch. 2*

The cooperatives' rules below that were temporarily excepted in 8§15 now enter into force. In order to create an equal level playing field between Design cooperatives and pre-transition enterprises, the legislation also applies for the latter.
• It is enacted that cooperatives shall be organised in no more than one single location (2§3.4). The same rule applies for pre-transition entities.

The rule implies that current multi-location workers-owned cooperatives (WOCs) and other entities (including banks) have to legally separate into single location ones.

For each entity at least one consequence of this rule is: that WOCs shall introduce a workers' council for each one location; that stock corporations shall partition the shares according to the new corporate entities; that firms shall adopt a ring-fenced bookkeeping for each location.
• It is enacted that banking cooperatives are required to build up a legally binding resistance buffer of 10% of their assets, and other cooperatives of 30%

of their assets.[30] Prior to having built up this buffer, workers shall receive no more than the minimum wage (2§7.0). The same rules apply for pre-transition entities. (Note that the rule applies for all workers, including those that have a management function.)

• *Entry into force.* The two clauses enter into force six months after the enactment (note that these rules were publicly communicated in phase 1 – 8§15).

8§36   *Physically circular production, safety of and information about output, and safety at work – full enactment*

• Legislation enacts the rules for 'physically circular production' (3§7) as including sector specific rules for the location of production near to where it is used. Depending on the state of the physically circular production at the time of the transition it also sets time-paths for reaching it.[31]

• Legislation also enacts the rules for the safety of output, for the information about output – as including the advertisement prohibition (3§8), and the safety at work (3§9). Regarding the advertisement prohibition, the transition rule is enacted that it overrules existing private contracts as including on sponsoring.

Many of the rules above (excluding on advertisement) might already be in force in the country at hand, in which case the relevant amount of legislation would be moderate. All these rules are initiated by a relevant ministry, and during the transition the rules also apply for pre-transition entities. Inspectorates see to the compliances (3§12).

• *Entry into force.* The legislation enters into force six months after the enactment; however, that on the advertisement prohibition enters into force three years after the enactment (esp. the latter should be widely communicated at the current point).

8§37   *Municipal and provincial democratic organs*

• Legislation enacts the democratic organisation and election procedures for municipalities (4§2) and provinces (4§4). Until phase 5 (8§56) the remuneration clauses 4§2-h and 4§4-g do not apply.

• *Entry into force.* The legislation enters into force six months after the enactment, which means that elections held from that point onwards fall under this enactment.

---

30   The Central Bank may propose that parliament adapt the buffer rates in general or in specific sectors (3§13-*l*).

31   See also 8§52 on the 'National institute for the advance of physically circular production' and 8§39 on 'mining and other extractions from the Earth'.

8§38 Real estate and the real estate agency – full enactment

The 'Real estate agency' (REA) was formally established in 8§3 and in 8§11 it was assigned limited tasks. Before setting out its full legislation, some comments are appropriate.

General aspects of the transition regarding the REA
• Under this heading I merely pre-empt that only the REA shall purchase or sell real estate.
• It is recalled that after the full transition, cooperatives can, of their choice, either own their self-occupied premises or rent these from the REA (agricultural land can be rented only). Except this ownership and the real estate owned by state institutions other than REA (mainly offices and the premises of the health and education sectors) the REA owns and manages all real estate. At that point the main task of the REA is to rent out dwellings to households, and premises to cooperatives, and to undertake any construction and maintenance for that purpose (carried out by cooperatives).
• At the current point REA owns no real estate apart from that consequent on the 8§11 construction, and from pre-transition state-owned real estate that might now be subsumed under the delegated REA ownership and management.
• During the transition REA gradually acquires households' dwellings that inheritors have to sell given the inheritance taxes.
• REA gradually acquires real estate owned by pension funds and life insurance companies because these gradually phase out (8§27).
• Probably far sooner REA acquires much of the rental property owned by enterprises (except pension funds and life insurance companies), in face of the considerable taxes on such property (8§9, Table 8.2, row 23). That tax enters into force in the first full calendar year after the current enactment.
• It is expected that due to the pre-transition turbulences real estate prices decline (ch. 7), and that they will further go down due to the previous point (though there will probably be demand from the side of pension funds and life insurance companies that are expected to shift assets from shares and bonds to real estate). This would mean that REA acquires real estate at relatively low or moderate prices.

Below the focus is on (to be) rented out dwellings.
• After the acquirement of dwellings REA renovates these when required (via cooperatives or other construction entities) and then rents these out. Rents will be set at reasonable prices that on average are expected to be lower than before the transition. During the transition the acquired stock of dwellings will keep pace with the *current* population. For expected population growth (as well

TRANSITION TO A WORKER COOPERATIVES SOCIETY 359

as any shortages at the start of the transition) REA plans a construction programme – as indicated at high standards of acclaimed urban and landscape designs, and provided in a variety of qualities and sizes.
• Finally, because the REA is probably a new institute in the country at hand, it will require quite some new staff. It – that is its workers' council – can (in part) appoint these from existing real estate companies that are being phased out.

REA and real estate legislation
• The permanent REA Design rules are enacted (3§37). Besides the following transition rules are enacted.
• The following REA tasks and competences are amended in comparison with 3§37 (the numbering of that section is maintained; amendments are in italics).
(a) Ownership and management [by REA] of the nation's real estate, except the real estate that is owned by other state institutions or the self-occupied premises that are owned by cooperatives. *During the transition real estate may also be owned by pre-transition enterprises and individuals.*
(c) Renting out [by REA] of self-occupied premises to cooperatives and of self-occupied dwellings to individual workers or pensioners. *Until the 'transition completion' such premises and dwellings may only be limitedly available.*
(d) Renting out [by REA] of land to agricultural cooperatives. *During the transition such land may only be limitedly available.*
(f) [about architectural design and construction] To this article is added:
> During the transition REA can make use of the services of cooperatives as well as pre-transition enterprises for architectural design, construction and maintenance. However, it is allowed to prioritise cooperatives given that it must develop long term relations with architects and contractors.

• All purchasing or selling of real estate shall uniquely be carried out by the REA; direct real estate transaction between cooperatives, pre-transition enterprises or individuals are prohibited.
• For owners of self-occupied dwellings that wish to move, REA can mediate for intended purchases and sales. (Given the inheritance taxes, this ownership category will gradually phase out.)
• Pre-transition owners of real estate may keep on renting out such estate, and without the intermediation of the REA. (Given the property and inheritance taxes, this ownership category will gradually phase out.)
• Owner-occupied agricultural land will usually only be offered for sale to REA on bequest. The land can then be rented out to inheritors and/or other indi-

viduals provided these establish a Design cooperative (inheritor-workers and other workers at the farm have a priority right).
• *Entry into force.* The legislation enters into force three months after the enactment.[32]

8§39   Mining and other Earth extractions – full enactment
The 'Mining and other Earth extractions agency' (MEA) was formally established in 8§3 with the then single task of preparing for the execution of the current legislation and for a reorganisation of a perhaps similar currently existing institution, or a split-off from a department of the relevant ministry.

'Mining and other extractions from the Earth' regard, usually exhaustible, 'free gifts of nature'. The MEA determines the limits of the yearly extractions that are sustainable. Within the limits, licensed cooperatives may via concession engage in the extractions for which they pay rent-like fees; concessions are awarded via tender procedures.
• Legislation enacts the 3§38 rules, together with the following transition rules.
• The legislation also applies for pre-transition enterprises.
• All pre-transition licences and concessions of pre-transition enterprises (as well as of the entities that already converted into Design cooperatives) are reconsidered in face of up-to-date sustainability standards, and if required adapted; as is the appropriate fee.
• The market share rules also apply for these concessions (8§6-c).
• Extractions that were not under concession but that require sustainability limits (perhaps fishing) shall require a concession awarded via tender (the appropriate fee will apply).
• It is also enacted that the MEA may take up to five years to phase-wise implement the rules for particular sectors and specific concessions. At the end of those five years, it reports to parliament about the extraction limits set at that point.
• *Entry into force.* The legislation enters into force three months after the enactment.

8§40   Infrastructure – full enactment
The 'National Infrastructure Agency' (NIA) was formally established in 8§3 with the then single task of preparing for the execution of the current legislation

---

32   The taxation legislation may have to be adapted for the year of entry into force of the taxation of rental property owned by enterprises – Table 8.2, row 23.

and for a reorganisation of a perhaps similar currently existing institution, or a split-off from a department of the relevant ministry.

Recall that in the Design the NIA is the owner of infrastructural transport networks (*interurban* waterways, railways, and roads, as well as the bridges, viaducts, railway stations and waterway ports – 3§39-f), as well as of the nationwide networks for communication, information and energy (3§39-h).

• Legislation enacts the 3§39 rules, together with the following transition rules.

• In case in the country at hand one or more networks (3§39-f; 3§39-h) is/are licensed or given in concession, then, first, a clause is added that this may temporarily be the case. Second – as indicated in 8§6-c – when the maximum market share rule applies (this will most often be the case) licences or concessions will expire three years after the enactment of 8§6 or with the entering into force of the current legislation;[33] at the expiration licences or concessions are not continued. Third, when a licence or concession expires for non-market share reasons, it is not continued at the relevant date.

• *Entry into force*. The legislation enters into force three months after the enactment.

8§41   *Patents and copyrights – full enactment*

The 'Patents and Copyrights Authority' was formally established in 8§3 with the then task of preparing for a reorganisation of a perhaps similar currently existing institution, or of a split-off from a department of the relevant ministry.

• Legislation enacts the 3§44 rules. It is added that the authority brings the pre-transition patents and copyrights in line with the Design's, by way of the maximum market share rules of 8§6-c.

• *Entry into force*. The legislation enters into force three months after the enactment.

8§42   *Concluding matters phase 3*

Economically the most far-reaching legislation of phase 3 regards, first, the 8§35 rule that entities shall be organised in one single location – which acts as a main lever for the transition. Secondly, the full enactment of the Real Estate Agency (8§38).

Table 8.12 lists the state expenditure due to the phase 3 legislation.

---

33   See 8§6 under 'entering into force'.

TABLE 8.12 *State expenditure due to phase 3 legislation*

Expenditure category	Finance of expenditure†		
	Phase 3	Further transition	After transition
general state administration‡	permanent taxes	permanent taxes	permanent taxes
real estate agency (8§38)	break-even*	break-even*	moderate surplus⁂
Earth extractions (8§39)	surplus running	surplus running	surplus running
infrastructure (8§40)	permanent taxes	permanent taxes	permanent taxes

† 'Permanent taxes' are mainly the turnover/production tax and the income tax.
‡ This includes the internal organisation of the agencies introduced in phase 3, excluding their payment of allowances or other transfers.
* This regards the running (or operating) expenditure. During the transition the assets are acquired via purchases that are financed by inheritance taxes and by rental property taxes. The end and after transition construction investments are recovered from rents.
⁂ The surplus regards rented out agricultural land (collective income for free gifts of nature). The remainder runs on average break-even basis.

Table 8.13 provides an indication of the sequentially measured amount of legislative work in phase 3. Measured simultaneously the phase 3 legislation would take about half a year.

TABLE 8.13 *Indication amount of legislative work phase 3: sequential measure in weeks*[34]

	Subject		Indication	Wk.
8§35	removal of exceptions economic domain	full legis.	mod/much	4.5
8§36	circular production & production safeties	full legis.	much	5.5
8§37	municipal and provincial democratic organs		much	5.5
8§38	Real Estate Agency	full legis.	much	5.5
8§39	Mining and other Earth extractions agency	full legis.	minor/mod	2.5

34 [The following explanatory note is abbreviated from a note to the phase 1 Table 8.7.] It is assumed that several enactments are in process at the same time. 'Minor' indicates on average 1½ full-time weeks; 'moderate' 3½ weeks; 'much' 5½ weeks; 'very much' 9 weeks. The drafting of an act could be done in half the time if a sufficient number of civil service officers work on it. It is assumed that groups of civil officers work on all of the five phases' acts concurrently.

TABLE 8.13   *Indication of legislative work phase 3: sequential measure (cont.)*

	Subject	Indication		Wk.
8§40	National Infrastructure Agency	full legis.	mod/much	4.5
8§41	Patents and copyrights authority	full legis.	moderate	3.5
	total weeks in the non-likely case of a complete sequential treatment			*31.5*
	total weeks in terms of the simultaneous measure (2/3 of previous row)			*21.0*

Division 4. Transitional legislation phase 4: advanced transition

It is assumed that the phase 4 legislation starts after the national elections and the adaptation period just before it (see the table below). In case in the country at hand the changes of the state's administration (8§1) would require a change of the constitution via a voting in two parliamentary rounds, this phase starts with a second round of voting about that change.

Phase 4 enacts three essential social-economic policies of the Design, all regarding the minimisation of joblessness. The first two regard the minimisation of joblessness due to either qualifications mismatches or to recessions (8§43), the third one regards regular jobs for people with restricted abilities to work (8§44). Especially the first two could or should not be legislated earlier, either for reasons of lack of information (the gathering of information by the jobs agency was enacted in phase 2, 3§30), or/and for the reason that economic entities (but also public sector entities) require time to gradually adapt to the requirements of the Design constellation (whence the adaptation period of about two years between phases 3 and 4 – the phases *Table 8.11* is repeated below).

TABLE 8.11   *The transition phases duration in years (repeat from introduction 8D3)*

	Transition phase	Duration in years	(Sub)total years
after the first transition elections	phase 1	1.1	
	phase 2	0.4	
	phase 3	0.5	
	overrun and adaptation period	2.0	4

TABLE 8.11 *Transition phases in years (repeat from introduction 8D3) (cont.)*

	Transition phase	Duration in years	(Sub)total years
after the second transition elections	phase 4	0.2	
	phase 5 (final)	0.6	
	overrun period	0.7	1.5
	total number of years		**5.5**

Phase 4 also enacts the procedure for the appointment of the judiciary and of administrative prosecutors (8§45), as well as public security (8§46) and the relevant parts of the chapter on international economic relations (8§47). In case in the country at hand public security would be inadequately regulated at the start of the transition, this regulation should be forwarded to an earlier phase.

8§43 *Joblessness due to qualifications mismatches and to recessions – full enactment*

The 'Job securities and jobs shortage agency' (JSA) was formally established in 8§3, and in phase 2 (8§30) it was assigned limited tasks in preparation for the execution of the regulation below.
• The tasks and competences of this agency (3§17) are now fully enacted. For 'cooperatives' read 'cooperatives and current pre-transition enterprises'.
• The non-explanatory parts of the rules regarding 'qualifications mismatch and recessional joblessness' (3§18–3§20) are enacted. For 'cooperatives' read 'cooperatives and current pre-transition enterprises'.
• The level of the compensations and allowances (end of 3§20) is enacted.
  Recall from ch. 3 that one of the rules entails that all cooperatives, current pre-transition enterprises, state institutions and 'workers' council governed foundations' with a workforce of 50 or more, should continuously offer potential traineeship positions of, as an indication, 5% of their workforce. If required, the JSA may adapt the 5% figure. It is recalled from 8§30 that already in phase 2 the JSA was assigned the task to inform the relevant entities about the potential traineeship positions. Finally it is recalled from ch. 3 that (1) jobless school-leavers, and persons that are jobless after having had a job for less than two years, may receive for max. two months a job search allowance of 60% MiW; (2) if after this period

they have no regular position, they shall adopt a traineeship at a compensation of 60% MiW; (3) jobless persons after having had a two years job may for maximum two months receive a job search allowance of 85% MiW; (4) if after this period they have no regular position, they shall adopt a traineeship at a compensation of 60% MiW, which the JSA makes up to 85% MiW.

As a result of the 8§30 legislation, the JSA has most information available to carry out its full tasks. However, jobless people still have to inform the JSA about their preferences for traineeships. By this time (phase 4) the JSA has published all the traineeships offered at its website (see the last sentence of 8§30).[35]

• *Entry into force.* The legislation enters into force three months after the enactment. (In case the JSA at the time of legislation informs parliament that it requires some more time to match traineeships, the date of entry into force may be adapted). With the entering into force any 'minimum costs of living allowances' (8§10) expire.

The implication is that soon after the entering into force no one is out of work for longer than two months – where 'work' includes permanent jobs, temporary jobs (during recessions), and paid traineeships (in non-recession periods), the latter being a lever to permanent jobs (3§20).

8§44   *Restricted abilities to work – full enactment*

In the Design the cooperatives and state institutions are required to provide work to those with restricted physical or mental abilities to work. The 'Job securities and jobs shortage agency' (JSA) is also responsible for the allocation of these jobs.

• Legislation enacts 3§21, together with the transition rule that also current pre-transition entities are, proportional to their workforce, required to provide work to those with restricted physical or mental abilities to work and that they shall be paid *at least* 1.5 times the minimum wage.

Recall from 8§30 (phase 2) that by now the 'Job securities and jobs shortage agency' has determined the proportions mentioned in the previous sentence. Recall also that already in phase 2 the JSA was assigned the task to inform all the entities about the main lines of the current legislation, as including the (then)

---

35   Prior to the start of phase 4, the JSA might have informed jobless people about the available traineeships, so that they can already state their preferences for traineeships. Depending on the date of enactment, the JSA may not yet have information on jobless recent school-leavers.

indication of jobs for the restricted ability persons of about 5% on top of their other workforce.

Recall from 3§21 that there will be a remaining category of disabled persons that are in no way able to work, at whatever quality or speed. Via the JSA these persons, or those caring them, receive a social security allowance of 120% of the minimum wage (this is exclusive of all medically prescribed extra provisions). Herewith any other currently existing allowances for these people terminate.

• *Entry into force.* The legislation enters into force one year after the enactment. With the entering into force any 'minimum costs of living allowances' (8§10) expire. (In principle, and given the warning referred to, an earlier date of entry into force might be possible. However, the introduction of the traineeships of the previous section, and soon after it the current legislation, might ask too much of the internal organisation of the regarding entities.)

8§45 Appointment procedure of the judiciary and administrative prosecutors – full enactment

• Legislation enacts the procedure for the appointment of the judiciary and of administrative prosecutors, as well as the organisation of the judiciary (3§6). The following transition regulation is also enacted.

• Regarding 3§6 clauses (c) and (d): In order to give the current parliament no predominant influence on the selection of judges (it is the first parliament after the start of the transition that is involved in the Design procedure), one half instead of one quarter of the 'judiciary committee' members (the external committee that selects judges) resigns after the next elections;[36] the resignation is – only this time – determined by lot.

• *Entry into force.* The legislation about the appointment of retiring or resigning judges and administrative prosecutors enters into force three months after the enactment (thus parliament has three months to constitute the 'judiciary committee'). Clauses 3§6 (i) and (k) (about remuneration matters) enter into force when 8§49 has been enacted (phase 5).

8§46 Public security – full enactment

• Legislation establishes the organisation of public security (3§5). Most of the organisation can probably built on the existing organisation, and on existing legislation.

---

36 To be sure (as phase 4 starts immediately after the elections), the next elections are after about four years.

• *Entry into force*. In case of minor changes, the legislation enters into force three months after the enactment (in case of considerable changes accordingly later). Clauses 3§5 (h) and (i) (about remuneration matters) enter into force when 8§49 has been enacted (phase 5).

8§47   International economic relations (ch. 5) and treaties – full enactment

• *International economic relations*. The relevant parts of the International economic relations chapter 5 are enacted (including its Appendix).
• *Entry into force*. The legislation of the main text and of the first section of the appendix enter into force immediately after the enactment. The second and third section of the appendix enter into force five months after the enactment.
• *Treaties*. In case the Constitution (Appendix 3C) has not yet been enacted and entered into force (8§1), ordinary legislation enacts the Constitution's article 33 on treaties. Transitory legislation enacts that in case current treaties – or provisions or resolutions of treaties – are inconsistent with the Design, the country at hand withdraws from these treaties at the earliest date in line with these treaties.
• *Entry into force*. Each of these legislations enters into force three months after the enactment.

8§48   Concluding matters phase 4

Socially and economically the most far-reaching legislation of phase 4 regards, first, the joblessness countering measures 8§43 – both for potentially jobless workers, and the requirements for the economic and public sector entities (temporary jobs during recessions and continuously the offering of traineeships). Second, the continuously offering of work to the people with restricted physical and mental abilities (8§44). Each of these are major socially progressive characteristics of the Design.

Table 8.14 lists the state expenditure due to the phase 4 legislation.

Table 8.15 provides an indication of the sequentially measured amount of legislative work in phase 4. Measured simultaneously, the phase 2 legislation would take about 2½ months.

TABLE 8.14   *State expenditure due to phase 4 legislation*

Expenditure category	Finance of expenditure†		
	Phase 4	Further transition	After transition
general state administration‡	permanent taxes	permanent taxes	permanent taxes
joblessness allowances (8§43)*	permanent taxes	permanent taxes	permanent taxes
restricted work abilities (8§44)⁑	permanent taxes	permanent taxes	permanent taxes

† 'Permanent taxes' are mainly the turnover/production tax and the income tax.
‡ This includes the internal organisation of the agencies introduced in phase 2, excluding their payment of allowances or other transfers.
* Note that in comparison with capitalism the number and the duration of allowances vastly decreases.
⁑ This regards only the disabled persons who are in no way able to work, at whatever quality or speed. (Presumably these received an allowance prior to the transition but possibly at a lower level. Most or many that due to the legislation now have a regular job, did (hopefully) receive some allowance prior to the transition.)

TABLE 8.15   *Indication amount of legislative work phase 4: sequential measure in weeks*[37]

	Subject		Indication	Wk.
8§43	regulation countering joblessness	full legis.	moderate	3.5
8§44	restricted physical abilities to work	full legis.	minor/mod	2.5
8§45	procedure appointment judiciary	full legis.	minor	1.5
8§46	public security	full legis.	minor/mod	2.5
8§47	international econ. relations; treaties	full legis.	minor/mod	2.5
	total weeks in the non-likely case of a complete sequential treatment			*12.5*
	total weeks in terms of the simultaneous measure (2/3 of previous row)			*8.3*

37   [The following explanatory note is abbreviated from a note to the phase 1 Table 8.7.] It is assumed that several enactments are in process at the same time. 'Minor' indicates on average 1½ full-time weeks; 'moderate' 3½ weeks; 'much' 5½ weeks; 'very much' 9 weeks. The drafting of an act could be done in half the time if a sufficient number of civil service officers work on it. It is assumed that groups of civil officers work on all of the five phases' acts concurrently.

Division 5. Transitional legislation phase 5: matured transition

This Division sets out the final transitional legislation phase 5 in nine sections. Only at this point do we get to one of the Design's key points that the average remuneration in each public sector institution is a derivative of the economic domain's average remuneration, and that the workers' councils of each institution decide on the wage scales within the institution (8§49). This is next applied to a number of institutions and sectors that had not yet been (fully) enacted. (Recall that for sectors that were fully enacted, the entering into force of the regarding clauses was postponed to the current phase.) The full enactment in this phase regards the health sector (8§50), the education sector (8§51), state-financed research institutes (8§52), the culture sector (8§53), national railway transport (8§54) and municipalities and provinces (8§56). At this point the regulation about the finance of the state and state institutions can also be fully enacted (8§55). Further, now that all of the Design's provisions and allowances have been fully established – the minimum work-time and the regulation about temporary part-time work is legislated (8§57). Finally the regulation about temporary work as organised through 'stand-in cooperatives' is enacted (8§58).

8§49 *Remuneration of public sector workers and full competences of their councils – full enactment*
When in 8§26 workers' councils for public sector institutions were established, institutions with fewer than 10 workers were not required to introduce councils.
• It is enacted that the 8§26 fewer than 10 workers exemption no longer applies.
   So far the remuneration of public sector workers has been left unaffected in comparison with the pre-transition period.[38] As a consequence, when their workers' councils were introduced, remuneration matters were yet exempted from their competences (8§26).
• It is enacted that the 8§26 remuneration exemption no longer applies.
• It is also enacted that public sector institutions receive wages sum budgets equal to their workforce in FTE times the economic domain's average remuneration of workers in FTE, the latter as determined by the General statistical office or its current equivalent – which was committed this task in 8§33.[39]

---

38   Sections 8§3 for ministries and state agencies; 8§4 for provincial/regional and municipal/local and similar administrations; 8§7 for Workers' council governed foundations.
39   Thus in terms of amendments of the Design text, the entities referred to receive wages sum budgets 'equal to their workforce in FTE' times the weighted average of, on the one hand, 'the wages and dividends of the nation's cooperatives in FTE (as including their "post-

As in the Design a number of people receive the average remuneration individually.[40] This implies that parliamentarians are to vote about, probably, a decrease in their before-tax remuneration (that is, in many countries).[41]
• *Entry into force*. The legislation enters into force in the first full calendar year that starts three months after the enactment.

8§50   The health sector – full enactment

Preliminaries. (a) The legislation set out in this section replaces the regulation of the health sector set out in phase 1 (8§12). However, all health services remain free of charge, that is, fully state-financed out of taxation. Recall that the earlier regulation entered into force (briefly) in the calendar year that started 12 months after the start of phase 1, and that the regarding contracts with insurance companies were given out for a period of five years, thus ending on the 31 December of the fifth year. This means that the current enactment should enter into force at the latter date (or later in case the insurance contracts were prolonged). (b) Recall that currently all medical health institutions have a workers' council (phase 2, 8§26), with full competences (phase 5, 8§49). (c) Recall that the National Health Agency already was given the duty of preparing for its tasks of current section (phase 1, 8§3).
• (*1*) *Tasks of the National Health Agency*. The tasks and the delegated authorities of the National Health Agency (NHA) are enacted (3§26). Regarding its clause (b) – budget and workforce allocation over the nation's medical institutions – the following transition sub-clause is added. 'A condition for receiving finance is that current medical institutions are legally converted into a 'workers' council governed foundation' (8§7; 3§25), and that they transfer the property of premises and fixed equipment to the NHA'. (It is not in the interest of the workers' councils to refuse this, given the finance guarantees that the legal form of a WGF provides.)
• (*2*) *Regulation of medical institutions*. Legislation establishes the rules for medical institutions as set out in 3§27, 3§28 and 3§29, as including relevant details of the organisation of these institutions as set out in chapter 3's Appendix to subdivision 7A. These include at least the latter's rules about the recordkeeping by, and the finance of, medical institutions.

---

poned dividends")' and the wages, plus perhaps other remunerations, of workers in the rest of the economic domain, on the other.
40   Parliamentarians, ministers, judges, administrative prosecutors, councillors and executives of municipalities and provinces.
41   The after-tax effect is probably minor in face of the taxation legislation.

Starting from the organisational structure of medical institutions in the country at hand, there should be a gradual movement towards the organisation set out in the appendix. The rules of this appendix are therefore medium-term strivings on which the NHA reports to parliament at least every three years, as including on:
- The size of the institutions and the ratios of institutions to inhabitants;
- The institutions' staff composition;
- The specifics about evening, night and weekend shifts (the actualisation of the principle that there should be shifts such that the services are sufficiently available is assumed).
- Further, until a date to be determined by the NHA, current primary medical treatment practices are exempted from the requirement to be organised in a Design 'primary medical treatment clinic'. This does not imply exemption from the required legal conversion into a 'workers' council governed foundation'.[42]

• *Entry into force.* The enactment (1) of 3§26, enters into force on 1 January after the end of the 8§12 contracts with insurance companies. (At the time of enactment, the date is exactly known).[43] The under heading (2) mentioned rules, as well as the strivings and the reporting about these, equally enter into force at the above-mentioned date.

8§51 *The education sector – full enactment*

Preliminaries. In phase 1 (8§3) the 'National Education Agency' (NEA) was formally established and given the duty of preparing for the current section's tasks. Provisional transition regulation of the education sector was enacted in phase 1 (8§13). Currently all educational institutions have a workers' council (phase 2, 8§26), with full competences (phase 5, 8§49; entering into force in the first full calendar year that starts three months after the enactment).

---

42 Especially the growth to Design 'primary medical treatment clinics' (MTC), with a staff of about 50 workers, will take time. In order to reach the MTC organisation, the NHA might proceed as follows. First, the NHA communicates to the non-specialist medical practitioners in cities and regions that MTCs will be in formation. Second, because a pharmacy is the pivot of an MTC, and because pharmacies are often already team institutions, the NHA might ask the pharmacists in cities/regions to take the lead for the formation of an MTC. Third, medical profession school-leavers might be enforced to associate with an MTC. Finally, after a lapse of time, the NHA gradually binds primary medical treatment licences to working in an MTC.

43 The contract started towards the end of phase 1. At the current point (phase 5) we are about three years and three months after the end of phase 1. Hence at the point of enactment, the remaining duration of the contracts is about one year and nine months.

- Legislation fully establishes the rules regarding the NEA 3§30. Its clause (c) implies that all primary, secondary and tertiary educational institutions are required to legally convert into a 'Workers' council governed foundation' (8§7; 3§25), and that they transfer the property of premises and fixed equipment to the NEA. (It is not in the interest of the workers' councils to refuse this, given the finance guarantees that the legal form of a WGF provides.)[44]
- Legislation also establishes the rules for educational institutions as set out in 3§32 as well as for university research and PhD programmes (3§33-A). The institutions' number of students are rough, indicative, long-term strivings (Table 3.12).
- *Entry into force.* The legislation of 3§30 enters into force in the first school/academic year that starts six months after the enactment, with the exception of clause (c) on the legal form of Workers' council governed foundation, which enters into force one year after the enactment (which does not prevent the institutions to convert their legal form earlier). The legislation of 3§32 and 3§33-A enters into force in the first school/academic year that starts six months after the enactment, with the exception of matters regarding Workers' council governed foundations, which enter into force one year after the enactment (however, the relevant budget matters in the first school/academic year after that date).

8§52   *State-financed research institutes – full enactment*

- The establishment of (at least) the following four state-financed applied-research institutes is enacted, cf. 3§33-B. (Other applied research is carried out by cooperatives; and during the transition perhaps by pre-transition entities.)
- A General statistical office.
- A National institute for the environment and public health.
- A National institute for the advance of physically circular production.
- A National institute for economic analysis and forecasts.

These four institutes shall have the legal form of a 'Workers' council governed foundation (WGF)' (3§25; 8§7).

All or most of these can be established by way of a reorganisation of pre-transition existing research institutes. To the extent that similar public sector institutes already exist, they currently have a workers' council (phase 2, 8§26) with full competences (phase 5, 8§49; entering into force at the start of the first full calendar year after that enactment).

---

44   To be sure, the WGF requirement also applies for institutions with fewer than 10 workers.

- *Entry into force.* The legislation enters into force in the first full calendar year that starts six months after the enactment.

8§53 *Regulation of the culture sector – full enactment*
In phase 1 (8§3) the 'Culture and cultural heritage agency' was formally established and given the duty of preparing for its tasks of the current section. To the extent cultural heritage and contemporary arts institutions are part of the public sector, or are fully or predominantly state-financed, they currently have a workers' council (phase 2, 8§26), with full competences (phase 5, 8§49; entering into force in the first full calendar year that starts three months after that enactment).
- *Legislation enacts the tasks of the 'Culture and cultural heritage agency'* (CHA; 3§34) together with the following transitional regulation.
- All institutions mentioned in the second sentence of the first paragraph above shall legally convert into a 'Workers' council governed foundation' (8§7; 3§25). This implies that they shall transfer the property of premises and fixed equipment to the CHA. State museums and state libraries and archives shall transfer the property of their collections to the CHA. The CHA immediately rents out the premises, fixed equipment and collections to the regarding institutions. (This, and all similar rules elsewhere, is a safety measure in the event an institution should go bankrupt.)
- The CHA allocates budgets to the institutions above, and sets quantitative workforce norms for the institutions.
- *Legislation enacts the principles of the regulation on 'State and non-state museums, and the national library and archives'* (3§35) together with the following transitional regulation.
- During the transition *non-state* museums or libraries may have the legal form of a cooperative or of a pre-transition entity. In case the latter have the legal form of a foundation these should introduce workers' councils with full competences (cf. 8§49).[45]
- The CHA develops criterions for what museums should be state museums in the medium and long run, and proposes these via the relevant minister to parliament.

---

45   In case a pre-transition entity has the legal form of a stock corporation and when the corporate shares are part of a bequest, the 'Agency for temporary workers' council governed foundations' (ATF) has a pre-emptive right to purchase these – against reasonable prices (8§8). Once the ATF is the majority shareholder it could insist on a legal conversion of the corporation into a cooperative (8§23 under heading 4-A 'Medium to large stock corporations').

- On the basis of the previous point, and when relevant, the CHA gradually sells or rents out the assets of a to be non-state museum to a new cooperative (similar as the 'Agency for temporary workers' council governed foundations' would do this – 8§8; 3§41).[46]
- The digitalisation tasks of the National Library (3§35-a) are, depending on the country at hand, a medium-term project. The National Library reports its progress every two years to the CHA.
- *Legislation enacts the principles of the regulation on 'Contemporary creative arts and arts performance'* (3§36) together with the following transitional regulation.
- Concert and theatre halls including opera houses (3§36-a) that currently are part of the public sector or that are fully or predominantly state-financed, shall convert into a 'Workers' council governed foundation' (WGF) on basis of the first part of the legislation above (under 3§34). The CHA gradually legally converts these into cooperatives by selling or renting out the assets of these institutions to the cooperative. In case the hall or house has the status of cultural heritage, the CHA shall not sell but only rent out these.
- In case concert and theatre halls including opera houses have the legal form of a foundation these should introduce workers' councils with full competences (cf. 8§49). See also the last but one footnote.
- Reproduction of artefacts: arts publishing (3§36-b) and artistic creations and performances (3§36-b). These categories are treated similarly as under the last but one bullet.
- *Entry into force.* All legislation above enters into force in the first full calendar year that starts six months after the enactment.

8§54   *National railway transport – full enactment*

In phase 1 (8§3) the 'National public transport agency' (NTA) was formally established and given the duty of preparing for its tasks of the current section.
- Legislation enacts the tasks of the NTA (3§40). This task exclusively regards the equally enacted National Railway Company (the latter carries out the interurban railway transport for passengers and freight, and it has the form of a full costs charging 'Workers' council governed foundation' – WGF, 3§40).

(a) In case in the country at hand the national railway transport is part of the public sector, the two entities can be established by way of a reorgan-

---

46 Note that prior to this action of the CHA, all relevant cultural entities have the form of a 'Workers' council governed foundation – on the basis of the first part of the current legislation.

isation of pre-transition institutions. In this case the legislation above *enters into force* in the first full calendar year that starts six months after the enactment.

(b) In case in the country at hand the national railway transport is carried out by pre-transition stock corporations via licences or concessions, there are two possibilities.

(b-1) First, when the corporate shares are part of a bequest, the 'Agency for temporary workers' council governed foundations' (ATF) has a pre-emptive right to purchase these – against reasonable prices (8§8).[47] Once the ATF is the majority shareholder it could insist on a legal conversion of the corporation into a WGF (8§23 under the heading 'Medium and large corporations'). In this case the legislation above (second paragraph) *enters into force* at that point.

(b-2) Second, at the current point (phase 5) the licences or concessions will have expired. (See 8§6-c, which states that the maximum market share regulation overrules licences or concessions – as entering into force from off three years after the phase 1 enactment of 8§6; or if this is later when the current enactment enters into force.) The NTA can then bargain about taking over these entities. The latter are then integrated into the National Railway Company. In this case the legislation above (second paragraph) *enters into force* in the first full calendar year that starts one year after the enactment. (This assumes that the integration takes considerable time.)

The costs for the state of the first alternative (b-1) are negligible.[48] (In the second alternative (b-2) the corporations will liquidate, the result accruing to their shareholders that will be taxed at the going income tax rates (8§9)). The choice between the alternatives then depends, first, on the prices that the corporations charge for the transport, and on how good or bad their services are (and in case of many suppliers on the burden of perhaps non-connecting changes between suppliers). This can only be judged during the actual transition. Secondly, however, in (b-1) – and in case more than one stock corporation held concessions – there will be a gradual integration into the National Railway Company. It is difficult to judge if this is an advantage or a disadvantage.

---

47 The reasonable prices do not matter for the inheritors given the inheritance taxes.
48 In the second alternative (b-2) the corporations will liquidate, the result accruing to their shareholders that will be taxed at the going income tax rates (8§9).

8§55   Finance of the state and state institutions – full enactment
• The regulation regarding the finance of the state and state institutions (3§4) is enacted. Some of this legislation anticipates the full enactment of the regulation about municipalities and provinces (8§56). Thus these should be enacted simultaneously.
• *Entry into force.* The legislation enters into force in the first full calendar year that starts two months after the enactment.

8§56   Municipalities and provinces (ch. 4) – full enactment
So far legislation on municipalities and provinces was enacted in 8§26 (workers' councils except remuneration matters), 8§37 (non-internal democratic organs) and 8§49 (remuneration of councillors and executives, and full competences of the workers' councils).
• Legislation now establishes the regulation for municipalities and provinces (ch. 4) that has as yet not been enacted. This regards especially their finance and budget, and their tasks and competences. In case municipalities and/or provinces levied taxes, these are abolished.
• In case a municipality maintains urban and suburban passenger railway transport, similar regulation applies as for the national railway transport (8§54). In case a pre-transition private railway entity would be taken over, the municipality deliberates with the minister of home affairs about transferring the relevant state tax receipts (8§54 under b-2).
• *Entry into force.* The legislation under the first bullet enters into force in the first full calendar year that starts two months after the enactment. That under the second bullet enters into force similar as 8§54.

8§57   Minimum work-time, and a temporary part-time position – full enactment
The taxes on the incomes of workers and pensioners (will) account for about 50% of the taxation revenue. Because at this point all provisions such as pensions, child-related allowances, healthcare and education have been enacted, and because those that would work part-time would nevertheless fully benefit from the provisions, a minimum work-time is legislated.
• It is enacted hat the number of hours per year that defines a 'full-time position' is also the minimum work-time in hours per year (3§10-c). Along with it, the regulation for a temporary part-time position is enacted (3§10-d).[49] The regulation applies for all workers.

---

49   Regarding the latter, temporary transition regulation establishes the fictitious presump-

TRANSITION TO A WORKER COOPERATIVES SOCIETY 377

Herewith all work-time regulation (3§10) has been enacted.
• *Entry into force.* The legislation enters into force in the first full calendar year that starts three months after the enactment.

8§58 *Temporary work as organised through 'stand-in cooperatives' – full enactment*

• Legislation finally enacts the non-explanatory parts of Appendix 3F on stand-in work/temporary work as organised in 'stand-in cooperatives'.

Recall that these cooperatives are organised like all other cooperatives (ch. 2) but their output regards a special service for other cooperatives (stand-in seekers) that is bound to a specific rule – the service being the standing-in for, or temporary replacing, workers of other cooperatives or of public sector institutions (the main specific rule for the replacement or standing-in they are required to charge the seeker *at least* 150% of the seeker's average wage as indicated in the latter's last audited annual report). Appendix 3F also includes the rule that only the 'stand-in cooperatives' (thus no other cooperatives nor 'single person enterprises') are allowed to provide the stand-in service.

• Three transitional rules are equally enacted. *First*, also current pre-transition entities such as 'employment agencies' are not (no longer) allowed to provide the stand-in or temporary work service (this implies that if employment agencies and the like would want to continue their service, they will have to legally convert into a Design cooperative). *Second*, the 'stand-in cooperatives' also provide their service for current pre-transition enterprises. *Third*, during a transition period of 15 months (see the entry into force) current 'employment agencies' and the like are required to charge the temporary work or stand-in seeking institutions *at least* 150% of the seeker's average wage as indicated in the latter's last audited annual report; concomitantly they are required to pay the stand-in/temporary workers 150% of the seeker's average wage.

• *Entry into force.* The legislation under the first bullet (Appendix 3F) enters into force 18 months after the enactment. However, at their earliest convenience prospect 'stand-in cooperatives' may already start their service, either for cooperatives or for current pre-transition enterprises. The transitional legislation of the second bullet, under 'first' and 'second' enters into force 18 months after the enactment; that under 'third' enters into force three months after the

---

tion that the regarding 10 years (work at 50% of the full-time position) was/will be proportionally spread over one's working life.

enactment (it should be widely communicated prior to the enactment that this rule is upcoming).

8§59   Concluding matters phase 5

The previous section completes the transitional legislation. The most important phase 5 legislation regards the establishment of the average remuneration in each public sector institution as a derivative of the economic domain's average remuneration, and that the workers' councils of each institution decide on the wage scales within the institution (8§49), which is a key characteristic of the Design.

Until this point the pre-taxation remuneration of public sector workers was left unaffected. However, notwithstanding the long-term importance of the previous point, its effect on the after-tax individual remunerations is presumably far less than the effect of the phase 1 taxation legislation.

A less far-reaching point, even if socio-economically important, is the legislation of the minimum FTE work-time in hours per year – together with the possibility of working part-time for a total equivalent of 10 years (8§57; 3§10). It is a consequence of the taxation systematic together with the free of charge provisions and (mainly) the pension allowances for all. Important is also the legislation about 'stand-in cooperatives' (8§58) because it prevents the evil of an echelon of workers with casual inferior jobs.

Table 8.16 lists the state expenditure due to the phase 5 legislation.

TABLE 8.16   *State expenditure due to phase 5 legislation*

Expenditure category[†]	Finance of expenditure[‡]	
	Phase 5	After transition
general state administration[*]	permanent taxes	permanent taxes
education sector: research (8§51)	permanent taxes	permanent taxes
research institutes (8§52)	permanent taxes	permanent taxes
culture sector (8§53)	permanent taxes	permanent taxes
municipalities and provinces (8§56)	permanent taxes	permanent taxes

[†] The full enactment of the health sectors requires no extra expenditure in comparison with its phase 1 legislation. For the educations sector the research of universities and their PhD programs has been added in comparison with its phase 2 legislation. Railway transport charges the full costs.
[‡] 'Permanent taxes' are mainly the turnover/production tax and the income tax.
[*] This includes the internal organisation of the agencies introduced in phase 5, excluding their payment of allowances or other transfers.

Table 8.17 provides an indication of the sequentially measured amount of legislative work in phase 5. Measured simultaneously, the phase 5 legislation would take just over half a year (Table 8.8, 8§24).

TABLE 8.17   *Indication amount of legislative work phase 5: sequential measure in weeks*[50]

	Subject		Indication	Wk.
8§49	remuneration and councils public sector	full legis.	minor	1.5
8§50	regulation health sector	full legis.	much	5.5
8§51	regulation education sector	full legis.	much	5.5
8§52	state-financed research institutes	full legis.	moderate	3.5
8§53	culture sector	full legis.	much	5.5
8§54	national railway transport	full legis.	moderate	3.5
8§55	finance of the state and state institutions	full legis.	minor/mod	2.5
8§56	municipalities and provinces	full legis.	much	5.5
8§57	minimum work-time and temporary part-time position	full legis.	minor	1.5
8§58	'stand-in cooperatives'	full legis.	minor	1.5
	total weeks in the unlikely case of a complete sequential treatment			36.0
	total weeks in terms of the simultaneous measure (2/3 of previous row)			24.0

Division 6. Full implementation in practice of the transition legislation

As mentioned before, the transition legislation period as set out in the previous Divisions is (as an indication) planned in five to six years. During this period a transition in practice – that is, an implementation of the legislation in practice – gradually emerges.

The transition of the public sector is after six years is almost entirely completed. (Some matters of the health, education and culture sectors regard medium-term strivings, without affecting their Design essence.) The gradual emergence of the transition in practice regards especially the economic domain, that is the legal conversion of capitalist entities into worker cooperatives (see also 8§23). It is impossible to predict how much of that transition

---

50   [The following explanatory note is abbreviated from a note to the phase 1 Table 8.7.] It is assumed that several enactments are in process at the same time. 'Minor' indicates on

will already be realised in those six years. This depends, first of all, on the relative sizes of the capitalist sector and the pre-transition sector of worker-owned cooperatives at the start of the transition. It also depends on the reactions of capitalist enterprises and their shareholders on the key levers for the transition (such as financial market restrictions, taxation, maximum market shares and the single location for entities). In face of these levers, they might either try to keep on competing with cooperatives, or give up and try to sell an entity to the 'Agency for temporary workers' council governed foundations' (8§8) before it goes bankrupt.

However, in case capitalist enterprises and their shareholders would persevere in their competition effort with cooperatives, the Design's inheritance taxes imply the capitalist enterprises' death-knell. This means that the transition will ultimately be completed within a generation.

Yet, individuals are free to run by themselves a registered 'single person enterprise'; once they wish to hire a person, the only possible legal form is that of a cooperative (2§2.2).

Concluding summary of chapter 8

Starting at the point when in a country there is parliamentary majority that aims to go for a transition, this chapter presented a transition path from capitalism to a Design worker cooperatives society. The path is divided into two broad periods. One in which all of Part One's Design has been put into legislation – in this period its implementation in practice already gradually emerges. Another in which that legislation becomes fully implemented in practice in the sense that all of the society's economic domain is organised in Design worker cooperatives. The most important point of the chapter is that such a transition seems possible along with a preservation of the degree of production and work as inherited from the immediate past – although I cannot prove that.

Contrary to this preservation posited, it might be argued that in the early phases of the transition the prevailing capitalist sector will begin to break down because of an investment stop by capitalist enterprises. However, this is not likely because – also from the part of the enterprises' shareholders – there is no better alternative than to keep on investing. (An investment stop because

---

average 1½ full-time weeks; 'moderate' 3½ weeks; 'much' 5½ weeks; 'very much' 9 weeks. The drafting of an act could be done in half the time if a sufficient number of civil service officers work on it. It is assumed that groups of civil officers work on all of the five phases' acts concurrently.

of revenge feelings does not bring in profits.[51] Moreover, if these enterprises' management or shareholders would want to show that capitalist enterprises are more vital than cooperatives, then an investment stop is rather counter-productive.)

This matter is to be distinguished from the likely inheritance of a recession due to the turbulences just before the transition (ch. 7) – recession countering policies were treated in 8§20.

TABLE 8.18 *The transition legislation phases and their implementation in practice*

		Duration in years (indication)	Implementation in practice
I	**transition legislation phases**		
	after first transition elections		
	phase 1: transition foundations	1.1	
	phase 2: completion elementary transition	0.4	
	phase 3: preconditions for mature transition	0.5	
	overrun and adaptation period	2.0	emerging transition in practice
	subtotal	4	
	after second transition elections		
	phase 4: advanced transition	0.2	
	phase 5 (final): matured transition	0.6	
	overrun period	0.7	
	subtotal	1.5	
	total number of legislation years	5.5	
II	**full implementation in practice**		full transition (in maximum one generation)

---

51   For shareholders, the dividends derived from profits are crucial. As indicated in 8§23 (under heading 4-A) the transitional constellation is such that the market-value of shares

Table 8.18 lists the above mentioned two broad transition periods, with for the first period an indication of the duration of the transition's five legislation phases. This first period has been detailed in the chapter's first five Divisions – together with an underpinning of the duration – the second one was briefly pointed out in Division 6.

1. Transition of the economic domain. The key policy instruments that bring about the transition path of the economic domain, are listed in the six points below.
• *First.* The Design's cooperative is enacted as legal entity, together with the enactment of the specific rules set out in chapter 2. In addition the following two transition rules are enacted. First, regarding the economic domain (and except for a 'single person enterprise') no new legal entity shall be established other than a Design cooperative. Second, the sole allowed non-public sector legal conversion of an entity is that into a Design cooperative (Phase 1, 8§14). These two transition rules, in combination with the rules below, are core to the transition.
• *Second.* In the Design there are no shares and bonds markets. For the transition it is enacted that *no new* shares or bonds shall be issued. In line with the Design, bank savings accounts must be terminated and be transferred to a savings account with the 'Savings and Loans Bank' (Phase 1, 8§16).
• *Third.* Taxation measures include steeply progressing individual income and inheritance brackets (each as in the Design). For corporations the income and property taxes are maintained as they are before the transition; those for cooperatives are nil (as in the Design). This implies a comparative advantage for the latter – note that under capitalism there are also different taxation regimes for different legal entities. (Phase 1, 8§9, Table 8.2.) The inheritance tax (with, as in the Design, a top bracket of 100% above twice the minimum wage) implies that after a generation the individual property ownership, in shares, bonds, non-incorporated firms, and in real estate will have evanesced.

The three sets of rules above are sufficient for a within one generation fading away of the capitalist sector and a complete transition to worker cooperatives. This hinges on the inheritance tax together with the rule that in the economic domain no legal entities other than Design cooperative can be established (first above). The rules below accelerate the transition process.

---

is not determined by the corporations' equity (and prospects) but by the present value of the expected future dividends during the lifetime of the average shareholder (an individual shareholder will calculate her/his expected lifetime, as well as the individual marginal tax rate).

• *Fourth*. The enactment of the Design's competition policy rule about maximum market shares, which for the transition implies that many current pre-transition enterprises will have to break up into two or more independent smaller legal entities (Phase 1, 8§6; this rule enters into force one year after the enactment.)

• *Fifth*. Enactment of the Design's rule that economic domain entities shall be organised in no more than one single location, which implies that current pre-transition multi-location enterprises will have to break up into two or more independent single location legal entities (Phase 3, 8§35; the rule enters into force six months after the enactment.)[52]

Rules four and five formally merely mean that capitalist enterprises lose a market power/dominance 'advantage' above Design cooperatives.

• *Sixth*. Enactment of the Design's 'Agency for temporary workers' council governed foundations' (Phase 1, 8§8). Amongst several other competences, the main one is that when during the transition corporate shares, or a firm, are part of a bequest, the agency has a pre-emptive right to purchase these – against reasonable prices. (Given the inheritance taxes the inheritors are required to sell anyway.) Once this agency acquires the majority of the shares in a corporation it can insist on the legal conversion into a cooperative (perhaps via the stage of a temporary workers' council governed foundation).

The general strategy for the gradual legal conversion of pre-transition capitalist enterprises into Design cooperatives was expanded on in 8§23.

2. Transition of the public sector. The rest of the transition's five legislation phases mainly concern an orderly transition of the state, the state institutions and the rest of the public sector. This mainly regards the enactment of the following items.

• The election and interconnection of the state's highest democratic organs as well as of the democratic organs of provinces and municipalities (Phase 1, 8§1; and Phase 3, 8§37).

• The workers' councils of ministries, the judiciary, state agencies, provinces and municipalities, as including the competences of these councils (Phase 2, 8§26; the competences regarding remuneration in Phase 5, 8§49).

• The free of charge health and education, and their institutions (Phase 1, 8§11 and 8§12) and their organisation through workers' council governed foundations (Phase 2, 8§26; the competences regarding remuneration in Phase 5, 8§49).

---

52   In phase 1 this rule was already publicly announced.

• The various allowances such as those for pensions and the child-related ones (Phase 2, 8§27–8§29) and for persons with restricted abilities to work (Phase 4, 8§44). (Until these are enacted, general allowances at a minimum level of 60% MiW apply for all from early on Phase 1, 8§10 – MiW abbreviates the minimum wage.)
• The minimisation of joblessness to a maximum of two months (Phase 4, 8§43).
• The average remuneration of workers in public sector institutions as a derivative of the average remuneration of workers in the economic domain (Phase 5, 8§48).

As it is, the transition path of chapter 8 shows that all issues mentioned under 1 and 2 (and those that are not mentioned in this Summary) cannot be transformed in one go; their transition not only takes time, but also requires a specific transition sequence. To take the last point above, the remunerations of public sector workers cannot be changed in one stroke; orderly change of these requires at least that the various provisions have reached a substantial quality and quantity level.

Generally, the main puzzle to solve for the transition in each of the economic and public sector domains is the specific transition sequence from capitalism to the Design's components, as well as the required transition time in between the introduction of the different components.

I do not claim that the transition path chosen in this chapter is the only possible one. My sole self-imposed task was to show that there is at least one, reasonably detailed, feasible transition path. One that does not result in an immediate collapse of pre-transition capitalist sectors, and thus one that keeps production and jobs going throughout the transition.

Appendix 8A. Various summarising tables

This appendix brings together five summarising tables.
• Summary of the transition's phase-wise enactment of allowances and compensations (Table 8.19).
• Summary of the entering into force of legislation (Table 8.20).
• Indication of the duration of the legislative transition phases 1–5 (Table 8.8). This is the same table as the one shown at the end of Division 1.
• Indication of the amount of legislative work in phases 1–5: sequential measure (Table 8.21). This table brings together the similar per phase tables at the end of Divisions 1–5.
• Legislative transition implementation of the Part One Design (Table 8.22). Starting from the systematic of Part One, this table shows the transition order of the former: sometimes in a single full enactment, often via temporary or partial enactments.

Three of these tables show 'phases columns'. Here the sign 'x' means 'full enactment' (from that phase onwards), and the sign 't' temporary or partial enactment in that phase. (A repeated 't' in a row means that there is more than one temporary enactment.)

TABLE 8.19 *Summary of the transition's phase-wise enactment of allowances and compensations* [FT = financed out of taxation; MR = required (minimum) remuneration by entities*])

Section	Subject		Indication of level (before tax)	Phases				
				1	2	3	4	5
8§10	minimum costs of living (MCL)		costs of living basket					
	minimum wage in FTE (MiW)		set by parliament; indication: 167% MCL					
	MCL in terms of MiW		60% MiW					
8§10	minimum wage	MR	see above	x				
8§10	minimum costs of living allowances	FT	60% MiW (100% MCL)	t				
8§10/8§27	pensions	FT	100% MiW (in phase 1: 60% MiW)	t	x			
8§12/8§50	health provisions	FT		t				x
8§13/8§51	formal education provisions	FT		t				x
8§28	child allowances	FT	child age dependent costs of living		x			

TABLE 8.19 *Summary of enactment of allowances and compensations (cont.)*

Section	Subject	Indication of level (before tax)		Phases				
				1	2	3	4	5
idem	childcare allowances	FT	equivalent of costs institutional childcare		x			
idem	parental leave allowances (total 31 weeks)	FT	100% MiW		x			
idem	orphan allowances	FT	twice the child cost of living allowances		x			
8§29	allowance students (usually max. 6 years)	FT	60% MiW (100% MCL)		x			
8§43	job search allowances (max. 2 months)†	FT	60% MiW (100% MCL)				x	
idem	traineeship persons previous row	MR	60% MiW (100% MCL)				x	
idem	job search after two-year job (max 2 months)	FT	85% MiW (142% MCL)				x	
idem	trainees after having had a two-year job	‡	85% MiW (142% MCL)				x	
idem	recessional work-time and wage reduction	MR	wage reduction equivalent to 0.5%-points above the rate of recessional joblessness				x	
idem	recessional additionally hired workers	MR	85% MiW (142% MCL) [preliminary]				x	
8§44	workers with restricted abilities	MR	at least 150% MiW (250% MCL)				x	
idem	those unable to work, at any quality or speed	FT	120% MiW (200% MCL)				x	

* Cooperatives, public sector institutions, pre-transition enterprises. Except transition matters this table is similar to Table 3.9.
† For school-leavers and those who had a job < two years.
‡ Remuneration for traineeships is paid by the regarding entity (previous row); the JSA makes this up to 85% of the minimum wage.

TABLE 8.20 *Summary of the entering into force of legislation* [The mark R in the last column indicates: considerable restructuring of pre-transition economic entities.]

Section	Subject	Phases					Entering into force (time after enactment)	
		1	2	3	4	5		
8§1	democratic organs state	x					country dependent	
8§2	judiciary	t					immediate	
8§45	judiciary				x		3 months	
8§3	ministries and state agencies: general	x					various	
8§4	four banking and fund agencies	x					4 months	
8§5	(no legislation)							
8§6	competition legislation	x					various[53]	R
8§7	workers' council gov. found. (WGF)	t					immediate	
8§49	workers' council gov. found. (WGF)				x		1 Jan. after 3 months	
8§8	rules Agency for temporary WGFs	x					immediate	
8§9	taxation	x					1 Jan. after 9 months[54]	R
8§10	minimum wages	x					2 months / immediate	
8§10	minimum costs of living allowances	t					2 months	
8§27–29;44	various allowances		x		x		various	
8§11	housing legislation: rents	x					immediate	
8§11	REA and legislation construction	t					immediate	
8§38	real estate legislation: full			x			3 months	
8§12	health sector: temporary	t					1 Jan. after 9 months[55]	
8§50	health sector: full				x		various	
8§13	education sector: temporary[56]	t					1 Jan. after 9 months[57]	
8§51	education sector: full				x		various	

---

53 Immediately: prohibition take-overs. One year after enactment: maximum market shares.
54 Inheritance and gift taxes: immediately. Rental property tax in/after phase 3.
55 This is the date of free health provisions (and insurance contracts). Other parts enter into force immediately.
56 Excluding research universities.
57 This is the date of free education provisions. Other parts enter into force at various other dates.

TABLE 8.20   *Summary of the entering into force of legislation (cont.)*

Section	Subject	Phases					Entering into force (time after enactment)	
		1	2	3	4	5		
8§14	Design worker coop economy	x					immediate (exc. 8§15)	
8§15	idem, entry into force exception	t					N.A.	
8§16	rules financial markets	x					immediate / 2 months	R
8§17	accommodation investment credit	t					immediate	
8§18	conversion entities (esp. WOCs)	t					immediate	
8§19–24	(no legislation)							
8§25	work-time maximum		x				3 months	R
8§26	public sector councils (except remuneration)		t				1 year[58]	
8§49	public sector councils: full legisl.					x	1 Jan. after 3 months	
8§27	pension allowances		x				year income tax 8§9	
8§28	four child-related allowances		x				year income tax 8§9	
8§29	allowance students		x				year income tax 8§9	
8§30	preparatory regulation about jobs		t				6 months / 3 years	
8§43	jobs agency: full enactment				x		3 months	
8§31	legislation auditing		x				3 months	
8§32	auditors/accountancy separation		x				6 months	
8§33	income accounts and balance sheets		x				1 year	
8§33	average remuneration econ. domain		x				1 Oct. after former	
8§34	(no legislation)							
8§35	removal temp. exceptions 8§15			x			6 months	R
8§36	physically circular production			x			6 months	R
8§36	safety & info output; safety at work			x			6 months / 3 years[59]	R
8§37	municipal & provincial democr. org.			t			6 months	
8§56	municipal & provincial: full enactment					x	various	

---

58   This is about two years after the start of the transition; or, towards the end of phase 3.
59   The latter for the advertisement prohibition.

TABLE 8.20 *Summary of the entering into force of legislation (cont.)*

Section	Subject	Phases					Entering into force (time after enactment)	
		1	2	3	4	5		
8§38	real estate legislation: full enactment			x			3 months	
8§39	mining & other Earth extractions			x			3 months	
8§40	infrastructure legislation			x			3 months	
8§41	patents & copyrights			x			3 months	
8§42	(no legislation)							
8§43	joblessness				x		3 months	R
8§44	restricted abilities to work				x		1 year	R
8§45	appointment judges & a-prosecutors				x		3 months	
8§46	public security				x		3 months	
8§47	international econ. relations; treaties				x		immediate / 5 months	
8§48	(no legislation)							
8§49	public sector remuneration					x	1 Jan. after 3 months	
8§50	regulation health sector					x	1 Jan. after 8§12 end	
8§51	regulation education sector[60]					x	various[61]	
8§52	state-financed research institutes					x	1 Jan. after 6 months	
8§53	regulation culture sector					x	1 Jan. after 6 months	
8§54	national railway transport					x	1 Jan. after 6 months[62]	
8§55	finance of state and state institutions					x	1 Jan. after 2 months	
8§56	municipalities and provinces					x	1 Jan. after 2 months	
8§57	work-time minimum					x	1 Jan. after 3 months	R
8§58	stand-in cooperatives					x	3 to 18 months	R

---

60 Including research universities.
61 Mainly the first school/academic year that starts six months after the enactment.
62 Main case; other cases enter into force later.

TABLE 8.8 *Indication of the duration of the legislative transition phases 1–5 (repeat from 8§24)*

	Phase	Duration in weeks		Duration in years
		Sequential	Simultaneous 2/3 previous column	Simultaneous at 40 weeks per year
	(1)	(2)	(3)	(4)
1	*after the first transition elections*			
2	transition legislation phase 1	67.0	44.7	1.1
3	transition legislation phase 2	23.5	15.7	0.4
4	transition legislation phase 3	31.5	21.0	0.5
5	*overrun and adaptation period*†			2.0
6	*subtotal*			4
7	*after the second transition elections*			
8	transition legislation phase 4	12.5	8.3	0.2
9	transition legislation phase 5 (final)	36.0	24.0	0.6
10	*overrun period*			0.7
11	*subtotal*			1.5
12	*total number of weeks*	170.5	113.7	
13	*total number of years*			5.5

† In case there is no overrun, an adaptation period of nearly two years is nevertheless required in view of phases 4–5. Thus phase 4 (row 8) should start after 4 years.

Table 8.21 takes together the similar per phase tables at the end of Division 1–5. of the main text.

TABLE 8.21 *Indication amount of legislative work phases 1–5: sequential and total simultaneous measure*[63]

	Subject		Indication	Wk.
	Phase 1			
	General legislative preparations by civil service workers			10
8§1	state's democratic organs	full legis.	much	5.5

---

63 [The following explanatory note is abbreviated from a note to the phase 1 Table 8.7.] It

TABLE 8.21   *Indication of legislative work phases 1–5 (cont.)*

	Subject		Indication	Wk.
8§2	judiciary		minor	1.5
8§3	ministries and state agencies (elementary)		moderate	3.5
8§5	four state's banking and fund agencies	full legis.	much	5.5
8§6	Competition authority	full legis.	moderate	3.5
8§7	workers' council governed foundations		moderate	3.5
8§8	Agency for temporary workers' council gov. foundations	full legis.	moderate	3.5
8§9	taxation		much	5.5
8§10	minimum wage; minimum cost of living allowances		minor	1.5
8§11	housing legislation		minor	1.5
8§12	health sector, temporary		moderate	3.5
8§13	education sector, temporary		moderate	3.5
8§14	Design ch. 2	full legis.	very much	9.0
8§15	idem, temporary exceptions		minor	1.5
8§16	financial markets		minor	1.5
8§17	accommodation banks' investment credit to cooperatives		minor	1.5
8§18	conversion legal form into Design coops (esp. WOCs)		minor	1.5
	total weeks in the non-likely case of a complete sequential treatment			67.0
	total weeks in terms of the simultaneous measure (2/3 of previous row)			44.7
	Phase 2			
8§25	full-time position and maximum work-time	full legis.	minor	1.5
8§26	workers' councils public sector inst. (restricted)		moderate	3.5
8§27	pension allowances	full legis.	moderate	3.5
8§28	child allowances	full legis.	moderate	3.5
8§29	costs of living allowances tertiary students	full legis.	minor	1.5
8§30	preparatory regulation about jobs		moderate	3.5

is assumed that several enactments are in process at the same time. 'Minor' indicates on average 1½ full-time weeks; 'moderate' 3½ weeks; 'much' 5½ weeks; 'very much' 9 weeks. The drafting of an act could be done in half the time if a sufficient number of civil service officers work on it. It is assumed that groups of civil officers work on all of the five phases' acts concurrently.

TABLE 8.21 *Indication of legislative work phases 1–5 (cont.)*

	Subject		Indication	Wk.
8§31	Registered external accountants authority	full legis.	minor/mod	2.5
8§32	Accountancy companies ring-fence		minor	1.5
8§33	income account & balance sheet economic domain entities	permanent	minor/mod	2.5
	total weeks in the unlikely case of a complete sequential treatment			*23.5*
	total weeks in terms of the simultaneous measure (2/3 of previous row)			*15.7*
	Phase 3			
8§35	removal of exceptions economic domain	full legis.	mod/much	4.5
8§36	circular production and production safeties	full legis.	much	5.5
8§37	municipal and provincial democratic organs		much	5.5
8§38	Real Estate Agency	full legis.	much	5.5
8§39	Mining and other Earth extractions agency	full legis.	minor/mod	2.5
8§40	National Infrastructure Agency	full legis.	mod/much	4.5
8§41	Patents and copyrights authority	full legis.	moderate	3.5
	total weeks in the unlikely case of a complete sequential treatment			*31.5*
	total weeks in terms of the simultaneous measure (2/3 of previous row)			*21.0*
	Phase 4			
8§43	Joblessness: qualifications mismatches; recessions	full legis.	moderate	3.5
8§44	restricted physical abilities to work	full legis.	minor/mod	2.5
8§45	procedure appointment judiciary	full legis.	minor	1.5
8§46	public security	full legis.	minor/mod	2.5
8§47	international economic relations; treaties	full legis.	minor/mod	2.5
	total weeks in the unlikely case of a complete sequential treatment			*12.5*
	total weeks in terms of the simultaneous measure (2/3 of previous row)			*8.3*
	Phase 5			
8§49	public sector remuneration and councils	full legis.	minor	1.5
8§50	regulation health sector	full legis.	much	5.5
8§51	regulation education sector	full legis.	much	5.5
8§52	state-financed research institutes	full legis.	moderate	3.5
8§53	regulation culture sector	full legis.	much	5.5

TRANSITION TO A WORKER COOPERATIVES SOCIETY

TABLE 8.21 *Indication of legislative work phases 1–5 (cont.)*

	Subject		Indication	Wk.
8§54	national railway transport	full legis.	moderate	3.5
8§55	finance of the state and state institutions	full legis.	minor/mod	2.5
8§56	municipalities and provinces	full legis.	much	5.5
8§57	minimum work-time and temporary part-time position	full legis.	minor	1.5
8§58	'stand-in cooperatives'	full legis.	minor	1.5
	total weeks in the unlikely case of a complete sequential treatment			36.0
	total weeks in terms of the simultaneous measure (2/3 of previous row)			24.0

The last table (Table 8.22) starts from the systematic of Part One and shows the transition order of the former: sometimes in a single full enactment, often via temporary or partial enactments.

TABLE 8.22 *Legislative transition implementation of the Part One Design*

Chs. 2–5	Ch. 8		Subject	Phases				
				1	2	3	4	5
ch. 2		8§14	Design worker coop economy	x				
ch. 2		8§15	idem, entry into force exception	t				
ch. 2		8D1-C	transition. regulation econ. domain					
	N.A.	8§16	rules financial markets	x				
	N.A.	8§17	accommodation banks' investment credit	x				
	N.A.	8§18	legal form conversion pre-trans. entities	x				
3D1	3§1	8§1	state's democratic organs	x				
	3§2	8§3	ministries and state agencies	x				
	3§3	8§26/8§49	public sector councils & remuneration			t		x
	3§4	8§55	finance state & state institutions					x
3D2	3§5	8§46	public security				x	
	3§6	8§2/8§45	judiciary & admin. prosecutors	t			x	
3D3	3§7	8§36	physically circular production			x		
	3§8	8§36	safety & information output			x		
	3§9	8§36	safety at work			x		

TABLE 8.22 *Legislative transition implementation Part One Design (cont.)*

Chs. 2–5	Ch. 8	Subject	Phases				
			1	2	3	4	5
	3§10	8§25	work-time maximum		x			
	3§10	8§57	work-time minimum					x
	3§11	8§10	minimum wages	x				
	3§12	8§34	inspectorates			x		
3D4	3§13	8§4	central bank	x				
	3§14	8§4	guardian bank	x				
	3§15	8§4	investment-credit guarantee fund	x				
	3§16	8§4	Savings and Loans Bank	x				
3D5	N.A.	8§10	minimum costs of living allowances	t				
	3§17	8§30/8§43	jobs agency			t	x	
	3§18	8§43	mismatches joblessness & allowances				x	
	3§20	8§29	recessional joblessness & allowances				x	
	3§21	8§44	restricted abilities to work				x	
3D6	3§22	8§28	child allowances		x			
	3§23	8§29	allowances tertiary students		x			
	3§24	8§27	pensions	x				
3D7	3§25	8§7/8§49	workers' council governed foundations	t				x
	N.A.	8§12	health sector temporary	t				
	3§26	8§50	health sector and health agency					x
	3§27	8§50	primary medical treatment					x
	3§28	8§50	hospitals					x
	3§29	8§50	other medical treatment and care					x
	3§30	8§13/8§51	education sector and education agency			t		x
	3§31	8§13/8§51	pre-primary education			t		x
	3§32	8§13/8§51	primary, secondary & tertiary education			t		x
	3§33	8§51	research universities					x
	3§33	8§52	State-financed research institutes					x
	3§34	8§53	culture and cultural heritage agency					x

TABLE 8.22 *Legislative transition implementation Part One Design (cont.)*

Chs. 2–5	Ch. 8	Subject	Phases				
			1	2	3	4	5
	3§35	8§53	museums, national library and archives					x
	3§36	8§53	contemporary arts and arts performance					x
3D8	3§37	8§38	real estate and real estate agency			x		
	3§38	8§39	mining & other Earth extractions			x		
	3§39	8§40	infrastructure and infrastructure agency			x		
3D9	3§40	8§54	public transport and railway transport					x
	3§41	8§8	agency for temporary WGFs	x				
	3§42		stagnant underinvestment					
3D10	3§43	8§31	auditing rules & auditing authority		x			
	3§44	8§41	patents and copyrights			x		
	3§45	8§6	competition and market power	x				
3D11	3§46	8§9	taxation	x				
App.	3F	8§59	stand-in cooperatives					x
ch. 4		8§37/8§56	municipal & provincial administrations				t	x
ch. 5		8§47	international economic relations				x	

This concludes the Appendices of Chapter 8.

General summary

As indicated in the General Introduction, for the judgement on the possible functioning of the in this book proposed 'worker cooperatives society' and the adequacy thereof, one needs a design of its full economic and state organisation that is blueprint-like in its detail – detailed such that the feasibility and consistency of the design can be fully scrutinised. This applies for the Design itself (Part One of the book), as well as for the transition to it (the third chapter of Part Two, i.e. chapter 8). Obviously, many details are absent from the current General Summary.

The text below is organised in two parts along the two parts of the book, together about 25 pages. Cross-references to the book text are as 2§1 (chapter 2 section 1) and 2D1 (chapter 2 division 1) etc.

A Summary of Part One: design of the organisation of a worker cooperatives society

The 17-page text on Part One is organised around the following themes. (1) Worker cooperatives; (2) Democracy; (3) Physical circular production and extractions from the Earth; (4) The cooperatives economy: from capital in monetary dimension, to conditional assets in monetary dimension; (5) Markets and competition in the cooperatives economy; (6) The single economic class and the unity of the cooperatives economy and state; (7) The distribution of income and wealth; (8) Hard budget constraints and workforce constraints for the public sector; (9) A summing up of the Design's main features.

1. Worker cooperatives. It was indicated in the General Introduction, and repeated several times, that the Design's worker cooperatives economy is such that workers constitute the single economic class. As against capitalism, there is no class of owners of means of production – hence no antagonism between those owners and workers. In contrast with state socialism, the state does not own the economy's reproducible means of production.[1]

The cooperative as legal entity holds a restricted ownership of the cooperative's assets – the right to alienation of the cooperative is excluded. This should guarantee that cooperatives are continuous between generations of workers. A cooperative is founded by a group of workers; the foundation requiring no own

---

1 The non-reproducible agricultural land, fishery waters and mines can be rented from a state institution. The criterium is that these are 'free gift of nature' that should never be the property of an individual or economic entity.

funds of the workers. Whereas workers collectively are the sole beneficiaries of the cooperative's distributable income – they are the usufructuaries of the cooperative – they have no direct or indirect ownership in the cooperative and its assets; nor is the membership of a cooperative bound to refundable or non-refundable dues.[2] Because workers constitute the single economic class, and given the ownership-like relations just outlined, there is no means of production owning class that exploits the working class (this is one main distinction from capitalism).

2. **Democracy.** At the basis of the Design's worker cooperatives society lies the moral value, and normative principle, of democratic decision-making at all of the society's levels and in all of its institutions – from the economic democracy in worker cooperatives, to the political democracy of the state and of state institutions (with the latter including workers' councils regarding their internal organisation).

After the most basic human survival elements of food shelter and bodily security as well as mutual love, democracy is the highest social virtue. However, democratic decision-making is not merely a moral fundament of the Design. Democratic decision-making regards first the continuous determination of social goals. That is, social goals at all of society's levels – and only a very limited part of people's lives is non-social or deemed non-social.[3] Next it generates a thorough involvement in those social goals and their everyday execution.

At the society's economic base level, the production (including of services) is carried out by a structure of numerous cooperatives. In each single cooperative the democratic decision-making regards the workers that carry out the production – the cooperative's workers' council being the highest governance body. This council sees to the common interests of the cooperative's workers. The council elects the management from its ranks, and can also remove the management. More specifically, democratic decision regards: (a) the policies of the cooperative, as including the techniques used (the specific inputs mix), the internal division of labour, and the planning of investments and the required

---

2   One similarity between a 'foundation' and a 'Design worker cooperative' is that these entities have no owners. One relevant distinction is that the cooperative has members, whereas a foundation has no members.
3   The Design focussed on the economic and state institutions; however much of the so-called private sphere of households and of leisure activities is also social; here democratic decision-making is equally important.

additional workers in face of expected sales; (b) the determination of the internal wage scales (in case these are not uniform in face of unpleasant work, an expertise that is (temporarily) scarce, or for other reasons that the council deems opportune); (c) the allocation of the cooperative's surplus, including the distribution of dividends.[4] (Chapter 2.)

Next to this base structure there is a superstructure of institutions that regard the common interests of individual cooperatives, their workers and the households of workers and pensioners. This superstructure is composed of the state, of state institutions (including the judiciary, ministries, state agencies, provinces and municipalities) and of 'workers' council governed foundations' – these together are called the public sector. (Note the distinction between 'state institutions' and its subcategory 'state agencies' – the latter were, together with the judiciary, presented in Divisions 2–10 of chapter 3.)

The parliament elected by all eligible voters is the state's highest governing body on all terrains – to which there are no executive or other exceptions. Parliament elects a government that it can also remove. (Division 1 of chapter 3 set out procedures that should guarantee proper election procedures.) Next to the judiciary and the government's ministries there are 18 state agencies that are responsible for the common social tasks (varying from public security, the financial constellation, job securities, health, education and pensions, to the management of real estate and infrastructure). These agencies are, inasmuch as the ministries, accountable to parliament that can also adjust the main lines of their policies. This means that within the institutional superstructure, and given the supreme power of parliament, there is quite some division of powers.

Notwithstanding parliament being the state's highest governance body, state institutions comprise workers' councils that are responsible for their internal work organisation (including remuneration matters – see below). The qua amount of labour force largest social common tasks – those of the free provided health and education – are carried out by 'workers' council governed foundations' in which workers' councils have full democratic powers (that is, within general rules set by parliament and within their budget and labour force constraints – see below). (Chapter 3.)

Table GS-1 summarises the worker cooperative society's legal entities and their governance, as well as their estimated workforce in percent of the total workforce (the estimates are detailed in Appendix 3A, subsection 3A-5).

---

4 Workers receive a wage (usually fixed for a year), and – depending on the reached size of the surplus – they may at the end of the year also receive a dividend (2§9.0).

TABLE GS-1 *Legal entities and their governance and percent of the workforce*

	Legal entities	Highest governance body (HGB)	Delegated governance: elected and removable by HGB; accountable to HGB	Estimated workforce of institutions as % total workforce		
1	cooperatives	workers' council	management	72.5%		
2	workers' council governed foundations	workers' council	management	21.0%		
3	state	parliament†	government	6.5%	general state	public sector
4	ministries and state agencies*	parliament	director general (appointed by government; accountable to parliament)			
5	municipalities	municipal council†	executive board			
6	provinces	provincial council‡	executive board			
7	entities rows 4–6 regarding their internal organisation	workers' council	secretary general and other management			

† Elected by the eligible voters.
‡ Indirectly elected by the province's municipal councillors.
* The judiciary is an extraordinary state institution; its internal organisation is as in row 7.

It has been mentioned, and it can be seen from *Table GS-1*, that all of the Design's institutions include a workers' council. These councils have in common that they decide on the internal organisation of the institution, as including the appointment (and removal) of the management, and the determination of the distribution of income among the workers. What there is to be distributed, depends for cooperatives (row 1) on their productivity and the market constellation. The latter results in some per annum average remuneration per worker for the cooperatives sector at large (in FTE). This average determines the wages budget that is allotted to each state institution according to their workforce in FTE. Next the workers' councils of all these other institutions (rows 2 and 4–6) decide on their internal wage scales. Thus the remuneration within those institutions is derived from the cooperatives sector. Members of the parliament, the government and the judiciary each individually receive the cooperatives' average remuneration. This allocation of the society's income is a core element of the Design.

One legal entity is not mentioned in *Table GS-1*. No one is forced to become member of a cooperative or to get a job in the public sector. Individuals are free to run by themselves a registered 'Single person enterprise'. However, 'hiring a worker' is not allowed; in the economic domain the only possible legal form for a multi-workers entity is that of a cooperative. This avoids exploitative relations, as in capitalist enterprise–employee relations. On the other hand, for a similar reason any individual services for households (such as childcare or repair) shall be provided by cooperatives only.[5]

3. Physical circular production and extractions from the Earth. The cooperatives' economy is vitally a physically circular one; each cooperative is required to further optimise it. Furthermore, the production is as much as possible located near to where it is used, which saves on transport of freight and on commuting (3§7).

Regarding mining and other extractions from the Earth, a state agency has the task to determine the limits of yearly extractions that are sustainable. Within these limits, the agency issues tendered extraction concessions to cooperatives. Because such extractions regard common 'free gifts of nature' licensed cooperatives shall pay a rent (3§38). The latter also applies for the use of agricultural land (3§37).

4. Tendential aim of cooperatives' councils; elimination of the categories of 'capital' and 'accumulation of capital'.[6] 'Value-added' is the sum of wages and the surplus. Given the Design's interconnections, councils of cooperatives tend to aim for, first, the preservation of the cooperative's jobs and, next, for a maximisation of the average value-added per worker – furthermore, the last can increase by expansion investments and workforce increases. The reserves of cooperatives are no aim, but an instrument for job preservation; the cooperative's assets are an instrument for the value-added per worker. Because, as mentioned in section 1, workers have no direct or indirect ownership in the cooperative, and neither invested funds in the cooperative, any aim of enhancement of such funds ('valorisation') can play no role. These considerations imply that the Design eliminates the capitalist economic categories of 'capital' and of the 'accumulation of capital' (2§10).[7] They also imply that the type of investment decisions by cooperatives are utmost different from those of capitalist enterprises (Addendum 2§19).

---

5   The latter have to pay at least the minimum wage (obviously the wage category does not apply for single person enterprises).
6   Identical to the similar named section of chapter 2's Concluding Summary.
7   The aim of capitalist enterprises is to accumulate capital and to maximise the profits as calculated over the equity capital – the profit rate. At a given profit rate, the accumulation of capital also maximises absolute profits. For these enterprises 'wages' are no aim but rather a cost, nor is 'employment' an aim but merely a profit instrument – thus employment and wages are a capitalist valorisation instrument. [continued on next page]

GENERAL SUMMARY 401

Table GS-2 lists the Design's economic characteristics mentioned above, as well as some other ones – each in comparison with a capitalist economy (identical to the ch. 2 summary's Table 2.7).

TABLE GS-2 *Key distinctions between the capitalist and the Design cooperatives economies*

Production relations	Capitalist economy	Design economy
economic classes	capitalist and labour	labour (single class) (2§1.0)
relation to means of production	property by members capitalist class	usufruct by labour (2§1.0; 2§3.0)
economic class relation	exploitative	not applicable: single class (2§1.0)
organisation units of production	authoritarian	democratic (addendum 2§5)
measure of value†	monetary	monetary (2§2.0)
general form efficient production	value output > value input	value output > value input (2§26 sub 2)
result of efficient production	value-added (VA)	value-added (VA) (2§1.0; 2§8.0)
producer of value-added	labour	labour (2§1.0)
core economic category	capital	labour; category capital eliminated (2§10.3)
aim of production	profit and accumulation of capital	work preservation and VA (2§10.0)
instrument for aim of production	labour employment and wages (costs)	cooperative assets and reserves (2§10.2)
internal finance	capital shareholders or owner(s) firm	no funds or dues of workers (2§3.0; 2§4)‡
Ownership and governance	**Capitalist stock corporation**	**Design worker cooperative**
legal form unit of production	stock corporation	cooperative (2§3.0)
foundation unit of production	finance-capital-owning shareholders	workers (2§4)
funds required for foundation	finance capital of shareholders	none (2§4)
highest governance body	general body of shareholders	cooperative council (2§5.0)
alteration governance body	purchase (and selling) shares	successful application (2§3.4)

The elimination the capitalist economic category of 'capital' is also one of the main distinctions between a Design cooperative and the 'worker-owned cooperative' as existing within capitalism (ch. 6).

TABLE GS-2 *Key distinctions (cont.)*

Ownership and governance	Capitalist stock corporation	Design worker cooperative
legal ownership of assets	corporation: full ownership right	cooperative: no alienation right (2§3.0)
final/effective ownership of entity	shareholders: full ownership	workers: collective usufruct (2§3.0)
appointment (top-)management	body of shareholders	council elects from its ranks (2§5.0)

† This regards the means of payment for – and the means of circulation of – commodities or other entities.
‡ Nevertheless the minimum wage related to the legally binding resistance buffer might be considered as a form of internal finance. This buffer cannot be alienated by individual workers, whereas capital shares can.

5. **Markets and competition in the cooperatives economy.** This section is divided in five subsections (a–e).

(*a*) *Free choice of specific consumption and of cooperative's investment.* Predicated on the Design's commodity markets for consumer goods, individuals have free choice of specific consumption. Predicated on commodity markets for means of production, cooperative councils have a free choice of (specific) investment and techniques – constrained by investment loans from cooperative banks. Thus the Design maintains commodification.

(*b*) *Quantitative aspect of a labour market.* Whereas the Design has no full-fledged labour market with price and quantity adaptation – only the latter applies (2§23), individuals have a free choice of occupation. Such a free choice is as limited in the Design as it is in capitalism. Someone may not find work in her/his profession if the demand is deficient.

However, whereas capitalist enterprises require a degree of unemployment so as to press down wages, no institution or person in the Design has a similar interest – on the contrary. More specifically, as set out in division 5 of chapter 3, the Design is such that school-leavers and those that had a job before may be out of work for a period of maximum two months. Apart from this period, everyone either has a regular job, or has temporarily work (during a recession), or participates in a traineeship. Moreover, workers with restricted physical or mental abilities will always have a permanent job – proportionally spread over all cooperatives and public sector institutions (at a remuneration of 150% of the minimum wage; the minimum wage is 167% of the minimum costs of living).

(c) *Two financial markets*. In the Design there are only two financial markets, a market for investment loans and a market for insurances. (There are no markets for shares, bonds or savings – all savings are collected by the state agency 'Savings and Loans Bank'.) On the demand side of investment loans, non-banking cooperatives call for investment loans, and cooperative banks compete for these (the latter provide these loans via the creation of new money – similar as this is the case for capitalist banks). Apart from payment transfers, investment loans are the sole business of these cooperative banks. (They are not allowed to engage in credit to any institution, including households, other than cooperatives; they shall not engage in insurance at all; the interest rate on payment accounts is nationwide uniformly zero – or near to zero depending on a rate of inflation/deflation, as specified by the Central Bank, the latter being an agency.)

The 'Savings and Loans Bank' (SLB) provides loans to the cooperative banks (without these loans, the banks would be ineffective given that there are no shares and bonds markets). This makes the SLB one of the Design's most prominent economic policy institutions as it can, by varying the rate of interest on the loans, directly and rather promptly affect the macro-economic investment. Parliament may temporary also authorise the SLB to adopt meso-economic investment policies. (3§16 under c and d; 3§47 under a-first and c.)

(d) *No real estate market*. One state agency is responsible for the nationwide real estate (3§37). Cooperatives that wish so, can own *self-occupied* premises as including the plot of land on which these are build. All other land (including agricultural land) and the waters, as well as all dwellings are owned by this agency. It is the only one institution from which or to which premises can be purchased or sold at 'reasonable prices'. This agency also rents out premises to cooperatives (including to agricultural cooperatives) and dwellings to individuals, each at costs covering or 'reasonable' prices. The effect is that there is no real estate market that speculatively drives up real estate prices. The maintenance and construction of buildings is carried out by cooperatives. For the construction of new premises and dwellings the agency is committed to acclaimed high standard urban and landscape designs, which makes that it has a huge impact on the beauty of cities, towns and villages. In its function of contracting authority for cooperatives, the agency bases itself on long-term and medium-term planning; which makes that it does not act pro-cyclically, whence is operates as a stabilising agent for the economy's construction sector.

(e) *Market dominance, technical change and competition.*[8] In the Design the possible market dominance of individual cooperatives is restricted by four

---

8 Including the table below, identical to the similar named section of chapter 2's Concluding Summary.

rules: first, they shall be organised in no more than one single location;[9] second, they are not allowed to found other cooperatives; third, they shall not take-over other cooperatives; fourth, they shall not expand beyond ceilings that in their relevant market would generate market power (as an indication, for cooperative banks in a 'large' country, the ceiling might be a nationwide market share of 1%).[10] Nevertheless these rules are not incompatible with large-scale production; country dependent a single cooperative might provide jobs to several tens of thousands of workers in a location of several hundred thousand m².

These restrictions – together with the in section 4 mentioned council's aims of preservation of the cooperative's jobs and of a maximisation of the average value-added per worker – mean that technical change has a very different role in comparison with capitalism. Whereas capitalist enterprises tend to use technical change as an instrument to squeeze out competitors, it is for cooperatives primarily an instrument for increasing their per worker value-added – usually leaving the production and jobs of competitors unaffected. In this respect the cooperatives' economic interaction tends to be non-aggressive and non-destructive regarding competitors. Comparatively this tends to result in less technical-change-induced joblessness; and to the extent that competitors' physical plants are not scrapped, less dwindling of environmental resources. (2§19 addendum.)

The restrictions mentioned under (e), together with other restrictions for cooperatives or their councils, are listed in *Table GS-3*.

TABLE GS-3 *Main requirements or restrictions for cooperatives and their councils*

	Foundation of cooperatives	
1	cooperatives are founded by workers; cooperatives shall not found cooperatives	2§4.0
2	foundation of cooperatives requires no funds of the workers	2§4.0
	Cooperatives	
3	a founded cooperative shall not be sold; nor shall it convert its juridical status	2§3.0

---

9   The primary reason for this rule is that a multitude of locations would dilute the power of the cooperative's council. The rule also affects potential market power.
10 All nationwide ceilings are indeed dependent on the size of a country. See further ch. 3, 3§45.

TABLE GS-3 *Main requirements (cont.)*

Cooperatives

4	take-overs are prohibited (implied by the previous point)	2§3.2
5	cooperatives are organised in no more than a single location	2§3.3
6	cooperatives pay at least the minimum wage (set by parliament)	2§8.0
7	a maximum labour-time duration per day, week and year applies (parliament sets)	2§8.1
8	cooperatives shall build up a legally binding resistance buffer, expressed as a percentage of the assets – 10% for COBs and on average 30% for other cooperatives; before meeting it, workers are paid no more than the minimum wage†	2§7.0
9	in face of market dominance, the cooperatives' expansion is restricted	2§14.0
10	cooperatives shall register their incomes and expenditures, and annually record an 'Income account' and a 'Balance sheet'	2§11.0

Additional workers

11	positions shall not be denied on ethnic, gender, social, political or religious grounds	2§3.4
12	any probation period for new workers is maximum two years	2§3.4

Cooperative banks, specifically

13	besides servicing payments, COBs uniquely provide investment loans to PWCs†	2§6.4

Councils

14	membership of councils is not bound to refundable or non-refundable dues	2§3.0
15	only the cooperative's workers can be members of its council	2§3.0
16	the council elects the management (removable) from its ranks	2§5.0
17	the council must approve of at least five key issues listed in 2§5.1, including the internal structure of the wages and dividend levels, and increases in investments or in the workforce, each beyond 5% of the past 5 years average	2§5.1

† COB: cooperative bank. PWC: all other cooperatives (production worker cooperatives; including services production).

6. The single economic class and the unity of the cooperatives economy and state.

In any stable mode of production 'the state' (or whatever a similar body is called) must be tailored to meeting the requirements of its particular economy. Thus the two spheres must constitute a unity. This applies for the Design's mode of production as much as for any other.

Because the capitalist economy is based on the class antagonism between owners of capital and labour, the capitalist state reflects and sustains this class antagonism. Specifically it grants in the form of capitalist *rights*, the capitalist enterprises' *claims* of entitlement to the private property of much of the earth; their *claims* of entitlement to private property in means of production other than for production by the claimant; and their *claims* of entitlement to employ labour as combined with the appropriation of the surplus-value (profit) produced by that labour.

Because in the cooperatives economy workers constitute the single economic class, the worker cooperatives state reflects and sustains the common interests of this single class. Such is the Design.[11]

It might be posited that even if the cooperatives state reflects and sustains the single economic class, there nevertheless is, or might be, separate interests between cooperatives workers and workers of state institutions or of the public sector at large (for 'public sector' see the outer right-hand side columns of *Table* GS-1). There are differences in work related circumstances (see the next paragraph), but public sector workers – including members of the parliament and the government – have a direct interest in the flourishing of the cooperatives economy. As indicated in section 2, the per worker average remuneration in each one public sector institution is equal to (and derived from) the per worker average of all cooperatives. On the other hand, cooperatives, their workers and workers' households have an interest in the flourishing of public sector institutions because the latter work in the formers' common interest. In this sense there is a unity between the cooperatives economy and state (and the public sector at large).

Nevertheless there are differences in work related circumstances. (a) Normally public sector workers have a permanent position. (Unless they obviously do not function according to their capacities – that also applies to cooperatives workers.) (b) Cooperatives workers, in contradistinction, can lose their position due to bankruptcy. However, as against public sector workers, these workers

---

11   I cannot understand the views holding that because economic relations and political relations are held to be bifurcated terrains in capitalism, this should be inevitable for any mode of production.

can – per individual cooperative – influence their income by being above average productive. (c) In case an individual (after leaving school or later in its career) makes the choice between the two sectors above – and if income would be the only one consideration – then the choice is not obvious. It would probably be character dependent (whether or not being risk-averse). (d) Nevertheless there is another difference between the two sectors. Within the constraints set by parliament (such as regarding physically circular production, safety of output, safety at work, the work-time duration, and minimum wages), cooperatives worker councils have complete democratic autonomy over the aims and arrangement of their cooperative. However, whereas councils of 'workers' council governed foundations' (mainly in the health and education sectors) have a considerable autonomy, the councils of other public sector institutions have far less autonomy. Parliament decides on the public sector aims and on the main line of the policies of state institutions, and all these are directly or indirectly accountable to parliament. Still, councils of public sector institutions elect their management, decide with the latter on the work organisation, and decide on the internal structure of the wages scales within the institution. How all of the points above (a–d) sum up for individual choices about preferred work is probably again character dependent.

In conclusion, there is a unity between the cooperatives economy and state (and the public sector at large), but also differences within this unity that may match individual professional preferences.

7. **The distribution of income and wealth.** Within cooperatives the distribution of income among workers is decided on by its workers' council. In case this does not result in equal remunerations, their distribution will nevertheless be far less skewed than in capitalism. The same applies for the public sector institutions where the distribution of income is similarly decided on by their workers' councils. (As mentioned above, the average per worker income in these institutions is equal to the total average per worker income in the economic sector cooperatives.) All pensioners individually, receive an equal income of around the minimum wage, the minimum wage being decided on by parliament (to be sure, this pension equally applies for parliamentarians when they retire). A caring parent receives child's costs of living and childcare allowances.

Taxation could minimise or even undo any remaining skewedness. This poses a potential conflict, because non-proportional taxation affects the democratic decisions of councils. However, for taxation there also counts the normative principle that 'the strongest bodies have to shoulder the heaviest burden'. Progressive income tax rates are therefore taken as a fairness principle, and the after-tax income differences amount to a ratio of about 1:2.5 (3§46, Table 3.7).

Any skewedness in the distribution of wealth is primarily limited by the distribution of income above. Cooperatives are not directly or indirectly owned by cooperative workers; no one can own bonds, shares or similar financial assets because these do not exist in the Design; no individual can own real estate. (Hence all these can also not have been inherited.) Thus there can be merely a very moderate skewedness in the distribution of wealth – one that is by far not as extreme as in capitalism.[12]

In the Design wealth is not taxed, however inheritances are heavily taxed, because of the normative principle that children deserve an equal treatment, independent of the wealth of their ancestors. A moderate tax exemption should be sufficient for treasured possessions. (All outlined and argued for in 3§46.)

8. Hard budget constraints and workforce constraints for the public sector. In Appendix 3A, estimates of the Design's total state expenditure in % of GDP are summarised in its Table 3A.1 and Table 3A.2, and estimates of the public sector workforce in % of the total labour force are summarised in its Table 3A.13.

So as to keep the size of the public sector limited, the Design includes budget and workforce constraints for public sector institutions (those listed in rows 2–6 of Table GS-1). A distinction is made between annual and structural (long-term) constraints.

Annual budget constraints. All public sector institutions receive their budget from the State via the Central Bank; these institutions 'bank' uniquely with the Central Bank; no such institution is allowed to run a bank overdraft. Only the State is allowed to borrow, and uniquely so by the selling of short-term or long-term debt paper to the 'Central Bank'.[13] The previous two sentences are key to the hard budget constraints. (For all institutions this requires tight income and expenditure planning, and the keeping of reserves for difficult to plan expenditures.)

In total the budgets' expenditures should result in a fixed percentage of GDP (with one qualification about education expenditure set out below).

Annual workforce constraints. Together with the budget, all public sector institutions are committed to hard ceilings regarding the amount of their workforce in FTE. This way the proportions indicated in the last column of *Table GS-1* should be maintained.

---

12   In the OECD countries in 2019 the top 10% owns 41% to 79% of total wealth, whereas the bottom 40% owns -7% to 9% of the total (Reuten 2023b, §2.3, Graph 5).

13   In case of emergency state institutions can borrow from the central state (if the latter consents).

Structural budget and workforce ceilings. In principle the annual budget ceilings, expressed as a percentage of GDP, and workforce ceilings as percent of the national workforce could be maintained structurally (that is, in the long run). However, the main problem for such ceilings regards formal education. The point is that the latter's ceilings are dependent, firstly, on the population of, roughly, younger than 25 years (with a balanced age composition this poses no problem), Secondly, however, the required expenditure and workforce depends on the average duration of schooling which tends to increase. This means that for this sector (current ceilings being estimated at 5.5% of GDP for expenditure, and at 6% of the total labour force) ceilings cannot be maintained. (Note that a similar problem occurs in capitalist countries regarding the sum of private and public education expenditure. There, however, it is not necessarily expressed in state expenditure.)[14]

It might be argued that increasing schooling generally results in average productivity increase. True, but for the public sector this is likely to lead mainly to, welcome, quality increase (this applies especially for its largest segment of health – estimated at 12% of GDP and 15% of the workforce) and in lesser extent to relative expenditure decreases.[15] For the cooperatives sector the *average* result would probably be declining prices (good for households) rather than increasing value-added.

Budget constraints in face of taxation. A final constraint on budgets and state expenditure regards the decision-making on these. This is a specific characteristic of the Design given, first, that the average workers remuneration in the public sector is equal to that of the cooperatives sector (members of parliament and government individually receive the cooperative sector's average), and, second, that about 50% of the taxes are levied on the workers' and pensioners' income. This means that, via taxation, increases or decreases in state expenditure are proportionally reflected in the after-tax income of the elected

---

14 For the average of 21 current OECD countries the number of years of schooling increased from 3.5 in 1870 to 11.9 in 2010. For these countries state expenditure on education in % of GDP increased from 0.6% in 1870 to 5.7% in 2014 (Reuten 2019, pp. 354–5).

15 Here Baumol's theorem of 'cost disease' is relevant. It refers to the phenomenon of structurally enduring productivity differences between particular economic sectors. The theorem originated with a paper by Baumol and Bowen (1965), which illustrated differences in labour productivity change with the example of a symphony orchestra whose productivity for performances today is pretty much the same as it was in 1870. In various degrees, similar labour productivity obstacles apply for many state expenditure categories, such as legislative processes, inspectorates, education and the care part of the health sector.

decision-makers. Given that increasing/decreasing state expenditure has well-being effects, the after-tax income effect is not the sole consideration, but it is suitable that it is one consideration.

9. A summing up of the Design's main features. This final section on Part One lists main features of the Design (quite some included in the points above). The list and its references serve as a guide for readers that jumped from the General Introduction to the current summary and that might want to read selective parts of the book.

General features
- Not only political but also deep economic democracy at the point of production (point 2 above; 3§1 and 2§5).
- Worker cooperatives are the economy's units. Workers constitute the single economic class, workers being the sole beneficiaries of the cooperatives' distributable income (2§1). As against capitalism, there is no class of owners of means of production. In contrast with state socialism, the state does not own the economy's means of production – except for rented out agricultural land. (Point 1 above; 3§37 on the renting out of agricultural land.)
- The worker cooperatives state reflects and sustains the common interests of this single class (point 6 above).
- Together with the abolition of the economic category of capital, the abolition of the exploitation of labour, the profit drive and the associated motive of the 'accumulation of capital' (2§10 and point 4 above).
- Instead (of the previous point), cooperatives aim at the preservation of their members jobs and the maximisation of the value-added per worker (2§10 and point 5-e above). Concomitantly the cooperatives' economic interaction tends to be non-aggressive and non-destructive regarding competitors (2§19 addendum, and point 5-e above).

Production, markets and measures countering joblessness
- Physical circular production and sustainable extractions from the Earth (3§7; 3§38; and point 3 above).
- No markets for shares, bonds, savings and real estate (2§17 addendum; 2§15 addendum; 3§16; 3§37; and point 5-c above).
- Via markets: free choice of specific consumption (2§23, and point 5-a above).
- Via the market: free choice of occupation, though limited as it is in capitalism (2§23, and point 5-b above).
- Permanent jobs for workers with restricted physical or mental abilities – spread over all cooperatives and state institutions, and remunerated at least

150% of the minimum wage; the minimum wage is 167% of the minimum costs of living (3§21, and point 5-b above).
• Regarding joblessness, including for reasons of qualifications mismatches, no one is out of work for longer than two months – where 'work' includes permanent jobs and paid traineeships, the latter being a lever to permanent jobs (3§18, and point 5-b above).
• Any recessional joblessness is allocated over cooperatives and, with some exceptions, state institutions, such that no one is without a job for longer than two months (3§19–3§20, and point 5-b above).
• The prevalence of non-desired uneven jobs distribution over regions is moderated by policies of the 'Investment-credit Guarantee Fund' (3§15-e).
• The market power of cooperatives is prevented by: market share ceilings (2§19; 3§45), the single location of cooperatives; and the ban on take-overs (2§3.2; 2§3.3; 2§14.0; and point 5-e above).

Distribution of income and wealth
• The remuneration of public sector workers (including members of parliament, of government and the judiciary) is derived from, and on average equal to that of cooperatives (3§3; 3§6; 3§25; 4§1; and point 2 above).
• Except for pensions that are equal for all (3§24), the per institution distribution of income is decided on by the workers' councils (2§5.1 and references previous point). In case this does not result in equal remunerations, their distribution will nevertheless be far less skewed than in capitalism (2§8 addendum).
• There can be a moderate skewedness in the distribution of wealth, but by far not to an extent as in capitalism (2§20).

Main other public sector aspects
• There is a strict borderline for production by worker cooperatives and by, or via, state institutions (3§2-g).
• Hard budget constraints and workforce constraints for the public sector (3§2 and point 8 above).
• The judiciary is an extraordinary state institution. Judges of the 'supreme court' and of the 'courts level just below it', as well as administrative prosecutors, are appointed by a judiciary committee of 16 members composed of – each for one quarter – former judges, lawyers, former ministers, former parliamentarians (3§6).
• The large macro- and meso-economic policy potential of the Savings and Loans Bank regarding especially investment (3§16, and the above point 5-c).
• A caring parent receives child's costs of living allowances and costs covering childcare allowances (3§22), each until the child reaches the age of 18 (or until the child starts working, if that is earlier).

- Students receive costs of living allowances from the age of 18 for usually a maximum of six years (3§23).
- Pensions are – on an individual basis – equal for all, at a level around the minimum wage (3§24). The pre-tax minimum wage is 167% of the minimum costs of living.
- Health and education are financed out of general taxation and provided free of charge for all; these provisions shall exclusively be provided by 'workers' council governed foundations' (ch. 3, subdivisions 7A and 7B).
- The culture sector is for one part organised in state-financed 'workers' council governed foundations', and for another part taken on by worker cooperatives – for which municipalities receive an earmarked subsidy budget (ch. 3, subdivision 7C).
- The elimination of a (speculative) real estate market, which has, within the Design's alternative, also great effect on the beauty of cities, towns and villages, as well as a stabilisation of the economy's construction sector (3§37, and the above point 5-d).
- Special judicial proceedings regarding the abuse of power and other improper behaviour by parliamentarians, ministers, others state workers and political parties (ch. 3, Appendix 3D)
- The administrative burden for cooperatives is (qualitatively estimated) probably less than that for capitalist enterprises (ch. 3, Appendix 3B).
- Stand-in work as organised in 'stand-in cooperatives', and the prevention of casual inferior jobs (ch. 3, Appendix 3F). Regards, among other, cooperatives with a seasonable work concentration; cooperatives and public sector institutions that are confronted with sickness of their workers for more than a brief period.

B Summary of Part Two: from modifying capitalism to transition

This summary encompasses about eight pages. Part Two consists of three chapters, its last one (chapter 8) being about the transition. The start of the transition in that chapter is defined as the point in time when there is a parliamentary majority that wishes to bring the Part One Design into practice. Qua book text – though not in practice – there is a fluent line from Part One to that chapter. This is not so for Part Two's other chapters (6 and 7) that set out a *possible* movement towards the chapter 8 transition. Given their character these three chapters will be summarised sequentially rather than integrated under three headings: (1) Modification of capitalist practices by 'worker-owned cooperatives' and similar democratic enterprises – chapter 6; (2) Circumstances just before the transition: financial and real estate markets and the scope of capital flight – chapter 7; (3) Transition to a worker cooperatives society – chapter 8.

1. **Modification of capitalist practices by 'worker-owned cooperatives' and similar democratic enterprises (chapter 6).** Chapter 6 – and apart from its conclusions – is the only empirical chapter of the book. It set out the functioning and performance of 'worker-*owned* cooperatives' (WOCs) and other democratic enterprises, as they exist around 2020 within capitalism, in comparison with 'conventional capitalist enterprises' (CCEs).

• *Amount of employment by WOCs (6D1).* Although there is quite a lot of case-study information on WOCs, data on the world-wide number of WOCs and their employment are scarce. A 2016 dataset of 156 countries on all types of cooperatives includes only for 51 countries information on WOCs (6§2, Table 6.4). Of the top-five countries qua relative WOC employment (Italy, Malaysia, Sweden, India and Spain) the WOC employment ranges around 2016 from no more than 3.9% to 1.0% of their labour force (6§2, Table 6.5). This means that, as yet, WOCs constitute on average no threat to conventional capitalist enterprises.

• *Performance of WOCs in comparison with CCEs (6D1).* Nevertheless WOCs outperform CCEs not only in their institutional democracy but also on the following main points.

- WOCs are present in most sectors of the economy; on average WOCs are larger than CCEs, and they survive at least as well.
- WOCs are at least as productive as CCEs, and more productive in some areas.
- Profit may not be higher in WOC than in CCEs, but WOCs may produce more and preserve their members' jobs better.
- Regarding unemployment and income risks, workers in WOCs are considerably better protected than workers in CCEs against the moral hazard potentially attached to management decisions over investment.
- When faced with demand shocks CCEs primarily adjust employment whereas WOCs primarily adjust remuneration.
- Recessions increase the number of firm *closures* among CCEs and WOCs alike. However, recessions decrease the number of *creations* among CCEs, whereas the creation of WOCs increases.

(Based on a review of empirical studies in the period 1950 to 2010 by Pérotin 2012; see more extensively 6§3; many of these points are confirmed by later studies.)

• *The case of the Spanish Mondragon WOCs (6D2).* This regards a federation of about 100 WOCs, employing together about 81,000 workers (2020). Within its space confines, chapter 6 treated this case rather extensively, because it shows the complexities of the functioning of WOCs within a capitalist constellation of international competition. The focus was on the quantitative employment performance of the Mondragon WOCs. The main findings are the following.

- In the period between 1983 and 2019 Mondragon's total employment grew by 335%, and its comparatively relevant employment in Spain by 258%. In the same period Spain's employment grew by 75%, and that of the aggregate of OECD countries by 41% (6§7, Table 6.8 and Graph 6.9).
- The group's survival record of almost 65 years is outstanding – the major exception being the bankruptcy of one large cooperative in 2013 (6§8, last paragraph).
- In comparison with CCEs, Mondragon's intra-cooperative income differences are remarkable – by 2019 a before-tax ratio of maximum 1:9, and for individual cooperatives on average about 1:5 (6§6).

A drawback of this excellent performance was that whilst the employment of WOC members was optimally secured, many of these WOCs also employed non-members with a less secure position, and that many also established non-cooperative subsidiaries in Spain and abroad (6§9). It is noted that also from the side of the Mondragon federation, and from the side of quite some individual cooperatives, these are considered as second-best practices in face of finding a modus between competitive pressures and the maintenance of employment within cooperatives (6§9).

- *Social and solidarity economy entities (6D3).* Cooperatives, as including WOCs, are part of the encompassing category of 'social and solidarity economy entities' (SSEs). Generally these produce goods, services and knowledge while pursuing economic and social aims and fostering solidarity. Cooperatives, mutual benefit societies and production/service associations do so for their members – thereby having only an indirect impact on the society or a community at large. A fairly recent category (late 1970s) is the 'social enterprise' (SE) which pursues an explicit social aim in the interests of the society or a community. Like the earlier mentioned categories it runs market-oriented production activities, and it likewise adopts an inclusive and participatory governance model (6§10).

Regarding the employment performance of all of the SSEs, data for cooperatives are available on a world scale (though still limited as mentioned above). Aggregate data beyond a single country are much more limited for the other categories. However, there are encompassing data for the European Union from 2002–2015 which show that in this period the aggregate employment performance of SSEs outran that of the EU at large by a factor 4.4; concomitantly the share of SSEs in the total EU employment increased from 5.5% to 6.4% (6§11, Table 6.24).

- *Some of the chapter 6 conclusions.* In comparison with capitalist enterprises, the employment record of WOCs – and of other worker-owned entities, as well as of 'social and solidarity economy' entities generally – is outstanding. The further growth of SSE entities might lead to a gradual expansion of the current islands of such entities, and this expansion would be an important lever to a 'beyond capitalism'. Whether the success of SSE entities would gradually undermine the legitimation for conventional capitalist enterprises is bare speculation. Anyway, the last two chapters of Part Two assumed that the SSE has expanded substantially (say to near one third of the employment in the private sector – although this number is no condition for the chapter 8 transition) and that along with it the said legitimation has indeed been undermined.

2. Circumstances just before the transition: financial and real estate markets and the scope of capital flight (chapter 7). For the take-off to the transition (chapter 8) it is important to have an idea about the economic and political constellation immediately before the take off. The brief chapter 7 tried to imagine that constellation. It starts from the point at which capitalist enterprises and their owners feel that there might be a reasonable chance that pro-worker cooperatives political parties are going to win the next elections. Assuming that this point emerges at least two years before these elections, it is analysed what effect this might have on the financial and real estate markets and on an ensuing capital flight. It is next considered what their effects are on the 'real economy' that will be the inheritance for the transition's actual take off. The following are the main conclusions of the analysis.

- *Value of financial assets.* After the full transition shares, bonds and the markets for these will no longer exist. Because of anxiety among owners of these financial capital assets, their prices will deeply fall (7§2).
- *Value of real estate.* After the full transition cooperatives that wish so can own self-occupied premises; all other real estate will be owned by the National real estate agency. This agency rents out (1) dwellings for self-occupation to households; (2) premises to cooperatives; (3) land to agricultural cooperatives. There will no longer be a real estate market (3§37). Just before the transition therefore, there will be a sharp fall in the prices of immovable property, with distinctive effects for owner-occupied dwellings, for rented out dwellings and for other real estate as set out in 7§3.
- *Capital flight.* During this period there is surely going to be capital flight. There are two possible forms of this: emigration, or international movement of assets without emigration. In each case capital owners must first try to sell financial or real estate assets; however, given the two previous points, there is not much value of home assets to substitute into foreign assets. Of what there might remain, the selling has no effect on the real economy because enterprises as structure cannot be moved abroad. (7§6.)

The chapter's Table 7.2 summarises the direct effects of the three points above. It is concluded that there are income and wealth effects but (so far) no effects on the production of enterprises. However, in face of the insecure future, capitalist enterprises will during this period of, say, two years, probably stop investing, or at least heavily cut investment, which will set in motion a serious recession. Its degree depends on the at this point reached relative sizes of the capitalist sector and the sector of WOCs and other SSE entities. (7§8.)

3. **Transition to a worker cooperatives society (chapter 8).**[16] Starting at the point when in a country there is parliamentary majority that aims to go for a transition, chapter 8 presented a transition path from capitalism to a Design worker cooperatives society. The path is divided in two broad periods. One in which all of the Part One's Design has been put into legislation – in this period its implementation in practice already gradually emerges. Another in which that legislation becomes fully implemented in practice in the sense that all of the society's economic domain is organised in Design worker cooperatives. The most important point of the chapter is that such a transition seems possible along with a preservation of the degree of production and work as inherited from the immediate past – although I cannot prove that.

Contrary to this preservation posited, it might be argued that in the early phases of the transition the prevailing capitalist sector will begin to break down because of an investment stop by capitalist enterprises. However, this is not likely because – also from the part of the enterprises' shareholders – there is no better alternative than to keep on investing. (An investment stop because of revenge feelings does not bring in profits.[17] Moreover, if these enterprises' management or shareholders would want to show that capitalist enterprises are more vital than cooperatives, then an investment stop is rather counterproductive.)

This matter is to be distinguished from the likely inheritance of a recession due to the turbulences just before the transition (ch. 7). Recession countering policies immediately from the start of the transition were treated in 8§20 (including: various measures that result in a consumption expenditure floor; an emergency programme of dwellings construction; a regular dwellings construction programme; policies regarding non-construction investment; and the forwarding of infrastructural projects).

---

16 This summary is almost identical to the concluding summary of chapter 8.
17 For shareholders, the dividends derived from profits are crucial. As indicated in 8§23 (under heading 4-A) the transitional constellation is such that the market-value of shares is not determined by the corporations' equity (and prospects) but by the present value of the expected future dividends during the lifetime of the average shareholder (an individual shareholder will calculate her/his expected lifetime, as well as the individual marginal tax rate).

GENERAL SUMMARY 417

TABLE GS-4 *The transition legislation phases and their implementation in practice*

		Duration in years (indication)	Implementation in practice
I	**transition legislation phases**		
	after first transition elections		
	phase 1: transition foundations	1.1	
	phase 2: completion elementary transition	0.4	
	phase 3: preconditions for mature transition	0.5	
	overrun and adaptation period	2.0	emerging transition in practice
	subtotal	4	
	after second transition elections		
	phase 4: advanced transition	0.2	
	phase 5 (final): matured transition	0.6	
	overrun period	0.7	
	subtotal	*1.5*	
	total number of legislation years	5.5	
II	**full implementation in practice**		full transition (in maximum one generation)

Table GS-4 lists the above mentioned two broad transition periods, with for the first period an indication of the duration of the transition's five legislation phases. This first period has been detailed in the chapter's first five divisions – together with an underpinning of the duration – the second one was briefly pointed out in 6D6.

(1) *Transition of the economic domain.* The key policy instruments that bring about the transition path of the economic domain are listed in the six points below.

• *First.* The Design's cooperative is enacted as legal entity, together with the enactment of the specific rules set out in chapter 2. In addition the following two transition rules are enacted. First, regarding the economic domain (and

except for a 'single person enterprise') no new legal entity shall be established other than a Design cooperative. Second, the sole allowed non-public sector legal conversion of an entity is that into a Design cooperative (Phase 1, 8§14). These two transition rules, in combination with the rules below, are core to the transition.
• *Second*. In the Design there are no shares and bonds markets. For the transition it is enacted that *no new* shares or bonds shall be issued. In line with the Design, bank savings accounts must be terminated and be transferred to a savings account with the 'Savings and Loans Bank' (Phase 1, 8§16).
• *Third*. Taxation measures include steeply progressing individual income and inheritance brackets (each as in the Design). For corporations the income and property taxes are maintained as they are before the transition; those for cooperatives are nil (as in the Design). This implies a comparative advantage for the latter – note that under capitalism there are also different taxation regimes for different legal entities. (Phase 1, 8§9, Table 8.2.) The inheritance tax (with, as in the Design, a top bracket of 100% above twice the equivalent of the minimum wage) implies that after a generation the individual property ownership, in shares, bonds, non-incorporated firms, and in real estate will have evanesced.

The three sets of rules above are sufficient for a within one generation fading away of the capitalist sector and a complete transition to worker cooperatives. This hinges on the inheritance tax together with the rule that in the economic domain no legal entities other than Design cooperative can be established (first above). The rules below accelerate the transition process.
• *Fourth*. The enactment of the Design's competition policy rule about maximum market shares, which for the transition implies that current pre-transition enterprises will have to break up into two or more independent smaller legal entities (Phase 1, 8§6; this rule enters into force one year after the enactment.)
• *Fifth*. Enactment of the Design's rule that economic domain entities shall be organised in no more than one single location, which implies that current pre-transition multi-location enterprises will have to break up into two or more independent single location legal entities (Phase 3, 8§35; the rule enters into force six months after the enactment.)

Rules four and five formally merely mean that capitalist enterprises lose a market power/dominance 'advantage' above Design cooperatives.
• *Sixth*. Enactment of the Design's 'Agency for temporary workers' council governed foundations' (Phase 1, 8§8). Amongst several other competences, the main one is that when during the transition corporate shares, or a firm, are part of a bequest, the agency has a pre-emptive right to purchase these – against

reasonable prices. (Given the inheritance taxes the inheritors are required to sell anyway.) Once this agency acquires the majority of the shares in a corporation it can insist on the legal conversion into a cooperative (perhaps via the stage of a temporary workers' council governed foundation).

The general strategy for the gradual legal conversion of pre-transition capitalist enterprises into Design cooperatives was expanded on in 8§23.

(2) *Transition of the public sector.* The rest of the transition's five legislation phases mainly concerns an orderly transition of the state, the state institutions and the rest of the public sector. This regards the enactment of mainly the following items.
• The election and interconnection of the state's highest democratic organs as well as of the democratic organs of provinces and municipalities (Phase 1, 8§1; and Phase 3, 8§37).
• The workers' councils of ministries, the judiciary, state agencies, provinces and municipalities, as including the competences of these councils (Phase 2, 8§26; the competences regarding remuneration in Phase 5, 8§49).
• The free of charge health and education, and their institutions (Phase 1, 8§11 and 8§12) and their organisation through workers' council governed foundations (Phase 2, 8§26; the competences regarding remuneration in Phase 5, 8§49).
• The various allowances such as those for pensions and the child-related ones (Phase 2, 8§27–8§29) and for persons with restricted abilities to work (Phase 4, 8§44). (Until these are enacted general allowances at a minimum level of 60% of the minimum wage apply for all from early on Phase 1, 8§10.) (Recall that the minimum wage is 167% of the minimum costs of living.)
• The minimisation of joblessness to a maximum of two months (Phase 4, 8§43).
• The average remuneration of workers in public sector institutions as a derivative of the average remuneration of workers in the economic domain (Phase 5, 8§48).

As it is, the transition path of chapter 8 shows that all these points sub 1 and 2 (and those that are not mentioned in this Summary) cannot be transformed in one go; their transition takes not only time, but also requires a specific transition sequence. To take the last point above, the remunerations of public sector workers cannot be changed in one stroke; orderly change of these requires at least that the various provisions have reached a substantial quality and quantity level.

Generally, the main puzzle to solve for the transition in each of the economic and public sector domains, is the specific transition sequence from capitalism to the Design's components, as well as the required adaptation time in between the introduction of the different components.

I do not claim that the transition path chosen in this chapter is the only possible one. My sole self-imposed task was to show that there is at least one, reasonably detailed, feasible transition path. One that does not result in an immediate collapse of pre-transition capitalist sector, and thus one that keeps production and jobs going throughout the transition.

∴

References

Aedes 2020. *Verplaatsbare woningen bouwen* (The building of movable dwellings); https://dkvwg750av2j6.cloudfront.net/m/5fea56e0bdff4eb7/original/Aedes_Verpla atsbare-woningen-bouwen_februari-2020.pdf

Anderson, Robert T. 1971, 'Voluntary Associations in History', *American Anthropologist*, New Series, 73, 1: 209–22. https://anthrosource.onlinelibrary.wiley.com/doi/pdf/10 .1525/aa.1971.73.1.02a00150

Arando, Saioa, Fred Freundlich, Monica Gago, Derek C. Jones and Takao Kato 2011, 'Assessing Mondragon: Stability and Managed Change in the Face of Globalization', in *Employee Ownership and Shared Capitalism: New Directions and Debates for the 21st Century* (pp. 241–27), edited by Edward Carberry, Ithaca, NY: ILR Press, Cornell University.[1] Quoted from paper under the same title, *William Davidson Institute Working Paper*, no. 1003: https://deepblue.lib.umich.edu/bitstream/handle/2027.42/ 133017/wp1003.pdf;jsessionid=1373326D08B938F02756DD43BC771DC6?sequence=1

Arando, Saioa, Monica Gago, Derek C. Jones and Takao Kato 2015, 'Efficiency in Employee-Owned Enterprises: An Econometric Case Study of Mondragon', *Industrial and Labor Relations Review*, 68, 2: 398–425. Quoted from: https://www.researchgate .net/publication/228252042

Arestis, Philip and Malcolm Sawyer (eds) 2006, *A handbook of alternative monetary economics*, Cheltenham: Edward Elgar.

Balestra, Carlotta, Richard Clarke, R. Fernandez, Sebastian Königs and Kamil Kouhen, forthcoming, 'Inequalities in household wealth – trends, drivers and policy implications', *OECD Social, Employment and Migration Working Papers*, Paris: OECD Publishing.

Barandiaran, Xabier, and Javier Lezaun 2017, 'The Mondragón experience', in *The Oxford Handbook of mutual, co-operative, and co-owned business* (pp. 279–94), edited by Jonathan Michie, Joseph R. Blasi and Carlo Borzaga, New York: Oxford University Press. https://www.researchgate.net/publication/320016464

Battilani, Patrizia, and Harm G. Schröter (eds) 2012, *The cooperative business movement, 1950 to the Present*. New York: Cambridge University Press.

Baumol, William J., and William G. Bowen 1965, 'On the performing arts: The anatomy of their economic problems', *The American Economic Review*, 55, 2: 495–502.

Bavel, Bas van 2016, *The invisible hand? How market economies have emerged and declined since AD 500*. Oxford: Oxford University Press.

---

1 https://ecommons.cornell.edu/handle/1813/74107 || https://ecommons.cornell.edu/bitstream /handle/1813/74107/Carberry_Employee_Ownership_and_Shared_Capitalism.pdf?sequence =1&isAllowed=y

Bellofiore, Riccardo 1989, 'A monetary labor theory of value', *Review of Radical Political Economics*, 21, 1–2: 1–26.

Bellofiore, Riccardo 2005, 'Monetary economics after Wicksell: Alternative perspectives within the theory of the monetary circuit', in *The Monetary Theory of Production – Traditions and Perspectives* (pp. 39–51), edited by Giuseppe Fontana and Riccardo Realfonzo, London/New York: Palgrave Macmillan.

Bindseil, Ulrich, and Philipp J. König 2013, 'Basil J. Moore's horizontalists and verticalists: An appraisal 25 years later', *Review of Keynesian Economics*, 1, 4: 383–90, available at: http://dx.doi.org/10.4337/roke.2013.04.01.

Bonnaud, Jean-Jacques 1975, 'Planning and industry in France', in *Planning, politics and public policy: The British, French and Italian experience*, edited by Jack Hayward and Michael Watson, Cambridge: Cambridge University Press.

Borzaga, Carlo, Giulia Galera, Barbara Franchini, Stefania Chiomento, Rocío Nogales and Chiara Carini 2020. See European Commission 2020.

Borzaga, Carlo, Gianluca Salvatori and Riccardo Bodini 2017, 'Social and Solidarity Economy and the Future of Work', *Euricse Working Paper* for the ILO/ International Labour Office. https://www.ilo.org/wcmsp5/groups/public/---ed_emp/---emp_ent/---coop/documents/publication/wcms_573160.pdf

Bosma, Niels, Thomas Schøtt, Siri A. Terjesen and Penny Kew 2016, *Global Entrepreneurship Monitor 2015 to 2016: Special Topic Report on Social Entrepreneurship*. https://papers.ssrn.com/sol3/papers.cfm?abstract_id=2786949

Bretos, Ignacio, and Anjel Errasti 2018, 'The challenges of managing across borders in worker cooperatives: Insights from the Mondragon cooperative group', *Journal of Co-operative Organization and Management*, 6, 1: 34–42. Quoted from: https://www.researchgate.net/publication/325545021

Bretos, Ignacio, Anjel Errasti and Carmen Marcuello 2019a, 'Is there life after degeneration? The organizational life cycle of cooperatives under a "grow-or-die" dichotomy', *Annals of Public and Cooperative Economics*, October, 1–26. https://www.researchgate.net/publication/336596972

Bretos, Ignacio, Anjel Errasti and Carmen Marcuello 2019b, 'Multinational expansion of worker cooperatives and their employment practices: Markets, institutions, and politics in Mondragon', *Industrial and Labor Relations Review*, 72, 3: 580–605. Quoted from https://www.researchgate.net/publication/325437137

Bretos, Ignacio, and Carmen Marcuello 2017, 'Revisiting globalization challenges and opportunities in the development of cooperatives', *Annals of Public and Cooperative Economics*, 88, 1: 47–73. Quoted from: https://www.researchgate.net/publication/307379635

Caves, Richard E., and Masu Uekusa 1976a, 'Industrial organization', in *Asia's New Giant: How the Japanese Economy Works*, edited by Hugh Patrick and Henry Rosovsky, Washington: The Brookings Institution.

Caves, Richard E. and Masu Uekusa 1976b, *Industrial organization in Japan*, Washington: The Brookings Institution.

CICOPA (International organisation of industrial and service cooperatives) 2017a,[2] *Cooperatives and Employment: Second Global Report 2017* (author: Hyungsik Eum) https://www.ica.coop/sites/default/files/publication-files/cooperatives-and-emplo yment-second-global-report-625518825.pdf

CICOPA 2017b, *Industrial and Service Cooperatives: Global Report 2015–2016* (authors: Elisa Terrasi and Hyungsik Eum) https://www.cicopa.coop/wp-content/uploads/201 9/07/Global-REPORT-2015-2016-2019-corrections.pdf

Cooperatives Europe 2015, *The power of cooperation – Cooperatives Europe key figures 2015*. https://coopseurope.coop/power-cooperation-%E2%80%93-cooperative s-europe-key-figures-2015

Cristea, Anca, David Hummels, Laura Puzzello and Misak Avetisyan 2013, 'Trade and the greenhouse gas emissions from international freight transport', *Journal of Environmental Economics and Management*, 65, 1: 153–73. https://www.sciencedirect.com /science/article/abs/pii/S0095069612000708
https://www.krannert.purdue.edu/faculty/hummelsd/research/YJEEM-1749_FINAL 082312.pdf page references are to this last version (pp. 1–21).

Dalton, George 1974, *Economic systems and society: Capitalism and the third world*, Harmondsworth: Penguin.

Deleplace, Ghislain, and Edward J. Nell (eds) 1996, *Money in motion: The post Keynesian and circulation approaches*, London/New York: Macmillan/St. Martin's Press.

Deloitte 2020, *Global Powers of Retailing 2020*. https://www2.deloitte.com/content/ dam/Deloitte/global/Documents/Consumer-Business/Report_GPR2020.pdf

Dijk, Gert van, Panagiota Sergaki and George Baourakis, 2019, *The cooperative enterprise; Practical evidence for a theory of cooperative entrepreneurship*, Cham: Springer.

EESC/CIRIEC 2017 (European Economic and Social Committee; International Centre of Research and Information on the Public, Social and Cooperative Economy), *Recent evolutions of the Social Economy in the European Union* (authors: Jose Luis Monzón and Rafael Chaves). https://www.eesc.europa.eu/sites/default/files/files/qe -04-17-875-en-n.pdf

EFES 2020 (European Federation of Employee Share Ownership), *Annual economic survey of employee share ownership in European countries 2019* (author: Marc Mathieu) Brussels, EFES. http://www.efesonline.org/Annual%20Economic%20Survey/2019/ Survey%202019.pdf

Eroski Group 2020, *Annual report 2019*. https://corporativo.eroski.es/wp-content/uploa ds/2020/08/Memoria-EROSKI-2019_en.pdf

---

2 Sector organisation of the *International Cooperative Alliance* (ICA).

Errasti, Anjel, Iñaki Heras, Baleren Bakaikoa and Pilar Elgoibar 2003, 'The internationalisation of cooperatives: The case of the Mondragon cooperative corporation', *Annals of Public and Cooperative Economics*, 74, 4: 553–84. https://www.researchgate.net/publication/247635511

Errasti, Anjel, Ignacio Bretos and Aitziber Nunez 2017, 'The viability of cooperatives: The fall of the Mondragon cooperative Fagor', *Review of Radical Political Economics*, 49, 2: 181–97; quoted from https://www.researchgate.net/publication/313292439

Eum, Hyungsik 2017, see CICOPA 2017a.

European Commission n.d., 'Cooperatives', https://ec.europa.eu/growth/sectors/social-economy/cooperatives_en

European Commission n.d., 'Social economy in the EU', https://ec.europa.eu/growth/sectors/social-economy_en

European Commission 2014, *The promotion of employee ownership and participation* (report by the Inter-University Centre for European Commission's DG MARKT; personal authors: Jens Lowitzsch, Iraj Hashi, Alban Hashani, Sabine Schneider, Lea Salathé and Dave Lemmens). https://op.europa.eu/en/publication-detail/-/publication/c184fcde-ecd7-11e5-8a81-01aa75ed71a1/language-en/format-PDF/source-194400715

European Commission 2020, *Social enterprises and their ecosystems in Europe. Comparative synthesis report*. (Authors: Carlo Borzaga, Giulia Galera, Barbara Franchini, Stefania Chiomento, Rocío Nogales and Chiara Carini). Luxembourg: Publications Office of the European Union. https://ec.europa.eu/social/BlobServlet?docId=22304&langId=en

European Council 2015, *The promotion of the social economy as a key driver of economic and social development in Europe*, Brussels: Council of the European Union. [3] https://data.consilium.europa.eu/doc/document/ST-15071-2015-INIT/en/pdf

European Parliament 2015, *Resolution of 10 September 2015 on Social Entrepreneurship and Social Innovation in combating unemployment* (2014/2236 (INI)). https://www.europarl.europa.eu/doceo/document/TA-8-2015-0320_EN.html

Eurostat 2019, *Manual on sources and methods for the compilation of COFOG statistics – Classification of the Functions of Government (COFOG) – 2019 edition* https://ec.europa.eu/eurostat/web/products-manuals-and-guidelines/-/KS-GQ-19-010

Eurostat – 2020, *Glossary: Classification of the functions of government (COFOG)*. https://ec.europa.eu/eurostat/statistics-explained/index.php?title=Glossary:Classification_of_the_functions_of_government_(COFOG)

---

[3] The Council of the EU represents the member states' governments; it consists of national ministers from each EU country and meets to adopt laws and coordinate policies.

Fakhfakh, Fathi, Virginie Pérotin, and Monica Gago 2012. 'Productivity, capital and labor in labor-managed and conventional firms', *Industrial and Labor Relations Review*, 65, 4: 847–79. Quoted from: https://www.researchgate.net/publication/2368 88727_Productivity_Capital_and_Labor_in_Labor-Managed_and_Conventional_Fir ms_An_Investigation_on_French_Data

Fennell, Lee Anne 2011, 'Ostrom's Law: "Property rights in the commons"', *International Journal of the Commons*, 5, 1: 9–27. file:///G:/Fennell%202011,%20Ostrom's%20law, %20property%20rights%20in%20the%20commons.pdf

Flecha, Ramon, and Pun Ngai 2014, 'The challenge for Mondragon: Searching for the cooperative values in times of internationalization', *Organization*, 21, 5: 666–82. https://sociology.hku.hk/wp-content/uploads/9.-Mondragonpaper2014.pdf

Flecha, Ramon, and Ignacio Santa Cruz 2011, 'Cooperation for economic success: the Mondragon case', *Analyse & Kritik*, 1: 157–70. http://www.analyse-und-kritik.net/ Dateien/5696575a8cb2e_ak_flecha_santa-cruz_2011.pdf

Fontana, Giuseppe, and Riccardo Realfonzo (eds) 2005, *The monetary theory of production – Traditions and perspectives*, London/New York: Palgrave Macmillan.

Fonteneau, Bénédicte, and Ignace Pollet 2020, see ILO 2020.

Fonteneau, Bénédicte, Fredrick Wanyama, Leandro Pereira Morais, Mathieu de Poorter, Carlo Borzaga, Giulia Galera, Tom Fox and Nathaneal Ojong 2011, see ILO 2011.

George, Donald A.R., Eddi Fontanari and Ermanno C. Tortia 2020, 'Finance, property rights and productivity in Italian cooperatives', *Euricse Working Paper Series 110|20*. https://www.euricse.eu/wp-content/uploads/2020/01/WP-110-20_George-et-al.pdf

Goodman, Peter S. 2020, 'Co-ops in Spain's Basque region soften capitalism's rough edges', *The New York Times*, 29 December. https://www.nytimes.com/2020/12/29/ business/cooperatives-basque-spain-economy.html

Government of the Netherlands 2012, *The constitution of the kingdom of the Netherlands 2008*. https://www.government.nl/documents/regulations/2012/10/18/the-constitut ion-of-the-kingdom-of-the-netherlands-2008

Grace, Dave 2014. *Measuring the size and scope of the cooperative economy; results of the 2014 Global census on co-operatives*. Report for the UN Department of Economic and Social Affairs. https://www.un.org/esa/socdev/documents/2014/coopsegm/grace.p df

Graziani, Augusto 1989, 'The theory of the monetary circuit', *Thames Papers in Political Economy*, 1, London, available at: http://www.gre.ac.uk/__data/assets/pdf_file/0009/ 1147581/TP_PPE_89_1.pdf, also in *Economies et Sociétés*, Série Monnaie et Production (1990), 7: 7–36.

Graziani, Augusto 2003, *The monetary theory of production*, Cambridge: Cambridge University Press.

Grigore, Alina-Aurelia 2013, 'Social economy entities: a worldwide overview', *Review of Applied Socio-Economic Research*, 6, 2: 111–20. http://reaser.eu/RePec/rse/wpaper/R6 _9_GrigoreAlina_p111-120.pdf

Heras-Saizarbitoria, Iñaki 2014, 'The ties that bind? Exploring the basic principles of worker-owned organizations in practice', *Organization* 21, 5: 645–65. Quoted from https://www.researchgate.net/publication/268278380

Herrera, David 2004, 'Mondragon: a for-profit organization that embodies Catholic social thought', *Review of Business*, 25, 1: 56–68. Quoted from: https://community-wealth.org/sites/clone.community-wealth.org/files/downloads/article-herrera.pdf

ICA and EURICSE 2021 ('International Co-operative Alliance' and 'European Research Institute on Cooperative and Social Enterprises'), *World Cooperative Monitor 2020; Exploring the cooperative economy*. https://monitor.coop/sites/default/files/publication-files/wcm2020-1727093359.pdf

ILO 2011 [International Labour Office], *Social and Solidarity Economy: Our common road towards decent work* (authors: Bénédicte Fonteneau, Fredrick Wanyama, Leandro Pereira Morais, Mathieu de Poorter, Carlo Borzaga, Giulia Galera, Tom Fox and Nathaneal Ojong). https://www.ilo.org/wcmsp5/groups/public/---ed_emp/---emp_ent/---coop/documents/instructionalmaterial/wcms_166301.pdf

ILO 2019, *Small matters; Global evidence on the contribution to employment by the self-employed, micro-enterprises and SMEs* (Executive summary). https://www.ilo.org/wcmsp5/groups/public/---dgreports/---dcomm/---publ/documents/publication/wcms_723314.pdf

ILO 2020, *The contribution of SSE and social finance to the future of work* (authors Bénédicte Fonteneau and Ignace Pollet), https://www.ilo.org/empent/areas/social-finance/publications/WCMS_739377/lang--en/index.htm

ITF 2019 (International Transport Forum at the OECD), *ITF Transport Outlook 2019*, Paris: OECD Publishing, https://doi.org/10.1787/transp_outlook-en-2019-en.

Jakab, Zoltan, and Michael Kumhof 2015, 'Banks are not intermediaries of loanable funds – and why this matters', *Bank of England Working Paper* No. 529, available at: http://z822j1x8tde3wuovlgo7ue15.wpengine.netdna-cdn.com/wp-content/uploads/2015/02/wp529.pdf

Kasmir, Sharryn 2016a, 'The Mondragon cooperatives and global capitalism: a critical analysis', *New Labor Forum*, 25, 1: 52–9. https://www.researchgate.net/publication/290978631

Kasmir, Sharryn 2016b, 'The Mondragon cooperatives: successes and challenges', *Global Dialogue*, 6, 1. https://globaldialogue.isa-sociology.org/the-mondragon-cooperatives-successes-and-challenges/

Kerlin, Janelle 2006, 'Social enterprise in the United States and Europe: Understanding and learning from the Differences', *International Journal of Voluntary and Nonprofit Organizations*, 17, 3: 246–62. https://www.researchgate.net/publication/225759566_Social_Enterprise_in_the_United_States_and_Europe_Understanding_and_Learning_From_the_Differences

Klikauer, Thomas, and Norman Simms 2020, Review of 'Adler, Paul S, 2019, *The 99 Percent Economy: How Democratic Socialism Can Overcome the Crises of Capitalism', *Marx & Philosophy Review of Books*, February. https://marxandphilosophy.org.uk/reviews/17778_the-99-percent-economy-how-democratic-socialism-can-overcome-the-crises-of-capitalism-by-paul-s-adler-reviewed-by-thomas-klikauer-norman-simms/

Kornai, János 1979. 'Resource-constrained versus demand-constrained systems', *Econometrica*, 47, 4: 801–19.

Kornai, János, 1986, 'The soft budget constraint', *Kyklos*, 39, 1: 3–30.

Kornai, János, Eric Maskin and Gérard Roland 2003, 'Understanding the soft budget constraint', *Journal of Economic Literature*, XLI (December): 1095–136. https://www.researchgate.net/profile/Gerard_Roland/publication/4981461_Understanding_the_Soft_Budget_Constraint/links/0046351cda41325010000000/Understanding-the-Soft-Budget-Constraint.pdf

Kruse, Douglas 2016, 'Does employee ownership improve performance?', *IZA World of Labor*, December. https://wol.iza.org/uploads/articles/311/pdfs/does-employee-ownership-improve-performance.pdf?v=1

Laboral Kutxa 2019 [Mondragon bank], Consolidated balance sheet and Profit and loss account 2018. https://corporative.laboralkutxa.com/src/uploads//2019/04/2018-CLP-Consolidado-ING-WEB.pdf

Lavoie, Marc 2003, 'A primer on endogenous credit-money', in *Modern theories of money: The nature and role of money in capitalist economies* (pp. 506–43), edited by Sergio Rossi and Louis-Philippe Rochon, Cheltenham and Northampton: Edward Elgar.

Lowitzsch, Jens, Iraj Hashi, Alban Hashani, Sabine Schneider, Lea Salathé and Dave Lemmens 2014, see European Commission 2014.

Luzarraga, José Maria 2008, *Mondragon multi-localisation strategy: innovating a human centred globalisation*, Doctoral thesis, Mondragon University. https://www.researchgate.net/publication/340594067

Luzarraga, José Maria, Dionisio Aranzadi and Iñazio Irizar 2007, 'Understanding Mondragon globalisation process: local job creation through multi-localization; Facing globalization threats to community stability', paper presented at 1st CIRIEC International research conference on the social economy, Victoria, BC, Canada, 22–25 October. https://www.researchgate.net/publication/237604098

Mathieu, Marc 2020, see EFES 2020.

Meade, James 1964, *Efficiency, equality and the ownership of property*, London: George Allen & Unwin.

Mellor, Mary, Janet Hannah, John Stirling 1988, *Worker cooperatives in theory and practice*, Milton Keynes: Open University Press.

Michie, Jonathan, Joseph R. Blasi and Carlo Borzaga (eds) 2017, *The Oxford handbook of mutual, co-operative, and co-owned business*, New York: Oxford University

Press. (Introduction and overview at: https://www.oxfordhandbooks.com/view/10.1093/oxfordhb/9780199684977.001.0001/oxfordhb-9780199684977-miscMatter-9.)

Monaco, Kristen 2020, 'Employer-provided bonuses: what are they, what types of businesses offer them, and who receives them?' *Beyond the Numbers: Employment and Unemployment*, 9, 19 (US Bureau of Labor Statistics, December 2020). https://www.bls.gov/opub/btn/volume-9/employer-provided-bonuses-what-are-they-what-types-of-businesses-offer-them-and-who-receives-them.htm

Mondragon n.d., 'About us', https://www.mondragon-corporation.com/en/about-us/; includes a document about Mondragon's history. https://www.mondragon-corporation.com/en/history (accessed 18 January 2021).

Mondragon n.d. 'Mondragon Corporation' (information on the Mondragon Divisions). https://www.mondragon-corporation.com/en/

Mondragon 1998–2019, Annual Reports. [The last report provides a reference to the PDFs of earlier reports. In the following link click on the top icon 'idioma' for the language.] https://www.mondragon-corporation.com/2019urtekotxostena/?l=en

Monzón, Jose Luis, and Rafael Chaves 2017, see EESC/CIRIEC 2017.

Mook, Laurie, John R. Whitman, Jack Quarter and Ann Armstrong 2015, *Understanding the social economy of the United States*, Toronto: University of Toronto Press.

Nielsen, Klaus 2008, 'Indicative planning', in *The new Palgrave dictionary of economics*, second edition, edited by Steven N. Durlauf and Lawrence E. Blume, Basingstoke: Palgrave Macmillan. *The new Palgrave dictionary of economics online*, Palgrave Macmillan, accessed 20 September 2014, available at: http://www.dictionaryofeconomics.com/article?id=pde2008_I000060.

OECD 2022, Specific wealth distribution dataset OECD countries around 2019, based on the OECD Wealth distribution database, and Balestra et al., forthcoming, (see reference above).

Pérotin, Virginie 2006, 'Entry, exit, and the business cycle: Are cooperatives different?' *Journal of Comparative Economics*, 34: 295–316. http://educ333b.pbworks.com/w/file/fetch/54071946/Business%20cycle.pdf

Pérotin, Virginie, 2012, 'The performance of workers' cooperatives', in *The cooperative business movement, 1950 to the present*, edited by P. Battilani and H. Schroeter (pp. 195–221), New York: Cambridge University Press. Quoted from: https://www.researchgate.net/publication/285356456_The_performance_of_worker_cooperatives

Pérotin, Virginie, 2014, 'Worker cooperatives: good, sustainable jobs in the community', *Journal of Entrepreneurial and Organizational Diversity*, 2, 2: 34–47. http://www.jeodonline.com/articles/invited-paper-worker-cooperatives-good-sustainable-jobs-community; also in *The Oxford Handbook of Mutual, Co-Operative, and Co-Owned Business* 2017, eds. Jonathan Michie, Joseph R. Blasi and Carlo Borzaga [references are to the 2014 version]

Pérotin, Virginie 2016, 'Democratic firms: assets for the long term', in *Institutions for Future Generations*, edited by A. Gosseries and I. Gonzalez (pp. 330–51), Oxford: Oxford University Press. Quoted from: https://www.researchgate.net/publication/312563888_Democratic_Firms

Pizzigati, Sam 2015, 'Alternate approaches: a manufacturer of equality; interview with Josu Ugarte', *Too Much*, June (Institute for Policy Studies). https://toomuchonline.org/this-business-manufactures-equality/

Rawls, John 2001, *Justice as fairness: a restatement*, edited by Erin Kelly, Cambridge, MA: Belknap Press.

Reuten, Geert 2019, *The unity of the capitalist economy and state; a systematic-dialectical exposition of the capitalist system*, Leiden/Boston: Brill. https://brill.com/view/title/38778 (open access).

Reuten, Geert 2023a, 'The Mondragon worker cooperatives' employment record 1983–2019', *Journal of Labor and Society* vol. 26/3, pp. 336–75 (pre-publication 28 July 2022) https://brill.com/view/journals/jlso/26/3/article-p336_003.xml (open access).

Reuten, Geert 2023b, 'On the distribution of wealth and capital ownership: an empirical application to OECD countries around 2019', *Historical Materialism*, pre-publication 5 June 2023 (25 pages). https://brill.com/view/journals/hima/aop/article-10.1163-1569206x-bja10005/article-10.1163-1569206x-bja10005.xml (open access)

Rochon, Louis-Philippe, and Sergio Rossi (eds) 2003a, *Modern theories of money: the nature and role of money in capitalist economies*, Cheltenham: Edward Elgar.

Roelants, Bruno, Hyungsik Eum and Elisa Terrasi 2014, *Cooperatives and employment: a global report*, CICOPA. https://www.cicopa.coop/wp-content/uploads/2018/03/cooperatives_and_employment_a_global_report_en__web_21-10_1pag.pdf

Santa Cruz Ayo, Ignacio, and Eva Alonso 2016, 'Mondragon's third way: reply to Sharryn Kasmir', *Global Dialogue*, 6, 3. https://globaldialogue.isa-sociology.org/mondragons-third-way-reply-to-sharryn-kasmir/

Saros, Daniel 2014, *Information technology and socialist construction: the end of capital and the transition to socialism*, London/New York: Routledge.

Schumpeter, Joseph A. 2003 [1943^1, 1954^4], *Capitalism, socialism and democracy*, London/New York: Taylor & Francis e-Library, available at: http://digamo.free.fr/capisoc.pdf.

Schweickart, David 2002, *After capitalism*, Lanham, MD: Rowman & Littlefield.

Schweickart, David, 2011, *After capitalism* (revision of the 2002 edition), Lanham, MD: Rowman & Littlefield.

Smith, Tony 2017, *Beyond liberal egalitarianism: Marx and normative social theory in the twenty-first century*, Leiden: Brill.

Smith, Tony, forthcoming, 'A socialism for the twenty-first century: The full and free development of every individual' (quoted from the book draft of October 2022).

Snowdon, Brian, and Howard Vane 2002, 'Aggregate demand management', in *Encyc-

lopedia of Macroeconomics, edited by B. Snowdon and Howard Vane (pp. 19–20), Aldershot: Edward Elgar.

Storey, John, Imanol Basterretxea, and Graeme Salaman 2014, 'Managing and resisting "degeneration" in employee-owned businesses: a comparative study of two large retailers in Spain and the United Kingdom', *Organization*, 21, 5: 626–44. Quoted from: https://papers.ssrn.com/sol3/papers.cfm?abstract_id=2690802

Surroca, Jordi, Miguel A. Garcia-Cestona and Lluís Santamaría 2006, 'Corporate governance and the Mondragón cooperatives', *Management Research*, 4, 2: 99–112. Quoted from: https://www.researchgate.net/publication/235323030

Suvin, Darko 2016, *Splendour, misery, and possibilities: an x-ray of socialist Yugoslavia*, Leiden/Boston: Brill.

Terrasi, Elisa, and Hyungsik Eum 2017, see CICOPA 2017b.

Thomas, Henk, and Chris Logan 1982, *Mondragon: an economic analysis*, London: Allen & Unwin. https://library.uniteddiversity.coop/Cooperatives/Mondragon/Mondragon_An_Economic_Analysis-1982.pdf || https://library.uniteddiversity.coop/Cooperatives/Mondragon/

Trezise, Philip H., and Yukio Suzuki 1976, 'Politics, government, and economic growth in Japan', in *Asia's new giant: how the Japanese economy works* (pp. 753–811), edited by Hugh Patrick and Henry Rosovsky, Washington: The Brookings Institution.

UK Parliament 2010, 'House of Commons information office', *Disciplinary and penal powers of the house*, Factsheet G6. https://www.parliament.uk/documents/commons-information-office/g06.pdf

UN 2008 (United Nations), *International Standard Industrial Classification of all economic activities, Rev. 4;* retrieved from UK ONS, Last updated 9 January 2018, https://www.gov.uk/government/publications/standard-industrial-classification-of-economic-activities-sic

UN 2009 (United Nations) [European Commission, International Monetary Fund, Organisation for Economic Co-operation and Development, United Nations and World Bank], *System of National Accounts 2008* [SNA 2008], available at: http://unstats.un.org/unsd/nationalaccount/sna2008.asp.

United Nations, General Assembly 2013, '*Cooperatives in Social Development*', resolution adopted on 18 December 2013. https://undocs.org/en/A/RES/68/133

Waldron, Jeremy 2016 [2004], 'Property and ownership', in *The Stanford Encyclopedia of Philosophy* (Winter 2016 Edition), edited by Edward N. Zalta, https://plato.stanford.edu/entries/property/

White, Allen 2015, 'Worker cooperatives in a globalizing world: interview with Josu Ugarte', *Great Transition Initiative*, October. https://community-wealth.org/sites/clone.community-wealth.org/files/downloads/paper-ugarte.pdf

REFERENCES

Websites cooperative organisations (world and regional)
  • *International Co-operative Alliance* (ICA) http://ica.coop/
worldwide organisation with the following four regional branches
    • *Cooperatives Europe* https://coopseurope.coop/
    • *Cooperatives of the Americas* http://www.aciamericas.coop/
    • *ICA Asia and the Pacific* http://www.icaap.coop/
    • *The Alliance Africa* https://icaafrica.coop/
    • *Committee for the Promotion and Advancement of Cooperatives* (COPAC)[4] http://www.copac.coop/about/

---

4 Current members (2021): UN Department of Economic and Social Affairs (UNDESA); International Labour Organization (ILO); International Co-operative Alliance (ICA); Food and Agriculture Organization of the United Nations (FAO); World Farmers' Organisation (WFO).

Index of names

Alonso, Eva   273 *n*35; 429
Anderson, Robert T.   285; 421
Arando, Saioa   263 *n*15 and *n*17; 264 *n*19; 272–73; 273 *n*34; 274 *n*37; 275; 275 *n*42; 276; 280; 421
Aranzadi, Dionisio   279–80; 427
Arestis, Philip   45 *n*22; 421
Armstrong, Ann   288 *n*57; 428
Avetisyan, Misak   423

Bakaikoa, Baleren   265 *n*22; 270 *n*31; 424
Baourakis, George   3 *n*2; 423
Barandiaran, Xabier   258; 260–62; 263 *n*15; 273; 279; 421
Basterretxea, Imanol   274; 430
Battilani, Patrizia   4; 421; 428
Baumol, William J.   409 *n*15; 421
Bavel, Bas van   68 *n*1; 421
Bellofiore, Riccardo   44 *n*22; 422
Bindseil, Ulrich   164 *n*77; 422
Blasi, Joseph R.   3 *n*2; 421; 427–28
Bodini, Riccardo   287 *n*57; 422
Bonnaud, Jean-Jacques   47 *n*26; 422
Borzaga, Carlo   3 *n*2; 285 *n*53; 286 *n*54; 288 *n*57; 421–22; 424–28
Bosma, Niels   288; 422
Bowen, William G.   409 *n*15; 421
Bretos, Ignacio   vii; 255; 258; 263 *n*17; 269 *n*29 and *n*32; 270; 272; 277 *n*43 and *n*44; 278–79; 281; 295; 422; 424

Carini, Chiara   285 *n*53; 286 *n*54; 422; 424
Caves, Richard E.   47 *n*26; 422–23
Chaves, Rafael   423; 428
Chiomento, Stefania   285 *n*53; 286 *n*54; 422; 424
Cristea, Anca   238 *n*1; 423

Dalton, George   47 *n*26; 423
Damsma, Dirk   vi
Deleplace, Ghislain   45 *n*22; 423
Dijk, Gert van   3 *n*2; 423

Elgoibar, Pilar   264 *n*22; 270 *n*31; 424
Errasti, Anjel   258; 263 *n*17; 265 *n*22; 269 *n*29, *n*31 and *n*32; 270; 272; 277 *n*43 and *n*44; 278–79; 281; 295; 422; 424

Eum, Hyungsik   249; 423–24; 429–30

Fakhfakh, Fathi   34 *n*12; 255; 257; 292 *n*63; 425
Fennell, Lee Anne   425
Flecha, Ramon   263 *n*15; 264 *n*21; 269 *n*28; 272–73; 275; 278–79; 425
Fontana, Giuseppe   45 *n*22; 422; 425
Fontanari, Eddi   255–56; 292 *n*64; 425
Fonteneau, Bénédicte   426
Fox, Tom   425–26
Franchini, Barbara   285 *n*53; 286 *n*54; 422; 424
Freundlich, Fred   263 *n*15 and *n*17; 264 *n*20; 272–73; 273 *n*34 and *n*37; 275; 280; 421

Gago, Monica   34 *n*12; 255; 257; 263 *n*15 and *n*17; 264 *n*20; 272–73; 275–76; 280; 293 *n*63; 421; 425
Galera, Giulia   285 *n*53; 286 *n*54; 422; 424–26
Garcia-Cestona, Miguel A.   261; 430
George, Donald A.R.   255–56; 292 *n*64; 425
Goodman, Peter S.   296; 425
Grace, Dave   251; 425
Graziani, Augusto   44 *n*22; 425
Grigore, Alina-Aurelia   288 *n*57; 425
Gunsteren, Herman van   vii

Hannah, Janet   3 *n*2; 427
Hashani, Alban   424; 427
Hashi, Iraj   424; 427
Hayward, Danny   vii
Heras, Iñaki   265 *n*22; 269 *n*31; 424
Heras-Saizarbitoria, Iñaki   273 *n*35; 426
Herrera, David   263 *n*15; 426
Hummels, David   423

Irizar, Iñazio   279–80; 427

Jakab, Zoltan   45; 426
Jones Derek C.   263 *n*15 and *n*17; 264 *n*20; 272–73; 275–76; 280; 421

Kasmir, Sharryn   273 *n*35; 426; 429
Kato, Takao   263 *n*15 and *n*17; 264 *n*20; 272–73; 275–76; 280; 421
Kerlin, Janelle   287 *n*56; 426

INDEX OF NAMES

Kew, Penny 288; 422
Klikauer, Thomas 305 n5; 426
König, Philipp J. 164 n77; 422
Kornai, János 79 n16; 427
Kruse, Douglas 255; 427
Kumhof, Michael 45; 426

Lavoie, Marc 65; 427
Lemmens, Dave 424; 427
Lezaun, Javier 258; 260–62; 263 n15; 273; 279; 421
Logan, Chris 265 n25; 430
Lowitzsch, Jens 424; 427
Luzarraga, José Maria 265 n22; 269 n30 and n31; 277 n44; 278–80; 427

Marcuello, Carmen 255; 258; 263 n17; 269 n29; 270 n32; 278–79; 281; 422
Maskin, Eric 79 n16; 427
Mathieu, Marc 423; 427
Meade, James 1 n1; 427
Mellor, Mary 3 n2; 427
Michie, Jonathan, 3 n2; 421; 427–28
Monaco, Kristen 297 n69; 428
Monzón, Jose Luis 423; 428
Mook, Laurie 288 n57; 428
Mussell, Simon vii

Nell, Edward J. 45 n22; 423
Ngai, Pun 269 n29; 272; 275; 278–79; 425
Nielsen, Klaus 47 n26; 428
Nijsten, Bart viii
Nogales, Rocío 285 n53; 286 n54; 422; 424
Nunez, Aitziber 270; 278; 295; 424

Ojong, Nathaneal 425–26

Pereira Morais, Leandro 425–26
Pérotin, Virginie 4; 34 n12; 46 n24; 193 n92; 254–55; 257–58; 291; 292 n63; 297; 413; 425; 428–29
Pizzigati, Sam 262; 278; 429
Pollet, Ignace 425–26
Poorter, Mathieu de 425–26
Puzzello, Laura 423

Quarter, Jack 288 n57; 428

Rawls, John 1 n1; 429
Realfonzo, Riccardo 45 n22; 422; 425
Rochon, Louis-Philippe 45 n22; 427; 429
Roelants, Bruno 249; 429
Roland, Gérard 79 n16; 427
Rossi, Sergio 45 n22; 427; 429
Rostow, Walt 5

Salaman, Graeme 274; 430
Salathé, Lea 424; 427
Salvatori, Gianluca 287 n57; 422
Santa Cruz Ayo, Ignacio 429
Santa Cruz, Ignacio 263 n15; 264 n21; 272–73; 425
Santamaría, Lluís 261; 430
Saros, Daniel 49 n28; 429
Sawyer, Malcolm 421
Schneider, Sabine 424; 427
Schøtt, Thomas 288; 422
Schröter, Harm G. 3 n2; 421
Schumpeter, Joseph A. 338 n22; 429
Schweickart, David 24 n1; 26 n4; 429
Sergaki, Panagiota 3 n2; 423
Simms, Norman 305 n5; 426
Smith, Tony vii; 1 n1; 34 n11; 51–53; 429
Snowdon, Brian 106 n30; 429
Stirling, John 3 n2; 427
Storey, John 274; 275 n40; 430
Surroca, Jordi 261; 430
Suvin, Darko 50 n30; 430
Suzuki, Yukio 47 n26; 430

Terjesen, Siri A. 288; 422
Terrasi, Elisa 249; 423; 429–30
Thomas, Henk 265 n25; 430
Tortia, Ermanno C. 255–56; 293 n64; 425
Trezise, Philip H. 47 n26; 430

Uekusa, Masu 47 n26; 422–23

Vane, Howard 106 n30; 430

Waldron, Jeremy 431
Wanyama, Fredrick 425–26
Went, Robert vii
White, Allen 259; 260 n13; 264; 278; 430
Whitman, John R. 288 n57; 428
Wit, Debbie de viii

Index of subjects

- In order to facilitate the finding of a lemma, the index is divided into eight rubrics:
  A. Cooperatives economy (pp. 434–39);
  B. State and state institutions (pp. 439–50);
  C. Interconnection economy, state and households (p. 450);
  D. International relations (p. 450);
  E. Modification capitalist practices: worker-owned cooperatives and other democratic enterprises (pp. 451–53);
  F. Period just before the transition (pp. 453–54);
  G. Transition:
      G1. General transition matters (pp. 454–55);
      G2. Enactment of design and transitional rules (pp. 456–58).
- This index is not exhaustive for each one (main) term, it rather focusses on references where a main term/concept is explained.
- Two general abbreviations are used: PWC for 'production worker cooperative' and COB for 'cooperative bank'.
- References are most often to sections of a chapter; for example, 2§5 stands for chapter 2, section 5; in case of a subsection, for example, 2§5.2.
- In case the reference is to a *full (sub)section*, it is followed by its page numbers in brackets; for example 2§5.2 (44–45).
- Reference to a *single page*, or some pages, are as, for example, 2§5.2: 44, or also ch. 2: 44, 49.
- References to *appendices* are as, for example, 3–App E, meaning appendix E of chapter 3.
- Most lemmas have sub-lemmas.
- Many lemmas have a cross-reference (see: ... see also: ...). In case this reference is to a sub-lemma this is indicated as, for example, see: 'state institutions' sub 'broadly categorised'. Only in case of *between* rubric cross-references these have a rubric indication; for example, see B: 'state institutions', or, see also B: 'state institutions'.

A. COOPERATIVES ECONOMY

Accumulation of capital
   see: 'capital and capital accumulation'
auditing
   see: 'cooperatives specialised in auditing'
Balance sheet of cooperatives   2–App A (59–64)
banks
   see: 'cooperative banks'
   see also B: 'Central Bank'; 'Guardian Bank'; 'Investment-credit Guarantee Fund'; 'Savings and Loans Bank'
Capital and capital accumulation
   eliminated in cooperatives economy   2§10.3: 35; 2§10–table 2.5: 35; ch. 2–Sum: 55
   see also: 'valorisation'
capitalism
   see: 'comparison economies of Design and capitalism'
class: social-economic
   workers constitute the single economic class   2§1.0: 24

INDEX OF SUBJECTS

circular production
    see: B 'physically circular production'
COB
    abbreviation for 'cooperative bank'
    see: 'cooperative banks'
comparison economies of Design and capitalism
    different aims and instruments   2§10.0–2§10.1: 34; 2§10–table 2.5: 35
    ownership relations   2§5–addendum: 28–29; 2§5–table 2.3: 30
    summary of key distinctions   ch. 2–Sum, table 2.7: 55–56
    wage differences   2§8–addendum: 32
comparison economies of Design and socialism
    aims for a socialist alternative to the Design   2§25 (47–48)
    central planning as alternative for cooperatives' local planning   2§26 (48–51)
    indicative planning: Tony Smith's proposed form   2§26–addendum: 51–53
competition between cooperatives
    general account   2§19.0–2§19.1: 39–40
    matters limiting market dominance individual coops   2§19.2: 40
    tendency non-aggressive and non-destructive competition   2§19–addendum: 40–41
    see also: 'markets'
    see also B: 'Competition authority'
contraction of cooperatives
    restructuring plan when 3y contraction resistance buffer   2§14.2 (37–38)
    see also: 'expansion of cooperatives'
cooperative banks
    single task cobs: investment loans pwcs and payment accounts pwcs and households   2§6.4: 31; 2§16.0: 39
    maximum sum on payment accounts of households   2§16.2: 39
    zero real rate of interest on payment accounts   2§16.1: 39
    see also: 'credit-debt relation between COBs and PWCs'
    see also B: 'Central Bank'
    see also B: 'Savings and Loans Bank'
cooperative: as legal entity   2§3 (26–27)
cooperative: foundation of
    general 2§4 (27–28)
    specifics of foundation cooperative banks   2–App B (64–66)
cooperative: governance of   2§5: (28–30)
cooperative: single location   2§3.3: 27
cooperative: two types of
    'production worker cooperatives'; 'cooperative banks'   2§2.0: 25
    see also: 'production: terminology'
cooperative's council
    see: 'council of cooperative'
cooperatives
    see A entries 'cooperative: …'
    see also B: 'stand-in cooperatives'
    see also: 'cooperatives economy'
    see also: 'cooperatives specialised in auditing'
    see also: 'cooperatives specialised in insurance'
    see also: 'council of cooperative'

see also: 'management of cooperatives'
see also: 'mergers between cooperatives'
see also: 'take-over prohibition'
cooperatives economy
    brief overview   1§1–1§6 (11–15)
    general characterisation   2§1 (24–25)
    summary of   ch. 2–Sum (53–59)
cooperatives specialised in auditing   2§18: 39
    see also B: 'Registered Auditors Authority'
cooperatives specialised in insurance
    general 2§17: 39
    prohibition cooperative banks to engage in insurance 2§6.4: 31
cooperatives' premises
    see: 'premises of cooperatives'
council of cooperative
    highest governance body of a cooperative   2§5.0: 28
    rights (minimum) and main authority: general account   2§5.1: 29
    tendential aim of councils: jobs preservation and maximisation of average value-added per worker   2§10.0: 34
credit-debt relation between cobs and pwcs   2§6 (31)
    see also: 'cooperative banks'
Distribution of income: pre-taxation
    dividends: decided on by council of cooperative 2§9.0 (33)
    wages: minimum wage   2§8.0 (32)
    wages: wage scales decided on by council of cooperative   2§8.0 (32)
    see also: 'dividend'
    see also B: 'minimum wage'
    see also B: 'taxation'
    see also: 'postponed dividends'
    see also: 'resistance buffer: legally binding'
    see also: 'uncommitted reserves'
    see also: 'value-added' sub 'from value-added to disposable surplus and dividends'
distribution of wealth: pre-taxation   2§20 (41)
    see also B: 'taxation'
dividend   ch. 2–Intro (terminology): 23
    see also: 'distribution of income: pre-taxation'
dwellings of households
    see: 'households' self-occupied dwellings'
Employment
    Design evades term: no social class that exploits (i.e. employs) another by appropriating the latter's surplus product   ch. 2–Intro (terminology): 22
    Design uses terms 'work' and 'job'
    see also B: 'constitution: constitutional rights' (art. 2 on slavery and employment)
expansion of cooperatives
    restricted expansion in face of dominant market power   2§14.0: 37
    see also B: 'Competition authority'
    see also: 'contraction of cooperatives'
Households' self-occupied dwellings
    rented from state's 'Real Estate Agency'   2§15.2: 38
    see also B: 'Real Estate Agency'

INDEX OF SUBJECTS 437

Income account of cooperatives   2–App A (59–63)
income of workers
    see: 'distribution of income: pre-taxation'
    see also B: 'taxation'
insurance
    see: 'cooperatives specialised in insurance'
Labour market, quantitative aspect
    see: 'markets'
labour-time: maximum duration
    see: 'work-time: maximum duration'
Macroeconomic connections
    between households and cooperatives   2§1, scheme 2.1: 25; 2§22, scheme 2.6: 43
management of cooperatives
    chosen (and removed) by council of cooperative   2§5.0: 28
    chosen from rank and file of the cooperative's workers   2§5.3: 29
    see also: 'council of cooperative'
markets
    financial markets for only investment loans by banks, and for insurance   2§17–addendum: 39
    no full-fledged labour market, only quantity aspect applies   2§23: 46
    no real estate market   2§15–addendum: 38
    no shares and bonds markets   2§3.0: 27; 2§6.1: 31
    product markets (output markets; consumer goods markets)   2§2.0–2§2.1 (25–26); 2§23: 45–46
    see also: 'competition between cooperatives'
    see also B: 'Competition authority'
    see also B: 'National Real Estate Agency'
membership of cooperative   2§3.4: 27
mergers between cooperatives   2§3.2: 27; 2§14: 38
Ownership of means of production
    cooperatives: restricted ownership   2§3.0: 26; 2§3–Addendum: 27
    workers are usufructuaries, not owners   2§1.0: 24; 2§3.0: 26
    see also: 'usufruct: defined'
Postponed dividends
    paid out share in uncommitted reserves   2§13.0: 37
    see also: 'dividend'
    see also: 'uncommitted reserves'
premises of cooperatives
    ownership or renting of self-occupied premises   2§15 (38)
    transactions operate via state's 'Real Estate Agency'   2§15 (38)
    see also B: 'National Real Estate Agency'
production: terminology
    used in wide sense, as including retail and other services   2§2.0 (25)
production worker cooperative (PWC) 2§2.0: 25
    see also: all lemmas 'cooperative ...'
    see also: 'cooperatives economy'
    see also: B 'physically circular production'
PWC
    abbreviation of 'production worker cooperative'

Record keeping (economy)
    items to be recorded   2§11.0 (36)
    serves also determination average remuneration public sector workers   2§11.1 (36)
    see also B: 'research: non-university, state-financed' sub 'General statistical office – special task: determination annual average remuneration of cooperatives' workers'
reserves
    see: 'resistance buffer' and 'uncommitted reserves'
resistance buffer: legally binding   2§7 (31–32)
restructuring of cooperatives   2§14.2 (37–38)
Selling of cooperative's assets
    generally requires assets purchase of at least equal value   2§14.2 (37–38)
    see also: 'contraction of cooperatives'
single location of cooperatives
    see: 'cooperative: single location'
single person enterprise
    defined   2§2.2 (26)
    general restrictions, esp. prohibition of hiring workers   2§2.2 (26)
    regulation of turnover tax for single person enterprises   3–App E (225–26)
socialism
    see: 'comparison economies of Design and socialism'
stand-in cooperatives
    see B: 'stand-in cooperatives'
summary ch. 2
    1. democracy at the point of production   ch. 2: 53
    2. ownership-like characteristics   ch. 2: 54
    3. tendential aim of cooperatives' councils; elimination of the categories of 'capital' and 'accumulation of capital'   ch. 2: 54
    4. free choice occupation, specific consumption and cooperative's investment   ch. 2: 56
    5. market dominance, technical change and competition   ch. 2: 56
    key distinctions between capitalist and cooperatives economies   ch. 2–table 2.7: 55–56
    main requirements or restrictions for cooperatives and councils   ch. 2–table 2.8: 57–58
Take-over prohibition   2§3.2: 27
Uncommitted reserves
    defined   2§9.0: 33
    aim for uncommitted reserves   2§9.1: 33–34
    individual workers future claim on uncommitted reserves   2§9.1: 33; 2§12.0: 36
    see also: 'postponed dividends'
unemployment
    term not used for the Design, see: 'employment'
usufruct: defined   1§1: 12; 2§1.0: 24
Valorisation
    can play no role in cooperatives economy   2§10.0 (34); ch. 2 Sum: 54
    contrasted with capitalist enterprises   2§10.1 (34)
    'valorisation' of inputs value: production of value-added   2§26: 49
    see also: 'capital and capital accumulation'
value-added
    from value-added to disposable surplus and dividends   2§9.0–table 2.4: 23
    labour the sole producer of value-added   2§1.0: 24
    see also: 'income account of cooperatives' (PWC; COB)

INDEX OF SUBJECTS 439

Wealth of workers
    see: 'distribution of wealth: pre-taxation'
    see also B: 'taxation'
work-time: maximum duration   2§8.1: 32
    see also B: 'work-time'

B.   STATE AND STATE INSTITUTIONS

Acts, laws and bills   ch. 3–Intro: 68 and 68 n3
administrative burden: estimates
    all burdens   3–App 3B (202–205)
    all burdens – introduction: comparison with capitalist entities   3–App 3B: 202
    cooperatives compared with capitalist enterprises   3–App 3B: 203–205
    cooperatives compared with capitalist enterprises: summary 3–App 3B–table 3B.1: 203
    main burden mutation for households or workers   3–App 3B: 204–205
    main burden mutation for ministries and state agencies   3–App 3B: 205
advertisement and output information
    advertisement prohibition (including internet)   3§8: 91
    consequences of advertisement prohibition   3§8–addendum: 91–92
    safety and information about output   3§8 (91–92)
Agency for temporary workers' council governed foundations
    agency acts when the required scale of production and/or the risk is too large to be undertaken by cooperatives   3§41: 118
    agency sets up temporary WGFs that fully charge for the costs of their production or services 3§41: 151–52
    when sufficiently running sold or rented out to PWCS   3§41: 152
    see also: 'workers' council governed foundations (WGFs)'
    see also: 'state agencies'
allowances (all summarised)
    see: 'income allowances and securities'
Central Bank
    being a state agency   3D4–Intro: 94–95
    budget and workforce constraints   3D4: 99–100
    task regarding all cooperatives (resistance buffer)   3§13-l: 96
    tasks regarding cooperative banks   3§13-d to i: 96
    tasks regarding insurance cooperatives   3§13-j to k: 96
    tasks regarding the state and state institutions   3§13-a to c: 95
    see also: 'Guardian Bank'; 'Investment-credit Guarantee Fund'; 'Savings and Loans Bank'
    see also: 'state agencies'
childcare allowances
    see: 'Pensions and child allowances agency'
child-related allowances (all)
    see: 'Pensions and child allowances agency'
child's costs of living allowances
    see: 'Pensions and child allowances agency'
circular production
    see: 'physically circular production'
climate and environment
    see: 'physically circular production'

COB
    abbreviation of 'cooperative bank'
    see A: 'cooperative banks'
competition and market power
    see: 'Competition authority'
Competition authority
    being a state agency   3§45: 155
    general tasks and delegated authority   3§45-a to h: 155–57
    prevention of dominant market power cooperatives   3§45-a: 155
    prohibition price and quantity cartels   3§45-g: 157
    sector specific maximum market share rules   3§45-c: 155–56
    see also: 'state agencies'
concluding summary ch. 3
    1. types of institutions, workforce and expenditure   ch. 3: 170
    2. parliamentary democracy   ch. 3: 170–71
    3. remuneration of public sector workers   ch. 3: 172
    4. unity worker cooperatives society's economy and state   ch. 3: 172–73
    5. further important characteristics   ch. 3: 173–74
    6. taxation   ch. 3: 174
    7. hard budget constraints and workforce constraints   ch. 3: 172–75
    8. classification of state agencies by their expenditure   ch. 3: 172
constitution: constitutional rights   3–App 3C(D1) (206–11)
constitutional rights and main other constitutional elements   3–App 3C (205–23)
costs of living allowances students
    see: 'Pensions and child allowances agency'
creative arts and arts performance
    activities below are institutionalised in PWCs or 'single person enterprises'   3§36: 141
    artistic creations and performances   3§36: 141–42
    arts publishing, film, television and radio   3§36: 141
    concert halls, theatre halls, cinemas   3§36: 141
    final finance of contemporary arts   3§36–table 3.13: 142
    subsidies creative arts and arts performance   3§36: 142
    summary of organisation and finance of culture sector   3§36–table 3.14: 143
    see also A: 'production worker cooperative' (PWC)
    see also A: 'single person enterprise'
    see also: 'Culture and cultural heritage agency'
Culture and cultural heritage agency
    agency's budget and amount of workforce   3§34: 139
    agency's duties regard National Library and State Museums   3§34: 139
    agency's tasks and delegated authority   3§34: 139
    National Library: collects all culturally, socially and scientifically relevant publications   3§34: 108
    National Library: digitalises publications and makes these freely available   3§34: 140
    National library's legal form: WGF (see: workers' council governed foundations)   3§34: 140
    non-state and state museums   3§34: 140
    non-state museums: run (and restrictively owned) by cooperatives   3§34: 141
    state museums: collections owned by the agency   3§34: 139
    state museums: criteria for collections   3§34: 140
    state museums: legal form of WGF (see: workers' council governed foundations)   3§34: 140
    see also: 'creative arts and arts performance'; and see also: 'state agencies'

INDEX OF SUBJECTS 441

culture sector
    see: 'creative arts and arts performance'
    see: 'Culture and cultural heritage agency'
Decrees
    (a) require parliamentary approval 3§1: 73
    (b) government issued high urgency decrees are legally binding for no more than 15 days 3§1: 73 n6
democratic organs
    of internal organisation state institutions, see: 'state institutions' sub 'workers' councils'
    of municipalities, see: 'municipalities' sub 'democratic organs and their election'
    of provinces, see: 'provinces' sub 'democratic organs and their election'
    of the state, see: 'parliament'; see: 'government'
    of workers' council governed foundations, see 'workers' council governed foundations' sub 'council of WGFs: tasks and competences'
    see also A: 'council of cooperative'; and see also: 'public sector: delineation'
dwellings
    see: 'National Real Estate Agency'
Economic policy instruments
    economic policy: evaluation key policy instruments   ch. 3 3D11–Intro: 157
    macroeconomic policy instruments   3§47-a (164–65)
    macro-policy: countering recessions and joblessness   3§47-a-second: 164
    macro-policy: direct influence on investment   3§47-a-first: 164
    policy instrument of general work-time variation   3§47-d (165)
    policy instrument of minimum wage variation (above costs of living threshold)   3§47-e (165–66)
    stagnation countering instruments   3§47-b (165)
    stimulation social priority investments   3§47-c: (165)
    see also (on 'macro-policy: direct influence on investment', and on 'stimulation social priority investments'): 'Savings and Loans Bank' sub 'grants loans to COBs for their investment loans to PWCs' and sub 'may grant loans selectively in face of social priorities'
    see also: taxation
education services
    see: 'National Education Agency'
employment
    see A: 'employment'
environment and climate
    see: 'physically circular production'
evaluation of ch. 3 in perspective ch. 2   ch. 3, General Addendum (167–69)
Finance of the state and state institutions
    borrowing and bank overdrafts: state and state institutions   3§4d-g: 82
    income and expenditure of the state: main line   3§4a-c: 82
    see also 'state institutions'; and see also: 'state';
    see also: 'taxation: categories and tax rates'
formal education
    see: 'National Education Agency'
Government
    accountable to parliament   3§1-c: 73
    elected (and removable) by parliament   3§1-c: 73
    rights of members of government on office termination   3§1-g: 75
    rules for members of government   3§1-e: 74

    see also: 'parliament'
    see also: 'state workers' sub 'judicial proceeding in case of improper behaviour'
Guardian Bank
    being a state agency   3D4–Intro: 94
    budget and workforce constraints   3D4: 100
    tasks   3§14 (97)
    see also: 'Central Bank'; 'Investment-credit Guarantee Fund'; 'Savings and Loans Bank'
    see also: 'state agencies'
Health services
    see: 'National Health Agency'
housing
    see: 'National Real Estate Agency'
Income allowances and securities
    levels summarised   3§24–table 3.9: 114–15
    summary in terms of percent annual state expenditure   3–App 3A–table 3A.1: 180–81
    summary of, regarding state expenditure compared to OECD average   3–App 3A–table 3A.2: 182
infrastructure
    see: 'National infrastructure agency'
inspectorates
    concerning: 'advertisement prohibition'; 'physically circular production'; 'safety at work'; 'safety of output'; 'work-time'   3§12 (94)
    inspectorates together constitute a 'state agency'   3§12: 94
    see also: 'state agencies'
interest rate
    see: rates of interest (summary Design's various interest rates)
internet
    see: 'National infrastructure agency' sub 'ownership of a digital network'
    see also: 'advertisement and output information' sub 'advertisement prohibition (including internet)'
Investment-credit Guarantee Fund
    being a state agency   3D4–Intro: 94
    budget and workforce constraints   3D4: 100
    tasks regarding pwc s in formation   3§15: 98
    tasks regarding regional discrepancies   3§15: 98
    see also: 'Central Bank'; 'Guardian Bank'; 'Savings and Loans Bank'
    see also: 'state agencies'
Job securities and jobs shortage agency: joblessness
    agency's general tasks   3§17 (101–02)
    kinds of joblessness (introduction)   3§18: 102
    regulation for non-recession joblessness: qualifications mismatch   3§18: 102–04
    regulation for recessional joblessness   3§19 (104–107)
    regulation regarding articulation of joblessness types   3§20: 107–09
    summary and conclusions on (regulation for) joblessness   3§20: 109–110
    wrap-up: no one out of work for longer than two months – where 'work' includes permanent jobs and paid traineeships   3D5–Intro: 101; 3§20 (summary): 109
    see also: 'Job securities and jobs shortage agency: restricted abilities'
Job securities and jobs shortage agency: restricted abilities
    regulation for those with restricted abilities to work 3§21: 110–111
    this and previous lemma: agency's budget and workforce 3§21: 111

INDEX OF SUBJECTS 443

  see also (this and previous lemma): 'state agencies'
  see also (this and previous lemma): 'income allowances and securities' sub 'levels summarised'
joblessness
  see: 'Job securities and jobs shortage agency'
judiciary
  extraordinary state institution   3§6: 88
  judiciary: courts' budget   3§6-j: 89
  non-interference by members elected state organs in cases under judicial consideration 3§5-f: 87
  power abuse by state workers: specific courts   3§6-g,h: 88–89
  procedures for appointment judges   3§6-a to e: 88
  remuneration of courts staff   3§6-k: 89
  remuneration of judges: average of worker cooperatives   3§6-i: 89
  workers' councils of courts   3§6-k: 89
  see also: 'prosecution' (two lemmas)
Labour force public sector
  see: 'public sector: labour force'
legislation and delegated regulation   ch. 3–Intro: 68
Market power
  see: 'Competition authority'
minimum wage   3§11 (94)
Mining and other Earth extractions agency
  agency's general tasks and delegated authority   3§38 (147)
  determination limits of yearly extractions   3§38-a: 147
  within the limits concessions: rents   3§38-b: 147
  see also: 'state agencies'
municipalities
  budget (no taxation)   4§1-b: 231
  democratic organs and their election   4§2 (232–34)
  remuneration of elected functionaries   4§2-h: 234
  tasks and authority of the municipal administration   4§3 (234–35)
  workers' councils of municipal institutions   4§6 (237)
  see also: 'state institutions' sub 'broadly categorised'
mutual flourishing state institutions and cooperatives   ch. 3–Intro: 67–68; 3§3-g: 81–82
National Education Agency
  agency's tasks, delegated authority and budget   3§30 (133–34)
  all primary, secondary and tertiary education provided free of charge   3D7B–Intro: 132
  argument for free of charge education provisions   3D7B–Intro: 132
  education institutions: spread, size and student/staff ratios   3§32–table 3.12: 135
  formal education provided by licensed institutions only   3§30-d: 133
  legal form of post-pre-primary education institutions: WGF (see: workers' council governed foundations)   3§30-c: 133
  number of education workers: criteria determination   3§32-d: 135
  pre-primary non-compulsory education   3§31 (134)
  primary, secondary and tertiary education   3§32 (134–37)
  state expenditure education sector   3§30–Intro: 133
  state expenditure education sector compared with OECD average   3–App 3A.3–table 3A.2: 182

state expenditure education sector: detailed per level   3–App 3A-3–table 3A.3: 189–190
see also: 'research by universities'; and see also: 'state agencies'
National Health Agency
　agency's tasks, delegated authority and budget   3§26 (118–120)
　all health institutions: legal form of WGF (see: workers' council governed foundations)
　　3§26-a: 119
　all health services free of charge   3D7A–Intro: 118
　all health workers: no free establishment   3§26-c: 119
　argument for free of charge health provisions   3D7A–Intro: 118
　care institutions   3§29 (121)
　care institutions: expanded   3D7A–App7A-3 (130–32)
　hospitals   3§28 (121)
　hospitals: expanded   3D7A–App7A-2 (126–29)
　primary medical treatment and prevention   3§27 (120–21)
　primary medical treatment and prevention: expanded   3D7A–App7A-1 (123–26)
　state expenditure and workforce health sector   3D7A–table 3.10: 122
　state expenditure compared with OECD average   3–App 3A.3–table 3A.2: 182
　state expenditure health sector: detailed per level   3–App 3A-3–table 3A.3: 187–89
　see also: 'state agencies'
National infrastructure agency
　agency's budget and estimated expenditure   3§39 (under conclusions): 149
　agency's general tasks   3§39-a to e: 148
　distinction infrastructural networks and supply (plant)   3§39: 147–48
　infra. networks: communication, information and energy   3§39-h to j: 149
　licences for mass energy generation   3§39-m: 149
　ownership of a digital network for communication   3§39-h: 149
　transport networks: interurban – ownership   3§39-f and g: 148
　see also: 'advertisement and output information' sub 'advertisement prohibition (including
　　internet)'
　see also: 'National Public Transport Agency'; and see also: 'state agencies'
National Public Transport Agency
　agency's delineation: interurban railway transport   3§40: 150
　agency's general tasks and delegated authority   3§40-a to f: 150–51
　argument for delineation   3§40: 150
　delineation *all* public transport categories (incl. carriers)   3§40–table 3.15: 151
　the agency institutes a National Railway Company   3§40-a: 150
　the National Railway Company is a customer charging WGF   3§40-a and c: 150 and 151
　see also (for networks): 'National infrastructure agency' sub 'transport networks'
　see also: 'state agencies'
　see also: WGF (abbreviation of 'workers' council governed foundation)
National Real Estate Agency (REA)
　agency's general tasks and delegated authority   3§37-a to d: 144–45
　argument for REA's tasks   3D8–Intro (first two paragraphs): 144
　budget: income and expenditure of the REA   3§37-r: 146–47
　construction of to be rented out premises and dwellings   3§37-e and f: 145
　construction: architectural design   3§37-f: 145; 146 n62
　land is not for sale   3D8–Intro (first two paragraphs): 144; 3§37-j: 145
　norms, publication and appeal regarding rents and real estate prices   3§37-n to p: 146
　renting out of dwellings, premises and land   3§37-g to i: 145

INDEX OF SUBJECTS 445

    sales and purchases of cooperatives' premises   3§37-j to m: 145–46
    the impact of the REA   3§37-q: 146
    wealth amount covered by the REA (estimate)   3§37-q: 146
    see also: 'state agencies'
Orphan allowances
    see: 'Pensions and child allowances agency'
output information
    see: 'advertisement and output information'
Parental leave allowances
    see: 'Pensions and child allowances agency'
parliament
    all legislation, as well as decrees, require its approval   3§1-a: 73
    election of parliament: procedures   3§1-d: 74
    election on proportional basis   3§1-b: 73
    elects (and may remove) government   3§1-c: 73
    highest governance organ of the nation   3§1-a: 73
    highest governance organ: schematic overview   3§1–scheme 3.3: 75; 3§1–scheme 3.4: 77
    rights of parliamentarians on office termination   3§1-g: 75
    rules for (candidate) parliamentarians   3§1-e: 74
    see also: 'decrees'; and see also: 'government'
    see also: 'state workers' sub 'judicial proceeding in case of improper behaviour'
Patents and copy rights authority
    being a state agency   3§44: 154
    tasks   3§44: 154–55
    see also: 'state agencies'
pensions
    see: 'Pensions and child allowances agency'
Pensions and child allowances agency
    agency's budget and amount of workforce   3D6–Intro: 77
    all child-related allowances   3§22 (86–87)
    childcare allowances   3§22: 86
    child's costs of living allowances   3§22: 86
    orphan allowances   3§22: 87
    parental leave allowances   3§22: 86–87
    pensions   3§24 (87–88)
    students: costs of living allowances   3§23 (87)
    see also: 'state agencies'
    see also: 'income allowances and securities', sub 'levels summarised'
physically circular production
    general   3§7 (90)
    role of Savings and Loans Bank   3§7-c: 90
    see also: 'Mining and other Earth extractions agency'
    see also: 'research: non-university, state-financed' sub 'National institute for the advance of
        physically circular production'
    see also: 'Savings and Loans Bank' sub 'may grant loans selectively in face of social priorities'
premisses of cooperatives
    see: 'National Real Estate Agency'
production
    types of, in state sector and non-state public sector   ch. 3–Intro (table 3.1): 69

user charged production and services, see: 'National Public Transport Agency', and see: 'Agency for temporary workers' council governed foundations'
    see also: 'public sector: delineation'
prosecution: administrative
    abuse of power by elected and other state workers   3§6: 89
    non-interference by members elected state organs in cases under judicial consideration 3§5-f: 87
    procedure appointment administrative prosecutors   3§6: 89
    remuneration administrative prosecutors   3§6: 89
    see also: 'judiciary' sub 'power abuse by state workers: specific courts'
    see also: 'state workers' sub 'defined' and sub 'judicial proceeding in case of improper behaviour'
prosecution: public
    minister of national public security is responsible   3§5-e: 64
    non-interference by members elected state organs in cases under judicial consideration 3§5-f: 66
provinces
    budget (no taxation)   4§1-b: 231
    democratic organs and their election   4§4 (235–36)
    remuneration of elected functionaries   4§2-h: 234
    tasks and authority of the provincial administration   4§5 (236–37)
    workers' councils of provincial institutions   4§6 (237)
    see also: 'state institutions' sub 'broadly categorised'
public sector: cases of user charged production and services
    see: 'National Public Transport Agency' and see: 'Agency for temporary workers' council governed foundations'
public sector: delineation   ch. 3–Intro (table 3.2): 70
public sector: labour force
    in % of total labour force (estimate)   3–App 3A.5–table 3A.13: 201
public sector: workers' remuneration
    members parliament, government, judges, administrative prosecutors, municipal and provincial councillors and executives: individually the average of worker cooperatives   3§3-a: 80; 3§6-i: 89; 4§2-h: 234
    workers of state institutions: per institution's FTE: the average of worker cooperatives   3§3-b: 80; 3§3-d (under fourth): 81
    workers of WGFs: per institution's FTE: the average of worker cooperatives   3§25-d: 117; 3§25-g (under second): 117
    see also: 'research: non-university, state-financed' sub 'General statistical office – special task: determination annual average remuneration of cooperatives' workers'
    see also: WGF (abbreviation of 'workers' council governed foundation)
public security
    general   3§5 (86–88)
    see also: 'judiciary', and see also: 'prosecution: public'
public transport
    carriers non-railway transport: by licensed cooperatives   3§40–table 3.15: 151
    carriers railway transport: by WGFs   3§40–table 3.15: 151
    see also (for networks): 'National infrastructure agency' sub 'transport networks'
    see also: 'National Public Transport Agency'
    see also: WGF (abbreviation of 'workers' council governed foundation)

INDEX OF SUBJECTS   447

PWC
　　abbreviation of 'production worker cooperative'
　　see A: 'production worker cooperative'
Rates of interest (summary Design's various interest rates)　　ch. 3–table 3.8: 100
real estate
　　see: 'National Real Estate Agency'
Registered Auditors Authority
　　being a state agency　　3§43: 154
　　tasks and delegated authority　　3§43: 154
　　see also: 'state agencies'
remuneration public sector workers
　　see: 'public sector: workers' remuneration'
research: categories and institutions
　　fundamental and applied research　　3§33: 137
　　fundamental and applied research institutions　　3§33: 137
research: non-university, state-financed
　　at least four state-financed research institutes　　3§33-B: 138
　　General statistical office　　3§33-B: 138
　　General statistical office – special task: determination annual average remuneration of co-
　　　　operatives' workers　　3§33-B: 138
　　National institute for economic analysis and forecasts　　3§33-B: 138
　　National institute for the advance of physically circular production　　3§33-B: 138
　　National institute for the environment and public health　　3§33-B: 138
　　state-financed research institutes: legal form of WGF　　3§33-B: 138
　　see also: workers' council governed foundations (WGFs)
research: universities
　　general 3§33-A (137–38)
　　staff requirement of combining education and research　　3§33-A-a: 137–38
　　workforce of universities and its research devoted part　　3§33: 137
　　see also: 'National Education Agency' sub lemmas 'tertiary ...'
Safety at work　　3§9 (92)
safety of output　　3§8 (first para): 91
　　see also: 'advertisement and output information'
Savings and Loans Bank (SLB)
　　being a state agency　　3D4–Intro: 94–95
　　budget and workforce constraints　　3D4: 100
　　collects savings　　3§16-a: 98
　　general tasks　　3§16-a to f: 98–99
　　grants loans to COBs for their investment loans to PWCs　　3§16-c: 99
　　may grant loans selectively in face of social priorities　　3§16-d: 99
　　mortgage loans provision to COBs and PWCs　　3§16-e: 99
　　outcome: SLB as a (or the) most influential economic policy institution　　3§16: 99
　　see also: 'Central Bank'; 'Guardian Bank'; 'Investment-credit Guarantee Fund'
　　see also: 'state agencies'
secretary general and director general
　　of ministries and state agencies: tasks　　3§3-c and e: 80–81 and 81
　　see also: 'state institutions' sub 'workers' councils'
sickness payments　　3§21: 111
stagnant underinvestment by PWCs
　　five policy measures in case of (regional) stagnation　　3§42 (152–53)

stand-in cooperatives
    introduction   3–App 3F: 226–27
    legislation stand-in cooperatives   3–App 3F: 227
    replacement seekers, consequences for   3–App 3F: 228–29
    stand-in cooperatives: consequences for   3–App 3F: 229
    workers of stand-in cooperatives: consequences for   3–App 3F: 229
state
    democratic organs of the state, see: 'parliament'; see: 'government'
    see also: 'finance of state and state institutions'
    see also: 'state expenditure (estimates)'; and see also: 'taxation'
    see also: 'Central Bank' sub 'tasks regarding the state and state institutions'
state (term without specification)
    refers to: 'state as legal entity' as governed by parliament and government   ch. 3–Intro: 70
state agencies
    subcategory of 'state institutions'   ch. 3–Intro–table 3.2: 70
    summary of the general regulation for state agencies   3§4–Addendum (85–86)
    the 18 state agencies appear under separate lemmas of the index of subjects
    the 18 state agencies listed   3–App 3G (229–30)
    see also: 'state institutions'
state expenditure (estimates)
    state expenditure – annual, summary   3–App 3A.2–table 3A.1: 180–81
    state expenditure – comparison with OECD average   3–App 3A.3–table 3A.2: 182
    state expenditure: COFOG 2nd digit in % GDP   3–App 3A.3–table 3A.3: 184–92
state institutions
    broadly categorised   3§2-a–table 3.5: 77
    budget and workforce constraints   3§2-d: 78; 3§2-h: 79
    delegated tasks   3§2-b: 78
    establishment of   3§2-a: 76
    institutions listed   3–App 3G (229–30)
    wages sum individual institutions   3§3-b: 80
    workers' councils: five main competences   3§3-d: 81
    workers' councils: large state institutions   3§3-f: 81
    see also: 'finance of the state and state institutions'
    see also: 'state agencies'; and see also: 'state workers'
state workers
    defined (elected and appointed workers)   ch. 3–Intro (under terminology): 71
    improper behaviour delineated   3§3-h: 82
    judicial proceeding in case of improper behaviour   3–App D (223–25)
    remuneration of state workers vis-à-vis cooperatives: comment (mutual flourishing)   3§3-g: 81–82
student allowances
    see: 'Pensions and child allowances agency'
summary ch. 3
    see: 'concluding summary ch. 3'
Taxation: briefly introduced
    categories and tax rates briefly introduced   3§4: 83
    categories of taxation and tax rates   3§4–table 3.7: 84–85
    see also: 'taxation: expanded on'

INDEX OF SUBJECTS 449

taxation: expanded on
    [a] carried out by taxation authority; status   3§46: 157
    [b] categories of taxation and tax rates   3§46–table 3.7: 158–59
    [c] four taxation principles   3§46: 158–60
    [d] four taxation categories: intro   3§46: 160
    [d-1] taxation of cooperatives: turnover tax   3§46: 160–61
    [d-2] income tax: on income workers and pensioners   3§46: 161
    [d-3] inheritance tax, levied on the receiver   3§46: 161
    [d-4] gift taxes   3§46: 161–62
    institutional prepayment of income taxes   3§46: 162
    regulation of turnover tax for single person enterprises   3–App E (225–26)
    transparent income tax assessment   3§46: 162–63
    see also A: 'single person enterprise'
    see also: 'taxation revenue from the income tax'
taxation revenue from the income tax (estimates)
    0. income taxation revenue   3–App 3A.4 (193–200)
    1. from GDP to the average taxable income   3–App 3A.4–table 3A.4: 193–94
    2. number of income receivers   3–App 3A.4–table 3A.5: 195
    3. tax rate: average rate on fixed income categories   3–App 3A.4–table 3A.6: 196
    4. tax rate: average of classes of fixed income   3–App 3A.4–table 3A.7: 196–97
    5. taxation revenue from receivers of fixed incomes   3–App 3A.4–table 3A.8: 197
    6. taxation revenue from receivers of non-fixed incomes: alternative 1   3–App 3A.4–table 3A.9: 198
    7. coverage of state expenditure by income taxes: alternative 1   3–App 3A.4–table 3A.10: 198
    8. taxation revenue from receivers of non-fixed incomes: alternative 2   3–App 3A.4–table 3A.11: 199
    9. coverage of state expenditure by income taxes: alternative 2   3–App 3A.4–table 3A.12: 200
Unemployment
    term not used for the Design, see A: 'employment'
    see also: 'Job securities and jobs shortage agency: joblessness'
unity of economy and state
    brief comparison Design and capitalism   ch. 3–Intro: 67–68
    unity worker cooperatives society's economy and state   ch. 3–Sum: 134; table 3.18: 172–73
universities' research
    see: 'research: universities'
user charged production and services
    see: 'National Public Transport Agency' and see: 'Agency for temporary workers' council governed foundations'
Wages: minimum wage
    see: 'minimum wage'
WGF
    abbreviation of 'workers' council governed foundation'
    see: 'workers' council governed foundations'
workers' council governed foundations (WGFs)
    all matters   3§25 (116–18)
    council of WGFs: tasks and competences   3§25-g: 117
    councils of large WGFs   3§25-h: 117
    legal form of WGF 3§25-a: 89
    ownership, finance and financial matters   3§25-b to f: 116–17

450   INDEX OF SUBJECTS

    remuneration WGF workers: per WGF the average of worker cooperatives   3§25-d: 117
    services of WGFS: most often free of charge   3§25-k: 118
workers' councils of state institutions
    see: 'state institutions' sub 'workers' councils'
workers: state workers defined (elected and appointed)   ch. 3–Intro (under terminology): 71
work-time
    determination of a full-time work position   3§10-a: 92
    maximum work-time   3§10-b: 92–93
    minimum work-time (equivalency of tax contribution)   3§10-c: 93
    temporary part-time position: right to   3§10-d: 93
    see also (on temp. part-time pos.): 'stand-in cooperatives'

C.   INTERCONNECTION ECONOMY, STATE AND HOUSEHOLDS

direct support of cooperatives by state institutions (summary)   2§21 (42)
macroeconomic flow schemes
    main flows (except savings): cooperatives and households   2§1–scheme 2.1: 25
    main flows (except savings): cooperatives, households, and state institutions   1D3–scheme 1.3: 21
    main flows: households coop workers, production coops, coop banks and 'Savings and loans bank'   2§22–scheme 2.6: 43
    elucidation scheme 2.6   2§22: 44
mutual flourishing state institutions and cooperatives   ch. 3–Intro: 67–68; 3§3-g: 81–82
summary
    • general summary of Part One (396–412)
    1. worker cooperatives   (396–97)
    2. democracy   (397–400)
    • legal entities: their governance and percent of the workforce   table GS-1: 399
    3. physical circular production and Earth extractions   (400)
    4. tendential aim of cooperatives' councils; elimination of the categories of 'capital' and 'accumulation of capital'   (400)
    • key distinctions between capitalist and cooperatives economies   table GS-2: 401–02
    5. markets and competition in the cooperatives economy   (402–04)
    • main requirements or restrictions for cooperatives and their councils   table GS-2: 404–05
    6. the single economic class and the unity of the cooperatives economy and state   (406–07)
    7. distribution of income and wealth   (407–08)
    8. hard budget and workforce constraints for the public sector   (408–10)
    9. summing up of the Design's main features   (410–12)

D.   INTERNATIONAL RELATIONS

balance of payments   5§4 (239)
development transfers   5§5 (239)
international migration   5§1 (238)
international ownership titles   5§3 (239); 5–App 5A: 239–40
international trade   5§2 (238–39); 5–App 5A: 240
international treaties   3–App 3A (constitution): 220–21

INDEX OF SUBJECTS 451

E.   MODIFICATION CAPITALIST PRACTICES: WORKER-OWNED COOPERATIVES AND
     OTHER DEMOCRATIC ENTERPRISES

Cooperatives, types of (within capitalism)
    classification and general characteristics: three types   6§2–table 6.1: 247–48
    producer-serving cooperatives   6§2: 247
    user-serving cooperatives' (incl. consumer coops)   6§2: 247
    worker-owned cooperatives [WOCS]   6§2: 247
    see also: 'hybrid cooperatives'
    see also: 'worker-owned coops: characteristics'
Employee-owned enterprises
    see: 'majority-employee-owned enterprises'
employment by cooperatives: world
    by type of coop, % of world employment (around 2016)   6§2–table 6.2: 249
    distinguished by world continents (2016)   6§2–table 6.3: 250
    scarceness of data on worker-owned coops (2016)   6§2–table 6.4: 251
    worker-owned coops: top 10 countries by employment   6§2–table 6.5: 251–52
    see also: 'cooperatives, types of'
Hybrid cooperatives
    also called: mixed coops or multi-stakeholder coops   6§2–table 6.1 (bottom row): 248
Majority-employee-owned enterprises
    number > 100 workers in 32 European countries   6§2: 252
members of cooperatives: number, world
    distinguished by cooperative types (around 2016)   6§2–table 6.2: 249
    idem for world continents   6§2–table 6.3: 250
    see also: 'cooperatives, types of'
Mondragon cooperatives
    organisational structure individual cooperatives   6§4–Scheme 6.6: 260
    salary differences of worker-members   6§6: 263 and 263 n15
    solidarity funds: inter-cooperative   6§6: 206
    worker-members' paid-in capital   6§6: 263–64
    see also: 'Mondragon Corporation'
    see also: 'Mondragon employment: …' (three lemmas)
    see also: 'Mondragon sales'
    see also: 'Mondragon: foreign subsidiaries'
Mondragon Corporation
    being the umbrella organisation for (in 2020) nearly 100 separate self-governing 'worker-
        owned cooperatives'   6D2–Intro (1st two paras): 258; 6§4: 259
    being the world's largest WOC group   6D2–Intro (1st para): 258
    divisions of Mondragon: finance, industry, retail, knowledge   6§7: 264
    organisational structure   6§4–Scheme 6.7: 261
    principles of Mondragon (from off 1987)   6§5 (262)
    see also: 'Mondragon cooperatives'
    see also: 'WOC' (abbreviates 'worker-owned cooperative')
Mondragon employment: quality
    employment types: general   6§9–1 (270–73)
    employment types: grouped by legal entity   6§9–table 6.14: 271
    industrial coops' employment worker-members and other: general   6§9–3 (276–81)
    industrial coops' national and international employment 2001–2019   6§9–3-graph 6.16: 277

industrial coops' proportion of worker-members 1995–2019   6§9–3-graph 6.17: 280
retail coops' employment worker-members and other: general   6§9–2 (273–76)
retail coops' proportion of worker-members 2000–2019   6§9-2-graph 6.15: 274
see also: 'Mondragon employment: quantity (1)' and (2)
Mondragon employment: quantity (1)
  employment 1983–2019: general   6§7 (264–66)
  employment performance compared with Spain and OECD average: 1983–2019   6§7–table 6.8: 265
  employment performance compared with Spain: 1983–2019   6§7–graph 6.9: 266
  employment performance: divisions: 1996–2019   6§7–graph 6.10: 266
  see also: 'Mondragon Corporation' sub 'divisions ...'
  see also: 'Mondragon employment: quality'
  see also: 'Mondragon employment: quantity (2)'
Mondragon employment: quantity (2)
  employment 2001–2019: in Spain and in foreign subsidiaries – latter gradually emerged from off 1989   6§9–3: 277 n44
  employment performance compared with Spain and OECD average, total and by divisions: 2001–2019   6§9–4-table 6.18: 282
  employment performance compared with Spain: industrial 2001–2019   6§9–4-graph 6.20: 284
  employment performance compared with Spain: retail 2001–2019   6§9-4-graph 6.19: 283
  summary and conclusions employment performance 2001–2019   6§9–4: 284
  see also: 'Mondragon: employment quality'
  see also: 'Mondragon: foreign subsidiaries'
Mondragon sales
  international sales include exports and sales by subsidiaries abroad   6§8 (1st para): 267
  sales 1996–2019: general   6§8 (267–70)
  sales 1996–2019: industry, retail and total   6§8–graph 6.11: 267
  sales 1996–2019: share of international sales   6§8–graph 6.12: 268
Mondragon: foreign subsidiaries
  foreign subsidiaries gradually emerged from off 1989   6§9–3: 277 n44
  general on foreign subsidiaries   6§8: 268–70
  number of cooperatives and subsidiaries 1998–2020   6§8–table 6.13: 269
Social and solidarity economy (SSE): classification
  • introduction   6D3–Intro: 284–85
  • delineation: general   6§10: 285–86
  • historical emergence SSE entities   6§10–table 6.21: 285
  categories (see sub-lemmas below)
  cooperative   6§10: 285–86
  cooperatives subclasses, see: 'cooperatives, types of ...'
  mutual benefit society   6§10: 286
  social enterprise (SE)   6§10: 286–87
  SSE association   6§10: 286
  SSE foundation   6§10: 286
social and solidarity economy (SSE): employment
  • general 6§11 (287–90)
  'social enterprises': indicator for the dispersal of SEs, world regions estimate 2014–2015   6§11–graph 6.22: 288
  sse entities (total): employment growth European Union: 2002–2015   6§11–graph 6.23: 289

INDEX OF SUBJECTS

SSEs by sub-entities: employment and its growth, European Union: 2002–2015   6§11–table 6.24: 289
SSEs: democratic enterprises and employment potential   6§11: 290
summary and conclusions chapter 6
   1. number and general performance of WOCs up to 2020   ch. 6–Sum: (291–92)
   2. complexities of WOCs' functioning within globalising capitalism: the Mondragon case ch. 6–Sum: (292–94)
   3. reflection on WOCs within capitalism as significant modification of capitalist practices ch. 6–Sum: (294–96)
   4. cooperatives as subcategory of 'social and solidarity economy entities' [SSEs]   ch. 6–Sum: (296)
   5. Future growth of number of WOCs and other SSE entities within capitalism   ch. 6–Sum: (297)
see also: 'WOC' (abbrev. 'worker-owned cooperative')
summary extract
   from General summary of Part Two   413–15
WOC
abbreviation of 'worker-owned cooperative'
worker-owned coops: characteristics
   four general characteristics 6§1 (246–47)
   performance of WOCs compared with conventional capitalist enterprises 6§3 (253–57)
   see also: 'woc' (abbrev. 'worker-owned cooperative')

F.   PERIOD JUST BEFORE THE TRANSITION

Delineation of start transition
   parliamentary majority in a country aims to go for the transition   Part Two–Intro (2nd para): 243
delineation period just before transition
   capitalist enterprises and capital owners realise that pro-worker cooperatives political parties might win next elections   ch. 7–Intro (298)
   object ch. 7: imagine regarding economic and political constellation   ch. 7–Intro (298)
development of assets value
   financial assets value   7§2 (298–300)
   real estate value   7§3 (300–01)
   value other assets   7§5 (301)
Effects of capital flight
   no effect on real economy   7§6 (302)
effects of value change assets
   enterprises' current production: none   7§7: 302–03
   labourers income: none   7§7: 303
   major assets value of banks, pension funds, insurance corp. and capital owners: all down 7§7: 303
   pensioners income: contract dependent fall   7§7: 303
   summary of effects   7§7–table 7.2: 303
Investment fall: recession effect   7§8 (303–04)
Reactions
   by Central Bank   7§9: 304

454   INDEX OF SUBJECTS

   by the government   7§9: 304–05
   ideological battle: press and other media releases   7§9: 305
Summarising appraisal   7§10 (305–06)
   from General summary of Part Two   415–16

G.   TRANSITION[1]

G1.   *GENERAL TRANSITION MATTERS*
Introductory items
   • introduction ch. 8: general   ch. 8–Intro (307–10)
   aim of transition: outline   ch. 8–Intro (2nd para): 307
   general periodisation of transition and objectives for the periods; five legislation phases
       ch. Intro: 307–08
   ideology of the 'general interest'   ch. 8–Intro: 308–09
   terminology and general matters   ch. 8–Intro: 309–10
   see also G1: 'legislation phases: enumerated'
   see also G1: 'terminology, general'
Legislation phases: duration
   listed   8§24–table 8.8: 347
   see also G1: 'legislative work: time per enactment'
   see also G1: 'legislation phases: enumerated'
legislation phases: duration and full implementation
   full implementation in practice   8D6 (379–80)
   phases duration and full implementation listed   ch. 8–Sum–table 8.18: 381
legislation phases: enumerated
   phase 1: transition foundations (38 pages)   8D1–Intro and 8§1–8§24 (311–48)
   phase 2: completion of elementary transition (8 pages)   8D2–Intro and 8§25–8§34 (348–55)
   phase 3: preconditions for mature transition (9 pages)   8D3–Intro and 8§35–8§42 (355–63)
   phase 4: advanced transition (6 pages)   8D4–Intro and 8§43–8§48 (363–68)
   phase 5: matured transition (11 pages)   8D5–Intro and 8§49–8§59 (369–79)
   see also G1: 'legislation phases: duration and full implementation'
   see also G1: 'legislation phases: duration'
legislation phases: phase-wise comments
   phase 1: aim   8D1–Intro: 311
   phase 1: general comments   8§19 (333)
   phase 2: conclusions on phase 2 and phases 1–2 together   8§34 (353–54)
   phase 3, 4, 5: constraints legislation order   8D3–Intro (355–56)
   phase 3: conclusion   8§42 (1st para): 361
   phase 4: introduction   8D4–Intro (363–64)
   phase 4: conclusions   8§48 (1st para): 367
   phase 5: introduction   8D5–Intro (369)
   phase 5: conclusions   8§59 (1st three paras): 378
legislative work: time per enactment
   general elucidation   8§24 (345–48)
   minor, moderate, much and very much enactment times   8§24: 346

---

1   Subdivided into: G1 General transition matters (pp. 454–55), and G2 Enactment of Design and transitional rules (pp. 456–58).

INDEX OF SUBJECTS   455

    sequential measure   8§24: 345 and the two bottom rows of table 8.7 (346)
    simultaneous measure   8§24: 345 and the two bottom rows of table 8.7 (346)
    see also G1: 'legislation phases: duration'
legislative work: total time per phase
    listed   ch. 8 App A–table 8.21 (390–93)
Recession countering policies (phase 1)   8§20 (333–35)
Sequential measure legislative work   8§24: 345 and the two bottom rows of table 8.7 (346)
simultaneous measure legislative work   8§24: 345 and the two bottom rows of table 8.7 (346)
state expenditure: mutation
    due to legislation phase 1: commented on   8§21: 336
    due to legislation phase 1: listed   8§21–table 8.4: 337
    due to legislation phase 2: listed   8§34–table 8.9: 354
    due to legislation phase 3: listed   8§42–table 8.12: 362
    due to legislation phase 4: listed   8§48–table 8.14: 368
    due to legislation phase 5: listed   8§59–table 8.16: 378
strategy of the transition
    see: 'transition strategy'
summary – overall
    legislation phases and their implementation in practice   ch. 8–Sum–table 8.18: 381
    legislation phases: duration   8§24–table 8.8: 347
    summary ch. 8   ch. 8–Sum (380–84)
summary of some details
    allowances and compensations: summary phase-wise enactment   8–App A–table 8.19 (385–86)
    legislation: amount legislative work   8–App A–table 8.21 (390–93)
    legislation: summary of its entering into force   8–App A–table 8.20 (387–89)
    legislation: transition implementation of the Part One Design   8–App A–table 8.22 (393–95)
Taxation revenue
    phase 1 and further transition: compared with the Design   8§21–table 8.3: 336
    see also G2: 'taxation'
terminology, general
    'full enactment'   ch. 8–Intro: 309
    'pre-transition capitalist enterprises/entities'   ch. 8–Intro: 309
    'pre-transition enterprises/entities'   ch. 8–Intro: 310
    'pre-transition worker-owned cooperatives' (WOCs)   ch. 8–Intro: 310
    'temporary enactment' 'phase x–y' preceding full enactment   ch. 8–Intro: 309
    entry into force of an enactment   ch. 8–Intro: 309
transition strategy
    for evanescence private property ownership, in enterprises, shares, bonds and real estate within a generation: ultimate requirement of taxation   8§22: 337–38
    general transition strategy: gradual change – taxation and competition policy necessary though not sufficient   8§23-3 (340)
    key role of 'Agency for temporary workers' council governed foundations'   8§23-3 (340)
    transition differences between stock corporations and firms; role of the 'Agency for temporary workers' council governed foundations'   8§23-4 (340–45)
    transition's impact on owners' capitalist enterprises during their lifetime   8§23-1 (338–39); 8§23-2 (339–40);
    see also G2: 'Agency for temporary workers' council governed foundations'
    see also G2: 'Competition authority'
    see also G2: 'taxation'

G2.   ENACTMENT OF THE DESIGN, AND TRANSITIONAL RULES

Advertisement and output information
    phase 3: full enactment   8§36 (357)

Agency for temporary workers' council governed foundations
    phase 1: full enactment, together with transitional legislation   8§8 (316–17)

allowances: non-work related
    phase 1: allowances at minimum cost of living level in phases 1–3 (phase 1 or 2 for allowances below)   8§10: 323–24
    phase 2: child-related allowances: full enactment   8§28 (350)
    phase 2: pensions, full enactment, together with transitory matters   8§27 (349–50)
    phase 2: students' costs of living allowances: full enactment   8§29 (350–51)
    see also (for work-related allowances) G2: 'Job securities and jobs shortage agency'
    see also G1: 'summary of some details' sub 'allowances and compensations: summary phase-wise enactment'

allowances: work-related
    see G2: 'Job securities and jobs shortage agency'

auditing
    phase 2: full enactment, together with transitory rules   8§31 (352)
    see also G2: 'auditing and accountancy companies'

auditing and accountancy companies
    phase 2: legal separation entities   8§32 (352)

Balance sheet and Income account economic domain entities
    phase 2: permanent rules   8§33 (352–53)

banking and fund agencies
    phase 1: full enactment, some items enter into force later   8§5 (314–15)

Competition authority (agency)
    phase 1: full enactment, some items enter into force later   8§6 (315–16)

conversion of legal form
    see G2: 'legal form conversion'

cooperatives
    phase 1: Design cooperative as legal entity   8§14 (328–29)
    phase 1: Design cooperative: unique form for newly established multi-worker legal entities in economic domain   8§14: 329
    phase 1: Design's cooperatives: temporary exceptions phases 1–2   8§15 (329)
    phase 3: termination of phases 1–2 exceptions   8§35 (356–57)
    see also G2: 'stand-in cooperatives'

culture sector
    phase 5: full enactment, together with transitional legislation   8§53 (373–74)

Democratic organs of the state
    phase 1: full enactment   8§1 (311–12)

Education provisions
    phase 1: temporary regulation phases 1–4   8§13 (326–28)
    phase 5: full enactment   8§51 (371–72)

Finance of state and state institutions
    phase 5: full enactment   8§55 (376)

financial markets
    phase 1: shares, bonds, mortgages and consumer credit: permanent transition rules   8§16 (329–30)

Health provisions
    phase 1: temporary regulation phases 1–4   8§12 (325–26)

INDEX OF SUBJECTS 457

phase 5: full enactment   8§50 (370–71)
housing
    phase 1: rented out dwellings owned by enterprises or individuals: permanent transition rules   8§11-a: 324
    see also G2: 'Real estate agency'
Income account economic domain entities
    see G2: 'Balance sheet and Income account economic domain entities'
international economic relations and treaties
    phase 4: full enactment   8§47 (367)
investment credit
    phase 1: accommodation by the 'Savings and loans bank' of banks' investment credit: permanent transition rules   8§17 (330–31)
Job securities and jobs shortage agency
    phase 2: preparatory regulation tasks during phases 2–3   8§30 (351–52)
    phase 4: full enactment   8§43 (364–65); 8§44 (365–66)
    see also G1: 'summary of some details' sub 'allowances and compensations: summary phase-wise enactment'
judiciary
    phase 1: competences of judiciary during phases 1–3   8§2 (312–13)
    phase 4: appointment procedure, full enactment   8§45 (366)
Legal form conversion
    phase 1: conversion pre-transition entities into Design entities (voluntary): permanent transition rules 8§18 (331–32)
Minimum wage
    phase 1: full enactment, together with transitional legislation   8§10: 322–23
Mining and other Earth extractions agency
    phase 3: full enactment together with transition rules   8§39 (360)
ministries
    phase 1: full enactment; some items enter into force later   8§3: 313
municipalities and provinces
    phase 1: administrations unchanged during phases 1–3   8§4 (314)
    phase 3: enactment democratic organs and election procedures   8§37 (357)
    phase 5: full enactment   8§56 (376)
National Infrastructure Agency
    phase 3: full enactment together with transition rules   8§40 (360–61)
national railway transport
    phase 5: full enactment, together with transitional legislation   8§54 (374–75)
Patents and Copyrights Authority
    phase 3: full enactment together with a transition rule   8§41 (361)
physically circular production
    phase 3: full enactment   8§36 (357)
public sector
    phase 5: remuneration matters enter into force   8§49 (369–70)
public sector: worker's councils
    see: worker's councils public sector
public security, organisation of
    phase 4: full enactment   8§46 (366–67)
Real estate agency (REA)
    phase 1: rental dwellings construction by REA during phases 1 and 2   8§11: 324–25
    phase 3: full enactment of REA   8§38 (358–60)

phase 3: transitional legislation, and comment on, REA   8§38 (1st subheading): 358–59
    see also G2: 'housing'
research institutes, state-financed
    phase 5: full enactment   8§52 (372–73)
Safety at work
    phase 3: full enactment   8§36 (283–84)
safety of output
    phase 3: full enactment   8§36 (357)
stand-in cooperatives
    phase 5: full enactment, together with transitional rules   8§58 (377–78)
state
    see G2: 'democratic organs of the state' and G2: 'state and state institutions, finance of'
state agencies
    phase 1: full enactment; some items enter into force later   8§3 (313–14)
    phase 1: on the status of 'full enactment' here   8§3: 314 (1st bullet)
state and state institutions, finance of
    phase 5: full enactment 8§55 (376)
Taxation
    phase 1: full enactment, together with transitional legislation   8§9 (317–22)
transport, national railway
    see G2: 'national railway transport'
workers' council governed foundations
    phase 1: full enactment; remuneration enters into force in phase 5   8§7 (316)
workers' councils: public sector
    phase 2: regulation phases 2–4   8§26 (348–49)
    phase 5: full enactment, including remuneration matters   8§49 (369–70)
work-time: maximum
    phase 2: full enactment   8§25 (348)
work-time: minimum
    phase 5: full enactment; together with regulation for a temporary part-time position   8§57 (376–77)

Abbreviations

Frequently used abbreviations (written out only on their first use)

COB	Cooperative Bank
FTE	Full-time equivalent
GDP	Gross domestic product
NA	Not applicable
PWC	Production Worker cooperative
WGF	Workers' council Governed Foundation

Infrequently used abbreviations (written out in section or division in which they are first and frequently used; fully written out in later sections or divisions); those with an asterisk (*) are chapter 3 'state agencies'[1]

ATF	*Agency for Temporary workers' council governed Foundations
CA	*Competition Authority
CB	*Central Bank
CCE	Conventional capitalist enterprise
CHA	*Culture and cultural Heritage Agency
GB	*Guardian Bank
IGF	*Investment-credit Guarantee Fund
JSA	*Job Securities and jobs shortage Agency
MEA	*Mining and other Earth extractions Agency
NEA	*National Education Agency
NHA	*National Health Agency
NIA	*National Infrastructure Agency
NTA	*National public Transport Agency
PCA	*Pensions and Child allowances Agency
PSC	Producer-serving cooperative
REA	*Real Estate Agency
SE	Social enterprise
SLB	*Savings and Loans Bank
USC	User-serving cooperative, a main subset being consumer cooperatives
WOC	Worker-owned cooperative

---

[1] Three non-abbreviated agencies are not mentioned here – see Appendix 3G.

Extended list of contents

General Introduction   1

PART ONE
Design of the organisation of a worker cooperatives society

Chapter 1. Preview of the main elements of the design's worker cooperatives society   11
  Introduction   11
  Division 1. Main elements of the organisation of the worker cooperatives economy   11
    1§1   The cooperative as legal entity and its democratic governance   11
    1§2   Markets, types of cooperatives and the 'single person enterprise'   13
    1§3   Membership of an existing cooperative and the foundation of a cooperative   13
    1§4   Legally required resistance buffer, 'uncommitted' reserves and dividends   14
    1§5   Credit-debt relation between cooperative banks and other cooperatives   14
    1§6   Competition between cooperatives   14
  Division 2. Description of the design's parliamentary democracy and state institutions   15
    1§7   Parliamentary democracy   15
    1§8   State institutions and the public sector   15
        Table 1.1. Public sector institutions, with estimates of their assigned state expenditure and workforce   16
    1§9   State expenditure and workforce of the public sector   17
    1§10 Functions of state agencies vis à vis cooperatives   17
        Table 1.2. Functions of state agencies vis à vis cooperatives   17
    1§11 Remuneration of public sector workers   18
    1§12 Taxation   18
  Division 3. Macroeconomic income and expenditure flows between cooperatives, households and state institutions   19

EXTENDED LIST OF CONTENTS 461

    Division 4. The design's legal entities 20
        Scheme 1.3. Main income and expenditure flows between aggregates of cooperatives, households and state institutions (abstracting from savings) 21

Chapter 2. Design of the economy of a worker cooperatives society: economic democracy and the organisation of cooperatives 22
    Introduction 22
    Division 1. Organisation of the cooperatives economy 24
    2§1   General characterisation of the cooperatives economy 24
        Scheme 2.1. Macroeconomic connections between households and cooperatives (abstracting from saving) 25
    2§2   Types of worker cooperatives 25
    2§3   The cooperative as legal entity 26
    2§4   Foundation of cooperatives 27
    2§5   Governance of cooperatives 28
        Addendum 2§5. Comparison of capitalist and cooperatives (non-)ownership relations 28
        Scheme 2.2. The cooperative and its council's rights and main authority 30
        Table 2.3. Summary memo of 2§3–2§5: legal and effective ownership and governance 30
    2§6   Credit-debt relation between cooperative banks and other cooperatives 31
    2§7   Distribution of income prior to taxation: (a) legally required resistance buffer 31
    2§8   Distribution of income prior to taxation: (b) wages 32
        Addendum 2§8. Likely moderate wage differences compared with capitalism 32
    2§9   Distribution of income prior to taxation: (c) dividends 33
        Table 2.4. From value-added to disposable surplus and dividends 33
    2§10   Intermediate conclusion: jobs preservation, maximisation value-added, and elimination of capital and the accumulation of capital 34
        Table 2.5. Summary memo of 2§10: assets dimension, and aims and instruments of production – comparison capitalist stock corporation and Design cooperative 35
    2§11   Recordkeeping 36
    2§12   Change of workforce: (a) additional workers 36

2§13 Change of workforce: (b) retirement or movements 37
2§14 Expansion and contraction of cooperatives 37
2§15 Cooperatives' ownership or renting of self-occupied premises 38
    Addendum 2§15. No real estate market 38
2§16 Bank payment accounts and their rate of interest 39
2§17 Cooperatives specialised in insurance 39
    Addendum 2§17. Exclusively financial markets for investment loans and insurances 39
2§18 Cooperatives specialised in auditing 39
2§19 Competition between cooperatives 39
    Addendum 2§19. Tendency for non-aggressive and non-destructive competitive interaction between cooperatives 40
2§20 Distribution of wealth prior to taxation 41

Division 2. Direct support of cooperatives by state institutions, and the macroeconomic connections between households and cooperatives 41

2§21 The direct support of cooperatives by state institutions 42
2§22 Macroeconomic monetary connections between households and cooperatives 42
    Scheme 2.6. Macroeconomic monetary connections between households and cooperatives, and interconnection with the state's 'Savings and Loans Bank' 43

Division 3. The cooperatives economy's markets; and reasons for the book's not taking the 'socialism' road 45

2§23 The Design's markets and commodification of products 45
2§24 A note on the ownership of means of production 47
2§25 Aims for a socialist alternative to the Design 47
2§26 Central planning as alternative for the cooperatives' local planning 48
    Addendum 2§26. Comments on Tony Smith's proposed form of socialist planning 51

Concluding summary chapter 2 53
    Table 2.7. Key distinctions between the capitalist and the Design cooperatives economies 55
    Table 2.8. Main requirements or restrictions for cooperatives and councils 57

Appendix 2A. Examples of Income accounts and Balance sheets for cooperatives 59
  Sheets 2A.1 Income account and balance sheet for a production worker cooperative 60
  Sheets 2A.2 Income account and balance sheet for a cooperative bank 62
Appendix 2B. Foundation of a cooperative bank 64
  Sheet 2B.1 COB founding balance sheet: money-creating loan to the Guardian Bank 64
  Sheet 2B.2 COB founding balance sheet: initial reserves of the COB 65
  Sheet 2B.3 COB balance sheet during its transition to full establishment 66

Chapter 3. Design of the state in a worker cooperatives society: democratic governance of the state and the organisation of state institutions 67
 Introduction 67
  Table 3.1. Types of production in the state sector and in a specific public sector institution 69
  Table 3.2. The Design's economic and public sector legal entities 70
 Division 1. The state's democratic organs and the general organisation of state institutions 72
  3§1 The democratic organs of the state 73
   Scheme 3.3. Democratic organs of the state and their election 75
   Scheme 3.4. Main tasks and powers of parliament and government 77
  3§2 State agencies and other state institutions: establishment, budget and amount of workforce 76
   Table 3.5. State and state institutions 77
   Table 3.6. Budget and workforce constraints 80
  3§3 Councils of state institutions and remuneration of parliamentarians, ministers and state workers 80
  3§4 Finance of the state and state institutions 82
   Table 3.7. Overview of the tax categories and tax rates 84
   Addendum 3§4. Summary of the general regulation for state agencies 85
 Division 2. Institutions safeguarding public security and justice 86
  3§5 Public security 86
  3§6 The judiciary, and administrative prosecution 88

Division 3. Protecting constraints: environment; safety output and work; work-time; minimum wages   90
3§7   Physically circular production   90
3§8   Safety of, and information about, output   91
         Addendum 3§8. Note on the consequences of advertisement prohibition   91
3§9   Safety at work   92
3§10   Work-time   92
3§11   Minimum wages   94
3§12   Inspectorates   94

Division 4. Institutions safeguarding the finance of cooperatives and the financial constellation at large   94
3§13   The Central Bank   95
3§14   The Guardian Bank   97
3§15   The Investment-credit Guarantee Fund   97
3§16   The Savings and Loans Bank   98
Table 3.8   Summary of the Design's various rates of interest   100

Division 5. Job securities, jobs shortages and restricted abilities to work   101
3§17   Job securities and jobs shortage agency   101
3§18   Qualifications mismatch and other non-recession joblessness   102
3§19   Recessional joblessness   104
3§20   The articulation of joblessness due to qualifications mismatches and to recessions, and conclusions on joblessness in general   107
3§21   Restricted abilities to work, and sickness payments   110

Division 6. Income allowances (exclusive work-related allowances)   112
3§22   Child-related allowances   112
3§23   Costs of living allowances for students   113
3§24   Pensions   113
Table 3.9   Summary of the Design's income securities and income allowances   114

Division 7. Wellbeing institutions: health, education, culture   115
3§25   Workers' council governed foundations   116
         Subdivision 7A. The health sector   118
3§26   National Health Agency: tasks and delegated authority   118
3§27   Primary medical treatment and prevention   120
3§28   Hospitals   121

3§29	Care institutions 121	

Table 3.10. Estimates of the state expenditure on, and the labour force of, the health sector   122

Appendix to subdivision 7A: Details of a possible organisation of the health sector   122

7A-1. Primary medical treatment and prevention   123

Table 3.11. Composition of a primary medical treatment clinic per about 10,000 inhabitants   123

7A-2. Hospitals   126

7A-3. Care institutions   130

Subdivision 7B. The education sector   132

3§30 National Education Agency: tasks and delegated authority   133

3§31 Pre-primary education   134

3§32 Primary, secondary and tertiary education   134

Table 3.12. Educational institutions qua level: spread, size and student/staff ratio   135

3§33 Research by universities and by other state-financed institutions   137

3§33-A Universities and university research   137

3§33-B State-financed research institutes   138

Subdivision 7C. Cultural heritage and contemporary creative arts and arts performance   139

3§34 Culture and cultural heritage agency: task and delegated authority   139

3§35 State and non-state museums, and the national library and archives   139

3§36 Contemporary creative arts and arts performance   141

Table 3.13. Final finance of contemporary arts in case of absence of subsidies   142

Table 3.14. Summary of the organisational form and the current expenditure finance of cultural heritage and of the main contemporary creative arts and arts performance   143

Division 8. Real estate, mining and infrastructure   144

3§37 Housing, real estate and the tasks and delegated authority of the 'national real estate agency'   144

3§38 Concessions for mining and other extractions from the Earth   147

3§39 Infrastructure and the 'national infrastructure agency'   147

Division 9. User charged production and services undertaken by 'Workers' council governed foundations' 149

3§40   Public transport and the special treatment of railway transport   150

         Table 3.15. Public transport: responsible administration, and carriers   151

3§41   Essential production or services that might possibly not be taken up by PWCs   151

3§42   Possible stagnant underinvestment by PWCs   152

Division 10. Regulation of auditing, of patents and copyrights, and of competition 153

3§43   Auditing rules and the supervision of registered auditors   153

3§44   Patents and copyrights   154

3§45   Competition and market power   155

Division 11. Taxation, and key macroeconomic and other social-economic policy instruments 157

3§46   Taxation   157

         Table 3.7. Overview of the tax categories and tax rates (repeat from 3§4)   158

         Table 3.16. Example of an income tax assessment sheet   162

3§47   Key macroeconomic and other economic policy instruments   164

General Addendum. An evaluation of chapter 3 in the perspective of chapter 2   167

         A. The initial goals and their implementation   167

         B. From deemed strong to weak points   168

Concluding summary chapter 3   170

         Table 3.17. Public sector institutions, with estimates of their assigned state expenditure and workforce   171

         Table 3.18. Functions of state institutions vis-à-vis cooperatives   172

         Table 3.19. Classification of state agencies by their expenditure: from surplus-running to big spending ones   176

Appendix 3A. Estimates of state expenditure, taxation revenue and the state's labour force   177

3A-1   Introduction and method   177

3A-2   Summary of the Design's state expenditure   179

         Table 3A.1. Summary of the annual state expenditure   180

3A-3   State expenditure according to the international 'classification of the functions of government' (COFOG)   182

Table 3A.2. Estimate of the Design's state expenditure in comparison with the OECD average: COFOG 1st digit in % GDP 182

Table 3A.3. Estimate of the Design's state expenditure: COFOG 2nd digit in % GDP 184

3A-4 Taxation revenue from the income tax 193

Table 3A.4. From GDP to the average taxable income: estimates 193

Table 3A.5. Calculation of the number of income receivers 195

Table 3A.6. The average tax rate on the fixed incomes 196

Table 3A.7. The average of the (median) tax rate on the fixed incomes 196

Table 3A.8. Taxation revenue from the receivers of fixed incomes 197

Table 3A.9. Taxation revenue from the receivers of non-fixed incomes (primary income, except income from savings): at an assumed distribution of income as decided on by workers councils – alternative 1 198

Table 3A.10. Coverage of state expenditure by income taxes: alternative 1 198

Table 3A.11. Taxation revenue from the receivers of non-fixed incomes (primary income, except income from savings): at an assumed distribution of income as decided on by workers councils – alternative 2 199

Table 3A.12. Coverage of state expenditure by income taxes: alternative 2 200

3A-5 Estimate of the labour force of the public sector 200

Table 3A.13. Estimate of the labour force of the public sector, in % of the total labour force 201

Appendix 3B. The administrative burden for cooperatives in comparison with capitalist enterprises 202

Table 3B.1. Number of administrative burden increases and decreases for comparatives in comparison with capitalist enterprises: qualitative estimate 203

Appendix 3C. Constitutional rights and main other constitutional elements 205

Division 1. Constitutional rights 206

Division 2. The Parliament and the Government 211

Section 2.1. Election and composition of the parliament 211

Section 2.2. Parliamentary procedures 213

Section 2.3. The government 214

Section 2.4. Legislation 215
Section 2.5. Relations between the parliament and the government 217
Division 3. The judiciary 218
Division 4. Miscellaneous institutions and provisions 219
Section 4.1. State agencies and other state institutions 219
Section 4.2. Workers council governed foundations 219
Section 4.3. Audit 220
Section 4.4. National Ombudsperson 220
Division 5. International matters 220
Division 6. Worker cooperatives, Single person enterprises, and individual services for households 222
Division 7. Revision of the Constitution 223

Appendix 3D. Abuse of power and other improper behaviour by parliamentarians, ministers, other state workers and political parties: judicial proceedings 223

Appendix 3E. Regulation of the turnover tax for 'Single person enterprises' 225

Appendix 3F. Stand-in work as organised in 'stand-in cooperatives', and the prevention of casual inferior jobs 226

Appendix 3G. List of separate accounting maintaining state agencies and other state institutions 229

Chapter 4. Municipal and provincial administrations 231

Introduction 231

4§1	Establishment and budget of municipalities and provinces	231
4§2	Municipal democratic organs	232
4§3	Tasks and authority of the municipal administration	234
4§4	Provincial democratic organs	235
4§5	Tasks and authority of the provincial administration	236
4§6	Workers councils of municipal and provincial institutions	237

Chapter 5. International economic relations 238

Introduction 238

5§1	International migration	238
5§2	International trade	238
5§3	International ownership titles	239
5§4	International balance of payments	239

5§5   International development transfers   239
Appendix 5A. Regulation of international ownership titles and of import duties   239

PART TWO
From modifying capitalism to transition

Introduction to Part Two   243

Chapter 6. The modification of capitalist practices by 'worker-owned cooperatives' and similar democratic enterprises   245
   Introduction   245
   Division 1. Worker-owned cooperatives within capitalism up to 2020: number and performance   246
      6§1   Worker-owned cooperatives (WOCs) and similar legal entities: general characteristics   246
      6§2   Worker-owned cooperatives and other cooperatives: terminology and quantifications   247
         Table 6.1. Classification of cooperatives as functioning within capitalism   247
         Table 6.2. World employment in or within the scope of cooperatives around 2016   249
         Table 6.3. Continental employment in or within the scope of cooperatives around 2016   250
         Table 6.4. Scarceness of data on WOCs around 2016   251
         Table 6.5. Country-wise employment in WOCs around 2016: world top-10's relative and absolute rank (out of 51 countries)   251
      6§3   The performance of worker-owned cooperatives: some key results of empirical research   253
         (1) A general summary of the economic performance of WOCs   253
         (2) The productivity and investment performances of WOCs   255
   Division 2. Complexities of worker-owned cooperatives' functioning within globalising capitalism: the case of Mondragon   258
      6§4   The organisational structure of individual Mondragon cooperatives and of the Mondragon umbrella   259
         Scheme 6.6. The organisational structure of the Mondragon cooperatives   260

	Scheme 6.7. Main organisational structure of the Mondragon Corporation 261
6§5	The ten 1987 principles of Mondragon 262
6§6	Worker-member salaries and paid-in capital, and inter-cooperative solidarity funds 262
6§7	The course of Mondragon's employment: general quantification 1983–2019 264
	Table 6.8. Employment of Mondragon, Spain and the aggregate of OECD countries: growth 1983–2019 265
	Graph 6.9. Total employment Mondragon in comparison with that of Spain: 1983–2019 266
	Graph 6.10. Employment Mondragon Corporation by divisions 1996–2019 266
6§8	Mondragon's sales 1996–2019 267
	Graph 6.11. Mondragon total sales and its industrial international sales 1996–2019 267
	Graph 6.12. Mondragon's industrial international sales proportions 1996–2019 268
	Table 6.13. Number of Mondragon cooperatives and subsidiaries 1998–2020 269
6§9	Mondragon's way of employment in face of globalising capitalism's competition 270
	(1) Types of employment 270
	Table 6.14. Main Mondragon legal entities and their types of employment 271
	(2) Retail cooperatives: worker-members and other employment 273
	Graph 6.15. Proportion of worker-members in the retail division employment: Eroski Group, 2000–2019 274
	(3) Industrial cooperatives: worker-members and other employment 276
	Graph 6.16. National and international employment of Mondragon's industry division 2001–2019 277
	Graph 6.17. Proportion of worker-members in industrial cooperatives 1995–2019 (with an indication of their proportion in the total industrial employment) 280
	(4) Comparative employment performance of Mondragon, Spain and the aggregate of OECD countries: 2001–2019 281
	Table 6.18. Comparison of the Mondragon employment in Spain, with that of Spain and the aggregate of OECD countries: 2001–2019 282

Graph 6.19. Comparison of Spain's retail employment with Mondragon's: 2001–2019 283

Graph 6.20. Comparison of Spain's industrial employment with Mondragon's industrial employment in Spain: 2001–2019 284

Division 3. Cooperatives as subcategory of 'social and solidarity economy entities' 284

6§10   Social and solidarity economy entities   285

Table 6.21. Social and solidarity economy entities as prevalent within capitalism: end 2nd decade 21st century 285

6§11   Employment by SSE entities – a geographically limited account   287

Graph 6.22. Persons that lead a 'social enterprise' as indicator for the dispersal of SEs: world regions estimates 2014–15 288

Graph 6.23. Employment growth in SSE entities within the EU in comparison with the total EU employment growth: 2002–2015 289

Table 6.24. Employment and employment growth in SSE entities within the EU in comparison with the total EU employment: 2002–2015 289

Concluding summary chapter 6   290

Chapter 7. Circumstances just before the transition: financial and real estate markets and the scope of capital flight   298

     Introduction   298

7§1   The 'critical period' just before the transition   298

7§2   The value of financial assets in the critical period   298

Graph 7.1. Distribution of net wealth, financial assets and capital ownership assets: average of 24 OECD countries around 2019, shares of quintiles and top 10%   299

7§3   The value of real estate in the critical period   300

7§4   Country dependent effect on taxation revenue   301

7§5   The value of other real assets (non-real-estate) in the critical period   301

7§6   Capital flight in the critical period   302

Table 7.2. Effects of turbulences financial and real estate markets during the 'critical period'   303

7§7   Direct effects of changes in assets value and capital flight   302

7§8 Turbulences' investment effects on production, employment and incomes   303
    Table 7.3. Turbulences' investment effects on production, employment and incomes: non-WOC sector   304
7§9 Reactions: the central bank, government and 'the public vote'   304
7§10 A concluding appraisal of the critical period   305

Chapter 8. Transition to a worker cooperatives society   307
Introduction   307
    Table 8.1. Legal entities during the transition: Design and Capitalist legal entities   310

Division 1. Transitional legislation phase 1: transition foundations   311
    Subdivision 1A. Institutional changes and regulation in the public sector domain   311

8§1 Democratic organs of the state (cf. 3§1) – full enactment   311
8§2 Competences of the judiciary – phases 1–3   312
8§3 Ministries and state agencies (cf. 3§2) – full enactment   313
8§4 Unchanged municipal and provincial administrations – phases 1–4 {*requires no legislation*}   314
8§5 The four banking and fund agencies – full enactment   314
8§6 Competition and the 'competition authority' – full enactment   315
8§7 Workers council governed foundations – phases 1–4   316
8§8 'Agency for temporary workers council governed foundations' – full enactment   316
8§9 Taxation during the transition – permanent transition legislation   317
    Table 8.2. Overview of tax categories and tax rates during the transition   318
    Subdivision 1B. Regulation of social-economic provisions   322
8§10 Minimum wage – full enactment – and temporary 'minimum costs of living allowances' – phases 1–3   322
8§11 Housing legislation: rental dwellings – permanent transition legislation; and rental dwellings construction – phases 1–2   324
8§12 Health provisions: temporary regulation – phases 1–4   325
8§13 Education provisions: temporary regulation – phases 1–4   326

Subdivision 1C. Institutional changes and regulation in the economic domain 328

8§14 The Design's cooperative as legal entity; unique form for newly established multi-worker legal entities in the non-public sector domain – full enactment 328

8§15 Temporary exceptions for the Design's cooperatives – phases 1–2 329

8§16 Financial markets: shares, bonds, mortgages and consumer credit – permanent transition rules 329

8§17 Accommodation by the SLB of banks' investment credit – permanent transition rules 330

8§18 Conversion of the legal form of pre-transition entities (those of WOCs in particular) into Design cooperatives – phases 1–3 and permanent transition rules 331

Subdivision 1D. Recession policy, the general transition strategy and concluding matters phase 1 {requires no legislation} 332

8§19 General comments on phase 1 333

8§20 Recession-countering policies 333

8§21 State expenditure and taxation revenue due to phase 1 legislation 335

Table 8.3. Extra taxation revenue due to phase 1 legislation in comparison with the Design 336

Table 8.4. State expenditure due to phase 1 legislation 337

8§22 Note on the transition in general in face of the 'phase 1 taxation measures' 337

8§23 The transition strategy for the gradual legal conversion of pre-transition capitalist enterprises into Design cooperatives 338

Table 8.5. Stock corporations (including banks): taxation, expansion, break up and continuity 342

Table 8.6. Firms and limited-owner incorporates: taxation, expansion and legal conversion upon retirement of owner 344

8§24 Amount of legislative work in phase 1, and the duration of the legislative transition phases 1–5 345

Table 8.7. Indication amount of legislative work phase 1: sequential measure 346

Table 8.8. Indication of the duration of the legislative transition phases 1–5 347

Division 2. Transitional legislation phase 2: completion of elementary transition 348

8§25 Full-time position and maximum work-time – full enactment 348
8§26 Workers' councils public sector, except remuneration matters – phases 2–4 348
8§27 Pension allowances – full enactment 349
8§28 Child-related allowances – full enactment 350
8§29 Costs of living allowances for students – full enactment 350
8§30 Preparatory regulation on job securities – phases 2–3 351
8§31 Auditing – full enactment 352
8§32 Legal separation audit and accountancy companies – full enactment 352
8§33 End of year income account and balance sheet of economic domain entities – permanent rules 352
8§34 Conclusions on phase 2 and phases 1–2 together 353
Table 8.9. State expenditure due to phase 2 legislation 354
Table 8.10. Indication amount of legislative work phase 2: sequential measure 354

Division 3. Transitional legislation phase 3: preconditions for mature transition 355

Table 8.11. The transition phases duration in years 356
8§35 Design cooperatives: termination of exceptions 8§15; rules for pre-transition entities – full entry into force Design ch. 2 356
8§36 Physically circular production, safety of and information about output, and safety at work – full enactment 357
8§37 Municipal and provincial democratic organs 357
8§38 Real estate and the real estate agency – full enactment 358
8§39 Mining and other Earth extractions – full enactment 360
8§40 Infrastructure – full enactment 360
8§41 Patents and copyrights – full enactment 361
8§42 Concluding matters phase 3 361
Table 8.12. State expenditure due to phase 3 legislation 362
Table 8.13. Indication amount of legislative work phase 3: sequential measure 362

Division 4. Transitional legislation phase 4: advanced transition 363

Table 8.11. The transition phases duration in years (repeat from introduction 8D3) 363
8§43 Joblessness due to qualifications mismatches and to recessions – full enactment 364

8§44   Restricted abilities to work – full enactment   365
8§45   Appointment procedure of the judiciary and administrative prosecutors – full enactment   366
8§46   Public security – full enactment   366
8§47   International economic relations (ch. 5) – full enactment   367
8§48   Concluding matters phase 4   367
   Table 8.14. State expenditure due to phase 4 legislation   368
   Table 8.15. Indication amount of legislative work phase 4: sequential measure   368

Division 5. Transitional legislation phase 5: matured transition   369

8§49   Remuneration of public sector workers and full competences of their councils – full enactment   369
8§50   The health sector – full enactment   370
8§51   The education sector – full enactment   371
8§52   State-financed research institutes – full enactment   372
8§53   Regulation of the culture sector – full enactment   373
8§54   National railway transport – full enactment   374
8§55   Finance of the state and state institutions – full enactment   376
8§56   Municipalities and provinces (ch. 4) – full enactment   376
8§57   Minimum work-time, and a temporary part-time position – full enactment   376
8§58   Temporary work as organised through 'stand-in cooperatives' – full enactment   377
8§59   Concluding matters phase 5   378
   Table 8.16. State expenditure due to phase 5 legislation   378
   Table 8.17. Indication amount of legislative work phase 5: sequential measure   379

Division 6. Full implementation in practice of the transition legislation   379

Concluding summary of chapter 8   380
   Table 8.18. The transition legislation phases and their implementation in practice   381

Appendix 8A. Various summarising tables   385
   Table 8.19. Summary of the transition's phase-wise enactment of allowances and compensations   385
   Table 8.20. Summary of the entering into force of legislation   387
   Table 8.8. Indication of the duration of the legislative transition phases 1–5 (repeat from 8§24)   347

Table 8.21. Indication amount of legislative work phases 1–5: sequential measure   390

Table 8.22. Legislative transition implementation of the Part One Design   393

General summary   396

    A. Summary of part one: design of the organisation of a worker cooperatives society   396

        Table GS-1. Legal entities and their governance and percent of the workforce   399

        Table GS-2. Key distinctions between the capitalist and the Design cooperatives economies   401

        Table GS-3. Main requirements or restrictions for cooperatives and their councils   404

    B. Summary of part two: from modifying capitalism to transition   412

        Table GS-4. The transition legislation phases and their implementation in practice   417

References   421
Index of names   432
Index of subjects   434
Abbreviations   459

www.ingramcontent.com/pod-product-compliance
Lightning Source LLC
Chambersburg PA
CBHW070606030426
42337CB00020B/3699